D1320352

Readings in SOVIET FOREIGN POLICY

Readings in SOVIET

FOREIGN

POLICY

Theory and Practice

ARTHUR E. ADAMS

Michigan State University

D. C. Heath and Company

BOSTON

PREFACE

This book represents an effort to provide the college student or intelligent lay-man with a coherent introduction to Soviet foreign policy since late 1917. The readings included are roughly of three types—narrative, documentary, and analytical.

Narrative analyses of significant events in Soviet foreign relations are arranged chronologically through fifteen chapters. These narratives have been painstakingly culled from the writings of the West's most authoritative scholars, journalists, and statesmen. The accounts used here are of particular value because they combine de-tailed description with their authors' considered judgments concerning the purposes and methods of Soviet foreign policy.

In order to set forth the Soviet point of view with as much authenticity as possible, the narrative sections of nine chapters are supplemented by pertinent Soviet-Communist documents. Whether the individual selections stem from Lenin or Khrushchev, or from the *Statutes* of the Communist International, they have been chosen because they are significant policy statements or because they present important Communist analyses of world affairs. These materials provide deep insight into the Soviets' interpretation of their relations with the outside world.

Finally, several chapters are illuminated by the efforts of competent specialists to construct a theory of Soviet foreign policy or to discern the pattern of recent develop-ments. These essays, attempting as they do to explain the motives and processes that determine Soviet policy, complement similar efforts embedded in the narratives and documents. Altogether, these materials present the major theories used to explain the conduct of the USSR in its relations with other powers. Thus, it is believed, the atten-tive reader of the following pages may acquire not only a substantial fund of factual information about the evolution of Soviet foreign policy, but also an understanding of the analytical techniques and conceptual tools which will help him to make his own analyses of Soviet intentions and actions valid.

Grateful acknowledgment is made to the authors, publishers, and editors who have permitted me to reprint their materials. While it is always impossible to thank all those who have contributed directly to one's work, my deepest thanks must go to the helpful and intelligent students on whom many of these readings have been tested through several years. Also I wish to express my special indebtedness to Allen K. Workman of D. C. Heath and Company for his skillful editorial aid, and to my wife, Janet, for her invaluable assistance in every phase of the work of preparing these readings for publication.

Arthur E. Adams

v

Table of Contents

Introduction

THE West's great need to understand the objectives, the ruling principles, and the processes of Soviet foreign policy cannot be overemphasized. It is the aim of this book to provide materials that will further the achievement of such understanding. More specifically, this work has three purposes: (1) to present a selective, chronological narrative of the most important events in the Soviet Union's relations with other nations since late 1917; (2) to furnish some of the best evidence available concerning the motives and principles that appear to govern Soviet foreign policy; and (3) to acquaint the reader with the chief theories or hypotheses by which the world's most authoritative students of these matters explain Soviet policy.

Many theories have been propounded as explanations of Soviet foreign policy, and a somewhat confusing number of the more important ones are presented in this book. For the sake of clarity and convenience, all such theories may be classified under four main categories. These categories are defined here in the hope that they will help the reader identify the theoretical position of each author or document in the following pages:

The Balance of Power. In general this term describes the relationship existing between sovereign national states, each of which practices power politics, or in other words, seeks by every means to preserve or increase its security, prestige, wealth, and power. In a world made up of sovereign states it is axiomatic that as soon as one nation significantly increases its power, others feeling themselves endangered by this action will seek ways to oppose it. Any state that wishes to preserve its own position must ally itself with opponents of the threatening nation, and when such an alliance becomes sufficiently strong to halt the threatening nation's expansion, a balance is reached. Always this is a precarious equilibrium, subject to the innumerable internal and external developments that continuously alter the relative power positions of all states. Though we refer to the operation of the balance of power as a "system," it would be more accurate to call it "systematized chaos." Each state, much like a beast in the jungle, is forced to judge every other nation a potential enemy. It must note and correctly interpret every significant event in the domestic life or international relations of its peers, and woe to the nation that fails to discover in time the secret meetings and coalitions of its enemies or the burgeoning economic might and political ambitions of its allies.

It is of special importance that in this system no nation may be said to "make" all of its own policy. Nations constantly respond to the conduct of their fellows. Since World War II, for example, with the struggle suddenly polarized between the Soviet Union and the United States, this reciprocal relationship has been particularly noticeable to Americans. A policy innovation by the United States compels Soviet leaders to devise a suitable response; in turn, the United States must revise its own policy to meet the Soviet response, and so on, ad infinitum. Beneath the shadows of the giants, lesser states grimly watch a game which they feel themselves helpless to influence, and develop policies in accord with their interpretation of the relationship between their own interests and those of the great powers. Meanwhile, other nations, some of them reviving from the war and some stretching their economic and political muscles for the first time in this century—Germany and France; China, India, and Indonesia—are increasing their strength and may soon break the present stalemate.

It is the assumption of most students of Soviet political affairs that at least to some degree the Soviet Union must be viewed as one national state among many, struggling to win security and power by conventional diplomatic maneuvering. Like other states, at different times in its history it has displayed varying degrees of aggressiveness and defensiveness, bumptiousness and cunning. While at the present time some observers believe that the development of inter-continental missiles carrying immensely destructive nuclear explosives may render meaningless the whole practice of power politics, up to this moment the USSR does not appear to have strayed a hair's breadth from the strictest defense of its "national interests."

Ideology. Although the balance of power concept is fundamental to the explanation of the conduct of any modern nation's foreign policy, it cannot by itself explain the unique character of Soviet relations with other states. One of the most important determinants of this uniqueness appears to be the Marxist-Leninist ideology, that is, the complex of theories and attitudes about life and the world peculiar to Soviet Communists. Since the Anglo-Saxon world seems to boggle almost unconsciously at the postulate that ideas influence or determine such important matters as the foreign policy

of a national state, it is necessary to insist emphatically that the communist ideology is and has been extremely influential in determining the Soviet Union's relations with the rest of the world. Indeed, unless one has studied the evolution of the ideology and its influence upon Soviet attitudes and behavior, it is impossible to comprehend Soviet foreign policy.

It is essential further to be aware of the several roles played by Soviet ideology during the forty-odd years of Communist rule in Russia. Of primary importance is the Communists' fervent belief that Marxism-Leninism is a scientific and absolutely accurate description of the inevitable march of proletarian revolution toward victory over the "capitalist" world. This utopian faith in world revolution and the concomitant conviction that the Soviet Communist party and the Soviet state are the instruments which will carry out the revolution have not changed significantly since 1917. These ideas form the foundation of the Soviet leaders' unchanging strategic aim —the eventual establishment of an all-Communist world.

But if the ideology provides a long-range grand strategy, it also provides a sizeable body of tactical devices—techniques for day-to-day use, designed to protect the state, to increase its power, or further the advance toward revolution. The Soviet Union's leaders pride themselves on the wide range and flexibility of their tactics, on their ability to zigzag, to take one step forward and two steps back, to ally with capitalist nations while working for their destruction, to retreat and patiently wait out defeats, to organize peace fronts and popular fronts, and to preach coexistence or rebellion as the situation demands. However, it should be remembered always that regardless of the current tactic, the Soviet leaders remain dedicated to the strategic goal. No matter what they may say today or tomorrow to win a current struggle, they believe in the ultimate victory of world communism over "capitalism," and seem never to tire of reiterating this belief.

The ideology has many other influences upon Soviet foreign policy, some of which may be mentioned here to illustrate further its general importance. By conditioning the minds of Soviet leaders to see the whole world and its events through Marxist-Leninist spectacles and to interpret all international developments in Marxist-Leninist terms, the ideology predetermines their responses, preventing them from seeing or comprehending things as they are. Since the very foundation of Marxist-Leninist thought is its expectation that the capitalist states must die and be replaced by a communist "classless society," in Soviet theory there can be no real hope of genuine or lasting friendship between the two camps. Thus, although Soviet leaders incessantly repeat and may sincerely believe that they stand for *peace*, their use of the word is peculiar to their ideological stance; the peace they envision can only be achieved by the victory of the proletariat under Soviet leadership.

Communist ideology also serves as an *instrument* of foreign policy. Exported through the auspices of international Communist organizations, innumerable propaganda agencies, and the speeches of Soviet leaders, it is an effective means of influencing political action around the world. It arouses colonial peoples to fight for liberation. In trying times it has successfully incited urban workers and even well-to-do intellectuals to act against their "bourgeois" governments. On the other hand, this export of ideology has negative consequences, for it rouses resentment among peoples and governments of non-Communist nations, intensifying suspicions of the Soviet Union's motives. Thus Communist intransigence abroad has sometimes crippled or destroyed concurrent Soviet diplomatic efforts to win alliance and friendship.

In sum, Soviet foreign policy as conventional power politics is distinct from and at the same time inseparable from communist ideology. The conventional policy is irrevocably wedded to the Communists' conviction that the hostile world must eventually succumb to the future Marx predicted for it. From this marriage of power politics and ideology stems the dualism that is the most obvious characteristic of Soviet foreign policy and the most important cause of much confused thinking about it. And from this dualism arise many of the perplexing vacillations, the alternation of peace talk and threats of violence, the self-hindering practice of propagating revolution while simultaneously attempting to establish firm alliances with bourgeois states.

Internal Organization. A nation's internal organization—its geographic and cultural inheritance, its economic, political, and social systems—obviously has a direct bearing upon its foreign policies. However, while this statement would be regarded by most students of international affairs as a truism, it is impossible to express the manifold relationships between internal and external affairs in simple formulas. There are, consequently, a wide variety of hypotheses about Soviet foreign policy based upon some feature or combination of features of Russian-Soviet internal organization. Russia's geography and history have given rise to a theory that Soviet policy has been determined by an "urge to the sea." A coordinate theory explains that much of the Soviet Union's interest in Asia is based on propinquity. Arnold Toynbee has argued that Russia's long historical experience of hostility toward the West, and her Orthodox (Byzantine), anti-Catholic and anti-Protestant religious culture are the foundations of the anti-Western and messianic characteristics of Soviet policy. Other theories emphasize the role of the development of economic and military strength, and still others see the evolving Soviet social system as the key to Soviet policy.

A most influential contemporary theory finds the determining factor of Soviet policy in the relationships between the Communists and the evolution and operation of the Soviet political system. This theory, argued most effectively in the following pages by W. W. Rostow, has many adherents. Briefly, Rostow believes that the power interests of the ruling clique—the Communist élite—are predominant in all policy making. Historically, Rostow argues, the Bolsheviks who carried out the revolution of 1917 found themselves threatened with imminent destruction from all sides, domestic and foreign. Struggling to preserve their new-found power *at all costs*, they learned to make every decision on the basis of what would best *maximize their power inside the Soviet Union*. In the early years, domestic chaos and poverty and the need to hold on determined their foreign policy. Later, the dynamic evolution of Soviet society into a highly-industrialized totalitarian state made new and tough demands upon the leaders, dictating to them at every moment what they must do at home *and abroad* in order to maximize their power *at home*. Thus the internal organization has played a very great role in the determination of Soviet foreign policy.

Personality and Character. It is impossible to argue that individual men, even men like Lenin and Stalin, actually determine a nation's foreign policy by virtue of superior intelligence or the special force of their personalities. It is evident that the many pressures of power politics, ideology, and internal organization severely limit the degree of influence one man may exercise. Yet the role of the leaders in the Soviet system has been one of immense authority. Somewhere within this system certain men make the calculations and decisions which constitute policy. The mentality of these men—their sensitivity or obtuseness to specific aspects of the ideology, their knowledge or ignorance of the rest of the world, the degree of forcefulness, ambition, or humanity they possess—must directly influence the calculation of which policy will most successfully achieve Soviet objectives. Many Western statesmen and scholars, as well as such important Soviet citizens as Joseph Stalin and Nikita Khrushchev, have

placed considerable emphasis on the role of the individual great man. Other competent students attempt to explain Soviet policy by studying the psychology and the "operational codes" of the élite group which shares Soviet power with the titular leader. Regardless of the approach—whether it be that of the anthropologist, the psychoanalyst, the historian, the intelligent layman, or the statesman—it seems obvious that the human factor must always be taken into account.

Such are the four principal categories. It should be noted that the champions of a theory falling under any one of these categories may argue that it explains the "whole truth" about Soviet foreign policy. Other students, more sophisticated, or perhaps only more cautious, combine theories and portions of theories from the several categories in various ways. Theories of both types are well represented in the following pages.

* * *

It must be admitted frankly that our knowledge of the principles and processes of Soviet foreign policy is inadequate. We are unable to define exactly the interrelations of the different influencing factors identified above or to measure accurately the relative influences of these factors. While such difficulties are familiar in all areas of social science, rather special problems are involved in the work of trying to get at the motives and institutional processes which determine Soviet policy. Since these difficulties are integral to the whole subject of Soviet foreign policy, they must be identified here.

First, for a number of reasons our evidence is less than satisfactory. In most countries outside the Soviet bloc it is possible to study popular opinion on current international issues in the public press and to follow the official debates concerning alternative policies in the published records of congresses and parliaments. But in the

Soviet Union the press is a government agency; there is no free public discussion of international issues, no open debate between competing leadership groups. Policies are determined in secret by means unknown to us. Once decided upon they are put into effect, and again there is no public discussion. When this phase of the process has been reached, Soviet public figures formally extol the decisions, and the Soviet press, speaking always with the government's words, praises the new policy for its "wisdom," "farsightedness," and so on.

In the West, we learn much from the memoirs of retired statesmen and diplomats. Men of stature and vast experience publish voluminous and well-documented accounts of the means by which they arrived at important diplomatic decisions in the recent past. But retired Soviet diplomats do not publish memoirs. And though Soviet diplomatic documents are being published, too often they are edited to present the official "line" of the moment rather than to reveal the truth about the events described. Granted, the situation is difficult, but it is not hopeless. Lacking better evidence we are compelled to study the available documents, to examine floods of propaganda, speeches, and the overt conduct of the leaders. From such study we at least learn what the Communists want us to think, what they are persuading other nations to think, what they say they hope to accomplish, and so on. Over a span of more than forty years we have acquired considerable facility at ferreting out the bits of truth embedded in Soviet words and deeds and piecing them together in a fairly accurate pattern.

The second chief difficulty in getting at the truth arises from the inevitable distortion of every judgment by the viewpoint of the judge. Given the xenophobic nationalist passions, suspicions, and prejudices of the present era, and the wide differences between the ideologies and political characters of the Soviet Union and the Western na-

tions, it is virtually impossible (some would even say, undesirable,) to achieve objectivity. The leaders and peoples of the Soviet Union appear incapable of understanding the West as it understands itself; nor can the most brilliant Soviet scholar study Soviet foreign relations with anything approaching what non-Communist scholars would term objectivity. For different reasons the reverse is true. The West simply cannot approach sympathetically the Soviet version of history or the Communist view of the Soviet state's role in history. Even the so-called "neutralists" of India and other Asian countries are trapped willy-nilly by their background, training, judgment, and taste. To paraphrase Mao Tse-tung, all men must lean to one side.

In late 1939 Winston Churchill created a striking and often repeated epigram when he characterized Soviet foreign policy as "a riddle wrapped in a mystery inside an enigma." As is the way with epigrams, his has received more credence than it deserves. Probably the best illustration of this fact is that the rest of his thought reads: "but perhaps there is a key. The key is Russian national interest."* Subsequently during his wartime negotiations with Stalin, while Churchill held to national self-interest as the key, he pondered long on the role of ideology and the impact of domestic affairs upon Soviet policy, and his reflections concerning the character and influence of Stalin himself are among the most penetrating and enlightening that we possess. This is only to say that a crystal ball is not in fact a necessity for the student of Soviet foreign policy. That policy is finite and man-made, complicated to be sure, but amenable to informed, rational analysis and practical judgment. We must make the best use of the information that we possess.

The following pages provide no easy guide-lines to a peaceful future, but their evidence indicates that if the Western na-

* Winston Churchill, *The Gathering Storm* (New York, 1948), p. 494, in which he quotes his speech of October 1, 1939.

tions hope for justice and peace in the world, they must look deep into the complexities of Soviet foreign policy and make honest and accurate assessments of its purposes and potentials. If the hard problems Soviet policy poses for the rest of the world are to be solved, surely, first of all, the policy itself must be understood.

A NOTE ON TECHNICALITIES

Scholars of the United States and Great Britain who use the Russian language are unable to agree upon a standard system of transliterating names from Russian to English. In consequence, proper names may be spelled in a number of ways; e.g., Trotzky, Trotsky, and Trotski. I have not changed the spellings which appear in the materials presented here, since to do so would be to violate the scholarly convictions of other men and would imply that I consider my own transliteration system perfection itself. Similarly, different writers employ widely varying techniques for making footnote citations. I have not presumed to standardize the footnotes throughout the book. Nor have I thought it essential to force British and American usage into one mold in spelling such words as *honour*, (*honor*). Finally, it must be emphasized that a single volume cannot adequately treat every significant event or influence in the Soviet Union's foreign relations. Important omissions here—the wartime meetings leading up to the Yalta Conference, postwar disarmament negotiations, pertinent twists and turns in Communist theory, etc.—underline the necessity for continued and extensive study by the person who would understand Soviet foreign policy.

Readings in SOVIET FOREIGN POLICY

The Peace with Germany 1917–1918

I

DECLARATION ON PEACE

VLADIMIR LENIN

Lenin's immense personal and intellectual influence upon the foreign policy of the Soviet state, both in its formative period and in later years, can hardly be exaggerated. The decree printed here, which he read to the All-Russian Congress of Soviets a day after the Bolsheviks' seizure of power at Petrograd, is, first of all, an illustration of his skill as a propagandist. Lenin knew that many of the people of Russia would support him because they desperately wanted peace. Similarly the "Declaration" was an appeal for sympathy from the war-weary populations of other nations. But this document is not propaganda alone; it is a sincere expression of Lenin's utopian faith that revolutionary ideals and diplomatic techniques could destroy the old patterns of international relations and achieve a just peace for all the peoples of the world.

THE Workers' and Peasants' Government, created by the revolution of November 6-7, and drawing its strength from the Soviets of Workers', Soldiers', and Peasants' Deputies, proposes to all warring peoples and their governments to begin at once negotiations leading to a just democratic peace.

A just and democratic peace for which the great majority of wearied, tormented, and war-exhausted toilers and laboring classes of all belligerent countries are thirsting, a peace which the Russian workers and peasants have so loudly and insistently demanded since the overthrow of the Tsar's monarchy, such a peace the government considers to be an immediate peace without annexations (i.e., without the seizure of foreign territory and the forcible annexation of foreign nationalities) and without indemnities.

The Russian Government proposes to all warring peoples that this kind of peace be concluded at once; it also expresses its readiness to take immediately, without the least delay, all decisive steps pending the final confirmation of all the terms of such a peace by the plenipotentiary assemblies of all countries and all nations.

By annexation or seizure of foreign territory the government, in accordance with the legal concepts of democracy in general and of the working class in particular, understands any incorporation of a

From "Lenin's Speech [November 8, 1917] on the Peace Declaration," reprinted from *The Bolshevik Revolution, 1917–1918* by James Bunyan and H. H. Fisher, pp. 125–128, with the permission of the publishers, Stanford University Press. Copyright 1934 by the Board of Trustees of Leland Stanford Junior University.

small and weak nationality by a large and powerful state without a clear, definite, and voluntary expression of agreement and desire by the weak nationality, regardless of the time when such forcible incorporation took place, regardless also of how developed or how backward is the nation forcibly attached or forcibly detained within the frontiers of the [larger] state, and, finally, regardless whether or not this large nation is located in Europe or in distant lands beyond the seas.

If any nation whatsoever is detained by force within the boundaries of a certain state, and if [that nation], contrary to its expressed desire—whether such desire is made manifest in the press, national assemblies, party relations, or in protests and uprisings against national oppression—is not given the right to determine the form of its state life by free voting and completely free from the presence of the troops of the annexing or stronger state and without the least pressure, then the adjoining of that nation by the stronger state is annexation, i.e., seizure by force and violence.

The government considers that to continue this war simply to decide how to divide the weak nationalities among the powerful and rich nations which had seized them would be the greatest crime against humanity, and it solemnly announces its readiness to sign at once the terms of peace which will end this war on the indicated conditions, equally just for all nationalities without exception.

At the same time the government declares that it does not regard the conditions of peace mentioned above as an ultimatum; that is, it is ready to consider any other conditions, insisting, however, that such be proposed by any of the belligerents as soon as possible, and that they be expressed in the clearest terms, without ambiguity or secrecy.

The government abolishes secret diplomacy, expressing, for its part, the firm determination to carry on all negotiations absolutely openly and in view of all the people. It will proceed at once to publish all secret treaties ratified or concluded by the government of landlords and capitalists from March to November 7, 1917. All the provisions of these secret treaties, in so far as they have for their object the securing of benefits and privileges to the Russian landlords and capitalists—which was true in a majority of cases—and retaining or increasing the annexation by the Great Russians, the government declares absolutely and immediately annulled.

While addressing to the governments and peoples of all countries the proposal to begin at once open peace negotiations, the government, for its part, expresses its readiness to carry on these negotiations by written communications, by telegraph, by parleys of the representatives of different countries, or at a conference of such representatives. To facilitate such negotiations the government appoints its plenipotentiary representative to neutral countries.

The government proposes to all governments and peoples of all belligerent countries to conclude an armistice at once; at the same time it considers it desirable that this armistice should be concluded for a period of not less than three months—that is, a period during which it would be entirely possible to complete the negotiations for peace with the participation of representatives of all peoples and nationalities which were drawn into the war or forced to take part in it, as well as to call the plenipotentiary assemblies of people's representatives in every country for the final ratification of the peace terms.

In making these peace proposals to the government and peoples of all warring countries, the Provisional Government of Workers and Peasants of Russia appeals particularly to the class-conscious workers of the three most advanced nations of mankind, who are also the largest states participating in the present war—England, France, and Germany. The workers of these countries have rendered the greatest possible service to the cause of progress and socialism by the great example of the Chartist movement in England, several revolutions of universal historic significance accomplished by the French proletariat, and, finally, the heroic struggle against the Law of Exceptions in Germany, a struggle which was prolonged, stubborn, and disciplined, which could be held up as an example for the workers of the whole world, and which aimed at the creation of proletarian mass organizations in Germany. All these examples of proletarian heroism and historic achievement serve us as a guaranty that the workers of these three countries will understand the tasks which lie before them by way of liberating humanity from the horrors of war and its consequences, and that by their resolute, unselfishly energetic efforts in various directions these workers will help us to bring to a successful end the cause of peace, and, together with this, the cause of the liberation of the toiling and exploited masses from all forms of slavery and all exploitation.

The Workers' and Peasants' Government created by the revolution of November 6-7 and drawing its strength from the Soviets of Workers', Soldiers', and Peasants' Deputies must begin peace negotiations at once. Our appeal must be directed to the governments as well as to the peoples. We cannot ignore the governments, because this would delay the conclusion of peace, a thing which a people's government does not dare to do, but at the same time we have no right not to appeal to the peoples. Everywhere governments and peoples are at arm's length; we must, therefore, help the peoples to take a hand in [settling] the question of peace and war. We shall of course stand by our program of peace without annexations and without indemnities. We shall not relinquish [that program], but we must deprive our enemies of the possibility of saying that their conditions are different and that they do not wish, therefore, to enter into negotiations with us. No, we must dislodge them from that advantageous position by not presenting them our conditions in the form of an ultimatum. For this reason we have included a statement to the effect that we are ready to consider any condition of peace, in fact, every proposal. Consideration, of course, does not necessarily mean acceptance. We shall submit [the proposals] for consideration to the Constituent Assembly, which will then decide, officially, what can and what cannot be granted. We have to fight against the hypocrisy of the governments, which, while talking about peace and justice, actually carry on wars of conquest and plunder. Not one single government will tell you what it really means. But we are opposed to secret diplomacy and can afford to act openly before all people. We do not now close nor have we ever closed our eyes to the difficulties. Wars cannot be ended by a refusal [to fight]; they cannot be ended by one side alone. We are proposing an armistice for three months—though we are not rejecting a shorter period—[in the hope] that this will give the suffering army at least a breathing spell and will make possible the calling of popular meetings in all civilized countries to discuss the conditions [of peace].

BREST-LITOVSK: THE STRUGGLE FOR PEACE

WILLIAM HENRY CHAMBERLIN

William Henry Chamberlin was born in Brooklyn and educated at Haverford College. He has had a long and active career as journalist, author, and historian. From 1922 to 1934 he was the Moscow correspondent of the *Christian Science Monitor*, an experience that undoubtedly aided him in writing his pioneering and valuable study, *The Russian Revolution*. This work, characterized throughout by an intense effort to achieve objectivity, has long been one of the best accounts of the revolution and the civil war published in this country. In the following extract, Chamberlin carefully recounts the diplomatic reverses and the ideological agonies suffered by the Bolsheviks during their first effort to adjust utopian theories and revolutionary hopes to the harsh realities of Russian military weakness. It is important to remember that such grim experiences are not soon forgotten; the negotiations at Brest-Litovsk and the treaty that followed had lasting impact upon the Bolsheviks' thinking about their relations with other nations.

THE peace negotiations at Brest-Litovsk represented at once one of the most vital and one of the most difficult problems of the new Soviet regime. It was a matter of life and death to win peace. The Bolshevik leaders and a comparatively small number of their convinced followers felt, of course, that there was a substantial difference between war in defense of the "capitalist" Provisional Government and war in defense of the Soviet Republic.

But the overwhelming majority of the Russian soldiers in the trenches were no more inclined to fight for Lenin than they were inclined to fight for Kerensky. Their sympathy for Lenin and against Kerensky was based on the belief that Lenin stood for peace and for giving land to the peasants. Peace, peace "without annexations and indemnities" if possible, but peace at any price, if necessary, was an indispensable condition of the survival of the Soviet Government; and no one saw this more clearly than Lenin, whose hard realistic mind was not intoxicated by the success of the Revolution in Russia and was not diverted by optimistic fantasies about the possible immediate spread of the revo-lutionary flame to Germany and Austria.

At the same time it was imperatively necessary to hold out as long as possible against German annexationist demands, to utilize the negotiations as a forum from which to proclaim to the world what the Soviet Government regarded as just peace conditions, to dispel, so far as circumstances would permit, the accusation that the Bolshe-viki were German agents, to give the Ger-man and Austrian workers an opportunity to react to the course of the negotiations and to protest against excessive demands of their own Governments. The question how far the Soviet Government was morally obligated to resist the demands of the Cen-tral powers was to be a subject of major disagreement between Lenin, who believed from the beginning that it was necessary to sign even a bad peace, and many of his associates in the Party Central Committee.

Two worlds, the world of old-fashioned diplomacy and militarism and the world of emerging revolutionism, met when the peace delegations held their first plenary session in Brest-Litovsk on December 22. The Soviet delegation had dropped its orna-mental worker, sailor and peasant, who were taken along to the armistice discussions, and consisted of men of high education and culture: A. A. Joffe, the President, L. B. Kamenev, M. N. Pokrovsky, the Bolshevik historian, and L. B. Karakhan, the future Assistant Foreign Commissar, who acted as Secretary. The Left Socialist Revolutionaries had a typical representative: Mme. A. A. Bitzenko, who had made herself a heroine in revolutionary circles by killing a Tsarist official and serving a long term in prison and exile.

The main figures in the delegations of the Central powers were the German Foreign Minister, von Kühlmann, the Austrian Foreign Minister, Count Ottokar Czernin, and the German Major-General Max Hoffman, who represented the German Supreme Command and more than once intervened brusquely in the discussions when he felt that the civilian negotiators were not showing sufficient energy and firmness. Count Czernin was the most conciliatory member of this triumvirate; Austria's psychological and physical need for peace and bread was second only to that of Russia itself, and Count Czernin was seriously afraid that a breakdown of the negotiations might lead to a collapse of the Dual Monarchy. But his influence on the course of affairs was slight; Austria was helplessly dependent on Germany for everything, from military support to assistance with food. The Bulgarian and Turkish delegates at the Conference played secondary rôles; both were anxious to obtain sanction for territorial expansion—Bulgaria at the expense of its Balkan neighbors, Rumania and Serbia, and Turkey in the Caucasus.

After demanding and obtaining consent for publicity in connection with the proceedings of the Conference, Joffe offered the following proposals as a basis for peace negotiations:

1. No forcible annexations of territories seized in time of war are permitted. Troops in occupation of these territories are withdrawn from them in the shortest period of time.

2. The political independence of those peoples who were deprived of it during the present war is fully restored.

3. National groups which did not enjoy political independence before the war are guaranteed the possibility of deciding the question of their attachment to one or another state or of their state independence by means of a referendum. This referendum must be organized in such a manner that complete freedom of voting will be assured to the whole population of the given territory, not excluding emigrants and fugitives.

4. In regard to territories which are inhabited by several nationalities the right of the minority is guarded by special laws, which guaranty it national cultural independence and, if possible, administrative autonomy.

5. No one of the belligerent countries is obligated to pay to other countries so-called "war expenditures"; contributions which have already been levied are to be returned. As for the compensation of private persons who have suffered from the war, this is to be made out of a special fund, created by means of proportionate contributions from all the belligerent countries.

6. Colonial problems are to be decided in accordance with the principles set forth in Points 1, 2, 3 and 4.

Joffe also suggested that such measures of pressure of strong on weak nations as economic boycott, naval blockade and discriminatory commercial agreements should be forbidden.

The negotiators of the Central powers were all apostles of *Realpolitik* and certainly had no intention of relaxing their grip on Poland and on the considerable part of Russia's Baltic Provinces which had been occupied in response to the moral exhortations of Russian revolutionaries who had behind them no serious armed force. But Kühlmann and Czernin believed that some diplomatic advantage might be gained by outwardly accepting the Soviet formulas. There was a faint chance that such a method would pave the way to peace negotiations with the Entente powers; there was also the possibility that the Bolsheviki, if they obtained the shadow of recognition of their theoretical principles, would be ready to surrender the substance of Russian territory, which they had no means of reconquering.

So, despite the private remonstrances and misgivings of the more downright and straightforward General Hoffmann, Kühlmann, in the name of the Quadruple Alliance (Germany, Austria-Hungary, Bulgaria and Turkey), delivered a very conciliatory reply to Joffe's proposals on December 25. He declared that the delegation of the Quadruple Alliance was ready to conclude immediately a general peace without forcible annexations and without contributions. For the sake of conquests the Quadruple Alliance would not prolong the War a single day. He added, however, the significant reservation that the proposals of the Russian delegation could be realized only if all the powers involved in the War bound themselves within a definite period of time to observe these same conditions. He renounced, on behalf of the Quadruple Alliance, any intention of forcibly annexing territories which had been occupied, and declared that the peace treaty should define the conditions of withdrawal of troops. He welcomed the Soviet proposal that colonies occupied during the War should be evacuated (a suggestion that would have benefited only Germany) and politely rejected as impracticable the application of Soviet ideas of selfdetermination to the native population of the German colonies.

At Joffe's suggestion it was decided to suspend the negotiations for ten days, in order to give the other belligerent powers an opportunity to participate in the negotiations. So far the course of the discussions had been unexpectedly harmonious. But on December 26 the blunt, outspoken General Hoffmann, who was not disposed to leave the Russian delegates in any doubt as to the firm intention of Germany to retain effective control of the territory which

had been conquered, took advantage of the first opportunity at luncheon to tell Joffe that the Central powers did not regard it as forcible annexation if some parts of the former Russian Empire, such as Poland, Lithuania and Courland (all occupied at this time by the German forces) decided to secede from Russia and to unite with Germany or with any other state.

It is not altogether clear whether the Soviet delegates had been so naïve as to believe that their proclamation of international socialist peace principles would induce the German Supreme Command to give up its conquests. But Hoffmann's statement excited great indignation and for a day or two the atmosphere at the conference was strained and uncertain. There was some talk on the Russian side of breaking off the conference; and Count Czernin declared in conversation with Kühlmann and Hoffmann that he would open up separate peace negotiations, if the general negotiations broke down.

Hoffmann, as much of a realist in his way as Lenin was on the other side, remained unmoved. He knew that Austria could always be browbeaten into submission. As for Russia, the masses were eager for peace, the army had fallen to pieces, the sole chance for the Bolsheviki to remain in power was to obtain peace. All this strengthened the Prussian General in his conviction that "the Bolsheviki must accept the conditions of the Central powers, however harsh they may be."

Hoffmann's confidence was justified when the Soviet delegation reappeared in Brest-Litovsk and formal negotiations were resumed on January 9, 1918. Trotzky replaced Joffe as head of the delegation and henceforward was far and away the dominant figure in the negotiations on the Soviet side. A sterner atmosphere prevailed in this second phase of the negotiations. Trotzky isolated the members of his delegation from the Germans and forbade the former practice of dining with the representatives of the Central powers.

The Soviet delegation again raised the question of transferring the sessions of the conference from Brest-Litovsk and suggested that Stockholm would be preferable. This proposal was firmly and definitely rejected. General Hoffmann seized the first opportunity on January 9 to lodge a protest against the circulation of revolutionary appeals, "full of abuse of the German Army and the German Supreme Command" and signed by representatives of the Russian Government and of the Russian Army, addressed to the troops of the Central powers.

Representatives of the Ukrainian Rada were now participating in the negotiations; and the German and Austrian diplomats were quick to grasp the favorable opportunity of denying Trotzky's right to speak for all Russia and to drive a wedge between Kiev and Petrograd. Ukraina was far richer in agricultural resources than Northern and Central Russia; and a separate peace with the Rada seemed to open up alluring possibilities, both political and economic, for the Central powers.

The Ukrainian delegates, conscious of the weakness of their Government's position before the rising wave of Bolshevism, were not hard bargainers, although in the beginning they put forward certain territorial demands, suggesting, as a compensation for food exports to hungry Germany and Austria, that Austria-Hungary should cede to Ukraina, East Galicia and Bukovina, with their predominantly Ukrainian population, and that the Kholm district of Poland, should also be allocated to Ukraina. The Germans and Austrians refused pointblank to consider any cession of Austrian territory; but a compromise was arranged under which Kholm was to go to Ukraina (Hoffmann was quite willing to weaken Poland and Czernin felt that Kholm would be a cheap price of Ukrainian bread), while a special Crown Land within the Austrian Empire was to be created out of East Galicia and Bukovina.

Kühlmann on January 10 asked Trotzky whether his delegation was to be the sole diplomatic representation of Russia, and Trotzky replied that he "had no objection to the participation of the Ukrainian delegation in the peace conference." At this time the Bolshevik offensive against Kiev had not advanced so far that Trotzky felt inclined to deny the right of the Rada to represent Ukraina.

The second phase of the Brest-Litovsk negotiations resolved itself largely into a verbal duel between Trotzky and Kühlmann, ranging around the subject of how the principle of selfdetermination should be applied in the regions which were occupied by German troops. Trotzky adopted the viewpoint that only a free referendum, taken without the presence of foreign military forces, would constitute a genuine expression of popular will. Kühlmann refused to consider the withdrawal of the German troops and argued that the occupied districts had already declared their will through the resolutions of bodies which had been created under the regime of occupation. He also insisted that the Soviet Government, in view of its professed willingness to permit any part of the former Russian Empire to secede, if the majority of its inhabitants so desired, had no right to interfere in the arrangements which Germany might reach with the population of the occupied territories. Trotzky's reply to this was:[1]

We defend not the possessions of Russia, but the rights of separate nationalities to free historical existence. We shall never in any case consent to recognize that all those decisions which are being taken, which have already, perhaps, been taken or will be taken in the near future, under the control of the German occupation authorities, through the medium of organizations which are created by the occupation authorities, or with their coöperation, or through institutions which are arbitrarily recognized as authoritative organizations, — that these decisions are an expression of the genuine will of these nationalities and can determine their historic fate. . . . We

[1] L. Trotsky, *Sobranie sochinenii* (Moscow, 1925–1927), XVII, Part I, 26–28.

are revolutionaries, but we are also realists, and we should prefer to talk directly about annexations, rather than to replace their real name with a pseudonym.

While Kühlmann endeavored to put the German case in diplomatic phraseology General Hoffmann, in his occasional interventions, talked the plain language of superior force. So, on January 12,[2] he complained that "the Russian delegation talks the language of a victor, invading our country. The facts contradict this; victorious German troops are on Russian territory." Hoffmann furthermore undertook to give the Bolsheviki a lecture on ethics, declaring that "the Soviet Government is based exclusively on force, and anyone who thinks otherwise is simply declared a counterrevolutionary and a bourgeois and outlawed." He cited as proof of his statement the armed dissolution of a White Russian Congress on December 30 and the employment of arms against the Rada. Finally he referred to the acts of such bodies as the Courland Popular Assembly, the Lithuanian Landrat, the municipal administration of Riga and others, which had repudiated all connection with Russia and appealed to Germany for defense.

Actually the bodies which Hoffmann mentioned could not reasonably be regarded as nationally representative. They were hand-picked bodies of delegates elected by the landlords and by the wealthier classes in the towns, and they contained a disproportionately large number of delegates elected by the German racial minorities in the Baltic States. Equally little could be said for the popular basis of the Government which had been created under German-Austrian auspices in occupied Poland. This regime disappeared immediately after the breakdown of the German military power. The Soviet delegates were indefatigable in denouncing the unrepresentative character of the Polish and Baltic govern-

mental bodies; several Socialists from Poland and the Baltic Provinces, including the brilliant and sharp-tongued Karl Radek, were attached to the delegation as "consultants on national questions."

Neither side in the wordy duel at Brest-Litovsk seriously expected to convince the other. Trotzky's policy was to play for time in the hope that some revolutionary sparks might be kindled in Germany and Austria. There were some rather faint and muffled responses to this policy; there were strikes and hunger demonstrations in Austria in mid-January; later in the month there were serious strikes in Berlin and in a number of provincial towns, such as Hamburg, Danzig and Kiel. These strikes aroused exaggerated hopes in Russia; but the discipline of the German Empire was proof against everything except definite military defeat, and the strike wave ebbed away without shaking the position of the Government.

Why the representatives of the Central powers allowed the negotiations to drag on so long is less comprehensible. The military leaders were eager for a swift decision in the East which would free their hands for the projected great spring offensive on the Western Front. But the civilian diplomats hoped, by the exercise of some patience, to obtain a settlement which would not be too obviously a mere product of superior military force. The parallel discussions with the Ukrainian delegates raised questions affecting the internal structure of Austria-Hungary and required time for solution.

By January 18, however, the patience of the negotiators of the Central powers, or at least of the German Supreme Command, had worn thin. At Kühlmann's invitation General Hoffmann, never loath to present an ultimatum, spread out a map of Eastern Europe on the table and pointed to a blue line, running north of Brest-Litovsk, as the future boundary of Russia. Hoffmann declared that territorial arrangements south of Brest-Litovsk would depend on the issue of negotiations with the delegates of the

[2] A. A. Joffe, ed., *Mirnie peregovori v Brest-Litovske* (Moscow, 1920), pp. 94ff.

Ukrainian Rada. Hoffman's line coincided precisely with the military line held by the German forces. It separated from Russia most of the territory now included in Poland, all Lithuania, western Latvia, including the city of Riga and the islands in Moon Sound, inhabited by Esthonians. In response to an ironical question from Trotzky as to what principles guided the drawing of the line Hoffmann said: "The indicated line is dictated by military considerations; it assures the peoples living on this side of the line a tranquil organization of state life and the realization of the right to selfdetermination."[3]

Confronted with this semi-ultimatum Trotzky maneuvered for time by proposing a suspension of the negotiations for some days. Apart from the desire to test out the effect of the sweeping German demands on the German working class and on world public opinion, Trotzky felt that it was necessary to return to Petrograd in order to participate in the shaping of the fateful decision as to what should be done, if, as seemed quite probable, the Germans should put their demands in more imperative form after the resumption of the negotiations.

Now that the question of war or peace had become urgent, three main viewpoints, along with several minor shadings, had developed among the Bolshevik leaders. Lenin, supported by Stalin, Zinoviev, Kamenev and Sokolnikov, stood for the signature of peace after all the resources of delay had been exhausted. At the other extreme were Bukharin, Lomov and some other "left-wing" Communists, who were especially strong in the Moscow Party organization. They favored absolute refusal to sign an annexationist peace and the proclamation of a "revolutionary war." Trotzky's position was an intermediate one. He does not seem to have cherished any illusions about the possibility of resuming war. But he was anxious to play out to the very end the appeal to international working class soli-

darity. What he advocated was a sort of demonstration of passive resistance: a refusal to sign peace on the terms of Hoffmann and Ludendorff, accompanied by a declaration that Russia no longer considered itself in a state of war and a demonstrative demobilization of the Russian army, which was already, to a very large extent, "self-demobilized."

There is an intoxication about successful revolution that makes retreat psychologically very difficult for the revolutionists. A period of only a little more than two months separated the seizure of power in November from the German demand for an annexationist peace, the signature of which seemed to many ardent Communists a betrayal of their international principles. It is not surprising, therefore, that even the weight of Lenin's personal authority was unable to bring about an immediate general acceptance of the necessity of agreeing to what he himself described as "a Tilsit Peace."

In his usual fashion Lenin had outlined his attitutde toward the problem of peace in a series of "theses," or argumentative propositions, written on January 20, but only published on February 24, when the situation had become much more critical. Lenin started out with the assumption that an interval of some months was necessary for the success of socialism in Russia, so that the Soviet Government might have a free hand in crushing the bourgeoisie and carrying out organizing work. He answered the criticism that acceptance of the German terms would be a breach with proletarian internationalism with the statement that workers who are obliged to accept unfavorable terms imposed by a capitalist do not betray socialism.

The socialist revolution in Europe must and would come; "all our hopes for the *final* victory of socialism are based on this conviction." But it would have been a blind gamble to try to determine precisely when the European, and especially the German, Revolution would come. The army could

[3] *Ibid.*, pp. 126ff.

not resist a German attack; any attempt to continue the War, unless it was accompanied by a speedy revolution in Germany, would merely mean that the Soviet Government would be swept away and a still more onerous peace would be imposed upon its successor. To stake the existence of the Soviet regime on the possibility that a revolution might break out in Germany within a few weeks was "a risk which we have not the right to take."

Lenin's theses, bitterly realistic and quite unsentimental, failed at this time to command general support. At a discussion in which Bolshevik delegates to the Third Congress of Soviets participated along with members of the Central Committee of the Party, fifteen votes were cast for his proposal to sign an annexationist peace, thirty-two for the slogan of "revolutionary war" and sixteen for Trotzky's idea: refusal to sign the peace, accompanied by a declaration that the state of war was ended.

Lenin again remained in the minority at a very important session of the Party Central Committee on January 24 which discussed the policy to be pursued at Brest-Litovsk. Lenin repeated his arguments about the exhaustion of the army and the certainty that any attempt to prolong hostilities would lead to the overthrow of the Soviet Government. He resorted to a homely metaphor, declaring: "Germany is still only pregnant with revolution; and a quite healthy child has been born to us—a socialist republic which we may kill if we begin war." He characterized Trotzky's proposal as an international political demonstration which would hand over Esthonia to the Germans. "If the Germans begin to attack," he predicted, "we shall be compelled to sign any peace, and then, of course, the terms will be worse."

Bukharin spoke in opposition to Lenin, recalling how Kornilov's forces had been demoralized by propaganda, hopefully mentioning the strike in Vienna, arguing that the prospects of international revolution should not be sacrificed to the preservation of the Soviet regime. Trotzky followed, advocating his "no war and no peace" formula, urging that only such a procedure could test out the forces of resistance to militarism in Germany. Stalin supported Lenin's views, emphatically declaring, in contravention of the internationalist views of Trotzky and Bukharin: "There is no revolutionary movement in the West. There are no facts; there is only a possibility, and with possibilities we cannot reckon."

Lenin, who was himself strongly convinced that the Russian Revolution was closely linked up with the international movement, dissented from Stalin's outspoken formula, remarking that "there is a mass movement in the West, but the revolution there has not begun," and adding: "If we should believe that the German movement may develop immediately in the event of an interruption of the peace negotiations, we should be obliged to sacrifice ourselves, because the German Revolution in its force will be greater than ours." It was only Lenin's doubt about the likelihood of an immediate outburst of insurrection against the Kaiser that made him insist on the necessity of purchasing a longer term of life for the Soviet Government by signing the peace.

At the end of the session three propositions were put to a vote. Revolutionary war was rejected by eleven votes to two, with one abstention; only one vote was cast against Lenin's proposal to put off the signing of the peace by dragging out the negotiations as much as possible; finally, Trotzky's "no war and no peace" slogan obtained the sanction of the Central Committee by nine votes to seven. So Trotzky's subsequent action in refusing to sign the peace at Brest-Litovsk was authorized by the Central Committee, although it was opposed to Lenin's recommendations.

The Third Congress of Soviets, which, like the Second, had an overwhelming majority of Bolshevik and Left Socialist Revolutionary delegates, holding its sessions in Petrograd from January 23 until

January 31, adopted a resolution approving the previous policy of the Soviet peace delegation and granting it practically a free hand in future negotiations. The peace negotiations in Brest-Litovsk were resumed on January 30, and Trotzky announced that the Soviet delegation now included two representatives of the Ukrainian Soviet Republic, Medvedev and Shakhrai.

The course of military operations at this time was definitely against the forces of the Kiev Rada; Kiev itself would soon fall into the hands of the Soviet troops. But this circumstance did not affect the attitude of the Central powers. Their leaders realized that a few second class German and Austrian divisions could easily restore the Rada and drive the disorderly Red Guards out of Ukraina. On February 1 Count Czernin, in the name of all the delegations of the Central powers, announced the recognition of the Ukrainian People's Republic "as a free sovereign state, fully authorized to enter into international relations." On the same day Czernin's diary contains the following entry:[4] "My design is to play the Petersburgers and the Ukrainians against each other and to come to a peace with at least one or the other of them."

Trotzky exhausted his batteries of sarcasm on "the non-existent Ukrainian Republic, the territory of which is restricted to the rooms which are assigned to their delegation in Brest-Litovsk." But the Ukrainian Rada at this moment was a useful pawn in the hands of the Germans and Austrians. Prodded by Ludendorff for quicker and more decisive action, Kühlmann promised a breach with Trotzky within twenty-four hours after the signature of peace with Ukraina.

The drama at Brest-Litovsk was now approaching its climax. Apparently Trotzky wavered somewhat between the possibility of obtaining peace, with perhaps a slight improvement of the original German terms, and plunging into the risks associated with his own policy of refusing to sign the peace. At any rate when Czernin talked with him on February 7 Trotzky admitted that Russia was too weak to regain the territory occupied by the Germans and laid stress on two points: the abandonment by the Central powers of a separate peace with Ukraina and the restoration of the Moon Sound Islands. About the same time Trotzky endeavored to sound out Kühlmann as to whether Riga and the Moon Sound Islands might be given back to Russia.

Kühlmann, eager for a peace which would bear some sign of agreement rather than for a breaking off of the negotiations, took Trotzky's suggestion so seriously that he proffered his resignation rather than deliver an ultimatum which the Kaiser, greatly incensed over one of the revolutionary proclamations which the Bolsheviki were addressing to the German soldiers, had demanded. The proposed ultimatum would have required the cession of the whole of Latvia and Esthonia. Kühlmann's resignation was not accepted and the ultimatum was not delivered.

But peace by agreement did not come about. The Ukrainians signed a treaty with the representatives of the Central powers on February 9, thereby paving the way for an exchange of German military assistance against the Bolsheviki for Ukrainian exports of grain, eggs and other foodstuffs to blockaded and hungry Germany and Austria. And Trotzky, after some delay, rejected Kühlmann's suggestion to discuss a settlement on the basis of possible concessions in connection with Riga and the Moon Sound Islands. The impulse to make a spectacular appeal to world opinion, to test the possibilities of international workingclass solidarity, was too strong. Trotzky chose February 10, the day after the conclusion of the separate peace between the Central powers and Ukraina, as the occasion for formally

---

[4] Count Ottokar Czernin, *Im Weltkriege* (Berlin and Vienna, 1919), p. 332.

breaking off negotiations. Always eloquent in moments of crisis, he announced his decision in a speech that made a profound impression upon the members of the hostile delegations in the council room.[5]

We no longer desire to take part in this purely imperialistic War, where the pretensions of the propertied classes are clearly paid for with human blood. We are equally uncompromising in regard to the imperialism of both camps, and we are no longer willing to shed the blood of our soldiers in defense of the interests of one camp of imperialists against the other.

In anticipation of that hour, which we hope is near, when the oppressed working classes of all countries will take power into their own hands, like the working people of Russia, we withdraw our army and our people from the War. . . .

We refuse to sanction the conditions which German and Austro-Hungarian imperialism is writing with the sword on the bodies of living peoples. We cannot place the signature of the Russian Revolution beneath conditions which bring oppression, sorrow and misfortune to millions of human beings.

The Governments of Germany and Austria-Hungary wish to rule lands and peoples by the right of military conquest. Let them do this openly. We cannot sanction violence. We withdraw from the War, but we are obliged to refuse to sign the peace treaty. . . .

Refusing to sign an annexationist treaty, Russia, on its side, declares the state of war with Germany, Austria-Hungary, Turkey and Bulgaria as ended. At the same time the Russian troops are ordered to demobilize entirely on the whole front.

The bold and unique experiment of thus ostentatiously throwing down arms while at the same time refusing to sign an objectionable peace was launched. The German reply was swift and crushing. On February 13 the highest German military and civilian authorities, Hindenburg, Ludendorff, the Chief of the Naval Staff, the Chancellor, Hertling, the Vice-Chan-

cellor and Foreign Minister Kühlmann met in council at Hamburg. The military men agreed that the situation in the East must be cleared up; otherwise a new front might arise and divisions which were needed in France would have to remain in Poland and the Baltic States. Moreover, Ukrainian grain was badly needed. It was decided, after a little half-hearted opposition on the part of the civilian participants in the council, to strike a brief hard blow, which would round out the German acquisitions in the East by advancing the line of occupation to the eastern boundaries of Latvia and Esthonia and which would bring in a quantity of booty in the shape of war material.

The original armistice had provided for a period of seven days' notice before the resumption of hostilities. The Germans interpreted Trotzky's refusal to sign the peace as an automatic denunciation of the armistice; and their advance began on February 18. Everything turned out as Lenin had foreseen. There was no refusal on the part of the German troops to march, and there was no organized Russian force to meet them. So complete was the disorganization of the Russian Front that there was little successful effort to carry out such passive defensive measures as the blowing up of bridges or the removal and destruction of munition stocks.

The German Military Command announced on February 16 that the armistice would come to an end at noon on the 18th. On the morning of the 18th the Bolshevik Party Central Committee met to consider the new situation. All the news was disquieting. German airplanes had appeared over Dvinsk; Prince Leopold of Bavaria, commander of the German Eastern Front, had broadcast a speech proclaiming that Germany's mission was to ward off the "moral infection" of Bolshevism; an offensive against Reval was expected at any moment. Lenin urged an immediate proposal to Germany to resume peace negotiations. Trotzky was in favor of holding out

5 Trotzky, *Soch.*, XVII, Part I, 103–104.

a little longer; the offensive might bring about a serious explosion in Germany. If this did not occur there would still be time to propose peace. Lenin was defeated on this issue by one vote; seven members of the Central Committee were against his proposal, while six voted for it.

This decision was reversed, however, on the evening of the same day. The Germans had already occupied Dvinsk and were advancing everywhere without meeting serious resistance. Lenin spoke passionately and bitterly, insisting that it was impossible "to play with war" and that the breakdown of the Revolution was inevitable, unless a clearcut decision were taken. If Esthonia, Latvia and Finland were given up the Revolution was still not lost.

Trotzky protested against the phrase "playing with war" and reminded Lenin that the latter had proposed "to feel out the Germans." Apparently, however, he believed that the demonstration had gone far enough, and by changing his vote he gave Lenin a majority for the proposal to make immediate peace overtures. A radio message was promptly despatched to Berlin, under the signatures of Lenin and Trotzky, protesting against the German troop movements, expressing readiness to sign peace on the terms proposed by the delegations of the Central Powers at Brest-Litovsk and promising to give without delay a reply to precise conditions of peace offered by the German Government.

This Soviet message was sent to Berlin on the 19th. For three anxious days no reply was received, while the Germans continued to advance. The council of People's Commissars appealed to the workers, peasants and soldiers "to let our enemies know that we are ready to defend the conquests of the Revolution to the last drop of blood" and a second appeal, written by Trotzky, called for the destruction of railroad communication, of food and munition stores, for the organization of workers' battalions to dig trenches, for the shooting of "enemy agents, speculators, bandits, hooligans,

counterrevolutionary agitators and German spies."

It is doubtful whether these appeals would have evoked any effective popular resistance if the Germans had endeavored to occupy Petrograd and Moscow. But such a large-scale operation, which would have involved the employment of considerable numbers of troops, did not enter into their plans. What the German Government and the German Supreme Command regarded as practicable and desirable was set forth plainly enough in the new peace conditions, which were received on February 22. They were considerably more unfavorable than the original conditions of Brest-Litovsk. The chief new demands were the evacuation of Latvia and Esthonia by Russian troops and Red Guards; the immediate conclusion of peace between Russia and the Ukrainian People's Republic and the withdrawal of Russian troops and Red Guards from Ukraina and Finland. All this pointed clearly to a German protectorate over Ukraina and Finland, combined with German annexation, in one form or another, of the Baltic Provinces.

The harsh new terms were accompanied by a sharp intimation that they must be accepted within forty-eight hours, that Soviet representatives must immediately set out for Brest-Litovsk and sign the treaty within three days. Ratification must follow within two weeks. There was to be no loophole for a repetition of Trotzky's former tactics of delay and evasion.

Lenin was heartily weary of what he called "the policy of the revolutionary phrase." At a session of the Central Committee on February 23 he reinforced the German ultimatum with one of his own. For a revolutionary war an army was necessary and Russia had no army. Therefore the terms must be accepted. Otherwise he would withdraw from the Central Committee and from the Soviet Government.

This threat was of decisive importance. Trotzky and Dzerzhinsky, who were both unreconciled to signing the peace, agreed that it was unthinkable to organize success-ful resistance if a considerable part of the Party, headed by Lenin, was unwilling to coöperate. When the question of accepting the German conditions was put to a vote seven of the fifteen members present voted in favor of acceptance. Four irreconcilable members, Bukharin, Lomov, Uritzky, and Bubnov, voted in the negative. Four others, Trotzky, Dzerzhinsky, Joffe, and Krestin-sky, abstained from voting. They would not support Lenin; but they would not assume the responsibility of causing his withdrawal from the Party and the Govern-ment.

In these last stages of the negotiations Trotzky had based some hope on military aid, at least of a passive character, from the Allies. The senior diplomats were all definitely anti-Bolshevik in sentiment; but such men as Colonel Raymond Robins, head of the American Red Cross Mission in Russia, R. H. Bruce Lockhart, formerly British Consul in Moscow, who was playing the difficult and thankless rôle of an un-official British diplomatic agent with vague and undefined powers, and Captain Jacques Sadoul, of the French Military Mission, believed in the stability of the Soviet regime and argued that a friendly policy on the part of the Allied Governments might keep Russia as at least a potential enemy of Germany. Some offers of limited and unofficial military cooperation apparently came from the French Military Mission; and at the height of the German offensive Colonel J. A. Ruggles, of the American Military Mission, and Captain Sadoul had a meeting with Lenin, where it was agreed that, if the Germans advanced beyond Pskov, Allied troop units would assist in blowing up bridges and destroying war material. About the same time Trotzky told Lockhart that, if an Allied promise of sup-port were forthcoming, he would sway the decision of the Soviet Government in favor of war. In view of the closeness of the division in the Central Committee Trotzky might easily have carried out this assur-ance. But the British Government was un-willing to commit itself and Lockhart's inquiry went unanswered.

The question of the propriety of ac-cepting military instructors and supplies from the "imperialistic" Allied Govern-ments was hotly debated within the Party Central Committee on February 22 and Trotzky obtained a majority of one vote for his view that aid should be accepted, on condition that the Bolsheviki retained complete independence in foreign policy and gave no political promises. Lenin was not present at this session, but, character-istically enough, he agreed with Trotzky's practical view on this question and put himself on record with a scribbled note which read: "I ask to add my vote in favor of taking potatoes and arms from the ban-dits of Anglo-French imperialism."

Even after the peace had been signed Trotzky seems to have kept in view the possibility of Allied military cooperation. On March 5, two days after the Treaty of Brest-Litovsk had been signed, but before it had been ratified, Trotzky gave Robins a written statement asking whether, in the event of a Soviet refusal to ratify the Peace or of a subsequent breach with Germany, "the Soviet Government could rely on the support of the United States, of Great Britain and of France in the struggle against Germany"; what would be the na-ture of this assistance; what would America do if Japan should occupy Siberia.

Lockhart talked with Trotzky on the same day and telegraphed to the British Foreign Office, recommending that aid should be extended to Russia on the ground that "if ever the Allies have had a chance in Russia since the Revolution the Germans have given it to them by the exorbitant peace terms they have imposed."[6]

The representations of Robins in Washington and of Lockhart in London did not lead to any positive results. Presi-

6 C. K. Cumming and W. W. Pettit, eds., *Russian-American Relations, March 1917–March 1920* (New York, 1920), p. 82.

dent Wilson did, indeed, make two sympathetic gestures in Russia's direction. One was in his famous "fourteen points" speech, delivered on January 8, in direct response to an appeal from Edgar Sisson, representative of the Committee on Public Information in Russia, couched in the following terms:[7] "If President will restate anti-imperialistic war aims and democratic peace requisites of America in thousand words or less, in short, almost placard paragraphs, short sentences, I can get it fed into Germany in great quantities in German translation, and can utilize Russian version potently in army and everywhere."

Wilson's reference to Russia in the sixth point of this speech was obviously designed to encourage the Soviet delegation at Brest-Litovsk to resist the German demands. It read as follows:

The evacuation of all Russian territory and such a settlement of all questions affecting Russia as will secure the best and freest cooperation of all the nations in the world in obtaining for her an unhampered and unembarrassed opportunity for the independent determination of her own political development and national policy and assure her of a sincere welcome into the society of free nations under institutions of her own choosing; and, more than a welcome, assistance also of every kind that she may need and may herself desire. The treatment accorded Russia by her sister nations in the months to come will be the acid test of their goodwill, of their comprehension of her needs as distinguished from their own interests, and of their intelligent and unselfish sympathy.

Wilson's second gesture took the form of a friendly message to the Fourth All-Russian Congress of Soviets, which opened on March 14 to discuss the ratification of the Peace of Brest-Litovsk. The message spoke of "the sincere sympathy which the people of the United States feel for the Russian people" and continued: "Although the Government of the United States is unhappily not in a position to render the direct and effective aid it would wish to render, I beg to assure the people of Russia through the Congress that it will avail itself of every opportunity to secure for Russia once more complete sovereignty and independence in her own affairs and full restoration to her great role in the life of Europe and the modern world."

The message had little immediate concrete significance, but it did seem to reflect a not unfriendly attitude on the part of Wilson toward the new regime. Whether from a sheer oversight on the part of the Soviet leaders or whether because of conviction that American and Allied aid was a mirage and an illusion, the Congress answered Wilson's soft words with a trumpet blast of uncompromising revolutionism,[8] "expressing to all the peoples which are perishing and suffering from the horrors of imperialist war its sympathy and its firm conviction that the happy time is not far away when the working masses of all bourgeois countries will overthrow the yoke of capital and establish the socialist order, which alone can assure a stable and just peace, and at the same time the culture and welfare of all the toilers."

The actions of the Soviet Government in quitting the War, repudiating Russia's foreign obligations and issuing appeals for world revolution had alienated the Allied Governments to such an extent that it is not surprising that proposals for collaboration with it fell on deaf and unfriendly ears. And indeed in retrospect it is difficult to see how the Allies could have effectively served their own cause by offering active military cooperation to the Soviet regime. The Russian masses obviously would not fight; the sending of small forces and quantities of war supplies would have been futile, while the despatch of a large expedi-

[7] Edgar G. Sisson, *One Hundred Red Days: A Personal Chronicle of the Bolshevik Revolution* (New Haven, 1931), p. 205.

[8] Yuri V. Kluchnikov and Andrei Sabanin, *Mezhdunarodnaya politika noveischego vremeni v dogovorakh, notakh i deklaratsiakh* (Moscow, 1925–1928), II (1926), 135.

tion or the sending into a disorganized and chaotic country of considerable stocks of munitions would have been a risky adventure.

After the decision to accept the German terms had been taken by the Bolshevik Party Central Committee there was a good deal of discussion as to who should assume the onerous and undesired function of going to Brest-Litovsk to sign the treaty. Trotzky refused to go; he had resigned as Commissar for Foreign Affairs and was preparing to devote his boundless energy to the new post, with which his name will always be associated, of Commissar for War. A delegation headed by G. Y. Sokolnikov, a member of the Central Committee who had supported Lenin's attitude on the question of the peace, proceeded to Brest-Litovsk and signed the Treaty on March 3. Sokolnikov ostentatiously refused to discuss or even to read with any care the terms of the document which was submitted for his signature, in order to emphasize the point that the Peace was a matter of pure dictation, not of agreement. The final text of the Treaty was made still worse from the Russian standpoint, by the insertion, at Turkey's request, of a new clause which provided for the evacuation of the Kars, Batum and Ardaghan districts of the Caucasus and the cession of this territory to Turkey.

To Russians who thought in nationalist terms the Brest-Litovsk Peace must have seemed the climax of the country's humiliation and misfortune. It swept away at one stroke the fruits of two centuries of expansion toward the West and South. It stripped the former Russian Empire of almost a third of its population; of almost eighty per cent of its iron and ninety per cent of its coal production, of about half its industrial plant and equipment. It threw Russia back from the Black and Baltic seas.

From a revolutionary, as well as from a nationalist, standpoint the Treaty was a cause for bitter heartburning, with its clauses demanding the withdrawal of Russian troops from Soviet Ukraina and Finland and cessation of revolutionary agitation and propaganda both in Germany and Austria-Hungary and in Ukraina and Finland. The Left-Socialist Revolutionaries were strongly opposed to the Treaty and quit the Government on this issue. Bukharin and his "Left" Communists continued to fulminate against Lenin's peace policy in their organ, *The Communist.*

But Lenin, after forcing through the decision to sign the Peace by the threat of his resignation, pushed steadily on toward ratification. A Party Congress, attended by a small number of delegates, met on March 6, 7, and 8. Here Lenin repeated his familiar arguments. There was no army; it was impossible to hold out. "We should have perished at the least attack of the Germans; we should have been the prey of the enemy within a few days." He compared Russia's position with that of Prussia when Napoleon imposed the Peace of Tilsit; and offered some consolation to the more militant delegates by saying: "Yes, of course we break the Treaty; we have already broken it thirty or forty times."[9] Probably Lenin had in mind the giving of aid with arms and military instructors to the Red Finns, which was, of course, a contravention of the terms of the Treaty.

Bukharin summed up the case for the critics of the Treaty: he argued that Lenin's theory of a "breathing-space" was unsound, because a short respite would not permit the reorganization of the railroads and the military training of the population. Bukharin also complained that the Peace compelled the Bolsheviki to renounce internationalist propaganda, "which is the sharpest weapon at our disposal."

The Congress upheld Lenin by 28 votes to 12, with four abstentions, passing a resolution to the effect that "the ratification of the most oppressive and humiliating Peace Treaty is necessary because of the

[9] *Sedmoi Syezd RKP(b): Stenograficheskii otchet* (Moscow, 1923), p. 29.

incapacity of our army and because of the necessity of exploiting even the slightest possibility of obtaining a breathing-space before the assault of imperialism upon the Soviet Republic." The Brest-Litovsk Peace had called not only for the cessation of revolutionary propaganda against the Governments of the Central Powers, but also for the demobilization of the Russian army; and therefore it is understandable why the Congress resolution on war and peace, which called for general military training and ended with the declaration that "the socialist proletariat of Russia with all its forces and all the resources at its disposal will support the brotherly revolutionary movement of the proletariat of all countries" was kept secret for almost a year, until the breakdown of the German Imperial regime had made it possible to end the Brest-Litovsk Treaty. The final ratification of the Treaty took place at the Fourth Congress of Soviets on March 15 by a vote of 784 to 261, with 115 abstentions. Among the latter were 64 "Left Communists."

* * *

At Brest-Litovsk the Russian Revolution, flushed with its easy triumphal march over the territory of the former Tsarist Empire, encountered embattled German militarism, and was obliged to retreat. The weapon of propaganda, effective enough against Kornilov and Kaledin, was of little avail against the gray-uniformed legions of Hindenburg and Ludendorff. It is a striking proof of Lenin's perspicacity and freedom from selfdelusion that he could reckon the chances against successful resistance to Germany just as accurately as a few months earlier he had calculated the

chances in favor of the overthrow of Kerensky. Seen in retrospect the signature of the Peace was inevitable; the only alternative would have been a collapse of the Soviet Government. Yet this inevitable act was so intensely distasteful that it required a strong combination of willpower and tact on Lenin's part to push through the ratification of the Peace without bringing about a split in the Party.

The consequences of Brest-Litovsk would have been far more serious for the Soviet regime if Germany had not been on the eve of decisive defeat on the Western Front. There is no convincing evidence to show that the Bolshevik propaganda which filtered in among the German troops on the Eastern Front or the surreptitious communications which passed between the Soviet Ambassador in Berlin, Joffe, and the left-wing leaders of the German Social Democrats played more than a minor role in undermining German morale and hastening the final debâcle. The German military Empire, and the Brest-Litovsk system for East Europe, which was one of its last diplomatic achievements, were broken on the battlefields of France. Had Germany emerged from the World War victorious or at least strong enough to bargain for a free hand in the East in exchange for territorial concessions in the West, it might well have gone hard with the Bolshevik Revolution. For the subsequent Allied intervention in Russia, feeble and halfhearted, intermittent and constantly thwarted by the cross-purposes and conflicting interests of its initiators, was a far less serious threat to Soviet existence than intervention of the type which Ludendorff and Hoffman would probably have sponsored, if their system had survived the shock of military defeat.

THESES ON THE QUESTION OF THE IMMEDIATE CONCLUSION OF A SEPARATE AND ANNEXATIONIST PEACE

VLADIMIR LENIN

Lenin's "Theses," presented to leading members of his party on January 21, 1918, embody the results of his strenuous efforts to develop a viable foreign policy guided by Marxist-Leninist theory. The objective of a "democratic peace," as proposed in his "Declaration on Peace" of November 1917, had been evaded by the Western Allies and rejected by the Germans. An unflinching realist, intent upon preserving the new Bolshevik power at any cost, Lenin was compelled to seek a new approach; in his "Theses" he developed several principles of utmost importance to subsequent Soviet policy. Thus. he concluded that since the exact date of the world revolution could not be calculated, it was necessary to dig in for a long, stubborn struggle. He also suggested that some Marxian principles might be reinterpreted or even set aside when they appeared to interfere with the central task of strengthening the socialist revolution, and he argued that preservation of the new socialist state in Russia might be the best of all possible ways to hasten the advent of world revolution. As William Henry Chamberlin has explained above, Lenin's colleagues rejected his arguments for immediate peace with the Germans until the actual advance of German troops forced them to capitulate.

1. THE position of the Russian revolution at the present moment is that nearly all the workers and the vast majority of the peasants are undoubtedly in favor of Soviet government and of the Socialist revolution which it has started. To that extent the socialist revolution in Russia is assured.

2. At the same time, the civil war, provoked by the frantic resistance of the wealthy classes, who fully realize that they are faced with the last, decisive fight for the preservation of private ownership of the land and means of production, has not yet reached its climax. The victory of Soviet government in this war is assured, but some time must inevitably elapse, no little exertion of effort will inevitably be demanded, a certain period of acute economic disruption and chaos, such as attend all wars, and civil war in particular, is inevitable, before the resistance of the bourgeoisie is crushed.

3. Furthermore, this resistance, in its less active and non-military forms—sabotage, corruption of the declassed elements and of agents of the bourgeoisie, who worm their way into the ranks of the Socialists in order to ruin their cause, and so on and so forth—has proved so stubborn and capable of assuming such diversified forms, that the fight to counter it will inevitably still take some time, and, in its main forms, is scarcely likely to end before several months. And unless the passive and covert resistance of the bourgeoisie and its supporters is definitely crushed, the Socialist revolution cannot possibly succeed.

4. Lastly, the organizational problems of the Socialist reformation of Russia are so immense and difficult that their solution—in view of the abundance of petty-bourgeois fellow-travellers of the Socialist proletariat, and of the latter's low cultural level—will demand a fairly long time.

From V. Lenin, "Theses on the Question of the Immediate Conclusion of a Separate and Annexationist Peace," trans. in Jane Degras, *Soviet Documents on Foreign Policy* (London and New York, 1951), I, 34–39. Published by the Oxford University Press for the Royal Institute of International Affairs and used with their permission.

5. All these circumstances taken together are such as to make it perfectly clear that for the success of Socialism in Russia a certain amount of time, not less than several months at least, will be necessary, during which the hands of the Socialist Government must be absolutely free for the job of vanquishing the bourgeoisie in our own country first, and of arranging widespread and far-reaching mass organizational work.

6. The situation of the Socialist revolution in Russia must form the basis of any definition of the international tasks of our Soviet state, for the international situation in the fourth year of the war is such that it is quite impossible to calculate the probable moment of outbreak of revolution or overthrow of any of the European imperialist governments (including the German). That the Socialist revolution in Europe must come, and will come, is beyond doubt. All our hopes for the *final* victory of Socialism are founded on this certainty and on this scientific prognosis. Our propagandist activities in general, and the organization of fraternization in particular, must be intensified and extended. But it would be a mistake to base the tactics of the Russian Socialist Government on an attempt to determine whether the European, and especially the German, Socialist revolution will take place in the next six months (or some such brief period), or not. Inasmuch as it is quite impossible to determine this, all such attempts, objectively speaking, would be nothing but a blind gamble.

7. The peace negotiations in Brest-Litovsk have by this date—7 [20] January 1918—made it perfectly clear that the upper hand in the German government (which leads the other governments of the Quadruple Alliance by the halter) has undoubtedly been gained by the military party, which has virtually already presented Russia with an ultimatum (and it is to be expected, most certainly to be expected, that any day now it will be presented formally). The ultimatum is as follows: either

the continuation of the war, or an annexationist peace, i.e., peace on condition that we surrender all the territory we occupy, while the Germans retain *all* the territory they occupy and impose upon us an indemnity (outwardly disguised as payment for the maintenance of prisoners)—an indemnity of about three thousand million rubles, payment over a period of several years.

8. The Socialist government of Russia is faced with the question—a question which brooks no postponement—of whether to accept this annexationist peace now, or at once to wage a revolutionary war. Actually speaking, no middle course is possible. No further postponement is now feasible, for we have *already* done everything possible and impossible artificially to protract the negotiations.

9. Examining the arguments in favor of an immediate revolutionary war, the first we encounter is the argument that a separate peace at this juncture would, objectively speaking, be tantamount to an agreement with the German imperialists, an "imperialistic deal," and so forth, and that, consequently, such a peace would be at complete variance with the fundamental principles of proletarian internationalism.

But this argument is clearly incorrect. Workers who lose a strike and sign terms for the resumption of work which are unfavorable to them and favorable to the capitalists, do not betray Socialism. Only those betray Socialism who barter to secure advantages for a section of the workers in exchange for advantages to the capitalists; only such agreements are impermissible in principle.

Whoever calls a war with German imperialism a defensive and just war, but actually receives support from the Anglo-French imperialists, and conceals from the people secret treaties concluded with them, betrays Socialism. Whoever, without concealing anything from the people, and without concluding any secret treaties with the imperialists, agrees to terms of peace which are unfavorable to the weak nation and favorable to the imperialists of one group, if at the given moment he has no strength to continue the war, does not betray Socialism in the slightest degree.

10. Another argument in favor of immediate war is that, by concluding peace, we, objectively speaking, become agents of German imperialism, for we afford it the opportunity to release troops from our front, surrender to it millions of prisoners, and the like. But this argument too is clearly incorrect, for a revolutionary war at the present juncture would, objectively speaking, make us agents of Anglo-French imperialism, by providing it with forces which would promote its aims. The British bluntly offered our commander-in-chief, Krylenko, one hundred rubles per month for every one of our soldiers provided we continued the war. Even if we did not take a single kopek from the Anglo-French, we nevertheless would be helping them, objectively speaking, by diverting part of the German army.

From that point of view, in neither case would we be entirely escaping some sort of imperialist tie, and it is obvious that it is impossible to do so entirely without overthrowing world imperialism. The correct conclusion from this is that the moment a Socialist government triumphs in any one country, questions must be decided, not from the point of view of whether this or that imperialism is preferable, but exclusively from the point of view of the conditions which best make for the development and consolidation of the Socialist revolution which has already begun.

In other words, the underlying principle of our tactics must not be, which of the two imperialisms is it more profitable to aid at this juncture, but rather, how can the Socialist revolution be most surely and reliably ensured the possibility of consolidating itself, or, at least, of maintaining itself in one country until it is joined by other countries.

11. It is said that the German Social-Democratic opponents of the war have now become "defeatists" and are requesting us not to yield to German imperialism. But we recognized defeatism only in respect to *one's own* imperialist bourgeoisie, and we have always discountenanced victory over an alien imperialism, victory attained in formal or actual alliance with a "friendly" imperialism, as a method impermissible in principle and generally obnoxious.

This argument is therefore only a modification of the previous one. If the German Left Social-Democrats were proposing that we delay concluding a separate peace for a *definite* period, and guaranteed revolutionary action in Germany in this period, the question *might* assume a different aspect for us. But far from saying this, the German Lefts formally declare: "Stick it out as long as you can, but decide the question from the standpoint of the state of affairs in the *Russian* Socialist revolution, for we cannot promise you anything positive regarding the German revolution."

12. It is said that in a number of party statements we positively "promised" a revolutionary war, and that by concluding a separate peace we would be going back on our word.

That is not true. We said that in the era of imperialism it was *necessary* for a Socialist government to *"prepare for and wage"* a revolutionary war; we said this as a means of countering abstract pacifism and the theory that "defense of the fatherland" must be completely rejected in the era of imperialism, and, lastly, as a means of countering the purely egoistical instincts of a part of the soldiery, but we never gave any pledge to start a revolutionary war without taking account of how far it is possible to wage it at any given moment.

Unquestionably, even at this juncture we must *prepare* for a revolutionary war. We are carrying out this promise, as we have in general carried out all our promises that could be carried out at once; we annulled the secret treaties, offered all nations a fair peace, and several times did our best to drag out peace negotiations so as to give other nations a chance to join us.

But the question whether it is possible to wage a revolutionary war *now and at once* must be decided exclusively from the standpoint of whether material conditions permit it, and of the interests of the Socialist revolution which has already begun.

13. Having weighed up the arguments in favor of an immediate revolutionary war, we are forced to the conclusion that such a policy might perhaps answer the human yearning for the beautiful, dramatic and striking, but that it would absolutely ignore the objective relation of class forces and material factors in the present stage of the Socialist revolution which has begun.

14. There can be no doubt but that our army is absolutely in no condition at the present moment, and will not be for the next few weeks (and probably for the next few months), to resist a German offensive successfully; firstly, owing to the extreme fatigue and exhaustion of the majority of the soldiers, coupled with the incredible chaos in the matter of victualling, replacement of the overfatigued, etc.: secondly, owing to the utter unfitness of our horses, which would doom our artillery to inevitable destruction; and thirdly, owing to the utter impossibility of defending the coast from Riga to Revel, which affords the enemy a certain chance of conquering the rest of Livonia, and then Estonia, and of outflanking a large part of our forces, and lastly, of capturing Petrograd.

15. Further, there is not the slightest doubt that the peasant majority of our army would at the present juncture unreservedly declare in favor of an annexationist peace, and not of an immediate revolutionary war; for the Socialist reorganization of the army, the merging of the Red Guard detachments with it, and the like, have only just begun.

With the army completely democratized, to wage war in defiance of the wishes of the majority of the soldiers would be sheer recklessness, while to create a really staunch and ideologically-strong Socialist workers' and peasants' army will require months and months, at least.

16. The poor peasants in Russia are capable of supporting a Socialist revolution led by the working class, but they are not capable of a serious revolutionary war immediately, at the present juncture. To ignore this objective relation of class forces in the present instance would be a fatal error.

17. Consequently, the situation at present in regard to a revolutionary war is as follows:

If the German revolution were to break out and triumph in the coming three or four months, the tactics of an immediate revolutionary war might perhaps not ruin our Socialist revolution.

If, however, the German revolution does not eventuate in the next few months, the course of events, if the war is continued, will inevitably be such that a smashing defeat will compel Russia to conclude a far more disadvantageous separate peace, a peace, moreover, which would be concluded, not by a Socialist government, but by some other (for example, a bloc of the bourgeois Rada and the Chernovites, or something similar). For the peasant army, which is unendurably exhausted by the war, will, after the first defeats—and very likely within a matter not of months but of weeks—overthrow the Socialist workers' government.

18. Such being the state of affairs, it would be absolutely impermissible tactics to stake the fate of the Socialist revolution which has begun in Russia merely on the chance that the German revolution may begin in the immediate future, within a period measurable in weeks. Such tactics would be a reckless gamble. We have no right to take such risks.

19. And the German revolution will not be jeopardized, as far as its objective foundations are concerned, if we conclude a separate peace. Probably the chauvinist intoxication will weaken it for a time, but Germany's position will remain extremely

grave, the war with Britain and America will be a protracted one, and the aggressive imperialism of both sides has been fully and completely exposed. A Socialist Soviet Republic in Russia will stand as a living example to the peoples of all countries, and the propaganda and revolutionizing effect of this example will be immense. There— the bourgeois system and an absolutely naked war of aggrandizement of two groups of marauders. Here—peace and a Socialist Soviet Republic.

20. In concluding a separate peace we free ourselves *as much as is possible at the present moment* from both hostile imperialist groups, we take advantage of their mutual enmity and warfare—which hamper concerted action on their part against us— and for a certain period have our hands free to advance and consolidate the Socialist revolution. The reorganization of Russia on the basis of the dictatorship of the proletariat, and the nationalization of the banks and large-scale industry, coupled with exchange of products in kind between the towns and the small peasants-consumers' societies, is economically quite feasible, provided we are assured a few months in which to work in peace. And such a reorganization will render Socialism invincible both in Russia and all over the world, and at the same time will create a solid economic basis for a mighty workers' and peasants' Red Army.

21. A really revolutionary war at this juncture would mean a war waged by a Socialist republic on the bourgeois countries, with the aim—an aim clearly defined and fully approved by the Socialist army— of overthrowing the bourgeoisie in other countries. However, we *obviously* cannot set ourselves this aim at the *given* moment. Objectively, we would be fighting now for the liberation of Poland, Lithuania and Courland. But no Marxist, without flying in the fact of the principles of Marxism and of Socialism generally, can deny that the interests of Socialism are higher than the interests of the right of nations to self-determination. Our Socialist republic has done all it could, and continues to do all it can to give effect to the right to self-determination of Finland, the Ukraine, etc. But if the concrete position of affairs is such that the existence of the Socialist republic is being imperilled at the present moment on account of the violation of the right to self-determination of several nations (Poland, Lithuania, Courland, etc.), naturally the preservation of the Socialist republic has the higher claim.

Consequently, whoever says, "We cannot sign a shameful, indecent, etc., peace, betray Poland, and so forth," fails to observe that by concluding peace on condition that Poland is liberated, he would only *still further* be strengthening German imperialism against England, Belgium, Serbia and other countries. Peace on condition of the liberation of Poland, Lithuania, and Courland would be a "patriotic" peace *from the point of view of Russia*, but would none the less be a peace with the *annexationists*, with the German imperialists.

The West and the Comintern 1917-1920

II

ISOLATION, AND PLANS FOR WORLD REVOLUTION

EDWARD HALLETT CARR

Edward Hallett Carr, one of Great Britain's most authoritative students of the Soviet Union, has had several distinguished careers. From 1916 to 1936 he served in the Foreign Office, and thus acquired extensive knowledge of diplomacy at first hand. In 1936 he entered the academic world, as Professor of International Politics at the University College of Wales, Aberystwyth; in 1953 he became Tutor in Politics at Balliol College, Oxford, and since 1955 he has been a Fellow of Trinity College, Cambridge. In his third profession, that of writer, he has won world-wide recognition, with works which range from studies of Dostoevsky, Bakunin, Alexander Herzen, and Karl Marx to a number of books on international relations and the Soviet Union. His major work, *A History of Russia*, of which six volumes have appeared, displays great erudition and originality. The following excerpts from Volume III of the *History* deal with the Bolsheviks' early relations with Western Europe, the Allied intervention and its diplomatic consequences, and the establishment of the Comintern—the Third (Communist) International. The latter organization deserves special attention as the coordinating organ of international communism and as an agency of Soviet foreign policy.

IMPROVED Soviet relations with Germany were the counterpart of deteriorating relations with the allies, which followed an inverse variation of the same pattern. In the Soviet attitude to Germany, the *leitmotif* of conciliation and accommodation gained ground throughout the summer of 1918. In the Soviet attitude to the allies, the abortive movement towards accommodation in February and March faded away in face of the uncompromising character of allied hostility and the imminent threat of allied intervention. After the summer of 1918 no serious doubt could be entertained of allied determination to destroy the regime and to give assistance to any who sought to destroy it. The British landing at Murmansk at the end of June was followed by a British and French landing at Archangel at the beginning of August; during August American troops joined the British and French in north Russia and the Japanese in Vladivostok; in south Russia the "white" forces coalesced under the leadership of Denikin with allied encouragement, and, a little later, active allied support. The counter-revolutionary conspiracies of July and August in central Russia were organized and financed from abroad. On August 31 the official British agent, Lockhart, was arrested on the charge of complicity in them, and two days later a detailed Soviet statement denounced "the conspiracy organized by Anglo-French diplomats." The last bridge had been broken. No form of appeasement or conciliation was any longer open to the Soviet Government.

This conclusion, while accepted without qualification in regard to Great Britain, France and Japan, was applied with the utmost reluctance to the United States. From the first days of the revolution the impression had prevailed that sentiment in the United States was more sympathetic to the Bolsheviks than in any other capitalist country. In November 1917 Trotsky had speculated that "American diplomats understand that they cannot defeat the Russian revolution and therefore want to enter into friendly relations with us, calculating that this will be an excellent means of competing with German and, in particular, with British capitalists after the war." Now Soviet policy, relying on the unconcealed American antipathy to Japan and on Wilson's obvious reluctance to participate in intervention, endeavoured to drive a wedge between the allied governments by ostentatious gestures of friendliness to the United States. When Robins returned to Washington in May 1918, he carried with him detailed offers of concessions in Soviet Russia for American capitalists. As late as August 4, 1918, a naïvely worded note was addressed to Poole, the American consul in Moscow, as "the representative of a nation which, to use your own words, will take no action against the Soviets," protesting against the intervention of "Anglo-French armed forces" in Soviet territory, and conveying assurances of unalterable friendship for the American people. A month later

Chicherin, in a speech to VTsIK,* explained that American citizens were not being interned with those of the other allied powers "because, although the United States Government was compelled by its allies to agree to participation in intervention, so far only formally, its decision is not regarded by us as irrevocable." But within a few weeks this agreeable fiction of American friendship had become untenable. Two American regiments had landed at Vladivostok; others were soon to join the allied forces on other fronts; and the RSFSR was faced with a solid phalanx of interventionist powers. At the beginning of October 1918 a resolution of VTsIK on the international situation grouped together "the Anglo-French, American and Japanese imperialist robbers" under a single rubric. The circle had been closed.

These catastrophic developments left a lasting mark on Soviet thought. The action of the allies confirmed and intensified the ideological aspect of Soviet foreign policy and made international revolution once more its principal plank, if only in the interest of national self-preservation. The vital question whether the coexistence of capitalist and socialist states was possible had at any rate been left open by the first pronouncements of the Soviet Government, and notably by the decree on peace; in some, at any rate, of the pronouncements of the spring and summer of 1918 it had been answered in the affirmative. Now it seemed irrefutably clear that this coexistence was impossible, at any rate with the countries of the Entente, and that revolutionary propaganda directed to the workers of these countries was the most effective, and indeed the only effective, weapon in the hands of a government whose military resources were still negligible. Soviet foreign policy from the autumn of 1918 to the end of 1920 was in all probability more specifi-

---

* The Central Executive Committee of the All-Russian Congress of Soviets. It was the supreme government body between sessions of the Congress of Soviets.—Ed.

cally and exclusively coloured by international and revolutionary aims than at any other time. World revolution was in a certain sense the counterpart in Soviet foreign policy of war communism in economic policy. In form a logical, though extreme, development of communist doctrine, it was in fact imposed on the regime, not so much by doctrinal orthodoxy, as by the desperate plight of the civil war.

The undeclared war which began with the allied military landings in the summer of 1918 meant a rupture of such quasi-diplomatic relations as had been established in the preceding winter and spring. At the end of July 1918 the allied representatives, who had retired from Petrograd to Vologda five months earlier, left Russia altogether or withdrew to occupied territory, taking with them the military missions through which some contact with the Soviet authorities had been maintained. After the assassination of Mirbach and the risings against the Soviet Government in July 1918, the few allied representatives, civil and military, left in Moscow were regarded as agents of counter-revolutionary conspiracy. Lockhart, after four weeks of confinement, was released and allowed to leave the country, and Litvinov was expelled from Great Britain as a reprisal for the expulsion of Lockhart. The closing of the channels of normal intercourse with the outside world stimulated the use of the weapons of "open diplomacy"; as Chicherin afterwards put it, "we write fewer notes to governments and more appeals to the working classes." On August 1, 1918, Sovnarkom issued an appeal to "the labouring masses of France, England, America, Italy and Japan," concluding with the words:

Compelled to struggle against allied capital, which to the chains imposed on us by German imperialism seeks to add new chains, we turn to you with the call:

Long live the solidarity of the workers of the whole world!

Long live the solidarity of the French,

English, American, Italian proletariat with the Russian!

Down with the gangsters of international imperialism!

Long live the international revolution!

Long live peace among the nations![1]

A few days later Chicherin commented in an official note to the American consul:

At this very moment we are speaking to the countries whose armies are taking the field against us with open violence, and we turn to their peoples with the call: "Peace to the cottages!"[2]

Towards the end of August *Pravda* published an open letter from Lenin himself to the American workers:

The American millionaires, those modern slave-owners, have opened a particularly tragic page in the bloody history of bloody imperialism by giving their consent . . . to the armed campaign of the Anglo-Japanese beasts for the purpose of crushing the first socialist republic. . . . We are in the position of a beleaguered fortress until other detachments of the international socialist revolution come to our aid. Such detachments exist, they are more numerous than ours. . . . We are unconquerable because the world proletarian revolution is unconquerable.[3]

Meanwhile the part played a year earlier by *Die Fackel* and *Der Völkerfriede* among the German invaders was now taken over by the innumerable pamphlets and broad-sheets in English and French distributed to the allied troops landed on Russian soil. The tale was still the same:

You will be fighting not against enemies [ran a sheet addressed to British and American troops in Archangel] but against working people like yourselves. We ask you, are you

[1] Yu. V. Klyuchnikov and A. V. Sabinin, *Mezhdunarodnaya politika noveishego vremeni v dogovorakh, notakh i deklaratsiyakh* (Moscow, 1925–1928), II, 161.

[2] *Ibid.*, p. 163; the concluding phrase is taken from the slogan of the armies of the French revolution: "War on the great houses! Peace to the cottages!"

[3] V. Lenin, *Sochineniya* (2nd ed.; Moscow, 1930–1935), XXIII, 176–189.

going to crush us? . . . Be loyal to your class and refuse to do the dirty work of your masters. . . . Go home and establish industrial republics in your own countries, and together we shall form a world-wide cooperative commonwealth.[4]

Tracts and journals prepared in the propaganda department of Narkomindel* were dropped by aeroplane over the enemy lines. The work of propaganda and indoctrination which had proved successful with German and Austrian prisoners of war was now undertaken among prisoners captured on the allied fronts. The number of prisoners was small, and the men had not experienced months or years of captivity, so that successes were relatively few. But they occurred, and were heralded as triumphs. This reversion to propaganda for world revolution in its crudest and most outspoken form was, however, part of a desperate defensive action by the forces of revolution against the embattled onslaught of the western capitalist world. It was the action of the western Powers, quite as much as of the Soviet Government, which had forced the international situation into a revolutionary setting. . . .

* * *

The year 1919 was the year of Soviet Russia's most complete isolation from the outside world. It was also the year in which Soviet foreign policy took on its most outspokenly revolutionary complexion. The two circumstances were interconnected, and it would be a mistake to attribute to premeditation the prominence assumed by the revolutionary aspect of Soviet policy at this time. Throughout 1919 the dominant factor in Soviet foreign policy, as in the Soviet economy, was the civil war, in which the enemies of the regime received the military, economic and moral support of Great Brit-

ain, France, Italy, Japan and the United States, as well as some of the lesser allies. When the war against Germany ended in November 1918, there seemed to be a good chance that allied intervention in the Russian civil war would also come to an end: the invariable pretext for this intervention up to the date of the armistice had been the need to counteract German designs. So long as this possibility existed, the Soviet Government showed itself eager to seize any opportunity for conciliation and negotiation. On November 8, 1918, the sixth All-Russian Congress of Soviets proposed to the five principal allied governments "before the whole world" to enter into negotiations for peace. Litvinov, recently expelled from Great Britain, was sent to Stockholm in the hope of establishing contact with the diplomats and journalists of western Europe; and from Stockholm on December 24, 1918, Litvinov addressed to President Wilson an appeal for peace, whose mild and deprecatory language, innocent even of the faintest allusion to the goal of world revolution, contrasted notably with Chicherin's ironical note of two months earlier or even with the original peace decree of October 26/November 8, 1917. The immediate sequel to this appeal was encouraging. A State Department official named Buckler, then at the American embassy in London, was instructed to visit Copenhagen where, in the middle of January 1919, he had three long interviews with Litvinov. Litvinov was conciliatory about the possibility of recognizing foreign debts, though Soviet Russia would want "foreign machinery and manufactured imports as a *quid pro quo.*" He undertook that propaganda against the western countries would cease when peace was made, adding explicitly that "the war declared on Russia by the allies called forth that revolutionary propaganda as a measure of retaliation," and that "Russians realize that in certain western countries conditions are not favourable for a revolution of the Russian type." When, therefore, the peace conference

[4] M. Fainsod, *International Socialism and the World War* (Cambridge, Mass., 1935), p. 184.
* The Commissariat of Foreign Affairs.—Ed.

assembled in Paris almost at the moment of the Litvinov-Buckler conversations, the prospects of an agreement seemed reasonably promising, especially as the Russian question was among the first to which the Council of Ten—the solemn conclave of the five principal allied Powers—devoted its attention. When on January 16, 1919, Lloyd George proposed to call for a "truce of God" between "all of the different governments now at war within what used to be the Russian Empire," he encountered warm sympathy from Wilson and veiled opposition from the French and Italian delegates. On January 21, when Wilson read to the council Buckler's report of his conversations with Litvinov, the proposal was approved in principle; and three days later the principal allied Powers issued an invitation by radio to "all organized groups exercising or attempting to exercise power in any part of former Russian territory" to attend a conference at Prinkipo. The Soviet Government accepted with alacrity. Its reply of February 4, 1919, showed an anxious readiness to come to terms on disputed issues. It announced that the Soviet Government "does not refuse to recognize its financial obligations to creditors who are nationals of the allied Powers"; that it "offers to guarantee the payment of interest on its loans by a certain quantity of raw materials"; and that it "is willing to grant to nationals of the allied Powers mining, timber and other concessions." It was, as Chicherin afterwards wrote, the first occasion of "an appeal to the Entente in the name of economic advantages"—an idea which became "one of the most outstanding in Lenin's foreign policy." The calculation was purely practical; the Soviet Government was prepared to pay a certain price in order to buy off the hostility of the capitalist world and obtain for itself a much-needed respite.

The Prinkipo proposal broke down owing to the refusal of "white" Russian groups, encouraged by covert French opposition; and this failure gave encouragement to the anti-Bolshevik wing of the British coalition, drawing its strength mainly from military and diplomatic circles which were most keenly conscious of the Russian defection in the war, and from financial and commercial circles which held assets and interests in Russia. Of both these groups Churchill became the outstanding spokesman. Lloyd George describes Curzon and Churchill at this time as the "two powerful men in the government who were zealous and untiring advocates of the policy of intervention." While Curzon remained in London, replacing Balfour at the Foreign Office, Churchill as Secretary of State for War made frequent journeys to Paris. On February 15, 1919, in the absence of Lloyd George and Wilson, Churchill made a strong appeal to the Council of Ten in favour of sending "volunteers, technical experts, arms, munitions, tanks, aeroplanes, etc." to Russia and "arming the anti-Bolshevik forces," and repeated the plea at length at a further meeting on the same afternoon. Balfour extricated himself from an awkward situation by proposing that the question should be adjourned till the following week. What exactly happened behind the scenes is unknown. But the discussion at the Council of Ten was never resumed. A week later the American delegation reported to Washington that "Churchill's project is dead and there is little danger that it will be revived again by the conference."

The defeat of the Churchill project balanced the failure of Prinkipo; and Lloyd George and Wilson, back in Paris, now initiated a further attempt at pacification. On March 8, 1919, William Bullitt, a junior official of the American delegation in Paris, arrived in Petrograd on a confidential mission with unofficial instructions from Lloyd George and Wilson to ascertain, without committing anyone, what peace terms would be accepted by the Soviet Government. Having conferred with Chicherin and Litvinov, he went on with them on March 10 to Moscow, where he had daily conversations with them as well as an interview with Lenin; and on March 14 he received from Chicherin a memorandum dated March 12, 1919, containing the text of proposals which, if made by the allied governments before April 10, the Soviet Government undertook to accept. The most important of the proposals were a cessation of all hostilities in Russia on lines of demarcation at present occupied by the contending armies, a withdrawal of all allied troops and cessation of allied assistance to anti-Soviet elements, a resumption of trade and official relations, and a recognition by Soviet Russia of financial obligations as offered in the note of February 4, 1919. When, however, Bullitt returned to Paris with these proposals in the latter part of March, the climate of opinion had radically changed, and was veering towards the policy of Churchill and the French. Neither Wilson nor Lloyd George was prepared to submit the Soviet proposals to the conference. The utmost secrecy was maintained about them; and Lloyd George publicly disowned any responsibility for Bullitt's mission. The die was now cast. A compromise was reached in the allied camp between those who desired to give full military backing to the "white" Russians and those who desired to stand aloof. It was decided to send no more allied troops to Russia and gradually to withdraw those already there, but at the same time to supply the Russian anti-Bolshevik forces with military and other material on as generous a scale as possible. The next three months were the period of Kolchak's most serious successes against the Red Army in Siberia and of the strongest and most enthusiastic allied support of his cause.

The Bullitt mission was the last attempt for more than six months to establish any kind of direct contact between Soviet Russia and the allies. The last allied diplomatic representatives had left Soviet territory in August 1918; unofficial or consular agents had been expelled or withdrawn after the arrest of Lockhart in September. The neutral representatives had one by one followed the example of their allied colleagues. The German embassy retired to occupied territory in August 1918, and the consular staff remaining in Moscow returned to Germany when Joffe was expelled from Berlin in November 1918. After the expulsion of Litvinov from Great Britain in September 1918, the Soviet representatives who had attempted to establish themselves in neutral countries suffered the same fate. In December 1918 a Russian Red Cross mission was expelled from Warsaw, and four out of its five members were assassinated on their way back to Moscow. A Soviet delegation sent to France at the beginning of February 1919 for the ostensible purpose of arranging for the repatriation of Russian soldiers in France was refused admission and ignominiously confined on a small island off Saint-Malo pending expulsion. In March 1919 Ludwig Martens, a Russian-born German resident in New York who had acquired Soviet citizenship, forwarded to the American State Department his credentials signed by Chicherin as Soviet representative in the United States. This communication, together with a memorandum containing proposals for Soviet-American trade, was ignored, and the only response was a search of his office by the police three months later for incriminating propaganda. By the beginning of 1919, Moscow was cut off from all normal contacts with the outside world. For a long while the only foreigner remaining there in an official capacity was a representative of the Danish Red Cross, who had undertaken the protection of the interests of citizens of all the Scandinavian and other western European countries, and of the United States. After the armistice of November 1918 and before the close of navigation, a few ships loaded with timber and flax had sailed from Petrograd in the endeavour to reestablish trade with Germany. These had been confiscated in Baltic ports; and since then the blockade had been maintained in all its rigour.

These measures, tantamount to war in all but name, put an end to the first tentative efforts of Soviet diplomacy. The division of the world into two hostile camps, which had been a favourite theme of Bolshevik speakers and writers since before the Bolshevik revolution, was now an accomplished fact. In March 1919, at the eighth party congress, Lenin defended the regime against Kautsky's charge of "militarism":

We are living not merely in a state, but in *a system of states; a*nd it is inconceivable that the Soviet republic should continue to exist for a long period side by side with imperialist states. Ultimately one or the other must conquer. Until this end occurs a number of terrible clashes between the Soviet republic and bourgeois states is inevitable.[5]

What first appeared as a civil war waged on Russian territory between the Red Army and the armies of the "white" generals now took on the shape of a war between the revolutionary Soviet regime and the principal Powers of the capitalist world; and against these Powers "political warfare" in the form of propaganda for world revolution was the most effective weapon in the Soviet armoury. Though it fell short of its announced objective, its use was justified by the results which it achieved. But, just as it would be mistaken to suppose that the revolutionary element in Soviet policy was ever absent even when diplomacy appeared to have the upper hand, so it would be wrong to treat it, even in moments of greatest tension, as the exclusive factor. It is symbolical of the constant juxtaposition of the two elements that Soviet acceptance of the allied invitation to Prinkipo came only a few days after the issue of invitations from Moscow to a founding congress of a Communist International, and that Bullitt reached Russia two days after the congress

had ended its sessions. The two elements could be kept in separate compartments without any sense of incongruity between them. Bullitt in his otherwise copious reports on his visit to Moscow does not mention the birth of the Communist International and may have been unaware of it, though *Pravda* was still carrying reports of the congress during his stay. The occasion attracted little attention at the time outside—or even inside—Russia. Only in the light of later developments and achievements can it justly be described in retrospect as one of the outstanding events of the year.

The task of creating a new International had first been proclaimed by Lenin in the autumn of 1914, and was an item in his "April theses" of 1917. But the victory of the October coup left the Bolsheviks with little time for anything that did not immediately bear on the consolidation of the revolution at home; the beginning of revolution elsewhere was disappointingly delayed; and, so long as the war lasted, it was materially impossible to bring together anything like a representative international group. Progress was for all these reasons slow. Throughout the first winter of the revolution peace was still the predominant aim. It was VTsIK which, at its meeting on December 22, 1917/January 4, 1918, made a first move. It decided to send a delegation to Stockholm "in order to establish a close link with all working elements of western Europe" and to "prepare for convening a Zimmerwald-Kienthal conference." But this was governmental, not party, action (the delegation, reflecting the current composition of the coalition, was to contain Left SRs as well as Bolsheviks); the Zimmerwald organization was still recognized; and this implied that peace rather than world revolution was the overriding aim. The mood was still cast in the radical bourgeois mould of the peace decree: the net was being cast widely for as large a catch as possible. On January 24/February

[5] Lenin, *Sochineniya*, XXIV, 122.

6, 1918, the project was pursued at an "international socialist conference" convened on the premises of Narkomindel. The conference was attended by Bolsheviks (Stalin was the leading party representative) and Left SRs, by several representatives of the border countries and of Scandinavia, and by Petrov and Reinstein, representing the British Socialist Party and the American Socialist Labor Party respectively, and passed a general resolution advocating "a revolutionary struggle . . . for immediate peace" and support for "the Russian October revolution and the Soviet Government." A few days later a delegation was appointed to proceed to Stockholm consisting of two Bolsheviks, Kollontai and Berzin, and two Left SRs. At the height of the Brest-Litovsk crisis the delegation set out on its mission, but was turned back in Finland; and the project fell to the ground.

The conclusion of the Brest-Litovsk treaty ruled out for some time any direct attempt to mobilize the international socialist movement in support of the Soviet Government, and communications with the outside world became increasingly precarious. It was only after the armistice of November 1918 that the obstacles seemed suddenly to melt away. Germany, far from being a barrier to the advance of revolution, was now a centre of the revolutionary ferment. The moment was ripe to raise high once more the banner of international socialism. On December 19, 1918, the Petrograd Soviet convened an "international meeting" which was presided over by Maxim Gorky. Gorky was an international figure of the Left, though at this time a strong anti-Bolshevik; and the company was doctrinally mixed.

> We have among us today [said Zinoviev in his opening speech] guests who are neither Marxists nor communists, but all of us here are agreed on one point, in our hatred of the bourgeoisie, in our hatred of a class guilty of the death of millions of men in the interests of a small group.

Reinstein spoke once more for the United States, and Fineberg, like him of Russian origin and recently returned to Russia, for Great Britain; Sadoul appeared for France; there were Serbian, Bulgarian, Turkish, Chinese, Hindu, Persian and Korean representatives; and speeches were also delivered by Scottish, English and American prisoners of war captured on the Archangel front (the first was introduced as the "delegate for Scotland"), and by a member of the Petrograd German Soldiers' and Workers' Council. The meeting lacked nothing in fervour, and lived up to Zinoviev's description of it as "the modest precursor of a future grand assembly."

Shortly after this demonstration external events gave concrete form to these aspirations for the establishment of a new International. About the time of the international meeting it became known that a conference was being convened in the near future at Berne for the purpose of reviving the Second International; and on December 24, 1918, the central committee of the party issued a broadcast to the world denouncing this project. At the end of December 1918 the foundation of a German Communist Party provided for the first time a respectable nucleus for an international communist organization. Early in January 1919 Lenin presided over a small meeting in the Kremlin, which decided without further delay to invite "all parties opposed to the Second International" to attend a congress in Moscow with a view to the creation of a Third International. The invitation was broadcast to the world from Moscow on January 24, 1919, three days before the date set for the Berne conference. It was signed in the names of the central committee of the Russian Communist Party (Lenin and Trotsky); of Polish, Hungarian, Austrian, Lettish and Finnish communist parties; of the Balkan Revolutionary Social-Democratic Federation (Rakovsky); and of the Socialist Labor Party of America (Reinstein). It was not specifically addressed to anyone, but named 39 parties or groups as eligible to attend the founding congress. Only one of these ("socialist groups in Tokyo and Yokohama") had its seat in Asia. Bolshevik thoughts of revolution were still confined mainly to Europe; and the principal appeal was to groups in revolt against the Second International. The invitation set forth principles purporting to be based on the programmes of the Spartakusbund and the Russian Communist Party. The division of professed socialists into Right, Centre and Left which had emerged during the war was maintained. Of the three elements included in the Second International, the "social-chauvinists" could be met only by an "unsparing struggle"; for the Centre there must be a "policy of splitting off its most revolutionary elements and of unsparing criticism and exposure of its leaders"; the "Left revolutionary wing" would, it was assumed, come over. The task of the proletariat was now "the immediate seizure of state power"; and the purpose of the congress was to create "a general fighting organ for permanent coordination and systematic leadership of the movement, the centre of a communist International, subordinating the interests of the movement in each particular country to the interests of the revolution on its international scale."

At the beginning of March 1919 more than 50 delegates assembled in Moscow, of whom 35, representing communist parties or groups in 19 different countries, were recognized as full delegates with voting rights, the others being admitted in a consultative capacity. A large majority of the delegates came from Russia or from smaller countries within the Russian orbit, since more distant countries were unable to fill the allotted quota of five delegates for large nations, three for medium and one for small. The Russian party was represented by Lenin (who was elected to the presidium of the congress together with the German and Swiss delegates), Trotsky, Zinoviev, Stalin, Bukharin and Chicherin. There were delegates representing communist parties of Poland, Finland, the Ukraine,

Armenia, Latvia, Estonia, and White Russia and Lithuania; and a "united group of the eastern peoples of Russia" had one full delegate. Turkestan, Azerbaijan and Georgia had "consultative" delegates. France and the United States had one full delegate each; the one British delegate, Fineberg, had no formal mandate and had only "consultative" status. The Swiss Social-Democratic Party was represented by Platten, famous in history as the organizer of Lenin's journey to Russia in April 1917. "Consultative" delegates appeared from China, Persia and Korea. Most of these were resident in Moscow, and some of them purported to speak for countries where no communist organization as yet existed. The large Norwegian Labour Party, the main workers' party in Norway, sent a delegate; and Dutch, Swedish, Hungarian and Austrian delegates represented tiny Left groups in their respective countries, not all of them unimpeachably communist in outlook. Rakovsky spoke for the Balkan Revolutionary Social-Democratic Federation. The language of the congress was German.

The attitude of the Germans was the crucial point for the future, as everyone knew. Of the two delegates chosen by the newly formed German Communist Party only one, Eberlein, had succeeded in eluding the German police: he appeared at the congress under the *nom de guerre* of Albert. He had, however, come with a mandate to oppose the creation of a new International as premature. The German communists, weak and persecuted at home, perceived clearly that an International founded in Moscow in existing conditions must be almost exclusively Russian in character and leadership; and they would have preferred to wait until communism had developed further in Germany and western Europe. These objections first appeared at an informal preliminary discussion between a few of the principal delegates on March 1, 1919. They were met to the extent that the delegates assembled on the following day not as a formal congress but as a "preparatory conference." Zinoviev was elected president, not yet of the future International, but of the conference, with Angelica Balabanov and Vorovsky as secretaries. Eberlein announced in the name of the KPD that he had "no objection of principle" to the creation of a Communist International, but asked that the present proceedings should be limited to a conference "to test the available strength and review the political foundations on which we can unite." The resistance of the one serious communist party outside Soviet territory seemed at first decisive. The Bolshevik delegation saw nothing for it but to yield, and a long speech made on its behalf by Bukharin, implied willingness to defer the vital decision. "The proposal to treat the meeting as the constituent assembly of a new International had," in Balabanov's words, "been generally abandoned," when the current of opinion was suddenly reversed by a fiery speech from the newly arrived Austrian delegate, Steinhardt, *alias* Gruber, which depicted the whole of central Europe on the verge of revolution. In the new mood further delay seemed pusillanimous, and Eberlein was completely isolated. When at the next meeting the formal constitution of a Communist International was proposed in the name of the delegates of Austria, Sweden, the Balkan federation and Hungary, Eberlein restated his objections:

Real communist parties exist in only a few countries; in most, they have been created only in the last few weeks; in many countries where there are communists today they have as yet no organization. . . . What is missing is the whole of western Europe. Belgium, Italy are not represented; the Swiss representative cannot speak in the name of the party; France, England, Spain, Portugal are missing; and America is equally not in a position to say what parties would support us.[6]

[6] *Der I. Congress der Kommunistischen Internationale* (Hamburg, 1921), p. 134.

But he was induced to abstain from voting in order not to mar the harmony of the proceedings; and on March 4, 1919, the conference by a unanimous resolution transformed itself into the first congress of the Communist International. The abstention of Germany (though Eberlein signed the manifesto of the congress) could do nothing to avert the danger which the German communists feared. Indeed wholehearted cooperation from the outset might at least have mitigated a Russian predominance which resulted from lack of serious competition rather than from any conscious Russian design.

The fact of the foundation of a Third or Communist International, henceforth familiarly known as Comintern, was more important than anything done at its first congress. It adopted a "platform" and a manifesto "To the Proletarians of the Whole World," which reviewed the rise and fall of capitalism and the development of communism in the seventy-two (or more accurately seventy-one) years since Marx and Engels issued the *Communist Manifesto*, and was afterwards described by Zinoviev as "a second *Communist Manifesto*." The congress approved a set of theses presented by Lenin in denunciation of bourgeois democracy and parliamentarianism and in defence of the dictatorship of the proletariat (this was the theme of Lenin's main speech at the congress); it derided the attempts of the Berne conference to revive the "yellow" Second International, and attacked the imperialism of the Entente Powers and the "white" terror. Finally, it issued an appeal "To the Workers of All Countries," whose urgent tone and topical content distinguished it from the other congress documents. This began by expressing the "gratitude and admiration" of the congress for "the Russian revolutionary proletariat and its directing party—the Communist Party of the Bolsheviks." The work of liberation and reform pursued by the Soviet power had, however, been interrupted by a civil war which was being waged with the aid of the Entente countries and would collapse at once without that aid. Hence it was the duty of the "working masses of all countries" to press upon their governments by all available means ("including, if necessary, revolutionary means") demands for the cessation of intervention, for the withdrawal of armies from Russia, for the recognition of the Soviet regime, for the establishment of diplomatic and commercial relations, and for the despatch to Russia of "some hundreds or even thousands" of engineers, instructors and skilled workers to assist in the restoration and reorganization of transport. The congress elected an "executive committee of the Communist International (IKKI or, by its English initials, ECCI) containing representatives of the communist parties of Russia, Germany, Austria, Hungary, the Balkan federation, Scandinavia and Switzerland, to act, like the central committee of the party, in the name of the institution in the intervals between congresses; other parties joining Comintern before the next congress were to receive a seat on IKKI. Zinoviev became its president, and Radek its secretary. The appointment of Radek, who seemed likely to remain for an indefinite period in his Berlin prison, was an empty gesture of defiance of the capitalist world. As soon as the congress separated, Angelica Balabanov took over the functions of secretary of IKKI, but held the post only for a few weeks. It was unthinkable for the present that IKKI should have its seat anywhere but in Moscow. But Zinoviev explained that this was temporary and that "we shall be glad if we can succeed in transferring the place of residence of the Third International and its executive committee as quickly as possible to another capital, for example, Paris."[7]

The appeal "To the Workers of All Countries" to rally to the support of the Soviet regime in Russia was in some respects the most significant document of the first Congress of the Communist International. Beyond question the new organization had been conceived by its founders as in the fullest sense international—a successor of the defunct and discredited "Second International." Lenin, in one of his rare flights of rhetoric, described it at the moment of its foundation as "the forerunner of the international republic of Soviets." But the conditions of its birth marked it out for a different destiny. The constant and ineradicable duality of purpose inherent in Lenin's outlook—the defence of the Soviet power in Russia and the furtherance of international revolution—coloured his view of the new instrument; and the partly unforeseen circumstances which put the effective control of it exclusively into Russian hands completed the organic link between Comintern and the Soviet regime. What had taken place in Moscow in March 1919 was not in fact the fusion of a number of national communist parties of approximately equal strength into an international organization, but the harnessing of a number of weak, in some cases embryonic and still unformed, groups to an organization whose main support and motive force was necessarily and inevitably the power of the Soviet state. It was Soviet power which created Comintern and gave it its influence and prestige; in return, it was natural to expect that international communist propaganda and action should help to defend

---

[7] This assurance did not appear in the record of the congress, but was reported by Zinoviev to the eighth party congress a few days later (*Vos'moi S"ezd RKP[B]* [1933], p. 139). This view was common to all the Bolshevik leaders. "If today," wrote

Trotsky in *Izvestiya* on May 1, 1919, "Moscow is the center of the Third International, tomorrow—we are profoundly convinced—this center will move to the west: to Berlin, Paris, London. However joyfully the Russian proletariat welcomed the representatives of the working class of the world in the walls of the Kremlin, it will with even greater joy send its representatives to the second congress of the Communist International in one of the western European centres. For an international communist congress in Berlin or Paris will mean the complete triumph of the proletarian revolution in Europe and, probably, in the whole world" (Trotsky *Sochineniya* [Moscow 1925–1927], XIII, 28).

that power at a moment when it was threatened by all the reactionary forces of the capitalist world. At this crucial moment of the civil war the supreme task naturally presented itself in Lenin's mind as "a struggle of the proletarian state surrounded by capitalist states." National and international aims, the security of the Soviet regime and the interests of the proletarian revolution, were once more inextricably blended. In an article contributed by Lenin to the first number of *Kommunisticheskii Internatsional*, the journal of the new organization, the simple truth was stated with the emphasis of italics:

> The new third "International Working-men's Association"[8] has *already begun to coincide* in a certain measure *with the Union of Soviet Socialist Republics.*

The struggle was waged simultaneously on the two planes—the revolutionary plane and the plane of state action—without any sense of incompatibility between them.

It would, therefore, be an error to suggest that the foundation of the Communist International marked any fresh departure in Soviet foreign policy, or had any immediate effect on its course. Once the civil war began, that policy was necessarily concerned to foster the disintegration of the enemy's power, both at home and in the field, through revolutionary propaganda. At the moment when Comintern came into being, the propaganda which had helped to destroy the war-weary German armies already threatened to have a similar effect on the victorious but equally war-weary forces of the allies. In January 1919 when the allied statesmen, assembled in Paris for the peace conference, discussed the occupation of Russia by allied troops, the British Prime Minister bluntly assured his colleagues that "if he now proposed to send a thousand British troops to Russia for that purpose, the armies would mutiny," and that, "if a military enterprise were started

against the Bolsheviki, that would make England Bolshevist and there would be a Soviet in London." Lloyd George was talking for effect, as was his manner. But his perceptive mind had correctly diagnosed the symptoms. Serious mutinies in the first months of 1919 in the French fleet and in French military units landed in Odessa and other Black Sea ports led to an enforced evacuation at the beginning of April. Of the troops of several nationalities under British command on the Archangel front the Director of Military Operations at the War Office reported in March 1919 that their morale was "so low as to render them a prey to the very active and insidious Bolshevik propaganda which the enemy are carrying out with increasing energy and skill." The details were disclosed much later through official American reports. On March 1, 1919, a mutiny occured among French troops ordered to go up to the line; several days earlier a British infantry company "refused to go to the front," and shortly afterwards an American company "refused for a time to return to duty at the front." It was in the light of such experience that the British Government decided in March 1919 to evacuate north Russia, though the evacuation was not in fact completed till six months later.

Mutiny among the troops was matched by widespread disaffection in the industrial centres of Great Britain. At the time of the armistice a report handed by the Foreign Office to the American embassy in London expressed the belief that "apart from certain centres, notably the Clyde and South Wales, Bolshevism as such is innocuous for the present." Nevertheless no chances were being taken:

> A careful watch is being maintained for such Bolshevik propaganda as may reach this country from abroad, in order that it may be intercepted and destroyed, and the same measures are being taken wherever possible in respect to inflammatory literature secretly printed at home. Counter-propaganda is meanwhile being conducted through the un-

---

[8] This was the official title of the First International founded in London in 1864.

ostentatious distribution of pamphlets designed to educate the people as to the true significance of Bolshevism, and appropriate articles appear in the Sunday papers customarily read by the working men.[9]

The first serious attempt to challenge public order by calling a general strike was made in Glasgow at the end of January 1919; and "Red Friday" was long remembered as the peak of the revolutionary movement on the Clyde. Political discontent was focused on the government's Russian policy by a meeting at the Albert Hall on February 9, 1919, which launched a "Hands off Russia" campaign. At the founding congress of Comintern a month later the British delegate, Fineberg, spoke in a language which seemed to find support in the facts:

> The strike movement is spreading all over England and is affecting every branch of industry. In the army discipline is much weakened, which in other countries was the first symptom of revolution.[10]

"England may seem to you untouched," Lenin told a British correspondent at this time, "but the microbe is already there."[11]

Meanwhile hunger was rife in central Europe, and disorganization was everywhere; strikes and disorders had occurred even in peaceful neutral countries like Holland and Switzerland. On March 21, 1919, just a fortnight after the founding congress of Comintern had dispersed, a Soviet republic was proclaimed in Budapest. On the next day House in Paris confided his apprehensions to his diary:

> Bolshevism is gaining everywhere. Hungary has just succumbed. We are sitting upon an open powder magazine and some day a spark may ignite it.[12]

Almost at the same moment Lloyd George dramatized the situation in a confidential memorandum designed to overcome Clemenceau's obstinacy at the peace conference:

> The whole of Europe is filled with the spirit of revolution. There is a deep sense not only of discontent but of anger and revolt amongst the workmen against pre-war conditions. The whole existing order in its political, social and economic aspects is questioned by the masses of the population from one end of Europe to the other.[13]

Early in April another Soviet republic was proclaimed in Munich. World revolution was on the march. Lenin, appealing to the central council of the trade unions in the same month to give their full support to the mobilization against Kolchak, referred to the French mutinies at Odessa and to the Soviet republics in central Europe as proof that "our victory on an international scale is completely secure"; and his May Day speech on the Red Square ended with the slogans: "Long live the international republic of Soviets! Long live communism!" Not only did Zinoviev in the first issue of the journal of Comintern make his famous prophecy that in a year's time one would begin to forget that there had ever been a struggle for communism in Europe, but the far more sober Lenin was inspired by the Versailles treaty to discover "an immense revolutionary movement" in Germany and to predict that "this July will be our last difficult July, and next July we shall greet the victory of the international Soviet republic.[14] Meanwhile the sapping of the hostile front by revolutionary action through every possible instrument—Comintern being merely the newest and most far-reaching—was the one effective foreign policy still open to the Soviet Government; and it seemed, in the summer of 1919, to be yielding excellent dividends.

It appeared, therefore, in no way

[9] *Foreign Relations of the United States, 1918: Russia* (Washington, D. C., 1931), I, 727–728.

[10] *Der 1. Kongress Der Kom. Int.*, p. 70.

[11] A. Ransome, *Six Weeks in Russia in 1919* (London, 1919), p. 149.

[12] C. Seymour, ed., *The Intimate Papers of Colonel House* (London, 1928), IV, 405.

[13] *Papers Respecting Negotiations for an Anglo-French Pact*, Cmd. 2169 (1924), p. 78.

[14] Lenin, *Sochineniya*, XXIV, 381.

anomalous that Chicherin, as head of Nar-komindel, should at this time work hand in glove with Zinoviev, as head of Comin-tern, and that the language of the two organs should be scarcely distinguishable. When a Soviet government was set up in Munich in April 1919, Chicherin greeted it in a message which was published in *Izvestiya:*

> We may rest assured that the day is not far off when revolutionary socialist allies will join forces with us and will give support to the Bavarian republic against any attack. Every blow aimed at you is aimed at us. In absolute unity we carry on our revolutionary struggle for the well-being of all workers and exploited peoples.[15]

And VTsIK, sending its greetings to the Soviet republics of Hungary and Bavaria, expressed the conviction that "the prole-tariat of the whole world, having before its eyes striking examples of the victorious insurrection of the workers in three coun-tries of Europe, will follow them with com-plete faith in victory."[16] Ten day later Chicherin signed an appeal to the workers of the allied countries protesting against the aid furnished by the allies to the "white" forces in the civil war and against the allied blockade.

A fresh opportunity was offered when the allied peace terms were first disclosed to Germany at Versailles. Zinoviev issued a proclamation on behalf of IKKI, which declared that "the proletarian revolution is the only salvation for the oppressed classes of the whole world" and concluded with the words:

> Down with the Versailles peace, down with the new Brest!
> Down with the government of the social traitors!

Long live the power of the Soviets in the whole world.[17]

At the same moment Chicherin issued a pamphlet, which was published in German and French by IKKI, *To the German Worker,* ending with the same revolution-ary appeal:

> In the ranks of the communist revolu-tionary fighters is your place; there you will find salvation from your present calamity.[18]

In Germany, as in Russia, only revo-lutionary action now seemed relevant to the position. Chicherin analysed *The Foreign Policy of the Two Internationals* in an article which appeared in the journal of Comintern in October 1919. He described the whole activity of Comintern as consti-tuting "a proletarian foreign policy—con-tact between workers' organizations and mutual help in all possible cases." In the optimistic mood of the summer of 1919 he wrote throughout of "Soviet governments" in the plural:

> Before the revolutionary proletarian par-ties and groups of all countries is set the task of struggling to guarantee and strengthen the international position of the revolutionary Soviet government. Only in this way is a new programme of foreign policy open to those parties and groups which take their stand on revolutionary Soviet ground.

He admitted that those governments, "as governments existing *de facto* among other existing governments, are compelled to place themselves in certain relations with the latter, and those relations impose on them obligations which have to be taken into account." But, on the other hand, Soviet governments—here Chicherin was probably thinking of the League of Na-tions—"keep aloof from all participation in any kind of combination of imperialist

---

[15] *Izvestiya,* April 9, 10, 1919, quoted in A. L. P. Dennis, *The Foreign Policies of Soviet Russia* (London, 1924), p. 352.

[16] Klyuchnikov and Sabanin, *Mezhdunarodnaya politika,* II, 237–238.

[17] *Kommunisticheskii Internatsional,* No. 2 (June 1919), cols. 149–150: it was published in German in *Die Internationale,* I, No. 11–12 (August 18, 1919), pp. 244–248.

[18] G. Chicherin, *An den Deutschen Arbeiter* (Mos-cow, 1919).

governments."[19] Mutual aid among workers and workers' governments seemed at this time to exhaust the content of a proletarian foreign policy. Nothing more was either necessary or practicable.

Yet the omens were by no means all propitious. On May 1, 1919, the ineffectual career of the Bavarian Soviet republic, left to its own devices and unsupported by any decisive action of the Prussian proletariat, had come to its inevitable end. In the middle of June an attempted communist rising in Vienna was ignominiously crushed. Early in August 1919 the slightly more substantial Hungarian Soviet regime succumbed to internal dissension and to the intervention of Rumanian troops, backed by the western allies. These defeats, and the delay in the time-table of world revolution, left the RSFSR cut off from all external aid in a hostile capitalist world. In the autumn of 1919 all the "white" forces arrayed against the Soviet power reached in turn the peak of their activity and of their success—Kolchak on the confines of Siberia, Yudenich in front of Petrograd, Denikin in the Ukraine and central Russia. The months of October and November marked the crucial point at which the continued existence of the regime hung by a thread. . . .

* * *

Throughout the year 1919 the weakness of the Soviet Government, threatened by enemies on all sides, deprived it of any power of initiative in foreign policy, and made its course of action dependent on the successive moves of its adversaries. The direct cause of the complete rupture of relations between Soviet Russia and the outside world was the decision of the allied governments to give active support to the "whites" in the civil war, and to treat the Soviet Government as a rebel and hostile faction. It was the allied governments

[19] *Kom. Int.*, No. 6 (October 1919), cols. 817–828.

which deliberately and successfully sought to isolate Moscow, not Moscow which sought to isolate itself from the world. Thus a breaking down of the barriers had to await a change of mood and policy in the allied camp and particularly in Great Britain, whose attitude to the Russian question throughout the year continued to be marked by glaring fluctuations and inconsistencies. These reflected acute differences, not only in public opinion, but in government circles. The turn of policy in April 1919, when attempts to establish relations with Soviet Russia were abandoned and all-out aid, short of direct military action, extended to the "whites," was never fully endorsed by Liberal and Labour opinion, which was in general anxious to cut commitments and to come to terms with the Soviet Government if this was in any way possible; and this anxiety was shared by Lloyd George, in so far as he could indulge it without upsetting the uneasy balance of the coalition. Fear of the spread of Bolshevism in Europe, and hopes of the overthrow of the Soviet Government by the "whites," had sufficed to give a fresh impetus in the summer of 1919 to anti-Bolshevik opinion. But this line, half-heartedly pursued in the face of growing public scepticism, failed in its purpose; and, when it became clear in the late autumn of 1919 that the main effort of all the "white" generals—Kolchak, Denikin and Yudenich—had exhausted itself without forcing a decision, opinion began to set strongly against a policy which had been reluctantly accepted when it seemed successful, and was readily abandoned once its futility was revealed.

The other factor which, combined with the patent failure of the "whites," at last brought a return to conciliation was the growing consciousness of economic needs. As the world groped its way back to what it thought of as "normal," recollections revived of Russia's former place in a now shattered world economy. It seemed increasingly difficult to maintain indefinitely a commercial boycott of one of the largest countries in the world merely because of objections to its form of government. On August 1, 1919, a letter in *The Times*, which at this period represented extreme anti-Bolshevik opinion, guardedly expressed anxiety about the future of British trade with Russia and stressed the need to consider "the new conditions which have been brought about by the war." After the Bolshevik revolution the blockade applied to Germany by the allied Powers was extended to Russia, and was silently maintained even after the conclusion of hostilities with Germany. At the beginning of October 1919 an attempt was made by the Supreme Council to meet an obvious criticism by requesting the principal neutral governments to join in the existing blockade of Soviet Russia, which in order to appease American susceptibilities was referred to euphemistically as "economic pressure;" and a similar note, rather clumsily embodying the terms of the note to the neutral governments and requesting compliance with them, was addressed to the German Government. The Soviet Government at once countered with a strong protest to the neutral governments and to the German Government, who were warned that compliance with the allied request would be regarded as a "consciously hostile act." The neutral answers to the allied request were evasive or frankly unfavourable. The German Government, while "fully conscious of the great danger threatening the culture and economic life of all peoples by the spread of Bolshevism," thought that the blockade would not serve the purpose in view, and excused itself on the ground that it had now no common frontier with Russia. The note ended with the complaint that, "whilst the Allied and Associated Powers propose to Germany that she should participate in the blockade of Russia, they are actually applying the policy of blockade to the German coasts and German ships."[20] No further attempt

[20] *The Times*, October 31, 1919.

was made by the allies to press the demand. Blockade or no blockade, trade with Soviet Russia was for the present impracticable. But nobody was prepared to prejudice future prospects.

The failure to generalize the blockade, coming at a moment of disillusionment with the prospects of the "white" armies, prepared the way for a radical change of front. At the end of October Krasin, a shrewd observer who knew western Europe, accurately diagnosed the new mood in a private letter:

The prospect of carrying on the war indefinitely will not appeal to the Powers, and if Denikin has not settled our hash by the beginning of winter, which is hardly likely, then England for one would deem it acceptable in her own interests to overpower the Bolsheviks in the domain of politics by coming to some agreement and entering into peaceful relations with Soviet Russia. Perhaps this plan of conquering Bolshevik Russia would have more chance of success than the fruitless military campaigns of the last two years.[21]

Lloyd George responded with his customary sensitiveness to the change of mood. In his Guildhall speech of November 8, 1919, he created something of a sensation by observing that "you cannot have peace unless you have peace in Russia."[22] He spoke significantly of the cost of "intervention in an interminable civil war," referred to Russia as "a dangerous land to intervene in," and expressed the hope that "an opportunity may offer itself for the great Powers of the world to promote peace and concord in the great country." Five days later in the House of Commons he openly attacked the blockade, describing Russia as "one of the great resources for the supply of food

[21] L. Krasin, *Leonid Krasin: His Life and Work* (n.d. [1929]), pp. 111–112; the originals of Krasin's letters quoted in translation in this volume have not been published.

[22] He had used almost the same words in a speech in the House of Commons on February 19, 1919 (*House of Commons: 5th Series*, CXII, 194): but that was before the change of policy in April.

and raw material."[23] Then, on November 17, 1919, in response to a challenge by his critics, he delivered a major speech which was evidently intended to prepare the way for the winding up of the policy of intervention and the substitution of a policy of commercial negotiations with Soviet Russia. In a much-quoted passage he invoked the memory of "Lord Beaconsfield, who regarded a great, gigantic, colossal, growing Russia rolling onwards like a glacier towards Persia and the borders of Afghanistan and India as the greatest menace the British Empire could be confronted with."[24] This argument spoke strongly against the "whites," who sought to reconstitute the former Russian Empire, and in favour of the Bolsheviks who were only too eager to promise self-determination to its constituent parts. Nor did these utterances pass unnoticed in Moscow, where Chicherin, in a broadcast statement, propounded a new and significant attitude to relations with the capitalist world:

Relations with Russia are quite possible in spite of the profound differences between Britain's and Russia's regime. . . . The British customer and purveyor are as necessary to us as we are to them. Not only do we desire peace and the possibility of internal development, but we also feel strongly the need of economic help from the more fully developed countries such as Great Britain. We are ready even to make sacrifices for the sake of a close

economic connection with Britain. . . . I, therefore, gladly welcome the declaration of the British Premier as the first step towards such a sane and real policy corresponding to the interests of both countries.[25]

It was only eight months since Lenin had explained that it was "inconceivable that the Soviet republic should continue to exist for a long period side by side with imperialist states," and that in the meanwhile "a number of terrible clashes between the Soviet republic and bourgeois states is inevitable." The doctrine was not abandoned. The Bolshevik leaders, from Lenin downwards, continued firmly to believe, not merely that revolution in Europe was necessary, but that it was imminent. But the change of mood in response to changing conditions was prompt and far-reaching.

With these new feelers put out from both sides, the situation was ripe for a renewal of contacts. The excuse was found in the need to negotiate an exchange of prisoners. Throughout the worst period, the British and Soviet governments had managed to effect occasional exchanges of important agents captured by one side or the other—a curious instance of professional reciprocity; and two British Red Cross representatives had continued to distribute relief to British prisoners in Soviet hands. The peace proposals handed to Bullitt in March 1919 included one for the mutual repatriation of prisoners and other nationals. In May 1919 the British Government in a radio message had proposed a general exchange of prisoners, and on June 10, 1919, Chicherin replied through the same channel that this proposal was acceptable only "if the Russian Government is allowed to send to London, or alternatively to some neutral country, a commission enabled to get in touch with Russians in Great Britain."[26] This condition caused pro-

---

[23] *Ibid.,* CXXI, 474. It was Russia as a supplier rather than Russia as a market which preoccupied the British Government at this time. A confidential Board of Trade memorandum of January 6, 1920, pointed out that Russia before 1914 had been the source of one quarter of the world's wheat exports, and that Great Britain had received from Russia one third of her imports of flax: the memorandum ended with the recommendation "definitely to abandon the blockade and to place no obstacles at all in the way of the restriction of commercial relations with the whole of Russia" (*Documents on British Foreign Policy, 1919–1939: First Series,* II [1948], 867–870). Lloyd George's much derided remark that "the corn bins of Russia are bulging with grain" occurred in a speech in the House of Commons on February 10, 1920 (*House of Commons: 5th Series,* CXXV, 45).
[24] *Ibid.,* CXXI, 723.

[25] Moscow radio of November 20, 1919, quoted in Dennis, *The Foreign Policies of Soviet Russia,* p. 380.
[26] *Documents on British Foreign Policy, 1919–1939: First Series,* III (1949), 343–344, 360.

longed embarrassment and procrastination, and it was not till the ice had begun to melt elsewhere that agreement was reached for a meeting between British and Soviet plenipotentiaries in Copenhagen, to be strictly confined to the discussion of questions relating to prisoners of war. The Soviet representative was Litvinov, the British representative a Labour M. P. named O'Grady; they met in Copenhagen on November 25, 1919—the first formal quasi-diplomatic contact for more than a year with any of the allied Powers.

The following month saw other significant developments. In September 1919 negotiations had been opened with the Estonian Government, which had, however, broken them off on the plea that it could not conclude peace with Soviet Russia except in conjunction with neighbouring states: this refusal was the result of British pressure on the eve of the Yudenich venture. The defeat of Yudenich in the second half of October threatened to produce a crisis in Soviet-Estonian relations. Trotsky voiced the desire of the Red Army to pursue Yudenich's beaten troops into Estonia, while Chicherin thought that the appearance of Soviet forces on Estonian soil would merely "antagonize English Liberals and moderate Conservatives" and "play Churchill's game." Lenin supported Chicherin, and the Red Army was restrained, though a warning was issued to the Estonian Government insisting on the disarmament of Yudenich's troops which took refuge in Estonia. These difficulties having been overcome, negotiations were opened at Dorpat on December 2, 1919, between an Estonian delegation and a Soviet delegation headed by Krasin.

Meanwhile negotiations had been proceeding in strict secrecy in a railway coach at a desolate spot in the Pinsk marches between Markhlevsky, the Polish communist who had appeared at the founding congress of Comintern but now acted in the capacity of a delegate of the Russian Red Cross, and Polish delegates holding credentials from the Polish Red Cross. This picturesque and little-known episode of Soviet diplomacy resulted in an agreement of November 2, 1919, for the release of Polish hostages held by Soviet Russia and for the renunciation by both sides of the practice of taking hostages, and in a second agreement a week later for the release of civilian prisoners on both sides. But these practical arrangements also served as a screen for more delicate discussions. When the negotiations began early in October 1919, the Red Army was in a precarious plight on two fronts—against Yudenich before Petrograd and against Denikin in central Russia; and it was necessary to buy off Polish intervention by a withdrawal which ceded further territory to the Polish forces. The success of this plan was due not so much to the skill and flexibility of the Soviet negotiators as to the unwillingness of Pilsudski to see the overthrow of the Soviet regime by "white" generals who seemed to represent in the long run a greater danger to Polish independence. On the other hand, not even the offer of much more extensive territorial concessions would induce Pilsudski to desert the western allies and conclude a formal peace with the Soviet Government; and in December, when the gravest danger for the Red Army had passed, the negotiations ended with no result other than the exchange of a few hundred Poles for a few hundred Bolsheviks. Polish passivity had been temporarily secured and beyond this Pilsudski would not go. After the failure of these secret negotiations the Soviet Government, noting that the Polish Minister for Foreign Affairs had officially denied that any peace overtures had been received from Soviet Russia, put forward a public proposal for peace negotiations which was ignored.

The new year of 1920, which saw the capture and execution of Kolchak in Siberia and the final discomfiture of Denikin in South Russia, brought to a head these tentative moves to break through the wall of isolation which separated Soviet Russia not only from the western Powers themselves, but from her smaller western neighbours under their patronage. On January 14, 1920, the Supreme Council meeting in Paris gave audience to two representatives of the Paris office of the Russian cooperatives, which by some strange anomaly had continued to exist throughout the revolutionary period: these stated that "the cooperative society had no politics," that it embraced 25,000,000 members, so that "practically the whole population of Russia was included," and that south Russia had a surplus of 10,000,000 tons of wheat for export. On the strength of these assurances, the Supreme Council announced two days later its decision to "permit the exchange of goods on the basis of reciprocity between the Russian people and allied and neutral countries;" the purpose was to provide "for the import into Russia of clothing, medicines, agricultural machinery and the other necessaries of which the Russian people are in sore need, in exchange for grain, flax, etc. of which Russia has surplus supplies." It was specifically added that "these arrangements imply no change in the policy of the allied governments towards the Soviet Government."[27] This decision, which amounted to a concentration of Russian imports and exports in the hands of the All-Russian Central Union of Cooperatives (Tsentrosoyuz), presented no embarrassments to the Soviet Government. It was a convenient means of enforcing the monopoly of foreign trade, since Tsentrosoyuz was by this time fully under Soviet control. On January 23, 1920, the president of Tsentrosoyuz telegraphed to the Paris office that this organ had been empowered by the Soviet authorities to enter into direct trade relations with the cooperatives, as well as with private firms, of western Europe, America and other countries. The lifting of the blockade was an event of great symbolical importance: it was greeted in

Soviet Russia as a declaration of the ending of the war with the western Powers. The practical difficulties in the way of a resumption of trade were to appear later.

This decision may well have hastened another. If Soviet Russia was to trade with western Europe, it was highly desirable to have a neutral, yet not unfriendly, port and clearing-house through which trade might pass. Tallinn, the Estonian capital, was well suited for the purpose. Soviet-Estonian negotiations proceeded rapidly and smoothly, and a treaty of peace was signed on February 2, 1920. A few days earlier Lloyd George had given pointed advice to the Polish Prime Minister to make peace with the Soviet Government; and three weeks later the Supreme Council sitting in London issued a statement that, if the allied Powers were asked for advice by any of "the communities which border on the frontiers of Russia," they would not be able "to take on themselves the responsibility of advising them to continue a war which may be injurious to their own interests."[28] Meanwhile the negotiations in progress with Litvinov in Copenhagen since November 1919 had after many difficult passages resulted in an Anglo-Soviet agreement for the repatriation of prisoners; this agreement was signed on February 12, 1920. Lenin briefly and without emphasis pointed the moral of these events: "We have shown that we know how to repel violence, but that we know, when victorious, how to renounce it." And again: "We have already opened a window on Europe which we shall try to utilize as extensively as possible."[29] It seemed as if, after the alarms and excursions of the civil war and the allied intervention on the side of the "whites," an interlude of peaceful cohabitation with the capitalist world was about to begin. The period of isolation was over.

The new attitude which began to develop in Soviet foreign policy in the first

[27] *Ibid.*, II, 912.

[28] *Foreign Relations of the United States, 1920* (Washington, D. C., 1936), III, 647.
[29] Lenin, *Sochineniya*, XXV, 21, 27.

months of 1920 arose automatically out of the continued existence of Soviet Russia in a world of capitalist states. The Soviet Government found itself almost involuntar- ily in the posture of defending, not the interests of world revolution, but national interests which any government of Russia would be obliged to defend.

STATUTES AND THESES OF THE THIRD (COMMUNIST) INTERNATIONAL

THE SECOND COMINTERN CONGRESS AND VLADIMIR LENIN

The Second Comintern Congress (July 17 to August 7, 1920) marked the early consolidation of this new organization. What the leading Bolshevik, Leo Kamenev, called "the General Staff for World Revolution" now made its objectives explicit, laid down its bylaws, and worked out the permanent principles that would govern its activities. The passages printed below include the "Statutes," worked out at the congress, and a portion of the "Theses on the Fundamental Tasks of the Communist International," drafted by Lenin and adopted by the congress. These represent only a part of the decisions of the congress, yet they very effectively portray the Communists' grim and militant determination to spread revolution around the world in the shortest time possible.

STATUTES OF THE COMMUNIST INTERNATIONAL

IN London in 1864 was established the first International Association of Workers, latterly known as the First International. The statute of the International Association of Workers reads as follows:

That the emancipation of the working class be attained by the working class itself;

That the struggle for the emancipation of the working class does not mean a struggle for class privileges and monopolies but a struggle for equal rights and equal obligations, for the abolition of every kind of class-domination;

That the economic subjection of the worker under the monopolists of the means of production, i.e., of the sources of life is the cause of servitude in all its forms, the cause of all social misery, all mental degradation and political dependence;

That the economic emancipation of the working class is therefore the great aim which every political movement must be subordinated to;

That all endeavors for this great aim have failed as yet because of the lack of solidarity between the various branches of industry in all countries, because of the absence of the fraternal tie of unity between the working classes of the different countries;

That the emancipation is neither a local nor a national problem but a problem of a social character embracing every civilized country, the solution of which depends on the theoretical and practical cooperation of the most progressive countries;

That the actual simultaneous revival of the workers' movement in the industrial countries of Europe, on the one hand, awakens

From "Theses and Statutes of the Third (Communist) International," *The Communist Conspiracy: Strategy and Tactics of World Communism*, Part I, Section C (Wash., D. C.: U. S. Government Printing Office, May 29, 1956), pp. 24–36.

new hopes, while, on the other hand, it is a solemn warning of the danger of relapse into the old errors and an appeal for an immediate union of the hitherto disconnected movement.

The Second International which was established in 1889 at Paris had undertaken to continue the work of the First International. In 1914, at the outbreak of the world slaughter, it suffered a complete failure. Undermined by opportunism and damaged by the treason of its leaders who had taken the side of the bourgeoisie—the Second International perished.

The Third Communist International which was established in March, 1919, in the capital of the Russian Socialist Federated Soviet Republic, in the city of Moscow, solemnly proclaims before the entire world that it takes upon itself to continue and to complete the great cause begun by the First International Workers' Association.

The Third Communist International was formed at a moment when the Imperialist slaughter of 1914–1918, in which the Imperialist bourgeoisie of the various countries had sacrificed twenty million men, came to an end.

Keep in mind the Imperialist war! This is the first appeal of the Communist International to every toiler wherever he may live and whatever language he may speak. Keep in mind that owing to the existence of the capitalist system a small group of Imperialists had the opportunity during four long years to compel the workers of various countries to cut each other's throats. Keep in mind that the bourgeois war has cast Europe and the entire world in a state of extreme destitution and starvation. Keep in mind that unless the capitalist system is overthrown the repetition of such criminal war is not only possible but inevitable.

The Communist International makes its aim to put up an armed struggle for the overthrow of the International bourgeoisie and to create an International Soviet Republic as a transition stage to the complete abolition of the State. The Communist International considers the dictatorship of the proletariat as the only means for the liberation of humanity from the horrors of capitalism. The Communist International considers the Soviet form of government as the historically evolved form of this dictatorship of the proletariat.

The Imperialist war is responsible for the close union of the fates of the workers of one country with the fates of the workers of all other countries. The imperialist war emphasizes once more what is pointed out in the statute of the First International: that the emancipation of labor is neither a local, nor a national task, but one of a social and international character.

The Communist International once for ever breaks with the traditions of the Second International which in reality only recognized the white race. The Communist International makes it its task to emancipate the workers of the entire world. The ranks of the Communist International fraternally unite men of all colors: white, yellow, and black—the toilers of the entire world.

The Communist International fully and unreservedly upholds the gains of the great proletarian revolution in Russia, the first victorious socialist revolution in the world's history, and calls upon all workers to follow the same road. The Communist International makes it its duty to support with all the power at its disposal every Soviet Republic, wherever it may be formed.

The Communist International is aware that for the purpose of a speedy achievement of victory the International Association of Workers, which is struggling for the abolition of capitalism and the establishment of Communism, should possess a firm and centralized organization. To all intents and purposes the Communist International should represent a single universal Communist party, of which the parties operating in every country form individual sections. The organized apparatus of the Communist International is to secure to the toilers of every country the possibility at any given moment of obtaining the maximum of aid from the organized workers of the other countries.

For this purpose the Communist International confirms the following items of its statutes:

1. The new International Association of Workers is established for the purpose of organizing the common activity of the workers of various countries who are striving towards a single aim: the overthrow of capitalism; the establishment of the dictatorship of the proletariat and of the International Soviet Republic; the complete abolition of classes, and the realization of socialism—the first step of Communist Society.

2. The new International Association of Workers has been given the name of The Communist International.

3. All the parties and organizations comprising the Communist International bear the name of the Communist party of the given country (section of the Communist International).

4. The World Congress of all parties and organizations which form part of the Communist International, is the supreme organ of this International. The World Congress confirms the programmes of the various parties comprising the Communist International. The World Congress discusses and decides the more important questions of programme and tactics, which are connected with the activity of the Communist International. The number of decisive votes at the World Congress for every party and organization is determined by a special regulation of the Congress; it is found necessary to strive for a speedy establishment of a standard of representation on the basis of the actual number of members of the organization and the real influence of the party in question.

5. The World Congress elects an Executive Committee of the Communist International which serves as the leading organ of the Communist International in the interval between the convention of

World Congresses, and is responsible only to the World Congress.

6. The residence of the Executive Committee of the Communist International is every time decided at the World Congress of the Communist International.

7. A Special World Congress of the Communist International may be convened either by regulation of the Executive Committee, or at the demand of one-half of the number of the parties which were part of the Communist International at the last World Congress.

8. The chief bulk of the work and greatest responsibility in the Executive Committee of the Communist International lie with the party of that country where, in keeping with the regulation of the World Congress, the Executive Committee finds its residence at the time. The party of the country in question sends to the Executive Committee not less than five members with a decisive vote. In addition to this, one representative with a decisive vote is sent to the Communist International from ten or twelve of the largest Communist parties. The list of these representatives is to be confirmed by the Universal Congress of the Communist International. The remaining parties and organizations forming part of the Communist International enjoy the right of sending to the Executive Committee one representative each with a consultative vote.

9. The Executive Committee is the leading organ of the Communist International between the conventions; the Executive Committee publishes in no less than four languages the central organ of the Communist International (the periodical "The Communist International"). The Executive Committee makes the necessary appeals on behalf of the Communist International, and issues instructions obligatory on all the parties and organizations which form part of the Communist International. The Executive Committee of the Communist International enjoys the right to demand from the affiliated parties the exclu-

sion of groups of members who are guilty of the infringement of international proletarian discipline, as well as the exclusion from the Communist International of parties guilty of the infringement of the regulations of the World Congress. In the event of necessity the Executive Committee organizes in various countries its technical and auxiliary bureaus, which are entirely under the control of the Executive Committee.

10. The Executive Committee of the Communist International enjoys the right to include in its ranks representatives of organizations and parties not accepted in the Communist International, but which are sympathetic towards communism; these are to have a consultative vote only.

11. The organs of all the parties and organizations forming part of the Communist International as well as of those which are recognized sympathizers of the Communist International, are obliged to publish all official regulations of the Communist International and of its Executive Committee.

12. The general state of things in the whole of Europe and of America makes necessary for the Communists of the whole world an obligatory formation of illegal communist organizations along with those existing legally. The Executive Committee should take charge of the universal application of this rule.

13. All the most important political relations between the individual parties forming part of the Communist International will generally be carried on through the medium of the Executive Committee of the Communist International. In cases of exigency direct relations will be established, with the provision, however, that the Executive Committee of the Communist International shall be informed of them at the same time.

14. The Trade Unions that have accepted the Communist platform and are united on an international scale under the control of the Executive Committee of the Communist International, form Trade Union Sections of the Communist International. The Communist Trade Unions send their representatives to the World Congresses of the Communist International through the medium of the Communist parties of their respective countries. Trade Union sections of the Communist International delegate a representative with decisive vote to the Executive Committee of the Communist International. The Executive Committee of the Communist International enjoys the right of sending a representative with decisive vote, to the Trade Union section of the Communist International.

15. The International League of Communist Youth is subordinate to the Communist International and its Executive Committee. One representative of the Executive Committee of the International League of Communist Youth with a decisive vote is delegated to the Executive Committee of the Communist International. The Executive Committee of the Communist International, on the other hand, enjoys the right of sending a representative with a decisive vote to the Executive organ of the International League of Youth. Organization relations between the League of Youth and the Communist party are basically defined in every country after the same system.

16. The Executive Committee of the Communist International confirms the International Secretary of the Communist Women's Movement, and organizes a women's section of the Communist International.

17. In case a member of the Communist International goes to another country, he is to have the fraternal support of the local members of the Third International.

THE FUNDAMENTAL TASKS OF THE COMMU-
NIST INTERNATIONAL: THESES ADOPTED
BY THE SECOND CONGRESS

1. A characteristic feature of the present moment in the development of the

international Communist movement is the fact that in all the capitalist countries the best representatives of the revolutionary proletariat have completely understood the fundamental principles of the Communist International, namely, the dictatorship of the proletariat and the power of the Soviets; and with a loyal enthusiasm have placed themselves on the side of the Communist International. A still more important and great step forward is the unlimited sympathy with these principles manifested by the wider masses not only of the proletariat of the towns, but also by the advanced portion of the agrarian workers.

On the other hand two mistakes or weaknesses in the extraordinarily rapidly increasing international Communist movement have shown themselves. One very serious weakness directly dangerous to the success of the cause of the liberation of the proletariat consists in the fact that some of the old leaders and old parties of the Second International—partly half-unconsciously yielding to the wishes and pressure of the masses, partly consciously deceiving them in order to preserve their former role of agents and supporters of the bourgeoisie inside the Labor movement—are declaring their conditional or even unconditional affiliation to the Third International, while remaining, in reality, in the whole practice of their party and political work, on the level of the Second International. Such a state of things is absolutely inadmissible, because it demoralizes the masses, hinders the development of a strong Communist Party, and lowers their respect for the Third International by threatening repetition of such betrayals as that of the Hungarian Social-Democrats, who had rapidly assumed the disguise of Communists. The second much less important mistake, which is, for the most part, a malady inherent in the party growth of the movement, is the tendency to be extremely "left," which leads to an erroneous valuation of the role and duties of the party in respect to the class and

to the mass, and of the obligation of the revolutionary Communists to work in the bourgeois parliaments and reactionary labor unions.

The duty of the Communists is not to gloss over any of the weaknesses of their movement, but to criticize them openly, in order to get rid of them promptly and radically. To this end it is necessary, 1) to establish concretely, especially on the basis of the already acquired practical experience, the meaning of the term: "Dictatorship of the Proletariat" and "Soviet Power," and, 2) to point out what could and should be in all countries the immediate and systematic preparatory work to realizing these formulas; and, 3) to indicate the ways and means of curing our movement of its defects.

I. THE SUBSTANCE OF THE DICTATORSHIP
OF THE PROLETARIAT AND OF
THE SOVIET POWER

2. The victory of Socialism over Capitalism—as the first step to Communism—demands the accomplishment of the three following tasks by the proletariat, as the only really revolutionary class:

The first task is to lay low the exploiters, and above all the bourgeoisie as their chief economic and political representative; to defeat them completely; to crush their resistance; to render impossible any attempts on their part to reimpose the yoke of capitalism and wage-slavery.

The second is to inspire and lead in the footsteps of the revolutionary advance guard of the proletariat, its Communist party—not only the whole proletariat or the great majority, but the entire mass of workers and those exploited by capital; to enlighten, organize, instruct, and discipline them during the course of the bold and mercilessly firm struggle against the exploiters; to wrench this enormous majority of the population in all the capitalist countries out of their state of dependence on the bourgeoisies; to instill in them, through practical experience, confidence in the leading role of the proletariat and its revolutionary advance guard. The third is to neutralize or render harmless the inevitable fluctuations between the bourgeoisie and the proletariat, between bourgeois democracy and Soviet Power, on the part of that rather numerous class in all advanced countries—although constituting a minority of the population—the small owners and proprietors in agriculture, industry, commerce, and the corresponding layers of intellectuals, employees, and so on.

The first and second tasks are independent ones, demanding each of them their special methods of action in respect to the exploiters and to the exploited. The third task results from the two first, demanding only a skillful, timely, supple combination of the methods of the first and second kind, depending on the concrete circumstances of each separate case of fluctuation.

3. Under the circumstances which have been created in the whole world, and especially in the most advanced, most powerful, most enlightened and freest capitalist countries by militarist imperialism—oppression of colonies and weaker nations, the universal imperialist slaughter, the "peace" of Versailles—to admit the idea of a voluntary submission of the capitalists to the will of the majority of the exploited, of a peaceful, reformist passage to Socialism, is not only to give proof of an extreme petty bourgeois stupidity, but it is a direct deception of the workmen, a disguisal of capitalist wage-slavery, a concealment of the truth. This truth is that the bourgeoisie, the most enlightened and democratic portion of the bourgeoisie, is even now not stopping at deceit and crime, at the slaughter of millions of workmen and peasants, in order to retain the right of private ownership over the means of production. Only a violent defeat of the bourgeoisie, the confiscation of its property, the annihilation of the entire bourgeois governmental apparatus, parliamentary, judicial, military, bureaucratic, administrative, municipal, etc., even the individual exile or internment of the most stubborn and dangerous exploiters, the establishment of a strict control over them for the repression of all inevitable attempts at resistance and restoration of capitalist slavery—only such measures will be able to guarantee the complete submission of the whole class of exploiters.

On the other hand, it is the same disguising of capitalism and bourgeois democracy, the same deceiving of the workmen, when the old parties and old leaders of the Second International admit the idea that the majority of the workers and exploited will be able to acquire a clear Socialist consciousness, firm Socialist convictions and character under the conditions of capitalist enslavement, under the yoke of the bourgeoisie, which assumes an endless variety of forms—the more refined and at the same time the more cruel and pitiless, the more cultured the given capitalist nation. In reality it is only when the advance guard of the proletariat, supported by the whole class as the only revolutionary one, or a majority of the same, will have overthrown the exploiters, crushed them, freed all the exploited from their position of slaves, improved their conditions of life immediately at the expense of the expropriated capitalists—only after that, and during the very course of the acute class struggle, it will be possible to bring about the enlightenment, education and organization of the widest masses of workers and exploited around the proletariat, under its influence and direction; to cure them of their egotism, their non-solidarity, their vices and weaknesses engendered by private ownership, and to transform them into free workers.

4. For victory over capitalism a correct correlation between the leading Communist party—the revolutionary class, the proletariat—and the masses, i.e., the whole

mass of workers and exploited, is essential. If the Communist party is really the advance guard of the revolutionary class, if it includes the best representatives of the class, if it consists of perfectly conscious and loyal Communists, enlightened by experience gained in the stubborn revolutionary struggle—if it can be bound indissolubly with the entire life of its class, and through the latter with the whole mass of the exploited, and if it can inspire full confidence in this class and this mass, only then is it capable of leading the proletariat in the pitiless, decisive, and final struggle against all the forces of capitalism. On the other hand, only under the leadership of such a party will the proletariat be able to employ all the forces of its revolutionary onslaught, nullifying the inevitable apathy and partial resistance of the insignificant minority of the demoralized labor aristocracy, the old trade-union and guild leaders, etc. Only then will the proletariat be able to display its power which is immeasurably greater than its share in the population, by reason of the economic organization of capitalist society itself. Lastly, only when practically freed from the yoke of the bourgeoisie and the bourgeois governing apparatus, only after acquiring the possibility of freely (from all capitalist exploitation) organizing into its own Soviets, will the mass—i.e., the total of all the workers and exploited—employ for the first time in history all the initiative and energy of tens of millions of people, formerly crushed by capitalism. Only when the Soviets will become the only State apparatus, will effectual participation in the administration be realized for the entire mass of the exploited, who, even under the most cultured and free bourgeois democracy, remain practically excluded from participation in the administration. Only in the Soviets does the mass really begin to study, not out of books, but out of its own practical experience, the work of Socialist construction, the creation of a new social discipline, a free union of free workers.

II. IN WHAT SHOULD THE IMMEDIATE PREPARATION FOR DICTATORSHIP OF THE PROLETARIAT CONSIST?

5. The present moment in the development of the International Communist movement is characterized by the fact that in a great majority of capitalist countries the preparation of the proletariat or the realization of its dictatorship is not yet completed—very often it has not even been begun systematically. It does not follow that the proletarian revolution is not possible, for the economic and political situation is extraordinarily rich in inflammable material which may cause a sudden flame; the other condition for a revolution, besides the preparedness of the proletariat, namely, the general state of crisis in all the ruling and all the bourgeois parties, is also at hand. But it follows from the above that for the moment the duty of the Communist parties consists in accelerating the revolution, without provoking it artificially until sufficient preparation has been made; such preparation is to be carried on and emphasized by revolutionary activity. On the other hand, the above instance in the history of many Socialist parties draws our attention to the fact that the "recognition" of the dictatorship of the proletariat should not remain only verbal.

Therefore the principal duty of the Communist parties, from the point of view of an international proletarian movement, is at the present moment the uniting of the dispersed Communist forces, the formation in each country of a single Communist party (or the strengthening and renovation of the already existing one) in order to perform the work of preparing the proletariat for the conquest of the governing power, and especially for the acquisition of power under the form of a dictatorship of the groups and parties that recognize the dictatorship of the proletariat. This work has not been sufficiently subjected to the radical reformation, the radical renovation, which is necessary for it to be recognized as Communist work, and as corresponding to the tasks on the eve of proletarian dictatorship.

6. The conquest of political power by the proletariat does not put a stop to its class struggle against the bourgeoisie; on the contrary, it makes the struggle especially broad, acute, and pitiless. All the groups, parties, leaders of the Labor movement, fully or partially on the side of reformism, the "center," and so on, turn inevitably, during the most acute periods of the struggle, either to the side of the bourgeoisie or to that of the wavering ones, and the most dangerous are added to the number of the unreliable friends of the vanquished proletariat. Therefore the preparation of the dictatorship of the proletariat demands not only an increased struggle against all reformists and "centrist" tendencies, but a modification of the nature of this struggle.

The struggle should not be limited to an explanation of the fallacy of such tendencies, but it should stubbornly and mercilessly denounce any leader in the Labor movement who may be manifesting such tendencies, otherwise the proletariat will not know whom it must trust in the most decisive struggle against the bourgeoisie. The struggle is such, that the slightest hesitation or weakness in the denunciation of those who show themselves to be reformists or "centrists," means a direct increase of the danger that the power of the proletariat may be overthrown by the bourgeoisie, which will on the morrow utilize in favor of the counter-revolution all that which to short-sighted people appears only as a "theoretical difference of opinion" today.

7. In particular one cannot stop at the usual doctrinaire refutation of all "collaboration" between the proletariat and the bourgeoisie:

The simple defense of "liberty and equality," under the condition of preserving the right of private ownership of the means of production, becomes transformed under the conditions of the dictatorship of the proletariat—which will never be able to suppress completely all private ownership—into a "collaboration" with the bourgeoisie, which undermines directly the power of the working class. The dictatorship of the proletariat means the strengthening and defense, by means of the ruling power of the State, of the "non-liberty" of the exploiter to continue his work of oppression and exploitation, the "inequality" of the proprietor (i.e., of the person who has taken for himself personally the means of production created by public labor and the proletariat). That which before the victory of the proletariat seems but a theoretical difference of opinion on the question of "democracy," becomes inevitably on the morrow of the victory, a question which can only be decided by force of arms. Consequently, without a radical modification of the whole nature of the struggle against the "centrists" and "defenders of democracy," even a preliminary preparation of the mass for the realization of a dictatorship of the proletariat is impossible.

8. The dictatorship of the proletariat is the most decisive and revolutionary form of class struggle between the proletariat and the bourgeoisie. Such a struggle can be successful only when the revolutionary advance guard of the proletariat leads the majority. The preparation of the dictatorship of the proletariat demands, therefore, not only the elucidation of the bourgeois nature of all reformism, all defense of "democracy," with the preservation of the right to the ownership of the means of production; not only the denunciation of such tendencies, which in practice mean the defense of the bourgeoisie inside the Labor movement—but it demands also the replacing of the old leaders by Communists in all kinds of proletarian organizations, not only political, but industrial, cooperative, educational, etc. The more lasting, complete, and solid the rule of the bourgeois democracy has been in any country, the more has it been possible for the bourgeoisie to appoint as labor leaders men who have been educated by it, imbued with its views and

prejudices and very frequently directly or indirectly bribed by it. It is necessary to remove all these representatives of the Labor aristocracy, all such "bourgeois" workmen, from their posts and replace them by even inexperienced workers, so long as these are in unity with the exploited masses, and enjoy the latter's confidence in the struggle against the exploiters. The dictatorship of the proletariat will demand the appointment of such inexperienced workmen to the most responsible State functions, otherwise the rule of the Labor government will be powerless and it will not have the support of the masses.

9. The dictatorship of the proletariat is the most complete realization of a leadership over all workers and exploited, who have been oppressed, beaten down, crushed, intimidated, dispersed, deceived by the class of capitalists, on the part of the only class prepared for such a leading role by the whole history of capitalism. Therefore the preparation of the dictatorship of the proletariat must begin immediately and in all places by means of the following methods among others:

In every organization, union, association—beginning with the proletarian ones at first, and afterwards in all those of the non-proletarian workers and exploited masses (political, professional, military, cooperative, educational, sporting, etc., etc.) must be formed groups or nuclei of Communists—mostly open ones, but also secret ones which become necessary in each case when the arrest or exile of their members or the dispersal of their organization is threatened; and these nuclei, in close contact with one another and with the central party, exchanging experiences, carrying on the work of propaganda, campaign, organization, adapting themselves to all the branches of social life, to all the various forms and subdivisions of the working masses, must systematically train themselves, the party, the class, and the masses by such multiform work.

At the same time it is most important to work out practically the necessary methods on the one hand in respect to the "leaders" or responsible representatives, who are very frequently hopelessly infected with petty bourgeois and imperialist prejudices; on the other hand, in respect to the masses, who, especially after the imperialist slaughter, are mostly inclined to listen to and accept the doctrine of the necessity of leadership of the proletariat as the only way out of capitalistic enslavement. The masses must be approached with patience and caution, and with an understanding of the peculiarities, the special psychology of each layer, each profession of these masses.

10. In particular one of the groups or nuclei of the Communists deserves the exclusive attention and care of the party, namely, the parliamentary faction, i.e., the group of members of the party who are members of bourgeois representative institutions (first of all state institutions, then local, municipal, and others). On the one hand, such a tribune has a special importance in the eyes of the wider circles of the backward or prejudiced working masses; therefore, from this very tribune, the Communists must carry on their work of propaganda, agitation, organization, explaining to the masses why the dissolution of the bourgeois parliament (Constituent Assembly) by the national Congress of Soviets was a legitimate proceeding at the time in Russia (as it will be in all countries in due time). On the other hand, the whole history of bourgeois democracy has made the parliamentary tribune, especially in the more advanced countries, the chief or one of the chief means of unbelievable financial and political swindles, the means of making a career out of hypocrisy and oppression of the workers. Therefore the deep hatred against all parliaments in the revolutionary proletariat is perfectly justified. Therefore the Communist parties, and all parties adhering to the Third International, especially in cases when such parties have been formed not by means of a division in the old parties and after a long stubborn strug-

gle against them, but by means of the old parties passing over (often nominally) to a new position, must be very strict in their attitude towards their parliamentary factions, demanding their complete subordination to the control and the direction of the Central Committee of the party; the inclusion in them chiefly of revolutionary workmen; the carrying out at party meetings of a most intensive analysis of the party press and of the parliamentary speeches, from the point of view of their Communist integrity; detailing of parliament members for propaganda among the masses; the exclusion from such groups of all those who show a tendency towards the Second International, and so forth.

11. One of the chief causes of difficulty in the revolutionary Labor movement in the advanced capitalist countries lies in the fact that owing to colonial dominions and super-dividends of a financial capital, etc., capital has been able to attract a comparatively more solid and broader group of a small minority of the labor aristocracy. The latter enjoy better conditions of pay and are most of all impregnated with the spirit of professional narrow-mindedness, bourgeois and imperialist prejudices. This is the true social "support" of the Second International reformists and centrists, and at the present moment almost the chief social support of the bourgeoisie.

Not even preliminary preparation of the proletariat for the overthrow of the bourgeoisie is possible without an immediate, systematic, widely organized and open struggle against the group which undoubtedly—as experience has already proved—will furnish plenty of men for the White Guards of the bourgeoisie after the victory of the proletariat. All the parties adhering to the Third International must at all costs put into practice the mottoes: "deeper into the masses," "in closer contact with the masses," understanding by the word "masses" the entire mass of workers and those exploited by capitalism, especially the less organized and enlightened, the most oppressed and less adaptable to organization.

The proletariat becomes revolutionary in so far as it is not enclosed within narrow guild limits, in so far as it participates in all the events and branches of public life, as a leader of the whole working and exploited mass; and it is completely impossible for it to realize its dictatorship unless it is ready for and capable of doing everything for the victory over the bourgeoisie. The experience of Russia in this respect has a theoretical and practical importance: where the proletariat could not have realized its dictatorship, nor acquired the respect and confidence of the whole working mass, if it had not borne most of the sacrifices and had not suffered from hunger more than all the other groups in this mass, during the most difficult moments of the onslaught, war and blockade on the part of the universal bourgeoisie.

In particular it is necessary for the Communist party and the whole advanced proletariat to give the most absolute and self-denying support to all the masses for a larger general strike movement, which is alone able under the yoke of capitalism to awaken properly, arouse, enlighten, and organize the masses, and develop in them a full confidence in the leading role of the revolutionary proletariat. Without such a preparation no dictatorship of the proletariat will be possible, and those who are capable of preaching against strikes, like Kautsky in Germany, Turati in Italy, are not to be suffered in the ranks of parties adhering to the Third International. This concerns still more, naturally, such trade-union and parliamentary leaders, as often betray the workingmen by teaching them to make the strike an instrument of reform and not of revolution (Jouhaux in France, Gompers in America, and Thomas in England).

12. For all countries, even for most free "legal" and "peaceful" ones in the sense of a lesser acuteness in the class struggle, the period has arrived, when it has

become absolutely necessary for every Communist party to join systematically lawful and unlawful work, lawful and unlawful organization.

In the most enlightened and free countries, with a most "solid bourgeois-democratic regime," the governments are systematically recurring, in spite of their false and hypocritical assurances, to the method of keeping secret lists of Communists; to endless violations of their constitutions for the semi-secret support of White Guards and the murder of Communists in all countries; to secret preparations for the arrest of Communists; the introduction of provocateurs among the Communists, etc. Only the most reactionary petty bourgeoisie, by whatever high-sounding "democratic" or pacifist phrases it might disguise its ideas, can dispute this fact or the necessary conclusion; an immediate formation by all lawful Communist parties of unlawful organizations for systematic unlawful work, for their complete preparation at any moment to thwart any steps on the part of the bourgeoisie. It is especially necessary to carry on unlawful work in the army, navy, and police, as, after the imperialist slaughter, all the governments in the world are becoming afraid of the national armies, open to all peasants and workingmen, and they are setting up in secret all kinds of select military organizations recruited from the bourgeoisie and especially provided with improved technical equipment.

On the other hand, it is also necessary, in all cases without exception, not to limit oneself to unlawful work, but to carry on also lawful work overcoming all difficulties, founding a lawful press and lawful organizations under the most diverse, and in case of need, frequently changing names. This is now being done by the illegal Communist parties in Finland, in part in Germany, Poland, Latvia, etc. It is thus that the I.W.W. in America should act, as well as all the lawful Communist parties at present, in case prosecutors start prosecutions on the basis of resolutions of the congresses of the Communist International, etc.

The absolute necessity of the principle of unlawful and lawful work is determined not only by the total aggregate of all the peculiarities of the given movement, on the very eve of a proletarian dictatorship, but by the necessity of proving to the bourgeoisie, that there is not and cannot be any branch of the work of which the Communists have not possessed themselves, and still more by the fact that everywhere there are still wide circles of the proletariat and greater ones of the non-proletarian workers and exploited masses, which still trust in the bourgeois democracy, the discussion of which is our most important duty.

13. In particular, the situation of the Labor press in the more advanced capitalist countries shows with special force both the falsity of liberty and equality under the bourgeois democracy, and the necessity of a systematic blending of the lawful and unlawful work. Both in vanquished Germany and in victorious America all the powers of the governmental apparatus of the bourgeoisie, and all the tricks of its financial kings are being set in motion in order to deprive the workingmen of their press; prosecutions and arrests (or murder by means of hired murderers) of the editors, denial of mailing privilege, curtailing of paper supply, etc. Moreover, the information necessary for a daily paper is in the hands of bourgeois telegraph agencies, and the advertisements, without which a large paper cannot pay its way, are at the "free" disposal of capitalists. On the whole, by means of deception, the pressure of capital, and the bourgeois government, the bourgeoisie deprives the revolutionary proletariat of its press.

For the struggle against this state of things the Communist parties must create a new type of periodical press for extensive circulation among the workmen:

1) Lawful publications, in which the Communists without calling themselves such and without mentioning their connection with the party, learn to utilize the

slightest liberty allowed by the laws, as the Bolsheviks did at the "time of the Tsar," after 1905.

2) Illegal sheets, although of the smallest dimensions and irregularly published, but reproduced in most of the printing offices by the workingmen (in secret, or if the movement has grown stronger by means of a revolutionary seizure of the printing offices) giving the proletariat undiluted revolutionary information and the revolutionary mottoes.

Without a Communist press the preparation for the dictatorship of the proletariat is impossible.

Dualism
in Peacetime
1921–1928

POWER POLITICS IN THE WEST

BARRINGTON MOORE, JR.

A brilliant sociologist and philosopher, Barrington Moore is a Senior Research Fellow at the Russian Research Center and Lecturer in the Department of Social Relations at Harvard University. A theme that deeply interests Dr. Moore is the influence of communist ideology upon Soviet policy. He is thoroughly aware of the sometimes unfathomable complexities of this problem, and he is equally conscious of the strongly pragmatic approach of the Bolsheviks to all matters concerned with the preservation of the Soviet state. From his analysis of the interaction of theory and reality, and the influence of this process upon the development of Soviet foreign policy in the 1920's, it becomes apparent that while the Bolsheviks continued to work for world revolution, they also practiced balance-of-power diplomacy in order to preserve the Soviet state. These essentially incompatible objectives form the basis of the dualism in Soviet policy that has perplexed so many observers. At one moment the Bolsheviks seem to be working to advance the world revolution, at another, they appear to be seeking to preserve or maximize the power of the Soviet Union by means of conventional diplomatic maneuvering. The Bolsheviks' own efforts to rationalize this dualism by arguing that strengthening the Soviet Union is the best way to advance world revolution, will be examined more fully in later sections of this chapter.

THE impact of political responsibility in the first months of the regime led to a temporary renunciation of revolutionary goals in favor of the preservation of the infant socialist state. This renunciation was not overtly recognized as such and was concealed through the rationalization that the strengthening of Russia inevitably implied the strengthening of the revolutionary forces. In addition, political responsibility very rapidly led to an awareness of splits in the enemy camp and to techniques for taking advantage of them, which received doctrinal sanction and recognition. The analysis of world politics hammered out in prewar years had been tried out in practice and found at least partly deficient, which Lenin himself was the first to admit.

REVOLUTIONARY HOPES AND DISAPPOINTMENTS

Despite their first disappointments, the new leaders of Russia continued to express

Reprinted by permission of the publishers from Barrington Moore, Jr., *Soviet Politics: The Dilemma of Power* (Cambridge, Mass.: Harvard University Press), pp. 195–208. Copyright, 1950, by The President and Fellows of Harvard College.

the opinion that they could not survive without revolutionary outbreaks in some more industrially advanced country. Shortly after the first anniversary of the November Revolution, Lenin told the Congress of Soviets that the complete victory of a socialist revolution was "unthinkable in a single country" and that it required "the most active cooperation of at least a few progressive countries in which we cannot include Russia."

As an advanced industrial country whose technology and highly skilled population would provide a tremendous asset in the Communist camp, Germany was widely regarded among the Russian leaders as the key to the international situation. Trotsky in a public speech on October 3, 1918, declared: "The German proletariat with all of its technical skill on the one hand and, on the other hand, our Russia—disorganized but extremely rich in natural resources and with 200 million inhabitants—present a most powerful bloc against which all the waves of imperialism will break. For us there can be no allies from the imperialist camp. The revolutionary camp of the proletarians, advancing in an open battle with imperialism—these are our allies."[1] Such responsible leaders as Trotsky and others predicted that the processes which brought the Bolsheviks to power in Russia would repeat themselves because of parallel and irresistible social forces, aided by only a minimum of Russian assistance. Their reliance on the logic of history may in this case have been an indirect confession of their inability to render more concrete assistance to their sympathizers in Germany, who became increasingly active with the collapse of German arms.

Nevertheless, the Russians did what they could. Adolph Joffe, the Soviet diplomatic representative in Berlin after the Treaty of Brest-Litovsk, behaved as a revolutionary agent rather than as an ordinary diplomat. More than ten Left Social Democratic newspapers were directed and supported by the Soviet Embassy in Berlin. In December 1918, Joffe admitted having paid 100,000 marks for the purchase of arms for German revolutionists, and claimed that he had established in Germany a 10 million ruble fund for the support of the German revolution.

Soviet financial assistance and conspiratorial advice failed to turn the upheavals in Germany into a copy of the November Revolution. In January 1919, the Spartacist Union, a group that had split off from the majority socialists and favored the seizure of power by violent means, was decapitated in an unsuccessful uprising by the killing of its two leaders, Rosa Luxemburg and Karl Liebknecht. The majority socialists turned to conservative forces in the army to suppress the uprising, and thereby saved their own position for the time being.

Similar outbreaks in Munich (April 7, 1919) and in Hungary (March 21, 1919) likewise ended in failure. These rebellions were led during their communist phases by flamboyant and doctrinaire revolutionaries who soon alienated local support by attempts to organize economic and political life on what they believed were Soviet models. This policy made it relatively easy for their internal and foreign enemies to crush them.

The communist phase of the Munich uprising lasted only two weeks, scarcely time for the Communist International to extend greetings. In the Hungarian revolt Lenin gave its leader, Béla Kun, tactical and general advice. But Lenin was in no position to enforce the acceptance of this advice. He lacked both the disciplinary power and the information upon which to make an informed judgment. Béla Kun sent flattering letters to Lenin, enclosing copies of his decrees and telling Lenin how his writings were serving as a model for the Hungarian proletarian revolution. From them it is clear that he was making most of

[1] L. Trotsky, *Kak vooruzhalas' revoliutsiya* (3 vols.; Moscow, 1923–1925), I, 372.

the decisions on his own, decisions that we need not record, but which ended disastrously for him and his followers.

The present-day concept of a tightly disciplined Communist Party blindly following detailed instructions from Moscow, a conception that distorts even the contemporary relationships between Moscow and its satellite parties, certainly does not apply to these early attempts to extend the Soviet system to other lands. At this time the leaders of the Russian Revolution served as inspirers, and as contributors of occasional advice and assistance, but not as directors. Although they often claimed they were riding the wave of the future, they were scarcely able to direct it into the channels they chose.

The only attempt to extend Soviet influence over which the Russian Communist leaders exercised considerable control took place in Poland, more or less by accident, during the spring and summer of 1920. What had begun as a defensive war against Pilsudski became transformed for a brief time by the military successes of the Red Army into a revolutionary crusade. The Russians established a Polish "Provisional Government" behind the lines of the Red Army and attempted to set up soviets as they went along. Local Polish support was not forthcoming, and the invasion of the Red Army unified Polish national sentiment behind Pilsudski, whose forces defeated the Red Army. A few months later Lenin confessed that he had made a political miscalculation.

A significant sidelight on Soviet foreign policy appears from the fact that, when the Red Army was at the height of its campaign against Poland, the Russians continued their negotiations with the British in an effort to bring to a close hostilities between the two countries, and to establish normal diplomatic relations. These actions indicate that the Communist leaders were anxious to keep a second string to their bow. They also suggest that the Bolsheviks had already begun to entertain serious doubts about the imminence of a world-wide revolutionary conflagration.

The revolutionary failures of 1918, 1919, and 1920 were attributed very largely by the Russian Communist leaders to a poor choice of tactics on the part of local leaders, over whom they felt they had inadequate control, and to a lack of disciplined organization in general. The Communist International had been founded formally at its opening Congress in March 1919. But as Zinoviev, the chairman of its Executive Committee, observed, the Comintern was merely a "propaganda society" during the entire first year of its existence. Now the time had come, the Russian leaders argued, for it to become something concrete. The Russian Party had succeeded in overthrowing the Tsarist autocracy by creating a strictly disciplined conspiratorial elite. Might not a similar organization be able to succeed on an international scale? In the spring of 1920 Lenin wrote that "the Russian model reveals to *all* countries something that is very essential in their near and inevitable future."[2] The experience of the victorious dictatorship of the proletariat in Russia," he added, "has clearly shown even to those who are unable to think . . . that absolute centralisation and the strictest discipline of the proletariat are one of the fundamental conditions for victory over the bourgeoisie." Similar arguments were hammered home by Zinoviev at the Second Congress of the Communist International, in July 1920. Waverers on both the Right and the Left, particularly those who wished to have dealings with the alleged traitors to the proletarian revolution among the moderate socialist parties, must be eliminated from Communist ranks.

Such was the background of thinking and circumstances that preceded the adoption of the famous "Twenty-One Conditions" for admission into the Communist

[2] V. I. Lenin, "Left Wing Communism," *Selected Works* (12 vols.; New York, n.d.), X, 58.

International at its Second Congress. On paper at least these conditions established a centralized organization very similar in structure to the Russian Communist Party. Henceforth the failures of the Comintern were to be rationalized by the explanation that they were due either to treachery or to the failure of various Communist leaders to understand Marxist-Leninist (later Marxist-Leninist-Stalinist) doctrine correctly and to apply it properly. The same argument was used against the leaders of the Comintern by those who lost power within its ranks. At no time was the suggestion made openly that the Russian experience might be irrelevant or that Lenin's conception of the dynamics of modern capitalist society could be seriously mistaken.

Despite the adoption of the Twenty-One Conditions in 1920, the Comintern remained for some time a loose gathering rather than a tightly centralized organization. As late as 1922, at the Fourth Congress, Zinoviev complained that the twenty-one points had not been "brought to life." He spoke bitterly about the misbehavior of the French and Italian Parties, and observed sadly that internal discipline was so weak it had not proved possible to carry out even such a minor festival as "Comintern Week" on an international scale. However, some improvement was noted by this time in Comintern connections with Germany. There, according to Zinoviev's claim, almost no political event took place without an exchange of opinions between the German Party and the Comintern Executive Committee.

In general, the Comintern was torn throughout its history by factional disputes frequently ending in wholesale expulsions. These disputes were the reflection of oppositional movements within the Communist Party of the Soviet Union, personal rivalries, and genuine differences of opinion over the correct policies to be adopted. Often these differences arose from the fact that the interests of the local Parties in adapting themselves to local conditions did not agree with the interests of the dominant Russian Party, or at least were interpreted in widely divergent fashions.

In the beginning, debates were often hot, long, and heavy at Comintern Congresses, where disagreements were brought out into the open. Such continued to be the case as late as the Fifth Congress in 1924. At the Sixth Congress in 1928 disagreements were largely prevented from coming out openly. However, the delegates were obviously concerned about rumors of differences within the Russia Politburo as Stalin prepared to liquidate the Right Opposition. The Seventh and last Congress in 1935, at which Comintern policy underwent one of its many sharp reversals, was a well-rehearsed affair in which policy was adopted without serious objection from the floor. These and many other facts show that the same process of transferring power to a narrower and narrower circle took place within the Comintern as well as in the Communist Party of the Soviet Union.

According to the Twenty-One Conditions, the formal procedure for reaching decisions within the Comintern was supposedly that of democratic centralism, as in the Russian Party. Actually, decisions were reached for the most part by prominent factional leaders taking their troubles to the top Russian authorities. Factional groups attempted to persuade the Russians that their policy was the correct one. If they succeeded, their policy was adopted as the formal line of the International. If they failed yet insisted on their point of view, they would, in time, be cast out as traitors to the working class. Naturally this situation put a great premium on personal contacts and accurate information on currents of opinion among the Russian leaders. A career and even survival often depended on guessing correctly which way the Soviet cat would jump. Those who out of principle disdained to make such guesses increasingly failed to survive. This situation has had important effects upon the present-day leaders of the Communist Parties outside the USSR. Most of them are skilled bureaucratic intriguers rather than flaming revolutionaries.

Thus the Russian Communists did not have at their command a revolutionary instrument until after the spontaneous postwar upheavals had died down. The earliest date at which the Russians may have attempted to direct a proletarian uprising was in March 1921, the time of an abortive outbreak in Germany. Even in this case the Russian role was at the very most no more than that of spurring on the German Communists to seize an apparently favorable moment for general strike throughout Germany. The attempt was a failure. By this time the pressure of domestic events, combined with the failure of world revolution to materialize, had forced Lenin to sound the signal for a general retreat. On March 8, 1921, he gave to the Tenth Party Congress the famous speech outlining the New Economic Policy.

Once again the revolution was postponed. Lenin conceded this frankly, both in public and in private. Other leaders adopted, officially at least, a more equivocal attitude. Trotsky's report to the Third Congress of the Communist International, held in the summer of 1921, and the Theses drafted by him which were adopted by that body, might be regarded as a model of political double talk. He argued that the conclusion of the peace treaties did not mean that the international bourgeoisie had renounced the goal of destroying the Soviet Republic. Future perspectives remained revolutionary. Capitalism was definitely not restored, and had instead entered a period of profound depression, according to Trotsky's interpretation. On the other hand, he conceded that capitalist equilibrium displayed great powers of resistance, that the bourgeoisie felt it had grown stronger, and that in the future the advance would not be so feverish, that there would be a slowing down of the revolutionary tempo. Therefore, he advised the Communist Parties to be ready for revolu-

tionary upheavals or for a period of gathering their forces and winning the support of the majority of the working class.

The equivocal nature of these statements and others of the same kind may be attributed to the conflicting pressures of the necessity for a new definition of political realities and the desire to cling to older definitions in the face of contradictory and refractory experiences. Even natural scientists have occasionally found themselves in this awkward predicament at the time of the breakup of one world view and the emergence of a new one.

On the whole, revolutionary hopes displayed a surprising tenacity in the face of repeated failures. Two more major attempts in Germany and China were undertaken before a long lull, lasting from 1927 until the Second World War, took place in Soviet endeavors to alter the social structure of the non-Soviet world. Before examining these attempts it is necessary to analyze the Soviet effort to adjust to a world of competing great powers by the more familiar methods of balance-of-power diplomacy, and its relationship to official Soviet doctrines.

MARX OR MACHIAVELLI?

Accepting in 1921 the supposedly temporary setback to the goal of self-preservation by revolution, the Communist leaders of Russia proceeded to display considerable skill in the techniques of balance-of-power diplomacy. As in the case of other contemporary states, the Soviets applied such techniques with but little open recognition that they were following an easily recognizable pattern of behavior. For the most part, their overt awareness of this fact was limited to statements about the necessity of splitting the imperialist camp, or to proclamations about their generally pacific intentions and willingness to cooperate with capitalist states "during a given historical period."

The Leninist conception of international relations, though it did not prevent the practice of balance-of-power politics on the part of the Communist elite, militated against any conception of international politics as a continuing system of political relationships, in which the participants themselves might change or change their positions, while the system itself remained relatively unchanged. Instead, the Russian leaders continued, though with decreasing frequency and emphasis, to predict the disappearance of the entire system and its replacement by an international proletarian community.

The first large-scale triumph won by the Soviets through the techniques of balance-of-power diplomacy was the detachment of Germany from a position of dependence on England and France by the Rapallo Treaty of April 16, 1922. The success of Rapallo appears to have been a hoped for, but unexpected, windfall. In the discussions that preceded Russia's participation in the Genoa Conference, Lenin continually emphasized Soviet economic rather than political goals. In fact, his published speeches contain no reference to the possibility of a Soviet-German rapprochement. The purpose of the Genoa Conference, as stated by its moving spirit, Lloyd George, was the restoration of European economy shattered by the war. From just such a conference Lenin apparently believed that Russia had much to gain. "From the very beginning we declared that *we welcomed Genoa and would attend it;* we understood perfectly well, and did not conceal it, that we were going there as merchants, because trade with capitalist countries is absolutely essential for us (until they have entirely collapsed), and that we were going to Genoa to discuss in the most correct and favorable manner the politically suitable terms of this trade, and nothing more."[3] There was, according to Lenin, no disagreement or controversy on this question in the Party Central Committee or among the rank and file, an indication of the extent to which the hopes and desires for a revolutionary crusade had died down.

Even though the restoration of trade relations appears to have been the primary Soviet objective, it is evident that political matters were also under consideration. On the way to Genoa the Soviet delegation stopped off in Berlin and engaged in conversations concerning the possibility of a Soviet-German agreement. Both sides had been feeling their way toward an agreement for some time in order to escape pressure from the victorious Allies. According to Louis Fischer, the conversations that ultimately led to Rapallo began as early as 1920 in a prison cell occupied by Karl Radek. They did not succeed until the Allies had been split by a combination of circumstances and Soviet-German diplomatic tactics.

In addition to England, the major participants in the Genoa Conference were Russia, France, Germany, and Italy. Certain economic interests temporarily united these countries against the Soviets before the conference. Various groups in England, France, and Germany joined together prior to the conference in a plan for dealing with the Russian problem that would in effect have resulted in the exploitation of Russian resources on what amounted to a basis of extraterritorial privileges. The hopes of these circles were perhaps unduly raised by the partial restoration of private property and private trade in Russia under the NEP, and by various official Soviet announcements concerning the opportunities for foreign capitalists to operate enterprises in the Soviet Republic in order to hasten the restoration of Russia's shattered economy. However, the powers were able to reach an agreement only on this extreme basis, which would have virtually ended

[3] "The International and Internal Position of the Soviet Republic," report delivered at a meeting of the Communist faction of the All-Russian Congress of Metal Workers' Union, March 6, 1922, *Selected Works*, IX, 306.

Russia's sovereignty. Other political factors divided them.

Chief among these factors were conflicting Anglo-French views on the German problem. The British were suspicious of French desires to achieve European hegemony. The French in turn were suspicious of British balance-of-power policies, and of the German desire to play off their former enemies against each other to increase their own freedom of action. The entire situation was further complicated by a division of opinion within each country, which was at least partly reflected in the delegations of each power, including the Soviet one.

At the opening of the conference Chicherin was careful not to create a common antagonistic front by revolutionary phrasemaking. Lenin had already advised him to "avoid big words" in discussing the text of his opening speech. Instead, and presumably taking his cue from Lenin, Chicherin opened his speech by declaring that the Russian delegation, while remaining true to the general principles of Communism, recognized the need for economic cooperation between the old and the new system of the world during the present historical epoch. This conception of the "peaceful co-existence of two social systems during a given historical epoch" was put forth on a number of subsequent occasions when the Soviet leaders were anxious to obtain the support of a specific capitalist country against other capitalist states. On this occasion, as on others, the search for support required the postponement or abjuring of revolutionary goals.

It is not possible to follow here in any further detail Soviet techniques at this conference, though they constitute a fascinating chapter in diplomatic history. Chicherin cleverly succeeded in splitting the Allies, so that they could not present a united opposition to Russian tactics. Then he managed to split the German delegation itself, which was divided between those favoring an Eastern and a Western orientation for German foreign policy. Finally, he telephoned a member of the German delegation at one-thirty Easter morning, saying the moment to sign was then or never. The same afternoon the Rapallo pact stunned other delegates to the conference.

The three-cornered diplomatic struggle among England, France, and Germany continued for several years, and again provided an opportunity for the Soviets to prevent capitalist unification directed against them. Among other incidents, the Bolshevik leaders feared that the Locarno pact of 1925, guaranteeing the Franco-German frontier, might be a move inimical to them. Before the treaty was signed, Chicherin stated to the German press that the "entire guarantee pact policy of England is an integral part of her basic anti-Soviet activity."[4] At the same time both the French leaders, Poincaré and Briand, feared that Locarno would make England the arbiter between France and Germany and hamper French freedom of action. They therefore made an unsuccessful attempt to effect a rapprochement with the Russians. Meanwhile the Germans, who were under pressure from the Russians to refuse Locarno, could not forfeit friendly relations with the Soviets, since this would weaken their bargaining position with the Western powers. Furthermore, there are indications that an arrangement was in effect at that time between Germany and the Soviet Union for an exchange of military experience, army experts, and munitions, though this fact has been denied by the Russians. For these reasons Stresemann and Chicherin reached an agreement, repeating the essentials of the Treaty of Rapallo, by October of 1925. The Locarno Treaty was signed on October 16, 1925, but the Russo-German treaty was kept secret in order to avoid spoiling Germany's chances in the West. It was not published until the League Council refused to allow Germany to enter the League of Nations in March of 1926.

[4] Quoted by L. Fischer from the *Berliner Tageblatt*, October 2, 1925, in *The Soviets in World Affairs* (London, 1930), II, 593.

This technique of pitting one power against another, the essence of balance-of-power diplomacy, was not confined to European affairs. It was also applied in the Near East, where the major antagonist again was England, and where the application of the policy also conflicted at times with revolutionary aspirations. Here, however, the conflict between doctrine and expediency was not so marked, since according to Leninist doctrine the forces opposed to colonial rule included local nationalist movements. After experimenting with propaganda appeals to throw off the imperialist yoke, and even in one case with the establishment of a Soviet regime in Northern Persia—the Gilan Republic which lasted until the autumn of 1921—the Russians contented themselves with the toleration or active support of local nationalist leaders such as Riza Shah Pahlavi in Persia or Kemal Atatürk in Turkey, who endeavored to westernize and modernize their countries. The anti-British policies of such leaders made them useful to the Soviets. Thus at the Lausanne Conference in 1923, called to discuss the status of the Dardanelles, Chicherin clashed with the British leader, Lord Curzon, and won the reputation of being "more Turkish than the Turks." Although Kemal used strong-arm measures to put down Russian Communist influence within his country, his actions had no appreciable effect upon the friendly relations between the two countries.

During the twenties the Soviets continued to waver between attempts to maximize their power and security by prolonging the truce, as they saw it, with the capitalist world, and attempts to find a more radical solution by revolutionary means. Among the devices used to prolong the truce was the series of disarmament proposals that won for the Soviets much sympathy in non-Communist circles opposed to war. The Soviet proposal, made on a number of occasions, amounted to complete and total disarmament. As a weak state in the military sense, the Soviets had much to gain from radical disarmament. They may also have anticipated gains from weakening what they regarded as the military props under capitalism, and have found some value in showing up the alleged hypocrisy of their capitalist opponents. Nevertheless, Soviet disarmament proposals were not merely propaganda statements, issued without any intention that they should be acted upon. As their actions show, the Russians regarded any step that might reduce the danger of armed attack on the USSR as desirable. They suggested partial steps, such as a mutual reduction of the Red Army and the armies of Russia's western border states to one quarter of their existing dimensions. After sharp initial criticisms, the Soviets participated in the Kellogg Pact (1929), sponsored by the United States in an effort to outlaw war as an instrument of national policy, and at a later date in the League of Nations. At the same time the Russians continued to make it clear that even though they welcomed partial, or indeed any, disarmament, they still regarded such measures as palliatives. Capitalism, they repeated, was bound to produce war.

Another aspect of the Soviet policy of prolonging the truce and seeking allies where they could be found was exemplified in their search for *de facto* and *de jure* recognition by the other powers. By 1924 recognition had been granted by the major powers except for the United States. In that year the Commissariat for Foreign Affairs could make the somewhat unrevolutionary claim in its annual report to the Congress of Soviets that "the USSR has taken its due place in the system of great world powers." In addition to the search for credits and other concrete advantages, the search for prestige—the desire to make the capitalist world and capitalist diplomats accept them as social equals—appears to have played no small role in this aspect of Soviet foreign policy. Italy, where Mussolini was one of the first dictators to succeed in suppressing the local Communist Party, managed to be the first country to grant *de jure* recognition, and thereby won a favorable trade agreement. Others followed rapidly.

As the Italian incident suggests, the search for allies and for recognition, conducted largely through the Commissariat for Foreign Affairs, conflicted on various occasions with the policy promoted through the Comintern. A frequently reproduced cartoon from *Pravda* shows Foreign Affairs Commissar Chicherin scratching his head in perspiring anxiety as Zinoviev, Comintern leader, thundered revolutionary phrases over the international air waves. Nor was the anxiety confined to Chicherin's organization. Bukharin found it necessary to reassure the delegates to the Fourth Congress of the Comintern that it was perfectly proper for proletarian states to accept loans and form alliances or blocs with bourgeois states, if the tactical situation of the moment demanded it. In such cases, he added, "it is the duty of foreign comrades to work for the victory of such a bloc. If in the future the bourgeoisie of such a country is itself defeated, then other tasks arise. *(Laughter.)*"[5] In other words, agreements with capitalist states were defended as one means among many for strengthening the socialist bulwark against the inevitable day of reckoning. Such statements were of course a repetition of Lenin's essential argument at Brest-Litovsk: that there could be no conflict between the national interests of the Soviet state and the ultimate interests of the world revolution.

[5] *IV Vsemirnyi Kongress Kommunisticheskogo Internatsionala, Izbrannye Doklady, Rechi i Rezoliutsii* (Moscow-Petrograd, 1923), pp. 195–196.

STALIN AND THE COMINTERN

ISAAC DEUTSCHER

Isaac Deutscher, born in Poland and educated at Cracow, was a member of the Communist party of Poland and an editor of its press from 1926 until 1932. In the latter year he was expelled from the party for opposition to Stalin. Gifted with a remarkable narrative style, he has made an enviable record as a journalist and editor in Great Britain and has published several authoritative works dealing with Soviet affairs. Among his most interesting recent books are: *The Prophet Armed: Trotsky, 1879–1921*, and *The Prophet Unarmed*. In the extracts from *Stalin* printed here, Deutscher examines the development of communist thought on foreign affairs after Lenin's death in early 1924, and shows how Stalin held Soviet policy away from aggressive efforts to bring about world revolution. Deutscher's explanation of Stalin's transformation of the Comintern into little more than an agency of Soviet foreign policy, while well-informed and accurate for the most part, is somewhat more conclusive than the available evidence justifies. In reality the machinery of the Comintern remained unwieldy and awkward. Continuous expulsions and purges were required to force the nationalist Communist parties to follow the Soviet line.

THE Comintern at first embodied the hope that the working classes of the west would, of their own accord, find their road to socialism.

From *Stalin: A Political Biography* by Isaac Deutscher, pp. 389–398, 404–405. Copyright 1949 by Oxford University Press, Inc. Reprinted by permission, with some of the author's footnotes omitted.

Very soon, however, the Soviet leaders were compelled in self-defence to resort to some of the conventional methods of diplomacy. They improvised a diplomatic doctrine which aimed at restoring a temporary European balance of power that would strengthen their position *vis-à-vis* the capitalist world. By the peace of Versailles the victors, and especially France, dominated the Continent. In the French system of alliances, Poland, Rumania, and Czechoslovakia were assigned a double role: they were to be the ramparts against the revolutionary menace from the east as well as against the pressure of any reviving German militarism. That system of alliances worked at first much more directly against Russia than against Germany. The Russian objective was to create a counter-balance to it. Soviet diplomacy achieved this by a partial alinement with the vanquished against the victors, with Germany against the Allies, especially against France. Curiously enough, British and Soviet policies, for all their ideological conflicts, developed in part along parallel lines. For different reasons, from opposite fringes of Europe, both Britain and Russia sought to counteract the domination of the Continent by a single military power. The parallelism can be found even in the attitudes of public opinion in the two countries towards the peace of Versailles. Both in Britain and Russia Versailles was denounced. The main arguments of J. M. Keynes's *Economic Consequences of the Peace* were expounded in the Marxist idiom by Soviet economists. But, unlike Britain, Bolshevik Russia was not encumbered by commitments to France and had a freer hand in playing for a balance of power. In 1922 Chicherin signed the Russo-German treaty of Rapallo. Even before that Russia had achieved friendship with Turkey, another vanquished country.

The Bolsheviks at first regarded their manoeuvres in the diplomatic field as temporary half-measures. They still expected social upheaval in the west. The Comintern was the main lever of their foreign policy; diplomacy was a poor auxiliary. The Politbureau sternly instructed the diplomats to say and do nothing that might embarrass the Communist parties abroad. Ambassadors were as a rule instructed to disregard etiquette and to speak like revolutionary agitators; at the most they were to engage in "sober, business-like" commercial deals with the capitalist states.

This trend had prevailed in foreign policy some time before Stalin stepped to the fore as one of the triumvirs. Lenin had shared the direction of foreign policy with Chicherin, the Commissar for Foreign Affairs, Kamenev, Trotsky, and Chicherin's assistants Karakhan and Litvinov, all former émigrés with a good knowledge of the western countries. Stalin had not been concerned with the conduct of foreign policy. It seems that the only time that he had been involved in a diplomatic incident was when Lord Curzon protested against one of his messages to Moslems, interpreting it as incitement of colonial peoples against His Majesty's Government. His role in the Comintern, too, had been altogether insignificant.

When, as one of the triumvirs, he became active in these fields also, he at first did nothing to alter the set course of foreign policy. Russia was then reaping the first fruits of Rapallo and widening the breaches in the *cordon sanitaire*. In 1923, 1924, and 1925 many countries resumed diplomatic and commercial relations with her. Every sign of an abatement in capitalist hostility was received in Moscow with genuine joy. The Soviets were gaining breathing space.

This hopeful development, however, demanded a new balance between the Soviet diplomacy and the Comintern. The two objectives, world revolution and normal or friendly relations between Russia and the capitalist countries, were *au fond* incompatible. One of them would have to be sacrificed or, at any rate, subordinated to the other. The choice emerged from the answer that events were giving to two questions: "What are the chances of world revolution?" and "Is stable peace between the Soviets and the capitalist world possible?" The dilemma did not arise suddenly. It was pressed home gradually by successive changes in the international situation. Nor did the solution take the form of a deliberate decision, adopted and recorded at any definite date. It was implicit in a series of shifts, now imperceptible and now dramatic.

After four years of Lenin's and Trotsky's leadership, the Politbureau could not view the prospects of world revolution without scepticism. Its scepticism, to be sure, was qualified by the Marxist conviction of all its members that it was as certain that socialism would in due course replace capitalism as it was that capitalism had already replaced feudalism. But Stalin was not content with broad historical perspectives which seemed to provide no answer to burning, topical questions. The process by which European feudalism was abolished lasted centuries. How long would capitalism be able to resist? Lenin had counted its lease of life in the major European countries first in weeks, then in months, and then in years. Prudence now seemed to counsel counting in decades. During all that time the fate of the Soviets would hang in the balance. Could Bolshevism hope for decades of peace? Recent successes of Soviet diplomacy induced Stalin to take the optimistic view. Thus extreme scepticism about world revolution and confidence in the reality of a long truce between Russia and the capitalist world were the twin premisses of his "socialism in one country."

Trotsky relates how contemptuously Stalin dismissed the potentialities of foreign communism. The Comintern, he allegedly held, would carry out no revolution for many decades. Lominadze, one of Stalin's close associates in the twenties, later attributed to Stalin the saying that "the Comintern represents nothing. It exists only because of our support." Stalin himself denied having made the remark. Lominadze may have referred to loose talk at a

session of the Politbureau. But most of Stalin's public statements in the middle twenties abound in broad, though much more cautious, hints to similar effect. The most illuminating of these can be found in his discourse to the students of the Sverdlov University on 9 June 1925. He described the domestic policies that Soviet Russia would have to adopt "if she was not backed by the social revolution of the western proletariat within the next fifteen years." Elaborating his point he then made the assumption of a peaceful isolation of Russia lasting twenty years, that is until 1945. Nor was this one of several alternative premises: it was the main premiss of his policy. His listeners were ardent young Communists, many of them sympathetic towards the left opposition, to whom the mere assumption of so long a hiatus in international revolution was shocking. The perspective of so long a peace also sounded incredible. The speaker had to take the mood of his audience into account and expound his views with caution. In his own mind he almost certainly reckoned with an even longer period of Russian isolation.

His attitude demanded the gradual subordination of Communist policies to the needs of Soviet diplomacy. In the Leninist period diplomacy had been, as it were, an auxiliary detachment of the Comintern. That relationship was to be reversed. From the "vanguards of world revolution" the Communist parties became, in Trotsky's words, the more or less pacifist "frontier guards" of Soviet Russia. From Stalin's viewpoint it would have been utter folly to risk the substance of socialism in one country for the shadow of revolution abroad. The main thing for the Bolshevik leaders was to make up their minds on how much substance there was in socialism in one country and whether international communism represented a mere shadow. Over these issues they split. To his last day Trotsky believed that there was more reality in international communism, despite all its weakness, than in socialism in one country, despite all its achievements. Most of the other leaders who vacillated between Stalin and Trotsky hesitated over this crucial issue. As to Stalin, this, the major premiss of his policy, remained unchanged throughout the period between the wars.

The peculiar point to be considered is that he was never free to lay bare his main premiss. The view that the world had entered into the era of Socialist revolution had been the mainspring of Leninism. The need for Stalin to pay lip-service to the expectation of revolution was the more pressing the more he was involved in the fight against the left Bolsheviks, who charged him with abandoning the Leninist heritage. It was mainly in the first phases of that struggle, in 1925 and 1926, that he could allow himself to argue publicly from the assumption that no Socialist upheaval in the west would occur for about twenty years. Then, pressed by his opponents, he either sought refuge in ambiguity or vied with them in prophesying the nearness of revolutionary events. Such prophesies represented the exoteric aspect of his policy, the coating without which a large section of the party would not have consented to swallow his ideas. His esoteric view he kept to himself: at the most, he discussed it with the leaders of his own faction; but it was always implied in what he did. The contradiction between the two sides of his policy gave to his behaviour that touch of insincerity and even duplicity which made his anti-Bolshevik critics accuse him of plotting for world revolution, while his Bolshevik critics charged him with plotting against it.

* * *

The débâcle of German communism in 1923 decisively speeded up the crystallization of the set of ideas associated with Stalinism. In the summer of that year the Politbureau and the Executive of the Comintern hotly debated the German crisis provoked by the French occupation of the Ruhr and the galloping devaluation of the German currency. Some of the Bolshevik leaders saw the approach of the "German October." Heinrich Brandler, the leader of the German Communist party, arrived in Moscow to consult the Executive of the Comintern on strategy and tactics. It was on that occasion that Stalin for the first time intervened with the weight of his growing influence in a major decision of the Comintern. His view on the German situation, which he set out in a letter to Zinoviev and Bukharin, was marked by a strong disbelief in the chances of German communism. He listed all the exceptional circumstances that favoured the Bolsheviks in the revolution of 1917 and concluded: "At the moment the German Communists have nothing of the kind. They have, of course, a Soviet country as neighbour, which we did not have. But what can we offer them? . . . Should the government in Germany topple over now . . . and the Communists seize hold of it, they would end up in a crash."[1] He warned the Politbureau against encouraging any risky Communist demonstrations in Germany, which the *bourgeoisie* and the right-wing Social Democrats ("at present all the odds are on their side") would turn into a general battle that might end in the extermination of the Communists. "In my opinion the Germans [that is the German Communists] should be restrained and not spurred on." The difference between the chances of the Bolsheviks in 1917 and those of the German Communists in 1923, as Stalin saw it, was that the Bolsheviks had the support of a people longing for peace and of a peasantry eager to seize the landlords' estates. What his argument implied was that the German Communists could not hope to seize power either

[1] L. Trotsky, *Stalin* (2nd ed.; New York, 1946), pp. 368–369. The authenticity of this letter is confirmed by the two rival leaders of German communism, Heinrich Brandler and Ruth Fischer. It has not been published in Stalin's *Works*, although Stalin has never denied its authenticity. A. Thalheimer, *1923: Eine Verpasste Revolution?* (Berlin, 1931), p. 31.

in 1923 or in any foreseeable future, because they could never obtain backing from the peasantry comparable to that received by Bolshevism, and that, at best, only a German defeat in another war might give them a chance. To the one circumstance that might have favoured them, the much greater role of the industrial working class in Germany than in Russia, Stalin paid no attention.

Later in the year, as the turmoil in Germany mounted, the Russian advocates of revolutionary action gained ground and began to "spur on" the Germans. Stalin ceased to air his scepticism and kept in the background. He let Trotsky, Zinoviev, and Radek, who did not see eye to eye with one another, commit themselves. Brandler returned to Germany with a set of incoherent and contradictory instructions: he was to organize a revolution against the Social Democrats and at the same time to enter the Social Democratic government of Saxony; he was to start the revolution in Saxony, not in the capital or any other decisive centre, &c.—instructions that would have made any insurrectionist party miss its best opportunities. The enterprise ended in a series of unco-ordinated moves, and in failure. The effect of the failure on Moscow was very great: the isolation of Russian communism was now sealed.

In the next few years the fate of the Comintern remained unsettled. Although Stalin believed the organization to be more or less useless as the instrument of revolution, he could not dissociate Russia's ruling party from it—the ties between Bolshevism and the Comintern had been too strong for that. The Comintern, on the other hand, was inspired by a sense of its mission. It spoke for only a minority of the European working classes; but that was a large and important minority comprising the most idealistic, active, and ardent elements of the western proletariat. Its activity could not but embarrass Soviet diplomacy. This was one motive which compelled Stalin to try to tame the unruly organization. An-

other was the influence which the Comintern might have on the internal struggles in Russia. In those years the European Communist leaders, though accepting guidance from the successful Bolshevik experts on revolution, still talked to them as equals and took for granted their own right to have a say in Russian affairs. Most of them at first sided with Trotsky against Stalin, with the European-minded Bolsheviks against the self-centred Russian hierarchy of secretaries. Thus, for domestic as well as diplomatic reasons, Stalin could not but extend to the Comintern, still accustomed to the interplay of various trends, traditions, and views in its midst, the methods by which he was remoulding the Russian party into a "monolithic" body.

He acted from behind the scenes, mainly through his lieutenants who sat on the Executive of the International. Unlike Lenin, who had addressed every congress of the Comintern and, though the official head of the Government, had publicly shouldered responsibility for its policy, Stalin, holding no post in the Government, never addressed any congress of the Comintern. During ceremonial meetings he sat silently on the platform to be acclaimed by multi-national crowds of delegates. Only the initiated knew that the public debates and votes were of little significance, and that no major decision of the Comintern had any validity unless it was approved by Stalin. He looked with disdain upon the great ideological debates, in which Lenin had indulged with eagerness and gusto, and he regarded the regular congresses as a waste of time. During the four years of Lenin's leadership, four fully fledged international congresses were convened; during the twenty-five years of Stalin's leadership only three: one in 1924, which endorsed the denunciation of Trotskyism, another in 1928, at which the influence of Bukharin and the right Bolsheviks was eliminated, and a third in 1935, which proclaimed the policy of Popular Fronts. The centre of gravity of the organization shifted to its

Executive Committee. As in the Russian party so in the Comintern, the caucus gained absolute predominance over the whole body of the movement.

Naturally most of the work that Stalin did in setting up that caucus was hidden in obscurity. He squeezed out the men who had independent minds, the rebels, the theoreticians, the radical *literati*, the leaders of European communism in its period of revolutionary spontaneity. Almost every one of them was involved in the reverses of the early twenties and therefore vulnerable; and Stalin made the most of their "errors" and "deviations" to discredit them. The emotional attachment of European Communists to the much-maligned and attacked Russian revolution was so great that almost any leader was undone if it was known that he had against him the authority of the Russian party. Stalin rarely used that authority directly. The verdicts and condemnations were passed by the Executive of the Comintern. The Executive was democratically elected at international congresses. But it was almost always swayed by the Russian delegation, on whom the views of the Russian Politbureau were binding. And inside the Politbureau Stalin swayed the majority. This was the mechanism through which he controlled the International. The Russian members of the Executive nominally had no prerogatives other than those possessed by representatives of foreign parties; but their moral pull was decisive. Where this was not enough, various forms of pressure were used to crush opposition. Rebellious foreign leaders were assigned with all honour to work at the headquarters of the International in Moscow, where they were easily controlled and cut off from their followers; public opinion in other Communist parties was mobilized against them; and their opponents and rivals in their own countries were encouraged and raised up. When, in spite of all the campaigning against them, in which calumny had its part, the "deviationists" still enjoyed authority in their own party, the cashiers of the Comintern withheld their subsidies from that party. But the effectiveness of this, the crudest means of pressure, was secondary.[2] It was the legend of the Russian revolution, its solid and permanent substance as well as the transitory myths woven into it, that gave Stalin his power over a vast agglomeration of foreign parties, in whose ranks the idealistic seekers for a new way of life were incomparably more numerous than the time-servers. And even the time-servers were time-servers only in a relative sense: they were ready to obey any master, but only if that master spoke with the authority of revolution. Over the years Stalin succeeded in drilling his hosts according to his own ideas, primarily because those hosts were willing to serve a great cause, a cause which, rightly or wrongly, they identified with the Soviets, a cause which seemed to them to be of much greater simplicity and magnitude than either the feuds in the Russian Politbureau or the shifts in the Comintern, than either the manœuvres of Russian diplomacy or even the dim shadows of a remote Russian reality.

Thus it came about that the Comintern not only shone with the reflected light of the Russian party, but that it reflected each of its internal alinements in turn. This was

[2] The subsidizing of the various branches of the Comintern was innocuous at first. Every section was to contribute its share to the treasury of the organization and to draw on it according to needs. In varying degrees this had also been the custom in the previous Internationals, the second and the first, without producing corruption. As the financial resources of the Russian party were incomparably greater than those of the other sections, the Comintern became up to a point dependent on them. Foreign parties with a large following could, of course, easily support themselves. But Moscow encouraged them to spend on organization and propaganda beyond their means: and the more they did so the bigger grew their bureaucratic establishments and their need for subsidies. Accustomed to easy money they then tended to neglect the collection of their own dues, which had a demoralizing effect on them. While the role of "Moscow gold" in fostering communism abroad has very often been melodramatically played up, it is true, nevertheless, that the subsidies did much to make the Communist hierarchies amenable to Stalin's guidance.

so much the case that anybody who would try to comprehend the history of any Communist party merely in the context of its own national environment would fail. He would not be able to account for the manifold changes of line, for the fading of some leaders and the emergence of others, or for the reforms in organizational structure. The origin of all these must most often be sought in the issues which preoccupied the Russian General Secretariat rather than in the social struggles on the spot. While the triumvirs were confronting Trotsky, Trotskyism haunted the Comintern. Then the leaders who by their views or sentiments had been tied to their President, Zinoviev, either joined in denouncing him or were effaced. During the years of his alliance with Stalin, Bukharin was the leading light of the International. He proclaimed the new policies and picked his staffs from among those foreign Communists who sympathized with the *bloc* of the centre faction and the right in the Bolshevik party. After that *bloc* had fallen asunder, the International laboured under new pangs of "Bolshevization."

* * *

In December 1927, immediately after Trotsky, Zinoviev, and Kamenev had been expelled from the party, Stalin surprised the fifteenth congress by stating that the "stabilization" of capitalism had come to an end. "Two years ago," he said, "one could talk about a period of relative balance between the Soviets and the capitalist countries and about their 'peaceful coexistence.'" Now we have every reason to say that the period of "peaceful coexistence" recedes into the past, giving place to a period of imperialist attacks and of preparation of intervention against the U.S.S.R.[3] He did not try to square this new view with his previous forecast of fifteen or twenty years

of "peaceful coexistence." His new thesis was finally accepted as the basis of a new policy at the sixth congress of the Comintern, in the summer of 1928, at which he surprised the foreign delegates by the virtual demotion of Bukharin, carried out behind the scenes.

The congress forecast the approach of a catastrophic economic crisis in the capitalist countries. (The forecast, authorized by Stalin, was strikingly confirmed, in the following year, by the great slump in the United States.) From these premisses new tactics were developed. A whole chain of revolutionary explosions was expected. The Communist parties in the west were to launch their final offensive against capitalism. The reformist Social Democratic parties, now labelled Social-Fascist, were to be regarded as the most dangerous enemies of communism. The left wings of the Social Democratic parties were to be regarded as even greater obstacles to Socialist revolution than the right ones—"the more to the left the more dangerous." Any cooperation or contact between Communists and Social Democratic leaders was contaminating. The Comintern was to muster its ranks for the world-wide struggle, relying exclusively upon its own strength and pull.

It is doubtful, to say the least, whether Stalin believed in the imminent eruption of all the revolutionary volcanoes, which his propagandists heralded. Though his grasp of conditions in foreign countries was poor, it was not so poor as to make him share the ultra-revolutionary illusions of the sixth congress of the Comintern. With even greater emphasis than hitherto, as if ignoring all the trumpets of the Comintern, he made "socialism in one country" the supreme article of faith, obligatory not only in his own party but in the Comintern as a whole. He now attached incomparably more importance to a single factory newly built in Russia than to all the great expectations of revolution abroad. His diplomacy was feeling its way even more cautiously than before and continued to work on the

[3] *15 Syezd VKP(b); Stenograficheskii otchet* (Moscow, 1928), p. 34.

assumption of Russia's prolonged isolation. There was an undeniable contradiction between his two lines of policy, the one he pursued in Russia and the one he inspired in the Comintern. It is easy to guess which of the two policies had the greater weight.

The Comintern was now indeed engaged in a mock fight. Its ultra-radicalism was so unreal that Stalin, in all probability, countenanced it only because he attributed very little practical significance to whatever the Comintern did in those years. If this was what he thought, he was profoundly mistaken, for the ultra-radicalism of the Comintern had important, though only negative, consequences.

THE THEORY OF "SOCIALISM IN ONE COUNTRY"

JOSEPH STALIN

Stalin was less able in theoretical debate than Lenin had been, and much less original. Yet because the party almost compulsively debated every policy in terms of its conformance with the principles of Marxism-Leninism, he was forced to seek theoretical bases for his own policies. In *The Question of the Victory of Socialism in One Country,* published in 1926, he elaborated upon Lenin's idea that the best tactic for the achievement of an international communist society was the strengthening of the Soviet state. Imputing to Leon Trotsky and other opponents a belief that to be completely successful socialism had to be international and that the Soviet Union should therefore aggressively spread revolution around the world, Stalin replied that it was both possible and imperative to build socialism in one country. Ultimately he won his point and concentrated the party's strength upon building a mighty communist nation. By doing this, he insisted, he was actually working for world revolution. The dualism of Soviet policy continued, but now national power was explicitly recognized as a legitimate communist objective.

WHAT do we mean by the *possibility* of the victory of Socialism in one country?

We mean the possibility of solving the contradictions between the proletariat and the peasantry with the aid of the internal forces of our country, the possibility of the proletariat assuming power and using that power to build a complete Socialist society in our country, with the sympathy and the support of the proletarians of other countries, but without the preliminary victory of the proletarian revolution in other countries.

Without such a possibility, the building of Socialism is building without prospects, building without being sure that Socialism will be built. It is no use building Socialism without being sure that we can build it, without being sure that the technical backwardness of our country is not an *insuperable* obstacle to the building of a complete Socialist society. To deny such a possibility is to display lack of faith in the cause of building Socialism, to abandon Leninism.

What do we mean by the *impossibility*

From J. Stalin, *Problems of Leninism* (Moscow: Foreign Languages Publishing House, 1947), pp. 159–166.

of the complete, final victory of Socialism in one country without the victory of the revolution in other countries?

We mean the impossibility of having full guarantees against intervention, and consequently against the restoration of the bourgeois order, without the victory of the revolution in at least a number of countries. To deny this indisputable thesis is to abandon internationalism, to abandon Leninism.

We are living [says Lenin] not merely in a state, but in a *system of states,* and the existence of the Soviet Republic side by side with imperialist states for a long time is unthinkable. One or the other must triumph in the end. And before that end supervenes a series of frightful collisions between the Soviet Republic and the bourgeois states will be inevitable. That means that if the ruling class, the proletariat, wants to hold sway, it must prove its capacity to do so by military organization also. (Lenin, *Selected Works,* Vol. VIII, p. 33.)

We now have before us [says Lenin in another place] an extremely unstable equilibrium, but an unquestionable, an indisputable, a certain equilibrium nevertheless. Will it last long? I cannot tell; nor, I think, can anyone tell. And therefore we must exercise the greatest possible caution. And the first precept of our policy, the first lesson to be learned from our governmental activities during the past year, the lesson which all the workers and peasants must learn, is that we must be on the alert, we must remember that we are surrounded by people, classes and governments who openly express their intense hatred for us. We must remember that we are at all times but a hair's breadth from every manner of invasion. (Lenin, *Collected Works,* Russian edition, Vol. XXVII, p. 117.)

Clear, one would think!

Where does Zinoviev stand on the question of the victory of Socialism in one country?

Listen:

When we speak of the final victory of Socialism we mean this much, at least: 1) the abolition of classes, and therefore 2) the abolition of the dictatorship of one class, in this case the dictatorship of the proletariat. . . . If we are to get a clearer idea of how the question stands here, in the U.S.S.R., in the year 1925 [says Zinoviev further], we must distinguish between two things: 1) the assured *possibility* of engaging in building Socialism—such a possibility, it stands to reason, is quite conceivable within the limits of one country; and 2) the complete construction and consolidation of Socialism, i.e., the achievement of a Socialist system, of a Socialist society.

What can all this signify?

It signifies that by the final victory of Socialism in one country Zinoviev means, not the guarantee against intervention and restoration, but the possibility of completely building Socialist society. And by the victory of Socialism in one country Zinoviev means the sort of Socialist construction which cannot and should not lead to the complete building of Socialism. Haphazard construction, construction without prospects, building Socialism although the complete construction of Socialist society is impossible—such is Zinoviev's position.

To build Socialism *without the possibility* of completing it; to build *knowing that it cannot be completed*—such are the absurdities in which Zinoviev has involved himself.

But this is a mockery of the question, not a solution of it!

Here is another extract from Zinoviev's concluding speech at the Fourteenth Party Congress:

Take, for instance, the things Comrade Yakovlev said at the last Kursk Provincial Party Conference. He asks: "Is it possible for us, surrounded as we are on all sides by capitalist enemies, to build Socialism in one country under such conditions?" And he answers: "On the basis of all that has been said we have a right to say not only that we are building Socialism, but that in spite of the fact that for the time being we are alone, that for the time being we are the only Soviet country, the only Soviet state in the world, we shall complete the building of Socialism." (*Kurskaya Pravda,* No. 279, December 8, 1925.) Is this the *Leninist method of presenting the question? Does not this smack of national narrow-mindedness?**

Thus, according to Zinoviev, the recognition of the possibility of building Socialism in one country signifies the adoption of the point of view of national narrow-mindedness, while the denial of such a possibility signifies the adoption of the point of view of internationalism.

But if this be true, is it at all worth while fighting for victory over the capitalist elements in our economy? Does it not follow from this that such a victory is impossible?

Capitulation to the capitalist elements in our economy—that is where the inherent logic of Zinoviev's line of argument leads us.

And this absurdity, which has nothing in common with Leninism, is presented to us by Zinoviev as "internationalism," as "hundred-per-cent Leninism!"

I assert that on this most important question of building Socialism Zinoviev is deserting Leninism and slipping to the standpoint of the Menshevik Sukhanov.

Let us turn to Lenin. Here is what he said about the victory of Socialism in one country even before the October Revolution in August 1915:

Uneven economic and political development is an absolute law of capitalism. Hence, the victory of Socialism is possible, first in several or even in one capitalist country, taken singly. The victorious proletariat of that country, having expropriated the capitalists and *organized its own Socialist production,** would stand up *against* the rest of the world, the capitalist world, attracting to its cause the oppressed classes of other countries, raising revolts in those countries against the capitalists, and in the event of necessity coming out even with armed force against the exploiting classes and their states. (Lenin, *Selected Works,* Vol. V, p. 141.)

What does Lenin mean by the phrase

"having . . . organized its own Socialist production," which I have emphasized? He means that the proletariat of the victorious country, having seized power, *can* and *must* organize Socialist production. And what does it mean to "organize Socialist production"? It means to build a Socialist society. It is hardly necessary to prove that Lenin's clear and definite statement needs no further comment. If it were otherwise, Lenin's call for seizure of power by the proletariat in October 1917 would be incomprehensible.

You see that Lenin's lucid thesis in comparison with Zinoviev's muddled and anti-Leninist "thesis" that we can engage in building Socialism "within the limits of one country," although it is *impossible* to build it, is as different from the latter as the sky from the earth.

The statement quoted above was made by Lenin in 1915, before the proletariat had taken power. But perhaps he modified his views after power had been taken, after 1917? Let us turn to his pamphlet *On Cooperation,* written in 1923.

As a matter of fact [says Lenin] the power of state over all large-scale means of production, the power of state in the hands of the proletariat, the alliance of this proletariat with the many millions of small and very small peasants, the assured leadership of the peasantry by the proletariat, etc. — *is not this all that is necessary in order to build a complete Socialist society* from the cooperatives, from the cooperatives alone, which we formerly treated as huckstering and which from a certain aspect we have the right to treat as such now, under NEP? Is this not all that is necessary for the purpose of building a complete Socialist society? This is not yet the building of Socialist society, but it is all that is *necessary and sufficient for this building.** (Lenin, *Selected Works,* Vol. IX, p. 403.)

In other words, we can and must build a complete Socialist society, for we have at our disposal all that is necessary and sufficient for this purpose.

* My italics.—J. S.

* My italics.—J. S.

I think it would be difficult to express oneself more clearly.

Compare Lenin's classical thesis with the anti-Leninist reproof Zinoviev hurled at Yakovlev, and you will realize that Yakovlev was only repeating Lenin's words about the possibility of building Socialism in one country, whereas Zinoviev, by attacking this thesis and castigating Yakovlev, deserted Lenin and adopted the point of view of the Menshevik Sukhanov, the point of view that it is impossible to build Socialism in our country owing to its technical backwardness.

One can only wonder why we took power in October 1917 if we did not count on completely building Socialism?

We should not have taken power in October 1917—this is the conclusion to which the inherent logic of Zinoviev's line of argument leads us.

I assert further that in this most important question of the victory of Socialism Zinoviev has gone *counter* to the definite decisions of our Party, as registered in the well-known resolution of the Fourteenth Party Conference *On the Tasks of the Communist International and of the Communist Party of Russia in Connection with the Enlarged Plenum of the Executive Committee of the Communist International.*

Let us refer to this resolution. Here is what it says about the victory of Socialism in one country:

The existence of two diametrically opposed social systems gives rise to the constant menace of capitalist blockade, of other forms of economic pressure, of armed intervention, of restoration. Consequently, the only guarantee of the *final victory of Socialism,* i.e., the *guarantee against restoration,** is a victorious Socialist revolution in a number of countries. . . . Leninism teaches that the *final* victory of Socialism, *in the sense of full guarantee against the restoration** of bourgeois relationships, is possible only on an international scale. . . . *But it does not follow** from this that it is impossible to build a *complete Social-*

*ist society** in a backward country like Russia, without the "state aid" (Trotsky) of countries more developed technically and economically.

As you see, the resolution regards the final victory of Socialism as a guarantee against intervention and restoration, which is the *very opposite* to the way Zinoviev regards it in his book, *Leninism.*

As you see, the resolution recognizes the possibility of building a complete Socialist society in a backward country like Russia, without "state aid" from countries that are technically and economically more developed, which is the *very opposite* to what Zinoviev said when he reproved Yakovlev in his concluding speech at the Fourteenth Party Congress.

How else can this be described if not as a struggle on Zinoviev's part *against* the resolution of the Fourteenth Party Conference?

Of course, Party resolutions are sometimes not free from error. Sometimes they contain mistakes. Speaking generally, one may assume that the resolution of the Fourteenth Party Conference also contains certain errors. Perhaps Zinoviev thinks that this resolution is erroneous. But then he should say so clearly and openly, as befits a Bolshevik. For some reason or other Zinoviev, however, does not do this. He prefers to choose another path, that of attacking the resolution of the Fourteenth Party Conference from the rear, while keeping silent about this resolution and refraining from any open criticism of the resolution. Zinoviev evidently thinks that this will be the best way of achieving his purpose. And he has but one purpose, namely —to "improve" the resolution, and to amend Lenin "just a little bit." It need hardly be proved that Zinoviev is mistaken in his calculations.

What is the source of Zinoviev's mistake? What is the root of this mistake?

* My italics.—J. S.

The root of this mistake, in my opinion, lies in Zinoviev's conviction that the technical backwardness of our country is an *insuperable* obstacle to the building of a complete Socialist society; that the proletariat cannot build Socialism owing to the technical backwardness of our country. Zinoviev and Kamenev once tried to raise this argument at a meeting of the Central Committee of the Party prior to the April Party Conference. But they received a rebuff and were compelled to retreat, and *formally* they submitted to the opposite point of view, the point of view of the majority of the Central Committee. But although he formally submitted, Zinoviev has continued the struggle against it all the time. Here is what the Moscow Committee of our Party has to say about this "incident" in the Central Committee of the C.P.S.U.(B.) in its *Reply* to the letter of the Leningrad Provincial Party Conference:

Recently, in the Political Bureau, Kamenev and Zinoviev advocated the point of view that we cannot cope with the internal difficulties owing to our technical and economic backwardness unless an international revolution comes to our rescue. We, however, with the majority of the members of the Central Committee, think that we can build Socialism, are building it, and will complete it, notwithstanding our technical backwardness and in spite of it. We think that the work of building will proceed far more slowly, of course, than it would have done had there been a world victory; nevertheless, we are making progress and will continue to do so. We also believe that the view held by Kamenev and Zinoviev expresses lack of faith in the intrinsic forces of our working class and of the peasant masses who follow its lead. We believe that it is a departure from the Leninist position.

This document appeared in the press during the first sessions of the Fourteenth Party Congress. Zinoviev, of course, had the opportunity of speaking against this document at the Congress. It is characteristic that Zinoviev and Kamenev found no arguments against the grave accusation directed against them by the Moscow Committee of our Party. Was this accidental? I think not. The accusation, apparently, hit the mark. Zinoviev and Kamenev "replied" to this accusation by silence, because they had no "card to beat it."

The New Opposition is offended because Zinoviev is accused of lacking faith in the victory of Socialist construction in our country. But if after a whole year of discussion on the question of the victory of Socialism in one country; after Zinoviev's viewpoint has been rejected by the Political Bureau of the Central Committee (April 1925); after the Party has arrived at a definite opinion on this question, recorded in the well-known resolution of the Fourteenth Party Conference (April 1925) —if, after all this, Zinoviev ventures to oppose the Party point of view in his book, *Leninism* (September 1925), if he then repeats this opposition at the Fourteenth Party Congress—how can his stubbornness, his persistence in his error, be explained if not by the fact that Zinoviev is infected, hopelessly infected, with scepticism as regards the victory of Socialist construction in our country?

It pleases Zinoviev to treat this scepticism as internationalism. But since when have we come to treat departure from Leninism on a cardinal problem of Leninism as internationalism?

Will it not be more correct to say that it is not the Party but Zinoviev who is sinning against internationalism and the international revolution? For what else is our country, "the country that is building Socialism," if not the base of the world revolution? But can it be a real base of the world revolution if it is incapable of building Socialist society? Can it remain the mighty center of attraction for the workers of all countries that it undoubtedly is now, if it is incapable of achieving victory over the capitalist elements in its economy, the victory of Socialist construction? I think not. But does it not follow from this that scepticism regarding the victory of Socialist construction, the dissemination of this scepticism, will lead to our country being discredited as the base of the world revolution? And if our country is discredited the world revolutionary movement will be weakened. How did Messrs. the Social-Democrats try to scare the workers away from us? By preaching that "the Russians will get nowhere." Wherewith do we beat the Social-Democrats now, when we attract numerous workers' delegations to our country and thereby strengthen the position of Communism all over the world? By our successes in building Socialism. Is it not obvious, then, that whoever disseminates scepticism regarding our successes in building Socialism thereby indirectly helps the Social-Democrats, reduces the sweep of the international revolutionary movement, and inevitably departs from internationalism?

You see that Zinoviev is in no better position in regard to his "internationalism" than in regard to his "hundred-per-cent Leninism" on the question of building Socialism in one country.

That is why the Fourteenth Party Congress rightly defined the views of the New Opposition as "lack of faith in the cause of Socialist construction," as "a distortion of Leninism."

CHINA: TRIAL, ERROR, AND FAILURE

FRANZ BORKENAU

From 1921 to 1929, Franz Borkenau was a member of the German Communist party. During the latter part of this period he worked for the Comintern as a researcher on the international labor movement and visited many Communist parties in Western Europe. Breaking with the party, he turned to writing on international communism in the belief that the Western world was failing to understand the importance of this subject. His works are based upon extensive study of printed sources and lighted by the insights gained from his own personal experience. The following excerpt from his book *The Communist International* is an account of the clumsy and ineffective Soviet efforts to direct the tragic coalition of Dr. Sun Yat-sen's nationalist movement with the Chinese Communists. In some ways Borkenau's description oversimplifies events that were immensely complicated, making them appear to be more orderly and comprehensible than they were. In general, however, he provides a brief and perceptive analysis of the events and their immediate significance.

. . . In revolutionary matters the Chinese naturally turned to their Russian neighbours and accepted, rather indiscriminately, the Russian version of Marxism. Characteristically, the birth of Chinese Marxism and communism is not linked in any way with the labour movement, but very directly linked with the literary movements of the Westernized Chinese intelligentsia. Chen-du-hsiu, the founder and, during the decisive phase, the leader of the Chinese Communist Party, was a man of fifty before he became a communist; he had been, during the earlier part of his life, the pioneer and leader of the Chinese literary *risorgimento,* the pioneer of a new literature based on Western models, and the editor of a paper called *Young China.* His first lieutenant, Li-tai-chao, was one of the leading professors of Pekin University, an economist. For them Marxism was the direct continuation of national revolutionism; the intelligentsia was going to find its ally, not so much, it is true, in the proletariat in particular, as in the people in general. But these were problems of the future. Initially the party consisted of a few dozen, and then a few hundred students, just as previously the revolutionary circles in Russia; there was hardly a single worker among them. And

From Franz Borkenau, *The Communist International* (London, 1938), pp. 302–318. Reprinted by permission of Faber & Faber, Ltd.

the first business of the new organization was not to organize masses but to liberate itself, in painful debates, from the presence of a welter of anti-political ideologies, among which anarchism was paramount.

One thing at least the fact of the foundation of a Communist Party in 1920 decided implicitly: the Chinese revolution would not be a fight of the whole nation against the foreigners, but only of its lower classes, to the exclusion of the militarists and the comprador class who financed them. But things did not at first go according to Marxist orthodoxy. The Chinese Communist Party had been founded in direct cooperation with representatives from Moscow. But, as in Turkey, Moscow wanted to achieve two aims at once, a Communist Party and cooperation with the militarists. The Communist Party, during the early years of the movement, seemed quite a minor force; the generals were very big forces and some of them were Russia's neighbours. True, some of them at least were agents of Japan, but this did not constitute a crime in the eyes of Moscow, as long as relations between Moscow and Tokyo were satisfactory; and they were, from the end of the Russian civil war to the Manchurian incidents of 1929. Moscow did all in its power to deprive the Chinese nationalist movement of its anti-Japanese character and to push it in the direction of an anti-British movement, though the points of divergence between Britain and China were insignificant compared with the Japanese danger. For years the Russians cooperated with General Wu-pei-fu, who, together with Chang-tso-lin, held Pekin. Wu-pei-fu was a ferocious enemy of the rising labour movement. Only later, when the nationalist movement grew stronger and clashed acutely with Wu did the Russians strengthen their ties with Feng-hiu-siang, another general of the north-east, a Christian who cleverly showed sympathy for the nationalist movement.

We must repeat: at that time the Kuomintang, Sun Yat Sen's Nationalist Party, nominally ruled Canton and the province of Kwantung, but was in fact a small group of ideologists without power, the real government of Kwantung being in the hands of militarists; and the Communist Party, hardly existing at all in the south, was in the north a circle of student conspirators without any influence whatsoever. But slowly the picture changed. The year 1922 saw the first big strike in China—there had been smaller strikes since 1911—the railwaymen of the Tientsin-Poukow line struck, not so much for better wages as for the recognition of a union they had formed. The movement was drowned in blood by Wu but made a tremendous impression. In Shanghai the textile workers started to organize; and in Hong Kong the sailors rose in a strike which closely resembled a revolt against the British. The strike lasted for many months and the strike committee, which was not tolerated in Hong Kong, went over to Canton. So did many of the strikers. They immediately strengthened the nationalist movement in Canton. Now, and only now, did Sun Yat Sen realize his opportunity. Here, and only here, might be a balancing power against both foreigners and militarists, an element able to stabilize his rule in Canton. After all, it was not he who had sought the support of the workers; they came, and only their coming made him aware of their importance.

But how to organize them? Sun Yat Sen throughout his life had borrowed every comma of his thought from some Western source, and he now looked for advice to the professional revolutionary organizers of the West. Here was a tremendous chance for Moscow. Canton was geographically remote from the Russian border, but if they succeeded in putting a reliable ally into power in Kwantung, it would enormously strengthen their position and the cause of revolution in China. It was the moment when the united-front tactics in the West were at their height. The idea of applying similar tactics in the East met no resistance. Adolf Joffe, one-time head of the Russian peace delegation at Brest-Litovsk in 1917, experienced diplomat and one of the closest friends of Trotsky, met Sun Yat Sen in secret conference at Shanghai in the summer of 1923. He gave detailed advice to his Chinese partner about the policy he ought to follow. This conference between Joffe and Sun resulted in a number of measures which, as a whole, have transformed the face of China. When Sun went back to Canton two Russian advisers followed him; Borodin, a close friend of Lenin and one of the chief agents of the Comintern, who in 1922 had represented the Comintern in Britain and there effected the turnover of the Communist Party to trade-union work, thus preparing the general strike; and General Galen-Bluecher, the most brilliant of all the Red guerrilla leaders of the civil war. Galen became chief adviser to General Chiang Kai-Shek, Sun Yat Sen's brother-in-law, who had just been named commander of the newly created military academy in Whampoa, which was to form officers for the intended revolutionary army of the Canton government. And Borodin became political adviser to this government itself. According to his suggestions, a trade-union council was formed in Canton, based upon the committee of the Hong Kong strikers. Out of these strikers and other elements of the same political opinions an armed workers' guard was formed in order to make the government independent of the whims of its generals. Peasant unions were created all over the province of Kwantung and the government tried to back them in the fight for lower rents. The Kuomintang called a congress, at which a central committee agreeing with Borodin's policy was elected; and the party launched a programme which, besides the national issues contained strong pledges to both workers and peasants. The whole of these measures was called "the reorganization of the Kuomintang." As a result the communists individually joined the Kuomintang, while the Communist Party as such remained independent. Many

of the Whampoa cadets, the chief military force of the movement, were communists; some communists were elected members of the central committee of the Kuomintang, whose majority consisted of members of the left wing of that party, favoring cooperation with the communists. Canton became a "Red" city.

The Kwantung government and the mass of its adherents were far from being socially homogeneous. The general revolutionary atmosphere of Canton made it easy to win over the numerous petty bourgeoisie of that town, and even a considerable number of the landowners consented to the change, which they regarded as capable of bringing increased power to their beloved south. Many of the higher officers, too, had voluntarily submitted, not because they agreed with social radicalism but because the reorganization of the Kuomintang gave the Canton militarists the hope of playing, with Russian help, a role in Chinese affairs very different from the insignificant efforts of the previous Canton governments. From this lack of homogeneity arose divergences, both in China and in Moscow.

Rebellion came first in China. The foreign merchants and Chinese capitalists who had hitherto supported the Kuomintang seceded almost immediately. This element counted for something, not so much in Canton, as in Shanghai and farther north. The right wing of the Kuomintang, thus constituted, proceeded to a conference at the "Western Hills," near Pekin, and seceded from the party. Sun Yat Sen went to the north in order to make the best of the situation there, but fell ill and died in Pekin in 1925. In the meantime a dramatic incident had happened in Canton. A secret society of the Canton merchants, the "Paper Tigers," rose against the reorganized government, but was put down by the Whampoa cadets and the workers' militia. The government took a course even more definitely to the left. After Sun's death Wang-Chin-Wei, the declared leader of the Kuomintang left, became president of the Canton government. Borodin and, at his advice, Wang-Chin-Wei, attempted to revolutionize Kwantung thoroughly before trying to extend the Kuomintang regime farther north.

In Moscow a certain amount of discussion had preceded the order to the Chinese communists to join the Kuomintang as individual members. Trotsky, much later, claimed to have voted against this step. But if he did so he did not mention the matter in public until 1926, when the situation had become very different. The very fact that Joffe, his closest associate, concluded the agreement with Sun, and that no quarrel between him and Trotsky ensued, shows clearly that no serious divergence of views existed between Trotsky and the other leaders of the Comintern upon the matter. If there is any truth in Trotsky's claim to have voted against the adhesion of the individual communists to the Kuomintang, he was certainly not opposed to a very close cooperation between the two parties. And, in fact, the policy followed by the Comintern was undoubtedly the only possible policy. As in other countries, so in China, the first stages of the revolution had to be carried through with the cooperation of all anti-militarist and—in the Chinese case—anti-foreign elements. The communists themselves could never have secured the support of the Cantonese petty bourgeois masses, of the Kuomintang generals, of many strata of the wealthy bourgeoisie, etc. The choice therefore simply lay between two things: either the communists must make an attempt to split the revolutionary movement from the outset, and then that movement would have remained ineffectual; the reorganization of the Kuomintang, the mass movements deriving from it, the conquest of China by the nationalists, would never have happened; or, if they had happened in spite of communist abstention, the communists, in a movement of mainly national impulses, would have remained an isolated

sect. But very likely neither the Kuomintang nor the communists would have achieved anything had they not almost merged in the first stages of the movement. The Kuomintang, for the masses, was essentially a small batch of intellectuals whose national ideals they vaguely shared, but who were otherwise incomprehensible. The cooperation of the communists testified to the social, immediate implications of the movement, lower rents, and better wages, which mattered for the masses. But the masses alone would have been helpless without the upper stratum represented by the Kuomintang. The pact between communists and Kuomintang symbolized the cooperation of both the higher and the lower stratum in the national cause.

Under the impulse of the revolutionary measures of the Canton government the movement spread to the north. General Feng, without officially adhering to the Kuomintang, espoused the national cause, and at one time took Pekin. And then followed the spark which set the powder-barrel alight. On 30th May 1925, a military cordon at the international settlement in Shanghai fired upon striking and demonstrating textile workers. Immediately a general strike and a boycott of British goods followed in Shanghai. As the Russian revolutionary strikes in 1905, so the Shanghai strike of 1925 was paid for by the mill-owners themselves, as far as they were Chinese. The movement immediately spread all over China; students' demonstrations and revolts, boycotts, strikes. The Hong Kong strike was resumed on an even broader basis than the first time. British trade in Hong Kong was nearly ruined. And the generals at Canton started to talk eagerly of an expedition northward.

Though the union of communists and nationalists had been necessary in order to bring a broad mass movement into being, the very appearance of this mass movement shattered their alliance. After a few months the Shanghai Chamber of Commerce, the most representative body of the

Chinese industrialists, sought and obtained a compromise with the administration of the international settlement. And in Canton the generals, landowners, and the moderates in general were thoroughly frightened by the revolutionary extremism of the movement. On 20th March 1926 something quite unexpected happened. Chiang Kai-Shek, the military commander of Canton, suddenly executed a coup against his own government. He dispersed the workers' militia, arrested many leading communists and communist Whampoa cadets, closed the offices of the trade unions, and even of the local Kuomintang, and was about to establish himself as military dictator. It was a turning-point of very wide bearing. How would the communists react?

The stroke was aimed at them. The natural reaction would have been to go into hiding, to break with Chiang Kai-Shek, who had broken with them, and, backed by the big mass movement which was approaching its climax, to try to extend the revolution. Former revolutions in other countries had been faced by similar events. In every revolution there comes a point when the moderates are frightened by the progress of the extremists and openly turn against them. It is an inevitable process, and it has been invariably the moment when the revolutionary front, united at first, broke in two. In China, up to that moment, the difference between the Kuomintang and communism had been abstract and theoretical only. Now it had acquired concrete meaning; it was time, from the communist point of view, to proceed one step further. The communists need not have broken with those who had no desire to break with them; they would naturally have been driven to break with those who were about to destroy them.

Why did they not do it? Who was responsible? Not even Borodin was the decisive person. During those years the most minute details of the policy of the Chinese communists were directed from Moscow. Stalin, with his profound distrust

of every living soul, did not allow any step to be taken without his personal orders and he did not see any difficulty in directing a revolution in Canton from Moscow: he had, however, considerations of his own. A break with Chiang Kai-Shek and an open struggle with all the moderates would entail a break with Feng in the north too. Then, Russia would be completely isolated in China, so far as the ruling powers were concerned; it would have to rely only on the revolutionary mass movement, with its dubious chances. The assets were big, the role of Russia in Chinese politics considerable. Up to then the interests of the Communist Party of China and of Russian foreign policy had coincided without difficulty. Now Stalin attempted to find an uneasy compromise between interests which were already divergent, a compromise which proved impossible.

And yet the way was open, would have been open at least, had there been no obstacles of an "ideological" character. Chiang Kai-Shek proclaimed repeatedly that he was quite prepared to cooperate with Russia provided the differences between the Kuomintang and the Chinese communists could be solved, or the Kuomintang itself admitted, as a "sympathizing" party, to the Comintern. For such an offer Chiang had very strong reasons. He could easily do without Borodin and Russian political influence, but he could not easily dispense with General Galen and Russian military and technical advice. Throughout the Canton crisis, and again during the 1927 crisis, Chiang offered much in order to keep Galen. The substance of his offer was that he would remain a reliable ally of Russia provided Russia left the Chinese communists to their fate. It was essentially the same policy as that followed by Kemal in Turkey six years earlier. Only the result would have been somewhat different. The Chinese communists, in an enormous country in disintegration and ruled by two dozen different rulers, and amidst a growing revolutionary mass movement, could better stand on their own feet than the Turkish communists. And Chiang, for many reasons, would find it more difficult to find alternative allies in place of Russia. To Stalin only two logical courses were open: either to drop the generals and support the communists, or to support the generals Chiang and Feng, and drop the communists. Both courses promised a certain amount of success. The course he chose presented no chance of success.

Instead of accepting Chiang's suggestion, one way or the other, he attempted to force a compromise upon Chiang. Chiang was ready to compromise on account of Galen and the other Russian technical advisers and on account of the prestige he derived from continued collaboration with the Russians. But in Canton he had won the fight, for the moment, and the Russians must cut their losses if they wanted to continue as allies. The compromise which was reached in May 1926 was very unfavourable for Borodin. Wang-Chin-Wei, hitherto president of the Canton government and leader of the left wing of the Kuomintang, who had fled on March 20th, would remain in exile; Chiang was recognized as head of the Canton government. The workers' militia was not reorganized. The number of communist officers in the Whampoan academy and in the army was strictly limited. So was the number of communist officials in the administration. They were no longer allowed to keep leading positions within the party. On the other hand, they must deliver a list of their members into the hands of Chiang, in order to enable him to control the carrying out of the compromise. The communists, moreover, were not allowed to win over new members in the army or in the administration. As to the workers and peasants, no limits were put to communist recruiting, but severe limits to the content of their slogans. They had formally to recognize Sun Yat Sen's programme of social peace and had to tone down their slogans until they became identical with those of the

Kuomintang. They had coincided with the Kuomintang slogans ever since 1923, but then before Chiang's coup the Kuomintang had been much to the left, whereas now its slogans were severely revised and moderated. All the communists could now offer the peasants was a 20 per cent reduction of rents. They were not permitted to carry out an agitation against landowners in general, but only against "bad landowners." Last but not least they had to consent to Chiang's plan of an expedition to the north. They had opposed such an expedition because in their opinion the Canton base was not yet socially strong enough. If successful, the expedition on its way north would induce very strong conservative elements to join the Kuomintang and thus deprive it of its revolutionary impulse. But this was exactly what Chiang wanted. Military glory, nationalism, social conservatism strengthened through the adherence of many militarists of the north to the Kuomintang, would safeguard his rule and put him in a position to make short shrift with the communists. Every step to the north would make him more independent of them, bring nearer the day of the final break and the extinction of the communists. The Russian and the Chinese communists, in agreeing to help him on his march to the north, prepared their own destruction.

True, Stalin and his advisers had one hope: the northern expedition would be a failure and bury under its ruins the prestige of Chiang. Galen in particular was strongly convinced of this, and in order to save his own prestige remained in Canton when the expedition started. But of all men the Russians were the last who were allowed to make such a mistake. The northern campaign proved to be, not a military, but a revolutionary affair. Stalin, Borodin, Galen, Chen-du-hsiu had grossly underestimated the impulse of the movement. Wherever the Cantonese armies went the road was opened to them by revolution. The students and middle-class people greeted them as national liberators; the peasants saw here the enemies of the hated tax-extorting generals; the workers hoped for a big change in their existence. The soldiers of the anti-Kuomintang generals ran away or deserted. Soon provincial governors, seeing the hopelessness of resistance, went over with their armies and their provinces, but without changing anything in the territory they ruled. In December the Cantonese took Hankow, the Yang-tse capital, and the Kuomintang government moved thither.

This brought things to a head. Hankow, renamed Wu-han, was a new revolutionary centre. It had been taken by the "Iron Division," the one communist army corp which still existed. In spite of all the restrictions imposed by the compromise of May 1926 the communists in their advance had made the best of the stipulations, and had organized in the regions where they passed peasant unions of a somewhat radical character. Notably in the province of Hu-nan the peasants started expropriating the land of the owners, with the connivance of the communists. Then, in January, the population of Wu-nan, in a big rising, assaulted and took the Hankow British settlement. When the government moved from Canton to Hankow it went from a place which had become thoroughly conservative to a centre of revolutionary ferment. Borodin went to Wu-han and with him those members of the government who inclined to the left.

Chiang protested immediately. Shanghai should be the new capital, or Nanking; for the time being he regarded Nanchang, the capital of the province of Kiangsi and his headquarters, as the capital of Kuomintang China. If the revolutionary wing had witnessed a certain increase of forces through the northern expedition Chiang could point to a much stronger increase. He held control over Canton, over most of the army, and all the more conservative leaders joined him in Nanchang.

There is no need to follow the crisscross of the negotiations which ensued between Wu-han and Nanchang. Chiang still bided his time, and Borodin, in an almost inexplicable blindness, and Stalin hoped for a continuance of the compromise while Chiang prepared the final coup. In February Chiang had approached Shanghai closely, but did not take it. The workers inside the town rose, in order to drive out the commander of Chang-tso-lin, who held the town. They were defeated, with the loss of many lives. Chiang hardly regretted it. Since the affair of 30th May 1925 the Shanghai trade unions had made tremendous progress and Shanghai had become the centre of the Chinese labour movement. The Chinese T.U.C. had its centre in Shanghai; it claimed to control two million members and was affiliated to the Red trade-union International. Chiang had certainly no objection to bleeding a labour movement of this type. After the February defeat the Shanghai labour movement seemed to be crushed for a time. But such was the *élan* of the revolutionary forces that in March they rose again, and this time they succeeded in driving out Chang-tso-lin's troops. During the last phase of the fight Chiang triumphantly entered Shanghai.

Now Chiang had reached his goal; he could no longer vacillate. Whatever nationalist bourgeoisie there was in China was concentrated in Shanghai. Shanghai was the right place in which to come to an understanding with Britain and to liberate himself from the anti-English fetters which the Russians had imposed upon him, only to their own advantage. Things now move at a breath-taking speed. Chiang, at the very moment of his entry into Shanghai, orders the workers to deliver their arms to the army. The communists delay and turn to Moscow; the local committee in Shanghai, feeling the axe over its head, implores Borodin and Chen in Wu-han and Stalin and Bukharin in Moscow to order the fight, which is anyway inevitable. Instead, Moscow orders them to bury the arms. The order is partly executed, partly sabotaged by the organization. The communists are left almost without arms. There are few parallels to this action in history. Had the leaders in Wu-han and Moscow believed in Chiang they would not have ordered the digging-in, but compliance with Chiang's demand. But at that moment they were already aware that something very serious was afoot. The meaningless order to bury the arms simply signified that Wu-han and Moscow realized the danger, but did not see a way out. And, in fact, it was very difficult or impossible now to find it. In Canton and Shanghai Chiang had all the trumps in his hands. Only Wu-han was out of his reach. Defeat was almost certain, by now. But the situation was made worse by the hesitating and two-faced attitude the communists took in front of the conflicts between peasants and owners which started to spread over central China. Then Chiang, having utilized his adversaries' indecision to the end, took action. Suddenly the Shanghai committee and all the known communists he could capture were arrested. The party had no choice left and rose, without arms, without organization, without preparation. The general strike broke down, the few nests where armed resistance was attempted were soon taken, and then an orgy of shooting, beheading, torturing, and all an Asiatic fancy can contrive in matters of cruelty ensued. A number of fighters and strikers were thrown into the boiling cauldrons of locomotives.

The Shanghai rising was immediately followed by open rupture between the Wu-han government and Chiang. Wang-Chin-Wei, the leader of the left wing of the Kuomintang, went back to China and became president of the Wu-han government. Open conflict broke out between the left Kuomintang at Wu-han and the right wing in Shanghai. Two communists joined the Wu-han government, and were restored in Wu-han to the position they had held in the Kuomintang in Canton before the coup of March 1926. But soon Wang-Chin-Wei and his men had to realize that a left policy was a thing more easily planned than carried out. Shanghai was the centre of the Kuomintang generals, who openly ruled there. In Wu-han civil revolutionary politicians ruled, but they were at the mercy of their generals. Apart from the "Iron Division" Wu-han was occupied by a few Canton troops and numerous corps which had gone over to the Kuomintang during the northern expedition and whose leaders were absolutely unreliable. At the head of this group of generals stood General Tang-Shen-Shi, a man rather to the right of Chiang and who had conspired with the left-wingers for the simple reason that he found himself in Wu-han and wanted to use his position against Chiang, for his own personal ends. There was only one way to break his dominating position, that of unleashing the mass movement. But the moment this was attempted Tang would certainly throw out the Wu-han government, which was at his mercy. Already the tide of revolution, after the Shanghai disaster and a subsequent coup of the same order in Canton, had visibly reached and overstepped its climax. On the narrow territory of the Wu-han government, consisting mainly of the provinces of Hu-peh and Hu-nan, the help of Tang could not be dispensed with. Wang-Chin-Wei was wavering between him, or rather between the pressure of the upper-class officers, and the communists. In order to break the enchanted circle the communists suggested that the territory of the Wu-han government be extended. While Chiang stopped in Shanghai the Wu-han government tried to carry out the original plan of the northern expedition and to take Pekin. But in the meantime General Feng had openly declared for the Kuomintang, had come to an understanding with Chiang, and after a very involved criss-cross of intrigues barred the way to Pekin against the Wu-han troops. The issue could no longer be avoided. The peasants, trusting in the "left" character of the Wu-han government, had risen all over Hu-nan, expropriating and killing owners and their guards, the "min-tuan," the local gendarmerie. The question was decisively put to Wang-Chin-Wei and to the communists; for or against the risings. The answer was half-hearted. Punitive expeditions were sent to the revolting districts, in which the communists actually participated. But their participation was rather formal and the troops under communist command tended to fire into the air. On the other hand the communists obtained the dispersal of the biggest peasant troop by means of persuasion. Very naturally, this did not transform the landowners into communists. In cooperation with the landowners the whole garrison of Chang-sha, the capital of Hu-nan, rose against the peasant unions. Communists and other active members of mass organizations were massacred in their hundreds: the terror spread to the countryside. Tang-Shen-Shi refused to interfere. The Wu-han government had to capitulate to its commander-in-chief and the communists received an ultimatum bidding them agree with the measures of repression of the peasant movement. They rejected it, the communist members of the Wu-han government and of the party central committee resigned, Borodin went back to Russia; and then the terror was unleashed in repression of communists and left-wingers all over the Wu-han territory. The episode in Wu-han had lasted less than four months. A few months later Wu-han capitulated to Chiang and Wang-Chin-Wei went once again into exile. The catastrophe of Chinese communism was complete and Chiang, its greatest adversary, triumphant.

The tremendous defeat had its effect on the Communist Party, which was nearly wrecked by the unimaginable tortures and persecutions to which the members were subjected. But the destruction of the party was not only physical. It had lost, once for all, the confidence of the workers. Wherever, in later days, the communists won a foothold, they were welcomed by a considerable section of the poor peasants; but the workers remained invariably indifferent. Instead of the Red trade unions the Kuomintang created official unions of the Italian type, which, there is no doubt about it, sometimes won the real allegiance of the workers. Occasionally these unions fought the communists, arms in hand. There was no longer any communist labour movement in China. For years the Chinese communists and the Comintern discussed how to win the proletariat again, admitting that they had lost contact with it almost completely. Then suddenly a certain Wan Min started writing articles about the big successes of communism in Chinese towns, claiming, at one time, no less than 60,000 urban members for the Chinese Communist Party. But there is also the report of Edgar Snow in his *Red Star over China;* Snow is the best expert on the matter and not suspect of an anti-communist bias. He simply calls Wan Min's reports "fantastic," without any further comment.

The policy of the Chinese Communist Party was suddenly and entirely reversed after the Wu-han disaster, and a course of civil war against all sections of the Kuomintang was initiated by orders from Moscow. At the same time Chen and his friends, who had made no step without the assent of Borodin, who, in his turn had acted according to detailed orders from Moscow, were accused of opportunism. Stalin wanted a scapegoat and, of course, wanted a confession from his subordinates that all his orders had been right and only their way of executing them wrong. The Russian Borodin submitted without any qualms, and, after only one year of disgrace, was again appointed as an official of the Comintern, though in a less outstanding capacity. Chen, however, who had a standing of his own as the founder of *Young China*, which had preceded his communism, with the pride of a Chinese intellectual refused to be the scapegoat for a policy which others had step by step evolved. He was ousted from the central committee and retired into hiding, shutting his lips.

The problem of the real causes of the disaster remains, and much ink has been spent by all communist groups in attempts to solve it. Trotsky, as was to be expected, vehemently accused Stalin of having betrayed the old revolutionary communist tradition. But this tradition was never so outright and unquestionable as Trotsky would like to assume after being chased from Russia. In fact, Lenin had first evolved the policy of a close alliance with *all* sections of the oppressed nations, and it was he who first, in the case of Turkey, subordinated the interests of communism to the interests of the Russian state. When Stalin, during the whole course of the Chinese revolution, tried to square Russian and communist interests and to maintain an alliance with the Chinese moderates, he was only in the tradition of Lenin.

Anyway, nobody considered the establishment of a pure dictatorship of the proletariat in China. Even the left-wing communists saw that for such a task the Chinese proletariat was too weak. They suggested that the revolution should aim at a "dictatorship of the proletariat and the peasantry," in other words a regime which would destroy the militarists, evict the foreign powers, abolish usury on the land, give protection to the workers, and create a centralized administration. The left-wing communists believed that for the carrying through of such a programme a break with even the left wing of the Kuomintang was necessary. It is doubtful whether such a policy would have been wise and whether the communists would have had any chance in a fight against all sections of the Kuomintang. While Trotsky accused Stalin of betraying the revolution, Chiang Kai-Shek accused him of subordinating the task of Chinese national liberation to that of social revolution. It would have been a consistent

policy to submit to Chiang and to leave the Chinese communists to their own devices; it would have been equally consistent to drop Chiang, follow Trotsky's advice, and choose the dangerous course of intransigent revolutionism. But it was impossible to be the ally of Chiang and at the same time prepare his overthrow, or play with the idea of his overthrow at least. It is this mistake which goes through all Comintern history: the desire to eat the cake and have it.

In the initial stages of the movement this was not altogether obvious. But the coup of Chiang in Canton on 20th March 1926 put the choice before the communists. They refused to choose. They made a "compromise" with Chiang which implied giving up their political and military independence. There was no further opportunity for them to break away from the chain by which Chiang held them without at once provoking a coup and frightful persecution. They had imagined that they would have the better of Chiang; but he was infinitely shrewder than Stalin and Borodin. Already they were his prisoners. He then manœuvred them into increasing difficulties, finally asking them to deliver even their arms. When they had done so he simply butchered them.

But this policy of compromise was not the simple result of the lack of understanding of foreign countries which Stalin shared with Lenin. Stalin has proved since that he is ready to forsake revolutionary policy completely. He could not do that, however, as long as the traditions of the revolution were strong and embodied in the powerful opposition of Sinovjev and Trotsky. Here the revolutionary past proved to be the biggest handicap of Russian policy, both at home and abroad, as it continues to be today. On the other hand, Russia was incapable of leading a revolution abroad. It had never been able to do so, because it had always identified Russian methods and necessities too directly with foreign ones. This tendency to transfer

Russian methods abroad, always naïve and very strong, had even increased with the emergence of a completely totalitarian dictatorship under Stalin.

This dictatorship had at the decisive moment shrunk from advancing revolution. Isn't this a splendid confirmation of Trotsky's view about "betrayal"? Hardly. The most revolutionary of revolutions cannot continue to be so indefinitely. The Russian revolution had ceased to be revolutionary precisely because, in many respects, its success had been so complete. A bureaucracy had emerged which had little in common with the Bolsheviks of the times of Tsarism. Again, the notorious "betrayal." Again, hardly. Socialism cannot help producing a bureaucratic system. How, in a system where everything is administered by the state, could the domination of the bureaucracy be avoided? Lenin had imagined that the Soviet system would avoid such a bureaucratic regime, but the Soviet system had never been a

reality and Lenin and Trotsky had been chief among those who destroyed every vestige of it. Trotsky, in shouting about treason, simply accuses the unsatisfactory reality of the system which he has himself helped to create; seeing what he has done, he accuses everybody but himself on account of the failure of a philistine, peace-loving, bureaucratic totalitarian regime, with its incapacity to lead to revolution, to correspond to his dreams. Yes, the new bureaucracy had shrunk from revolution in China, had shrunk from its big international implications, had distrusted, hampered, destroyed the mass movement. But what else does this prove but the complete unfitness of the doctrine of international Bolshevism? In the West the Comintern had invented revolutionary situations where there were none. In China the Russian bureaucracy, the legitimate child of the Russian revolution, had wasted the one big revolutionary chance it had ever had.

STRATEGY AND TACTICS

JOSEPH STALIN

Lenin's vigorously creative and subtle mind devised new theoretical justifications for whatever policy he wished to implement, but Lenin refused to be ruled by any dogma or principle that did not suit his immediate needs. Stalin, faithful lieutenant and wily successor, possessed less intellectual subtlety and theoretical inventiveness. Searching through the sophisticated thought of Lenin like any scholastic, he codified Lenin's ideas into relatively crude and rigid systems of maxims and rules. In April 1924 he delivered a series of lectures on "The Foundations of Leninism" to the students of Sverdlov University. The Seventh Lecture, printed here, replete with numbered definitions and principles, reads like a manual on military tactics. In a sense, this is what it is, for Stalin meant to provide an exact description of the strategy and tactics by means of which communism would conquer the world. In the extract from the Eighth Lecture, Stalin defines the role of the party as the director of the world struggle. Stalin's writings became the official interpretation of Leninism, which all loyal Communists were required to study, believe, and practice.

FROM this theme I take six questions:

1) strategy and tactics as the science of leadership in the class struggle of the proletariat;

2) stages of the revolution, and strategy;

3) the flow and ebb of the movement, and tactics;

4) strategic leadership;

5) tactical leadership;

6) reformism and revolutionism.

1) *Strategy and tactics as the science of leadership in the class struggle of the proletariat.* The period of the domination of the Second International was mainly a period of the formation and training of the proletarian political armies under conditions of more or less peaceful development. It was the period of parliamentarism as the predominant form of the class struggle. Questions of great class conflicts, of preparing the proletariat for revolutionary clashes, of the means of achieving the dictatorship of the proletariat, did not seem to be on the order of the day at that time. The task was confined to utilizing all means of legal development for the purpose of forming and training the proletarian armies, to utilizing parliamentarism in conformity with the conditions under which the status of the proletariat remained, and, as it seemed, had to remain, that of an opposition. It scarcely needs proof that in such a period and with such a conception of the tasks of the proletariat there could be neither an integral strategy nor any elaborated tactics. There were fragmentary and detached ideas about tactics and strategy, but no tactics or strategy as such.

The mortal sin of the Second International was not that it pursued at that time the tactics of utilizing parliamentary forms of struggle, but that it overestimated the importance of these forms, that it considered them virtually the only forms; and that when the period of open revolutionary battles set in and the question of extraparliamentary forms of struggle came to the fore, the parties of the Second International turned their backs on these new tasks, refused to shoulder them.

Only in the subsequent period, the period of direct action by the proletariat, the

From Stalin's "Lectures Delivered at Sverdlov University," April 1924, "The Foundations of Leninism," as translated in J. V. Stalin, *Works* (Moscow: Foreign Languages Publishing House, 1953), VI, 155–175, 176–179.

period of proletarian revolution, when the question of overthrowing the bourgeoisie became a question of immediate practical action; when the question of the reserves of the proletariat (strategy) became one of the most burning questions; when all forms of struggle and of organization, parliamentary and extra-parliamentary (tactics), had quite clearly manifested themselves—only in this period could an integral strategy and elaborated tactics for the struggle of the proletariat be worked out. It was precisely in this period that Lenin brought out into the light of day the brilliant ideas of Marx and Engels on tactics and strategy that had been suppressed by the opportunists of the Second International. But Lenin did not confine himself to restoring particular tactical propositions of Marx and Engels. He developed them further and supplemented them with new ideas and propositions, combining them all into a system of rules and guiding principles for the leadership of the class struggle of the proletariat. Lenin's pamphlets, such as *What Is To Be Done?*, *Two Tactics*, *Imperialism*, *The State and Revolution*, *The Proletarian Revolution and the Renegade Kautsky*, "*Left-Wing*" *Communism*, undoubtedly constitute priceless contributions to the general treasury of Marxism, to its revolutionary arsenal. The strategy and tactics of Leninism constitute the science of leadership in the revolutionary struggle of the proletariat.

2) *Stages of the revolution, and strategy.* Strategy is the determination of the direction of the main blow of the proletariat at a given stage of the revolution, the elaboration of a corresponding plan for the disposition of the revolutionary forces (main and secondary reserves), the fight to carry out this plan throughout the given stage of the revolution.

Our revolution had already passed through two stages, and after the October Revolution it entered a third one. Our strategy changed accordingly.

First stage. 1903 to February 1917. Objective: to overthrow tsarism and completely wipe out the survivals of medievalism. The main force of the revolution: the proletariat. Immediate reserves: the peasantry. Direction of the main blow: the isolation of the liberal-monarchist bourgeoisie, which was striving to win over the peasantry and liquidate the revolution by a *compromise* with tsarism. Plan for the disposition of forces: alliance of the working class with the peasantry. "The proletariat must carry to completion the democratic revolution, by allying to itself the mass of the peasantry in order to crush by force the resistance of the autocracy and to paralyze the instability of the bourgeoisie" (see Lenin, *Works*, 4th Russ. ed., VIII, 96).

Second stage. March 1917 to October 1917. Objective: to overthrow imperialism in Russia and to withdraw from the imperialist war. The main force of the revolution: the proletariat. Immediate reserves: the poor peasantry. The proletariat of neighboring countries as probable reserves. The protracted war and the crisis of imperialism as a favorable factor. Direction of the main blow: isolation of the petty-bourgeois democrats (Mensheviks and Socialist-Revolutionaries), who were striving to win over the toiling masses of the peasantry and to put an end to the revolution by a *compromise* with imperialism. Plan for the disposition of forces: alliance of the proletariat with the poor peasantry. "The proletariat must accomplish the socialist revolution, by allying to itself the mass of the semi-proletarian elements of the population in order to crush by force the resistance of the bourgeoisie and to paralyze the instability of the peasantry and the petty bourgeoisie" (*ibid.*).

Third stage. Began after the October Revolution. Objective: to consolidate the dictatorship of the proletariat in one country, using it as a base for the defeat of imperialism in all countries. The revolution spreads beyond the confines of one country; the epoch of world revolution has begun. The main forces of the revolution: the dictatorship of the proletariat in one country, the revolutionary movement of the proletariat in all countries. Main reserves: the semi-proletarian and small-peasant masses in the developed countries, the liberation movement in the colonies and dependent countries. Direction of the main blow: isolation of the petty-bourgeois democrats, isolation of the parties of the Second International, which constitute the main support of the policy of *compromise* with imperialism. Plan for the disposition of forces: alliance of the proletarian revolution with the liberation movement in the colonies and the dependent countries.

Strategy deals with the main forces of the revolution and their reserves. It changes with the passing of the revolution from one stage to another, but remains basically unchanged throughout a given stage.

3) *The flow and ebb of the movement, and tactics.* Tactics are the determination of the line of conduct of the proletariat in the comparatively short period of the flow or ebb of the movement, of the rise or decline of the revolution, the fight to carry out this line by means of replacing old forms of struggle and organization by new ones, old slogans by new ones, by combining these forms, etc. While the object of strategy is to win the war against tsarism, let us say, or against the bourgeoisie, to carry through the struggle against tsarism or against the bourgeoisie to its end, tactics pursue less important objects, for their aim is not the winning of the war as a whole, but the winning of some particular engagements or some particular battles, the carrying through successfully of some particular campaigns or actions corresponding to the concrete circumstances in the given period of rise or decline of the revolution. Tactics are a part of strategy, subordinate to it and serving it.

Tactics change according to flow and ebb. While the strategic plan remained unchanged during the first stage of the revolution (1903 to February 1917), tactics

changed several times during that period. In the period from 1903 to 1905 the Party pursued offensive tactics, for the tide of the revolution was rising, the movement was on the upgrade, and tactics had to proceed from this fact. Accordingly, the forms of struggle were revolutionary, corresponding to the requirements of the rising tide of the revolution. Local political strikes, political demonstrations, the general political strike, boycott of the Duma, uprising, revolutionary fighting slogans— such were the successive forms of struggle during that period. These changes in the form of struggle were accompanied by corresponding changes in the forms of organization. Factory committees, revolutionary peasant committees, strike committees, Soviets of workers' deputies, a workers' party operating more or less openly—such were the forms of organization during that period.

In the period from 1907 to 1912 the Party was compelled to resort to tactics of retreat; for we then experienced a decline in the revolutionary movement, the ebb of the revolution, and tactics necessarily had to take this fact into consideration. The forms of struggle, as well as the forms of organization, changed accordingly: instead of the boycott of the Duma—participation in the Duma; instead of open revolutionary actions outside the Duma— actions and work in the Duma; instead of general political strikes—partial economic strikes, or simply a lull in activities. Of course, the Party had to go underground during that period, while the revolutionary mass organizations were replaced by cultural, educational, co-operative, insurance and other legal organizations.

The same must be said of the second and third stages of the revolution, during which tactics changed dozens of times, whereas the strategic plans remained unchanged.

Tactics deal with the forms of struggle and the forms of organization of the proletariat, with their changes and combinations.

During a given stage of the revolution tactics may change several times, depending on the flow or ebb, the rise or decline, of the revolution.

4) *Strategic leadership.* The reserves of the revolution can be:

direct: a) the peasantry and in general the intermediate strata of the population within the country; b) the proletariat of neighboring countries; c) the revolutionary movement in the colonies and dependent countries; d) the conquests and gains of the dictatorship of the proletariat —part of which the proletariat may give up temporarily, while retaining superiority of forces, in order to buy off a powerful enemy and gain a respite; and

indirect: a) the contradictions and conflicts among the non-proletarian classes within the country, which can be utilized by the proletariat to weaken the enemy and to strengthen its own reserves; b) contradictions, conflicts and wars (the imperialist war, for instance) among the bourgeois states hostile to the proletarian state, which can be utilized by the proletariat in its offensive or in maneuvering in the event of a forced retreat.

There is no need to speak at length about the reserves of the first category, as their significance is clear to everyone. As for the reserves of the second category, whose significance is not always clear, it must be said that sometimes they are of prime importance for the progress of the revolution. One can hardly deny the enormous importance, for example, of the conflict between the petty-bourgeois democrats (Socialist-Revolutionaries) and the liberal-monarchist bourgeoisie (the Cadets) during and after the first revolution, which undoubtedly played its part in freeing the peasantry from the influence of the bourgeoisie. Still less reason is there for denying the colossal importance of the fact that the principal groups of imperialists were engaged in a deadly war during the period of the October Revolution, when the imperialists, engrossed in war among them-

selves, were unable to concentrate their forces against the young Soviet power, and the proletariat, for this very reason, was able to get down to the work of organizing its forces and consolidating its power, and to prepare the rout of Kolchak and Denikin. It must be presumed that now, when the contradictions among the imperialist groups are becoming more and more profound, and when a new war among them is becoming inevitable, reserves of this description will assume even greater importance for the proletariat.

The task of strategic leadership is to make proper use of all these reserves for the achievement of the main object of the revolution at the given stage of its development.

What does making proper use of reserves mean?

It means fulfilling certain necessary conditions, of which the following must be regarded as the principal ones:

Firstly. The concentration of the main forces of the revolution at the enemy's most vulnerable spot at the decisive moment, when the revolution has already become ripe, when the offensive is going full-steam ahead, when insurrection is knocking at the door, and when bringing the reserves up to the vanguard is the decisive condition of success. The Party's strategy during the period from April to October 1917 can be taken as an example of this manner of utilizing reserves. Undoubtedly, the enemy's most vulnerable spot at that time was the war. Undoubtedly, it was on this question, as the fundamental one, that the Party rallied the broadest masses of the population around the proletarian vanguard. The Party's strategy during that period was, while training the vanguard for street action by means of manifestations and demonstrations, to bring the reserves up to the vanguard through the medium of the Soviets in the rear and the soldiers' committees at the front. The outcome of the revolution has shown that the reserves were properly utilized.

Here is what Lenin, paraphrasing the well-known theses of Marx and Engels on insurrection, says about this condition of the strategic utilization of the forces of the revolution:

1) Never *play* with insurrection, but when beginning it firmly realize that you must *go to the end*.

2) Concentrate a great *superiority of forces* at the decisive point, at the decisive moment, otherwise the enemy, who has the advantage of better preparation and organization, will destroy the insurgents.

3) Once the insurrection has begun, you must act with the greatest *determination*, and by all means, without fail, take the *offensive*. "The defensive is the death of every armed rising."

4) You must try to take the enemy by surprise and seize the moment when his forces are scattered.

5) You must strive for *daily* successes, even if small (one might say hourly, if it is the case of one town), and at all costs retain the *"moral ascendancy"* [see Vol. XXI, pp. 319–20].

Secondly. The selection of the moment for the decisive blow, of the moment for starting the insurrection, so timed as to coincide with the moment when the crisis has reached its climax, when it is already the case that the vanguard is prepared to fight to the end, the reserves are prepared to support the vanguard, and maximum consternation reigns in the ranks of the enemy.

The decisive battle, says Lenin, may be deemed to have fully matured *if*

(1) all the class forces hostile to us have become sufficiently entangled, are sufficiently at loggerheads, have sufficiently weakened themselves in a struggle which is beyond their strength;

if

(2) all the vacillating, wavering, unstable, intermediate elements—the petty bourgeoisie, the petty-bourgeois democrats as distinct from the bourgeoisie—have sufficiently exposed themselves in the eyes of the people, have sufficiently disgraced themselves through their practical bankruptcy;

if

(3) among the proletariat a mass sentiment in favor of supporting the most determined, supremely bold, revolutionary action against the bourgeoisie has arisen and begun vigorously to grow. Then revolution is indeed ripe; then, indeed, if we have correctly gauged all the conditions indicated above . . . and if we have chosen the moment rightly, our victory is assured [see Vol. XXV, p. 229].

The manner in which the October uprising was carried out may be taken as a model of such strategy.

Failure to observe this condition leads to a dangerous error called "loss of tempo," when the Party lags behind the movement or runs far ahead of it, courting the danger of failure. An example of such "loss of tempo," of how the moment for an uprising should not be chosen, may be seen in the attempt made by a section of our comrades to begin the uprising by arresting the Democratic Conference in September 1917, when wavering was still apparent in the Soviets, when the armies at the front were still at the crossroads, when the reserves had not yet been brought up to the vanguard.

Thirdly. Undeviating pursuit of the course adopted, no matter what difficulties and complications are encountered on the road towards the goal; this is necessary in order that the vanguard may not lose sight of the main goal of the struggle and that the masses may not stray from the road while marching towards that goal and striving to rally around the vanguard. Failure to observe this condition leads to a grave error, well known to sailors as "losing one's bearings." As an example of this "losing one's bearings" we may take the erroneous conduct of our Party when, immediately after the Democratic Conference, it adopted a resolution to participate in the Pre-parliament. For the moment the Party, as it were, forgot that the Pre-parliament was an attempt of the bourgeoisie to switch the country from the path of the Soviets to the path of bourgeois parliamentarism, that the Party's participation in such a body might result in mixing everything up and confusing the workers and peasants, who were waging a revolutionary struggle under the slogan: "All Power to the Soviets." This mistake was rectified by the withdrawal of the Bolsheviks from the Pre-parliament.

Fourthly. Maneuvering the reserves with a view to effecting a proper retreat when the enemy is strong, when retreat is inevitable, when to accept battle forced upon us by the enemy is obviously disadvantageous, when, with the given relation of forces, retreat becomes the only way to escape a blow against the vanguard and to retain the reserves for the latter.

The revolutionary parties [says Lenin] must complete their education. They have learned to attack. Now they have to realize that this knowledge must be supplemented with the knowledge how to retreat properly. They have to realize—and the revolutionary class is taught to realize it by its own bitter experience—that victory is impossible unless they have learned both how to attack and how to retreat properly [see Vol. XXV, p. 177].

The object of this strategy is to gain time, to disrupt the enemy, and to accumulate forces in order later to assume the offensive.

The signing of the Brest Peace may be taken as a model of this strategy, for it enabled the Party to gain time, to take advantage of the conflicts in the camp of the imperialists, to disrupt the forces of the enemy, to retain the support of the peasantry, and to accumulate forces in preparation for the offensive against Kolchak and Denikin.

In concluding a separate peace [said Lenin at that time] we free ourselves as much *as is possible at the present moment* from both warring imperialist groups, we take advantage of their mutual enmity and warfare, which

hinder them from making a deal against us, and for a certain period have our hands free to advance and to consolidate the socialist revolution [see Vol. XXII, p. 198].

Now even the biggest fool [said Lenin three years after the Brest Peace] can see that the "Brest Peace" was a concession that strengthened us and broke up the forces of international imperialism [see Vol. XXVII, p. 7].

Such are the principal conditions which ensure correct strategic leadership.

5) *Tactical leadership.* Tactical leadership is a part of strategic leadership, subordinated to the tasks and the requirements of the latter. The task of tactical leadership is to master all forms of struggle and organization of the proletariat and to ensure that they are used properly so as to achieve, with the given relation of forces, the maximum results necessary to prepare for strategic success.

What is meant by making proper use of the forms of struggle and organization of the proletariat?

It means fulfilling certain necessary conditions of which the following must be regarded as the principal ones:

Firstly. To put in the forefront precisely those forms of struggle and organization which are best suited to the conditions prevailing during the flow or ebb of the movement at a given moment, and which therefore can facilitate and ensure the bringing of the masses to the revolutionary positions, the bringing of the millions to the revolutionary front, and their disposition at the revolutionary front.

The point here is not that the vanguard should realize the impossibility of preserving the old regime and the inevitability of its overthrow. The point is that the masses, the millions, should understand this inevitability and display their readiness to support the vanguard. But the masses can understand this only from their own experience. The task is to enable the vast masses to realize from their own experience the inevitability of the overthrow of the old regime, to promote such methods of struggle and forms of organization as will make it easier for the masses to realize from experience the correctness of the revolutionary slogans.

The vanguard would have become detached from the working class, and the working class would have lost contact with the masses, if the Party had not decided at the time to participate in the Duma, if it had not decided to concentrate its forces on work in the Duma and to develop a struggle on the basis of this work, in order to make it easier for the masses to realize from their own experience the futility of the Duma, the falsity of the promises of the Cadets, the impossibility of compromise with tsarism, and the inevitability of an alliance between the peasantry and the working class. Had the masses not gained their experience during the period of the Duma, the exposure of the Cadets and the hegemony of the proletariat would have been impossible.

The danger of the "Otzovist" tactics was that they threatened to detach the vanguard from the millions of its reserves.

The Party would have become detached from the working class, and the working class would have lost its influence among the broad masses of the peasants and soldiers, if the proletariat had followed the "Left" Communists, who called for an uprising in April 1917, when the Mensheviks and Socialist-Revolutionaries had not yet exposed themselves as advocates of war and imperialism, when the masses had not yet realized from their own experience the falsity of the speeches of the Mensheviks and Socialist-Revolutionaries about peace, land and freedom. Had the masses not gained this experience during the Kerensky period, the Mensheviks and Socialist-Revolutionaries would not have been isolated and the dictatorship of the proletariat would have been impossible. Therefore, the tactics of "patiently explaining" the mistakes of the petty-bourgeois parties and of open struggle in the Soviets were the only correct tactics.

The danger of the tactics of the "Left" Communists was that they threatened to transform the Party from the leader of the proletarian revolution into a handful of futile conspirators with no ground to stand on.

Victory cannot be won with the vanguard alone [says Lenin]. To throw the vanguard alone into the decisive battle, before the whole class, before the broad masses have taken up a position either of direct support of the vanguard, or at least of benevolent neutrality towards it . . . would be not merely folly but a crime. And in order that actually the whole class, that actually the broad masses of the working people and those oppressed by capital may take up such a position, propaganda and agitation alone are not enough. For this the masses must have their own political experience. Such is the fundamental law of all great revolutions, now confirmed with astonishing force and vividness not only in Russia but also in Germany. Not only the uncultured, often illiterate masses of Russia, but the highly cultured, entirely literate masses of Germany had to realize through their own painful experience the absolute impotence and spinelessness, the absolute helplessness and servility to the bourgeoisie, the utter vileness, of the government of the knights of the Second International, the absolute inevitability of a dictatorship of the extreme reactionaries (Kornilov in Russia, Kapp and Co. in Germany) as the only alternative to a dictatorship of the proletariat, in order to turn resolutely towards communism [see Vol. XXV, p. 228].

Secondly. To locate at any given moment the particular link in the chain of processes which, if grasped, will enable us to keep hold of the whole chain and to prepare the conditions for achieving strategic success.

The point here is to single out from all the tasks confronting the Party the particular immediate task, the fulfillment of which constitutes the central point, and the accomplishment of which ensures the successful fulfillment of the other immediate tasks.

The importance of this thesis may be illustrated by two examples, one of which could be taken from the remote past (the period of the formation of the Party) and the other from the immediate present (the period of the NEP).

In the period of the formation of the Party, when the innumerable circles and organizations had not yet been linked together, when amateurishness and the parochial outlook of the circles were corroding the Party from top to bottom, when ideological confusion was the characteristic feature of the internal life of the Party, the main link and the main task in the chain of links and in the chain of tasks then confronting the Party proved to be the establishment of an all-Russian illegal newspaper (*Iskra*). Why? Because, under the conditions then prevailing, only by means of an all-Russian illegal newspaper was it possible to create a solid core of the Party capable of uniting the innumerable circles and organizations into one whole, to prepare the conditions for ideological and tactical unity, and thus to build the foundations for the formation of a real party.

During the period of transition from war to economic construction, when industry was vegetating in the grip of disruption and agriculture was suffering from a shortage of urban manufactured goods, when the establishment of a bond between state industry and peasant economy became the fundamental condition for successful socialist construction—in that period it turned out that the main link in the chain of processes, the main task among a number of tasks, was to develop trade. Why? Because under the conditions of the NEP the bond between industry and peasant economy cannot be established except through trade; because under the conditions of the NEP production without sale is fatal for industry; because industry can be expanded only by the expansion of sales as a result of developing trade; because only after we have consolidated our position in the sphere of trade, only after we have secured control of trade, only after we have secured this link can there be any hope of linking industry with the peasant market and successfully fulfilling the other immediate tasks in order to create the conditions for building the foundations of socialist economy.

It is not enough to be a revolutionary and an adherent of socialism or a Communist in general [says Lenin]. One must be able at each particular moment to find the particular link in the chain which one must grasp with all one's might in order to keep hold of the whole chain and to prepare firmly for the transition to the next link . . .

At the present time . . . this link is the revival of internal *trade* under proper state regulation (direction). Trade—that is the "link" in the historical chain of events, in the transitional forms of our socialist construction in 1921-22, *"which we must grasp with all our might"* . . . [see Vol. XXVII, p. 82].

Such are the principal conditions which ensure correct tactical leadership.

6) *Reformism and revolutionism.* What is the difference between revolutionary tactics and reformist tactics?

Some think that Leninism is opposed to reforms, opposed to compromises and to agreements in general. This is absolutely wrong. Bolsheviks know as well as anybody else that in a certain sense "every little bit helps," that under certain conditions reforms in general, and compromises and agreements in particular, are necessary and useful.

To carry on a war for the overthrow of the international bourgeoisie [says Lenin], a war which is a hundred times more difficult, protracted and complicated than the most stubborn of ordinary wars between states, and to refuse beforehand to maneuver, to utilize the conflict of interests (even though temporary) among one's enemies, to reject agreements and compromises with possible (even though temporary, unstable, vacillating and conditional) allies—is not this ridiculous in the extreme? Is it not as though, when making a difficult ascent of an unexplored and hitherto inaccessible mountain, we were to refuse beforehand ever to move in zigzags, ever to retrace our steps, ever to abandon the course once selected and to try others? [see Vol. XXV, p. 210].

Obviously, therefore, it is not a matter of reforms or of compromises and agreements, but of the use people make of reforms and agreements.

To a reformist, reforms are everything, while revolutionary work is something incidental, something just to talk about, mere eyewash. That is why, with reformist tactics under the conditions of bourgeois rule, reforms are inevitably transformed into an instrument for strengthening that rule, an instrument for disintegrating the revolution.

To a revolutionary, on the contrary, the main thing is revolutionary work and not reforms; to him reforms are a by-product of the revolution. That is why, with revolutionary tactics under the conditions of bourgeois rule, reforms are naturally transformed into an instrument for disintegrating that rule, into an instrument for strengthening the revolution, into a strongpoint for the further development of the revolutionary movement.

The revolutionary will accept a reform in order to use it as an aid in combining legal work with illegal work and to intensify, under its cover, the illegal work for the revolutionary preparation of the masses for the overthrow of the bourgeoisie.

That is the essence of making revolutionary use of reforms and agreements under the conditions of imperialism.

The reformist, on the contrary, will accept reforms in order to renounce all illegal work, to thwart the preparation of the masses for the revolution and to rest in the shade of "bestowed" reforms.

That is the essence of reformist tactics.

Such is the position in regard to reforms and agreements under the conditions of imperialism.

The situation changes somewhat, however, after the overthrow of imperialism, under the dictatorship of the proletariat. Under certain conditions, in a certain situation, the proletarian power may find itself compelled temporarily to leave the path of the revolutionary reconstruction of the existing order of things and to take the path of its gradual transformation, the "reformist path," as Lenin says in his well-known article "The Importance of Gold," the path of flanking movements, of reforms and concessions to the non-proletarian classes—in order to disintegrate these classes, to give the revolution a respite, to recuperate one's forces and prepare the conditions for a new offensive. It cannot be denied that in a sense this is a "reformist" path. But it must be borne in mind that there is a fundamental distinction here, which consists in the fact that in this case the reform emanates from the proletarian power, it strengthens the proletarian power, it procures for it a necessary respite; its purpose is to disintegrate, not the revolution, but the non-proletarian classes.

Under such conditions a reform is thus transformed into its opposite.

The proletarian power is able to adopt such a policy because, and only because, the sweep of the revolution in the preceding period was great enough and therefore provided a sufficiently wide expanse within which to retreat, substituting for offensive tactics the tactics of temporary retreat, the tactics of flanking movements.

Thus, while formerly, under bourgeois rule, reforms were a by-product of revolution, now, under the dictatorship of the proletariat, the source of reforms is the revolutionary gains of the proletariat, the reserves accumulated in the hands of the proletariat and consisting of these gains.

Only Marxism [says Lenin] has precisely and correctly defined the relation of reforms to revolution. However, Marx was able to see this relation only from one aspect, namely, under the conditions preceding the first to any extent permanent and lasting victory of the proletariat, if only in a single country. Under those conditions, the basis of the proper relation was: reforms are a by-product of the revolutionary class struggle of the proletariat.... After the victory of the proletariat, if only in a single country, something new enters into the relation between reforms and revolution. In principle, it is the same as before, but a change in form takes place, which Marx himself could not foresee, but which can be appreciated only on the basis of the philosophy and politics of Marxism.... After the victory (while still remaining a "by-product" on an international scale) they [i.e., reforms — *J. St.*] are, in addition, for the country in which victory has been achieved, a necessary and legitimate respite in those cases when, after the utmost exertion of effort, it becomes obvious that sufficient strength is lacking for the revolutionary accomplishment of this or that transition. Victory creates such a "reserve of strength" that it is possible to hold out even in a forced retreat, to hold out both materially and morally [see Vol. XXVII, pp. 84–85].

THE PARTY

.... The new period is one of open class collisions, of revolutionary action by the proletariat, of proletarian revolution, a period when forces are being directly mustered for the overthrow of imperialism and the seizure of power by the proletariat. In this period the proletariat is confronted with new tasks, the tasks of reorganizing all party work on new, revolutionary lines; of educating the workers in the spirit of revolutionary struggle for power; of preparing and moving up reserves; of establishing an alliance with the proletarians of neighboring countries; of establishing firm ties with the liberation movement in the colonies and dependent countries, etc., etc. To think that these new tasks can be performed by the old Social-Democratic parties, brought up as they were in the peaceful conditions of parliamentarism, is to doom oneself to hopeless despair, to inevitable defeat. If, with such tasks to shoulder, the proletariat remained under the leadership of the old parties, it would be completely unarmed. It scarcely needs proof that the proletariat could not consent to such a state of affairs.

Hence the necessity for a new party, a militant party, a revolutionary party, one bold enough to lead the proletarians in the struggle for power, sufficiently experienced to find its bearings amidst the complex conditions of a revolutionary situation, and sufficiently flexible to steer clear of all submerged rocks in the path to its goal.

Without such a party it is useless even to think of overthrowing imperialism, of achieving the dictatorship of the proletariat.

This new party is the party of Leninism.

What are the specific features of this new party?

1) *The Party as the advanced detachment of the working class.* The Party must be, first of all, the *advanced* detachment of the working class. The Party must absorb all the best elements of the working class, their experience, their revolutionary spirit, their selfless devotion to the cause of the proletariat. But in order that it may really be the advanced detachment, the Party must be armed with revolutionary theory, with a knowledge of the laws of the movement, with a knowledge of the laws of revolution. Without this it will be incapable of directing the struggle of the proletariat, of leading the proletariat. The Party cannot be a real party if it limits itself to registering what the masses of the working class feel and think, if it drags at the tail of the spontaneous movement, if it is unable to overcome the inertia and the political indifference of the spontaneous movement, if it is unable to rise above the momentary interests of the proletariat, if it is unable to raise the masses to the level of understanding the class interests of the proletariat. The Party must stand at the head of the working class; it must see farther than the working class; it must lead the proletariat, and not drag at the tail of the

spontaneous movement. The parties of the Second International, which preach "khvostism," are vehicles of bourgeois policy, which condemns the proletariat to the role of a tool in the hands of the bourgeoisie. Only a party which adopts the standpoint of advanced detachment of the proletariat and is able to raise the masses to the level of understanding the class interests of the proletariat—only such a party can divert the working class from the path of trade unionism and convert it into an independent political force.

The Party is the political leader of the working class.

I have already spoken of the difficulties of the struggle of the working class, of the complicated conditions of the struggle, of strategy and tactics, of reserves and maneuvering, of attack and retreat. These conditions are no less complicated, if not more so, than the conditions of war. Who can see clearly in these conditions, who can give correct guidance to the proletarian millions? No army at war can dispense with an experienced General Staff if it does not want to be doomed to defeat. Is it not clear that the proletariat can still less dispense with such a General Staff if it does not want to allow itself to be devoured by its mortal enemies? But where is this General Staff? Only the revolutionary party of the proletariat can serve as this General Staff. The working class without a revolutionary party is an army without a General Staff.

The Party is the General Staff of the proletariat.

But the Party cannot be only an *advanced* detachment. It must at the same time be a detachment of the *class*, part of the class, closely bound up with it by all the fibers of its being. The distinction between the advanced detachment and the rest of the working class, between Party members and non-Party people, cannot disappear until classes disappear; it will exist as long as the ranks of the proletariat continue to be replenished with former members of other classes, as long as the working class as a whole is not in a position to rise to the level of the advanced detachment.

The Search for Security 1928–1939

V

FEAR, FASCISM, AND APPEASEMENT

FREDERICK L. SCHUMAN

Frederick L. Schuman, Woodrow Wilson Professor of Government at Williams College, has achieved great distinction as an American student of international politics. Living through the events of the twenties and thirties he describes here, he formed very firm convictions about the issues involved, and he assigns blame for misjudgments and errors mercilessly, writing always with dramatic eloquence and sometimes with a pen that appears to have been dipped in vitriol. His readiness to condemn the Western nations and his sympathy for the Communists have made him the center of fierce controversy; yet, while the reader may question some of Schuman's moral judgments about this tragic period in the world's history, he cannot but be stimulated and enlightened by the writer's provocative analyses.

IN QUEST OF SECURITY

THE *modus vivendi* achieved between Marxist Muscovy and its neighbors in the aftermath of the First War of East and West persisted throughout the 1920's to the tune of various vicissitudes and occasional crises, but with no renewal of violence. The post-Versailles "stabilization of capitalism" sent Communist dreams of World Revolution glimmering. The consolidation of the Soviet order, the success of the NEP, and the later "building of socialism" thwarted Western prayers for the downfall of the Red regime. On both sides hope continued to spring eternally from reciprocal suspicion. But in fact no practical alternative to peace was available.

For the men in the Kremlin, as for any group of policymakers ruling a "Great Power" in a State System comprising a multiplicity of rival sovereignties, the gravest danger and the recurrent nightmare of all *Realpolitik* has always been the possibility of finding themselves alone in the face of a hostile combination of all other Powers. Since the USSR was the only "socialist" State in the world of "bourgeois" States during the long armistice between World Wars, this peril loomed large in the minds of the Communist powerholders who had inherited the Tsarist empire. Their prescription for minimizing the hazard was compounded of diplomatic support to the vanquished and "revisionist" States of Europe against the dominant French bloc, championship of disarmament

Reprinted from *Russia Since 1917* by Frederick L. Schuman (New York, 1957), pp. 156–169, 170–182, 197–200, by permission of Alfred A. Knopf, Inc. Copyright 1957 by Frederick L. Schuman.

and outlawry of war, and sponsorship of bilateral non-aggression and neutrality pacts pledging the signatories to non-participation in any hostilities initiated by others. For more than a decade this formula served the purposes of Soviet security. To outline its application is our present concern.

The Narkomindel was ably directed by Chicherin, who later retired in ill-health and died on July 7, 1936, and by his shrewd helpmate Litvinov, who succeeded him as Commissar for Foreign Affairs on July 25, 1930. Both continued to seek recognition from the USA, but without success, for the America of the 1920's was as determined never to acknowledge the fact of Communist rule of Russia as the America of the 1950's was determined never to acknowledge the fact of Communist rule of China. This attitude, usually futile in relations among Great Powers, was a legacy of Woodrow Wilson's aberration in confusing diplomatic recognition (always a convenience and often a necessity) with moral or political approbation and in using non-recognition as a weapon to punish Evil and foster Good. When Litvinov in March 1921 sent a message from Kalinin to President Harding soliciting negotiations, Secretary of State Hughes replied that "this Government is unable to perceive that there is any proper basis for considering trade relations" pending "convincing evidence" of a restoration of "private property, the sanctity of contracts and the rights of free labor." Russia, said the Secretary, was "a gigantic economic vacuum" and would remain so as long as "the present political and economic system continued." Despite the anomaly of no official relations between the only two Great Powers that held the League of Nations in contempt and ardently championed disarmament and neutrality, Soviet-American trade flourished in a modest way, with Amtorg handling most of the exchanges of machinery, metals, cotton, and motor cars for furs, manganese, flax, and caviar.

The curious pattern of concords and clashes between Washington and Moscow during the '20's is worth recalling in view of later relationships. Although American policy-makers were eager for disarmament by international agreement, they were as shocked as were their Western European counterparts when the wily Litvinov, with tongue in cheek, appeared in Geneva in November 1927 at the fourth session of the League Preparatory Commission to arrange a general disarmament conference and there slyly suggested that the way to disarm was to disarm. He urged an immediate global accord for the total demobilization of all land, sea, and air forces, the scrapping of all weapons, the cessation of military training, and the abolition of general staffs, defense ministries, and military budgets. This "breach of all the proprieties," as he himself said, was "received as a sacrilege." His appeal for American support was rebuffed by Hugh Gibson. When his plea was rejected, he proposed limited disarmament by degrees on a quota basis — which was also rejected. The League's General Disarmament Conference did not meet until February 2, 1932, when the Japanese Navy was bombarding Shanghai. In a maladjusted world again on the road to war, all such efforts were doomed.

When a peace-seeking America sponsored the Kellogg-Briand Pact of Paris of August 27, 1928, renouncing war as an instrument of national policy and pledging the signatories to settle disputes by peaceful means, Litvinov at once signed (August 31) and saw to it that the USSR was the first Power to ratify. He further persuaded Poland, Rumania, Estonia, and Latvia to sign the "Litvinov Protocol" (February 9, 1929), to which Lithuania, Danzig, Turkey, and Iran soon adhered, putting the pact into effect at once between them and the USSR. This apparent parallelism of American and Soviet policies had a paradoxical sequel. Washington had protested in vain to China against a Sino-Soviet accord of May 31, 1924, signed by Wellington Koo and Leo Karakhan, whereby the USSR renounced all Russian concessions, privileges, and rights of extraterritoriality in China and agreed to joint control of the Chinese Eastern Railway to the exclusion of other Powers. When the young Manchurian warlord, Chang Hsueh-liang, arbitrarily seized the railway in the summer of 1929, Moscow sent troops across the frontier to protect Soviet interests. Washington espoused "internationalization" and "neutralization" of the line. Chang yielded to Soviet pressure and agreed on December 3 to a restoration of joint Russian-Chinese management. On the preceding day Secretary of State Henry L. Stimson had "invoked" the Kellogg Pact, with the implication that Moscow had violated its pledges. Litvinov at once denounced such "unjustified pressure" and unwelcome "advice and counsel" from a government that refused to maintain diplomatic relations with the USSR.

The Kremlin meanwhile quarreled bitterly, albeit non-violently, with Britain, where Churchill (November 28, 1925) said "the dark power of Moscow" was based upon "a band of cosmopolitan conspirators gathered from the underworld" and Lord Birkenhead described the Soviet regime as "a junta of assassins and thieves." On August 8, 1924, the first Labor Cabinet signed two treaties, subject to parliamentary approval, contemplating a loan to Moscow as a condition of compensation to British property-owners and bondholders for their losses in Russia. The Tories were outraged and the Liberals, under Asquith and Lloyd George, resentful. The Cabinet fell on October 8, 1924. Four days before the election set for October 29 the Foreign Office published a protest to Moscow against an alleged appeal by Zinoviev to British Communists for "armed insurrection." The "Zinoviev Letter" was a Tory device to discredit the Laborites. Ramsay McDonald, as usual, fumbled the ball. The polling reduced Labor from 191 to 151 seats in Commons, and the Liberals, who never

recovered, from 159 to 40. The triumphant Tories named a Cabinet headed by Stanley Baldwin, with Sir Austen Chamberlain as Foreign Secretary. The treaties were dropped and an attitude of unyielding hostility was assumed in the face of repeated Soviet efforts to negotiate a settlement of all disputes.

On May 26, 1927, following a Home Office raid on the HQ of Arcos, Ltd. and the Soviet Trade Delegation, London severed diplomatic relations with Moscow, while Lord Birkenhead vainly strove to effect an Anglo-French-German coalition against the USSR. The election of May 30, 1929, returned the Laborites to power. A new pact of October 1, 1929, approved in Commons on November 5, provided for a resumption of diplomatic relations, subsequently effected with the exchange of Ambassadors Sir Esmond Ovey and Gregory Sokolnikov. A commercial accord of April 16, 1930, provided for most-favored-nation treatment and the restoration in London of a Soviet Trade Delegation with diplomatic immunities. For the first time, but by no means the last, the politics of a democratic Great Power had been set askew by fear of Red radicalism and by fabricated crises in relations with the USSR.

The men of Moscow, in the interim, had viewed with alarm the British proposals of 1924 for a Western European security pact, lest it presage an anti-Soviet coalition. During the 1920's the Kremlin cultivated Berlin in the "spirit of Rapallo" and enabled the Weimar Republic to evade the Treaty of Versailles by sending officers to Russia for training in military tactics and techniques. When a Treaty of Mutual Guarantee was signed at Locarno, October 16, 1925, by Stresemann, Briand, Sir Austen Chamberlain, Benito Mussolini, and other Western statesmen, Chicherin pressed Stresemann to enter into Bismarckian "reinsurance" arrangements with Russia. The result was the German-Soviet treaty of April 24, 1926.

This agreement embodied the basic formula of all Soviet peace pacts during these years. It was foreshadowed by the treaty of December 17, 1925, signed in Paris by Chicherin and Tewfik Rushdi Bey, Foreign Minister of Turkey, who was smarting from the award of Mosul to Iraq by the League Council two days previously. Turkey and the USSR each agreed to remain neutral in any war involving the other and pledged themselves not to attack each other or to enter into any blocs, coalitions, or agreements against each other. The Soviet-German treaty, concluded for five years and subsequently extended, reaffirmed the Treaty of Rapallo and specified that "should one of the Contracting Parties, despite its peaceful attitude, be attacked by one or more third Powers, the other Contracting Party shall observe neutrality for the whole duration of the conflict" (Art. 2). If such a conflict should occur or a coalition be formed "with a view to the economic or financial boycott of either of the Contracting Parties, the other Contracting Party undertakes not to adhere to such coalition" (Art. 3). Stresemann further pledged his Government to oppose any anti-Soviet moves at Geneva and to decide for itself whether the USSR should ever be deemed an aggressor and to what extent, if any, the Reich would apply League sanctions. Moscow concluded similar non-aggression and neutrality pacts with Lithuania (September 28, 1926), Afghanistan (August 31, 1926), Iran (October 1, 1927), Estonia (May 2, 1932), Latvia (February 5, 1932), Finland (January 21, 1932), Poland (July 25, 1932, extended May 5, 1934, to December 31, 1945), and finally with France (November 29, 1932).

Neutrality is the antithesis of collective security. The Soviet peace pacts of the 1920's were in principle and purpose the negation of the League Covenant. The latter sought to generalize war by obligating all States to join forces against aggressors. The former sought to localize war by obligating each signatory to remain aloof from any conflict in which the other might be involved. For Moscow, as for Washington, the formula for peace was not the Wilsonian precept of "making any war everybody's business," but rather the injunction of "keeping out of other people's wars." American isolationism and Soviet fear of hostile coalitions led to a similar result in foreign policy. Moscow was in no sense "isolationist." But under the conditions of the time it correctly envisaged its security in terms of pledging as many other States as possible to refrain from aggression and to observe neutrality in any armed clash in which the USSR might be involved.

Litvinov crowned his structure of peace pacts by negotiating at the otherwise fruitless London Economic Conference of 1933 "a Convention for the Definition of Aggression," signed on July 4–6 by envoys of the USSR, Estonia, Latvia, Lithuania, Poland, Rumania, Czechoslovakia, Jugoslavia, Turkey, Iran, and Afghanistan. Aggression was defined as declaration of war, invasion, attack on territory, vessels, or aircraft, naval blockade, and support of armed bands invading another State. "No political, military, economic or other considerations may serve as an excuse or justification for aggression."

Peace was thus sought by legalistic formulas equally beloved by Soviet and American diplomats. The long armistice was, in fact, about to come to an end by virtue of a real, rather than imaginary, "collapse of capitalism," with political and military consequences wholly and horribly different from those forecast in the Marxist prognosis. Adolf Hitler became Chancellor of Germany on January 30, 1933. In the sequel the rulers and the ruled of Russia had desperate need of new devices for national survival.

* * *

DEFENSE AGAINST FASCISM

To convert imperialist war into civil war was Lenin's favorite formula for international peace and global proletarian revolution. To convert civil war into imperialist war became the formula of Fascism in the 1930's for the solution of the problems posed by the catastrophic breakdown and prolonged stagnation of capitalistic economy. In none of the afflicted societies did the debacle foreseen by Marx and Lenin create favorable conditions for the proletarian revolt which they and their followers anticipated. In several national communities it produced new despotisms brought to power by frightened industrialists and aristocrats, and fanatically supported in the name of anti-Bolshevism by the desperately insecure and neurotic masses of the lower middle class. The new tyrants restored production by programs of colossal rearmament. They kept peace at home by waging war abroad. First and last, the major target of their plans for aggression was the Soviet Union—as they never tired of boasting, once they discovered that those with wealth and influence in the "decadent" democracies were favorably impressed by such advertising. The anatomy of disaster is still fresh in many memories.

On "Black Thursday" in late October 1929 the American Dream of endless inflationary prosperity through stock speculation and installment buying came to an end with a panic-stricken fall of prices on the New York Stock Exchange. By month's end, the bottom had fallen out of the market. By year's end, corporate shares had declined in value by $15,000,000,000. Within two years the slump had wiped out $50,-000,000,000 of paper values, bankrupted millions of Americans, and reduced the richest country on earth to beggary, with 13,000,000 unemployed by 1933. At the close of the Hoover Administration every bank in the USA closed its doors. The American economy was prostrate. This "collapse of capitalism," hailed with joy by all Communists, was scarcely attributable to the "causes" alleged in the Marxist-Leninist analysis, but was rather due to the inability of statesmen in America and else-

where to comprehend the sources of the disaster and to resort boldly to Keynesian measures of amelioration.

The ensuing "World Depression" grievously afflicted every community in the world save only the Soviet Union, whose totally socialized and planned economy was, for all its ills, immune to "business cycles." The USSR, to be sure, was adversely affected by the drastic decline of prices for raw materials coupled with a slower decline of prices for manufactures. More goods had to be exported to pay for the same amounts of imports. Otherwise the effects of the slump were negligible. Elsewhere they proved disastrous, with the political beneficiaries of mass misery everywhere sworn to Holy War against Bolshevism.

"Fascism" had already conquered Italy in 1922 under the leadership of an ex-Marxist turned demagogue and dictator. The burghers of Germany, facing bankruptcy and confronted by 6,000,000 jobless, cast 6,400,000 votes for Hitler's Nazis in the *Reichstag* election of September 14, 1930; 13,400,000 in the presidential election of April 10, 1932; and 13,745,000 (37% of the total) in the *Reichstag* election of July 31, 1932. Through a conspiracy of industrialists, bankers, and militarists, Hitler became *Reichskanzler* on January 30, 1933, and proceeded in six months to do what Mussolini had taken three years to accomplish: the suppression of all other parties, the creation of a totalitarian dictatorship on the Soviet model, and the restoration of prosperity through public spending on armaments in preparation for wars of conquest to come. The warlords of Japan effected, more slowly, a like transfer of power in Tokyo. Similar groups arose and flourished in Austria, Hungary, the Balkans, Spain, France, and elsewhere.

The crisis found all Communists, bewitched by their vision of "proletarian revolution" and absorbed in their war against Social Democrats as "traitors" to Marxism, totally incapable of comprehending political realities. In most of Europe political liberals did no better, for many among them agreed with conservatives that Fascism was a bulwark against Bolshevism. The black magic of an evil time made politics a hopeless contest between the discouraged and the demented, with the former often regarding the latter as guardians of civilization against Communism. The outcome posed to the USSR a mortal threat of assault from abroad.

The masters of Muscovy, reduced to consternation by the demonstrated falsity of their own dogma, strove to meet the danger by abandoning the formula of "neutrality" and embracing the concept of "collective security" in the hope of somehow organizing a Grand Alliance against Fascism. Had this effort succeeded, World War II would never have been fought, for the aggregation of superior power confronting the Fascist Caesars would have convinced them, for all their delusions and ambitions, that they had no chance of victory in their bid for world conquest. Even madmen in power do not unleash war unless they believe that their prospects of winning are good. The Soviet effort failed, partly because of continued Muscovite suspicion of the motives of the Western Powers but chiefly because Anglo-French policy-makers hoped, to the ghastly end, that Fascist aggression could be deflected against the USSR. The record of the failure of statesmen, in East and West alike, to meet the challenge of the new nihilists has elsewhere been recounted at length. It is enough for the task in hand to outline the responses of the Kremlin Commissars to the successive crises of a decade of disaster.

On September 18, 1931, Lieut. Gen. Honjo's Imperial Japanese Kwantung Army, using as a pretext a bomb explosion on the tracks of the South Manchuria Railway near Mukden, began the seizure of China's rich northeastern provinces. A year later Henry Pu-yi, last of the Manchus, was set up as "Emperor Kang Teh" in the Japanese puppet state of "Manchukuo." Neither

League resolutions at Geneva nor America's "Stimson Doctrine" of non-recognition of the results of aggression changed Tokyo's course. *Izvestia* (September 21, 1931) opined that Chinese inability to defend Manchuria revealed "the depths of the collapse and the degree of weakness to which China has been brought by the Kuomintang feudal-bourgeois reaction." Litvinov voiced "serious alarm." Molotov in December asserted that the League Powers had shown "complete lack of desire and ability" to end the conflict, which he termed "the most important problem of our foreign policy."

The Narkomindel's devices for countering the danger of Japanese aggression were several. A new offer of a neutrality pact was evaded by Tokyo. Chinese proposals for a resumption of diplomatic relations, severed in 1927, were accepted by Moscow in December 1932. When Geneva invited the USSR to become a member of the League Advisory Committee of February 1933 to seek acceptance of the proposals of the belated and futile Lytton Commission, Litvinov declined on the ground that the USSR was pledged to "strict neutrality" and that most of the other members "do not maintain any relations with the Soviet Union and consequently are hostile to it." Since Japanese interruption of traffic on the Chinese Eastern Railway was now chronic, Litvinov on May 2, 1933, proposed the sale of Russian rights in the line. After much Oriental haggling, "Manchukuo" (i.e., Japan) agreed on March 23, 1935, to pay 170,-000,000 yen. A valuable Soviet property on Chinese soil was thus sacrificed at a fraction of its worth in the hope of minimizing friction with Tokyo. But it soon became apparent that the militarists of Japan understood only the language of force. Said Litvinov to the Central Executive Committee in December, 1933:

Along with infringing our rights on the railroad, political figures in Japan, including official representatives of the Japanese Government, began to discuss openly and even in the press the question of war against the Soviet for the purpose of seizing the Primore and the whole Far Eastern Krai. . . . In Manchuria near our border a large number of Japanese troops were concentrated, war materials were brought, railroads and highways were built, etc. In this way the danger not only of the seizure of our railroad by Japanese arms, but a direct danger to our frontier was created. Under these circumstances there was nothing left for our Government to do but to begin to fortify our frontier, transferring the necessary forces for that purpose and taking other military measures.[1]

Soviet-Japanese tension, coupled with American-Japanese friction, the rise of Hitler, and the advent of the "New Deal," contributed to Washington's belated recognition of the USSR. Senator William E. Borah had long urged a facing of facts. Franklin D. Roosevelt was favorably disposed. Business interests were sympathetic, the more so as exports to the USSR had declined from $100,000,000 in 1931 to $9,000,000 in 1933. Raymond Robins, long an advocate of recognition, visited Moscow early in the year, traveled through the Ukraine and Siberia, and had a long interview with Stalin on May 13, 1933. In June, Raymond Moley and William C. Bullitt conferred with Litvinov in London. Bullitt subsequently returned to Moscow, where Wilson had sent him in 1919. The Administration's course was much influenced by Robert F. Kelley, Chief of the Eastern European Division of the State Department since 1926. His memorandum of July 27, 1933, urged that recognition be withheld until Moscow should agree to a cessation of revolutionary propaganda, payment of repudiated debts, and compensation for confiscated property.[2]

On October 10, 1933, Roosevelt invited Kalinin to send an envoy "to end the present abnormal relations" between the two countries. Litvinov reached Washington on November 7, staying with Boris Skvirsky, head of the Russian Information Bureau, and telling newsmen that all questions could be settled in half an hour. His prime purpose was to promote American-Soviet collaboration to checkmate Japan and Germany. Roosevelt and Hull, unwilling and unable to assume any such commitments, concentrated on the problems of propaganda, debts, and claims. Long discussions ensued, unhappily lacking in precision, as later controversies were to reveal. On November 16, 1933, texts of accords were issued.

President and Commissar agreed to an exchange of Ambassadors (William C. Bullitt and Alexander Troyanovsky) and expressed the hope that diplomatic relations would lead to cooperation for "mutual benefit and for the preservation of the peace of the world." Litvinov agreed that the USSR should refrain "from interfering in any manner in the internal affairs of the United States"; should restrain all persons and organizations under its control from all agitation or propaganda aimed at "bringing about by force a change in the political or social order of the whole or any part of the United States, its territories or possessions"; and should not permit on its territory any organization or group aiming at intervention in, or revolutionary propaganda against, the United States. Roosevelt accepted reciprocal obligations and included in the compact a guarantee (willingly accepted by Litvinov to the tune of relevant citations from Soviet legislation) that Americans in the Soviet Union would be granted complete and unqualified religious liberty and would enjoy most-favored-nation treatment in legal protection. Questions of financial claims and counter-

---

[1] Maxim Litvinov, *Against Aggression* (International Publishers, 1939), pp. 76 ff. Cf. Arthur Upham Pope, *Maxim Litvinoff* (Fischer, 1943) and Harriet Moore, *Soviet Far Eastern Policy, 1931–1945* (Princeton University Press, 1945).

[2] See William Appleman Williams, *American-Russian Relations, 1781–1947* (Rinehart, 1952),

pp. 231–255, and Marshall Knappen, *An Introduction to American Foreign Policy* (Harper, 1956), pp. 238 f.

claims were deferred. But Litvinov expressly agreed to waive all counter-claims arising out of intervention in Siberia, thanks to his "examination of certain documents of the years 1918 to 1921 relating to the attitude of the American Government toward the expedition into Siberia, the operations there of foreign military forces and the inviolability of the territory of the USSR."

The sequel was not cooperation against the rising tide of Fascism, equally menacing to Russia and America, but petty squabbling over irrelevancies. Litvinov and Troyanovsky contended that it had been agreed that new American loans to finance trade were to precede Soviet payments on old debts and claims. Hull and Bullitt (who, when he discovered that his Soviet hosts ignored his advise, soon became an ardent crusader against Communism) insisted that Soviet payments must precede any new credit. Parleys over this issue ended in deadlock on February 1, 1935, with no payment ever made on either the Kerensky war debts and claims for nationalized properties or on Soviet counter-claims for damages arising out of an Archangel expedition of 1918. In July 1935, under the terms of the Reciprocal Trade Agreement Act of 1934, Moscow agreed to buy $30,000,000 worth of American goods annually. When the Seventh (and last) Congress of the Comintern met in Moscow, July 25–August 20, 1935, to renounce "World Revolution" in favor of a "Peoples' Front" against Fascism, Earl Browder appeared on behalf of the pathetic Communist Party of the USA. Hull at once ordered Bullitt to protest against Soviet violation of Litvinov's anti-propaganda pledge of 1933. The Narkomindel disclaimed all responsibility for the Comintern. Hull rejoined that in the event of continued propaganda "the friendly and official relations between the two countries cannot but be impaired." Said Litvinov, bitterly, to Bullitt: "No nation ever starts talking about the activities of the Comintern unless it wishes to have as bad relations as possible with us. The activities of the Comintern are merely an excuse for breaking diplomatic relations."[3]

Bullitt withdrew in the summer of 1936 to become Ambassador to France, where he had propagandized against any French-Soviet *rapprochement*. His wealthy successor, Joseph E. Davies, reached Moscow in January 1937 and compensated for Bullitt's embittered anti-Sovietism by a naive pro-Sovietism. Both attitudes ill served the cause of American interests and of Soviet-American collaboration. Chargé Loy W. Henderson reported to Hull on May 14, 1937, that secret Soviet microphones had been discovered in both the office and the residence of Ambassador Davies. "The discovery of the wiring and other traces of eavesdropping is being kept secret and it is hoped that following the Ambassador's return it may be possible to ascertain whether or not the Soviet agents have actually been endeavoring from the attic to listen to the various important and frequently confidential conversations which have taken place in the Ambassador's office." In late 1938 a firm of naval architects, with FDR's approval, presented blueprints for a Soviet "super-battleship." They were rejected by the Kremlin in favor of a standard capital ship to be built in the USA. American suspicions that Moscow desired such a vessel only to copy American secrets of construction killed the contract.

Lawrence Steinhardt succeeded Davies in March 1939, but did not arrive until August, by which time all hope of East-West collaboration against Fascism had waned. A major source of failure was symbolized by an utterance in mid-year 1935 of Rear Admiral Yates Sterling, Jr., USN, echoing sentiments widely shared in America and Western Europe. He called for support of Hitler in a "great crusade

[3] For full documentation on this and other aspects of American-Soviet relations see *Foreign Relations of the United States: Soviet Union, 1933–1939* (Government Printing Office, 1952).

led by Germany . . . not only forever laying the ghost of Bolshevism, but opening up the fertile land of Russia to a crowded and industrially hungry Europe."

* * *

The melancholy drama of aggression and appeasement proceeded, act by act, to its inevitable dénouement through a dismal calendar of wasted years. On March 16, 1935, Hitler repudiated the disarmament clauses of Versailles and decreed the restoration of military conscription. Litvinov at Geneva (April 17) called for action, contending that the Nazi step was "a violation of the Covenant" and "a threat to peace." London and Paris consulted, sent notes, and did nothing. Sir John Simon and Sir Samuel Hoare negotiated with Ribbentrop and signed, June 18, 1935, an Anglo-German naval pact conceding the "right" to rearm and granting to Hitler's Reich parity with Britain in submarines, plus a new navy one-third the size of Britain's and easily capable of controlling the Baltic.

On October 3, 1935, Mussolini, carefully noting the success of Tokyo in conquest and of Berlin in treaty-breaking, invaded Ethiopia. Laval had approved in advance. Hoare had agreed with Laval in September that while League sanctions should be imposed for the sake of appearances, none should be contemplated which might halt the invasion or provoke Italian resistance. Baldwin's Tories won an overwhelming majority in the British election of November 14, 1935, by pledging full support of the League Covenant. A fortnight later Hoare and Laval agreed to restore "peace" by giving Mussolini Ethiopia. The American Congress, by the "Neutrality" Act of 1935, forbade Americans to sell arms to belligerents. Ethiopia was in desperate need of foreign arms. Italy needed none. *Il Duce* floated to victory on a sea of American oil. The United States, in its befuddled anxiety to "keep out of

other peoples' wars," helped to make the world safe for aggression.

Litvinov's appeals at Geneva for aid to Ethiopia were ignored. Black men died in agony from Fascist poison gas. Badoglio entered Addis Ababa in triumph on May 5, 1936. The farce of sanctions was abandoned. The League died at Geneva on the 4th of July. Blum and Halifax urged "peace." Haile Selassie spoke in bitterness: "God and history will remember your judgment. . . . What reply have I to take back to my people?" The answer was betrayal and desertion. Litvinov spoke to a hall of shame, pleading in vain for obligatory sanctions against aggressors or, at least, for European regional security pacts under the Covenant. No one listened.

Hitler had meanwhile (March 7, 1936) ordered the remilitarization of the Rhineland, in violation of Versailles and Locarno. London and Paris sent protests and passed resolutions. At the League Council meeting in London on March 17, Litvinov quoted *Mein Kampf* and declared:

One cannot fight for the collective organization of security without taking measures against the violation of international obligations. We, however, do not count among such measures collective capitulation to the aggressor, capitulation in the face of the violation of treaties, or the collective encouragement of such violations. . . . I declare on behalf of my Government that it is ready to take part in all measures that may be proposed to the Council of the League by the Locarno Powers and will be acceptable to the other members of the Council.

The only answers were empty echoes, words without content, gestures without motion. Hitler began the building of the Siegfried Line. Belgium resumed neutrality. French power to aid France's eastern allies was at an end.

The next test was posed by the Fascist attack on the Spanish Republic, unleashed by Franco's rebellion of July 18, 1936. Blum proposed "non-intervention"—i.e., a common policy of forbidding the Spanish

Republic to buy arms abroad for its own defense. The London "Non-Intervention" Committee did what it could to see that the Loyalists received no aid. It concealed and even promoted a steady flow of troops, planes, tanks, and guns to Franco from Lisbon, Rome, and Berlin. The Roosevelt Administration, obedient to Downing Street and the wishes of the Vatican, saw to it that Madrid could buy no American arms. Asserted Litvinov:

Here is an attempt at a forcible implantation in Spain from without of a Fascist system, an attempt to force upon the Spanish people a Fascist Government with the aid of bayonet, hand-grenade and bomb. If this attempt were to succeed, there would be no guarantees against its repetition on a wider scale in relation to other states. . . . I would like to express the confidence that the League Council, not only in the interests of Spain, but in the interests of international justice and the preservation of peace, and also in the interests of the League itself, will throw its word into the scale and render all possible support to the Spanish people.

The League Powers preferred to render all possible support to the aggressors. The USSR sought to save the Spanish Republic by counter-intervention. The effort failed in the face of the determination of the Western democracies that Fascism should conquer Spain. At the end of March 1939 the heroic resistance of the Loyalists, deserted and betrayed to the Axis by Paris, London, and Washington, was at last beaten down. At the funeral of Spanish democracy the voice of John Donne came singing down the centuries to Frenchmen, Britons, and Americans: "Send not to know for whom the bell tolls. It tolls for thee. . . ."

A further test was posed by the resumption of the Japanese attack on China in July 1937. *Pravda* (September 22) declared that "the blood of whole peoples" was being spilled and that aggression could be halted only by the "collective repulse of the Fascists by all the Governments interested in peace, the collective defense of

indivisible peace." Once more the democratic Powers acted on the premises that peace was divisible, that aggression should be appeased, and that collective action would involve greater risks than inaction. In the apt words of Arnold J. Toynbee:

They made their momentous choice neither on the absolute criterion of morality nor on the relative criterion of expediency, but on that trivial distinction between this moment and the next which keeps the sluggard cowering between the blankets when the house is burning over his head.

The Fascist "Axis" and then the "Triplice" meanwhile took form under the guise of "protecting civilization from Communism," a theme always warmly endorsed by many persons of wealth and influence in the Western democracies. At the London Economic Conference, Alfred Hugenberg had circulated a memorandum demanding the return of the German colonies and a "mandate" to the Reich to "reorganize" Russia through German "constructive and creative genius." Dr. Schacht told the Governor of the Bank of France, according to Pertinax (*Echo de Paris*, November 3, 1935), that "we have no intention to change our Western frontiers. Sooner or later Germany and Poland will share the Ukraine, but for the moment we shall be satisfied with making our strength felt over the Baltic provinces."

The shape and size of the menace to be met are best suggested by noting the milestones of Fascist diplomacy. Following the German-Italian quarrel over Austria in 1934, negotiations were initiated in search of a basis of cooperation. The Berlin-Vienna Accord of July 11, 1936, and the joint German-Italian attack on the Spanish Republic launched a week later, paved the way for the formation of the "Axis." Before massed thousands of goose-stepping fanatics and civilian hysterics, Hitler at Nuremberg declared in September that "if I had the Ural Mountains with their incalculable store of treasure in raw materials,

Siberia with its vast forests, and the Ukraine with its tremendous wheat fields, Germany under Nationalsocialist leadership would swim in plenty." Said Rosenberg: "The Soviet Union's Government is controlled by Jewish interests and it is money stolen from the Russian people by the Jews that is being used in an attempt to awaken the underworld in all nations to march against European culture." Added Göbbels: "Bolshevism must be annihilated." On October 25, 1936, Ciano and Ribbentrop signed a secret pact. Commented *Il Duce:* "It is no wonder if today we raise the banner of anti-Bolshevism. This is our old banner!" On November 18 the two Caesars of Fascism took their first joint step in diplomacy: simultaneous recognition of Franco's rebels as the Government of Spain.

Less than a week later, on November 25, 1936, Ribbentrop and Mushakoji, Japanese Ambassador in Berlin, signed the five-year "Anti-Comintern Pact," pledging collaboration between their States against "Communist subversive activity." Italy adhered on November 6, 1937. Tokyo recognized Italian title to Ethiopia. Rome recognized Manchukuo. Trade agreements followed. On the first anniversary of the Pact, Matsuzo Nagai sent greetings to Göbbels: "The Sino-Japanese conflict is for us a holy war to free the Chinese people from the Red Peril." The Reich recognized Manchukuo on May 12, 1938. The German-Italian treaty of military alliance (May 22, 1939) and the Tripartite Pact (September 27, 1940), threatening the United States with war, were the capstones of the Fascist coalition.

Four days before the Anti-Comintern Pact was signed, *Izvestia* (November 21, 1936) declared that "the two most aggressive Powers in the world have formed a bloc" and are engaged in a "conspiracy against peace," directed as much against Britain and America as against the USSR. The answer must be "organization of collective security and real protection for peace." Moscow feared attack in the East from a Japan in control of Manchuria, Inner Mongolia, and much of China. Moscow feared attack in the West from an Axis in control of truncated Austria, feudal-Fascist Hungary, corrupt Rumania, helpless Bulgaria, and wavering Jugoslavia. Despite Warsaw's alliance with Paris and its peace pacts with the USSR, Poland veered toward the Axis camp. Pilsudski was less anti-German than anti-Russian. His friend, Josef Beck, became Foreign Minister, November 2, 1932. Warsaw and Berlin signed a ten-year non-aggression pact on January 26, 1934. At Pilsudski's funeral in Cracow, May 18, 1935, Laval, fresh from a hurried visit to Moscow, conferred at length with Göring. The orientation of Pilsudski's Colonels, who continued to rule Poland, is suggested by the widely circulated book of Wladimir Studnicki, *Poland's Political Aims* (1935):

Poland has the strongest interest in a victory of Japan over Russia. Participation in a Russo-Japanese war would be possible if Poland were to ally itself with Germany with this in view. No attention need be paid to France which occupies today a secondary position. Poland and Germany could lay the foundations of a great Central European bloc.

The Second and Third Five Year Plans made provision for a vast Soviet war industry capable of supplying a modern, mechanized defense force. In the Maritime Provinces a self-sufficient Red Banner Army of 250,000, under General Vasily Bluecher (Galen), was established to parry a possible Japanese attack from Manchukuo. A thousand bombing planes based at Vladivostok were calculated to impress Tokyo with the unwisdom of aggression. The Trans-Siberian was double-tracked. A new railroad was laid north of Lake Baikal to Komsomolsk on the lower Amur, with branches southward to Khabarovsk and eastward to the coast opposite Japanese Sakhalin. Frontier defenses were everywhere strengthened. Alone among European military forces, the Red Army kept pace with the growth of the *Wehrmacht* by expanding its regular troops to a million men by 1935, to two millions by 1937, and to almost three millions by 1939, all equipped with guns, tanks, and planes turned out by the new heavy industries. Said Defense Commissar Voroshilov in 1936: "When the enemy attacks the Soviet Ukraine or Soviet Byelorussia or any other part of the Soviet Union, we will not only prevent his invading our own country but will defeat him in the territory whence he came."

Against the Japanese danger it was impossible to make even a beginning of organizing an effective coalition. America, Britain, and France, though all threatened by Tokyo, were paralyzed. While their diplomats appeased the aggressors, their exporters supplied the Japanese war machine with oil, rubber, scrap iron, and all else needed to continue aggression. *Izvestia* (May 21, 1937) endorsed the Australian project of a Pacific security pact, but warned that such a policy required "that the Powers do not refuse ahead of time to participate in a real struggle for peace in the Pacific, that they do not prefer their attempts to reach agreements with the aggressor, and that they do not retreat before his impudent demands."

China, the first victim of attack, was as helpless as the Western Powers. Rather than resist Japan, Chiang Kai-shek preferred to conduct annual crusades against the peasant Soviets of the northern provinces. Extreme measures were required to change his mind. When he visited Sian Fu in Shensi in December 1936 he was kidnapped by the troops of Chang Hsueh-liang, who freed him only on condition that he cease his war against Red China, work for anti-Japanese unity, and cooperate with the Communists and northern warlords against the invader. As a result of this prospect, and of their own defeat at the polls at home, the Nipponese militarists launched a new and murderous assault on China, beginning with the clash on the Marco Polo Bridge near Lukouchiao, southwest of Peking, on July 7, 1937.

The initial Chinese protest at Japanese aggression was sent to the USSR as well as to the signatories of the Nine Power Pact. An American squadron, for the first time since the Revolution, made a courtesy call at Vladivostok at the end of July. In pursuit of their new program of conquering all of China, Japanese forces machine-gunned the British Ambassador, bombed and sank the U.S.S. *Panay*, and raided Soviet Consulates at Tientsin and Shanghai. Now, if ever, a Four-Power coalition was called for to halt the madmen of Tokyo. But the only result of the crisis was the signature of a five-year Sino-Soviet neutrality pact on August 21, 1937, by which the signatories renounced aggression and agreed "not to render assistance of any kind, either directly or indirectly," to any third Power which might attack the other. Litvinov's pleas at Geneva for effective League action against Japan came to nothing. The USSR accepted the invitation to attend the Brussels Conference of the signatories of the Nine Power Pact. But Litvinov soon left the Belgian capital and reported to his people what had happened:

China applies to the League of Nations for protection, referring to the corresponding points in the Covenant. The League forms a committee, the committee appoints a sub-committee, and the latter elects an editorial committee. A paper is drafted and addressed to Japan: "We do not approve of your offensive. Probably it is based on a misunderstanding. Please come to confirm this and, lest you feel lonely among us, we are inviting your kindred spirit and friend, Germany." From Japan comes confirmation that there is no misunderstanding at all, that she is on the war-path quite deliberately and agrees to discuss matters only with China and only on terms of the latter's surrender. Disarmed by this reply, the League decides to refer the question to the Powers most concerned in Far Eastern affairs, signatories to the so-called Washington Treaty which is violated by Japan for the second time. (It was violated the first time by the occupation of Manchuria.) And so the Brussels Conference is called, and the Soviet Union is also invited, although she is not a signatory to the Washington Treaty. What does this conference do? Its activity was very neatly hit off in a cartoon which I saw in a foreign newspaper. This shows the honorable delegates of eighteen States, not without great effort and strain, dragging a letter to the postbox for Japan. In this letter, as you know, they again demand Japan's confirmation whether she is deliberately committing her aggression in China and request her to stop and accept mediation. Confirmation is not long in coming. Japan, even with an inflection of resentment, replies that there is no need to bother her; she has repeatedly stated that she is attacking China quite deliberately and for quite definite aims. She does not need anybody's mediation; she is ready to negotiate only with China — about capitulation, of course — and the only thing the conference can do is to make China agree to this capitulation. This reply disarmed the Brussels Conference, just as the first reply disarmed the League of Nations, and the Conference was closed.

Only in Outer Mongolia did it prove possible for Moscow to acquire an "ally" against Japan. After the Chinese Revolution of 1911, the ancient land of Ghenghis Khan, under the leadership of the Khutukhta or "Living Buddha," had broken away from Chinese control. Between 1921, when the regime of Baron Ungern-Sternberg was liquidated and a Soviet-Mongol treaty of friendship was signed, and 1925, Soviet troops had remained in Mongolia. With the death of the last Khutukhta in 1924, after twenty-three earthly incarnations, a popular revolution against the feudal-theocratic rule of the Lamas and princes led to the establishment of a "People's Republic" fashioned on Soviet models. The northwestern area of Tannu-Tuva had already become an "independent" Soviet protectorate in 1923. The People's Republic, with its capital at Ulan Bator, was still nominally under Chinese suzerainty, but looked to the USSR for protection

against Japanese pressure, which became heavy in 1936. On March 1 Stalin told Roy Howard that "if Japan should venture to attack the Mongolian People's Republic and encroach upon its independence, we will have to help the Mongolian People's Republic. Stomoniakov, Litvinov's assistant, recently informed the Japanese Ambassador in Moscow of this and pointed to the immutable friendly relations which the USSR has maintained with the Mongolian People's Republic since 1921."

On March 12, 1936, at Ulan Bator, a Soviet-Mongolian Protocol was signed, putting into formal effect a "gentlemen's agreement" of November 27, 1934. For a period of ten years "the Governments of the USSR and of the Mongolian People's Republic undertake in the event of military aggression against one of the Contracting Parties to give each other every assistance, including military assistance" (Art. 2). Troops stationed by one State in the territory of the other by mutual agreement would be withdrawn, as in 1925, as soon as the necessity had passed (Art. 3). China protested on the ground that the Protocol violated Article 5 of the Sino-Soviet treaty of 1924. Litvinov retorted that the pact did not "violate to the slightest degree the sovereignty of China." Moscow charged that Tokyo had inspired the protest. A Soviet-Japanese press war raged throughout the year and thereafter. But Japanese-Manchukuo forces were halted at the Mongolian border by the knowledge that the Red Army would resist any farther advance.

The militarists of Tokyo persistently refused to negotiate a non-aggression pact, arguing that all outstanding issues should first be settled. Involved negotiations over fisheries and frontiers pursued their tedious course. With the signature of the Anti-Comintern Pact, Moscow refused to revise or replace the fisheries convention of 1928 and made Japanese rights dependent upon annual agreements. The Kwantung Army and the soldiers of Henry Pu-yi indulged in cautious experimentation to test the will and the power of Moscow to defend the Soviet and Mongolian frontiers. This policy was safe since Tokyo knew that the Kremlin would not take the initiative in precipitating a full-scale war. This policy was also conclusive; all the experiments had the same outcome.

Soviet diplomacy was supplemented by force. Arms achieved that which diplomacy alone could not have accomplished: the prevention of open war. The major clashes which convinced the Sons of Heaven that war with Russia would be unwise were interspersed among hundreds of border incidents. During the spring and summer of 1937 Japanese units on the Amur River south of Blagoveshchensk sought to occupy various islands claimed by the USSR. The incident was publicized throughout the world out of all proportion to its significance. In January 1938 Zhdanov criticized the Narkomindel before the first session of the newly elected Supreme Soviet, contending that it "should be more resolute in its attitude toward the arrogant, hooligan and provocative conduct of the agents of Japan and of that puppet State called Manchukuo." At the end of July, in the region southwest of Vladivostok, a Japanese division occupied Chankufeng Hill and another eminence to the north, both west of Lake Hassan near the juncture of Korea, Manchukuo, and the Soviet hinterland of Possiet Bay. Early in August a Soviet division, aided by tanks and bombers, drove out the intruders with several hundred casualties on both sides. Litvinov and Ambassador Shigemitsu signed an armistice on August 11, 1938, restoring the *status quo*.

Early in May 1939 new hostilities began in the district of Nomonhan, southeast of Lake Bui-Nor along the Khalka River, easternmost point of Outer Mongolia. Moscow came at once to the defense of the People's Republic. Intermittent fighting continued through the summer until Soviet-Mongol forces routed the invaders at the end of August, destroying or capturing 8 tanks, 144 guns, and 600 planes. A truce of September 16 restored the *status quo*. Having learned a costly lesson, the men of Nippon henceforth refrained from challenging Red forces to battle. Less resistance was to be encountered in other directions.

If the geopolitics of Soviet strategy called in the Orient for that which was unattainable—alliances with China, Britain, and America to checkmate Japanese ambitions—it called in the West for allies on Germany's flank and rear. The French post-Versailles alliance system already embraced Belgium, Poland, Czechoslovakia, Jugoslavia, and Rumania. British and Soviet support of this bloc would have rendered the Nazi Reich helpless. Moscow was willing and anxious to effect such a combination. London, Paris, and Warsaw were befogged in illusions and evasions. Yet the effort was persistent.

Soviet entry into the League of Nations was the point of departure for the attempts of the Narkomindel to organize collective security against aggression. Little progress was made until the coming to the Quai d'Orsay of Louis Barthou in the wake of the Fascist riots in Paris of February 6, 1934, and the ensuing resignation of the Daladier cabinet. Barthou, serving under Premier Gaston Doumergue, was 72 years old and a staunch conservative. He was the only French Foreign Minister during a fateful decade who understood the nature of the Nazi menace and saw how it might be met. The French-Soviet non-aggression pact of November 29, 1932, had paved the way for a *rapprochement*, as had the visit of Litvinov to Paris in July 1933 and the September journeys to Moscow of Edouard Herriot and Pierre Cot. Barthou spent the spring of 1934 visiting Warsaw, Prague, Geneva (where he conferred with Litvinov), Bucharest, and Belgrade, hoping to strengthen the French-Polish alliance and to weld the "Little Entente" and "Balkan Entente" into a firm structure of security.

Litvinov, like Barthou, realized that the safety of France and the USSR required an alliance. Without illusions, he had accepted Nazi renewal (May 5, 1933) of the 1926 neutrality treaty. In September 1933 he concluded a non-aggression pact with Italy. But he ignored overtures from the Wilhelmstrasse during his passage through Berlin in December. He took it for granted that in the end nothing would halt the Axis drive to war save a counter-mobilization of superior force. He now endorsed the familiar French view that security must be organized in concentric circles, and argued (May 18, 1934) that in the first circle must stand France, the USSR, the Baltic States, Poland, and the Little Entente; in the second, the Mediterranean Powers; and in the third, the Pacific Powers. His fears of a German-Polish-Finnish bloc against Muscovy were enhanced by the Polish-German pact of January 1934 and German rejection of his proposals of March 28, 1934, for a joint guarantee of the four Baltic States. He therefore supported Barthou's project of a mutual-assistance pact on the Locarno model among France, Germany, Poland, Czechoslovakia, the Soviet Union, and the Baltic States.

But the project failed, despite the blessing of Sir John Simon in July. Berlin and Warsaw both refused to participate save on conditions that would have made the arrangement meaningless. The attempt at least demonstrated, even to the British Cabinet, that there was no workable alternative to a French-Soviet alliance. Soviet membership in the League, it was agreed, should be a first step. Chicherin had opposed the Geneva organization with what he called "absolutely undiluted, unmixed, unwavering, unswerving" enmity. But Stalin told Walter Duranty on Christmas Day, 1933, that "notwithstanding the withdrawal of Germany and Japan—or perhaps just because of this—the League may become something of a check to retard the outbreak of military actions or to hinder them. . . . If historical events should follow such a course, then it is not impossible that

we should support the League of Nations despite its colossal defects."

Barthou had induced Prague and Bucharest to grant full recognition to Moscow on June 9, 1934. Bulgaria and Hungary did likewise, but not Jugoslavia, whose King Alexander had a horror of "regicides"—though his own father had come to the Serbian throne in 1903 through the murder of his predecessors. By the end of August, Barthou had secured general assent to an invitation to the Kremlin to join the League and to take a permanent seat on the Council. Swiss, Portuguese, and Irish objections could be ignored. Polish objections were more serious. Pilsudski's henchmen, already notorious for their oppression of the Byelorussians and Ukrainian populations of the eastern provinces, feared that Litvinov at Geneva might raise the question of the Polish treatment of minorities. They distrusted Soviet disclaimers of any such intention. On September 13, 1934, at the 15th League Assembly, Josef Beck declared that "pending the introduction of a general and uniform system for the protection of minorities, my Government is compelled to refuse, as from today, all cooperation with the international organizations in the matter of the supervision of the application by Poland of the system of minority protection."

In the sequel the Western Powers acquiesced in Polish repudiation of the minority treaty as the price of Polish support of Soviet membership in the League. On September 12 Barthou had sent Litvinov a formal invitation from the Council. On September 15, despite De Valera's protest, letters were exchanged and the Council voted to invite the Assembly to approve. On September 18, 1934, third anniversary of the Mukden Incident, the Assembly voted to approve Soviet admission, 38 against 3 (Switzerland, Portugal, and the Netherlands), with 7 abstentions (Argentina, Belgium, Cuba, Luxembourg, Panama, Peru, and Venezuela). Marcel Houden of the League Secretariat sought to embarrass

Litvinov and his colleagues by bringing them into the gloomy Bâtiment Electoral ten minutes before the Assembly President, R. J. Sandler of Sweden, had concluded his welcoming speech. (Such petty spite found later expression in assigning to Litvinov the chairmanship of the Committee on Sea-weeds.) Josef Beck sneered at the whole proceeding. But Litvinov's words from the rostrum were a clarion call to a world that might have saved itself infinite suffering had its leaders listened and acted:

The Soviet State has never excluded the possibility of some form or other of associating with States having a different political and social system, so long as there is no mutual hostility and if it is for the attainment of common aims. . . . The organization of peace! Could there be a loftier and at the same time more practical and urgent task for the co-operation of all nations? . . .

One thing is quite clear to me, and that is that peace and security cannot be organized on the shifting sands of verbal promises and declarations. The nations are not to be soothed into a feeling of security by assurances of peaceful intentions, however often they are repeated, especially in those places where there are grounds for expecting aggression or where, only the day before, there have been talk and publications about wars of conquest in all directions, for which both ideological and material preparations are being made. . . . Far be it from me to overrate the opportunities and means of the League of Nations for the organization of peace. I realize, perhaps better than any of you, how limited these means are. I am aware that the League does not possess the means for the complete abolition of war. I am, however, convinced that, with the firm will and close cooperation of all its members, a great deal could be done at any given moment for the utmost diminution of the danger of war, and this is sufficiently honorable and lofty a task, the fulfillment of which would be of incalculable advantage to humanity.

The Kremlin was now fully committed to collective security. The enterprise was auspiciously begun. But the obstructionism of the Polish Colonels, who were to persist to the end in their anti-Soviet orientation, was an evil augury. Still more ominous was the tragedy which brought Pierre Laval to the Quai d'Orsay: on October 9, 1934, one Vlada Georgiev, a Macedonian terrorist in the pay of Ante Pavelich's Croatian *Ustaschi*, a revolutionary movement linked with Fascist conspirators in Budapest, Rome, and Berlin, perpetrated a double assassination in Marseilles. The victims were King Alexander of Jugoslavia and Foreign Minister Louis Barthou of France.

* * *

On March 12, 1938, the new *Wehrmacht* marched unresisted into Austria, followed by Hitler, the Austrian Corporal of 1914 and now *Führer* of the Nazi Reich, who proclaimed *Anschluss* in Vienna before madly cheering throngs while Jews and Slavs fled for their lives as best they could. Czechoslovakia was now outflanked, but Prague and Paris did nothing. Lord Halifax had visited Hitler in Berchtesgaden in the preceding November and convinced *Der Führer* that Britain would not oppose the Nazi *Drang nach Osten*. On February 20, 1938, Hitler had publicly demanded that Eden resign as Foreign Minister. In protest against Neville Chamberlain's appeasement policy, Eden resigned the same night. Halifax succeeded. When informed of the rape of Austria, he exclaimed: "Horrible, horrible, I never thought they would do it!" On March 17 Litvinov warned that Czechoslovakia was in danger and proposed a conference to discuss collective means of "checking the further development of aggression and eliminating an aggravated danger of a new world massacre." In a statement to the press he asserted: "Tomorrow might be too late, but today there is time yet, if all States, particularly great States, take up a firm, unambiguous stand on the problem of the collective salvation of peace." But the British Cabinet declined to assume any new commitments. The Soviet proposal was dismissed as "premature."

The next test was posed by the unleashing, through propaganda, diplomacy, and terrorism, of the Nazi campaign against Prague in the summer of 1938. Moscow was pledged to the defense of Czechoslovakia. Tukhachevsky had conferred with Beneš and General Sirovy—and then allegedly disclosed the plans of joint defense to Berlin. The revelation of his treason by Czech agents led to his speedy arrest, trial, and execution. Moscow remained pledged to the defense of Czechoslovakia. Paris was likewise pledged. The Quai d'Orsay and Downing Street, however, had other plans and hopes that required the betrayal and destruction of the Czechoslovak Republic. Chamberlain flew three times to Germany on the principle that "if you don't concede the first time, fly, fly again."

On September 19 the Prague Cabinet received an ultimatum demanding that it surrender Sudetenland to Hitler, along with all the Czech border fortifications. The source of the ultimatum, incredibly, was not Berlin but Paris and London. Moscow offered to defend Czechoslovakia even after the French betrayal had released the USSR from any such obligations under the pacts of 1935. Amid the ruin of his hopes, Litvinov spoke with heavy heart at Geneva on September 21, 1938:

The League was created as a reaction to the World War and its countless quarrels; its object was to make that the last war, to safeguard all nations against aggression, and to replace the system of military alliances by the collective organization of assistance to the victim of aggression. In this sphere the League has done nothing. Two States — Ethiopia and Austria — have lost their independent existence in consequence of violent aggression. A third State, China, is now a victim of aggression and foreign invasion for the second time in seven years, and a fourth State, Spain, is in the third year of a sanguinary war, owing to the armed intervention of two aggressors in its internal affairs. The

League of Nations has not carried out its obligations to these States. At the present time a fifth State, Czechoslovakia, is suffering interference in its internal affairs at the hands of a neighboring State, and is publicly and loudly menaced with attack. . . .

A fire-brigade was set up in the innocent hope that, by some lucky chance, there would be no fires. Things turned out differently, however. Fires have broken out in defiance of our hopes, but luckily not in our immediate vicinity. So (say some) let us dissolve the fire brigade — of course not forever, but merely temporarily. Directly the danger of any fire disappears, we shall reassemble the fire brigade without a moment's delay. . . .

At a time when there is being drawn up a further list of sacrifices to the god of aggression and a line is under the annals of all post-war international history, with the sole conclusion that nothing succeeds like aggression — at such a moment, every State must define its role and its responsibility before its contemporaries and before history. That is why I must plainly declare here that the Soviet Government bears no responsibility whatsoever for the events now taking place, and for the fatal consequences which may inexorably ensue.

The fruit of Anglo-French policy was the "Peace" of Munich of October 1, 1938, concluded at a Four-Power conference to which the USSR was not invited and from which the Czechs were excluded. Having consummated the ruin of Czechoslovakia, Prime Minister Neville Chamberlain concluded a non-aggression pact with Hitler and returned to London with happy words: "I have brought back peace with honor. I think it is peace for our time." In December, Foreign Minister Georges Bonnet, with the blessing of Premier Edouard Daladier, signed a non-aggression pact with Ribbentrop in Paris. With the reduction of the Czech army to helplessness, General Gamelin, top commander of the military forces of the French Republic, lost 45 divisions without lifting a finger to save them. London and Paris were now committed to the "localization" of future wars and to the deflection of Axis aggression eastward.

Said Hugo Vavrecka, member of the Czech Cabinet:

It is a case without parallel in history that our allies and friends should impose conditions upon us which are usually imposed upon vanquished enemies. It is not a lack of courage that induced our Government to take the decision which grips our hearts. . . . God knows that more courage is needed for living than for committing suicide. . . . We shall not blame those who left us in the lurch, but history will pronounce a judgment about these days.

Said Winston Churchill: "France and Britain had to choose between war and dishonor. They chose dishonor. They will have war."

The entire French alliance system was now destroyed. All Danubia and Balkania were at the mercy of the Axis. Czechoslovakia had been outflanked by the Nazi occupation of Austria. Poland was now outflanked by the Nazi victory at Munich. Far from appreciating the fact, the Warsaw Colonels joined Hitler in destroying Czechoslovakia through their armed seizure of Teschen on October 2. Two days later *Le Journal de Moscou* stated:

In effect France has with its own hands and without having consulted the USSR annulled the Soviet-Czech pact which was a corollary to the French-Soviet pact and one of the important elements of a regional eastern pact. . . . The loss of its allies and isolation — this is the price which France will have to pay for capitulation before the aggressor.

The great democracies had all but lost World War II before it had begun. No comparable instance of folly and perfidy on the part of the responsible leaders of self-governing peoples is available in all the past records of human weakness, stupidity, and crime.

THE INTERNATIONAL SITUATION

JOSEPH STALIN

Early 1934 saw the world still in the grip of the Great Depression. Japan was aggressively extending her authority in Manchuria, threatening Russian borders, and Hitler was firmly seated in the German saddle. This was a time fraught with international stresses. One year of the Second Five-Year Plan had passed, but the USSR still had much to accomplish if it were to achieve the great economic and military strength it desired. On January 26, Stalin presented his "Report on the Work of the Central Committee to the Seventeenth Congress of the Communist Party of the Soviet Union," in which he reviewed the international situation and its meaning for the USSR. The extracts printed here are from this official report.

A RESULT of the protracted economic crisis has been the hitherto unprecedented tension in the political situation in capitalist countries, both within these countries and in their mutual relations.

The intensified struggle for foreign markets, the disappearance of the last vestiges of free trade, prohibitive tariffs, trade war, currency war, dumping, and many other analogous measures which demon-

From Stalin's "Report on the Work of the Central Committee to the Seventeenth Congress of the CPSU(b)," January 26, 1934, *Problems of Leninism* (Moscow: Foreign Languages Publishing House, 1947), pp. 460–469.

strate extreme *nationalism* in economic policy have made the relations among the various countries extremely strained, have prepared the ground for military conflicts, and have put war on the order of the day as a means for a new redivision of the world and of spheres of influence in favor of the stronger states.

Japan's war against China, the occupation of Manchuria, Japan's withdrawal from the League of Nations, and her advance in North China have made the situation still more tense. The intensified struggle for the Pacific and the growth of naval armaments in Japan, the United States, Great Britain and France are results of this increased tension.

Germany's withdrawal from the League of Nations and the spectre of revenge have further added to the tension and have given a fresh impetus to the growth of armaments in Europe.

It is not surprising that bourgeois pacifism is now dragging out a miserable existence, and that idle talk of disarmament is giving way to "business-like" talk about armament and re-armament.

Again, as in 1914, the parties of bellicose imperialism, the parties of war and revenge are coming into the foreground.

Quite clearly things are heading for a new war.

The internal situation of the capitalist countries, in view of the operation of these same factors, is becoming even more tense. Four years of industrial crisis have exhausted the working class and reduced it to despair. Four years of agricultural crisis have utterly ruined the poorer strata of the peasantry, not only in the principal capitalist countries, but also—and particularly—in the dependent and colonial countries. It is a fact that, notwithstanding all attempts to manipulate statistics in order to show a drop in unemployment, the number of unemployed, according to the official figures of bourgeois institutions, reaches 3,000,000 in Great Britain, 5,000,000 in Germany and 10,000,000 in the United States, not to mention the other European countries. Add to this the more than ten million part-time workers; add the millions of ruined peasants—and you will get an approximate picture of the poverty and despair of the laboring masses. The masses of the people have not yet reached the stage when they are ready to storm capitalism; but the idea of storming it is maturing in the minds of the masses—of that there can hardly be any doubt. This is eloquently testified to by such facts as, say, the Spanish revolution which overthrew the fascist regime, and the expansion of the Soviet districts in China, which the united counter-revolution of the Chinese and foreign bourgeoisie is unable to stop.

This, indeed, explains why the ruling classes in the capitalist countries are so zealously destroying or nullifying the last vestiges of parliamentarism and bourgeois democracy which might be used by the working class in its struggle against the oppressors; why they are driving the Communist Parties underground and resorting to open terrorist methods to maintain their dictatorship.

Chauvinism and preparation for war as the main elements of foreign policy; repression of the working class and terrorism in the sphere of home policy as a necessary means for strengthening the rear with a view to future wars—that is what is now particularly engaging the minds of contemporary imperialist politicians.

It is not surprising that fascism has now become the most fashionable commodity among bellicose bourgeois politicians. I am referring not only to fascism in general, but, primarily, to fascism of the German type, which is wrongly called National-Socialism—wrongly because the most searching examination will fail to reveal even an atom of Socialism in it.

In this connection the victory of fascism in Germany must be regarded not only as a system of the weakness of the working class and a result of the betrayals of the working class by the Social-Democratic

Party, which paved the way for fascism; it must also be regarded as a symptom of the weakness of the bourgeoisie, of the fact that the bourgeoisie is already unable to rule by the old methods of parliamentarism and bourgeois democracy, and, as a consequence, is compelled in its home policy to resort to terroristic methods of rule— as a symptom of the fact that it is no longer able to find a way out of the present situation on the basis of a peaceful foreign policy, and that, as a consequence, it is compelled to resort to a policy of war.

That is the situation.

As you see, things are heading towards a new imperialist war as a way out of the present situation.

Of course, there are no grounds for assuming that a war can provide a real way out. On the contrary, it will confuse the situation still more. More than that, it is sure to unleash revolution and jeopardize the very existence of capitalism in a number of countries, as was the case in the course of the first imperialist war. And if, notwithstanding the experience of the first imperialist war, the bourgeois politicians clutch at war as a drowning man clutches at a straw, that shows that they have gotten into a hopeless mess, have reached an impasse, and are ready to rush headlong over the precipice.

It will not be amiss, therefore, briefly to examine the plans for the organization of war which are now being hatched in the circles of bourgeois politicians.

Some think that war should be organized against some one of the Great Powers. They think of inflicting a crushing defeat upon that power and of improving their own affairs at its expense. Let us assume that they organize such a war. What may be the upshot? As is well known, during the first imperialist war it was also intended to destroy one of the Great Powers, *viz.*, Germany, and to profit at her expense. And what was the upshot of this? They did not destroy Germany; but they sowed such a hatred for the victors in Germany, and

created such a rich soil for revenge, that they have not been able to clear up the revolting mess they made even to this day, and will not, perhaps, be able to do so for quite some time. But they did get the smash-up of capitalism in Russia, the victory of the proletarian revolution in Russia, and—of course—the Soviet Union. What guarantee is there that the second imperialist war will produce "better" results for them than the first? Would it not be more correct to assume that the opposite will be the case?

Others think that war should be organized against a country that is weak in the military sense, but represents an extensive market—for example, against China, which, it transpires, cannot even be described as a state in the strict sense of the word, but is merely "unorganized territory" which needs to be seized by strong states. They evidently want to divide her up completely and improve their affairs at her expense. Let us assume that they organize such a war. What may be the upshot? It is well known that at the beginning of the nineteenth century Italy and Germany were regarded in the same light as China is today, i.e., they were considered "unorganized territories" and not states, and they were subjugated. But what was the upshot of this? As is well known, the upshot was wars for independence waged by Germany and Italy, and the amalgamation of these countries into independent states. The upshot was increased hatred for the oppressors in the hearts of the peoples of these countries, the results of which have not been removed to this day and will not, perhaps, be removed for quite some time. The question arises: What guarantee is there that the same thing will not result from an imperialist war against China?

Still others think that war should be organized by a "superior race," say, the German "race," against an "inferior race," primarily against the Slavs; that only such a war can provide a way out of the situation, for it is the mission of the "superior race" to fructify the "inferior race" and rule over it. Let us assume that this queer theory, which is as far removed from science as the sky from earth, let us assume that this queer theory is put into practice. What may be the upshot? It is well known that ancient Rome looked upon the ancestors of the present-day Germans and French in the same way as the representatives of the "superior race" now look upon the Slavonic tribes. It is well known that ancient Rome treated them as an "inferior race," as "barbarians," destined to live in eternal subordination to the "superior race," to "great Rome"; and between ourselves be it said, ancient Rome had some grounds for this, which cannot be said of the representatives of the "superior race" of today. [*Loud applause.*] But what was the upshot of this? The upshot was that the non-Romans, i.e., all the "barbarians," united against the common enemy, hurled themselves against Rome, and bore her down with a crash. The question arises: What guarantee is there that the claims of the representatives of the "superior race" of today will not lead to the same deplorable results? What guarantee is there that the fascist literary politicians in Berlin will be more fortunate than the old and experienced conquerors in Rome? Would it not be more correct to assume that the opposite will be the case?

Still others, again, think that war should be organized against the U.S.S.R. Their plan is to defeat the U.S.S.R., divide up its territory, and profit at its expense. It would be a mistake to believe that it is only certain military circles in Japan who think in this way. We know that similar plans are being hatched in the leading political circles of certain states in Europe. Let us assume that these gentlemen pass from words to deeds. What may be the upshot? There can hardly be any doubt that such a war would be the most dangerous war for the bourgeoisie. It would be the most dangerous war, not only because the peoples of the U.S.S.R. would fight to the very

death to preserve the gains of the revolution; it would be the most dangerous war for the bourgeoisie for the added reason that it would be waged not only at the fronts, but also behind the enemy's lines. The bourgeoisie need have no doubt that the numerous friends of the working class of the U.S.S.R. in Europe and in Asia will do their best to strike a blow in the rear at their oppressors who start a criminal war against the fatherland of the working class of all countries. And let not Messieurs the bourgeoisie blame us if some of the governments so near and dear to them, which today rule happily "by the grace of God," are missing on the morrow after such a war. [*Thunderous applause.*] One such war against the U.S.S.R. has been waged already, if you remember, fifteen years ago. As is well known, the universally esteemed Churchill clothed this war in a poetic formula—"the march of fourteen states." You remember, of course, that this war rallied the working people of our country into one united camp of heroic warriors, who stalwartly defended their workers' and peasants' homeland against the foreign foe. You know how it ended. It ended in the ejection of the invaders from our country and the establishment of revolutionary Councils of Action in Europe. It can hardly be doubted that a second war against the U.S.S.R. will lead to the complete defeat of the aggressors, to revolution in a number of countries in Europe and in Asia, and to the destruction of the bourgeois-landlord governments in those countries.

Such are the war plans of the perplexed bourgeois politicians.

As you see, they are not distinguished either for their brilliance or for their valor. [*Applause.*]

But while the bourgeoisie chooses the path of war, the working class in the capitalist countries, brought to despair by four years of crisis and unemployment, is taking the path of revolution. This means that a revolutionary crisis is maturing and will continue to mature. And the more the bourgeoisie becomes entangled in its war combinations, the more frequently it resorts to terroristic methods in its fight against the working class and the laboring peasantry, the more rapidly will the revolutionary crisis develop.

Some comrades think that, once there is a revolutionary crisis, the bourgeoisie must be in a hopeless position; that its end is therefore predetermined; that the victory of the revolution is thus assured, and that all they have to do is to wait for the fall of the bourgeoisie and to draw up victorious resolutions. This is a profound mistake. The victory of the revolution never comes by itself. It must be prepared for and won. And only a strong proletarian revolutionary party can prepare for and win victory. Moments occur when the situation is revolutionary, when the rule of the bourgeoisie is shaken to its very foundations, and yet the victory of the revolution does not come, because there is no revolutionary party of the proletariat sufficiently strong and influential to lead the masses and to take power. It would be unwise to believe that such "cases" cannot occur.

It will not be amiss in this connection to recall Lenin's prophetic words on revolutionary crises, uttered at the Second Congress of the Communist International:

We have now come to the question of the revolutionary crisis as the basis of our revolutionary action. And here we must first of all note two widespread errors. On the one hand, the bourgeois economists represent this crisis simply as "unrest," as the English so elegantly express it. On the other hand, revolutionaries sometimes try to prove that the crisis is absolutely hopeless. That is a mistake. There is no such thing as an absolutely hopeless situation. The bourgeoisie is behaving like an arrant brigand who has lost his head; it commits blunder after blunder, thus making the situation more acute and hastening its own doom. All this is true. But it cannot be "proved" that there is absolutely no chance of its gulling some minority of the exploited with some concessions or other, or of suppressing some movement or uprising of some sec-

tion or another of the oppressed and exploited. To try to "prove" beforehand that a situation is "absolutely" hopeless would be sheer pedantry, or juggling with concepts and catchwords. In this and similar questions the only real "proof" is practice. The bourgeois system all over the world is experiencing a most profound revolutionary crisis. And the revolutionary parties must now "prove" by their practical actions that they are intelligent and organized enough, are in contact enough with the exploited masses, are determined and skillful enough to utilize this crisis for a successful and victorious revolution. [Lenin, *Selected Works*, Vol. X, p. 192.]

THE RELATIONS BETWEEN THE U.S.S.R. AND THE CAPITALIST STATES

It is quite easy to understand how difficult it has been for the U.S.S.R. to pursue its peace policy in this atmosphere which is poisoned with the miasma of war combinations.

In the midst of this eve-of-the-war hullabaloo which is going on in a number of countries, the U.S.S.R. during these years has stood firmly and indomitably by its position of peace: fighting against the menace of war; fighting to preserve peace; meeting half way those countries which for one reason or another stand for the preservation of peace; exposing and tearing the masks from those who are preparing for and provoking war.

What did the U.S.S.R. rely on in this difficult and complicated struggle for peace?

a) On its growing economic and political might.

b) On the moral support of the vast masses of the working class in every country, who are vitally interested in the preservation of peace.

c) On the prudence of those countries which for one motive or another are not interested in disturbing the peace, and which want to develop commercial relations with such a punctual client as the U.S.S.R.

d) Finally — on our glorious army, which stands ready to defend our country against attacks from without.

It was on this basis that we began our campaign for the conclusion of pacts of non-aggression and of pacts defining the aggressor with neighboring states. You know that this campaign has been successful. As you know, pacts of non-aggression have been concluded not only with the majority of our neighbors in the West and in the South, including Finland and Poland, but also with such countries as France and Italy; and pacts defining the aggressor have been concluded with those same neighboring states, including the Little Entente.

On this basis, also, the friendship between the U.S.S.R. and Turkey has been consolidated; relations between the U.S.S.R. and Italy have been improved and have become indisputably satisfactory; relations with France, Poland and other Baltic states have improved; relations have been restored with the U.S.A., China, etc.

Of the many facts reflecting the successes of the peace policy of the U.S.S.R. two facts of indisputably material significance should be noted and singled out.

1. I have in mind, first, the change for the better that has taken place recently in the relations between the U.S.S.R. and Poland and between the U.S.S.R. and France. As is well known, our relations with Poland in the past were not at all good. Representatives of our state were assassinated in Poland. Poland regarded herself as the barrier of the Western states against the U.S.S.R. All and sundry imperialists counted on Poland as their vanguard in the event of a military attack upon the U.S.S.R. The relations between the U.S.S.R. and France were no better. We need only recall the facts relating to the trial of the Ramzin wreckers' group in Moscow to bring back the picture of the relations between the U.S.S.R. and France. But now these undesirable relations are gradually beginning to disappear. They are giving way to other relations, which cannot be otherwise described than as relations of rapprochement. It is not only that we have concluded pacts of non-aggression with these countries, although these pacts in themselves are of great importance. The point is, primarily, that the atmosphere of mutual distrust is beginning to be dissipated. This does not mean of course, that the incipient process of rapprochement can be regarded as sufficiently stable and as guaranteeing ultimate success. Surprises and zigzags in policy, for example in Poland, where anti-Soviet sentiments are still strong, cannot by far be regarded as precluded. But a change for the better in our relations, irrespective of its results in the future, is a fact worthy of being noted and singled out as a factor in the advancement of the cause of peace.

What is the cause of this change? What stimulates it?

Primarily, the growth of the strength and might of the U.S.S.R.

In our times it is not the custom to give any consideration to the weak—consideration is given only to the strong. Besides, there have been some changes in the policy of Germany which reflect the growth of imperialist and revenge sentiments in Germany.

In this connection some German politicians say that the U.S.S.R. has now taken an orientation towards France and Poland; that from an opponent of the Versailles Treaty it has become a supporter of that treaty, and that this change is to be explained by the establishment of the fascist regime in Germany. That is not true. Of course, we are far from being enthusiastic about the fascist regime in Germany. But fascism is not the issue here, if only for the reason that fascism in Italy, for example, has not prevented the U.S.S.R. from establishing the best relations with that country. Nor is it a question of any alleged change in our attitude towards the Versailles Treaty. It is not for us, who have experienced the shame of the Brest Litovsk Peace, to sing the praises of the Versailles

Treaty. We merely do not agree to the world being flung into the abyss of a new war on account of this treaty. The same must be said of the alleged new orientation taken by the U.S.S.R. We never had any orientation towards Germany, nor have we any orientation towards Poland and France. Our orientation in the past and our orientation at the present time is towards the U.S.S.R., and towards the U.S.S.R. alone. [*Loud applause.*] And if the interests of the U.S.S.R. demand rapprochement with one country or another which is not interested in disturbing peace, we take this step without hesitation.

No, that is not the point. The point is that Germany's policy has changed. The point is that even before the present German politicians came into power, and particularly after they came into power, a fight began in Germany between two political lines: between the old policy, which was reflected in the well-known treaties between the U.S.S.R. and Germany, and the "new" policy, which, in the main, recalls the policy of the former German Kaiser, who at one time occupied the Ukraine, marched against Leningrad, and converted the Baltic countries into a *place d'armes* for this march; and this "new" policy is obviously gaining the upper hand over the old policy. The fact that the supporters of the "new" policy are gaining supremacy in all things, while the supporters of the old policy are in disfavor, cannot be regarded as an accident. Nor can the well-known statements made by Hugenberg in London, nor the equally well-known declarations of Rosenberg, who directs the foreign policy of the ruling party in Germany, be regarded as accidents. That is the point, comrades.

2. Secondly, I have in mind the restoration of normal relations between the U.S.S.R. and the United States. There cannot be any doubt that this act is of great significance for the whole system of international relations. It is not only that it improves the chances of preserving peace, and that it improves the relations between

the two countries, strengthens commercial intercourse between them, and creates a base for their mutual collaboration. The point is that it is a landmark between the old position, when in various countries the United States was regarded as the bulwark for all sorts of anti-Soviet trends, and the new position, when this bulwark has been voluntarily removed, to the mutual advantage of both countries.

Such are the two main facts which reflect the successes of the Soviet peace policy.

It would be wrong, however, to think that everything went smoothly in the period under review. No, not everything went smoothly, by a long way.

Recall, say, the pressure that was brought to bear upon us by England; the embargo on our exports, the attempt to interfere in our internal affairs and thereby test our power of resistance. True, nothing came of this attempt, and later the embargo was lifted; but the unpleasant taste left after these sallies is still felt in everything affecting the relations between England and the U.S.S.R., including the negotiations for a commercial treaty. And these sallies against the U.S.S.R. must not be regarded as accidental. It is well known that a certain section of the English conservatives cannot live without such sallies. And precisely because they are not accidental we must bear in mind that in the future, too, sallies will be made against the U.S.S.R., all sorts of menaces will be created, attempts will be undertaken to damage the U.S.S.R., etc.

Nor can we lose sight of the relations between the U.S.S.R. and Japan, which stand in need of very considerable improvement. Japan's refusal to conclude a pact of non-aggression, of which Japan stands in no less need than the U.S.S.R., once again emphasizes the fact that all is not well in the sphere of our relations. The same must be said of the rupture of negotiations concerning the Chinese-Eastern Railway due to no fault of the U.S.S.R.;

and also of the outrageous actions of the Japanese agents on the C.E.R., the illegal arrests of Soviet employees on the C.E.R., etc. All this apart from the fact that one section of the military in Japan, with the avowed approval of another section of the military, is openly advocating in the press the necessity for a war against the U.S.S.R. and the seizure of the Maritime Province; while the government of Japan, instead of calling these instigators of war to order, pretends that it has nothing to do with the matter. It is not difficult to understand that such circumstances cannot but create an atmosphere of uneasiness and uncertainty. Of course, we will persistently continue our policy of peace and will strive to bring about an improvement in our relations with Japan, because we want to improve these relations. But it does not depend entirely upon us. That is why we must at the same time take all measures to guard our country against surprises, and be prepared to defend it in the event of attack. [*Loud applause.*]

As you see, besides successes in our peace policy we also have a number of negative phenomena.

Such is the situation as regards the foreign relations of the U.S.S.R.

Our foreign policy is clear. It is a policy of preserving peace and strengthening commercial relations with all countries. The U.S.S.R. does not think of threatening anybody—let alone of attacking anybody. We stand for peace and champion the cause of peace. But we are not afraid of threats and are prepared to answer the instigators of war blow for blow. [*Loud applause.*] Those who want peace and seek business relations with us will always have our support. But those who try to attack our country will receive a crushing repulse to teach them not to poke their pig snouts into our Soviet garden. [*Thunderous applause.*]

Such is our foreign policy. [*Thunderous applause.*]

The task is to continue this policy persistently and consistently.

Dualism in Distress 1935–1939

VI

THE POPULAR FRONT TACTIC

HUGH SETON-WATSON

Hugh Seton-Watson was attached to the British Legations in Rumania and Yugo-slavia (1940–1941), and served in the Special Forces G.H.Q. of the Middle East (1941–1944). He is the author of several excellent books, among them *Eastern Europe Between the Wars*, *The East European Revolution*, *The Pattern of Communist Revolution*, and *From Lenin to Malenkov*. At present he is Professor of Russian History at the School of Slavonic and East European Studies of the University of London. In the sections of *From Lenin to Malenkov* printed below, he succinctly defines the Communists' Popular Front movement and explains the reasons for its failures in France and in other nations around the world.

THE significance of Hitler's triumph was at first lost on the communist leaders in Moscow and their German subordinates. Neither Comintern nor K.P.D. would admit that the German working class had suffered a disaster. On 15th February 1933, Radek wrote: "A party that receives six million votes, deeply linked with the whole history of the German working class, cannot be dismissed from the balance-sheet of history." The Comintern organ *Rundschau* declared on 1st April 1933: "The momentary calm after the victory of fascism is only a passing phenomenon. The rise of the revolutionary tide will inevitably continue. The resistance of the masses against fascism will inevitably increase. The open dictatorship of fascism destroys all democratic illusions, frees the masses from the influence of the social democrats, and thus accelerates the speed of Germany's march towards the proletarian revolution."[1] This eloquent April-foolery was poor consolation to the communist leaders in Hitler's prisons and concentration-camps. The Reichstag fire, the expulsion of the Communists from the cowed assembly, the mass arrests and the Brown Terror made little impression on Comintern. Refusing to admit defeat, Moscow ordered the party to ignore the terror and act openly, to hold street demonstrations and distribute leaflets as if a revolutionary situation still existed. Thus hundreds of party organizers who might have been saved for underground work were

[1] Quoted in Max Beloff, *The Foreign Policy of Soviet Russia, 1929–1941*, Vol. I, p. 67.

From Hugh Seton-Watson, *From Lenin to Malenkov: The History of World Communism* (New York, 1954), pp. 176–182, 188–199. Reprinted by permission of Frederick A. Praeger, Inc.

exposed and arrested. Within a few months the once impressive K.P.D. ceased to be a force of any importance. Small illegal groups continued to exist under the Nazi regime, but their efforts, however heroic, had not the slightest effect on German policy. Not until 1945 was a German Communist Party created from nothing by the Soviet military authorities.

Communist policy changed only after the policy of the Soviet government had changed. This did not happen for some time. Hitherto, as we have seen, it had been a dogma in Moscow that the only kind of German government it need fear was one friendly to the Versailles victors. Hitler was clearly hostile to the West: therefore Hitler, for all his persecution of communists, might be useful to Moscow. During 1933 public speeches and newspaper articles in the Soviet Union stressed the desire for friendly relations with Germany. During 1934 however relations deteriorated. Soviet hopes received a shock when Hitler made a non-aggression pact with Poland. In view of the traditional Soviet view of Poland, and especially of Marshal Pilsudski, it was not surprising that Moscow should believe—though wrongly—that these two states could only have come to terms at the expense of Russia. Hereafter it seemed probable that Hitler was even more hostile to the Soviet Union than to the West. Soviet policy kept the same aim—to exploit the hostility between Germany and the West. But whereas hitherto its method had been to encourage Germany to resist the Western Powers, it was now to encourage the Western Powers to resist Germany. Bolshevik blandishments were now addressed not to Berlin but to Paris. Meanwhile in France, not only on the left but among the disciples of Poincaré, alliance with Russia became attractive. In May the French Foreign Minister, Louis Barthou, suggested that the U.S.S.R. should join the League of Nations. Moscow decided to agree, and on 10th September was formally admitted. In the following year Soviet collaboration with the West formally reached its climax with the signature of the Franco-Soviet pact (2nd May) and the Soviet-Czechoslovak pact (16th May).

The new course in Soviet foreign policy required a new "line" for the Comintern. This was provided at the 7th Congress, which met in Moscow in July-August 1935. It proclaimed the tactic of the Popular Front, the most perfect form yet devised of the "united front from above." In order to resist the threat of fascism at home and abroad, and especially the threat of fascist Germany to the toilers' fatherland, the U.S.S.R., communists were to combine not only with the masses but also with the leaders, not only of the social democrats but also of any non-socialist or even right-wing groups that were opposed to the fascists and to Nazi Germany or Japan.

The Popular Front policy brought the communists, whose prestige and influence had reached a low ebb by 1933, great popularity among the more or less non-political masses in many European and even Asiatic countries. The Comintern's new slogans expressed the genuine feelings of millions of workers, intellectuals and peasants in countries misruled by dictatorial cliques or menaced by German, Italian or Japanese aggression. Judged by its propaganda appeal, the Popular Front was the most successful tactic ever adopted by the Comintern in peacetime. Its adoption was in fact a concession made by Moscow to the mood of the masses, which Moscow for once accurately diagnosed. It may in fact be argued that the Popular Front was imposed not by the communist parties on the masses but by the masses on the communist parties.

Nevertheless the period of the Popular Front was a period of defeats for international communism.

This was in part due to the failure of the governments of France and Britain to offer political resistance to the three aggressive Powers at a time when political resistance could still have achieved results. The weakness shown in London and Paris caused many smaller states to choose the attractive but disastrous policy of cooperation with the fascist Powers. The years 1935–9 were a period of bloodless victories for Hitler and Mussolini and of cheap military triumphs for Japan. Millions of persons throughout the world—from politicians and intellectuals to simple peasants and workers—were convinced that fascism was the "idea of the future." The greatest blow dealt by the Western Powers to the will to resist fascism was, of course, the 1938 surrender at Munich.

But the failures of the Popular Front tactic were also due to internal disunity, to the mutual suspicion between the communists and their partners. Retrospectively it has of course become a dogma in communist circles that this suspicion was solely due to the treason of the social democrats. The truth is that the communists themselves were principally to blame. They were determined to enjoy both the pleasures of leadership and the pleasures of opposition. They could not bring themselves to cease their demagogic agitation against the socialists and democrats whom they were supposed to support. They never gave up their aim of winning the socialist and democratic masses away from their leaders. Though appearing in public as allies and colleagues of these leaders, they took every opportunity to undermine their authority. One may doubt whether mass agitation can be conducted by discreet means, even when the agitators are steel-hard Bolshevik conspirators equipped with Marxist-Leninist-Stalinist methodology. Certainly there was nothing discreet about the methods of the communist agitators in Western Europe during the Popular Front period. The socialist and democratic leaders soon became aware of the communists' disloyal behavior, which inevitably diminished their enthusiasm for the Popular Front and weakened the common resistance to fascism and to the enemies of the Soviet Union.

A third cause for the failures of the Popular Front was the course of internal policy in the Soviet Union. The vast purges of party, administration and armed forces in 1937–8 bewildered the potential friends of the U.S.S.R. among the masses—and even among the members of communist parties—of other countries. They also made the political and military leaders of the Western Powers doubt the value of Soviet Russia as an ally. This doubt of course strengthened the arguments of the "appeasers" in the West.

The first important success of the Popular Front was in France. Since the 6th Congress of the Comintern relations between French socialists and communists had been extremely bitter. The socialists were supported by the bulk of the French workers, while the communists were a small implacable faction. The economic depression, which came somewhat later to France than to most other European countries, had two important political effects. Economic hardships fell with special severity on the workers, who were less well protected by social legislation than the workers of most West European countries, and created a more bitter class feeling than had been known in France for many years, perhaps ever. At the same time, exploiting the discontent in all classes of the population but perhaps especially in the lower middle class, and pointing to the examples of Germany and Italy, fascist organizations made their appearance in France and won considerable support.

The danger signal was given by the riots of 6th February 1934, when fascist-inspired demonstrators attempted to march on the Chamber of Deputies. This incident was followed by a communist counter-demonstration on 9th February, and a big demonstration by the C.G.T. on 12th February, in which the communists instructed their followers to take part. After this, though the communist leaders continued to denounce the socialists, a spontaneous movement for unity between all working-class parties and organizations developed, with mass support from within both socialist and communist ranks. In June 1934 socialist and communist leaders made a pact of common action in defense of democratic liberties, opposition to rearmament and hostility to fascism in Germany and Austria. When, during the visit of Prime Minister Laval to Moscow to sign the Franco-Soviet pact, Stalin and Laval issued on 15th May 1935 a joint statement to the effect that Stalin approved French measures of defense, the French communists dropped their opposition to rearmament. In this they were followed more hesitantly by the socialists, who still had an important pacifist wing. In the first months of 1935 cooperation of the parties of the left became a reality. A *Comité national de rassemblement populaire* was created to formulate a common program. The unity of action of socialists, communists and radicals was formally asserted on 14th July 1935. The traditional commemoration of the fall of the Bastille was held in common. A great procession marched from the Place de la Bastille to the Place de la République, headed by the chief socialist and communist leaders and by the Radical Party leader Daladier. Negotiations for reunification of the two trade union organizations, socialist-led C.G.T. and communist-controlled C.G.T.U., had begun in October 1934, had been broken off, but were resumed with greater energy after the 14th July demonstration. In September 1935 congresses of both organizations approved the principle of reunification, and this was achieved in March 1936. The C.G.T.U. representatives argued fiercely for the specific communist points of view on trade union organization, and on the internal and international political affiliations of the future united body. But on all three points they were outvoted by two-thirds majorities. Such was the determination of Moscow to secure unity of action that the C.G.T.U. was allowed to accept reunion on the old C.G.T.U.'s terms rather than on its own.

The essential preliminary work for the formation of the French Popular Front had thus been accomplished, in response to the needs of the French political situation, before the 7th Congress of the Comintern met in Moscow. At the Congress in fact the agreement reached in France was held up as a model to other communist parties.

At the parliamentary election of 3rd May 1936 the parties of the Popular Front won 386 seats, and the various groups of the Right 222. Of the three parties the socialists had 149 seats, the radicals 109 and the communists 72. Whereas the number of votes cast for the socialists was almost exactly the same as at the last general election in 1932, the communists almost doubled their poll—from 800,000 to 1,500,000. A Popular Front ministry was formed on 5th June, with the socialist leader Léon Blum as Premier. The Communist Party however decided that its leaders should not accept cabinet office: the party pledged its support provided that the government would carry out the Popular Front program. This equivocal and distrustful attitude of the communists weakened the Blum ministry from its first day.

The left were now in power, and the communists were stronger than ever before. But the new government's relations with its working-class supporters soon proved extremely delicate. The workers awaited great social changes. Already before the Blum ministry was formed they began to strike, and the movement did not stop when Blum took office. In mid-May "sit-in" strikes took place in several provincial industrial centers, and at the end of the month they spread through the Paris region, especially affecting metallurgical and engineering plants. At the beginning of June the movement spread back to the provinces. At its peak it affected not much less than a million workers. The "sit-in" strike, by which the workers occupied their factories, was a new phenomenon in France. The only historical parallel was the occupation of factories in north Italy in August 1920. But the circumstances of France in 1936 were different from those of Italy in

1920. In Italy the socialists had been in at least verbally revolutionary opposition to the government: in France the socialists were in power. In Italy the internal situation was foremost in all minds: in France the internal situation was overshadowed by the dangers of the international situation. The most important difference of all, however, was that whereas the Italian strikes had been ordered by the trade unions, those in France were the result of spontaneous movement, and the trade unions' main concern was to get them under control. The origins of the 1936 strike wave still remain a mystery. The most probable explanation is that they were a genuine popular reaction: none of the hypotheses attributing them to secret and sinister influences are convincing. They were certainly not a bid for dictatorial power by the communists. The communists in fact were placed in an embarrassing position. As usual they tried to have their cake and eat it. Communist deputies made speeches in the occupied factories, and communist spokesmen declared on all possible occasions that the correct way to solve the crisis was to grant all the demands of the workers. But at the same time the communists were pledged to minimize class hatred and to maintain French national unity, in alliance with Soviet Russia against Nazi Germany.

The strike wave came to an end when the government imposed arbitration on employers and workers by the "Matignon agreements" of June. These were however modest gains. In the following months prices rose and there were important exports of capital. In October it became necessary to devalue the franc. In March 1937 Blum announced a "pause" in his reform program. This disappointed his working-class supporters without reconciling his business-class opponents. In June Blum resigned when the Senate refused his request for exchange control, designed to stop the continuing export of capital. This was really the end of the Popular Front. The governments led by the radicals Chau-

temps and Daladier were supported by the left until the autumn of 1938, but their policy was cautious and conservative. The hopes of an increased influence in policy for the working class in general and the communists in particular were not fulfilled.

The failure of its social and economic policy was not however the only reason for the Popular Front's defeat. Equally important were its defeats in foreign policy, and especially in the Spanish Civil War. Sympathy for the rival forces in Spain greatly widened the breach between left and right in France. It gave to French internal politics in these years a quality of ideological fanaticism such as had not been seen in France for a long time. It helped to undermine the democratic foundations of French government and morally to disarm France in the face of fascist aggression. . . .

* * *

If the Popular Fronts of France and Spain had ended in defeat, the first in confusion and the second in tragedy, in other West European countries there was not even temporary success. In Britain and Scandinavia, though Popular Front anti-fascist slogans made an impression on liberal and socialist intellectuals, the socialist parties refused to make common cause with the communists, and no Popular Fronts were formed. In Germany and Italy all anti-fascist groups were helpless.

In the Balkans the Popular Front period brought a small but substantial increase of strength to the communists. In Yugoslavia, where the Communist Party was still illegal, it recruited numerous and courageous members among university students and graduates, and enjoyed a measure of vague sympathy from a much wider section of the population. No Popular Front was formally created, but members and sympathizers of the Communist Party played a part in bringing together various democratic bourgeois and peasant parties in opposition to the dictatorial and increasingly pro-Axis government. The association of communism with Russia and France, the two foreign states most popular among the Serbs, assisted the communist cause. In Bulgaria the same tendency existed on a smaller scale. The international background was less favorable, for although most Bulgarians loved Russia there was much less fear of Germany than in Yugoslavia. The dictatorship of King Boris was however about as unpopular with the Bulgarians as was that of Milan Stojadinovic with the Yugoslavs. There was no formal Popular Front in Bulgaria, but the left wing of the Agrarian movement cooperated more closely with the communists. Both parties were illegal and persecuted, and both attracted support from the intelligentsia as well as from peasants and workers. In Greece the Communist Party became for the first time an important factor during the brief period of free parliamentary government which followed the restoration of King George II in November 1935. In the parliament elected in 1936 the communists had fifteen seats, and held a commanding position as the two major parties were almost exactly equal. The communists drew most of their support from industrial workers, especially in the north of Greece. They gained wider sympathy not only from economic discontent and from fear of the fascist Powers, but also from growing disillusionment among the younger intellectuals with the sterile quarrel between royalists and republicans that had bedevilled Greek politics since 1922 and made social progress impossible. No Popular Front was formed in Greece, and in August 1936 the establishment, with the King's consent, of General Metaxas' dictatorship, deprived the communists of all legal means of activity.

In Central Europe communism was weaker, and Popular Front tactics were more unsuccessful, than in the Balkans.

In Poland there was closer cooperation between the socialist and peasant movements. This was an example of greater unity on the left, but it owed nothing to communist influence. In 1937 the peasant strike in Galicia and "sit-in" strikes in the factories of Cracow were signs of growing social discontent. The government's benevolent neutrality towards Nazi Germany was unpopular with the Polish People. The growth of fascism, both on the government side and in the ranks of the right wing of the opposition, though confined to a section of the middle class—business, bureaucratic and intellectual—and deprived of mass support, was nevertheless alarming. There was no Popular Front in Poland, but the trend of public opinion was in that direction. This was the result of conditions in and around Poland: it was not due to communist influence. The Polish Communist Party was very weak. As we have seen, its leaders in exile in Russia fell victims to the purge of 1937–8, and the party was formally disbanded by the Comintern in 1938.

In Czechoslovakia, where the Communist Party could function legally, it had the support of about half the working class and of some intellectuals. The political parties did not create a Popular Front, but the idea of anti-fascist unity was popular among Czechs, though much less so among Slovaks.

In Hungary and Roumania communist influence was negligible. Both countries were ruled by Whiggish oligarchies, the Hungarian decked in quasi-liberal trappings, the Roumanian in quasi-fascist. Both regimes were evolving towards a more genuinely fascist form of bureaucratic dictatorship. In both countries the democratic forces were on the defensive. In Hungary the social democrats stood solidly for democracy, but they were unable to influence more than the working class of the capital and a few other towns. The Hungarian peasants had no effective representation: the Independent Small Farmers' Party was a curious assortment of peasant tribunes, bourgeois radicals and romantic reactionary nationalists. In Roumania the main democratic force, the National Peasant Party, had disintegrated under the pressure of the economic depression and the intrigues of King Carol II. In both countries the rising revolutionary movement was fascist. The anti-semitic pro-Nazi Iron Guard in Roumania used slogans of both national and social revolution to attract both the university youth and a large part of the peasants and workers. Though subsidized by Roumanian industrialists and landowners and by emissaries of Nazi Germany, it cannot be regarded as a mere tool of capitalists or of Berlin: it enlisted much genuine revolutionary enthusiasm. In the autumn of 1938 its leaders were shot by Carol II's police, and its supporters were fiercely pursued. Fascist groups in Hungary appeared later, and were at first too disunited to be strong. But in August 1938 the two main groups fused to form the Arrow Cross Party. Subsidized from Germany and mildly combated by the Hungarian government, this party made some appeal to discontented peasants and miners, though it could not shake the hold of the socialists on the factory workers.

The first communist experiment with a Popular Front tactic thus proved a failure in Europe. The Popular Front was successful only where a genuine and effective demand for unity of democratic forces already existed, and where national resistance to the fascist Powers was a real issue. The communists did not create the demand, but yielded to it. Having thereby won much popularity for themselves, they tried to exploit the Popular Front for their party aims, and failed. One is tempted to conclude that the Popular Front would have been more successful if the communists had had nothing to do with it. This conclusion however misses the point. It would be justified if the communists had been mainly concerned to ensure the triumph of the democratic forces in countries threatened internally or externally by fascism. For most members of communist parties in such countries this was no doubt the principal

aim, but for Moscow it was only a secondary consideration. Moscow's aim was to strengthen the position of Soviet Russia. Alliance with the Western Powers was one possible course: another was alliance with Nazi Germany. When the first did not produce results, the second was adopted. The Popular Fronts were intended, if circumstances were favorable, to give the communists—and so Moscow—a share, perhaps even a major share, in the government of their countries: if circumstances were unfavorable they could pursue useful rearguard actions. Democratic unity and resistance to fascism would have gained if the communist parties had dissolved themselves. But this would have deprived Moscow of an instrument of policy that might prove valuable later. Moscow never considered giving it up, and subsequent events showed that from the point of view of its own interests Moscow was right. The experience gained during the Popular Front years, especially in Spain, proved valuable in 1944-8, when the opportunity came to do what the Soviet leaders had come to understand by the notion "spreading world revolution"—to export the ready-made Stalinist regime by force of arms.

UNITED FRONT IN CHINA

The Popular Front policy achieved more substantial success in China. While the communists completed their Long March, and defended their newly-won territory in the north-west against Chiang Kai-shek's attacks, the Japanese, who had seized Manchuria in 1931, were steadily encroaching on northern China. To Chinese patriots it became increasingly clear that the civil war between Chiang and the communists was a tragic waste of lives and resources. From all sides the demand grew that civil strife be replaced by national unity against the invader. In the cities, businessmen, intellectuals and workers shared hatred of the Japanese. As on earlier occasions, university students played a leading part in the anti-Japanese movement. Chiang's armed forces were affected. The troops of the "Young Marshal," Chang Hsueh-liang, which occupied some of the territory nearest to the communist region, were especially affected. They were mostly recruited from Manchuria, and passionately wished to see their homeland freed of the Japanese. They were ever more reluctant to be used by Chiang against the communists. In southern China too leading warlords urged Chiang to resist Japan.

The communists made much better use of the new patriotic mood of the people than did Chiang. Soon after the 7th Comintern Congress, at which the Popular Front policy had been forcibly defended by Wang Ming, now the party's delegate in Moscow, on 1st August 1935 the Chinese Communist Party launched an appeal for a united front of Communists and Kuomintang against the invaders. Chiang ignored the offer, and persisted in his plans to destroy the communists. In his view, the admittedly desirable aim of unity against Japan could only be achieved when the "Red Bandits" had been wiped out. He professed to believe that this could soon be done. The historian may recognize that there was much to be said for Chiang's basic attitude: he was head of the legal government, the communists were rebels, and they, not he, were obstructing national unity. But Chiang's tactics and propaganda were foolish. By refusing to begin resistance to Japan, he enabled the communists to appear as the true patriots, and made himself appear the obstacle to unity and the persecutor of patriotism.

The patriotic movement gathered strength despite Chiang Kai-shek. On 9th December 1935 the Peking students organized a demonstration which demanded an end to civil war, restoration of civil liberties and resistance to Japan. Similar demonstrations took place in other university towns of China in the following weeks. In a speech to Communist Party "activists" on 27th December 1935 Mao Tse-tung for-

mulated in greater detail the united front policy. "The task before the Party," he said, "is to integrate the activities of the Red Army with all the activities of the workers, peasants, students, the petty bourgeoisie and the national bourgeoisie of the whole country and to form out of this integration a united national-revolutionary front."[2] During the first half of 1936 the communists helped to form a "National Salvation" movement. This was designed to enlist persons of all social classes, and of most political opinions and of none. Its greatest successes were won among workers and students in the towns. On 31st May it held a meeting in Shanghai to found an "All-China Federation of National Salvation Unions." This movement, in which communist influence was strong, was persecuted by Chiang, but won some public sympathy.

On 12th December 1936, while Chiang was visiting the headquarters of Chang Hsueh-liang at Sian, he was arrested by his host. He was visited in his captivity by the leading communist Chou En-lai, who joined the Young Marshal in urging him to resist Japan, promising if he would do this that the communists would accept him as their supreme commander. The communists were at this time convinced that only Chiang could lead the Chinese people. His person was essential for the short- and long-term policies of the communists, and he must therefore not be harmed. The communists, who for some time had been on fairly good terms with Chang Hsueh-liang, agreed with him that Chiang should be allowed to return safely to Nanking, even though he had given no formal pledge to change his policy. Chiang was undoubtedly impressed by the evidence of popular feeling that had been put before him. He consented to negotiate with the communists early in 1937.

Agreement between the communists and Chiang was achieved by the action of

[2] Quoted in Hu Chiao-mu, *Thirty Years of the Communist Party of China* (Peking, 1951), p. 42.

the Japanese, who began large-scale military action against China on 7th July. The announcement that agreement had been reached was issued from communist headquarters on 22nd September. In their manifesto the communists formally accepted the Kuomintang program and the "Three People's Principles" of Sun Yat-sen; promised to stop confiscation of land from landowners; renamed the Red Army "National Revolutionary Army"; and recognized the authority of the Military Affairs Commission of the Nanking government. The land policy in the communist regions was really changed: landowners kept their property, and were obliged only to lower rents to a fixed maximum. But the Communist Party's military and political hold was not relaxed in the regions it controlled. The communists continued to build the cadres of their own military and civil administration, disciplined and indoctrinated on communist principles. Nevertheless relations with Nanking improved, and the Chinese united front worked fairly well during the year that passed between the Japanese attack and the fall of Hankow in October 1938.

MIDDLE EAST AND FAR EAST

Faint echoes of the Popular Front were heard in the Arab lands. The *coup d'état* of October 1936 in Iraq was the joint work of discontented officers and the *Ahali* group of left intellectuals. Soon after the seizure of power, however, the military dictator Bekr Sidki broke with *Ahali*. In French North Africa and in the French mandated territories of Syria and Lebanon, the victory of the Popular Front in France encouraged hopes of reform and somewhat strengthened the influence of those members of the Arab intelligentsia who were attracted by the ideas of the left. But this was only a passing phase. After the general failure of Blum's government, the French parliament rejected the proposed reforms, and in France's Moslem territories nationalism triumphed over left trends, and to some extent sought inspiration from fascist Italy or Nazi Germany. Nowhere in the Middle East or North Africa was communism a force of any importance.

In the Far East outside China communist influence was very small but perhaps increasing. Young Indian intellectuals were attracted by the anti-fascist slogans of the Popular Front. In Japan a Japan Masses Party was formed in February 1937, with a Popular Front tendency, and undoubtedly influenced by communist tactics. The social democratic Social Masses Party rejected proposals for a Popular Front. At the March 1937 election to the Japanese parliament, the two parties together polled twice as many votes as the socialists had won at the preceding election in 1936. The Japan Masses Party was however banned in December 1937, while the Social Masses Party came under militarist and nationalist influence, and dissolved itself in July 1940.

In Indonesia a small illegal communist party was organized in 1935. There was also a small heretical communist group which supported Tan Malaka, a Comintern veteran who since 1928 had been regarded by Moscow as a Trotskist. In April 1937 was formed a legal party of the left, the Indonesian People's Movement (*Gerindo*). Its leaders, who included the socialist Sjarifoeddin, followed the Popular Front line, regarded fascism and Japanese imperialism as the main enemies, and were even willing to cooperate with the Dutch.

LATIN AMERICA

During the 1930's the Comintern began to pay attention to Latin America. Great contrasts in wealth, racial differences and habits of dictatorship and palace revolution made this vast region seem attractive ground for revolutionary activities. The Spanish civil war naturally made an impression on the Spanish-speaking peoples of America. Fascist movements made their appearance on the continent, and were strengthened both by the growing economic influence of Germany and Japan and by the presence of large communities of German, Italian and Japanese origin that had been hardly or not at all assimilated by their new homelands. Thus internal conflicts offered an opportunity to communists, while the strategic importance of Latin America was an incentive to Moscow to press the local communist parties into a more active policy. The years of the Popular Front did achieve some small successes.

Latin America was overwhelmingly agricultural. Industry was principally based on mineral resources—Mexican and Venezuelan oil, Chilean nitrates and Bolivian tin. Only in a few big urban centers —Buenos Aires, Rio de Janeiro, Sao Paulo, Mexico City—had some progress recently been made in manufacturing industry. Agriculture was mostly based on great landed estates, which owed their origin to the Spanish conquest. The dominant social problem was the peasants' need for land. The conflict between industrial labor and capital was in an early stage, overshadowed by the conflict between landowner and agricultural laborer. This social conflict was complicated by the racial issue, which deepened the gulf between rich and poor but also made the poor less capable of defending their interests.

The racial composition of the Latin American countries varied. Bolivia, Peru and Ecuador were essentially Indian states: only the ruling minority were European or of mixed origin (*mestizo*). In Mexico, Paraguay, Colombia, Venezuela and most of the Central American states the Indians were an important minority, but the most numerous element were the *mestizos*, while the more or less pure Europeans provided the ruling group. Chile and Brazil differed from the second category in that the European and mixed merged into each other, while the pure Indians were a relatively unimportant minority. In Brazil European stock was mixed with negro even more than with Indian: the same was true of

some of the Central American and Caribbean republics. Finally in three states— Argentine, Uruguay and Costa Rica—the great majority of the population was pure European.

The normal type of government in Latin America was an oligarchic dictatorship, more liberal in the more European states, more despotic in the more Indian. In the Argentine there was a certain habit of Whiggish liberalism, as in England before 1832 or in Hungary in 1900. Bolivia and Peru somewhat resembled European colonies of the nineteenth century: great landowners or mine-owners held in their hands the lives of thousands of Indian semi-slaves. Throughout the continent the army and the Catholic Church played an important part. Neither was necessarily identified with conservatism. There were liberal generals, and the church had at times fought fiercely and successfully to protect the Indians from exploitation. But by the twentieth century both were usually on the side of the ruling class.

The exception that did not fit this pattern was Mexico. Here in 1910 an armed revolt by an upright and moderate constitutionalist against the long dictatorship of Porfirio Diaz had let loose a social revolution. The peasants had fought a long and cruel guerrilla war for the land. The assassination of the peasant leader Zapata in 1919 marked the defeat of the extremists. The new rulers settled down to enjoy the fruits of power. Like the colonels who had made their career under the revolutionary banner of Pilsudski in Poland, the victors of the Mexican revolution lost much of their fervor and almost all their purity. Yet the revolution had done more than replace one ruling clique by another. The political power of the landlords and of the Catholic Church was broken: the process involved years of cruel religious persecution. Some land was redistributed to the peasants. The industrial workers began to play a part: the government created trade unions and gave them a privileged position in the state. A Mexican bourgeoisie was in formation, and differed fundamentally from the former ruling class by its fierce nationalism. Whereas the old rulers had felt themselves Europeans, and had never been quite sure whether Mexico was their home, the new leaders and the *mestizo* masses who supported them were quite sure that they were Mexicans, were fiercely "anti-imperialist" and distrustful of Europe and especially of the United States. In short, in Leninist terms, Mexico had made her bourgeois revolution. Mexico was a sort of democracy, turbulent and tough, but with the same sort of freedom as, for instance, the Serbia of 1903-14.

In the mid-1930's the three most interesting countries from the point of view of communist opportunities were Brazil, Mexico and Peru. In Brazil Getulio Vargas had established a dictatorship in 1930. His regime was something new. The old oligarchy of wealthy magnates from Sao Paulo state had been defeated. Vargas appealed to the middle class and to some extent to the poor. His social demagogy had a mildly fascist flavor. The economic hardships of the world depression brought him both his supporters and his enemies. In Brazil there was a small Communist Party. Its leader was Luis Carlos Prestes, formerly an army officer, who already in 1924 had made a small revolt and led a small force on a Long March through the wilds of the western provinces, and had later spent some years in Moscow. General economic misery, peasant land hunger, and discontent with Vargas within the army, offered the Brazilian communists some opportunities.

In Mexico the process of revolution, which had been very slow if not quite stationary from 1928 to 1934, gathered speed again when General Lazaro Cárdenas became President in 1934. Cárdenas greatly accelerated the distribution of land to the peasants, and favored a semi-communal form of cultivation known as the *ejido*. Already in the Mexican Constitution of 1917

ownership of land had been defined in a manner that recalls the Russian Populist conception of "labor-ownership." The rights of individuals were limited by an overriding right of the nation and the state to dispose of land. This conception was emphasized under Cárdenas. In 1940, at the end of his term of office, 51 per cent of the agricultural population of Mexico lived in *ejidos*, and owned 47 per cent of the country's arable land. Cárdenas also gave greater powers and greater independence to the trade unions, and within these communist influence began to make itself felt. Cárdenas expropriated the oil-fields in 1938, and this brought him into conflict with the United States and Britain. The nationalist and anti-imperialist trend of Cárdenas' policy was very acceptable to Moscow. In general, though Cárdenas and his closest collaborators were not communists, or even Marxists, there were better opportunities of communist action in Mexico than elsewhere on the continent.

In Peru the new factor was the appearance in 1931 of a movement called *Alianza Popular Revolucionaria Americana* (A.P.R.A.), led by Haya de la Torre. This was a socialist movement, of a Populist rather than Marxist type. Its leader had been much influenced by the Mexican revolution. The special feature of A.P.R.A. was that it stressed the rights of the Indians. It aimed not only at social justice for the people of Peru but at a new order for the Europeans, *mestizos* and Indians of the whole continent. The continent, in the A.P.R.A. view, was not Latin America but *Indo-america*. The enemy of all Indo-americans was foreign imperialism. In its first years A.P.R.A.'s wrath was directed mainly at the United States, but later the Axis Powers became its chief bogey. A.P.R.A. has some slight resemblance to such movements as Kemalism, the early Kuomintang or the early Wafd: political democracy, social revolution and nationalism were combined in its program. The attitude of the communists to A.P.R.A. was similar to their attitude to the Kuomintang in the 1920's: they considered it a petty bourgeois movement capable of serving the interests of the proletariat and in particular capable of damaging the imperialist enemy of Soviet Russia.

In the autumn of 1934 a secret conference of Latin American communists was held in Montevideo. The conference made the diagnosis that could be expected. It noted three main conflicts. The first was the internal class struggle, of workers against capitalists and especially of peasants against landowners. The second was the conflict of the Indians and *mestizos* with the European ruling classes. The third was the conflict of the bourgeoisies of the Latin American nations with foreign imperialist interests which were dictating to them unfavorable conditions of trade, and were hindering their industrialization. The conference expected that, in their struggle with the imperialists, the bourgeoisies would be compelled to conciliate the masses, and that this would make the task of the communists easier. The conference produced the well-worn Leninist phrases on the land question and the national question, and its slogans about the struggle of the masses and the national bourgeoisie against the imperialists and their latifundiary-compradore agents recall the experience of China. It is not without significance that at the 7th Congress of the Comintern in July 1935 it was Wang Ming who spoke on the Latin American situation.

The first attempt at a Popular Front in Latin America was the National Liberation Alliance formed in 1935 in Brazil. This was inspired by communists, included non-communist trade union and army officer groups, and had Luis Carlos Prestes for its chairman. The Comintern's hopes of this movement were however quickly destroyed. The Brazilian dictator Vargas claimed to have unravelled a communist plot of rebellion, arrested the Alliance's leaders and imprisoned Prestes for ten years. Vargas used the plot to strengthen his own legal powers, and in 1937 illegally prolonged his presidency and introduced a more or less fascist constitution. He made use in 1937 of a fascist movement called *Integralistas*, led by Plinio Salgado, but having won complete power he broke with them. The *Integralistas* in some ways resembled the Roumanian Iron Guard: their fascist doctrines included both social revolutionary demagogy and an emphasis on religion. Vargas' tactics towards them also recall the tactics of King Carol towards the Iron Guard: Vargas was less brutal and more successful than Carol, but this must be attributed at least as much to his more favorable geographical situation as to his superior wisdom or virtue.

The second Latin American Popular Front appeared in Chile. It was formed in 1936 in opposition to the measures of repression adopted by President Alessandri, formerly a man of the moderate left but now both conservative and dictatorial. The Front included radicals, socialists and communists. In 1938 the parties of the Front agreed to support the Radical Party leader Aguirre as presidential candidate. The Front was strengthened by a breach between the conservative candidate and the fascists. The election was held in December 1938, and Aguirre won by a small majority.

RUSSIA AND THE SPANISH CIVIL WAR

MAX BELOFF

Max Beloff is Gladstone Professor of Government and Public Administration at
Oxford and Fellow of All Souls' College. His numerous books range from studies in
American history and government to Soviet policy in the Far East. In his analysis of
the Soviet Union's role in Spain from 1936 to 1939, he delineates the mystifying intrica-
cies of Soviet policy as it was implemented simultaneously through the Comintern and
through Soviet party, military, and diplomatic channels. The result in this case was an
almost incredible display of conflict and confusion within the communist ranks. One
theme ultimately predominated. The national security of the Soviet Union was far more
important to Stalin than immediate revolutionary successes in Spain. And because
Soviet security seemed to depend upon the alliance with France and the good will of
other democratic nations, Russia's agents labored to stem the Spanish revolution,
presenting themselves as defenders of democracy against fascism. While the Spanish
affair stunned many Communists with its forceful demonstration that Soviet policy was
anti-revolutionary, it had the paradoxical effect of strengthening the Western democracies' conviction that the Soviet Union was interested solely in spreading communism.

EVEN more clearly than events in
France, the Spanish Civil War served to
illumine the contradictions inherent in the
Soviet attempt to combine diplomatic action
at the side of the Western democracies with
an active "popular front" policy on the
part of the Comintern. But both the motives and the nature of intervention in Spain
by the Comintern and the Soviet Union
were so largely misunderstood at the time
that it is essential to consider briefly not
only its diplomatic repercussions but also
its actual influence on the Spanish situation itself.

It is necessary to begin by trying to
rectify some errors about the war and foreign intervention which still persist from
the disputes of the time. The right considered it necessary to obscure the fact that
Franco was incapable of winning without
foreign backing, even at a time when Hitler
and Mussolini themselves had long thrown
off the pretense of non-intervention. Similarly, the left in Britain and France was
forced to ignore Russia's role in order to
represent the Spanish Republic as a freely-
functioning liberal democracy of the Western type. One side called the Spanish Republic "Bolshevist," "Moscow-controlled"
and "Red" in order to blacken its reputation among upholders of the existing social
order everywhere; the other was not in a
position to point out that in so far as the
Communists were in control, their power
was a guarantee against any large scale
internal changes. Russia was not in Spain
to endow it with an immediate Communist
revolution.

The fact that the popular front triumphs in Spain and France occurred within
so short a time of one another, should not
have blinded anyone, and probably did not
blind Moscow, to the essential differences
between the situation in the two countries
in the summer of 1936; it is certainly far
from easy to trace any exact parallelism in
the conduct of the Communist Parties of
the two countries—although there can be
no doubt that both were thoroughly responsive to Moscow's direction. The comparative weakness of Marxist as compared with
Anarcho-Syndicalist ideas in most of Spain,

From Max Beloff, *The Foreign Policy of Soviet Russia, 1929–1941* (London and New York: Oxford
University Press, 1949), II, 28–38. By permission of John Brown, Publisher.

and the fact that it was agrarian and not industrial relations which furnished the greater scope for agitation, largely explain the failure of the Spanish Communist Party to acquire a mass following in the pre-Civil War period.

Nevertheless, Spanish politics were not unaffected by the ideological conflicts which developed during the course of the Russian Revolution. The first impulse of the anarchist trade unions, the C.N.T.,[1] towards associating themselves with the Comintern in 1920 was weakened by the repercussions of the suppression of the Kronstadt rising in March 1921. In 1922, the C.N.T. declined all further contact with Moscow, a decision in which they were preceded by the Spanish Socialist Party. A small Communist Party was founded from exile by Nin and Maurin, ex-members of the C.N.T., in company with some Socialists. But the Party remained insignificant and was indeed too weak for Primo de Rivera to trouble to suppress it during the dictatorship. At the end of 1931, Nin and Maurin, with most of the Catalan membership of the Party, left it to form a left Marxist (Trotskyist) group and as such took part in the Catalin rising of 1932. This group itself split after the 1933 elections on the question of whether to cooperate with the Socialists. In February 1934, Largo Caballero's *Alianza Obrera*, an attempt at a united front under left-wing Socialist leadership, was joined by the Trotskyists but not by the Anarcho-Syndicalists or the Communists. The Communists eventually acceded to it in accordance with the new Comintern line a few days before the Asturias rising in October 1934. The dissident left Marxists also joined. The conduct of the Communists during the Asturias rising added to their following—they had returned only one member to the 1933 Cortes—but they were still numerically insignificant. They remained until 1936, when the popular front was formed, a sternly revolutionary party, rather reluctantly following the new path taken by the Comintern. Their working-class following outside the Asturias was confined to Seville and their membership in March 1936 has not been reckoned at more than 3,000. The rise in their representation in the Cortes to 14, must be attributed in large measure to their electoral coalition with the Socialists and Republicans. On the other hand, in Spain, as elsewhere, Communist influence extended well outside the ranks of the Party itself. The amalgamation of the Socialist and Communist youth organizations which Alvarez del Vayo carried through after his return from Russia in April 1936 gave the Communists control of the united organization. In Catalonia, where local separatism further complicated political issues, the Socialists and Communists were united in July 1936 into a single party, the P.S.U.C.,[2] which accepted the authority of the Comintern. The two minor Marxist factions in Catalonia had come together in February to form the P.O.U.M.[3] The Party was criticized by Trotsky, who retained a small Catalonian following outside it, but it was denounced as "Trotskyist" by the Communists and their associates.

For, in addition to the Marxist-Bakuninist feud, which lived on in Spain, the rivalry of the Stalinist and anti-Stalinist competitors for the Marxist heritage was also projected onto the Spanish scene. It is indeed just possible that this alone would have caused some Russian intervention in Spanish affairs, even had there not been the compelling political and strategic motives provided by Spain's geographical position. The Soviet public proved receptive to the enthusiasm for revolutionary Spain enjoyed by the Soviet press from August 1936. But from the Soviet viewpoint it was essential that the ideology of the Spanish Republic should have no room for trends hostile to those dominant at

[1] The National Confederation of Labor.—Ed.

[2] United Socialist Party of Catalonia.—Ed.
[3] Party of Marxist Unification.—Ed.

Moscow. "So far as Catalonia is concerned," wrote *Pravda* on 17 December 1936, "the cleaning up of the Trotskyist and Anarcho-Syndicalist elements has already begun and it will be carried out with the same energy as in the U.S.S.R." The price of Communist support for the Spanish Government was hostility to the Anarcho-Syndicalist program, even though the C.N.T. was represented in the Caballero Government between its reconstruction on 4 November 1936 and its fall on 15 May 1937, and again in Dr. Negrin's Government after 5 April 1938. If a *modus vivendi* with the Spanish disciples of Bakunin had to be found after the revelation of the C.N.T.'s strength in the Catalan crisis of December 1936, Soviet hostility towards those tarred with the Trotskyist brush was implacable. The severe action taken against the P.O.U.M. after the Barcelona rising of May 1937 was wholly in accordance with Soviet wishes. This does not, however, exhaust the connection between the internal politics of the Soviet Union and those of loyalist Spain. If the great Russian "purge" provided a sombre background to events abroad, it was the more important in its Spanish context, in that many of the victims were prominent figures in the world of international Socialism. The charges brought against them did nothing to cement and much to disrupt the forces of the left in Spain as elsewhere. It should also be noted that the "purge" sooner or later engulfed almost all those who had played a leading role in the Soviet Union's assistance to Spain, in its earliest and most intense phase from October 1936 to February 1937. The public figures of this period, the Ambassador Rosenberg, his second-in-command and successor Gaikis, Michael Koltsov, nominally correspondent of *Pravda*, Generals Kléber and Goriev disappeared, and the political direction of affairs in Spain was left to secondary Comintern figures like André Marty whose influence was wholly unhealthy.

The information at present available permits nothing like a detailed account of Soviet intervention; and even its main phases can be distinguished only with difficulty. The first decision, influenced no doubt by the wish to maintain collaboration with France, was not to intervene. There seems no doubt that the Soviet Government would have preferred to keep to non-intervention had it been possible to secure the withdrawal of foreign aid from the other side, and with it the collapse of the rebellion. Indeed the first Russian ships which arrived in Spain at the end of October were laden with food, the same sort of humanitarian assistance for which the Communists were later to scoff at the parties of the Second International. When it became clear that while the French Government was not going to assist the Spanish Government, the London committee would not prevent foreign help going to the rebels, the Soviet Government decided to take action. The revised attitude of the Soviet Government, of which there had been hints earlier in the month, was first made public on 23 October, when M. Maisky informed the Non-Intervention Committee that the Soviet Government could not consider themselves "bound by the agreement for non-intervention to a greater extent than any of the remaining participants." But the decision at Moscow was obviously taken at an earlier date. On 16 October Stalin sent the first public message of Soviet sympathy for the Spanish cause in a telegram to José Diaz, the secretary of the Spanish Communist Party. On 28 October, Russian tanks were in action in Spain for the first time, and on 8 November the International Brigade arrived on the Madrid front. Recruited through the machinery of the Comintern, but including no Russians—there was a nucleus of foreign Communists long resident in Russia— the Brigade deserves to be regarded as a very important part of the Soviet contribution to the Republican military strength. Whatever may have been true at later stages of the war, there can be little doubt that

it was Soviet intervention which, in the autumn of 1936, prevented the fall of Madrid. The importance of Soviet help at this stage meant that the Russians had for a time the main responsibility for military operations on the central front. The field commander from November was General Kléber. Russian military personnel was always limited in numbers. Krivitsky's maximum estimate is 2,000; Fischer declares that there were never more than 700 Russians in Spain at any one time. After the first months of the war, the most important aspect of Soviet aid was the fact that Comintern agents were available to assist in the purchase of arms—with Spanish funds. These arms were mostly not of Russian manufacture, but were purchased in different parts of Europe and America as occasion afforded. The chief difficulty throughout was one of transport rather than of supply or finance. The Russians were guaranteed against financial loss by the deposit in Moscow at the beginning of November 1936, of a large part of the gold reserve of the Bank of Spain.

There is no reason to doubt that political developments on the Republican side were conditioned by the importance of Soviet help. This was the easier to achieve in that the local and party nature of the early military formations enabled arms shipments to be directed to specific ports where they would come into the hands of elements which the Soviet authorities regarded as reliable. The Communists had two main political aims. The first was to increase the importance of the Party and its weight in the administration and in the armed forces. From the beginning they opposed the setting up of Revolutionary Committees and the creation of a workmen's militia. They stood for the creation of a centralized, disciplined, professionalized army. In the autumn of 1936, when Alvarez del Vayo was General Commissar for the Army, they secured the institution of a body of political commissars (with functions similar to those of their proto-

types in the Red Army) who were the main agents of Communist influence in the Spanish forces. It has been suggested that the cancellation of some of these appointments by Largo Caballero was one of the reasons for his overthrow by the Communists in favour of the Negrin-Prieto combination. The discipline and feeling for organization of the Spanish Communists made them an invaluable toughening element on the Republican side from the beginning of the war. Afterwards, however, the revelation of their complete lack of any principle other than their devotion to the policy of the Soviet Union and of their apparently limitless opportunism lost them the respect which they had gained. But numerically their advance in the early part of the war was striking.

The second political task assigned to the Spanish Communists was to prevent any large-scale social upheaval on the Republican side, which might detract from military efficiency and further prejudice the Western democracies against the Republic. This was true from the beginning of the rising. The Communists' first slogan was: "This is not a proletarian revolution; it is only a democratic movement." After a few days this was altered to: "This is not a revolution at all; it is only the defence of the legal government." The visit of Rosenberg to Moscow in December 1936 resulted in a letter to Largo Caballero, dated the 21st, and signed by Stalin, Voroshilov and Molotov. In it they suggested that special consideration should be given to peasant interests, that the middle and lesser bourgeoisie should be attracted to the side of the Government or at least kept neutral by guaranteeing their economic interests, that nothing should be done to alienate the Republican (non-Socialist) leaders, so as to prevent Spain from being branded as a Communist State, and that assurances should be given regarding foreign property and interests in Spain. At the same time the Soviet leaders promised to send further military specialists to help the Spaniards. It is a little difficult to accept the rather disingenuous argument of Alvarez del Vayo that the moderation of Stalin's advice proves that the Soviet Union did not intervene in Spanish internal affairs. On the other hand it is arguable that it was not Russian pressure which prevented the Republican regime from developing on more radical lines. The Russians merely assisted Caballero in his task of imposing internal discipline on the Republican side. The measures taken included the dissolution of the Revolutionary Police which had organized the execution of right-wing elements in the first few weeks of the rising, and the reinstatement of the old police who were used against the Communists' political rivals on the left.

The most active period of Russian intervention came to an end in February 1937 with the replacement of Rosenberg by Gaikis and the removal of General Kléber. On 4 February Stalin sent Largo Caballero a further letter promising "help in the future within the measure of our possibilities."

The results of the Communists' acting as the right wing of the Republican coalition, protecting the peasants against collectivization and even the Church against anarchist excesses, could be seen in the character of their newly increased membership.

Unable to draw to themselves the manual workers who remained firmly fixed in their unions, the Communists found themselves the refuge for all those who had suffered from the excesses of the Revolution or who feared where it might lead them. Well-to-do Catholic orange growers in Valencia, peasants in Catalonia, small shopkeepers and business men, Army officers and Government officials enrolled in their ranks.[4]

The Comintern view of events in Spain and of the position in the early spring of 1937 may be gathered from the report of the general secretary of the Spanish Communist Party made to the enlarged Plenum of the Executive on 5 March.[5]

We are fighting for a democratic republic, for a *democratic republic of a new type.* The object of the struggle in Spain is not the setting up of a democratic republic on the model of the French or similar republics in the other capitalist countries. No, the democratic republic for which we fight is another republic. We fight in order to destroy that material foundation on which was based reaction and Fascism, for without the destruction of this foundation a real political democracy is impossible.

We are fighting for the *destruction* of the material basis of semi-feudal Spain, in order finally to tear out the roots of Fascism.

We must liquidate the class of great landowners, who have all without exception taken part in the military-Fascist coup; we must nationalize their lands and hand them over to the agricultural labourers and peasants, so that they can utilize them as they wish—individually or collectively.

It is essential to destroy the economic and political power of the Church, which was the centre of the Fascist plot and the main stronghold of semi-feudal Spain, and to do that the property of the Church must be confiscated and nationalized. The struggle against the semi-feudal economic and political role of the Church does not signify a war against religion — on the contrary, only a republican and democratic Spain can guarantee the freedom of religion.

We must also strive to liquidate the caste spirit of the old army, which was at the service of semi-feudal Spain and was the weapon used to destroy progressive movements.

We must put an end to the financial oligarchy of bankers and manufacturers, which is closely connected with the landowners and the hierarchy, and which has hampered the growth of the national economy. We must proceed to the nationalization of the Bank of Spain and the main branches of

[4] Gerald Brenan, *The Spanish Labyrinth* (Cambridge, 1943), p. 325.

[5] José Diaz, in *Kommunisticheski Internatsional,* 1937, No. 3, reprinted in *O Mezhdunarodnom Polozhenie* (Moscow, 1937), pp. 135–136.

the country's industry. That is the only way of meeting the needs of the front and the country.

Apart from these fundamental points, which when accomplished will have wiped out the semi-feudal castes which rule in Spain, and lead to the rebuilding of the material and social bases of our new democratic parliamentary republic, we must also have a truly universal franchise, so that the whole people may participate in the political and economic life of the country.

This is the new kind of democratic and parliamentary republic for which our Party is fighting, and with our Party the whole of the Spanish people.

In all the provinces under the authority of the Government there are no more big landowners, no more big churches as ruling powers, no more big bankers and big manufacturers. The best guarantee that we shall retain what we have won is the fact that there are arms in the hands of the people, in the hands of the anti-Fascists, in the hands of workers, peasants, intellectuals and petty bourgeoisie. And in that lies the best pledge that there will be no return to the past. And just because our gains are guaranteed, we must not lose our heads and leap beyond the bounds of reality, attempting to instal "libertarian Communism" (anarchism), or busy ourselves with "socialization" in the factories and villages. The stage of the establishment of a democratic republic through which we are now passing makes it necessary for all anti-Fascist forces to take part in the struggle, and such experiments could only turn them aside from it.

It has been suggested that Russian supplies were deliberately held back in order to secure the fall of Largo Caballero and his replacement by Negrin and Prieto. Prieto himself is said to have advocated fusion between the Socialist and Communist Parties in the summer of 1937, a move which other Socialist leaders had contemplated earlier. The Comintern's "line" had swung so far in a popular-front direction that the Comintern was apparently prepared, so Dimitrov indicated to Fischer, to allow such a new combination to join the

Second International, in order to overcome the objections of Negrin, who feared that Communist domination of the united party would be inevitable. (At the same time, Dimitrov himself was using the Spanish situation to argue in the Russian press that United fronts were necessary everywhere and that the Second International was the chief obstacle to their conclusion.) Eventually Prieto would seem to have shown too much independence for the Communists' liking, and it has been suggested that Russian supplies were once more held up in order to secure his departure from the Government in April 1938. It was after his fall that Communist influence reached its height, but it declined with the falling off of Russian supplies later in the year.

The fluctuation in the Soviet attitude towards the war in Spain must be considered in the light of the general political situation. There seems no reason to doubt that at the beginning of the war, the Russians hoped that the Western Powers would intervene and thus further strengthen the combination against Germany. As Dr. Negrin put it later:

Moscow tried to do for France and Britain what they should have done for themselves. The promise of Soviet aid to the Spanish Republic was that ultimately Paris and London would awake to the risks involved to themselves in Italian and German intervention in Spain and join the U.S.S.R. in supporting us.[6]

Instead of this, the progress of the war witnessed two simultaneous processes, both equally unwelcome to the Russians: the drawing together of Germany and Italy as aggressor States and the step-by-step retreat of the Western democracies before this threat.

At the same time as the hostility of the European Axis became more and more open, Russia's fears of developments on

[6] Quoted in J. Alvarez del Vayo, *Freedom's Battle* (Heinemann, 1940), p. 76, from an address given in New York in May 1939.

her eastern frontier became still more acute. Help for Spain had to be balanced against other calls on Russian resources and suffered from the continual disadvantage of obstacles placed by the French on the transit of arms by land, while the Russians could not themselves keep open the Mediterranean route to Spain.

The Russians were no doubt influenced in their policy after the early months of the war by the knowledge of the growth of a spirit of compromise among some circles on the Republican side.

Having become convinced [writes Luis Araquistain] that the inhibitions of the democracies in the face of the Spanish war and the drop-by-drop help that Russia gave us — little war material and a good deal of it useless — made almost impossible a Republican victory, I started negotiations at the beginning of 1937, from Paris, to obtain through possible concessions, the withdrawal of Italy and Germany. . . . On one occasion in Paris I informed Alvarez del Vayo, Foreign Minister, about the negotiations I had undertaken on my own initiative. He said they were "very interesting." He went to Geneva . . . and on his return to Paris he had changed his mind. "Litvinov," he said, "says that an arrangement of this nature would be a bonus paid to the aggressor."[7]

[7] *The Philadelphia Evening Bulletin*, May 23, 1939.

In May 1937, President Azana himself is said to have tried to get the Western Powers to take up the question of mediation, approaching them through Julian Besteiro, Spain's representative at the coronation of King George VI.

By 1938 the tide of aggression had swept much closer to the Soviet Union's own frontiers, and Spain became a mere diversionary side-show. The ultimate importance of the Spanish War is its role in sowing distrust between the Soviet Union and the Western democracies. The word "non-intervention" itself came to be used by the Russians as symbolic of the attitude which had made the Litvinov policy of "collective security" impossible of fulfilment.

Far be it from me [said Stalin in his speech of 10 March 1939] to moralize on the policy of non-intervention, to talk of treason, treachery and so on. It would be naive to preach morals to people who recognize no human morality. Politics is politics, as the old case-hardened bourgeois diplomats say. It must be remarked, however, that the big and dangerous political game started by the supporters of the policy of non-intervention may end in a serious fiasco for them.[8]

[8] J. Stalin, *Leninism* (Allen and Unwin, 1940), pp. 627–628.

THE MESSIANIC URGE

KERMIT E. MC KENZIE

International communism is messianic—its adherents firmly believe that they will bring about man's earthly salvation from the "horrors" of capitalism by ushering in the classless society. Plunging deeply into the theoretical connotations of the Popular Front movement, Kermit McKenzie examines the role of messianism in this new tactic of the mid-thirties. The chief practical purposes of the Popular Front were to strengthen the democracies' opposition to fascism and to secure victory in the new "imperialist war" anticipated by the Communists. Allies were necessary; therefore, Communists who heretofore had dreamed of destroying bourgeois capitalist governments now joined them to work for the short-range salvation promised by the preservation and improvement of these multi-class democracies. This dramatic change of direction, however, did not shake the basic faith that ultimate salvation would come through proletarian revolution. Dr. McKenzie's analysis demonstrates the Communists' ability to fit any expedient policy into their theory of world revolution and their capacity for rationalizing every policy in such a way that they may always see themselves as fighters for man's salvation.

I

In the history of the Communist International, the period opened by its Seventh Congress in 1935 and closed by the outbreak of the Second World War stands as one of the most noteworthy phases of the Communist-led world revolutionary movement. Achievements were registered in theory and in practice alike. In terms of the latter, it is well known that Communist parties of several countries temporarily enjoyed a very considerable growth in membership, often accompanied by a disproportionate increase in political influence. In the realm of theory, a more meaningful development was the presentation of a complex messianism which sought not only to justify the immediate practical activity of the Communist parties, but also to preserve unaltered the ultimate goals of the Comintern. This paper seeks to present and analyze the content of this modified messianic concept as it emanated from the Comintern leadership during that period.

Stated in simplest terms, the reformulation which was given the messianic idea in the late thirties resulted in an extension of the concept of the Comintern's mission beyond the traditional definition and in the elaboration of appropriately enabling strategical and tactical concepts. Perhaps the most important thing about the reformulation is that it not only was valid from 1935 through 1939 but also holds true in a broad sense for the present day. Indeed, the years of Comintern and post-Comintern history which follow 1935 constitute a phase clearly distinguishable from the first fifteen years of the Comintern—from 1917 to 1934. In other words, the late thirties laid the major ideological foundations of an era having an inner unity that demarcates it from the pre-1935 period of the Third International.

What were the essential elements embraced within the messianic concept prior to 1935? In what fashion was the messianic concept broadened during 1935–1939? The answers to these questions serve to define the basic principles of the new era. It may safely be said that the traditional messianic concept involved a revo-

From Kermit E. McKenzie, "The Messianic Concept in the Third International, 1935–1939," reprinted by permission of the publishers from Ernest J. Simmons (editor), *Continuity and Change in Russian and Soviet Thought* (Cambridge, Mass.: Harvard University Press), pp. 516–526, 529–530. Copyright 1955 by The President and Fellows of Harvard College.

lutionary reconstruction of society by the Communist-led working class, during which the bourgeois state would be smashed and its social and economic structure transformed, all to the end of building a new society along the lines of Lenin's, and later Stalin's, interpretation of the principles of Marxism. However, during the late thirties, the messianic idea was elaborated in such a fashion that it also included, given certain conditions, the salvation of "bourgeois" democracy and "bourgeois" culture in the form of a somewhat socialized democracy —the "democracy of a new type," neither purely bourgeois nor completely socialist. The promise of an improved version of bourgeois democracy was offered in mass propaganda to broad categories of the population—the proletariat, the peasantry, and much of the middle class. The impermanence of this "new democracy" was fully explained in Communist theory, but seldom mentioned in mass propaganda except in vague terms. Correspondingly, talk of revolution and proletarian democracy was deëmphasized in propaganda.

The Comintern presented itself as the stalwart defender of bourgeois democratic achievements, as the advocate of moderate change, and as the champion of the interests of many classes. Thus its leadership became more palatable to many who had formerly looked askance. To Communists analyzing the course of world affairs, the enlargement of their mission was frankly regarded as an expedient measure. For the Comintern, the mission of world revolution and world Communism remained as real as ever.

To understand the international Communist movement during the late thirties it is necessary to have in mind the essential elements of the Comintern's appreciation of current history. Underlying the thinking of Moscow and the Comintern in 1935 was the threat of German aggression and the growth of fascism and fascist tendencies in other countries. War against the Soviet Union must have appeared as a grave possibility. The course of events seemed about to confirm what theory had predicted earlier. According to Comintern periodization of history since the First World War, a "third period" of postwar development had begun by 1928. It was defined as a period of "intense development of the contradictions of world capitalism," which would give rise to a new round of wars and revolutions. A first period of "extremely acute crisis of the capitalist system, and of direct revolutionary action on the part of the proletariat," had ended in 1923, and had been followed by a second period of "gradual and partial stabilization of the capitalist system," during which the proletariat was restricted to "defensive battles" and the possibility of a seizure of power seemed relatively remote.

In the absence of evidence to the contrary, the idea of a third postwar period appears to have been considered by the Communists as valid for the remainder of the Comintern's existence, or until May 1943. It is a matter of record that the congress meeting in 1935 considered its most important task to be the discovery of the best means "to secure victory in the second round of revolutions and wars." In Communist thinking, the subsequent developments in Spain and China, to mention only a few, coupled with the Second World War, constituted sufficient proof of the accuracy of its earlier analysis.

The anticipated economic crisis of the third period (which opportunely occurred and doubtless strengthened the confidence of the Comintern), was expected to result in attempts to solve the crisis by substituting fascism for bourgeois democracy and by preparing and conducting wars for a fresh repartition of colonial empires. From 1928 through 1933, the official Comintern viewpoint dictated that fascism and imperialist war should be answered by proletarian revolution and civil war. "The Communist parties must with full decisiveness set before the masses the task of a revolutionary way out of the crisis of capitalism." Thus declared the Thirteenth Plenum of the Executive Committee of the Comintern in December 1933. Otto Kuusinen's report on fascism and the war danger sanctioned the slogan of "revolutionary civil war" as appropriate if war should break out.

A much revised solution was elaborated in 1935. The term "fascist," loosely applied in former years to bourgeois governments in general, was now given a restricted and more precise meaning. Fascism, defined as the "power of finance capital," was carefully distinguished from traditional bourgeois rule. "The accession to power of fascism is not an *ordinary succession* of one bourgeois government by another, but a substitution of one state form of class domination of the bourgeoisie —bourgeois democracy—by another form —open terrorist dictatorship."[1] This concept of two separate forms of bourgeois rule was sharpened by Dimitrov's charge that the "fascist counterrevolution" was attacking bourgeois democracy in order to establish "the most barbaric regime of exploitation and suppression of the toiling masses."[2] Dimitrov's reconstruction of the whole problem is fundamental to an understanding of the period under survey: the choice to be made by the "toiling masses" was "not between proletarian dictatorship and bourgeois democracy, but between bourgeois democracy and fascism."[3]

Justification of the new mission followed several themes. In terms of the internal situation within the capitalist countries, it was frequently argued that the weakness of the Communist parties and their followings dictated a solution to fascism other than by way of a proletarian revolution.

Even before the new line was enunciated, the judgment of one of the most authoritative Comintern leaders, Dmitrii Manuil'skii, was that "In the overwhelming majority of capitalist countries the Communists have not yet won over the majority of the working class."[4] In similar vein, the Seventh Congress freely admitted that only a minority of the working class had accepted the Communist outlook. Maurice Thorez declared bluntly that the proletarian revolution could not be the immediate goal of the present struggle. The admitted failure up to that time to capture a mass basis was utilized to justify the temporary postponement of proletarian revolution. In such a negative fashion the longstanding weakness of the Communist parties was exploited as evidence of the rationality of a more modest policy.

Lenin's comments on the relative merits of democracy in the presocialist era were mustered in support of the new orientation. Karl Radek, pointing to Lenin's appreciation of the progressive features of bourgeois democracy, wrote: "We must keep these words of Lenin's clearly before us, if we do not wish to fall into the mistake of a summary, antihistorical denial of bourgeois democracy."[5] Another writer acknowledged Lenin's criticism of the "restricted character" of bourgeois democracy, but pointed out that Lenin regarded bourgeois political liberty as a useful "weapon for struggle" against exploitation and poverty.[6]

Accompanying the revision of the pattern of domestic tactics in capitalist countries was a similar reappraisal of the threat of a new imperialist war. As late as the Seventeenth Congress of the Communist Party of the Soviet Union in 1934, Manuil'-

[1] George Dimitrov, *The United Front* (New York, 1938), pp. 11–12.

[2] *Ibid.*, p. 110.

[3] *Ibid.* One year later, at the Ninth Convention of the American Communist Party, Earl Browder announced that "the direct issue of the 1936 elections is not socialism or capitalism, but rather democracy or fascism" (*The People's Front* [New York, 1938], p. 32).

[4] From his report to the Seventeenth Congress of the Soviet Communist Party (January-February 1934) on behalf of the Soviet delegation in the ECCI (*Socialism Victorious* [Moscow-Leningrad, n.d.], p. 319).

[5] *International Press Correspondence* (August 15, 1936), p. 1006.

[6] *Ibid.* (January 23, 1937), p. 62.

skii's report in the traditional vein defined all capitalist countries as predatory and imperialistic. "Imperialist war," he declared, "is the order of the day for all capitalist governments of the world."[7] In particular, England was credited with "the leading role in the preparations for war against the U.S.S.R."[8] Nor does Stalin's report to the same Congress preview the later temporary division by the Comintern of the capitalist world into "nonaggressive" states and "aggressive" states.

Such a division was made by Dimitrov at the Seventh Congress of the Comintern and remained generally characteristic of Comintern thinking until late fall of 1939. Dimitrov sought, moreover, to distinguish the current international scene from the situation in 1914:

. . . the world at that time was divided into two military-imperialist coalitions which were equally striving to establish their world hegemony and which had equally prepared and provoked the imperialist war. At that time there were neither countries where the proletariat had conquered, nor countries with a fascist dictatorship.[9]

The world picture in 1935–1939 included not only *aggressive* fascist states (Germany, Italy, and Japan), but also a proletarian state (U.S.S.R.) and a number of *nonaggressive* capitalist states (Britain, France, the United States, and small countries fearful of losing their independence), which for the moment were interested in the maintenance of peace. Only after the outbreak of war between Germany and the Western Powers in September 1939 was this picture revised by Dimitrov, although it is anticipated earlier in 1939 by increasing reference to the "reactionary ruling circles" of Britain and France.

In the light of this appraisal of the situation in the capitalist world in 1935, the Comintern defined its tasks as the defense of peace and democracy, of the U.S. S.R. and the international working class, against the onslaught of fascism and imperialist war.

The messianic theme was explicitly and frequently utilized by Dimitrov at the Seventh Congress in 1935, when it became his duty to outline what he termed the "*new tactical orientation for the Communist International.*" Dimitrov spoke of "the most important, the greatest class of modern society—the working class, to whose destiny it falls to free mankind from the sufferings of the capitalist system. . . ." This class, having partially realized its mission in one-sixth of the world where it "has already cast off the yoke of capitalism and constitutes the ruling class," was confronted with great obstacles in the middle thirties—the immediate challenge of fascism and imperialist war, against which above all else the Comintern had to devise a suitable policy.

The mission to save the world from fascism did not entail, for the time being, the method of revolutionary overthrow of capitalism, but rather the defense of bourgeois democracy. In the capitalist countries, Dimitrov explained, "we defend and shall continue to defend every inch of bourgeois-democratic liberties, which are being attacked by fascism and bourgeois reaction, because the interests of the class struggle of the proletariat so dictate."[10] Rejecting any "cut-and-dried approach to the question of defense of bourgeois democracy,"[11] Dimitrov made clear that changing conditions required a change in Comintern attitude. It had been perfectly valid for the German Communist Party to fight against the Weimar Republic in the twenties, when it represented counterrevolution, but the Party had erred in 1932 when, with the rise of fascism, it continued its tactics

---

[7] *Socialism Victorious*, p. 303.
[8] *Ibid.*, p. 305.
[9] *Inprecor* (May 16, 1936), p. 613.

[10] Dimitrov, *The United Front*, p. 111.
[11] *Ibid.*, p. 34.

unchanged.[12] Moreover, Dimitrov denied that the Comintern, in proposing joint action by all working class parties against fascism, intended to proclaim the dictatorship of the proletariat. "We make no such proposal now," he declared.[13] Immediate tasks dictated otherwise.

II

It is in the selection of adequate forms for the implementation of the messianic concept that the Seventh Congress developed several concepts, which, still utilized today, served then to introduce a new era of Comintern phraseology. The terminological revolution was revealed in the new phrases, "people's front," "government of people's front," and "democracy of a new type." One well-worn concept, the "united front," was refashioned.

The term "popular front" apparently does not exist in Comintern literature before 1934, while the term "united front" can be traced back to 1921 and the Third Congress of the Comintern. At that time the failure of the European revolutionary movement to meet Communist expectations produced a retreat to the more limited goal of winning mass working-class support, chiefly at the expense of those Social Democratic parties which had been accused since 1919 of splitting the labor movement. The tactics of the united front, operating strictly within a proletarian framework, called for joint action between working-class parties for the achievement of specific short-range aims. The application of the united front tactic "from above" was to be based on an agreement between the Communist Party and the Social Democratic leadership, while the united front "from below" was an attempt to win the rank-and-file of social democracy away from its leaders. In anticipation of the Seventh Congress, a shift was

made in 1934 to the united front "from above," reversing the form preferred since the Sixth Congress of the Comintern in 1928.

The popular or people's front was given its first clear exposition by Dimitrov at the Seventh Congress. It transcended a purely working-class arrangement and sought to compose an alliance with peasant, petty-bourgeois, and bourgeois parties for immediate aims of a specific nature. The people's front presupposed the existence of the proletarian united front which it resembled in structure. It was composed of an extragovernmental hierarchy of popularly elected committees from the local to the national level. Inevitably, the original Russian soviets come to mind. Regardless of the varieties of political alignments and group interests that might be represented, these committees were dedicated to the support of mutually agreeable aims, usually embodied in a written program to which the several party leaderships had formally subscribed.

The later history of the people's front can be briefly sketched. In November 1939, with a new turn in Comintern policy, the slogan of the "popular front" was reinterpreted to mean necessarily a people's front "from below," and the leaders of the democratic and Social Democratic parties were condemned as "traitors." Only after the Nazi invasion of the Soviet Union was the people's front resumed in its original form, that is, "from above." During the struggle against Hitler, the people's or national fronts reappeared, later to become transformed in Eastern Europe into new types of governments, the "people's democracies."

Satisfactory evidence is not available with respect to the role of certain personalities in the Comintern's decision to adopt the people's front policy. The attitudes of Stalin, Dimitrov, and Manuil'skii have not been fully clarified. Dimitrov's name was necessarily linked with the new "line" in his capacity as Secretary-General of the Comintern. There is considerable differ-

12 *Ibid.*, p. 110–111.
13 *VII Congress of the Communist International: Abridged Stenographic Report of the Proceedings* (Moscow, 1939), p. 126.

ence of opinion among authors, including ex-Communists, concerning the power position of Dimitrov and Manuil'skii in the Comintern and their relation to Stalin. Whether Manuil'skii was fully sympathetic to the new line has been answered variously.

Attempts were made, however, to place the people's front on a Leninist and Stalinist foundation. An editorial in the *Communist International* could do little more than indicate a parallel in Lenin's concern for a united movement in the struggle against tsarist autocracy. "For the realization of this task Lenin united all toilers, all democratic forces, able to fight for the victory of the bourgeois-democratic revolution." Another writer cited Lenin's approval of Communist agreement and compromises with other working-class parties and petty-bourgeois parties, if such tactics raised, rather than lowered, the political consciousness of the worker and his capacity for revolutionary struggle. Manuil'skii pieced together the essentials of the people's front from various elements emphasized in Stalin's writings: the utilization of the slightest opportunity to secure a mass ally, the need of the masses for political experience, and the importance of the middle strata of society.

The concept of a government of the people's front proved to be one of the most fruitful ideas advanced in this period. Dimitrov provided an initial exposition of the general conditions under which it was possible to form a government of the people's front. In effect, he appreciated that there might arise a political situation sufficiently unstable to be exploited by the Communists but not to the point of a direct seizure of power by armed uprising. He postulated an intermediate situation between that relative stability which would permit no opportunity for an effective challenge to bourgeois rule and an unstable situation fully vulnerable to revolution.

His "half-way house" abandoned Communist exclusiveness in relation to other parties and to prerevolutionary governments. His conceptual scheme permitted a

tapping of hitherto untouched mass support and opened at once new approaches to power that had been entirely lacking in preceding years. Formerly the question had been whether or not a revolutionary situation existed. Bound by traditional concepts of "objective" and "subjective" conditions with which to estimate a political situation, the Communists more often than not found themselves in a situation that was by definition "non-revolutionary." Their activity was confined to struggle for the daily interests of the working class and to propaganda about ultimate aims. The reception of their claims to leadership was severely restricted by their exclusiveness and extreme radicalism. The postulation of an intermediate situation now permitted temporary activity *through* a prerevolutionary governmental structure and not *outside* it, on behalf of several social groups and not for one alone, before the final move was made toward a Communist seizure of power. This gradualistic approach performed the function of pushing the distasteful specter of street barricades into a more remote future.

The prerequisites for a people's front government which seemed most important to Dimitrov were three: first, the bourgeois state apparatus must be "disorganized and paralyzed" to such an extent that the bourgeoisie cannot prevent such a people's front government; second, popular feeling must be in a state of "vehement revolt *against fascism and reaction*" though not ready for an armed uprising against capitalism; third, the leftward movement in the ranks of the parties participating in the united front must be sufficiently vigorous so that a "considerable proportion" demand "*ruthless measures against the fascists and other reactionaries,*" and are willing to work with the Communists and against the anti-Communist wing within their own parties.[14] That such prerequisites are vague does not cancel the fact that a new channel for Communist activity had been opened. These

[14] Dimitrov, *The United Front*, p. 71.

preconditions might possibly develop in any capitalist country involved in political crisis. Such a crisis, for Dimitrov, appears to mean simply the threat of fascist dictatorship at home or fascist aggression from another country.

Specific limitations were placed by the Communists on the capacity of the people's front government to achieve ultimate aims. "*Final salvation* this government *cannot bring*," Dimitrov warned. It could not overthrow the class rule of the exploiters, though it was designed to limit its worse features. It could not insure against fascist counterrevolution. "Consequently," the Secretary-General emphasized, "it is necessary to prepare for the socialist revolution! Soviet power and *only* Soviet power can bring salvation!"[15] Such exhortations demonstrate that within the dualistic messianism of the late thirties the "salvation" promised to non-Communists hardly had a permanent character in the eyes of members of the Third International.

The people's front was obviously not a government to be formed after the proletarian revolution but on the eve of and before the victory of revolution. The people's front government would, therefore, constitute a transitional form, following Lenin's idea, to the proletarian revolution. However, it was not regarded as indispensable or inevitable, but rather as strongly probable. Where fascist dictatorship existed, the united front government would be created as the result of the overthrow of fascism. It does not appear from Dimitrov's analysis that he excluded the possibility that a dictatorship of the proletariat might directly replace the fascist dictatorship, but later Communist statements seem to rule this out. In countries where the so-called bourgeois-democratic revolution was still uncompleted, Dimitrov suggested that the people's front government might become a "democratic dicta-

torship of the proletariat and the peasantry."[16] In the event that a number of important bourgeois reforms had not yet been achieved, the people's front government would effect such reforms.

As a *sine qua non,* the people's front government must allow full freedom to the Communist Party and other organizations of the working class. The government, which might not necessarily include Communists, was promised the support of the Communist Party if it implemented the "anti-fascist" program upon which the parties of the people's front had agreed. In this connection, the hierarchy of united front and people's front committees was to be used as an extraparliamentary vehicle for mass activity and Communist propaganda, agitation, and pressure. The importance of such committees in Communist eyes would, of course, depend on whether and to what extent Communists held posts in the national government.

It is interesting to observe that Dimitrov in 1937 considered it necessary to caution the members of the Third International against allowing the new tactics to mislead them into a relaxation of their revolutionary principles. He warned:

When carrying out the policy of the People's Front against fascism and war . . . the Communists do not lose sight of the historic need for the revolutionary overthrow of capitalism which has outlived its day and for the achievement of socialism which brings emancipation to the working class and the whole of mankind.[17]

---

[15] *Ibid.,* p. 76. "Soviet power" does not seem to mean here the power of the Soviet Union, but rather a domestic dictatorship of the proletariat in Soviet form.

[16] *Ibid.,* p. 108. Conceivably, Dimitrov may have believed also that even in an advanced capitalist country a lengthy rule of fascism could cause a "completed" bourgeois-democratic revolution to revert to an "uncompleted" condition through the abolition of democratic gains and thus require a "democratic dictatorship of the proletariat and peasantry." For Lenin's invention of this term, see Bertram D. Wolfe, *Three Who Made a Revolution* (New York, 1948), pp. 291–298. There is a clear consistency in the Comintern's view that a people's front government and not a proletarian dictatorship should succeed fascism.

[17] *Inprecor* (May 8, 1937), p. 468. This important May Day article, "Unity of the International Pro-

Citing the position of the Seventh Congress on the duty of Communists to criticize their allies within the people's front, Dimitrov warned that joint action with the socialist parties rendered even more necessary the "serious and well-founded criticism of reformism, of social-democracy as the ideology and practice of class collaboration. . . ." He regarded as mistaken the view that the existence of a people's front freed the Communists from the need to conduct a struggle for the basic principles of the working-class movement.

The term "new democracy" was applied to the society which would result from and, at the same time, would nourish the government of the people's front. The application of the tactics of the people's front assumed a variety of forms, depending on the economic and political structure of the country and upon its foreign policy, especially with reference to the existing attitude of the Soviet Union to world problems. The numerous programs of economic and political reform, proposed by Communists as minimum demands for a people's front, suggest some features of the "democracy of a new type" which was to emerge. This term, apparently not used by Dimitrov himself, came into increasing usage as a label for what was considered by the Comintern in the late thirties to be its most urgent short-term mission—the salvation and improvement of bourgeois democracy. The "new democracy" thus was to occupy temporarily a middle position between bourgeois and Soviet democracy.

Yet this concept—perhaps the most important theoretical contribution of the Comintern in this period—should not be interpreted as a static but rather as a dynamic stage in the advance toward other aims. Its duration was never precisely defined, but its function was frequently made clear. According to Maurice Thorez, the government of the people's front would be

a government for the purpose of leading the masses to the dictatorship of the proletariat, to the Soviet Republic. The "new democracy" was repeatedly characterized, in rather vague terminology, as one in which "fascism" and the "economic basis of fascism" would be destroyed and never allowed to reappear. . .

* * *

III

The features of the messianic concept, as it has emerged thus far in the description of the background of the third period, its tasks, and the techniques developed for the solution of those tasks, are the characteristic features of a secular, political messianism. "Instead of a next world, there is an earthly future," writes Jules Monnerot in his excellent study.[18] The ingredients of the messianism of the Comintern are clear: one truly creative social group (the proletariat), a general will expressed through an elite (the Communists), the harmony of interests between leader and led, the monopoly of truth (dialectical and historical materialism), the evil (capitalist society) from which salvation will bring deliverance.[19]

As Professor J. T. Halmon indicates, secular messianism replaces empirical thinking "with reasoning by definition, based on a priori collective concepts which must be accepted whatever the evidence of the senses. . . ."[20] So it was in the Comintern. By Communist definition, an identity of interests existed for the time being between the Soviet Union, the working class, and the cause of peace. One could not oppose the U.S.S.R. without being an enemy of the latter. Dimitrov is quite specific on this point:

letariat Is the Supreme Demand of the Present Moment," was printed also in *Kommunisticheski Internatsional* (May 1937), and in Soviet newspapers on May Day.

[18] Jules Monnerot, *Sociology and Psychology of Communism* (Boston, 1953), p. 156.
[19] Compare especially the recent study of Professor J. L. Talmon, *The Rise of Totalitarian Democracy* (Boston, 1952). Part III, "The Babouvist Crystallization," is penetrating and rewarding.
[20] *Ibid.*, p. 253.

In the present situation there is not, nor can there be any other more certain criterion than one's attitude toward the Soviet Union in determining who is the friend and who is the enemy of the cause of the working class and socialism, of determining who is a supporter and who an opponent of democracy and peace.[21]

The exalted position accorded the Soviet Union in the struggle "for democracy and peace" merely reëmphasized in another fashion its hegemony in Comintern mythology as the locus of the partially realized mission of the proletariat. Stalin himself held an unchallenged position as the fourth great teacher of dialectical materialism, following Marx, Engels, and Lenin.

The universality of the struggle at hand is another theme in messianic schemes. Defense of peace and resistance to fascism were considered to be as valid in Asia and Latin America as in Europe. Resistance against the fascists in Spain was the "common cause of advanced and progressive mankind" and helped at the same moment to aid Czechoslovakia against fascist Germany and to bolster China against imperialist Japan.[22]

An inevitable accompaniment of the messianic outlook is a bisection of the world into two hostile camps and the impossibility of a middle or neutral position. Such was the case in the 1930's. Even the neutrality of the Scandinavian states was attacked as, in effect, hostility to the cause of democracy and peace. A denial of the necessity of the people's front was equated with the encouragement of war; but whoever stood with the people's front stood, by definition, on the side of peace.

It should not be overlooked that member sections of the Comintern, encouraged by the blessing given to "national forms of the proletarian class struggle," took up the messianic idea in terms of their national heritages. A resolution of the German Communist Party spoke of the "historical mission" of the German working class in the struggle to preserve peace and to secure the future of Germany. Frequently the proletariat was replaced as the instrument of salvation by a larger entity, the nation. One writer spoke of the need for France to return to "its old traditions and remain true to its great past" and to its "historical mission of liberator." An entire section of Thorez's speech at the Ninth Congress of the French Party in December 1937 was devoted to "the mission of France in the world." Bourgeois tradition was freely exploited. The "principles of 1789" were appealed to in French Communist literature and throughout Europe. Earl Browder spoke of the American Party as "destined to carry on and complete the work begun by Tom Paine, George Washington, Thomas Jefferson, and Abraham Lincoln," and admitted that the American revolutionary heritage had long been neglected by the Party.[23]

Comintern messianism, it may be stated in conclusion, was presented on two levels during the late 1930's. On one level, the ultimate goals were maintained intact for the elite, that is, the Communist parties of the world. But on another level, the Comintern offered salvation from imperialist war and fascism, and extended the hand of fellowship to broad categories of the population for the satisfaction of common interests. In doing so, Dimitrov and the Comintern spokesmen elaborated new and fruitful techniques for the exercise of influence and control over non-Party allies.

Throughout the period from 1935 through 1939, the continuing validity of the mission of the Communist-led proletariat to transform society by revolutionary action was upheld. World revolution and the violent overthrow of capitalism were not regarded as immediate tasks; but in the struggle against fascism the proletariat was expected to achieve unity and experience, prerequisites for the fulfillment of its historical mission.

---

[21] *Inprecor* (November 13, 1937), p. 1179.

[22] Dimitrov, "Ko vtoroi godovshchine geroicheskoi bor'by ispanskogo naroda," *KI* (July 1938), p. 21.

[23] Browder, *The People's Front*, p. 235.

The Great Reversal 1939–1941

VII

A STATEMENT OF POLICY

JOSEPH STALIN

Stalin's "Report on the Work of the Central Committee to the Eighteenth Congress of the Communist Party of the Soviet Union," March 10, 1939, is justly famous as a cautious indication that Soviet policy was preparing to veer toward friendship with Nazi Germany. It also provides a most revealing insight into the interpretation of international events which Stalin and his followers found acceptable at that moment. Finally, it embodies a typically Stalinist, numbered statement of Soviet foreign policy and of the party's tasks in the sphere of foreign policy.

HERE is a list of the most important events during the period under review which mark the beginning of the new imperialist war. In 1935 Italy attacked and seized Abyssinia. In the summer of 1936 Germany and Italy organized military intervention in Spain, Germany entrenching herself in the north of Spain and in Spanish Morocco, and Italy in the south of Spain and in the Balearic Islands. Having seized Manchuria, Japan in 1937 invaded North and Central China, occupied Peking, Tientsin and Shanghai and began to oust her foreign competitors from the occupied zone. In the beginning of 1938 Germany seized Austria, and in the autumn of 1938 the Sudeten region of Czechoslovakia. At the end of 1938 Japan seized Canton, and at the beginning of 1939 the Island of Hainan.

Thus the war, which has stolen so imperceptibly upon the nations, has drawn over five hundred million people into its orbit and has extended its sphere of action over a vast territory, stretching from Tientsin, Shanghai and Canton, through Abyssinia, to Gibraltar.

After the first imperialist war the victor states, primarily Britain, France and the United States, had set up a new regime in the relations between countries, the postwar regime of peace. The main props of this regime were the Nine-Power Pact in the Far East, and the Versailles Treaty and a number of other treaties in Europe. The League of Nations was set up to regulate relations between countries within the framework of this regime, on the basis of a united front of states, of collective defense of the security of states. However, three aggressive states, and the new imperialist war launched by them, have upset the entire system of this postwar peace regime. Japan

From J. Stalin, "Report on the Work of the Central Committee to the Eighteenth Congress of the CPSU(b)," March 10, 1939, *Problems of Leninism* (Moscow: Foreign Languages Publishing House, 1947), pp. 600–606.

tore up the Nine-Power Pact, and Germany and Italy the Versailles Treaty. In order to have their hands free, these three states withdrew from the League of Nations.

The new imperialist war became a fact.

It is not so easy in our day to suddenly break loose and plunge straight into war without regard for treaties of any kind or for public opinion. Bourgeois politicians know this very well. So do the fascist rulers. That is why the fascist rulers decided, before plunging into war, to frame public opinion to suit their ends, that is, to mislead it, to deceive it.

A military bloc of Germany and Italy against the interests of England and France in Europe? Bless us, do you call that a bloc? "We" have no military bloc. All "we" have is an innocuous "Berlin-Rome axis"; that is, just a geometrical equation for an axis. [*Laughter.*]

A military bloc of Germany, Italy and Japan against the interests of the United States, Great Britain and France in the Far East? Nothing of the kind! "We" have no military bloc. All "we" have is an innocuous "Berlin-Rome-Tokyo triangle"; that is, a slight penchant for geometry. [*General laughter.*]

A war against the interests of England, France, the United States? Nonsense! "We" are waging war on the Comintern, not on these states. If you don't believe it, read the "anti-Comintern pact" concluded between Italy, Germany and Japan.

That is how Messieurs the aggressors thought of framing public opinion, although it was not hard to see how preposterous this whole clumsy game of camouflage was; for it is ridiculous to look for Comintern "hotbeds" in the deserts of Mongolia, in the mountains of Abyssinia, or in the wilds of Spanish Morocco. [*Laughter.*]

But war is inexorable. It cannot be hidden under any guise. For no "axes," "triangles" or "anti-Comintern pacts" can hide the fact that in this period Japan has seized a vast stretch of territory in China,

that Italy has seized Abyssinia, that Germany has seized Austria and the Sudeten region, that Germany and Italy together have seized Spain—and all this in defiance of the interests of the non-aggressive states. The war remains a war; the military bloc of aggressors remains a military bloc; and the aggressors remain aggressors.

It is a distinguishing feature of the new imperialist war that it has not yet become universal, a world war. The war is being waged by aggressor states, who in every way infringe upon the interests of the non-aggressive states, primarily England, France and the U.S.A., while the latter draw back and retreat, making concession after concession to the aggressors.

Thus we are witnessing an open redivision of the world and spheres of influence at the expense of the non-aggressive states, without the least attempt at resistance, and even with a certain amount of connivance, on the part of the latter.

Incredible, but true.

To what are we to attribute this one-sided and strange character of the new imperialist war?

How is it that the non-aggressive countries, which possess such vast opportunities, have so easily, and without any resistance, abandoned their positions and their obligations to please the aggressors?

Is it to be attributed to the weakness of the non-aggressive states? Of course not! Combined, the non-aggressive, democratic states are unquestionably stronger than the fascist states, both economically and in the military sense.

To what then are we to attribute the systematic concessions made by these states to the aggressors?

It might be attributed, for example, to the fear that a revolution might break out if the non-aggressive states were to go to war and the war were to assume worldwide proportions. The bourgeois politicians know, of course, that the first imperialist world war led to the victory of the revolution in one of the largest countries. They are afraid that the second imperialist world war may also lead to the victory of the revolution in one or several countries.

But at present this is not the sole or even the chief reason. The chief reason is that the majority of the non-aggressive countries, particularly England and France, have rejected the policy of collective security, the policy of collective resistance to the aggressors, and have taken up a position of non-intervention, a position of "neutrality."

Formally speaking, the policy of non-intervention might be defined as follows: "Let each country defend itself from the aggressors as it likes and as best it can. That is not our affair. We shall trade both with the aggressors and with their victims." But actually speaking, the policy of non-intervention means conniving at aggression, giving free rein to war, and, consequently, transforming the war into a world war. The policy of non-intervention reveals an eagerness, a desire, not to hinder the aggressors in their nefarious work; not to hinder Japan, say, from embroiling herself in a war with China, or, better still, with the Soviet Union; not to hinder Germany, say, from enmeshing herself in European affairs, from embroiling herself in a war with the Soviet Union: to allow all the belligerents to sink deeply into the mire of war, to encourage them surreptitiously in this; to allow them to weaken and exhaust one another; and then, when they have become weak enough, to appear on the scene with fresh strength, to appear, of course, "in the interests of peace," and to dictate conditions to the enfeebled belligerents.

Cheap and easy!

Take Japan, for instance. It is characteristic that before Japan invaded North China all the influential French and British newspapers shouted about China's weakness and her inability to offer resistance, and declared that Japan with her army could subjugate China in two or three months.

Then the European and American politicians began to watch and wait. And then, when Japan started military operations, they let her have Shanghai, the vital center of foreign capital in China; they let her have Canton, a center of Britain's monopoly influence in South China; they let her have Hainan, and they allowed her to surround Hongkong. Does not this look very much like encouraging the aggressor? It is as though they were saying: "Embroil yourself deeper in war; then we shall see."

Or take Germany, for instance. They let her have Austria, despite the undertaking to defend her independence; they let her have the Sudeten region; they abandoned Czechoslovakia to her fate, thereby violating all their obligations; and then began to lie vociferously in the press about "the weakness of the Russian army," "the demoralization of the Russian air force," and "riots" in the Soviet Union, egging the Germans on to march farther east, promising them easy pickings, and prompting them: "Just start war on the Bolsheviks, and everything will be all right." It must be admitted that this too looks very much like egging on and encouraging the aggressor.

The hullabaloo raised by the British, French and American press over the Soviet Ukraine is characteristic. The gentlemen of the press there shouted until they were hoarse that the Germans were marching on Soviet Ukraine, that they now had what is called the Carpathian Ukraine, with a population of some seven hundred thousand, and that not later than this spring the Germans would annex the Soviet Ukraine, which has a population of over thirty million, to this so-called Carpathian Ukraine. It looks as if the object of this suspicious hullabaloo was to incense the Soviet Union against Germany, to poison the atmosphere and to provoke a conflict with Germany without any visible grounds.

It is quite possible, of course, that there are madmen in Germany who dream of annexing the elephant, that is, the Soviet

Ukraine, to the gnat, namely, the so-called Carpathian Ukraine. If there really are such lunatics in Germany, rest assured that we shall find enough strait jackets for them in our country. [*Thunderous applause.*] But if we ignore the madmen and turn to normal people, is it not clearly absurd and foolish to seriously talk of annexing the Soviet Ukraine to this so-called Carpathian Ukraine? Imagine: The gnat comes to the elephant and says perkily: "Ah, brother, how sorry I am for you. . . . Here you are without any landlords, without any capitalists, with no national oppression, without any fascist bosses. Is that a way to live? . . . As I look at you I can't help thinking that there is no hope for you unless you annex yourself to me. . . . [*General laughter.*] Well, so be it: I allow you to annex your tiny domain to my vast territories. . . ." [*General laughter and applause.*]

Even more characteristic is the fact that certain European and American politicians and pressmen, having lost patience waiting for "the march on the Soviet Ukraine," are themselves beginning to disclose what is really behind the policy of non-intervention. They are saying quite openly, putting it down in black and white, that the Germans have cruelly "disappointed" them, for instead of marching farther east, against the Soviet Union, they have turned, you see, to the west and are demanding colonies. One might think that the districts of Czechoslovakia were yielded to Germany as the price of an undertaking to launch war on the Soviet Union, but that now the Germans are refusing to meet their bills and are sending them to Hades.

Far be it from me to moralize on the policy of non-intervention, to talk of treason, treachery and so on. It would be naïve to preach morals to people who recognize no human morality. Politics is politics, as the old, case-hardened bourgeois diplomats say. It must be remarked, however, that the big and dangerous political game started by the supporters of the policy of non-intervention may end in a serious fiasco for them.

Such is the true face of the prevailing policy of non-intervention.

Such is the political situation in the capitalist countries.

THE SOVIET UNION AND THE CAPITALIST COUNTRIES

The war has created a new situation with regard to the relations between countries. It has enveloped them in an atmosphere of alarm and uncertainty. By undermining the postwar peace regime and overriding the elementary principles of international law, it has cast doubt on the value of international treaties and obligations. Pacifism and disarmament schemes are dead and buried. Feverish arming has taken their place. Everybody is arming, small states and big states, including primarily those which practice the policy of non-intervention. Nobody believes any longer in the unctuous speeches which claim that the Munich concessions to the aggressors and the Munich agreement opened a new era of "appeasement." They are disbelieved even by the signatories to the Munich agreement, Britain and France, who are increasing their armaments no less than other countries.

Naturally, the U.S.S.R. could not ignore these ominous events. There is no doubt that any war, however small, started by the aggressors in any remote corner of the world constitutes a danger to the peaceable countries. All the more serious then is the danger arising from the new imperialist war, which has already drawn into its orbit over five hundred million people in Asia, Africa and Europe. In view of this, while our country is unswervingly pursuing a policy of preserving peace, it is at the same time doing a great deal to increase the preparedness of our Red Army and our Red Navy.

At the same time, in order to

strengthen its international position, the Soviet Union decided to take certain other steps. At the end of 1934 our country joined the League of Nations, considering that despite its weakness the League might nevertheless serve as a place where aggressors can be exposed, and as a certain instrument of peace, however feeble, that might hinder the outbreak of war. The Soviet Union considers that in alarming times like these even so weak an international organization as the League of Nations should not be ignored. In May 1935 a treaty of mutual assistance against possible attack by aggressors was signed between France and the Soviet Union. A similar treaty was simultaneously concluded with Czechoslovakia. In March 1936 the Soviet Union concluded a treaty of mutual assistance with the Mongolian People's Republic. In August 1937 the Soviet Union concluded a pact of non-aggression with the Chinese Republic.

It was in such difficult international conditions that the Soviet Union pursued its foreign policy of upholding the cause of peace.

The foreign policy of the Soviet Union is clear and explicit.

1. We stand for peace and the strengthening of business relations with all countries. That is our position; and we shall adhere to this position as long as these countries maintain like relations with the Soviet Union, and as long as they make no attempt to trespass on the interests of our country.

2. We stand for peaceful, close and friendly relations with all the neighboring countries which have common frontiers with the U.S.S.R. That is our position; and we shall adhere to this position as long as these countries maintain like relations with the Soviet Union, and as long as they make no attempt to trespass, directly or indirectly, on the integrity and inviolability

of the frontiers of the Soviet state.

3. We stand for the support of nations which are the victims of aggression and are fighting for the independence of their country.

4. We are not afraid of the threats of aggressors, and are ready to deal two blows for every blow delivered by instigators of war who attempt to violate the Soviet borders.

Such is the foreign policy of the Soviet Union. [*Loud and prolonged applause.*]

In its foreign policy the Soviet Union relies upon:

1. Its growing economic, political and cultural might;

2. The moral and political unity of our Soviet society;

3. The mutual friendship of the nations of our country;

4. Its Red Army and Red Navy;

5. Its policy of peace;

6. The moral support of the working people of all countries, who are vitally concerned in the preservation of peace;

7. The good sense of the countries which for one reason or another have no interest in the violation of peace.

* * *

The tasks of the Party in the sphere of foreign policy are:

1. To continue the policy of peace and of strengthening business relations with all countries;

2. To be cautious and not allow our country to be drawn into conflicts by warmongers who are accustomed to have others pull the chestnuts out of the fire for them;

3. To strengthen the might of our Red Army and Red Navy to the utmost;

4. To strengthen the international bonds of friendship with the working people of all countries, who are interested in peace and friendship among nations.

THE NAZI-SOVIET PACT

EDWARD HALLETT CARR

After the Western nations' appeasement of Hitler at Munich (September 1938), Soviet policy-makers appear finally to have concluded that the achievement of an effective alliance with France and England was highly unlikely. The subsequent rapprochement between the two "natural" enemies, Nazi Germany and Communist Russia, was carried out by the most devious and circumspect maneuvering, marked by extreme suspiciousness on both sides. The Communists had come far along the road of formal and secret diplomacy since Trotsky's fiery revolutionary speeches at Brest-Litovsk. So successfully did they play England and France against Germany that when at last the pact was announced, there were loud cries of surprise and dismay from the West. The Soviet Union has provided very little detailed information about these negotiations. E. H. Carr's account, based primarily on Nazi-Soviet diplomatic exchanges captured in Germany and published by the United States Department of State, sets forth the main outlines of what we know about this crucial phase of Soviet foreign policy.

IN Soviet Russia, though the decision of November 1937 remained of course unknown, it had been an axiom since 1935 that Hitler would start a war somewhere in Europe. The bugbear of Soviet statesmen was that it might be a war between Hitler and Soviet Russia with the western Powers neutral or tacitly favourable to Hitler. In order to conjure this bugbear one of two main alternatives had to be envisaged: either a war against Germany in which Soviet Russia would be allied with the western Powers, or a war between Germany and the western Powers in which Soviet Russia would remain neutral or tacitly favourable to Germany. It is fundamental to an understanding of Soviet policy at this time that the Soviet leaders thought an aggressive war by Hitler certain, and were determined at all costs to avoid having to face Hitler alone. If the alliance with the west failed, then neutrality in a war between Germany and the west, or at the worst alliance with Hitler, were the only ways out. The first alternative—alliance with the west against Hitler—had been forced on the Soviet leaders by Hitler's implacable hostility rather than spontaneously

chosen by them. But, once adopted, this line was consistently pursued from 1934 to 1938, both through the League of Nations and through specific pacts such as those with France and Czechoslovakia. At intervals during this time—and particularly in the first half of 1937 when the purges were at their height—circumstantial rumours circulated of approaches made to Hitler by secret emissaries of Stalin in the hope of healing the breach. Nothing to confirm these rumours has been found in any German documents captured in 1945; and, if such approaches occurred, they did not deflect the main line of Soviet policy.

What caused a change of atmosphere to set in during 1938 was the growth of doubts as to the willingness of the western Powers to enter into effective alliance with Soviet Russia. The vacillations of the west in face of Mussolini's aggression against Abyssinia and Hitler's coup in the Rhineland created in Moscow exactly the same impression of weakness as they created in Berlin. Developments in Great Britain during the winter of 1937-1938 intensified these fears which received their fullest confirmation in the Munich crisis of September

From E. H. Carr, *German-Soviet Relations Between the Two World Wars, 1919–1939* (Baltimore, 1951), pp. 123–135. Reprinted by permission of the Johns Hopkins Press.

1938. At the height of the crisis a leading article in *Pravda*—the first for many weeks on foreign affairs—struck almost casually in its last paragraph a new note:

> The Soviet Union examines with composure the question which particular imperialist robber stretches out his hand for this or that colony or vassal state; for it sees no difference between German and English robbers. But the "democratic" states in western Europe cannot regard these questions with indifference. In consenting to the dismemberment of Czechoslovakia, in blessing this dismemberment, England and France are playing with fire.

To see "no difference between English and German robbers" was the first hint of a potential shift from a policy of cooperation with the west to a policy of neutrality —a reversion to the old habit of regarding all imperialist Powers as equally wicked. Having dropped this barely audible hint, the Soviet press returned to its advocacy of a common front against Hitler, and approvingly quoted Litvinov's speech at the League of Nations in which he had declared that Soviet Russia would fulfill her obligations "in all ways available to us"—a hint at the opposition of Poland and Rumania to the passage of Soviet forces across their territories. Then on September 29, 1938, the Munich agreement was concluded without further consultation with the Soviet Government. No overt move was made. But the chagrin felt in Moscow was not concealed, and the conclusions were left to ripen.

Thus, at a time when Hitler was still undecided whether to move first against the east or against the west, and was bound to weigh the contingency, if he decided to move west, of having to patch up his tattered relations with Soviet Russia, Soviet Russia was also being driven to contemplate the apparent bankruptcy of her western policy and the necessity, if this were confirmed, of coming to terms with Hitler. It is a tribute to the depth and tenacity of the ill feeling between the two countries that it

took so long to bridge the gulf between them. The denunciations of Bolshevism in Hitler's Nuremberg speech in September 1938 were far less vitriolic than those of the previous year. After Munich, Hitler's increasingly bitter references to the west were matched by a corresponding diminution of acrimony, quantitive and qualitative, in regard to Soviet Russia. In October 1938 Schulenburg, the German Ambassador in Moscow, apparently on his own initiative, suggested an agreement to keep the names and personalities of Hitler and Stalin out of the mutual press polemics; and both sides rather unexpectedly agreed to this. The prelude to the events of the spring and summer of 1939 was a speech by Stalin at the party congress on March 10th, 1939. This speech was an extraordinarily astute exercise in political tight-rope walking, from which it would be rash to draw any confident conclusion other than the indeterminate and embarrassed state of Soviet foreign policy at the time. Only about one-sixth of the whole speech was devoted to the subject, but the passage was placed at the beginning of the speech to indicate its importance. Stalin began by stating that an imperialist war was already in progress, and naming Japan, Germany and Italy as aggressors:

> The three aggressive states and the imperialist war started by them have turned upside down the whole system of the post-war regime. . . . The aggressor states carry on war everywhere injuring the interests of the non-aggressive states, primarily England, France and the U.S.A., and the latter give ground and retreat, making one concession after another to the aggressors.

This attack on the aggressors was, however, carefully balanced by an attack on England and France, whose abandonment of collective security in favour of "non-intervention" and "neutrality" was, in Stalin's words, tantamount to saying: "Let every country defend itself against the aggressor as it will and can, our interest is not at stake, we shall bargain both with the aggressors and with their victims." This was "something very like encouragement of the aggresssor," and was equal to saying to Germany: "Start a war with the Bolsheviks and all will be well." Stalin concluded the foreign policy section of his speech by laying down four tasks for the party:

(1) To carry out and continue a policy of peace and strengthening commercial relations with all countries;
(2) To observe caution and not to allow our country to be drawn into war by warmongers who are accustomed to "rake the fire with other people's hands";
(3) By all means to strengthen the fighting powers of our Red Army and Red Fleet;
(4) To strengthen the international ties of friendship with the workers of all countries who are interested in peace and friendship between nations.

In spite of a divergence in the Russian idiom, the second of these items contained an obvious echo of the current American accusation against Great Britain of expecting others to "pull her chestnuts out of the fire for her"; this was its main significance.

Statesmen, like private individuals, sometimes betray the subconscious processes of their own minds by the motives which they attribute to others. In retrospect the most striking sentence in the speech was perhaps the one in which Stalin summed up his diagnosis of the attitude of the western Powers: "Let every country defend itself against the aggressor as it will and can, our interest is not at stake, we shall bargain with the aggressors and with their victims." Stalin's speech of March 10th, 1939, clearly did not announce any positive decision of Soviet policy; what it did was to keep all options open and to hint more plainly than before that they were open. Five days after the speech Hitler occupied Prague; and on March 18th, 1939, encouraged no doubt by the more vigorous reaction of British opinion and (after two days' hesitation) of the British Government to this coup, the Soviet Government handed to the German Ambassador in Moscow an exceedingly strong note, which was published, protesting against the German action and refusing to recognize the incorporation of the Czech lands in the Reich. Some tentative exchanges now occurred between the Soviet and British Governments. But a Soviet proposal for an immediate conference of the anti-Fascist Powers at Bukharest to concert military measures was rejected by Great Britain; and a British proposal for a pact between Great Britain, France, Soviet Russia and Poland for mutual consultation in the event of an act of aggression, though accepted by Moscow, was rejected by Poland. A British minister, who was in Moscow at the time for trade talks, declined to enter into any political discussions. Then on March 31, 1939, without any further approach to the Soviet Government, Great Britain gave to Poland a unilateral guarantee to come to her assistance if she were attacked. In the circumstances, the Soviet Government could hardly fail to deduce that Great Britain preferred the Polish to the Soviet alliance, and desired, as at Munich, to keep Soviet Russia out of major discussions affecting the peace of Europe.

The first formal step toward a Soviet *rapprochement* with Germany came a fortnight later in the form of an interview of the Soviet Ambassador in Berlin, Merekalov, with the German State-Secretary, Weizsäcker, on April 17th, 1939. Having discussed a routine question, Merekalov led the conversation to political matters and, after some beating about the bush, bluntly asked Weizsäcker what he thought of German-Russian relations. Weizsäcker cautiously observed that "the Russian press was not fully participating in the anti-German tone of the American and some of the English papers" and hinted at a similar restraint in the German press in regard to Russia. Thus encouraged Merekalov made the following statement:

Russian policy had always moved in a straight line. Ideological differences of opinion had hardly influenced the Italian-Russian relationship, and they did not have to prove a stumbling block with regard to Germany either. Soviet Russia had not exploited the present friction between Germany and the western democracies against us, nor did she desire to do so. There exists for Russia no reason why she should not live with us on a normal footing. And from normal, the relations might become better and better.

This rather clumsy confidential approach was followed by an exchange of public gestures. The first sign came in Hitler's speech of April 28, 1939, which was devoted to an attack on Poland; contrary to custom, it contained no word of abuse of Bolshevism or of Russia. The significance of this omission was underlined some days later by a prominent Nazi to a member of the French Embassy; and it seems not unlikely that a similar hint had already been conveyed to the Soviet Embassy by way of rejoinder to the *démarche* of April 17, 1939. The answer followed promptly. On May 3, 1939, Litvinov resigned the office of People's Commissar for Foreign Affairs and was succeeded by Molotov. Litvinov had been closely associated with the policy of collective security and was a Jew. The sudden decision, as officials correctly proclaimed, did not in itself herald a change of policy. Since Stalin's speech of March 10, 1939, had made it clear that two options were open, the presence at the head of Narkomindel of a commissar so publicly and conspicuously committed to one of them had become an anomaly; in this sense the change was a gesture of friendliness to Germany. Lest its significance be lost, Astakhov, the Soviet chargé d'affaires in Berlin, in the words of a German report, "tried without asking questions to learn" from the German Foreign Office on May 5 "whether this event would cause a change in our position toward the Soviet Union."

The next three months—May, June and July—saw the forefront of the stage occupied by the increasingly involved and difficult Soviet negotiations with Britain and France, negotiations with Germany being relegated to the twilight of secret diplomacy in the background. They advanced with a slowness which testified to the depth of mutual suspicion. On May 20, 1939, the new Commissar for Foreign Affairs received the German Ambassador for the first time. After a discussion about economic affairs, Molotov observed that "the Soviet Government could only agree to a resumption of the (economic) negotiations if the necessary 'political bases' for them had been constructed." Schulenburg, having tried in vain to probe what lay behind these words, took his leave: "Herr Molotov had apparently determined to say just so much and no more." The German Foreign Office, apprised of this conversation, replied on the following day that "we must now sit tight and wait to see if the Russians will speak more openly." It soon transpired, however, that Molotov's taciturnity had won the first round of this waiting game. At a conference on May 23, 1939, disclosed at the Nuremberg trials, Hitler announced his intention "to attack Poland at the first suitable opportunity"; and into the next few days we can now fit an episode described by Gaus, legal adviser to the German Foreign Office, in his Nuremberg affidavit. Gaus and Weizsäcker were summoned to Ribbentrop's country house, and informed that Hitler wanted "to establish more tolerable relations between Germany and the USSR." Some pretext should be found in the way of current affairs to explore the possibility of political talks: it was decided to use for this purpose the question of Soviet consular representation in Prague. Draft instructions to Schulenburg were prepared, but when submitted to Hitler were found to be "too explicit." His hesitations were apparently due to Chamberlain's highly optimistic statement in the House of Commons on May 24 that agreement on essentials had been reached between Soviet Russia and the western

Powers. A rebuff was now feared, and a more cautious approach decided on. On May 30, 1939, Weizsäcker sent for Astakhov and, after broaching the questions of the Prague consulate and the economic negotiations, expressed agreement with "Herr Molotov" that "politics and economics could not be entirely separated in our relations," reverted to the Soviet Ambassador's remarks in April about the "normalization and even further improvement of German-Russian political relations," and, having "changed over to a purely conversational tone," remarked *inter alia* that "the development of our relations with Poland . . . had actually made our hitherto restricted policy in the east freer." So far as the records show, this would-be subtle approach produced no visible effect. For a month discussions with Germany about economic negotiations proceeded without results. In interviews with Molotov on June 29 and July 3 Schulenburg still struggled in vain to secure from the costive commissar some amplification of his phrase of May 20 about "political bases." At the first of these conversations Molotov was particularly spiky; a reference by Schulenburg to Germany's non-aggression treaties with the Baltic states provoked the retort that "he had to doubt the permanence of such treaties after the experience which Poland had had." The impression left by these records is partly of a holding back for tactical reasons but also partly of a profound and ineradicable mistrust of German policy in the minds of the Soviet leaders.

It was not till the end of July that the ice began to melt; and this was plainly connected on the Soviet side with the deadlock in the political negotiations with Britain and France and the visit to London of a German economic commission headed by Wohltat. On July 22 it was announced that Soviet-German trade negotiations had been resumed in Berlin. The Germans now decided to speak more frankly, but through an informal channel. Schnurre, the German trade expert, was instructed to invite Asta-

khov and Babanin, the head of the Soviet trade delegation, to dinner; and the conversation, which took place on July 27, ranged far. For the first time the alternative was clearly put:

What could England offer Russia? At best, participation in a European war and the hostility of Germany, but not a single desirable end for Russia. What could we offer on the other hand? Neutrality and staying out of a possible European conflict, and if Moscow wished, a German-Russian understanding on mutual interests which, just as in former times, would work out to the advantage of both countries.

Three days later Weizsäcker in an instruction to Schulenburg added some further precision:

In any development of the Polish question, either in a peaceful manner as we desire it or in any other way that is forced on us, we would be prepared to safeguard all Soviet interests and to reach an understanding with the Moscow government. If the talk proceeds positively in the Baltic question too, the idea could be advanced that we will adjust our stand with regard to the Baltic in such a manner as to respect the vital Soviet interests in the Baltic.

Thus armed, Schulenburg had a conversation on August 3 with Molotov, who seems to have spoken most fully and eloquently on Germany's support of "the aggressive attitude of Japan towards the Soviet Union." An undeclared frontier war in the Far East between Soviet Russia and Japan had been in progress since May 1939, and had a substantial influence on the Soviet-German negotiations. If the avoidance of a war on two fronts was the compelling motive of the Germans in the *rapprochement* with Russia, it was also constantly present in the thoughts of the Soviet negotiators. Schulenburg's summary of the situation after the conversation was as follows:

My overall impression is that the Soviet Government is at present determined to sign with England and France if they fulfill all Soviet wishes. Negotiations, to be sure, might still last a long time, especially since mistrust of England is still great. I believe that my statements made an impression on M.; it will nevertheless take a considerable effort on our part to cause the Soviet Government to swing about.

But by this time the race between the two bidders for Soviet friendship had become altogether uneven; the impression could not be avoided at Moscow that one side was trying very hard and the other side not trying at all. This impression was merely strengthened by the undistinguished galaxy of military, naval and air talent which constituted the Anglo-French military mission, and by their choice of the slow sea route for their journey to Moscow—which seemed yet another public demonstration of a fundamental lack of interest on the British side. The military conversations began on August 12 and proceeded uneventfully till, on the third day, Voroshilov punctured the whole pretence by openly raising the unsolved question—the hidden crux of the whole negotiation—of the passage of Soviet troops across Polish territory in the event of German aggression, adding that it was useless to continue the discussions till that was settled. This move was clearly intended as a sign-off. On August 12 Astakhov in Berlin had conveyed the agreement of the Soviet Government to a conference in Moscow to discuss Soviet-German relations; and two days later Ribbentrop telegraphed his own readiness to come to Moscow. "An extended conference with Stalin" was the only condition laid down.

With the game in the bag, the Soviet Government could afford to keep the Germans on the doorstep; and the last stages still betray a strong element of mistrust in Moscow. After a further exhibition of the hedging and stalling in which Molotov was a master, the Soviet Government on August 19 agreed to a visit "one week after the

proclamation of the signing of the economic agreement." This was still too slow for the German military programme. Impatience at Berlin was expressed in a shower of telegrams and a personal message of August 20 from the Führer to "Herr Stalin," begging that "my Foreign Minister" should be received on August 22 or at the latest on August 23. Thus pressed Stalin accepted the second date. Ribbentrop arrived in Moscow on August 23, and the non-aggression pact and secret protocol were signed the same evening. The protocol fixed the division between Soviet and German spheres of influence "in the event of a territorial and political transformation of these areas," in the Baltic states along the northern frontier of Lithuania (Molotov particularly stressed Soviet interest in the ice-free ports of Windau and Libau, and Hitler was consulted by telephone before agreement was given) and in Poland along the line of the Narew, Vistula and San; the Soviet Government affirmed its interest, the German Government its "political disinterestedness," in Bessarabia. On the next day Ribbentrop returned to Berlin. The British and French military missions bowed themselves out of Moscow thirty-six hours later; and on August 27 Molotov pronounced to the French Ambassador his obituary on the negotiations:

The Soviet Government, having found that, in spite of the efforts of the three governments, the obstinate refusal of Poland made impossible a tripartite pact of mutual assistance, had for its part to settle the question by concluding a non-aggression pact with Germany. . . . A great country like the USSR could not beg Poland to accept help which she did not want at any price.

In his speech to the Supreme Soviet on August 31st, 1939, Molotov also named Polish objections as the chief cause of the breakdown. On the next day the German assault on Poland, and with it the second world war, began.

THE DIPLOMATIC ROAD TO WAR

ISAAC DEUTSCHER

Having signed the Nazi-Soviet Pact, the two new allies found it impossible to get along with one another. The story of the swift deterioration of relations leading up to Hitler's invasion of Russia on June 22, 1941, is brilliantly narrated here by Isaac Deutscher. These events have long been a focus of controversy, for their interpretation is made difficult by a dearth of Soviet evidence. Although Mr. Deutscher is thoroughly justified in puzzling over Stalin's conduct and motives, particularly in the early months of 1941, it may be that as Stalin's biographer he somewhat overestimates Stalin's ability to influence the course of international events and the economic-military situation at home. An inexorable chain of events in the West thwarted Stalin's diplomatic and organizational efforts. Heroic British resistance to Hitler through early 1940 forced the German Führer to give up his plans to invade England and to decide, in July 1940, upon a move against Russia. Though the signs thereafter were easy to read, and though Stalin was repeatedly warned that invasion was coming, there was little he could do. Hampered by domestic, economic, and political conditions, and by an army recently purged of its leaders and disgraced by its Finnish campaign, he could only continue his efforts to delay war as long as possible and hope for some development on the world scene that might offer him a new loophole.

STALIN's first, not very important, miscalculation was already apparent in the first days of September. He was surprised by the rapidity with which Polish armed resistance collapsed. When, on 5 September, Ribbentrop began to press the Russians to march into their share of Poland, Stalin was not yet ready to issue the marching orders. He was now given over to scruples and second thoughts. He would not openly lend a hand in defeating Poland, and he refused to budge before Poland's collapse was complete beyond doubt. His second thoughts concerned the fixed demarcation line which left part of ethnical Poland on the Russian side. This he was in no mood now to annex, for that would be too flagrant a violation of the professed principles of Bolshevik policy. He now preferred to shift the demarcation line farther east, from the Vistula to the Bug, so that only lands with a predominantly Ukrainian and Byelorussian population should be left on the Russian side. The

reunion of those lands with the Soviet Ukraine and Byelorussia could be politically justified. It would permit the Red Army to cross the frontier not as a conqueror of Poland but as the liberator of the Ukrainians and the Byelorussians, the "blood brethren" as he now called them, having caught a germ of racialism from his Nazi partners. While Stalin delayed action, Ribbentrop began blackmailing him with a political "vacuum" in eastern Poland, in which "new states" might spring into being. The "new states" could be headed only by anti-Soviet Ukrainian nationalists. Hitler also objected to a communiqué proposed by Stalin, which was to state that the Red Army had crossed the border to protect the Ukrainians and the Byelorussians from the Nazis. Meanwhile, Stalin became uneasy as he saw the Wehrmacht operating already in eastern Poland; and he asked the German Asbassador for a reassurance that it would withdraw from there. For a while he reflected whether a

From *Stalin: A Political Biography* by Isaac Deutscher, pp. 441–460. Copyright 1949 by Oxford University Press, Inc. Reprinted by permission, with some of the author's footnotes omitted.

Polish rump state should not be set up. Then he gave up the idea and issued the marching orders for the Red Army.

At the end of September Ribbentrop was again in the Kremlin, banqueting all night and listening to Stalin's second thoughts. A new bargain was made: Germany retained the whole of ethnical Poland, and Lithuania was allotted to the Soviet zone.

Impressed by Hitler's lightning victory over Poland, Stalin lost much of his self-confidence. The phoney war in the west made him apprehensive: were the British and the French not holding back their fire in order to encourage Hitler to attack Russia? Now it was he who was zealously offering friendly services to Hitler. The pact of non-aggression was supplemented by a treaty of friendship, which declared that it was an exclusive Russo-German task "to re-establish peace and order" in Poland and "to assure to the peoples living there a peaceful life in keeping with their national character." The western powers had no right to dispute German and Russian acquisitions. Gone was Stalin's cool reserve. Before the whole world he now assumed co-responsibility for the horrors of the Nazi occupation of Poland. He showed himself not merely Hitler's business partner, but also his accomplice. In a special secret protocol both governments obliged themselves to work hand in hand to suppress Polish propaganda for the restoration of Poland's independence. Crowning the work was a joint declaration which called for immediate peace and shifted responsibility for the continuation of war on England and France. In lending his support to this "peace offensive" of Hitler's, Stalin surpassed himself in hypocrisy. Nobody was now praying for the prolongation of war more ardently than he. If the western powers had now concluded an armistice and acquiesced in the German conquest of Poland, Hitler would probably have attacked Russia in the summer of 1940.

This dissimulation was to characterize Stalin's behaviour towards Hitler right up to June 1941: the more acutely he distrusted the Führer and feared his aggression, the louder and the more ostentatious were his declarations of friendship. His talk grew less friendly and his gestures stiffer whenever Hitler's forces seemed to be pinned down far from Russia's frontiers. There was to be give and take in their deal. Stalin, of course, wished to give as little as possible and take as much as he could. Russia was to supply Germany with grain and raw materials and to receive German machines and machine tools. One of the first things Stalin did, after the conclusion of the pact, was to dispatch his military missions to Germany. With what avidity those missions tried, in the first flush of friendship, to ferret out the German war factories can be seen from the complaints about their "excessive curiosity," which Göring, Keitel, and Räder were already lodging at the beginning of October. A little later the Nazi economic leaders complained that the Russians wanted too many machine tools for the production of artillery and too much other war material.

No sooner had the Polish campaign been finished than Stalin began to cast uneasy glances at the vast no-man's land that lay between Russia and Germany. Since August, in fact, the Baltic countries had ceased to be a no-man's land. In September and October Russian troops were already garrisoned in Estonia, Latvia, and Lithuania. The three countries still retained their old regimes and governments; and Stalin acted as if he had no intention of doing more than secure strategic bases. For the first time he now betrayed a passing anxiety about the Balkans, the real no-man's land. In October, Molotov asked the Bulgarians to conclude an alliance with Russia. The Bulgarians refused, and Stalin did not pursue the matter. His attention was now absorbed by the embarrassing conflict with Finland, which had refused to grant Russia strategic bases, needed for the defence of Leningrad, or to regard herself as part of the Russian sphere of influence.

The Russo-Finnish war broke out on 30 November, 1939. That military expediency should impel Stalin to wage this war was one of history's malicious whims: for it was he who had, in the first week after the October Revolution, proclaimed Finland's independence. The Finns now defended themselves tooth and nail. At first the war brought them important successes. These were in part due to accidents of climate and in part to the weakness of the Russian command after the recent purges. Russia's prestige and bargaining power sharply declined for a time. The adventure threatened grave complications. In Britain and France sympathy for Finland ran high; the two allied Governments officially promised military aid; armies of volunteers were recruited in both countries; and, while an uncanny calm reigned over the Siegfried Line and the Maginot Line, the French Government announced that a numerous army under General Weygand was concentrated in the Middle East, opposite Russia's vulnerable Caucasian frontier. On 14 December Russia was expelled from the League of Nations, which had always been so indulgent towards the Third Reich and Fascist Italy. Stalin had some ground for wondering whether the western powers were not going to "switch" the war from Germany to Russia. The Finnish game was not worth the candle; but he was so deeply involved that he could not withdraw from it. It was in this mood of uncertainty that he celebrated his sixtieth birthday in December 1939. He used the opportunity to assure Hitler of his friendship in a manner as ridiculous as it was unworthy: "The friendship of the peoples of Germany and the Soviet Union," he cabled Hitler in reply to a birthday message, "cemented by blood, has every reason to be lasting and firm."[1] How much would Stalin have given later to have this phrase deleted from the records.

In March 1940 the Finnish war was over. The prestige of Russian arms was in part restored. Hitler was now preparing his invasions in western Europe; and the fear of a "stab in the back" from Stalin was probably not completely absent from his mind. Once again the two changed roles. On 28 March Ribbentrop cabled his ambassador in Moscow: "The Führer will not only be particularly happy to welcome Stalin in Berlin, but he would also see to it that he would get a reception commensurate with his position and importance. And he would extend to him all the honours that the occasion demanded."[2] Stalin was in no hurry to receive the honours or, like another Duce, to review parades by Hitler's side. Not even Molotov hastened to accept the invitation. Count von Schulenburg sweetened the pill for the Führer and explained Stalin's reserve by his "inhibitions against appearing in strange surroundings."[3]

Soon came the events that gave Stalin the rudest shock—the rapid collapse and surrender of France and the withdrawal of the British from the Continent. Stalin's strategic calculations, too, now collapsed. Fearing a *tête-à-tête* with Hitler in Europe, he bolted the Baltic door to Russia without a moment's delay. Distrusting the Baltic governments, who looked ideologically to Berlin rather than to Moscow, he dispatched Zhdanov to Estonia, Vyshinsky to Latvia, and Dekanozov to Lithuania, with orders to overthrow the governments on the spot, to set up new Communist-controlled administrations and to prepare the incorporation of the three republics in the Soviet Union.

A new and important shift thus occurred in Stalin's foreign policy. His first move in the Baltic lands, the establishment of bases, had been dictated solely by strategic expediency. He had apparently had no

---

[1] *Pravda*, December 25, 1939.

[2] R. J. Sontag and J. S. Beddie, eds., *Nazi-Soviet Relations, 1939–1941* (Washington, D. C., 1948), p. 135.

[3] *Ibid.*, p. 136.

intention of tampering with their social system. His sense of danger, heightened and intensified by the collapse of France, now impelled him to stage revolutions in the three small countries. For the first time he now departed, in a small way, from his own doctrine of socialism in one country, the doctrine that he had so relentlessly inculcated into a whole Russian generation. He departed from it in the same unpremeditated, pragmatic manner in which he had arrived at it. But what he did was very different from the spread of revolution of which the old Bolsheviks had dreamt. He carried revolution abroad on the point of the bayonet or rather on the caterpillars of his tanks. The Baltic working classes probably supported the socialization of industry he decreed; but what was decisive was Russia's armed power, not the popular sentiment on the spot. The old Bolsheviks had, as a rule, imagined revolution primarily as a popular movement, as the work of the toiling masses, organized and led by their own party. Now, the Red Army substituted itself for that party. The upheaval was a mechanical by-product of the strategy of a great power.

Such upheavals could hardly have been carried through in any great or even medium-sized country, whose social organism pulsated with its own life blood. The three tiny republics with their expensive, comic-opera police regimes, were simply crushed by the stirring of their great neighbour. They had owed their existence in part to Russia's weakness in 1918 and in part to early Bolshevik generosity. Stalin's Russia was neither weak nor generous; and so Stalin appeared on the Baltic coast as the collector of old Russian possessions, the claimant to a portion of the Tsarist patrimony. *Vis-à-vis* the outside world he, now, in 1940, impersonated that role for the first time. The September before he still shrank before the annexation of a slice of ethnical Poland which had belonged to the Tsars and he had contented himself with lands to which Russia's ethnical claim was at least

as valid as Poland's. Now he annexed the Baltic states to which Russia neither had nor pretended to have any ethnical claim whatsoever. Yet he could not openly refer to the Tsarist title-deeds—Bolshevik orthodoxy still forbade him to do that. Nor did that orthodoxy allow him to admit that he was overruling the will of small and weak neighbours for strategic reasons, for, by Leninist standards, this smacked of imperialism. To save appearances, he falsified the popular will and staged plebiscites, in which Estonians, Latvians, and Lithuanians begged to be absorbed in the Soviet Union. His conduct was not more reprehensible than that of any other leader of a great power holding fast to or seizing strategic bases. But in appearance it was more odious, because it contrasted so sharply with the principles he professed and because he resorted to such crude tricks to cover up that contrast.[4]

Throughout the summer he watched vigilantly Hitler's reaction to the sovietization of the Baltic states. On the whole, Hitler still kept his part of the bargain and did not interfere. Nor did he put obstacles in Stalin's way when Stalin detached Bessarabia and northern Bukovina from Rumania. These were the last acts of their smooth cooperation.

Late in the summer of 1940, during the Battle of Britain, Stalin's tactics became even more tortuous than hitherto. He was still sceptical about Hitler's victories, sweeping and overwhelming as these

[4] Stalin's treatment of Finland was, of course, different. By the peace of 1940 Finland had ceded the strategic bases demanded from her, but she was not then absorbed in the Soviet Union. In part this was due to the Finn's own attitude—an attempt to absorb their country might have led to another war —and to the sympathy which the west had shown for their fight. In part, however, Stalin's exceptional "mildness" toward Finland, now and in 1945, may have been due to the fact that he himself had proclaimed her independence. This had been his first important appearance as Commissar of Nationalities. To this feat he may have looked back with enough pride and sentiment to prevent his disavowing his own pledge.

were; but he apparently also reckoned with the possibility of Britain's surrender. At any rate, he did his best to give Hitler the impression that he, Stalin, believed Hitler's triumph to be almost final and that Russia was ready to adjust herself to, and to settle down in, the Nazi "new order." Soon after the French surrender, Molotov, knowing well that his words would at once be reported to Hitler, told the Italian Ambassador that his Government regarded the war as nearly finished and that Russia's main interest was now in the Balkans, where she wanted to spread her influence to Bulgaria and to deprive Turkey of exclusive control over the Straits. Ostensibly, Stalin was thus claiming his share in the spoils of Hitler's "final" victory. Actually, his claims were dictated by his fear of German encirclement in the south. To Hitler they looked like Russian attempts at the encirclement of Germany. Jockeying for positions in the Balkans filled the second year of their *soi-disant* friendship.

While to Hitler Stalin was expressing confidence in a rapid conclusion of the war, his diplomatic envoys and agents abroad encouraged every sign of resistance to the "new order." The newspapers of Moscow, which hitherto had only disparaging remarks for the allies, began to report sympathetically the Battle of Britain and to call upon French patriots to resist the subjugation of their country. Even before this the German Foreign Office had had to protest against the anti-Nazi propaganda in which Madame Kollontai, the Soviet Minister in Sweden, had indulged.

Such sallies, however, were made stealthily or by people for whom Stalin could disclaim responsibility. The dominant tone was still one of friendship for Germany. Above all Stalin carefully avoided giving Hitler the impression that he was seeking contact with Great Britain, Hitler's only enemy erect and fighting. On the other hand, he had every reason to keep in touch with the British. In the beginning of July 1940 he personally received the new British Ambassador, Sir Stafford Cripps, an honour which, since Ribbbentrop's visit, he had bestowed on no other foreign envoy. The new Ambassador had distinguished himself as a champion of Anglo-Russian friendship; and his appointment was a mark of the importance that Winston Churchill even now attached to good relations with Russia. It was as awkward for Stalin to acknowledge this gesture as not to do so. He listened to the British Ambassador on the danger that German imperialism spelt to Russia, a danger of which he was only too well aware, and—this was more novel—on Russia's exclusive right to maintain the *status quo* in the Balkans and to safeguard her interests in the Straits and in the Black Sea. But he refused to show his hand. He denied that there was any German threat to Russia and rejected the suggestion of Russia's exclusive rights in the Balkans, though he confirmed his desire for a new settlement in the Straits. Wary of dropping a single word that could be interpreted as an expression of sympathy, he talked in an evasive though not unfriendly manner. He held that it was natural for the British to want to embroil Russia with Germany and that a single incautious phrase of his, especially if it were reported in the British newspapers, might precipitate the Russo-German conflict. He carried his caution so far as to instruct Molotov to give Count Schulenburg an appropriate version of his conversation with the British Ambassador. In that version Stalin was reported to have talked much more harshly than he did and to have uttered flattering remarks about "leading German statesmen."

Even before the Battle of Britain was over, the competition between Russia and Germany for the Balkan no-man's land became open. Without consulting the Kremlin, Hitler drew new frontiers for Hungary and Rumania. He also gave Rumania a guarantee of her changed frontiers, which was implicitly directed against Russia. German troops appeared in Rumania and in Finland. When Molotov protested against these breaches of previous agreements, he was told that the Wehrmacht had moved into the two countries to forestall the "English menace." Throughout the no-man's land points of friction multiplied. Eastern and south-eastern Europe was rapidly becoming too small to hold both Hitler and Stalin; and it was Hitler who was saying: *ôte-toi pour que je m'y mette.*

Stalemated in the war against Britain, Hitler could no longer look with indifference on the might of the Red Army in the east. He could now remain at peace with Russia only if Stalin agreed to join his camp and thus become his satellite. He made an attempt to reduce Stalin to that role, trying to make it as attractive as possible. "In the opinion of the Führer . . . ," Ribbentrop wrote to "My dear Herr Stalin" on 13 October 1940, ". . . it appears to be the historical mission of . . . the Soviet Union, Italy, Japan, and Germany to adopt a long range policy" and to carry out a "delimitation of their interests on a world-wide scale."[5] Hitler did not repeat his once rejected invitation to Stalin. Instead, he asked Molotov to come to Berlin and let Ribbentrop try to fix a date to talk with Stalin in the Kremlin. Assuming that the proposal for a pact of four powers would be accepted, Ribbentrop informed Stalin that he was ready to come to Moscow for the great occasion, along with Japanese and Italian envoys.

To Ribbentrop's long and bombastic message Stalin replied briefly, drily, and with a week's delay. He was not "in principle" opposed to Ribbentrop's suggestion, but would not be rushed. He was willing to send Molotov to Berlin and to see Ribbentrop in Moscow, but "joint deliberations with the Japanese and the Italians" must—the favourite excuse again!—be preceded by much "previous examination."[6] From the accounts of Molotov's behaviour in Berlin it is easy to infer how Stalin

[5] Sontag and Beddie, *Nazi-Soviet Relations*, p. 213.
[6] *Ibid.*, p. 216.

briefed him for the mission: Molotov was to listen attentively, with a friendly mien, to all suggestions, to accept no new commitments, and to bargain hard over Balkan stakes.   .

The tale with which Molotov returned from Berlin was briefly this: Hitler in person had repeated the proposal for the pact of four powers, evidently hoping that Russia's adherence might move Britain to surrender. Russia would be rewarded with a portion of the British Empire, that "gigantic world-wide estate in bankruptcy, of forty million square kilometres." The four powers that would partition the "bankrupt estate" should stop quarrelling among themselves. The Führer held that in the long run, the interests of Germany, Russia, Japan, and Italy required expansion in one direction only—southward. Germany and Italy would build their colonial empires in Africa; Japan was building hers in south Asia; and Russia should expand in the direction of India. Molotov had tried hard to turn the conversation from the alluring vistas painted by Hitler to smaller matters nearer home. To him one Balkan bird in the hand was worth all the oriental birds in all the bushes of the British Empire. He tried to get Hitler to disentangle the Russian and the German spheres of influence in south-eastern Europe. In this he failed.

The step that Stalin now took was of the gravest consequence. It amounted to a rejection of Hitler's proposals. Nominally, he agreed to join in the pact of the four powers, but before he did so he wanted Hitler to withdraw troops from Finland, to recognize that Bulgaria belonged to the Russian sphere of influence, to help Russia in obtaining a long-term lease of bases in the Straits, and so on. Hitler could have accepted such terms only if he had given up all plans to attack Russia and if he himself had not feared any Russian attack. Neither was the case. The idea of a four-power pact was dropped and never mentioned again. Three weeks after he had received Stalin's reply Hitler gave his chiefs of staff his first instruction on the campaign against Russia, the directive "Barbarossa."

In the first few months of 1941 Russia was completely squeezed out of the Balkans; and the Kremlin vented its displeasure. In January it suddenly announced that it had not been consulted about the entry of German troops to Bulgaria and had not agreed to it. In March the protest was repeated in even blunter terms. Every sign of opposition to Hitler was now encouraged. The Yugoslav Ambassador in Moscow, Gavrilovich, was received at the Kremlin "as a brother; there he discussed, plotted and signed agreements in all confidence. Stalin . . . had himself photographed at his side and . . . discussed the friendly prospects with him throughout the night. 'And if the Germans, displeased, turn against you?' . . . asked the Yugoslav Minister. . . . 'Let them come!' . . . replied the dictator, smiling."[7] On 4 April 1941 Russia concluded a pact of friendship with Yugoslavia; and Molotov told the German Ambassador that he expected Germany to keep peace with the southern Slavs, only to hear from the Ambassador two days later that the Wehrmacht was about to attack both Greece and Yugoslavia.

There was only one march that Stalin still succeeded in stealing on Hitler before they confronted one another as open enemies. On 13 April 1941 he received Matsuoka, the Japanese Foreign Minister, and negotiated a pact of neutrality. That pact freed Russia from the danger of a war on two fronts; and it also untied Japan's hands for the war in the Pacific. Matsuoka had just come back from Berlin, where Hitler and Ribbentrop had given him broad hints of the forthcoming German attack on Russia and had urged him to refrain from concluding any pact in Moscow. But Japan as well as Russia now feared war on two fronts; and that fear was stronger than ideological friendships and antagonisms.

[7] G. Gafencu, *Prelude to the Russian Campaign* (London, 1945), p. 192.

During Matsuoka's visits to Moscow— the first in November 1940 and the second in April 1941—Stalin was unusually animated and even talkative. "We both are Asiatics," he told his visitor. He took up that motif repeatedly. In part this was diplomatic cant. In part Stalin was preening himself on his descent. The Asiatic element in Russia had been exalted ever since his ascendancy; and now he himself carried that exaltation to the highest pitch. It was as if he were seeking to remind people that Russia owed her precious peace to him, who had risen from the borderland between Asia and Europe. He delighted in demonstrating his Asiatic outlook to his Japanese guest. Both had a peculiar way of wearing their hearts on their sleeves and holding their daggers up their sleeves. Matsuoka, the scion of a great feudal family, introduced himself as a "moral communist." Stalin listened to the stories about the heroic exploits of Matsuoka's ancestors and to his assurance that Japan was fighting in China not the Chinese, but Anglo-Saxon liberalism bent on overthrowing Japan's "moral communism." From political philosophy the two men turned to bargaining over concessions in northern Sakhalin. They bargained hard, in oriental fashion; and Stalin gesticulated to show that Matsuoka—the heartless creature—was out to strangle him.

In his "Asiatic" *panache* Stalin had an ulterior motive. He had just drawn his conclusions from the fact that, despite his resistance, Germany had become the master of the Balkans and had not left an inch of European land open to the expansion of Russian influence. He had had to put up with his reverse. Six months before he had sent Molotov to haggle with Hitler over Russian interests in Europe. Now he was trying, in his cryptic manner, to convey to Hitler that he, Stalin, had withdrawn from the contest and that he was ready to content himself, as Hitler had advised him through Molotov, with advantages in Asia. On the day of Matsuoka's departure from Moscow,

18 April, he made an ostentatious gesture calculated to bring his new attitude to Hitler's notice. Quite unexpectedly, he emerged from his seclusion to see off the Japanese Minister at the railway station. In the presence of a large gathering of foreign correspondents and astonished diplomats, he embraced his "fellow Asiatic"; and then, to quote Schulenburg, he "publicly asked for me and when he found me came up to me and threw his arm around my shoulders: 'We must remain friends and you must now do everything to that end!' Somewhat later Stalin turned to the German . . . military attaché, Colonel Krebs, first made sure that he was a German, and then said to him: 'We will remain friends with you in any event.' "[8] Hitler and Ribbentrop could not possibly have missed the meaning of all this. Stalin was, as it were, taking up their proposals of November and indicating his desire to negotiate.

Too late! In the next few weeks Moscow and Berlin fired protests at each other against violations of the frontier. German planes were flying over Russian territory and Russian planes were reconnoitring German terrain. About 150 German divisions were concentrated on the frontier. They were confronted by a slightly superior number of Russian divisions. It was in those days, about the end of April, that Stalin received the British message, which Churchill was to mention in his speech of 22 June, warning him of the imminence of the German attack. So precise was the warning, according to some versions, that it mentioned 22 June, the anniversary of Napoleon's invasion of Russia, as the probable date of the German invasion.

At least two men in Moscow refused to take the warning seriously: Stalin and von Schulenburg. The German Ambassador's mistake is understandable. He was true to his Bismarckian tradition and hoped that the friction between Germany and Russia

would not lead to war. In the last days of April he went to Hitler to plead for peace, just as another Ambassador, Caulaincourt, had pleaded with Napoleon against the invasion of Russia, 130 years before. Schulenburg brought with him a Russian offer of five million tons of grain to be delivered to Germany next year; and he tried to explain to Hitler the concentration of Russian troops on the frontier by the "well-known Russian urge for three hundred per cent. security. If for any reason we sent *one* German division, they would send ten for the same purpose in order to be completely safe. I could not believe that Russia would ever attack Germany."[9] But Hitler was not to be moved.

That Stalin, too, hoped that the peace between Russia and Germany could still be saved may seem almost incredible. Yet this follows from his whole behaviour in these critical weeks. He now committed one of those errors to which the overcunning are sometimes liable. He dismissed all ill omens and was confident that he, by himself, with his tactical skill and flair for sharp political turns, could retrieve the situation.

On 6 May Moscow was startled by the news that Stalin had become Prime Minister. What made him step out of the General Secretariat, for the first time since 1923, and assume direct responsibility for the Government? Grave, fateful decisions were in the balance. What were they to be? The last May Day parade had been turned into an unusual display of military power. On the eve of his appointment Stalin had attended military exercises at the War Academy and had made a long, secret speech to the graduating officers, extolling the valour of the Red Army. Was it war then? Hitler's opponents watched with bated breath the first steps of Stalin, the Prime Minister; and they were appalled. He denied the rumours of strong military concentrations on the frontier; he resumed diplomatic relations with the pro-German Government of

---

[8] Sontag and Beddie, *Nazi-Soviet Relations*, p. 324.

[9] *Ibid.*, pp. 331–332.

Iraq, which he had previously refused to recognize; and—most amazing of all—he asked the Belgian, Norwegian, and Yugoslav envoys in Moscow to close their embassies and leave Russia, because their Governments had ceased to exist. This last act, and even more so the allegation by which he supported it, was obviously meant to placate Hitler; and it is difficult to say which was more astounding in them: his lack of scruple or his short-sightedness. Yet, while going out of his way to regain Hitler's confidence, he also feared that in doing so he might infect his own people with weakness and defeatism. He therefore kept secret from the Russian people and the Red Army his decision to wind up the three embassies. Then he waited a whole month to see whether Hitler would show any sign of appreciation. No sign came.

He made one last desperate and tragicomic effort. On 14 June, exactly one week before the German invasion, he authorized his news agency to publish a statement which, against all diplomatic custom, violently attacked the British Ambassador for spreading rumours of an "impending Russo-German war." The statement, in which Stalin's hand could easily be recognized, denied that Germany had made any economic or territorial demands on Russia, and that, because Russia had rejected them, the two countries were completing their preparations for war. Contradicting several of Molotov's secret notes to Ribbentrop, Stalin now credited Germany with "fulfilling to the letter" her agreements with Russia; and, though he no longer denied that great armies were standing on both sides of the frontier, he described as "false, nonsensical and provocative" all suggestions that either the German or the Russian troops were there to wage war.[10]

It would be difficult to find, even in the diplomatic records of the Second World War, anything quite as pathetic. And yet

this bizarre statement, where Stalin praised before the whole world those who next week were to unmask themselves as Russia's mortal enemies and taunted those who next week would be her only allies, this bizarre statement was not wholly false. It was true, as Stalin claimed, that Germany had made no demands on Russia. He evidently expected Hitler to raise demands over which it would be possible to bargain. German attacks on Austria, Czechoslovakia, and Poland had indeed been preceded by open claims and loud threats. Stalin apparently thought that Hitler would act according to precedent. Because he did not see the usual danger signals he refused to admit the imminent danger. In his statement he invited Hitler, in that devious manner which Hitler understood so well in March 1939, to put forward his claims and to start negotiations. Hitler did not take the hint.

But why did not Stalin spare the British his taunts even now? He believed, and in this he was right, that the British were interested to frustrate his plans for a last-minute conciliation of Hitler. He was incensed by what he believed to be the British Ambassador's indiscretion. But even if the British had been completely unselfish in the matter, they would probably still have aroused his anger: the mere forecast of the storm seemed to him to bring the storm nearer. He could well afford, on the other hand, to hurt British susceptibilities. Now, after Britain had stood alone against Germany for a year, he knew that he had no need to sue for British friendship, that the alliance between Russia and Britain would be established almost automatically once hostilities had broken out; and then bygones would be bygones.

* * *

Very few of Stalin's deeds have given rise to so many passionate disputes as his dealings with Hitler between 1939 and 1941. It was in those years, so his critics say, that, low as had been his previous

[10] *Ibid.*, pp. 345–346.

record of political morality, he descended to even lower depths of treachery. His apologists retort that though his path was full of twists and turns, he acted from legitimate expediency, never losing sight of his ultimate objectives, never discarding his principles.

Stalin himself made his own apology soon after the outbreak of hostilities. "It may be asked," he said on 3 July 1941, "how could the Soviet Government have consented to conclude a non-aggression pact with such perfidious people, such fiends as Hitler and Ribbentrop? Was this not an error on the part of the Soviet Government?"[11] He denied the "error" and pointed to the advantages of his policy: "We secured to our country peace for a year and a half and the opportunity of preparing our forces." Apart from time Russia had, of course, also gained territory, the much desired defensive *glacis*. Her moral gain consisted in the clear awareness of her peoples that Germany was the aggressor and that their own Government had pursued peace to the very end.

Of these three alleged gains—in time, space, and morale—the gain in morale was the most real. It had been a peculiar feature of Russian military history that the Russian soldier had, unlike the German, fought best in the defence of his native soil; and the clear conviction that the fight for national survival had been forced upon Russia brought out the best qualities in him in the years that followed. The strategic value of Russia's territorial acquisitions appears far less certain. The military outposts in the Baltic states and in former eastern Poland were lost by Russia a few days after hostilities began. Yet to build up these outposts had been so arduous and ugly a job; it had caused so much resentment among so many small nationalities, especially after the mass deportations of "unreliable" Poles and Balts into the in-

terior of Russia; in a word, the strategic advantages of those outposts were so negligible or, at any rate, so quickly lost, and the moral and the political disadvantages arising from the acquisition were so great, that on balance the whole undertaking was a costly and dismal failure.

Nor was the gain in time more positive. To be sure, Stalin used the twenty-two months of the respite for an intensive development of Russian war industries and for retraining the armed forces in the light of fresh military experience. But Hitler, too, used these twenty-two months. Freed from the nightmare of war on two fronts, he subjugated nearly the whole of Europe and harnessed the economic resources and the manpower of a dozen countries to the German war machine. No matter how great and important was the fresh accumulation of war stocks and the expansion of armament plant achieved in Russia between 1939 and 1941, it could not match the additional power that accrued to Hitler in the same period. For three long years now, the Red Army was to confront almost single-handed Hitler's forces on the land, to cede vast and most valuable territory, to bleed more profusely than any army had ever bled, and to watch in anxious and frustrating suspense for the opening of a second front in the west. Yet that second front had been there in 1939 and 1940; and it might still have been there later, had Stalin thrown Russia's weight into the struggle during one of its earlier phases.

Nor is it true that he used his respite as fully as he might have used it. Hoping till the last minute to avert the war and disregarding the omens that showed it inevitable and imminent, he refrained from mobilizing sufficient strength to prevent the Wehrmacht from scoring its great initial victories. He met Hitler's onslaught only half mobilized. In June 1941 the number of mobilized Russian and German divisions was almost equal, but only part of the Russian divisions were ready to meet their experienced and well-equipped opponent,

11 J. V. Stalin, *War Speeches, Orders of the Day* (London, 1945[?]), p. 8.

to whom a long succession of brilliant victories had given high self-assurance. Yet the Red Army could have had strong superiority in numbers. The excessive complexity of his political game led Stalin to put himself at a military disadvantage. He had been uneasy enough to mobilize 170 divisions and to move most of these to the frontier; but he had still been too complacent, or too wary of "provoking" Hitler, to carry out the mobilization on the scale required. For this we have his own authority: "The fact of the matter is," he stated (3 July 1941), "that the troops of Germany, a country at war, were already fully mobilized, . . . and in a state of complete readiness, only awaiting the signal to move into action, whereas the Soviet troops had still to effect mobilization and to move up to the frontiers."[12] What Stalin in fact admitted was that in the last weeks before the invasion he had squandered much of that precious time, the gain of which he still pointed to as the justification of his policy. "Of no little importance," he added, ". . . was the fact that Fascist Germany suddenly and treacherously violated the non-aggression pact." The world was told then that "vizor'd falsehood and base forgery" betrayed his "credulous innocence."

When the balance of those strange twenty-two months is drawn, it is impossible to overlook the gratuitous service which the Comintern unwittingly rendered to Hitler. No sooner had Molotov and Ribbentrop put their signatures to the Pact of August 1939 than the Comintern called

off the anti-Hitler crusade to which its trumpeters had so long summoned governments and peoples. All the strategy and tactics of anti-fascism, all its elaborate arguments and slogans, were scrapped. The European shadows of the Russian General Secretary adopted an ambiguous pose of neutrality. Both belligerent camps, it was now said, pursued imperialist aims, and there was nothing to choose between them. The working classes were called upon to resist war and fight for peace. Outwardly, these appeals resembled the policy of revolutionary defeatism which Lenin had pursued in the First World War. The resemblance was deceptive. In Lenin's opposition to war there was revolutionary integrity and consistency, while the policy of the Comintern merely suited the temporary convenience of Stalin's diplomacy and was as tortuous as that diplomacy. At times the opposition to war had an unmistakably pro-German twist as, for instance, in October 1939, when the Comintern echoed Molotov's and Ribbentrop's call for a negotiated peace and blamed France and Britain for the war. The effect of that policy, especially in France, was merely defeatist, not revolutionary. It supplemented the defeatism that corroded the top of French society with a quasi-popular brand of defeatism coming from below. Only after the harm had been done, when Moscow, alarmed by Hitler's victories, began to encourage resistance to Nazi occupation, did the French Communist party switch over to a new policy. Less obvious, though not unimportant, was the effect of the Ribbentrop-Molotov pact upon anti-Nazi elements in Germany; it made their confusion worse confounded, it deepened their sense of defeat and induced some of them to reconcile themselves to Hitler's war.

It would be naïve to suppose that Stalin was not aware of those results of his "friendship" with Hitler. But he almost certainly thought them of little importance in comparison with the tangible advantages he had obtained. His pragmatic mind stuck

---

[12] *Ibid.*, pp. 7–8. Stalin admitted the fact even more explicitly to Harry Hopkins. See Robert E. Sherwood, *Roosevelt and Hopkins* (New York, 1948), pp. 333 and 335. Not only the mobilization of the army but the final conversion of industry to war was also unduly delayed. It was only in 1948 that the chief of the State Planning Commission, Vice-Premier N. Voznesensky, disclosed that the economic plans for the third quarter of 1941 had been based on the assumption of peace, and that a new plan, suited for war, had been drafted only after the outbreak of hostilities. N. Voznesensky, *Voennaya Ekonomika SSSR* (Moscow, 1948), p. 37.

to concrete, strategic conceptions, to military bases, rivers, salients, and rounded-off frontiers, all the elements of defence, the value of which had been so greatly reduced by modern military technique. He disregarded such imponderables as the mood of the French or the German working classes or the national resentments of Poles, Finns, and other Baltic nationalities. Yet all those imponderables were to take, and some of them are taking even now, their revenge on Russia. In this, his disregard of the immaterial factors in great political processes, lay the main weakness of his strong but limited realism.

The Wartime Alliance 1941–1943

THE FIRST MONTHS

CORDELL HULL

Cordell Hull began his career as a Tennessee lawyer, went on to serve seventeen years as a Member of the House of Representatives of the United States, and was later elected Senator from Tennessee. He was appointed Secretary of State on March 4, 1933, and held this office until November 1944, when illness forced his retirement. Here, in an excerpt from his *Memoirs*, he describes the first steps in the formation of the alliance that was eventually to defeat Germany and Japan. From the first, it will be noted, the United States was inclined to be a little imperious and self-righteous; Stalin, while displaying the same characteristics, was also aggressive and demanding. Mr. Hull, suspicious of Soviet intentions and determined to hold to his principles, nevertheless clearly recognized the need for cooperative effort.

ON the eve of Hitler's invasion of Russia, our policy toward the Soviet Union embraced these points:

Make no approaches to Russia.

Treat any approaches toward us with reserve until the Russians satisfied us they were not maneuvering merely to obtain unilateral concessions for themselves.

Reject any Soviet suggestions that we make concessions for the sake of improving American-Soviet relations, and require a strict *quid pro quo*.

Make no sacrifices of principle in order to better relations.

Let Russia understand that we considered an improvement in relations to be just as important, if not more so, to Russia than to the United States.

Make the principle of reciprocity the basis of our day-to-day relations.

In general our policy toward Russia was one of firmness but friendliness.

The first week in June we received convincing cables from our Legations in Bucharest and Stockholm that Germany would invade Russia within a fortnight. The Department sent these reports to Ambassador Steinhardt in Moscow.

Eight days before Hitler marched into Russia, Prime Minister Churchill sent the President a message saying that, from every source at his disposal, it looked to him as if a vast German onslaught on Russia were imminent. If the new war broke out, he said, Britain would of course give all encouragement and any help she could spare to the Russians, on the principle that Hitler was the foe she had to beat. He said he did not expect any class political reactions in England and trusted that a German-Russian conflict would not cause us any embarrassment.

The conflict caused us no embarrassment, and gave us renewed hope of overcoming Hitlerism. From White Sulphur Springs I was in constant touch with the President and Welles, urging that we give Russia the most vigorous assurances of all the help we could extend. The President sent Harry Hopkins from London to Moscow to survey Russia's military needs. Mr. Roosevelt released Soviet blocked funds, and decided not to apply the Neutrality Act. On August 2 Acting Secretary Welles and Ambassador Oumansky exchanged letters, we promising "to give all economic assistance practicable for the purpose of strengthening the Soviet Union in its struggle against armed aggression."

Immediately upon my return to Washington on August 4, I issued a statement saying that "no rational person needs any argument to convince him that during the weeks of my absence the most clinching demonstration has been given of what some of us for some years have insisted was being planned. That is, that there is a world movement of conquest by force, accompanied by methods of governing the conquered peoples that are rooted mainly in savagery and barbarism. That situation calls for . . . ever increasing production of military supplies both for ourselves and for those who are resisting the would-be world conquerors. . . . I feel very strongly that with unity of purpose, maximum effort, and firm determination, the remaining free peoples of the world will win."

At about the same hour I saw Oumansky, who brought with him Soviet General Golikov. Oumansky's attitude was now quite different from what it had been at our last interview. It told him of the interest I had taken while I was away, and especially since my return, in seeing that Russia

got all the military supplies we could spare. General Golikov said he had presented the needs of his Government to the State Department two weeks before, but the only result had been the shipment of sixty planes to Russia, and that Russia needed antiaircraft and antitank guns most of all. I offered to redouble my efforts to aid in speeding the delivery of these weapons.

As I talked to my Soviet visitors, the President was engaging in his Atlantic Conference with Prime Minister Churchill. Russia attracted an important segment of attention at the Atlantic Conference. After Harry Hopkins, who was present at the meeting, made an optimistic report on the Soviet Union's ability to resist Hitler's invasion, the President and the Prime Minister agreed on a statement to be given Stalin. The President wirelessed this to me on August 13, asking me to cable it to Moscow.

The two leaders assured Stalin: "We are at the moment cooperating to provide you with the very maximum of supplies that you most urgently need. Already many shiploads have left our shores and more will leave in the immediate future." They proposed a conference in Moscow to analyze Russia's needs, with high representatives of the United States and Britain going to Russia for this purpose.

The story of the Atlantic Conference has been narrated elsewhere at various times. While it was being prepared I was recuperating at White Sulphur Springs, and when I returned to Washington the President was already en route to his rendezvous. Mr. Roosevelt had cherished for several months the idea of a personal conference with Churchill. I first became aware of it the end of May.

Welles wrote me at White Sulphur Springs on July 28, stating that the conference had been arranged for August 8, 9, and 10, and telling me that he intended to urge the President, if he expected to discuss more than purely military problems, to take someone with him who could keep a precise record of the conversations and of the agreements that might be reached.

Much was accomplished at the conference in the way of bringing the President and the Prime Minister into close personal touch with each other's ideas. On the British battleship *Prince of Wales* and on our cruiser *Augusta* began that unique intimate relationship between two great men which did so much to speed the outcome of the war.

Their statement of the aims of the two countries set us a high goal. These aims embraced the right of peoples to choose their own form of government; no aggrandizement; no territorial changes opposed by the peoples concerned; access to trade and raw materials; improved labor standards, economic advancement, and social security; international security; freedom of the seas; and disarmament.

I publicly stated my reaction to the Atlantic Charter on August 14 by saying: "It is a statement of basic principles and fundamental ideas and policies that are universal in their practical application. They have heretofore been generally accepted by all civilized nations and were being strongly supported until certain countries decided to launch a universal movement to destroy the whole structure of civilized relations. . . . They are the basic doctrines and policies that have received the support of all civilized nations and should continue to receive their support until they are completely restored throughout the world."

I felt that our two nations could go no further in their statement of war or peace aims. In preceding months I had been asked frequently to bring pressure by this Government on Britain to make a formal statement of her war aims. I invariably replied to this effect: "If you see a peacefully disposed citizen engaged in a death grapple with another person, with pistols drawn and dirks raised, can you tap the peaceful man on the shoulder and ask him to stop and state his purposes before he goes any further defending himself?"

I was keenly disappointed, however, in the fourth article of the Atlantic Charter, referring to international trade. This stated that the two nations would endeavor, with due respect for their existing obligations, to further the enjoyment by all States, great or small, victor or vanquished, of access, on equal terms, to the trade and to the raw materials of the world which were needed for their economic prosperity. Unfortunately the phrase "with due respect for their existing obligations" deprived the article of virtually all significance since it meant that Britain would continue to retain her Empire tariff preferences against which I had been fighting for eight years. Mr. Churchill had insisted on this qualification; Welles had argued for a stronger declaration; but Churchill said he could not abandon Empire preference and, in any event, he would have to communicate on this point with the Dominions, which fact would delay the issuance of the Atlantic Charter. The President gave in.

After I learned the background of this article, I began negotiations with Britain, through Halifax here and Ambassador Winant in London, to work out a better understanding on this point. These negotiations bore fruit in the Lend-Lease agreement with Britain in 1942 which promised the elimination of all forms of discriminatory treatment in international commerce.

The Atlantic meeting stimulated yet more our efforts to get military supplies to Russia. The President and I were carefully following the cables telling of the extent of Hitler's advances into Russia. Already our original estimate that the Russians could hold out seemed likely to be proven true.

At this point Russia and Britain on August 25 jointly occupied Iran as it became evident that Nazi propaganda and other means had undermined some of the leaders of the Iranian Government. The Allies could not permit this dangerous situation to continue because of Iran's strategic position in the Middle East to the south of Russia.

I felt it was important, however, that Russia and Britain should make clear to the world that they had no intention to occupy Iran permanently. On August 27 I spoke to Soviet Ambassador Oumansky and to British Chargé Sir Ronald Campbell on this score. Referring to the assurances Britain and Russia had given to the Iranian Government that they were in Iran solely because of the war with Hitler, with no purpose of infringing on Iran's sovereignty or of remaining longer than military necessity required, I suggested: "Russia and Britain should repeat this same assurance to all peaceful nations and all other nations opposed to aggression. Such a statement would have a very healthy and wholesome effect on the entire Moslem world, even as it would be stimulating to the peoples of small countries everywhere."

This suggestion was duly carried out by Britain and Russia.

The question of credits for Russia to enable her to cover large purchases in the United States proved a difficult one at the beginning. When Oumansky asked to see the President on this subject, Mr. Roosevelt asked Harry Hopkins and me to take part in the discussion on September 11.

The President frankly explained to Oumansky the extreme difficulty of getting the necessary Lend-Lease appropriations from Congress for Russia because of the unpopularity of Russia among large groups in the United States which exercised great political power in Congress. Referring to the fact that Russia did have churches and did permit religious worship under the 1936 Constitution, the President suggested that if Moscow could get some publicity back to this country regarding freedom of religion it might have a fine educational effect. He added the further suggestion that this publicity begin before the next Lend-Lease appropriations bill came up in Congress and before the mission he had named, headed by W. Averell Harriman, arrived in Moscow to discuss Soviet needs. Oumansky said he would attend to it.

(Harriman was bringing to the public service a vast experience in our business and industrial life. In working for the Government he exhibited a ready grasp of the important phases of international problems, and this equipment stood him and the Government in good stead when in 1943 he went to Moscow as United States Ambassador.)

The President said also to Oumansky that, to get a Lend-Lease proposal for Russia through Congress, we should have to have an official statement showing Russian assets, the amount of gold on hand, and also the barter that could be carried on between the two countries. He offered to purchase the maximum quantities of Russian manganese, chromium, and other commodities with the understanding that production and delivery need not take place until after the war.

Oumansky said he preferred a direct credit, but, if this were not possible, then his Government very earnestly would ask for Lend-Lease aid. We finally agreed on a credit and barter arrangement for $75,-000,000 through the Reconstruction Finance Corporation to cover a few months during which adequate arrangements for Russian military supplies could be worked out.

We sought to aid Russia in another way by pulling off the two little countries that were clawing at her sides—Finland in the north and Rumania in the south. We had previously brought what pressure we could on Japan, through a message from President Roosevelt to Premier Konoye on July 6, to induce Japan to refrain from driving at Russia's back. . . .

*   *   *

Our relations with Russia became ever closer in the autumn of 1941. American and British missions—ours headed by W. Averell Harriman—met with the Russians at Moscow from September 29 to October 1 and made arrangements to fill practically all Soviet requests for supplies. The President extended initial Lend-Lease aid to Russia in the amount of $1,000,000,000.

In token of Russia's appreciation of the importance of United States aid in her desperate struggle to resist the German advances, Stalin named a new Ambassador to the United States, the former Foreign Commissar Maxim Litvinov, whom I had come to know on several occasions. He arrived in Washington at almost the hour of the attack on Pearl Harbor. . . .

* * *

One of the greatest preoccupations of the President and me during the first half of 1942 was Russia's suddenly revealed territorial aims in Europe, coupled with her determination to induce the Western Allies to guarantee them in advance.

This important and troublesome development came to light during British Foreign Secretary Eden's visit to Moscow in December, 1941.

Several months prior to this visit we began to learn from Ambassador Steinhardt in Moscow that relations between Britain and Russia were strained over the fact that Prime Minister Churchill had not acquiesced in Stalin's insistence that a British army be sent to Murmansk or Rostov to relieve pressure on the Red Army.

Then on December 4, 1941, Ambassador Winant in London cabled the President and me that Eden was leaving for Moscow on Sunday (Pearl Harbor Sunday). Stalin had cabled Churchill that an understanding should be reached not only on military matters but also on war aims and on plans for a postwar organization of the peace. Stalin, Winant said, seemed in a suspicious, even resentful mood.

The Soviet Ambassador in London, Ivan M. Maisky, according to Winant, had already indicated that his Government felt it should have been consulted beforehand regarding the Atlantic Charter, although Maisky in September announced his Government's agreement with the fundamental principles set forth therein. Russia, Winant reported, was suspicious that the British and ourselves aimed at excluding her from the peace and postwar settlement, and that we would not be prepared to take sufficiently harsh measures in that settlement to render Germany harmless.

When this telegram arrived I was intensely absorbed in the rush of events immediately preceding Pearl Harbor. I therefore asked Ray Atherton, Chief of the European Division, to draft a reply along lines we agreed to. I read this over, approved it and sent it and Winant's message to the President, who returned it with his O.K.

In this telegram, which we asked Winant to read to Eden personally, we said that, as proof of our policy of aid to Russia, we had recently sent representatives (the Harriman Mission) to the Soviet Union who had entered into an agreement with the Soviet Government on our furnishing of supplies.

We said it was our conviction that the test of our good faith with regard to the Soviet Union was the measure of our fulfillment of this agreement.

As for our postwar policies, we pointed out that these had been outlined in the Atlantic Charter which represented the attitude also of Great Britain and the Soviet Union.

We then concluded that it would be unfortunate were any of these three Governments to express any willingness to enter into commitments regarding specific terms of the postwar settlement. We would, of course, expect a continuation of discussions among the several Governments toward the fullest possible agreement on basic policies and toward later arrangements at the proper time and with full public knowledge. When Hitler was defeated, the Soviet Government would participate no less than Britain and the United States in an effort to restore peace and order. But no commitments as to individual countries should be entered into at this time lest they jeopardize the aims we all shared in common, looking toward an enduring peace. It would be unfortunate if we approached the peace conference thus hampered. Above all, there must be no secret accords.

Furthermore, we pointed out the constitutional limitation by which this Government was bound, meaning the necessity for Senate approval of treaties. We said it would be difficult if not impossible for us to implement the common understanding among the three big powers by a more detailed agreement at this time.

We assured Britain that our basic policy of aid to her was no less strong than our policy of aid to Russia. And we concluded that we were thus very frankly indicating our position on the eve of Eden's departure for Moscow so that he would have no misunderstanding on that score.

It was clear to us that Eden would be confronted at Moscow with specific territorial demands. Stalin did lay such demands before Eden in their first conversations. He wanted Britain's immediate agreement to the restoration of Russia's borders to what they were prior to Hitler's attack. Concretely, the Baltic States of Estonia, Latvia, and Lithuania, also portions of Finland, Poland, and Rumania would be incorporated in the U.S.S.R. The Polish border would be based on the "Curzon Line" which was approximately the Russo-German boundary following the partition of Poland in 1939. Rumania should also give Russia special facilities for bases, and in return receive certain Hungarian territory.

Stalin also proposed the restoration of Austria as an independent state; the detachment of the Rhineland from Germany as an independent state or protectorate; possibly the constitution of an independent state of Bavaria; the transfer of East Prussia to Poland; the return of the Sudetenland to Czechoslovakia; Yugoslavia should be restored and receive certain additional territory from Italy; Albania should be reconstituted as an independent state; Turkey

should receive the Dodecanese islands, with possible readjustments of Aegean islands in favor of Greece; Turkey might also receive some territory from Bulgaria and in Northern Syria; Germany should pay reparations in kind, particularly in machine tools, but not in money.

Stalin said to Eden that the conclusion of any Anglo-Soviet agreement would depend on whether the two countries reached an agreement on the future Soviet frontiers, particularly the inclusion of the Baltic States and the restoration of the Finnish-Soviet frontier of 1940.

Stalin said he was willing to support any arrangements Britain might make for securing bases in the Western European countries, France, Belgium, The Netherlands, Norway, and Denmark.

Eden parried these demands by saying that for many reasons it was impossible for him to enter into a secret agreement, one of which was that he was pledged to the United States Government not to do so. Stalin said he agreed that Eden should take these provisions back to London for discussion with the British Cabinet, and they should be communicated to the United States.

When Eden returned to London he loaned his papers and notes to Ambassador Winant, who sent us a comprehensive account of the conversations in a series of cables.

At the State Department we gave intensive study to these cables. Two of our most capable officers, James C. Dunn, Political Adviser on European Affairs, and Ray Atherton, headed this study. Following several conversations, I requested them to draw up a full memorandum for the President along lines we agreed to.

I sent this to the President on February 4, 1942. In an accompanying letter I referred to the telegram I had sent Ambassador Winant on December 5, and said:

I am inclined to the opinion that the policies which we outlined in our telegram to

Ambassador Winant are sound and that a deviation therefrom would be unfortunate, particularly just now when we are endeavoring to unite all forces opposed to the Axis on the primary task of defeating the enemy.

In that telegram we took the position that the test of our good faith with regard to the Soviet Union should not be our willingness to agree to the recognition of extended Soviet frontiers at this time, but rather the degree of determination which we show loyally to carry out our promises to aid the Soviet Government with equipment and supplies.

I am sure that you will agree with me that by our actions we should make it clear to the Soviet Government in the future to an ever greater degree that we are doing our utmost to live up to our promises.

In the memorandum to the President we pointed out that Stalin had attached so much importance to the question of an immediate settlement of boundaries that Eden had indicated to Stalin he would endeavor to obtain a favorable decision from his Government. We therefore considered it likely that the British Government would approach our Government shortly and request that we state our position with regard to Britain's making certain territorial commitments to the Soviet Union or that we approve certain commitments which Britain might desire to make.

We recalled to the President that our Government thus far had not recognized as Soviet territory any of the areas that had been annexed to the Soviet Union since the outbreak of the European War. Our attitude had been predicated on our general policy not to recognize any territorial changes that had been made in European frontiers since the outbreak of the war and not to enter into any territorial commitments that might hamper the proceedings of the postwar peace conference.

It is believed [we said] that it would be unfortunate if, at the present time, an ally of the American Government of such standing as Great Britain, which also has thus far refused to make any commitments of a territorial nature on the European continent, should begin bargaining with the Soviet Union or any other continental country with regard to frontiers. There is little doubt that if the principle is once admitted that agreements relating to frontiers may be entered into prior to the peace conference, the association of nations opposed to the Axis, which thus far has been based upon the common aim of defeating the enemy, may be weakened by the introduction among its members of mutual suspicion and by efforts of various members to intrigue in order to obtain commitments with regard to territory at the expense of other members.

We further stated our belief that Britain's assent to Stalin's territorial demands would result in only temporary improvement in relations between Britain and Russia.

If the British Government [we said] with the tacit or expressed approval of this Government, should abandon the principle of no territorial commitments prior to the peace conference, it would be placed in a difficult position to resist additional Soviet demands relating to frontiers, territory, or to spheres of influence which would almost certainly follow whenever the Soviet Government would find itself in a favorable bargaining position.

There is no doubt that the Soviet Government has tremendous ambitions with regard to Europe and that at some time or other the United States and Great Britain will be forced to state that they cannot agree, at least in advance, to all of its demands. It would seem that it is preferable to take a firm attitude now, rather than to retreat and to be compelled to take a firm attitude later when our position had been weakened by the abandonment of the general principles referred to above.

We thought it likely that Stalin would make use of all the weapons at his disposal to attain immediate recognition of some territorial gains. He might refuse at least temporarily to cooperate with Britain and the United States. He might insinuate that he would make a separate peace with Germany. He would no doubt endeavor, through the Communist Parties in the

United States and Britain, to bring pressure on the British and American Governments. But we warned that, if those Governments succumbed to such pressure, Stalin would be encouraged to resort to similar tactics later in order to obtain further and more far-reaching demands.

We pointed out that Stalin's insistence on obtaining at least certain territorial commitments at this time could be ascribed to three desires. One was to break down the principle of not making any territorial commitments prior to the peace conference. The second was to use such recognition as justification of the Soviet invasion of Poland and the Baltic States and the 1939–1940 war against Finland. The third was to have promises with regard to Soviet frontiers which might be useful to him at the peace conference in case the war should end with a weakened Soviet Union not occupying the territories he was demanding.

Our agreeing to Stalin's demands, we added, would have an unfortunate effect upon the attitude of small countries everywhere toward the United States and Britain and also of countries that were especially opposed to the spread of Communism. It might well be regarded by the Latin American Republics as a departure from the principles we had hitherto advocated. It would give concern to the Vatican. It would affect the integrity of the Atlantic Charter. (In the first two clauses of the Charter the signatories declared that they sought no aggrandizement, territorial or other, and that they desired to see no territorial changes that did not accord with the freely expressed wishes of the peoples concerned.) And it would afford a wonderful opportunity to German propaganda.

In handing this memorandum to the President, I hoped he would be able to discuss it with Prime Minister Churchill in the course of the direct exchanges they were constantly having on the progress of the war. It seemed to me we were in great danger of relapsing into the practice of the Allies during the First World War, when they concluded a series of secret treaties splitting up among themselves territories belonging to the Central Powers. These secret treaties had become one of the principal weapons of the isolationists in the United States in the period between the two wars. At least one of the provisions of the Atlantic Charter had been especially devised to prevent the same old device of power politics from being revived.

I could sympathize fully with Stalin's desire to protect his western borders from future attack. But I felt that this security could best be obtained through a strong postwar peace organization. And it certainly could be achieved without the necessity of absorbing the life of the Baltic peoples, who possessed a strong feeling of independence, into that of the U.S.S.R.

The President felt that the Soviet Union was legitimately entitled to obtain full security at the end of the war, but this security would necessarily depend on the solution of many problems still outstanding, one of which was the status of Germany. The security that the Soviet Union should rightly obtain would depend upon the type of Germany to be established after the war, and he recalled that the Atlantic Charter had clearly called for the disarmament of Germany.

Thus the matter stood when I became ill in February. After I returned to my office on April 20 I found that events had moved in the wrong direction. Prime Minister Churchill seemed reluctantly determined to go ahead with the accord, and Stalin continued to press for an immediate signature.

THE QUARRELSOME ALLIANCE

WINSTON CHURCHILL

During the first year after Hitler's invasion of the Soviet Union, Stalin pressed his new allies, Britain and the United States, for recognition of the western borders he had established just prior to the invasion. And until early 1944 he demanded that they mount a second front in France in order to draw German divisions away from the Russian front. In June 1942, President Roosevelt and Prime Minister Churchill agreed to attempt to create a second front. Then, as the months wore on and it became evident that this project could not be carried out in 1942, Churchill drew the bitterly unpleasant task of journeying to Stalin with the bad news. Here, he describes the early Soviet efforts to win recognition of their new western boundaries and his interviews with Stalin concerning the second front. Churchill movingly portrays Stalin's desperate need for help, his deep distrust of the Western powers. The reader will perceive that what Britain's wartime Prime Minister has called the "Grand Alliance" depended upon a delicate balancing of interests between three great powers of diverse character. That the alliance worked at all must be attributed in considerable degree to the sagacity and indomitable courage of Churchill, Stalin, and Roosevelt, and to their willingness to overlook for the moment their profound ideological differences.

WHEN Mr. Eden had visited Moscow in December, 1941, he had been confronted by specific demands from the Russian Government for the recognition of the Soviet frontiers in the West as they stood at that time. The Russians were particularly anxious to secure within the frame of any general treaty of alliance an explicit recognition of their occupation of the Baltic States and of their new frontier with Finland. Mr. Eden had refused to make any commitments on this subject, stressing, among other things, the pledge we had given to the United States Government not to enter into any secret agreement for territorial revision during the course of the war.

At the end of this conference it was agreed that Mr. Eden should convey the Soviet demands both to the British Cabinet and to the United States, and that they should be considered in the future negotiations for a formal Anglo-Soviet treaty. The

United States Government were fully informed of what had passed. Their attitude to the Russian proposals was sharp and negative. In the American view any acceptance of such requests would be a direct violation of the principles of the Atlantic Charter.

When I was at Washington on the morrow of the American entry into the war, and Mr. Eden had reported the wishes of the Soviet Government to absorb the Baltic States, I had reacted unfavourably, as the telegrams already printed show. But now, three months later, under the pressure of events, I did not feel that this moral position could be physically maintained. In a deadly struggle it is not right to assume more burdens than those who are fighting for a great cause can bear. My opinions about the Baltic States were, and are, unaltered, but I felt that I could not carry them farther forward at this time.

The selections from Winston S. Churchill, *The Hinge of Fate* (1950), pp. 326–336, 339, 341–342, 477–483, 486–498, 499, 500, are reprinted by permission of and arrangement with Houghton Mifflin Company, the authorized publishers, and Cassell and Company, Ltd. Documents in this excerpt are British Crown copyright and are used with permission of the Controller of Her Brittannic Majesty's Stationery Office.

Former Naval Person to President Roosevelt
7 Mar. 42

If Winant is with you now, he will no doubt explain the Foreign Office view about Russia. The increasing gravity of the war has led me to feel that the principles of the Atlantic Charter ought not to be construed so as to deny Russia the frontiers she occupied when Germany attacked her. This was the basis on which Russia acceded to the Charter, and I expect that a severe process of liquidating hostile elements in the Baltic States, etc., was employed by the Russians when they took these regions at the beginning of the war. I hope therefore that you will be able to give us a free hand to sign the treaty which Stalin desires as soon as possible. Everything portends an immense renewal of the German invasion of Russia in the spring, and there is very little we can do to help the only country that is heavily engaged with the German armies.

The President and the State Department however held to their position, and as will be seen we eventually arrived at a better conclusion.

* * *

A more cordial period now intervened in Anglo-Russian relations.

Prime Minister to Premier Stalin   9 Mar. 42

I have sent a message to President Roosevelt urging him to approve our signing the agreement with you about the frontiers of Russia at the end of the war.

2. I have given express directions that the supplies promised by us shall not in any way be interrupted or delayed.

3. Now that the season is improving we are resuming heavy air offensive both by day and night upon Germany. We are continuing to study other measures for taking some of the weight off you.

4. The continued progress of the Russian armies and the known terrible losses of the enemy are naturally our sources of greatest encouragement in this trying period.

Premier Stalin to Prime Minister   15 Mar. 42

I am very grateful to you for your message handed in at Kuibyshev on March 12.

I express to you the appreciation of the Soviet Government for your communication regarding measures you have taken to ensure supplies to U.S.S.R. and to intensify air attacks on Germany.

I express the firm conviction that the combined actions of our troops, in spite of incidental reverses, will in the end defeat the forces of our mutual enemy, and that the year 1942 will be decisive in the turn of events at the battle-front against Hitlerism.

As regards the first point of your letter, dealing with frontiers of U.S.S.R., I think that it will still be necessary to exchange views regarding the text of a respective suitable agreement, in the event of its being accepted for the signature of both parties.

* * *

In the general desire to find ways of helping the Soviet armies in the forthcoming German offensive, and the fear that gas, probably mustard gas, would be used upon them, I procured the consent of the Cabinet to our making a public declaration that if gas were used by the Germans against the Russians we would retaliate by gas attacks on Germany.

Prime Minister to Premier Stalin   20 Mar. 42

Many thanks for your reply of the 15th to my latest telegram. Beaverbrook is off to Washington, where he will help smooth out the treaty question with the President in accordance with the communications which have passed between us and between our Governments.

2. Ambassador Maisky lunched with me last week, and mentioned some evidences that the Germans may use gas upon you in their attempted spring offensive. After consulting my colleagues and the Chiefs of Staff, I wish to assure you that His Majesty's Government will treat any use of this weapon of poison gas against Russia exactly as if it was directed against ourselves. I have been building up an immense store of gas bombs for discharge from aircraft, and we shall not hesitate to use these over all suitable objectives in Western Germany from the moment that your armies and people are assaulted in this way.

3. It is a question to be considered whether at the right time we should not give a public warning that such is our resolve, as the warning might deter the Germans from adding this new horror to the many they have loosed upon the world. Please let me know what you think about this, and whether the evidence of German preparations warrants the warning.

4. There is no immediate hurry, and before I take a step which may draw upon our cities this new form of attack I must of course have ample time to bring all our anti-gas precautions to extreme readiness.

5. I trust you will give our new Ambassador the opportunity of presenting this message himself, and the advantage of personal discussion with you. He comes, as you know, almost direct from close personal contact with General Chiang Kai-shek, which he has maintained during the last four years. He enjoyed, I believe, the General's high regard and confidence; I hope and believe that he will equally gain yours. He is a personal friend of mine of many years' standing.

Premier Stalin to Prime Minister 30 Mar. 42
I thank you for the message recently transmitted to me by Sir A. Clark Kerr. I have had a long talk with Sir A. Clark Kerr, and I am convinced that our joint work will proceed in an atmosphere of perfect mutual confidence.

2. I wish to express to you the Soviet Government's gratitude for the assurance that the British Government will look upon any use by the Germans of poison gas against the U.S.S.R. in the same light as if this weapon had been used against Great Britain, [and] that the British Air Force will immediately use against suitable objectives in Germany the large stocks of gas bombs held in England.

* * *

The President was also at this time in pleasant relations with the Soviets, and we have seen in the last chapter his reference to a visit by Molotov to Washington. He would have preferred the envoy to come first to the United States, but Stalin planned otherwise.

Premier Stalin to Prime Minister 23 Apr. 42
Recently the Soviet Government received from Mr. Eden the drafts of two agreements between the U.S.S.R. and Great Britain which differed in some material respects from the text of agreements which were under discussion while Mr. Eden was in Moscow. In view of the fact that these drafts reveal fresh divergences of opinion which it would be difficult to solve by correspondence, the Soviet Government have decided, despite all the obstacles, to send Mr. Molotov to London, in order, by means of personal discussion, to dispose of all the matters which stand in the way of the signing of the agreements. This is all the more necessary because the question of opening a second front in Europe (which was raised in the last message addressed to me by the President of the United States, in which he invited Mr. Molotov to go to Washington to discuss this matter) calls for a preliminary exchange of views between representatives of our two Governments.

Accept my greetings and my wishes for success in your fight against the enemies of Great Britain.

Former Naval Person to President Roosevelt 24 Apr. 42
With regard to what you say in your telegram about Molotov's journeyings, I have had a message from Stalin saying he is sending M. here to discuss certain divergences in the draft texts of our agreement, which he wants settled as soon as possible. He may even be already on his way. You will understand that I cannot now suggest to him a change in the order of his visits. If and when therefore Molotov bears down upon us, I propose to agree to a discussion of our drafts, and would hope to clear main difficulties out of the way. But I will suggest to him that he should then go on to Washington and see you before anything is finally signed.

Prime Minister to Premier Stalin 24 Apr. 42
I am very grateful to you for your message of April 23, and we shall of course welcome M. Molotov, with whom I am confident we shall be able to do much useful work. I am very glad that you feel able to allow this visit, which I am sure will be most valuable.

Molotov did not arrive until May 20, and formal discussions began the following morning. On that day and at the two following meetings the Russians maintained their original position, and even brought up specifically the question of agreeing to the Russian occupation of Eastern Poland. This was rejected as incompatible with the Anglo-Polish Agreement of August, 1939. Molotov also put forward a case for the recognition in a secret agreement of Russia's claims on Rumania. This also was contrary to our understanding with the United States. The conversations at the Foreign Office, which Mr. Eden conducted, though most friendly, therefore moved towards a deadlock.

Apart from the question of the treaty, Molotov had come to London to learn our views upon the opening of a second front. On the morning of May 22 therefore, I had a formal conversation with him.

Molotov began by saying that he had been charged by the Soviet Government to come to London to discuss the question of the establishment of a second front. This was no new problem. It had first been raised nearly ten months ago, and now, more recently, the impetus had come from President Roosevelt, who had suggested to M. Stalin, that he (M. Molotov) should go to the United States to discuss this question. Though the initiative for the present inquiry had come from the United States, the Soviet Government had thought it right that he should proceed to the United States via London, since it was upon Great Britain that the main task of organising the second front would initially fall. The coming weeks and months on the Russian front were fraught with serious consequence to the Soviet Union and their Allies. The material aid rendered by Great Britain and the United States was highly prized and appreciated by the Soviet Government. Nevertheless the most urgent issues were involved in the establishment of a second front.

The object of his visit was to learn how the British Government viewed the prospects of drawing off in 1942 at least forty German divisions from the U.S.S.R., where it seemed that at the present time the balance of advantage in armed strength lay with the Germans.

In reply I gave Molotov the essence of our combined thought upon future operations on the Continent. In all previous wars control of the sea had given the Power possessing it the great advantage of being able to land at will on the enemy's coast, since it was impossible for the enemy to be prepared at every point to meet seaborne invasion. The advent of air-power had altered the whole situation. For example, in France and the Low Countries the enemy could move his Air Force in a few hours to threatened points anywhere along the coast; and bitter experience had shown that landing in the teeth of enemy air opposition was not a sound military proposition. The inescapable consequence was that large portions of the Continental coastline were denied to us as places for disembarkation. We were forced therefore to study our chances at those parts of the coast where our superior fighter force would give us control in the air. Our choice was, in fact, narrowed down to the Pas de Calais, the Cherbourg tip, and part of the Brest area. The problem of landing a force this year in one or more of these areas was being studied, and preparations were being made. Our plans were being based on the assumption that the landing of successive waves of assault troops would bring about air battles which, if continued over a week or ten days, would lead to the virtual destruction of the enemy's air-power on the Continent. Once this was achieved and the air opposition removed, landings at other points on the coast could be effected under cover of our superior sea-power. The crucial point in making our plans and preparations was the availability of the special landing-craft required for effecting the initial landing on the very heavily defended enemy coastline. Unfortunately, our resources in this special type of craft were for the time being strictly limited. I said that as far back as last August, at the Atlantic meeting, I had impressed upon President Roosevelt the urgent need for the United States to build as large a number of tank-landing and other assault craft as possible. Later, in January of this year, the President had agreed that the United States should make an even larger effort to construct these craft. We, for our part, for more than a year had been turning out as large a number of assault craft as our need for constructing ships for the Navy and mercantile marine, which had suffered grievous losses, permitted.

Two points should however be borne in mind. First, with the best will and endeavour, it was unlikely that any move we could make in 1942, even if it were successful, would draw off large numbers of enemy land forces from the Eastern Front. In the air however the position was different; in the various theatres of war we were already containing about one-half of the fighter and one-third of the German bomber strength. If our plan for forcing air battles over the Continent proved successful, the Germans might be faced with the choice either of seeing the whole of their fighter air force in the West destroyed in action or of making withdrawals from their air strength in the East.

The second point related to M. Molotov's proposition that our aim should be to draw off (including those now in the West) not less than forty German divisions from Russia. It should be noted that at the present time we had confronting us in Libya eleven Axis divisions, of which three were German, the equivalent of eight German divisions in Norway, and twenty-five German divisions in France and the Low Countries. These totalled forty-four divisions.

But we were not satisfied with that, and if any further effort could be made or plan devised, provided it was sound and sensible, for drawing the weight off Russia this year, we should not hesitate to put it

into effect. Clearly, it would not further either the Russian cause or that of the Allies as a whole if, for the sake of action at any price, we embarked on some operation which ended in disaster and gave the enemy an opportunity for glorification at our discomfiture.

Molotov said that he had no doubt that Great Britain genuinely wished for the success of the Soviet Army against the Germans this summer. What, in the view of the British Government, were the prospects of Soviet success? Whatever their views might be, he would be glad to have a frank expression of opinion—good or bad.

I said that, without detailed knowledge of the resources and reserves on both sides, it was difficult to form a firm judgment on this question. Last year the military experts, including those of Germany, had thought that the Soviet Army might be borne down and overcome. They had proved quite wrong. In the event the Soviet forces had defeated Hitler and nearly brought his Army to disaster. Consequently Russia's Allies felt great confidence in the strength and ability of the Soviet Army. The Intelligence available to the British Government did not indicate the massing of vast German forces at any particular point on the Eastern Front. Moreover, the full-scale offensive heralded for May now seemed unlikely to take place before June. In any event, it did not seem that Hitler's attack this year could be as strong or so menacing as that of 1941.

Molotov then asked what, if the Soviet Army failed to hold out during 1942, would be the position and the attitude of the British Government.

I said that if the Soviet military power was seriously reduced by the German onslaught, Hitler would in all probability move as many troops and air forces as possible back to the West, with the object of invading Great Britain. He might also strike down through Baku to the Caucasus and Persia. This latter thrust would expose us to the gravest dangers, and we should by no means feel satisfied that we had sufficient forces to ward it off. Therefore our fortunes were bound up with the resistance of the Soviet Army. Nevertheless, if, contrary to expectation, they were defeated, and the worst came to the worst, we should fight on, and, with the help of the United States, hope to build up overwhelming air superiority, which in the course of the next eighteen months or two years would enable us to put down a devastating weight of air attack on the German cities and industries. We should moreover maintain the blockade and make landings on the Continent against an increasingly enfeebled opposition. Ultimately the power of Great Britain and the United States would prevail. It should not be overlooked that after the fall of France Great Britain had stood alone for a whole year with but a handful of ill-equipped troops between her and Hitler's victorious and numerous divisions. But what a tragedy for mankind would be this prolongation of the war, and how earnest was the hope for Russian victory, and how ardent the desire that we should take our share in conquering the evil foe!

At the end of our talk I asked M. Molotov to bear in mind the difficulty of oversea invasions. After France fell out of the war we in Great Britain were almost naked —a few ill-equipped divisions, less than a hundred tanks and less than two hundred field guns. And yet Hitler had not attempted an invasion, by reason of the fact that he could not get command of the air. The same sort of difficulties confronted us at the present time.

* * *

On May 23 Mr. Eden proposed to substitute for a territorial agreement a general and public Treaty of Alliance for twenty years, omitting all reference to frontiers. By that evening the Russians showed signs of giving way. They were impressed by the solidarity of view of the British and

American Governments with which they had been confronted. The following morning Molotov requested permission from Stalin to negotiate on the basis of Mr. Eden's draft. Minor modifications were suggested from Moscow, mainly stressing the long-term character of the proposed alliance. The treaty, without any territorial provisions, was signed on May 26. This was a great relief to me, and a far better solution than I had dared to hope. Eden showed much skill in the timing of his new suggestion.

With this grave issue settled, Molotov left for Washington to begin general military talks with the President and his advisers on the question of opening a second front. It had been agreed that, having heard the American view, he should return to London for final discussions upon this matter before going back to Moscow.

* * *

I duly reported to the President.

Former Naval Person to President Roosevelt
27 May 42

We have done very good work this and last week with Molotov, and, as Winant will no doubt have informed you, we have completely transformed the treaty proposals. They are now, in my judgment, free from the objections we both entertained, and are entirely compatible with our Atlantic Charter. The treaty was signed yesterday afternoon, with great cordiality on both sides. Molotov is a statesman, and has a freedom of action very different from what you and I saw with Litvinov. I am very sure you will be able to reach good understandings with him. Please let me know your impressions.

* * *

When Molotov returned to London after his American visit he was naturally full of the plans for creating a second front by a cross-Channel operation in 1942. We ourselves were still actively studying this in conjunction with the American Staff, and nothing but difficulties had as yet emerged. There could be no harm in a public statement, which might make the Germans apprehensive and consequently hold as many of their troops in the West as possible. We therefore agreed with Molotov to the issue of a communiqué, which was published on June 11, containing the following sentence: "In the course of the conversations full understanding was reached with regard to the urgent task of creating a second front in Europe in 1942."

I felt it above all important that in this effort to mislead the enemy we should not mislead our Ally. At the time of drafting the communiqué, therefore, I handed Molotov personally in the Cabinet Room, and in the presence of some of my colleagues an *aide-mémoire* which made it clear that while we were trying our best to make plans we were not committed to action and that we could give no promise. When subsequent reproaches were made by the Soviet Government, and when Stalin himself raised the point personally with me, we always produced the *aide-mémoire* and pointed to the words *"we can therefore give no promise."*

Aide-Mémoire

We are making preparations for a landing on the Continent in August or September, 1942. As already explained, the main limiting factor to the size of the landing-force is the availability of special landing-craft. Clearly however it would not further either the Russian cause or that of the Allies as a whole if, for the sake of action at any price, we embarked on some operation which ended in disaster and gave the enemy an opportunity for glorification at our discomfiture. It is impossible to say in advance whether the situation will be such as to make this operation feasible when the time comes. *We can therefore give no promise in the matter,* but provided that it appears sound and sensible we shall not hesitate to put our plans into effect.

Molotov sailed off into the air on his somewhat dangerous homeward flight, apparently well satisfied with the results of

his mission. Certainly an atmosphere of friendliness had been created between us. He had been deeply interested in his visit to Washington. There was the Twenty Years Anglo-Russian Treaty, upon which high hopes were at that time set by all. . . .

* * *

I reached the Kremlin,* and met for the first time the great Revolutionary Chief and profound Russian statesman and warrior with whom for the next three years I was to be in intimate, rigorous, but always exciting, and at times even genial, association. Our Conference lasted nearly four hours. As our second airplane had not arrived with Brooke, Wavell, and Cadogan, there were present only Stalin, Molotov, Voroshilov, myself, Harriman, and our Ambassador, with interpreters. I have based this account upon the record which we kept, subject to my own memory, and to the telegrams I sent home at the time.

The first two hours were bleak and sombre. I began at once with the question of the Second Front, saying that I wished to speak frankly and would like to invite complete frankness from Stalin. I would not have come to Moscow unless he had felt sure that he would be able to discuss realities. When M. Molotov had come to London I had told him that we were trying to make plans for a diversion in France. I had also made it clear to M. Molotov that I could make no promises about 1942, and had given M. Molotov a memorandum to this effect. Since then an exhaustive Anglo-American examination of the problem had been carried out. The British and American Governments did not feel themselves able to undertake a major operation in September, which was the latest month in which the weather was to be counted upon. But, as M. Stalin knew, they were preparing for a very great operation in 1943. For this purpose a million American troops were now scheduled to reach the United Kingdom at their point of assembly in the

* August 12, 1942—Ed.

spring of 1943, making an expeditionary force of twenty-seven divisions, to which the British Government were prepared to add twenty-one divisions. Nearly half of this force would be armoured. So far only two and a half American divisions had reached the United Kingdom, but the big transportation would take place in October, November, and December.

I told Stalin that I was well aware that this plan offered no help to Russia in 1942, but thought it possible that when the 1943 plan was ready it might well be that the Germans would have a stronger army in the West than they now had. At this point Stalin's face crumpled up into a frown, but he did not interrupt. I then said I had good reasons against an attack on the French coast in 1942. We had only enough landing-craft for an assault landing on a fortified coast—enough to throw ashore six divisions and maintain them. If it were successful, more divisions might be sent, but the limiting factor was landing-craft, which were now being built in very large numbers in the United Kingdom, and especially in the United States. For one division which could be carried this year it would be possible next year to carry eight or ten times as many.

Stalin, who had begun to look very glum, seemed unconvinced by my argument, and asked if it was impossible to attack any part of the French coast. I showed him a map which indicated the difficulties of making an air umbrella anywhere except actually across the Straits. He did not seem to understand, and asked some questions about the range of fighter planes. Could they not, for instance, come and go all the time? I explained that they could indeed come and go, but at this range they would have no time to fight, and I added that an air umbrella to be of any use had to be kept open. He then said that there was not a single German division in France of any value, a statement which I contested. There were in France twenty-five German divisions, nine of which were

of the first line. He shook his head. I said that I had brought the Chief of the Imperial General Staff and General Sir Archibald Wavell with me in order that such points might be examined in detail with the Russian General Staff. There was a point beyond which statesmen could not carry discussions of this kind.

Stalin, whose glumness had by now increased, said that, as he understood it, we were unable to create a second front with any large force and unwilling even to land six divisions. I said that this was so. We could land six divisions, but the landing of them would be more harmful than helpful, for it would greatly injure the big operation planned for next year. War was war but not folly, and it would be folly to invite a disaster which would help nobody. I said I feared the news I brought was not good news. If by throwing in 150,000 to 200,000 men we could render him aid by drawing away from the Russian front appreciable German forces, we would not shrink from this course on the grounds of loss. But if it drew no men away and spoiled the prospects for 1943 it would be a great error.

Stalin, who had become restless, said that his view about war was different. A man who was not prepared to take risks could not win a war. Why were we so afraid of the Germans? He could not understand. His experience showed that troops must be blooded in battle. If you did not blood your troops you had no idea what their value was. I inquired whether he had ever asked himself why Hitler did not come to England in 1940, when he was at the height of his power and we had only 20,000 trained troops, 200 guns, and 50 tanks. He did not come. The fact was that Hitler was afraid of the operation. It is not so easy to cross the Channel. Stalin replied that this was no analogy. The landing of Hitler in England would have been resisted by the people, whereas in the case of a British landing in France the people would be on the side of the British. I pointed out that it was all the more important therefore not to expose the people of France, by a withdrawal, to the vengeance of Hitler and to waste them when they would be needed in the big operation in 1943.

There was an oppressive silence. Stalin, at length said that if we could not make a landing in France this year he was not entitled to demand it or to insist upon it, but he was bound to say that he did not agree with my arguments.

* * *

I then unfolded a map of Southern Europe, the Mediterranean, and North Africa. What was "A Second Front"? Was it only a landing on a fortified coast opposite England? Or could it take the form of some other great enterprise which might be useful to the common cause? I thought it better to bring him southward by steps. If, for instance, we could hold the enemy in the Pas de Calais by our concentration in Britain, and at the same time attack elsewhere—for instance, in the Loire, the Gironde, or alternatively the Scheldt—this was full of promise. There indeed was a general picture of next year's big operation. Stalin feared that it was not practicable. I said that it would indeed be difficult to land a million men, but that we should have to persevere and try.

We then passed on to the bombing of Germany, which gave general satisfaction. M. Stalin emphasised the importance of striking at the morale of the German population. He said he attached the greatest importance to bombing, and that he knew our raids were having a tremendous effect in Germany.

After this interlude which relieved the tension, Stalin observed that from our long talk, it seemed that all we were going to do was no "Sledgehammer," no "Round-up," and pay our way by bombing Germany. I decided to get the worst over first and to create a suitable background for the

project I had come to unfold. I did not therefore try at once to relieve the gloom. Indeed I asked specially that there should be the plainest speaking between friends and comrades in peril. However, courtesy and dignity prevailed.

* * *

The moment had now come to bring "Torch" into action. I said that I wanted to revert to the question of a second front in 1942, which was what I had come for. I did not think France was the only place for such an operation. There were other places, and we and the Americans had decided upon another plan, which I was authorised by the American President to impart to Stalin secretly. I would now proceed to do so. I emphasised the vital need of secrecy. At this Stalin sat up and grinned and said that he hoped that nothing about it would appear in the British press.

I then explained precisely Operation "Torch."

As I told the whole story Stalin became intensely interested. His first question was what would happen in Spain and Vichy France. A little later on he remarked that the operation was militarily right, but he had political doubts about the effect on France. He asked particularly about the timing, and I said not later than October 30, but the President and all of us were trying to pull it forward to October 7. This seemed a great relief to the three Russians.

I then described the military advantages of freeing the Mediterranean, whence still another front could be opened. In September we must win in Egypt, and in October in North Africa, all the time holding the enemy in Northern France. If we could end the year in possession of North Africa we could threaten the belly of Hitler's Europe, and this operation should be considered in conjunction with the 1943 operation. That was what we and the Americans had decided to do.

To illustrate my point I had meanwhile drawn a picture of a crocodile, and explained to Stalin with the help of this picture how it was our intention to attack the soft belly of the crocodile as we attacked his hard snout. And Stalin, whose interest was now at high pitch, said: "May God prosper this undertaking."

I emphasised that we wanted to take the strain off the Russians. If we attempted that in Northern France we should meet with a rebuff. If we tried in North Africa we had a good chance of victory, and then we could help in Europe. If we could gain North Africa Hitler would have to bring his Air Force back, or otherwise we would destroy his allies, even, for instance, Italy, and make a landing. The operation would have an important influence on Turkey and on the whole of Southern Europe, and all I was afraid of was that we might be forestalled. If North Africa were won this year we could make a deadly attack upon Hitler next year. This marked the turning-point in our conversation.

Stalin then began to present various political difficulties. Would not an Anglo-American seizure of "Torch" regions be misunderstood in France? What were we doing about de Gaulle? I said that at this stage we did not wish him to intervene in the operation. The [Vichy] French were likely to fire on de Gaullists but unlikely to fire on Americans. Harriman backed this very strongly by referring to reports, on which the President relied, by American agents all over "Torch" territories and also to Admiral Leahy's opinion.

* * *

At this point Stalin seemed suddenly to grasp the strategic advantages of "Torch." He recounted four main reasons for it.

First, it would hit Rommel in the back;

Second, it would overawe Spain;

Third, it would produce fighting between Germans and Frenchmen in France; and,

Fourth, it would expose Italy to the whole brunt of the war.

I was deeply impressed with this remarkable statement. It showed the Russian Dictator's swift and complete mastery of a problem hitherto novel to him. Very few people alive could have comprehended in so few minutes the reasons which we had all so busily been wrestling with for months. He saw it all in a flash.

I mentioned a fifth reason, namely, the shortening of the sea route through the Mediterranean. Stalin was concerned to know whether we were able to pass through the Straits of Gibraltar. I said, it would be all right. I also told him about the changes of command in Egypt, and of our determination to fight a decisive battle there in late August or September. Finally, it was clear that they all liked "Torch," though Molotov asked whether it could not be in September.

I then added: "France is down and we want to cheer her up." France had understood Madagascar and Syria. The arrival of the Americans would send the French nation over to our side. It would intimidate Franco. The Germans might well say at once to the French, "Give us your fleet and Toulon." This would stir anew the antagonisms between Vichy and Hitler.

I then opened the prospect of our placing an Anglo-American Air Force on the southern flank of the Russian armies in order to defend the Caspian and the Caucasian mountains and generally to fight in this theatre. I did not however go into details, as of course we had to win our battle in Egypt first, and I had not the President's plans for the American contribution. If Stalin liked the idea we would set to work in detail upon it. He replied that they would be most grateful for this aid, but that the details of location, etc., would require study. I was very keen on this project, because it would bring about more hard fighting between the Anglo-American air-power and the Germans, all of which aided the gaining of mastery in the air under more fertile conditions than looking for trouble over the Pas de Calais.

We than gathered round a large globe, and I explained to Stalin the immense advantages of clearing the enemy out of the Mediterranean. I told Stalin I should be available should he wish to see me again. He replied that the Russian custom was that the visitor should state his wishes and that he was ready to receive me at any time. He now knew the worst and yet we parted in an atmosphere of good will.

The meeting had now lasted nearly four hours. It took half an hour or more to reach State Villa No. 7. Tired as I was, I dictated my telegram to the War Cabinet and President Roosevelt after midnight, and then, with the feeling that at least the ice was broken and a human contact established, I slept soundly and long.

* * *

We all repaired to the Kremlin at 11 P.M., and were received only by Stalin and Molotov, with their interpreter. Then began a most unpleasant discussion. Stalin handed me a document. When it was translated I said I would answer it in writing, and that he must understand we had made up our minds upon the course to be pursued and that reproaches were vain. Thereafter we argued for about two hours, during which he said a great many disagreeable things, especially about our being too much afraid of fighting the Germans, and if we tried it like the Russians we should find it not so bad; that we had broken our promise about "Sledgehammer"; that we had failed in delivering the supplies promised to Russia and only sent remnants after we had taken all we needed for ourselves. Apparently these complaints were addressed as much to the United States as to Britain.

I repulsed all his contentions squarely, but without taunts of any kind. I suppose he is not used to being contradicted repeatedly, but he did not become at all angry, or even animated. He reiterated his view that it should be possible for the British and Americans to land six or eight divisions on the Cherbourg peninsula, since they had domination of the air. He felt that if the British Army had been fighting the Germans as much as the Russian Army it would not be so frightened of them. The Russians, and indeed the R.A.F., had shown that it was possible to beat the Germans. The British infantry could do the same provided they acted at the same time as the Russians.

I interposed that I pardoned the remarks which Stalin had made on account of the bravery of the Russian Army. The proposal for a landing in Cherbourg overlooked the existence of the Channel. Finally Stalin said we could carry it no further. He must accept our decision. He then abruptly invited us to dinner at eight o'clock the next night.

Accepting the invitation, I said I would leave by plane at dawn the following morning—i.e., 15th. Joe seemed somewhat concerned at this, and asked could I not stay longer. I said certainly, if there was any good to be done, and that I would wait one more day anyhow. I then exclaimed there was no ring of comradeship in his attitude. I had travelled far to establish good working relations. We had done our utmost to help Russia, and would continue to do so. We had been left entirely alone for a year against Germany and Italy. Now that the three great nations were allied, victory was certain, provided we did not fall apart, and so forth. I was somewhat animated in this passage, and before it could be translated he made the remark that he liked the tone of my utterance. Thereafter the talk began in a somewhat less tense atmosphere.

He plunged into a long discussion of two Russian trench mortars firing rockets, which he declared were devastating in their effects, and which he offered to demonstrate to our experts if they could wait. He said he would let us have all information about them, but should there not be something in return? Should there not be an agreement to exchange information about inventions? I said that we would give them everything without any bargaining, except only those devices which, if carried in aeroplanes over the enemy lines and shot down, would make our bombing of Germany more difficult. He accepted this. He also agreed that his military authorities should meet our generals, and this was arranged for three o'clock in the afternoon. I said they would require at least four hours to go fully into the various technical questions involved in "Sledgehammer," "Round-up," and "Torch." He observed at one moment that "Torch" was "militarily correct," but that the political side required more delicacy —i.e., more careful handling. From time to time he returned to "Sledgehammer," grumbling about it. When he said our promise had not been kept I replied, "I repudiate that statement. Every promise has been kept," and I pointed to the *aide-mémoire* I gave Molotov. He made a sort of apology, saying that he was expressing his sincere and honest opinions, that there was no mistrust between us, but only a difference of view.

Finally I asked about the Caucasus. Was he going to defend the mountain chain, and with how many divisions? At this he sent for a relief model, and, with apparent frankness and evident knowledge, explained the strength of this barrier, for which he said twenty-five divisions were available. He pointed to the various passes and said they would be defended. I asked were they fortified, and he said, "Yes, certainly." The Russian front line, which the enemy had not yet reached, was north of the main range. He said they would have to hold out for two months, when the snow would make the mountains impassable. He declared himself quite confident of their ability to do this, and also recounted in detail the strength of the Black Sea Fleet, which was gathered at Batum.

All this part of the talk was easier, but when Harriman asked about the plans for bringing American aircraft across Siberia, to which the Russians had only recently consented after long American pressing, he replied, curtly, "Wars are not won with plans." Harriman backed me up throughout, and we neither of us yielded an inch nor spoke a bitter word.

Stalin made his salute and held out his hand to me on leaving, and I took it.

* * *

I reported to the War Cabinet on August 14:

We asked ourselves what was the explanation of this performance and transformation from the good ground we had reached the night before. I think the most probable is that his Council of Commissars did not take the news I brought as well as he did. They may have more power than we suppose, and less knowledge. Perhaps he was putting himself on the record for future purposes and for their benefit, and also letting off steam for his own. Cadogan says a similar hardening up followed the opening of the Eden interview at Christmas, and Harriman says that this technique was also used at the beginning of the Beaverbrook mission.

It is my considered opinion that in his heart, so far as he has one, Stalin knows we are right, and that six divisions on "Sledgehammer" would do him no good this year. Moreover, I am certain that his surefooted and quick military judgment makes him a strong supporter of "Torch." I think it not impossible that he will make amends. In that hope I persevere. Anyhow, I am sure it was better to have it out this way than any other. There was never at any time the slightest suggestion of their not fighting on, and I think myself that Stalin has good confidence that he will win.

When I thanked Stalin for the forty Boston aircraft he made a half-disdainful gesture, saying, "They are American planes. When I give you Russian planes then you may thank me." By this he did not mean to disparage the American planes, but said that he counted on his own strength.

I make great allowances for the stresses through which they are passing. Finally, I think they want full publicity for the visit.

* * *

The following was the *aide-mémoire* which Stalin had handed me:

13 *Aug.* 42

As the result of an exchange of views in Moscow which took place on August 12 of this year, I ascertained that the Prime Minister of Great Britain, Mr. Churchill, considered the organisation of a second front in Europe in 1942 to be impossible. As is well known, the organisation of a second front in Europe in 1942 was pre-decided during the sojourn of Molotov in London, and it found expression in the agreed Anglo-Soviet communiqué published on June 12 last. It is also known that the organisation of a second front in Europe has as its object the withdrawal of German forces from the Eastern Front to the West and the creation in the West of a serious base of resistance to the German-Fascist forces, and the affording of relief by this means to the situation of the Soviet forces on the Soviet-German front in 1942. It is easy to grasp that the refusal of the Government of Great Britain to create a second front in 1942 in Europe inflicts a mortal blow to the whole of Soviet public opinion, which calculates on the creation of of a second front, and that it complicates the situation of the Red Army at the front and prejudices the plan of the Soviet command. I am not referring to the fact that the difficulties arising for the Red Army as a result of the refusal to create a second front in 1942 will undoubtedly be detrimental to the military situation of England and all the remaining Allies. It appears to me *and my colleagues*[1] that the most favourable conditions exist in 1942 for the creation of a second front in Europe, inasmuch as almost all the forces of the German Army, and the best forces to boot, have been withdrawn to the Eastern Front, leaving in Europe an inconsiderable amount of forces, and these of inferior quality. It is unknown whether the year of 1943

[1] My italics—Author.

will offer conditions for the creation of a second front as favourable as 1942.

We are of the opinion therefore that it is particularly in 1942 that the creation of a second front in Europe is possible and should be effective. I was however unfortunately unsuccessful in convincing Mr. Prime Minister of Great Britain thereof, while Mr. Harriman, the representative of the President of the United States, fully supported Mr. Prime Minister in the negotiations held in Moscow.

The next morning, August 14, having rested well, I prepared, with the aid of the C.I.G.S. and Cadogan, the following reply, which seemed to me suitable and conclusive:

The best second front in 1942 and the only large-scale operation possible from the Atlantic is "Torch." If this can be effected in October it will give more aid to Russia than any other plan. It also prepares the way for 1943, and has the four advantages mentioned by Premier Stalin in the conversation of August 12. The British and United States Governments have made up their minds about this, and all preparations are proceeding with the utmost speed.

2. Compared with "Torch," the attack with six or eight Anglo-American divisions on the Cherbourg peninsula and the Channel Islands would be a hazardous and futile operation. The Germans have enough troops in the West to block us in this narrow peninsula with fortified lines, and would concentrate all their air forces in the West upon us. In the opinion of all the British naval, military, and air authorities, the operation could only end in disaster. Even if the lodgment were made it would not bring a single division back from Russia. It would also be far more a running sore for us than for the enemy, and would use up wastefully and wantonly the key men and the landing-craft required for real action in 1943. This is our settled view. The C.I.G.S. will go into details with the Russian commanders to any extent that may be desired.

3. No promise has been broken by Great Britain or the United States. I point to paragraph 5 of my *aide-mémoire* given to Mr. Molotov on June 10, 1942, which distinctly says, "We can therefore give no promise."

This *aide-mémoire* followed upon lengthy conversations, in which the very small chance of such a plan being adopted was made abundantly clear. Several of these conversations are on record.

4. However, all the talk about an Anglo-American invasion of France this year has misled the enemy, and has held large air forces and considerable military forces on the French Channel coast. It would be injurious to all common interests, especially Russian interests, if any public controversy arose in which it would be necessary for the British Government to unfold to the nation the crushing arguments which they conceive themselves to possess against "Sledgehammer." Widespread discouragement would be caused to the Russian armies, who have been buoyed up on this subject, and the enemy would be free to withdraw further forces from the West. The wisest course is to use "Sledgehammer" as a blind for "Torch," and proclaim "Torch" when it begins as the second front. This is what we ourselves mean to do.

5. We cannot admit that the conversations with M. Molotov about the second front, safeguarded as they were by reservations both oral and written, formed any ground for altering the strategic plans of the Russian High Command.

6. We reaffirm our resolve to aid our Russian Allies by every practicable means.

* * *

That evening we attended the official dinner at the Kremlin, where about forty people, including several of the military commanders, members of Politburo, and other high officials were present. Stalin and Molotov did the honours in cordial fashion. These dinners were lengthy, and from the beginning many toasts were proposed and responded to in very short speeches. Silly tales have been told of how these Soviet dinners became drinking-bouts. There is no truth whatever in this. The Marshal and his colleagues invariably drank their toasts from tiny glasses, taking only a sip on each occasion. I had been well brought up.

During the dinner Stalin talked to me in lively fashion through the interpreter Pavlov. "Some years ago," he said, "we had a visit from Mr. George Bernard Shaw and Lady Astor." Lady Astor suggested that Mr. Lloyd George should be invited to visit Moscow, to which Stalin had replied, "Why should we ask him? He was the head of the intervention." On this Lady Astor said, "That is not true. It was Churchill who misled him." "Anyhow," said Stalin, "Lloyd George was head of the Government and belonged to the Left. He was responsible, and we like a downright enemy better than a pretending friend." "Well, Churchill is finished finally," said Lady Astor. "I am not so sure," Stalin had answered. "If a great crisis comes, the English people might turn to the old war-horse." At this point I interrupted, saying, "There is much in what she said. I was very active in the intervention, and I do not wish you to think otherwise." He smiled amicably, so I said, "Have you forgiven me?" "Premier Stalin, he say," said Interpreter Pavlov, "all that is in the past, and the past belongs to God."

* * *

In the course of one of my later talks with Stalin I said, "Lord Beaverbrook has told me that when he was on his mission to Moscow in October, 1941, you asked him, 'What did Churchill mean by saying in Parliament that he had given me warnings of the impending German attack?' I was of course," said I, "referring to the telegram I sent you in April '41," and I produced the telegram which Sir Stafford Cripps had tardily delivered. When it was read and translated to him Stalin shrugged his shoulders. "I remember it. I did not need any warnings. I knew war would come, but I thought I might gain another six months or so." In the common cause I refrained from asking what would have happened to us all if we had gone down for ever while he was giving Hitler so much valuable material, time, and aid.

As soon as I could I gave a more formal account of the banquet to Mr. Attlee and the President.

Former Naval Person to Deputy Prime Minister and President Roosevelt   17 Aug. 42

The dinner passed off in a very friendly atmosphere and the usual Russian ceremonies. Wavell made an excellent speech in Russian. I proposed Stalin's health, and Alexander Cadogan proposed death and damnation to the Nazis. Though I sat on Stalin's right I got no opportunity of talking about serious things. Stalin and I were photographed together, also with Harriman. Stalin made quite a long speech proposing the "Intelligence Service," in the course of which he made a curious reference to the Dardanelles in 1915, saying that the British had won and the Germans and Turks were already retreating, but we did not know because the intelligence was faulty. This picture, though inaccurate, was evidently meant to be complimentary to me.

2. I left about 1.30 A.M., as I was afraid we should be drawn into a lengthy film and was fatigued. When I said good-bye to Stalin he said that any differences that existed were only of method. I said we would try to remove even those differences by deeds. After a cordial handshake I then took my departure, and got some way down the crowded room, but he hurried after me and accompanied me an immense distance through corridors and staircases to the front door, where we again shook hands.

3. Perhaps in my account to you of the Thursday night meeting I took too gloomy a view. I feel I must make full allowance for the really grievous disappointment which they feel here that we can do nothing more to help them in their immense struggle. In the upshot they have swallowed this bitter pill. Everything for us now turns on hastening "Torch" and defeating Rommel.

* * *

It had been agreed between Stalin and me that there should also be meetings between the high military authorities on both sides. Two conferences were held on August 15.

I reported the results to Mr. Attlee and President Roosevelt as follows:

At a conference in Moscow on Saturday [August 15], Voroshilov and Shaposhnikov[2] met Brooke, Wavell, and Tedder, who offered detailed reasons about no "Sledgehammer." No impression was made, as the Russians, though entirely good-humoured, were acting under strict instructions. They did not even attempt to argue the matter in serious detail. After some time C.I.G.S. asked for details about the Caucasus position, to which Voroshilov replied he had no authority to speak on this point, but would ask for it. Accordingly, in the afternoon a second meeting was held, at which the Russians repeated what Stalin had said to us, to the effect that twenty-five divisions would be assigned to the defence of the Caucasus mountain line and the passages at either end, and that they believed they could hold both Batum and Baku and the Caucasus range until the winter snows greatly improved their position. However, C.I.G.S. is by no means reassured. For instance, Voroshilov stated that all the passes were fortified, but when C.I.G.S. had flown at 150 feet all up the west bank of the Caspian he only saw the northern line of defence being begun with anti-tank obstacles, pill-boxes, etc. In my private conversation with Stalin he revealed to me other solid reasons for his confidence, including a counter-offensive on a great scale, but as he asked me to keep this specially secret I will not refer to it further here. My own feeling is that it is an even chance they will hold, but C.I.G.S. will not go so far as this.

* * *

I had been offended by many things which had been said at our conferences. I made every allowance for the strain under which the Soviet leaders lay, with their vast front flaming and bleeding along nearly two thousand miles, and the Germans but fifty miles from Moscow and advancing towards the Caspian Sea. The technical military discussions had not gone well.

[2] The Russian Chief of Staff.

Our generals had asked all sorts of questions to which their Soviet colleagues were not authorised to give answers. The only Soviet demand was for "A Second Front *now*." In the end Brooke was rather blunt, and the military conference came to a somewhat abrupt conclusion.

We were to start at dawn on the 16th. On the evening before, I went at seven o'clock to say good-bye to Stalin. We had a useful and important talk. I asked particularly whether he would be able to hold the Caucasus mountain passes, and also prevent the Germans reaching the Caspian, taking the oilfields round Baku, with all that meant, and then driving southward through Turkey or Persia. He spread out the map, and then said with quiet confidence, "We shall stop them. They will not cross the mountains." He added, "There are rumours that the Turks will attack us in Turkestan. If they do I shall be able to deal with them as well." I said there was no danger of this. The Turks meant to keep out, and would certainly not quarrel with England.

Our hour's conversation drew to its close, and I got up to say good-bye. Stalin seemed suddenly embarrassed, and said in a more cordial tone than he had yet used with me, "You are leaving at daybreak. Why should we not go to my house and have some drinks?" I said that I was in principle always in favour of such a policy. So he led the way through many passages and rooms till we came out into a still roadway within the Kremlin, and in a couple of hundred yards gained the apartment where he lived. He showed me his own rooms, which were of moderate size, simple, dignified, and four in number—a dining-room, working-room, bedroom, and a large bathroom. Presently there appeared, first a very aged housekeeper and later a handsome red-haired girl, who kissed her father dutifully. He looked at me with a twinkle in his eye, as if, so I thought, to convey, "You see, even we Bolsheviks have family life." Stalin's daughter started lay-ing the table, and in a short time the housekeeper appeared with a few dishes. Meanwhile Stalin had been uncorking various bottles, which began to make an imposing array. Then he said, "Why should we not have Molotov? He is worrying about the communiqué. We could settle it here. There is one thing about Molotov—he can drink." I then realised that there was to be a dinner. I had planned to dine at State Villa No. 7, where General Anders, the Polish commander, was awaiting me, but I told my new and excellent interpreter, Major Birse, to telephone that I should not be back till after midnight. Presently Molotov arrived. We sat down, and, with the two interpreters, were five in number. Major Birse had lived twenty years in Moscow, and got on very well with the Marshal, with whom he for some time kept up a running conversation, in which I could not share.

We actually sat at this table from 8.30 till 2.30 the next morning, which, with my previous interview, made a total of more than seven hours. The dinner was evidently improvised on the spur of the moment, but gradually more and more food arrived. We pecked and picked, as seemed to be the Russian fashion, at a long succession of choice dishes, and sipped a variety of excellent wines. Molotov assumed his most affable manner, and Stalin, to make things go, chaffed him unmercifully.

Presently we talked about the convoys to Russia. This led him to make a rough and rude remark about the almost total destruction of the Arctic convoy in June. I have recounted this incident in its place. I did not know so much about it then as I do now.

"Mr. Stalin asks," said Pavlov, with some hesitation, "has the British Navy no sense of glory?" I answered, "You must take it from me that what was done was right. I really do know a lot about the Navy and sea war." "Meaning," said Stalin, "that I know nothing." "Russia is a land animal," I said; "the British are sea animals." He fell silent and recovered his good-humour. I turned the talk on to Molotov. "Was the Marshal aware that his Foreign Secretary on his recent visit to Washington had said he was determined to pay a visit to New York entirely by himself, and that the delay in his return was not due to any defect in the aeroplane, but because he was off on his own?"

Although almost anything can be said in fun at a Russian dinner, Molotov looked rather serious at this. But Stalin's face lit with merriment as he said:

"It was not to New York he went. He went to Chicago, where the other gangsters live."

Relations having thus been entirely restored, the talk ran on. I opened the question of a British landing in Norway with Russian support, and explained how, if we could take the North Cape in the winter and destroy the Germans there, the path of the convoys would henceforth be open. This idea was always, as has been seen, one of my favourite plans. Stalin seemed much attracted by it, and, after talking of ways and means, we agreed we must do it if possible.

* * *

About 1 A.M. Cadogan arrived with the draft, and we set to work to put it into final form. A considerable sucking-pig was brought to the table. Hitherto Stalin had only tasted the dishes, but now it was half-past one in the morning and around his usual dinner hour. He invited Cadogan to join him in the conflict, and when my friend excused himself, our host fell upon the victim single-handed. After this had been achieved he went abruptly into the next room to receive the reports from all

sectors of the front, which were delivered to him from 2 A.M. onwards. It was about twenty minutes before he returned, and by that time we had the communiqué agreed.

* * *

The following was the published text of the communiqué.

Prime Minister of Great Britain, Mr. Winston Churchill, with the President of the Council of the People's Commissars of U.S.S.R., J. V. Stalin.

Negotiations have taken place in Moscow between President of the Council of the People's Commissars of U.S.S.R., J. V. Stalin, and Prime Minister of Great Britain, Mr. Winston Churchill, in which Mr. Harriman, representing the President of the United States of America, participated. There took part in the discussions the People's Commissar for Foreign Affairs, V. M. Molotov, Marshal K. E. Voroshilov, from the Soviet side; the British Ambassador, Sir A. Clark Kerr, C.I.G.S. Sir A. Brooke, and other responsible representatives of the British armed forces, and the Permanent Under-Secretary of State for Foreign Affairs, Sir A. Cadogan, from the British side.

A number of decisions were reached covering the field of the war against Hitlerite Germany and her associates in Europe. This just war of liberation both Governments are determined to carry on with all their power and energy until the complete destruction of Hitlerism and any similar tyranny has been achieved. The discussions, which were carried on in an atmosphere of cordiality and complete sincerity, provided an opportunity of reaffirming the existence of the close friendships and understanding between the Soviet Union, Great Britain, and the United States of America, in entire accordance with the Allied relationships existing between them.

THE SECOND FRONT IN EUROPE

JOSEPH STALIN

Whatever Stalin's personal feelings about Prime Minister Churchill after their August discussions concerning the second front, the fact remained: there was no second front. The great majority of Hitler's divisions still pounded at Soviet troops and ravaged Soviet lands. Yet in November 1942, Stalin boldly announced his complete confidence that his allies would open a new front. Indeed, he emphasized with a hint of menace, they must open it, if only for their own good; and he prophesied that the Anglo-Soviet-American "fighting alliance" would ultimately triumph.

How are we to explain the fact that the Germans this year were still able to take the initiative of military operations into their hands, and to achieve substantial tactical successes on our front?

It is to be explained by the fact that the Germans and their allies succeeded in mustering all their available reserves, hurling them on the eastern front and creating a large superiority of forces in one of the directions.

There can be no doubt that but for these measures the Germans could not have achieved any success on our front.

But why were they able to muster all their reserves and hurl them on to the eastern front? Because the absence of a second front in Europe enabled them to carry out this operation without any risk to themselves.

Hence the chief reason for the tactical successes of the Germans on our front this year is that the absence of a second front in Europe enabled them to hurl on to our front all their available reserves and to create a large superiority of forces in the south-western direction.

Suppose a second front existed in Europe, as it existed in the first World War, and that the second front were diverting, say, sixty German divisions and twenty divisions of Germany's allies. What would have been the position of the German troops on our front then?

It is not difficult to guess that their position would have been deplorable. More than that, it would have been the beginning of the end of the German-Fascist troops, for in that case the Red Army would not be where it is now, but somewhere near Pskov, Minsk, Zhitomir and Odessa.

That means that in the summer of this year the German-Fascist army would already have been on the verge of disaster. If that has not occurred, it is because the Germans were saved by the absence of a second front in Europe.

Let us examine the question of a second front in Europe in its historical aspect. In the first World War Germany had to fight on two fronts: in the west, chiefly against Great Britain and France, and in the east against the Russian troops. Thus in the first World War there existed a second front against Germany.

Of the 220 divisions which Germany had then, not more than 85 German divisions were stationed on the Russian front. If to this we add the troops of Germany's allies then facing the Russian front—namely 37 Austro-Hungarian divisions, 2 Bulgarian divisions and 3 Turkish divisions—we get a total of 127 divisions facing Russian troops.

From J. V. Stalin, "Report by the Chairman of the State Committee for Defence at ceremonial session of the Moscow Soviet of Working People's Deputies, jointly with Party and public organizations of Moscow City, 6 November, 1942," in *Soviet Foreign Policy during the Patriotic War*, trans. by Andrew Rothstein (London and New York, 1946), I, 45–49, by permission of Hutchinson & Co., Ltd.

The rest of the divisions of Germany and her allies mainly held the front against the Anglo-French troops, while part of them performed garrison service in occupied territories of Europe. Such was the position in the first World War.

What is the position now, in the second World War, in September of this year, let us say? According to authenticated information which is beyond all doubt, of the 256 divisions which Germany now has, not less than 179 German divisions are on our front.

If to this we add 22 Rumanian divisions, 14 Finnish divisions, 10 Italian divisions, 13 Hungarian divisions, 1 Slovak and 1 Spanish division, we get a total of 240 divisions which are now fighting on our front.

The remaining divisions of Germany and her allies are performing garrison service in the occupied countries (France, Belgium, Norway, Holland, Yugoslavia, Poland, Czechoslovakia, etc.), while part of them are fighting in Libya or Egypt against Great Britain, the Libyan front diverting in all 4 German divisions and 11 Italian divisions.

Hence, instead of the 127 divisions as in the first World War, we are now facing on our front no less than 240 divisions, and, instead of 85 German divisions, we now have 179 German divisions fighting the Red Army.

There you have the chief reason and foundation for the tactical success of the German-Fascist troops on our front in the summer of this year.

The German invasion of our country is often compared to Napoleon's invasion of Russia. But this comparison will not bear criticism. Of the 600,000 troops which began the campaign against Russia, Napoleon scarcely brought 130,000 or 140,000 as far as Borodino. That was all he had at his disposal at Moscow.

Well, we now have over 3,000,000 troops facing the front of the Red Army and armed with all the implements of modern warfare. What comparison can there be here?

The German invasion of our country is also sometimes compared to the German invasion of Russia at the time of the first World War. But neither will this comparison bear criticism. First, in that World War there was a second front in Europe which rendered the Germans' position very difficult, whereas in this war there is no second front in Europe.

Secondly, in this war, twice as many troops are facing our front as in the first World War. Obviously the comparison is not appropriate. You can now conceive how serious and extraordinary are the difficulties confronting the Red Army, and how great is the heroism displayed by the Red Army in its war of liberation against the German-Fascist troops.

I think that no other country and no other army could have withstood such an onslaught of the brutalized bands of the German-Fascist brigands and their allies. Only our Soviet country and only our Red Army are capable of withstanding such an onslaught (*loud applause*). And not only withstanding it but also overpowering it.

It is often asked: But will there be a second front in Europe after all? Yes, there will be; sooner or later, there will be one. And it will be not only because we need it, but above all because our Allies need it no less than we do.

Our Allies cannot fail to realize that since France has been put out of action, the absence of a second front against Fascist Germany may end badly for all freedom-loving countries, including the Allies themselves.

THE FIGHTING ALLIANCE OF THE U.S.S.R., GREAT BRITAIN AND THE U.S.A. AGAINST HITLERITE GERMANY AND HER ALLIES IN EUROPE

It may now be considered indisputable that, in the course of the war imposed upon the nations by Hitlerite Germany, a radical demarcation of forces and the formation of two opposite camps have taken place: the camp of the Italo-German coalition and the camp of the Anglo-Soviet-American coalition. It is equally indisputable that these two opposite coalitions are guided by two different and opposite programmes of action.

The programme of action of the Italo-German coalition may be described by the following points: racial hatred, supremacy of "chosen" nations; subjugation of other nations and seizure of their territories; economic enslavement of subjugated nations and plunder of their national wealth; destruction of democratic liberties; the institution of the Hitlerite regime everywhere.

The programme of action of the Anglo-Soviet-American coalition is: the abolition of racial exclusiveness; the equality of nations and the inviolability of their territories; the liberation of the enslaved nations and the restoration of their sovereign rights; the right of every nation to arrange its affairs as it wishes; economic aid to the nations that have suffered, and assistance to them in achieving their material welfare; the restoration of democratic liberties; the destruction of the Hitlerite regime.

The effect of the programme of action of the Italo-German coalition has been that all the occupied countries of Europe— Norway, Denmark, Belgium, Holland, France, Poland, Czechoslovakia, Yugoslavia, Greece and the occupied regions of the U.S.S.R.—are burning with hatred of the Italo-German tyranny, are doing all the damage they can to the Germans and their allies, and are waiting for a favourable opportunity to take revenge on their enslavers for the humiliations and outrages which they are suffering.

In this connection, one of the characteristic features of the present moment is the progressively growing isolation of the Italo-German coalition and the depletion of its moral and political reserves in Europe, its growing weakness and disintegration.

The effect of the programme of action of the Anglo-Soviet-American coalition has been that all the occupied countries in Europe are full of sympathy for the members of this coalition and are prepared to render them all the help of which they are capable.

In this connection, another characteristic feature of the present moment is that the moral and political reserves of this coalition are growing from day to day in Europe—and not only in Europe—and that this coalition is progressively winning millions of sympathizers ready to join in the fighting against Hitler's tyranny.

If the relative strength of these two coalitions is examined from the standpoint of human and material resources, one cannot help reaching the conclusion that the Anglo-Soviet-American coalition has an indisputable advantage.

But here the question arises: is this advantage alone sufficient for victory? There are occasions, as we know, when resources are abundant, but are expended so unwisely that the advantage is nullified. Obviously, what is needed in addition to resources is the capacity to mobilize these resources and the ability to make the correct use of them.

Is there any reason for doubting the existence of such ability and such capacity on the part of the people of the Anglo-Soviet-American coalition? There are some who doubt this. But what grounds have they for their doubts?

In the past the people of this coalition have displayed their ability and capacity to mobilize the resources of their countries and to use them correctly for purposes of economic, cultural and political development.

Then what grounds are there for doubting that men who have displayed capacity and ability in mobilizing and distributing resources for economic, cultural and political purposes will prove incapable of doing the same thing for purposes of war? I think there are no such grounds.

It is said by some that the Anglo-Soviet-American coalition has every chance of winning and would certainly win, if it did not have one organic defect which is capable of weakening and disintegrating it. This defect, in the opinion of these people, is that the coalition consists of heterogeneous elements with different ideologies, and that this circumstance will prevent their organizing joint action against the common enemy.

I think that this assertion is incorrect.

It would be ridiculous to deny the difference in the ideologies and social systems of the States composing the Anglo-Soviet-American coalition. But does this preclude the possibility and expediency of joint action on the part of the members of the coalition against a common enemy who holds out the threat of enslavement for them? It certainly does not preclude it.

More than that, the existence of this threat imperatively imposes the necessity of joint action upon the members of the coalition, in order to save mankind from reverting to savagery and medieval barbarism.

Is not the programme of action of the Anglo-Soviet-American coalition a sufficient basis for the organization of the joint struggle against Hitlerite tyranny and for the achievement of victory over it? I think that it is quite sufficient.

The assumption of these people is incorrect also because of the fact that it is completely refuted by the events of the past year. Indeed, if these people were right we should be observing a progressive mutual alienation of the members of the Anglo-Soviet-American coalition.

Yet, far from observing this, we have facts and events indicative of progressive rapprochement between the members of the Anglo-Soviet-American coalition, and their unification into a single fighting alliance. The events of the past year supply direct proof of this.

In July, 1941, several weeks after Germany attacked the U.S.S.R., Great Britain concluded with us an agreement on "joint action in the war against Germany." At that time we had not yet any agreement with the United States of America on this subject.

Ten months later, on May 26, 1942, during Comrade Molotov's visit to Great Britain, the latter concluded with us a Treaty for an Alliance in the war against Hitlerite Germany and her associates in Europe and for collaboration and mutual assistance after the war. This Treaty was concluded for a period of twenty years. It marks an historic turning-point in the relations between our country and Great Britain.

In June, 1942, during Comrade Molotov's visit to the United States, the United States of America concluded with us an Agreement on the principles applying to mutual aid in the prosecution of the war against aggression, an agreement representing an important step forward in the relations between the U.S.S.R. and the United States.

Finally, one should mention so important a fact as the visit to Moscow of the Prime Minister of Great Britain, Mr. Churchill, which established complete mutual understanding between the leaders of the two countries.

There can be no doubt that all these facts point to a progressive rapprochement between the U.S.S.R., Great Britain and the United States of America, and to their uniting in a fighting alliance against the Italo-German coalition.

It follows that the logic of things is stronger than any other logic. There can be only one conclusion, namely that the Anglo-Soviet-American coalition has every chance of vanquishing the Italo-German coalition and undoubtedly will vanquish it.

Yalta, Potsdam, and the New, Bipolar World 1945

IX

THE YALTA CONFERENCE

WILLIAM L. NEUMANN

William Neumann's account of the Yalta Conference is based upon the principal sources and documents available in 1950 and reflects in considerable degree the inclination of many Americans to conclude that something went wrong at Yalta, that Roosevelt and Churchill made serious errors in their dealings with Stalin, for which the world has had to pay in subsequent years. Undoubtedly errors of judgment and execution were made during the wartime negotiations, and have had grave consequences for the world, but the problem of the precise degree of naïveté or wisdom displayed by Roosevelt and Churchill at Yalta is not the main concern here. More important from the point of view of the student of Soviet foreign policy are the demands Stalin presented and the concessions he made, the concrete terms of the agreements reached, and the nature of the difficult problems put off for later discussion. Somewhere along the road from Stalingrad the Soviet Union had become one of the world's greatest powers. At Yalta Stalin negotiated from a position of strength he had never before enjoyed; both he and his allies were thoroughly conscious of this fact.

THE most controversial of the wartime conferences is that commonly named for the small Russian town of Yalta. Roosevelt, Churchill and Stalin met there for the last time, February 3–11, 1945, and for the only conference in which all three were accompanied by their foreign ministers. The location of the conference on Soviet soil was again due to Stalin's reluctance to travel far from Moscow. Roosevelt chose the warm water coast of the Crimea for the meeting and Stalin selected the port of Yalta in that area. Churchill reluctantly agreed, complaining that the climate was not warm enough and that the comforts would be too few. Ten years of research, Churchill said, could not have located a worse place for a conference than Yalta.

Roosevelt was accompanied by Harry Hopkins; Edward Stettinius, the new Secretary of State; James Byrnes, the latter's successor-to-be; and by General Marshall, Admirals Leahy and King. Averell Harriman, Ambassador to Moscow, attended the conference as a consultant along with Alger Hiss, then Deputy Director of the Office of

From William L. Neumann, *Making the Peace, 1941–1945* (Washington, D. C., 1950), pp. 78–101. Reprinted by permission of the Foundation for Foreign Affairs, Inc.

Special Political Affairs. Some social life was contributed to the conference by the presence of the Democratic Party boss, Edward Flynn and the President's daughter, Anna Boettiger. Mr. Harriman's daughter and Churchill's daughter completed the female guest list.

The President was not in good health on his trip across the Atlantic. He neither spent much time in conferring with his advisers, nor did he read the policy papers prepared for his guidance at the conference. Questions have been raised, as a result, about the President's physical and mental competence at the conference. Stettinius believes that Roosevelt was fully capable of dealing with each situation throughout the meetings, although he agrees that the President's health had deteriorated in the previous two months. Others argue that Roosevelt seldom relied on his advisers for opinions on basic problems and that his lack of preparation had no effect on the decisions taken at Yalta.

The conference ran for eight days, and at its conclusion a lengthy report was issued jointly by the three powers. Policy statements on the United Nations, Germany, Poland and Yugoslavia were all included in this, the fullest official account of any of the wartime conferences.

Secret agreements were made, however, the texts of which were not released at that time. Early in March 1945, the agreement to call the San Francisco Conference was given to the press along with the decision on the voting procedures in the proposed Security Council. On February 11, 1946, the secret agreement by which the Soviet Union was to enter the war against Japan was published. On March 24, 1947, the texts of fourteen other agreements were given to the press by the State Department. Supplementing the official texts are the published memoirs of Byrnes, Hopkins and Stettinius. The result has been to make available a much fuller, but still a controversial picture of the last wartime conference.

GERMANY

Occupation and Control

We have agreed on common policies and plans for enforcing the unconditional surrender terms which we shall impose together on Nazi Germany after German armed resistance has been finally crushed. These terms will not be made known until the final defeat of Germany has been accomplished. Under the agreed plan, the forces of the three powers will each occupy a separate zone of Germany. Coordinated administration and control has been provided for under the plan through a central control commission consisting of the Supreme Commanders of the three powers with headquarters in Berlin. It has been agreed that France should be invited by the three powers, if she should so desire, to take over a zone of occupation, and to participate as a fourth member of the control commission. The limits of the French Zone will be agreed by the four governments concerned through their representatives on the European Advisory Commission.

It is our inflexible purpose to destroy German militarism and Nazism and to ensure that Germany will never again be able to disturb the peace of the world. We are determined to disarm and disband all German armed forces; break up for all time the German General Staff that has repeatedly contrived the resurgence of German militarism; remove or destroy all German military equipment; eliminate or control all German industry that could be used for military production; bring all war criminals to just and swift punishment and exact reparation in kind for the destruction wrought by the Germans; wipe out the Nazi Party, Nazi laws, organizations and institutions, remove all Nazi and militarist influences from public office and from cultural and economic life of the German people; and take in harmony such other measures in Germany as may be necessary to the future peace and safety of the world. It is not our purpose to destroy the people of Germany, but only when Nazism and militarism have been extirpated will there be hope for a decent life for Germans, and a place for them in the comity of nations.

Joint Communique

The dismemberment of Germany, suggested by Stalin and agreed upon by Roosevelt and Eden as early as March 1943, was the first German question raised by Stalin. Churchill in his visit to Moscow in October 1944 had suggested replacing Roosevelt's 5-part division by separating Germany into Prussia and Bavaria with the Ruhr and Westphalia under international control. Stalin felt that the time had come at Yalta for a final decision. Churchill still accepted dismemberment in principle, but parried any drawing of boundaries which he felt required lengthy study of details by a special committee.

No decision was reached, but the word "dismemberment" was to be included in the surrender terms for Germany. It was to be one of the steps deemed "requisite for future peace and security." No mention of this word was included in the official release in order to avoid any stiffening of German resistance. In May 1945 when Hopkins again visited Stalin in Moscow, the Soviet chief had decided that both Britain and the United States were against partition of the German Reich. Hopkins assured him that this was not true and Stalin agreed to keep an open mind on this question. By the time of the Potsdam Conference in July 1945, both Britain and the United States had shifted views and dismemberment plans were dropped.

The second question raised by Stalin involved the occupation program. France had been pressing Britain for a share in the occupation and control of Germany so Churchill asked Roosevelt and Stalin to make this concession. The area to be given France, he suggested, could be carved out of the American and British zones. Stalin opposed and jokingly spoke of keeping the Big Three an exclusive club, limited in membership to nations with five millions or more soldiers.[1] Stalin also argued that including France would establish a precedent and other nations would ask for occupation zones. Roosevelt who earlier said that he favored a French zone only out of "kindness," at first agreed with Stalin's position. Stalin asked him how long American troops would stay in Germany and Roosevelt answered that he did not think that he could hold public and Congressional support for American occupation forces for more than two years. Churchill then used this statement to argue the importance of using French troops. A concession was finally made to Churchill on the marking out of a French zone, but Stalin still did not want France to participate in the Allied Control Council. Roosevelt's change of mind on this question won another concession from Stalin and France was given a seat on the Council.

The actual drawing up of the boundaries of the occupation zones, according to Stettinius, was done in London by the European Advisory Commission in September and November 1944. The decision to make Berlin the headquarters of the Control Commission was made at Yalta, but there is no evidence of any discussion of future British and American access to this island in the Soviet zone.

Reparations

We have considered the question of the damage caused by Germany to the allied nations in this war and recognized it as just that Germany be obliged to make compensation for this damage in kind to the greatest extent possible. A commission for the compensation of damage will be established. The commission will be instructed to consider the question of the extent and methods for compensating damage caused by Germany to the allied countries. The commission will work in Moscow.

Joint Communique

1. Germany must pay in kind for the losses caused by her to the Allied nations in the course of the war. Reparations are to be re-

[1] Edward R. Stettinius, *Roosevelt and the Russians* (New York, 1949), p. 128, attributes this remark to Stalin, but James Byrnes, *Speaking Frankly* (New York, 1947), p. 25, reports that this witticism came from Churchill.

ceived in the first instance by those countries which have borne the main burden of the war, have suffered the heaviest losses and have organized victory over the enemy.

2. Reparation in kind is to be exacted from Germany in three following forms:

(a) Removals within two years from the surrender of Germany or the cessation of organized resistance from the national wealth of Germany located on the territory of Germany herself as well as outside her territory (equipment, machine tools, ships, rolling stock, German investments abroad, shares of industrial, transport and other enterprises in Germany, etc.), these removals to be carried out chiefly for the purpose of destroying the war potential of Germany.

(b) Annual deliveries of goods from current production for a period to be fixed.

(c) Use of German labor.

3. For the working out on the above principles of a detailed plan for exaction of reparation from Germany an Allied reparation commission will be set up in Moscow. It will consist of three representatives — one from the Union of Soviet Socialist Republics, one from the United Kingdom and one from the United States of America.

4. With regard to the fixing of the total sum of the reparation as well as the distribution of it among the countries which suffered from the German aggression, the Soviet and American delegations agreed as follows:

The Moscow reparation commission should take in its initial studies as a basis for discussion the suggestion of the Soviet Government that the total sum of the reparation in accordance with the points (a) and (b) of Paragraph 2 should be 20 billion dollars and that 50 percent of it should go to the Union of Soviet Socialist Republics.

The British delegation was of the opinion that, pending consideration of the reparation question by the Moscow reparation commission, no figures of reparation should be mentioned.

The above Soviet-American proposal has been passed to the Moscow reparation commission as one of the proposals to be considered by the commission.

Secret Protocol

The reparation discussions were initiated by the Russians. Stalin had wanted to discuss this question as early as September 1941, and at Yalta, Maisky, Deputy Commissar for Foreign Affairs, presented a specific proposal. He asked for reparations in kind, to be withdrawn from Germany in two ways. The first was capital reparations directly from Germany's national wealth in the form of factories, machinery, etc. This was to be completed in two years and to leave Germany with only 20 percent of her heavy industry. The second form of reparations was to be taken from current production over a period of ten years. Amounts were to be apportioned on the basis of a country's contribution to the winning of the war as well as its material war losses. The Russian representative set the total amount of reparations at twenty billions with half to go to the USSR, eight billions to Britain and the United States, and the remaining two billions to other allied countries.

The British raised the chief objections to the Russian proposals. Churchill said that he would like to get some benefits for his country from reparations, but recalling the failure of the reparations system after the first World War, he doubted if benefits would follow. He objected to apportionment on the basis of contributions to the war effort, and mentioned instead, "each according to his needs." The strongest of the British objections was to naming any specific sum, especially the proposed twenty billions.

Roosevelt did not stand behind Churchill on his objections. He believed that a specific figure should be mentioned and was willing to use twenty billions "as a basis" for the discussions of the Moscow reparations commission. The British remained adamant on this point and the final protocol included both the Soviet-American and British point of view. According to a later Soviet interpretation, the United States stood committed to the twenty billion figure with half of that sum going to the USSR. Roosevelt did not object to the Soviet estimates, but it was a strained interpretation to call his position a commitment.

The clause in the secret protocol including German labor in reparations marked a shocking return to the barbaric practice by which the victor exacted forced labor from the conquered. No mention of labor had been made in the Soviet proposal and Stalin said that he was not prepared to talk about the use of manpower. Roosevelt had suggested this form of reparations in his talks with Hull in October 1943 and it was included in the Morgenthau plan. But at Yalta Roosevelt said that the United States for its part did not want any German labor. He was also sure that Britain felt the same way. However, the British proposal, which countered the Russian draft, introduced the use of German labor and lorry service as a form of reparations. Possibly this was an attempt to win concessions from the Russians on the total reparations figure. Byrnes was unaware of the inclusion of the labor clause at Yalta, but states that he later learned that Mr. Maisky had added human beings to the reparation list. Whether a British or Russian proposal, there is no evidence that the United States raised any objections. Stettinius states only that his country had "great misgivings" about labor reparations. Sherwood ascribes to Roosevelt the hope that reparations in all forms would be discarded, but such an interpretation conflicts with Roosevelt's attitudes documented by other memoirs. In any event, the labor clause was not included in the postwar reparations agreements made at the Potsdam conference.

The suggestion of Britain that France be included on the Reparations Commission as a major recipient was strongly rejected by Stalin who pointed to the insignificance of France's contribution to the war effort. It was therefore agreed to include only the three major powers on the Reparations Commission. The subsequent breakdown of the reparations agreements and the inclusion of France at the suggestion of the United States, was to become a Soviet griev-

ance. Stalin told Hopkins in May 1945 that Poland and Yugoslavia both deserved a place on the commission more than France. Continued Soviet complaints about the implementation of the reparations program were to mark the early postwar years.

POLAND

Provisional Government

A new situation has been created in Poland as a result of her complete liberation by the Red Army. This calls for the establishment of a Polish Provisional Government which can be more broadly based than was possible before the recent liberation of Western Poland. The Provisional Government which is now functioning in Poland should therefore be reorganized on a broader democratic basis with the inclusion of democratic leaders from Poland itself and from Poles abroad. This new Government should then be called the Polish Provisional Government of National Unity.

M. Molotov, Mr. Harriman and Sir A. Clark Kerr are authorized as a commission to consult in the first instance in Moscow with members of the present Provisional Government and with other Polish democratic leaders from within Poland and from abroad, with a view to the reorganization of the present Government along the above lines. This Polish Provisional Government of National Unity shall be pledged to the holding of free and unfettered elections as soon as possible on the basis of universal suffrage and secret ballot. In these elections all democratic and anti-Nazi parties shall have the right to take part and put forward candidates.

Joint Communique

One of the Polish problems on the Yalta agenda was the existence of two groups of Poles, both claiming to be the legitimate government of Poland. One group, formed at Lublin under Soviet sponsorship and heavily weighted with Communists, declared itself the provisional government on January 1, 1945 and was recognized by the USSR. Soviet troops as they pushed the Germans out of Poland made it possible for this Lublin Committee of National Liberation to become the *de facto* government. In London, the Polish Government-in-exile, which included many anti-Communist Poles, also claimed the right to rule. Since Britain and the United States had given strong verbal support to the London Poles, the problem was one of reconciling the interests of this group with the Soviet-sponsored regime and of constructing a Polish government which would be acceptable to both the USSR and the western powers.

Stettinius brought to Yalta a State Department recommendation that a Polish government of national unity be created out of representative members of five Polish political parties, including the Communists. Mikolajczyk and other London Poles were to be included in the new government, but an amalgamation of the London and Lublin governments was to be opposed. Elections, supervised by outside powers, including the United States, were to decide on the presidency and the character of the permanent government. The interim government was to be pledged to the holding of these free elections. These recommendations were given to President Roosevelt.

In the first day's discussion of Poland, Churchill named three London Poles, Mikolajczyk, Grabski and Romer, and suggested creating a new government which included these men and which would then be recognized by all three powers. Stalin came back at Churchill at this point, saying that although he had been called a dictator he had enough democratic feeling to refuse to create a Polish government without consulting the Poles. Roosevelt apparently took this remark of the Marshal at its face value and that night sent him a long letter, suggesting that a number of specific Poles be invited to Yalta from Lublin and London to confer on the new government's formation. Stalin subsequently claimed to have tried unsuccessfully to telephone the Lublin Poles to get their reactions to this sugges-

tion. Decisions were therefore made without any direct referral to either the London or Lublin group.

Roosevelt's letter stated that the United States could not recognize the Lublin government "as now composed," but neither would support be given in any way to a provisional government inimical to Soviet interests. Stalin had made clear that a government dominated by some members of the London group would be anti-Soviet, and this he could not permit for military as well as political reasons.

The Soviet proposals stated it was desirable "to add to the Provisional Polish Government some democratic leaders from Polish émigré circles." The "enlarged Provisional Polish Government" would then be recognized by the Allied Governments. Both Roosevelt and Churchill objected to the use of the word "émigré" with its French Revolution connotations. Counterproposals were subsequently submitted by Roosevelt and Churchill. The American declaration asked for a Presidential Committee formed from members of the *de facto* government in Warsaw, from "other democratic elements inside Poland, and from Polish democratic leaders abroad." The interim government would be pledged to the holding of free elections for members of a constituent assembly and a permanent government. The British proposal asked for the establishment of a provisional government based upon "all the democratic and anti-Fascist forces in Poland and including democratic leaders from abroad."

The key point in this maneuvering for a formula was the extent to which the *de facto* Communist-run government would be able to transfer its point of view to the new government. Molotov charged that the British and American proposals ignored the existence of the present government and argued that the real objective was the *enlarging* of the existing government. It was at this point that the British and Russians clashed over the extent of popular support which the existing government enjoyed. Churchill claimed that the Soviet-favored government did not represent the interests of the Polish people and to brush aside the London Poles would be a great betrayal. Stalin replied that the government did have popular support and was at least as democratic as the government of de Gaulle which was not based on elections, yet recognized by Britain and the United States.

Stettinius attempted a compromise formula by which the existent government would have been "reorganized into a fully representative government." Eden expressed a much stronger British view to the effect that a new start must be made on a Polish Government and both the London and Lublin groups replaced. Molotov suggested a few changes in the American wording, but it remained for the British to present a revised formula which was accepted as the final text. By taking the *de facto* Soviet-sponsored government as the basis for the reorganization, the British finally made the major concession which made it possible for the Polish Communists to retain the upper hand in the reorganized government. In practice, the difference between *"enlarging"* (the Soviet formula) and "reorganizing" (the British-American term) the existent government was small. Stettinius, however, feels this was not a "sellout" of democratic Poland, but a Soviet concession even if it was not exactly what the United States wanted.

Along with the discussion of the character of the new Polish government went the consideration of the elections and of their supervision, as suggested by the original American proposal. In the revised American formula, the term "supervision" was dropped; instead, the ambassadors of the three major powers were charged with the responsibility of "observing and reporting" how well the pledge of free elections was carried out. Molotov suggested that this sentence, which he said might offend the Poles, be omitted from the text. The ambassadors could still observe and

report in line of their regular duty. He also suggested that the words "non-Fascist and anti-Fascist" be added in describing the "democratic parties" which would have a right to participate in the elections. Both Churchill and Roosevelt objected to dropping the sentence describing the role of the ambassadors, but when their objection threatened to delay agreement on Poland, Roosevelt took the lead in making this concession to Molotov.

Churchill and Stalin worked out a new statement in the final text which mentioned the role of the ambassadors, but in a manner which had no direct bearing on the elections. They also included a statement limiting the elections to "all democratic and anti-Nazi parties," a phrase which received little attention until it was so interpreted as to exclude numerous anti-Communist rightist parties from the polls. The Soviet by this wording had official support for the concept of "limited democracy" which it was henceforth to use against opposition parties in eastern Europe.

Polish Boundaries

The three Heads of Government consider that the Eastern frontier of Poland should follow the Curzon line with digressions from it in some regions of five to eight kilometres in favour of Poland. They recognize that Poland must receive substantial accessions of territory in the North and West. They feel that the opinion of the new Polish Provisional Government of National Unity should be sought in due course on the extent of these accessions and that the final delimitation of the Western frontier of Poland should thereafter await the Peace Conference.

Joint Communique

Both Roosevelt and Churchill, early in the Yalta Conference, expressed the opinion that the Polish frontiers were a much less important question than the character of the Polish government. The State Department's memorandum accepted the Curzon Line, proposed by the British Foreign Secretary in 1919, as the basis for the Russo-Polish frontier. Some modifications were suggested in the south so as to leave the city of Lwow and the nearby oil fields to Poland. Neither Roosevelt nor Churchill insisted on this southern deviation from the Curzon Line, but both felt that it would be a nice magnanimous gesture for the USSR to accept it. Stalin objected to not winning greater gains for his country than those given it by an Englishman in 1919, but he did accept the Curzon Line for the most part. Certain minor exceptions were made in favor of Poland, but Lwow and the oil fields were to remain in Soviet hands.

The Polish-German frontier was a more difficult question. The State Department memorandum proposed compensating Poland with East Prussia, a segment of German Pomerania on the Baltic coast, and Upper Silesia. This territory included eight million Germans, and both Eden and Stettinius recognized that this would result in mass population transfers. The State Department memorandum for President Roosevelt stated the United States position as opposing "so far as possible, indiscriminate" mass transfers of population and suggested international supervision.

The Soviet proposal for Poland's western boundary was, for obvious political reasons, more generous in annexing German territory. Molotov traced the future Polish border from the town of Stettin up the River Oder and to the Czechoslovakian frontier on the River Neisse. Churchill said that he personally favored moving the Polish border westward and that he would not be shocked by mass evacuation of Germans, but he thought the Soviet proposal went too far and would arouse public opposition in Britain. Stalin said that the most of the Germans in this area had already run away. Churchill agreed that this simplified the problem and added that German casualties would provide space in the remainder of Germany for the deportees.

None of the memoirs testify to any

opposition from President Roosevelt on this point, and both the American and British counter-proposals conceded up to the River Oder, but questioned the Neisse line in the south. It was finally agreed that Poland should get "substantial accessions of territory" with the actual delimitation of the western frontier to be decided upon at the peace conference with Germany. Poland nevertheless occupied with Soviet authorization the territory to the Oder and Neisse line, deporting the German residents who had not already fled. According to Sherwood, the Americans and British left Yalta feeling that the Polish boundary question had reached "an honorable and equitable solution." But, by the time of the Potsdam conference, the representatives of both countries were lamenting a state of affairs created in large part by their decisions at Yalta. The mass transfers of populations which President Roosevelt had suggested in November 1944 were carried out with little regard for humane considerations and added greatly to the economic burden of the western zones of Germany. At Potsdam the United States and Britain recognized a *fait accompli* in agreeing to Polish administration of the area already occupied while reserving final delimitation for the peace conference.

DECLARATION ON LIBERATED EUROPE

We have drawn up and subscribed to a Declaration on liberated Europe. This Declaration provides for concerting the policies of the three Powers and for joint action by them in meeting the political and economic problems of liberated Europe in accordance with democratic principles. The text of the Declaration is as follows:

The Premier of the Union of Soviet Socialist Republics, the Prime Minister of the United Kingdom, and the President of the United States of America have consulted with each other in the common interests of the peoples of their countries and those of liberated Europe. They jointly declare their mutual agreement to concert during the temporary period of instability in liberated Europe the policies of their three governments in assisting the peoples liberated from the domination of Nazi Germany and the peoples of the former Axis satellite states of Europe to solve by democratic means their pressing political and economic problems.

The establishment of order in Europe and the rebuilding of national economic life must be achieved by processes which will enable the liberated peoples to destroy the last vestiges of Nazism and Fascism and to create democratic institutions of their own choice. This is a principle of the Atlantic Charter — the right of all peoples to choose the form of government under which they will live — the restoration of sovereign rights and self government to those peoples who have been forcibly deprived of them by the aggressor nations.

To foster the conditions in which the liberated peoples may exercise these rights, the three governments will jointly assist the people in any European liberated state or former Axis satellite state in Europe where in their judgment conditions require (a) to establish conditions of internal peace; (b) to carry out emergency measures for the relief of distressed people; (c) to form interim governmental authorities broadly representative of all democratic elements in the population and pledged to the earliest possible establishment through free elections of governments responsive to the will of the people; and (d) to facilitate where necessary the holding of such elections.

The three governments will consult the other United Nations and provisional authorities or other governments in Europe when matters of direct interest to them are under consideration.

When, in the opinion of the three governments, conditions in any European liberated state or any former Axis satellite state in Europe make such action necessary, they will immediately consult together on the measures necessary to discharge the joint responsibilities set forth in this declaration.

By this Declaration we reaffirm our faith in the principles of the Atlantic Charter, our pledge in the Declaration by the United Nations, and our determination to build in cooperation with other peace-loving nations a world order under law, dedicated to peace, security, freedom and the general well-being of all mankind.

In issuing this Declaration, the Three Powers express the hope that the Provisional Government of the French Republic may be associated with them in the procedure suggested.

The declaration on the other countries occupied by the Axis powers followed the Polish agreement in its ambiguities. Once more the principles of the Atlantic Charter were invoked and applied to situations where they proved unworkable. Russian acceptance of this Declaration was conditioned by the October 1944 division of the Balkans. The "restoration of sovereign rights," promised the liberated countries, did not mean as events were to demonstrate that the Soviet Union was willing to tolerate an anti-Communist or even a non-Communist government on its European borders.

YUGOSLAVIA

We have agreed to recommend to Marshal Tito and Dr. Subasic that the agreement between them should be put into effect immediately, and that a new government should be formed on the basis of that agreement.

We also recommend that as soon as the new government has been formed it should declare that:

(1) The anti-Fascist assembly of the National Liberation (Avnoj) should be extended to include members of the last Yugoslav Parliament (Skupschina) who have not compromised themselves by collaboration with the enemy, thus forming a body to be known as a temporary Parliament; and,

(2) Legislative acts passed by the anti-Fascist Assembly of National Liberation will be subject to subsequent ratification by a constituent assembly.

The agreement on Yugoslavia, like that on Poland, was an attempt to get out of a situation in which the USSR and her western allies were backing rival governments. Like the Polish formula, it provided in effect for a Communist government led by Tito who was then receiving the full backing of Moscow.

THE UNITED NATIONS

Security Council Veto

We are resolved upon the earliest possible establishment with our allies of a general international organization to maintain peace and security. We believe that this is essential both to prevent aggression and to remove the political, economic and social causes of war through the close and continuing collaboration of all peace-loving peoples.

The foundations were laid at Dumbarton Oaks. On the important question of voting procedure, however, agreement was not there reached. The present conference has been able to resolve this difficulty.

Joint Communique

The above named governments (United States, United Kingdom, USSR, China and France) suggest that the Conference consider as affording a basis for such a Charter the Proposals for the Establishment of a General International Organization, which were made public last October as a result of the Dumbarton Oaks Conference, and which have now been supplemented by the following provisions for Section C of Chapter VI:

C. Voting

1. Each member of the Security Council should have one vote.
2. Decisions of the Security Council on procedural matters should be made by an affirmative vote of seven members.
3. Decisions of the Security Council on all other matters should be made by an affirmative vote of seven members including the concurring votes of the permanent members; provided that, in decisons under Chapter VIII, Section A, and under the second sentence of paragraph 1 of Chapter VIII, Section C, a party to a dispute should abstain from voting.

Secret Protocol

The Yalta decision on voting in the Security Council provided for the big-power veto on any matters involving eco-

nomic and military sanctions. When this was announced on March 5, 1945, it was at once interpreted as a great concession to the Soviet Union. Subsequent use of the veto by the USSR has increased the criticism of this decision. It is now clear, however, that both Britain and the United States favored the veto on all but procedural matters. Britain looked upon the veto as a check against encroachments on the interests of the Empire while the United States saw the veto as a check against American involvement in war. The Soviet Union accepted without a single change the American proposal on voting procedures and this became the text of the secret protocol. The only limitation on the veto was that which called upon the parties to a dispute to refrain from voting on a decision relating to that dispute as long as the decision referred to proceedings for peaceful adjustment.

Another voting decision was made in regard to the Assembly when Britain and the United States agreed to support the Soviet request for membership for two of its republics, the Ukraine and White Russia. This concession was made without argument on the part of Roosevelt and Churchill, although the Soviet claim that these two republics should be classified as sovereign states had no foundation. Since the USSR at the Dumbarton Oaks conferences in 1944 had asked for 16 votes or a membership for each of the Soviet Socialist Republics, the granting of three votes was defended as a minor concession.

The Stettinius memoirs reject the contention of Byrnes that the Russians were not greatly interested in the character of the United Nations. According to the former, Stalin argued the importance of a world organization to prevent disputes among the Big Three from leading to war. Churchill was much more sceptical of this aspect of the United Nations and expressed his belief that big power quarrels would still have to be settled by routine forms of diplomacy. Churchill also objected to setting any early date for the holding of the San Francisco conference and apparently preferred to delay such a meeting until the conclusion of the war.

Territorial Trusteeship

It was agreed that the five Nations which will have permanent seats on the Security Council should consult each other prior to the United Nations Conference on the question of territorial trusteeship.

The acceptance of this recommendation is subject to its being made clear that territorial trusteeship will only apply to (a) existing mandates of the League of Nations; (b) territories detached from the enemy as a result of the present war; (c) any other territory which might voluntarily be placed under trusteeship; and (d) no discussion of actual territories is contemplated at the forthcoming United Nations Conference or in the preliminary consultations, and it will be a matter for subsequent agreement which territories within the above categories will be placed under trusteeship.

Secret Protocol

On the question of trusteeship, Churchill proved to be as sensitive as was Stalin on Poland. On the other hand, the concept of transferring colonial holdings into trusteeships was a favorite dream of Roosevelt's. As soon as Churchill heard the American proposals, he exploded, and according to Stettinius, he said he would never consent to having "the fumbling fingers of forty or fifty nations" prying into the British Empire. The Prime Minister was assured that the proposals did not have the British Empire in mind, but he felt it would be better to make a specific reference to that fact in the agreement. The Russians, holding no colonial territories, had no objections and the agreement was reached on the basis of the American text.

THE USSR AND THE PACIFIC WAR

Terms for Entry of the Soviet Union into the War Against Japan

The leaders of the three Great Powers — the Soviet Union, the United States of America and Great Britain — have agreed that in two or three months after Germany has surrendered and the war in Europe has terminated, the Soviet Union shall enter into the war against Japan on the side of the Allies on condition that:

1. The status quo in Outer-Mongolia (the Mongolian People's Republic) shall be preserved;

2. The former rights of Russia violated by the treacherous attack of Japan in 1904 shall be restored, viz:

(a) the southern part of Sakhalin as well as all the islands adjacent to it shall be returned to the Soviet Union.

(b) the commercial port of Dairen shall be internationalized, the preeminent interests of the Soviet Union in this port being safeguarded, and the lease of Port Arthur as a naval base of the USSR restored.

(c) the Chinese-Eastern Railroad and the South-Manchurian Railroad, which provide an outlet to Dairen, shall be jointly operated by the establishment of a joint Soviet-Chinese Company, it being understood that the preeminent interests of the Soviet Union shall be safeguarded and that China shall retain full sovereignty in Manchuria.

3. The Kurile Islands shall be handed over to the Soviet Union. It is understood that the agreement concerning Outer-Mongolia and the ports and railroads referred to above will require concurrence of Generalissimo Chiang Kai-shek. The President will take measures in order to obtain this concurrence on advice from Marshal Stalin.

For its part the Soviet Union expresses its readiness to conclude with the National Government of China a pact of friendship and alliance between the USSR and China in order to render assistance to China with its armed forces for the purpose of liberating China from the Japanese yoke.

After the agreements on Poland, the terms by which the Soviet Union was pledged to make war upon Japan have been the most criticized aspect of Yalta. Despite Stalin's earlier promises to join in the Pacific War, Roosevelt was determined at Yalta to secure a written pledge even if the concessions made were great. According to Stettinius, the State Department took no part in this decision and the conversations to this end were carried on by Stalin and Roosevelt outside the plenary sessions of the Big Three. Byrnes knew nothing of the agreement even after he became Secretary of State and it was some months after Roosevelt's death before this outstanding IOU was discovered in the White House safe. Stettinius places the responsibility on the American military for insisting that the USSR be drawn into the war, and upon Harriman for an estimate of the concessions necessary to achieve the military objective.

In any event, the decision was based on a grave underestimate of the effect of the atomic bomb and an overestimate of the state of Japanese morale. The strategic plans of the Army did not expect the fall of the main Japanese islands until the spring of 1946 and ignored the estimates of the Foreign Morale Analysis Division of OWI, which early in 1945 pointed to Japanese surrender by fall of the same year. From several other sources there have been reports of Japanese peace overtures to Washington before the Yalta Conference began. If these reports are verified, the extent of American miscalculation was even greater than semi-official accounts indicate. By acting on faulty military intelligence, Franklin Roosevelt was restoring to Russia what his predecessor Theodore Roosevelt had helped to secure for Japan at Portsmouth in 1905. His decision at Yalta, at least, hastened the fall of China into the Soviet orbit.

IRAN

Mr. Eden, Mr. Stettinius and M. Molotov exchanged views on the situation in Iran. It was agreed that this matter should be pursued through the diplomatic channel.
Secret Protocol

Stettinius came to Yalta with the intention of securing some Soviet agreement to implement the Tehran Big Three declaration on Iran, which favored the maintenance of the political independence of that state. Soviet pressure beginning in 1944 was put on Iran for oil concessions and there was fear of Soviet political influence. Eden was also anxious to end the joint military occupation of Iran initiated by British and Soviet troops in 1941. According to the terms of the agreement signed by the Allied Powers with Iran, all troops were to be evacuated not later than six months after the end of hostilities with Germany. Eden further claimed that Britain did not want spheres of influence for any nation in Iran such as that established by the Anglo-Russian agreement of 1907 when Iran (then called Persia), was carved up by these two powers.

Not only were American oil companies (Socony Vacuum and Sinclair) interested in Iran, but Roosevelt also had plans for Iran's future. In January 1944 the President had prepared a memorandum proposing to use Iran as an example of what could be done for an undeveloped backward country by "an unselfish American policy." The selection of a nation, bordering on the USSR, in an area of traditional Anglo-Russian conflict, and having potential oil wealth, was not a tribute to Roosevelt's perspicacity in finding an area in which to demonstrate a disinterested policy. Stalin could not have helped but suspect an underlying motivation when Roosevelt began to discuss the reforestation of Iran at the Yalta conference.

Molotov accepted the assurances of Eden that there was no objection to the USSR obtaining oil from Iran, and Eden even went so far as to say that Russia was the natural consumer of Iranian oil. But Molotov was unwilling to make any pledges that the oil negotiations would be delayed until the end of the war, or to make any statement on troop withdrawal. An exchange of views was therefore all that was possible. No agreement on the date of troop withdrawal was reached at Potsdam and the Iranian Government finally brought the issue before the United Nations Security Council in January 1946.

THE YALTA CONTROVERSY

There are numerous explanations and theories concerning the significance of Yalta. As a key conference in the peace-making process, its every agreement has been carefully analyzed and discussed at length. For the most part these discussions have been either strongly defensive in tone or highly critical. In the United States, "Yalta" has become a word around which the supporters of Roosevelt's foreign policy rally and against which his critics rail. Both sides agree that on its interpretation rest the merits or demerits of the wartime diplomacy of the United States.

The arguments of the defenders of Yalta fall into patterns which are supplementary, but at some points contradictory. The most detailed defense is that presented by Stettinius. According to his interpretation, Roosevelt was in full possession of his physical and mental powers at Yalta and there negotiated the best of possible agreements. Many more concessions were extracted from Stalin by Roosevelt's firmness than the Russian leader received from the United States and Britain. The extent of these Soviet concessions is overlooked by Yalta's critics, Stettinius says, because of Soviet misinterpretations of the intent of the agreements. The failure of the USSR to live faithfully by its pledges cannot be properly blamed on the other parties to the agreements. This line of reasoning is also that of the Sherwood-Hopkins interpretation of Yalta, rating the conference itself as a great achievement which was marred by the subsequent actions of the Kremlin.

The State Department explanation of the Far Eastern agreements, stated in the China White Paper, uses this type of defensive argument in dealing with details.

Although the leaders of the three powers agreed to preserve the status quo in Outer Mongolia—since the mid-1920's under *de facto* Soviet control—the White Paper points out that an interpretation favorable to the Soviet Union has to take into consideration Chinese claims to sovereignty based on the Sino-Soviet Treaty of 1924. Averell Harriman, one of the key figures at Yalta who has yet to publish his memoirs, is also quoted in this official defense. According to Harriman, the agreement to safeguard Soviet preeminent interests in the port of Dairen and in both the Chinese-Eastern and South Manchurian Railroads did not carry with it the intention of weakening Chinese control over Manchuria. It was only to guarantee Soviet interests in the free transit of goods through the port of Dairen and across the railroads.

The State Department document admits that failure to consult China was "unfortunate" but was more than balanced by the military exigencies. Consultation with China might have meant a "leak" which would have involved the Soviet Union prematurely in the war with Japan and enabled the Japanese to prepare for this conflict. On the other hand, the assumed great potential of the Japanese Army in Manchuria and the price in American lives if Russian action did not hold this Army in Asia during the invasion of Japan was considered important enough to justify some concessions to the Soviet Union in the Far East. President Roosevelt, according to this official view, did not consider that he was at any point "compromising vital Chinese interests."

Another pattern of defense stresses the realism of Yalta. With the possible exception of the Kurile Islands, the United States is said to have handed nothing over to the USSR which would not have been acquired anyway. The Polish settlement is considered as the strongest example of this realistic view. Stettinius stated that it was not a question of what the British and Americans would permit the Russians to do in this country, but of what they could persuade the Russians to accept. Anthony Eden seems to have held the same view, admitting to Stettinius privately that it was asking "rather a lot" of the USSR to get assurances of really free elections in Poland. President Roosevelt also gave some recognition of this point of view in his address to Congress when he spoke of the Polish decision as being, "under the circumstances . . . the most hopeful agreement possible. . . ."

James Byrnes has presented a third type of defense for Yalta in his book, *Speaking Frankly*. Regardless of the way in which the agreements have been applied, Byrnes feels that it was valuable to get the Soviet pledges on paper as formal evidence to the rest of the world that Russian actions in eastern Europe, at least, have been in violation of written commitments.

In the first months after Yalta, its critics centered their fire on the secret pledge to the Soviet Union in support of three votes for the USSR in the United Nations. In practice, however, these additional votes have been too few to overcome the Anglo-American predominance through the votes of the British Dominions and of the Latin American states, which for the most part vote with the United States on all important questions.

The release of the secret agreements on the Far East in February 1946 brought about one of the major attacks on the Roosevelt-Churchill concessions to the Soviet Union. Roosevelt was charged with following the pattern of the secret treaties of the first World War in "selling out" China without even consulting this member of the United Nations. The text itself was written with "careless informality" and "execrable draftsmanship," leaving unanswered a number of pertinent questions.[2] It purports to be an agreement between the "leaders" or "Heads" of the three

[2] Herbert W. Briggs, "The Leaders' Agreement at Yalta," *American Journal of International Law*, Vol. 40 (April 1946), pp. 376–383.

powers, terms which have no meanings in American constitutional law. It speaks of *returning* southern Sakhalin, *restoring* the lease on the Port Arthur naval base to the Soviet Union when neither has ever been in the possession of that government. Certain obligations are vaguely stated, questioning whether they have been executed or remain executory.

So strong has been the criticism of the Far Eastern agreement in the United States that question has been raised as to whether it is legally binding on this country. President Roosevelt in the draft of his last address to Congress stated that the United Nations Charter must be approved by two-thirds of the Senate of the United States, "as well as some of the other agreements made at Yalta." Although he dropped this phrase from his speech in delivery, it suggests that he considered this arrangement to have been a form of treaty. Byrnes, however, takes the position that it was only a military agreement, committing the United States to support Soviet claims to Japanese territory at the peace conference where the authority for final cessions would be given.

The agreements on Poland and eastern Europe have also been key issues in the charges that British-American diplomacy failed at Yalta. The claim of Yalta's defenders that the Soviet Union was pledged to support the creation of a new government in which the Communist-dominated Lublin government would only be one of several equal groups is held to be unjustified by the "letter" of the agreement. The insertion of the term "free and unfettered election" in regard to Poland and other liberated countries of eastern Europe is dismissed as only a face-saving gesture which could have no meaning within the political framework of the countries to which it was to be applied. The previous military arrangement had allotted the whole area, with the exception of Greece, to the Red Army. The political predominance of the Soviet Union could not be replaced by ambiguous formulas sponsored by the United States and Britain. The official assumption that coalition governments in which the Communists participated would not in time necessarily become Communist-dominated, ignored Communist tactics.

This type of attack on the Yalta agreement is based on one or the other of two general critical interpretations of Roosevelt's role at Yalta. According to the one, he was inexcusably naïve if he honestly believed that a victorious Soviet Union was making real concessions to its rivals, particularly in areas which were considered important for the security of the USSR. According to the other interpretation, Roosevelt accepted the realities of Soviet victory, but with political duplicity concealed the significance of Yalta from his constituents and instead voiced hopes which he knew were false. Depending upon which of these interpretations is accepted, critics characterize Roosevelt's own evaluation of Yalta before Congress on March 1, 1945. At that time he said that the Big Three had "achieved a unity of thought and a way of getting along together," and that "a common ground" had been found for the solution of the Polish question. These statements are, accordingly, either expressions of political innocence, unforgivable in a man of Roosevelt's experience and responsibility, or political deviations from truth to hide diplomatic failure.

To apply the politically innocent characterization to Churchill's assurances to Parliament on February 27, 1945, that the Polish settlement was "simple, direct and trustworthy," critics find more difficult. Churchill himself at that time raised many of the possible interpretations of the eastern European formula which favored Soviet predominance. There is evidence to support the critical view that Churchill at Tehran, if not earlier, had accepted the partition of Europe into eastern and western spheres. On his return from Tehran he told Polish representatives in London that they must be prepared to accept political dependency on the Soviet Union as though they had been defeated in a war by their powerful neighbor.

Whatever the point of view taken, defensive or critical, it is generally agreed that Yalta has had results which do not conform to the officially proclaimed interests of the United States. Poland has become a Soviet satellite; the Declaration on Liberated Europe has been used in eastern Europe to defend the establishment of a chain of Soviet satellites; while in the Far East the concessions made have facilitated the establishment of Communist China and the growth of Soviet power on the Pacific shores.

* * *

The Yalta Conference brought to an end the wartime meetings of the Big Three powers. President Roosevelt died on April 12, 1945, and on July 26 Churchill resigned from office in the face of a British Labor Party victory at the polls. The Potsdam Conference, opening on July 17, 1945, brought President Truman and finally Prime Minister Clement Attlee to carry on negotiations with Stalin. The outlines of the peace had already been established and many of the major issues of the subsequent Big Three meetings involved decisions or understandings already reached by Roosevelt, Churchill and Stalin.

It is obvious that World War II failed to achieve the hopes and aspirations voiced by Roosevelt and Churchill in August of 1941. Roosevelt's attempt to better the record of President Wilson was a failure. While Wilson remained aloof from political bargaining until he was forced to bargain at Versailles, Roosevelt began to bargain with his allies in the first year of the war. Whereas Wilson expressed only disdain for power politics and championed the cause of small nations, Roosevelt sought to create a world based on the domination of the big powers who would act as guardians for the small nations. Wilson's peace was to be a peace without vengeance with European boundaries drawn on strictly ethnic lines. Roosevelt's peace was to reduce Germany to a predominantly agricultural nation with its boundaries drawn to meet the demands of Big Three strategy. Despite the differences in methods and ends, neither President was able to find a working solution to the problem of international peace.

Any evaluation of the failure of World War II to achieve a lasting peace must first of all measure what was achieved against what was achievable. The latter, essentially based on hypotheses, must therefore be a matter of opinion and be subject to questioning and reevaluation. But some picture can be constructed of the framework in which Roosevelt and Churchill had to operate and of the practical objectives which the wisest methods could have achieved.

World War II was a coalition war, fought by dissimilar powers with conflicting interests and often with no more in common than their interest in stopping German expansion. Taking this into consideration as well as the political course of the world since 1919, it was a childish dream to expect that the Four Freedoms and the Atlantic Charter had any possibility of achievement through war. Decades of peacetime international cooperation and billions of dollars and millions of lives spent in prosaic pursuit of these goals may have brought the world closer to their fulfillment, but no one would claim war as the most desirable means to that end. Those who sponsored this dream could not have been sincere in their hopes, and if millions believed, their faith is only a testimony to the power of propaganda.

If the achievement of the whole loaf was impossible, there must still be some examination of the failure to win half the loaf or more than a few crumbs. One explanation of this failure attacks American and British diplomacy for its lack of "toughmindedness" and for confusing war aims propaganda with realistic objectives. Proponents of this view believe that a stronger stand on the part of the United States in dealing with its Allies could have saved the world from the terrifying prospect of a third world war. It is argued that Lend-Lease and United States military strength should have been used not only to defeat the enemy but also to force acceptance of different terms of the peace on America's allies, particularly the Soviet Union. In 1942, when German armies were pressing hard on Soviet defenses, the threat of cutting off supplies and a hands-off attitude toward the eastern front might have secured greater concessions from Stalin than those of Tehran and Yalta. Even in 1945, it is charged, American military strategy blundered in not pushing beyond the Elbe in Germany or further into Czechoslovakia, and thus holding a stronger military position in the final settlements in Europe.

Supporters of Churchill and the wartime leader himself make similar arguments in regard to the failure to follow Churchill's military strategy. Instead of paper guarantees in eastern Europe, a Balkan invasion would have built a military barrier against Russian expansion and have given Britain and the United States a lever by which eastern Europe's orientation could have been turned westward. Instead, President Roosevelt and his military advisers let purely military strategy determine an invasion of France.

Whatever their position on these arguments, future historians will be likely to recognize that certain results were intrinsic in the character of the war itself. Total warfare, the decisions in favor of strategic bombing and the unconditional surrender formula in regard to Germany all had results which Roosevelt and Churchill should have foreseen. The destruction of German power and the devastation of that country by strategic bombing, although they may have considered it necessary for a complete military victory, involved high political costs. The elimination of one major power inevitably contributes to the aggrandizement of other powers and to its rivals in particular. Only one of Germany's neighbors was in a position to utilize this aggrandizement. Britain was beset by economic problems and France by political problems and stagnation. The result was inevitable; a Tsarist or a Communist Russia would spread its influence in Europe, particularly in the areas occupied by Russian troops. The removal of the old ruling classes from power, either by flight or by their collaboration with the Nazis during the occupation, made a return to the prewar status quo in eastern Europe impossible, if even desirable in all states. The economic chaos in which the war left Europe as a whole was a milieu unfitted for the growth of those free democratic institutions towards which Roosevelt and Churchill professed to be working.

The reason for the failure of western diplomacy is made even clearer by Winston Churchill himself. On February 27, 1945, he told Parliament that two principles were guiding his approach to the problems of the continent. "While the war is on, we give help to anyone who can kill a Hun; when the war is over we look to the solution of a free, unfettered democratic election." To believe that those who claimed to have killed the most "Huns" would not also look to solutions of their own was the greatest delusion under which British and American statesmanship could fall.

THE POTSDAM CONFERENCE

JAMES F. BYRNES

James F. Byrnes has enjoyed a long and exceptionally distinguished career as public servant. He has been a Member of the United States House of Representatives, Senator from South Carolina, and Justice of the United States Supreme Court. During the war years he was Director of the Office of Economic Stabilization, Chairman of the Economic Stabilization Board, and Director of the Office of War Mobilization. He accompanied President Roosevelt to the Yalta Conference as an adviser. Appointed Secretary of State on July 3, 1945, by President Truman, he was one of the principal participants at the Potsdam Conference (July 17–August 2, 1945). In the following passage, written in part from shorthand notes he made on the spot, Byrnes describes the events of the conference.

THE group that sat down at the large oaken table at 5:10 P.M. on July 17 included, besides the President and me, former ambassador Joseph E. Davies, Admiral Leahy and Chip Bohlen from the United States delegation; Prime Minister Churchill, Foreign Minister Anthony Eden, Mr. Attlee, Sir Alexander Cadogan, and an interpreter from the United Kingdom delegation; and from the Soviet Union, Generalissimo Stalin, Foreign Minister Molotov, Mr. Vyshinski, Mr. Andrei A. Gromyko, who was then the Soviet Ambassador in the United States, the Soviet Ambassador to Great Britain, F. T. Gousev, and Mr. Pavlov.

From James F. Byrnes, *Speaking Frankly* (New York and London, 1947), pp. 69–87. Copyright 1947 by Donald S. Russell, Trustee of the James F. Byrnes Foundation. Reprinted by permission of Harper & Brothers and William Heinemann, Ltd.

It was fortunate that the room was large because each of these delegations had grouped behind them other members of their delegations. This group would change as various issues before the conference called for the aid of different technical advisers. As I recall it, our delegation that opening day included Ambassador Averell Harriman, Under Secretary William L. Clayton, Reparations Commissioner Edwin W. Pauley, Counselor Ben Cohen, Assistant Secretary of State James C. Dunn and Doc Matthews.

At Stalin's suggestion, President Truman was made chairman and he immediately presented for consideration some of the proposals we had prepared aboard the *Augusta*. It was evident that the other heads of government appreciated the President's efforts in having proposals ready for discussion.

The first of these papers was the proposal to establish the Council of Foreign Ministers. It had been agreed at Yalta that there should be regular consultation of the Foreign Ministers to deal with the difficulties we knew would arise after the war. But it had not been intended that those meetings should be concerned with peace treaties. At Yalta, peace had still seemed so remote that the question of how it should be brought about was not, to my knowledge, ever discussed. The machinery for making the peace was, therefore, one of the first things we began to work on in planning for the Berlin Conference.

As a Member of Congress I had followed closely the peace conference proceedings at the end of World War I and I was convinced that this time we had to follow a different procedure. If we waited until the end of the war with Japan and then held one peace conference, attended by all the states at war, with no preliminary draft to use as a basis for the treaties, there would be endless bickering. The logrolling, the interplay of conflicting interests, plus the sheer number of issues and people, would result, I was sure, in such confu-

sion that the conference would last a year if, indeed, it could ever end successfully. Even the Versailles Conference had finally found it necessary to assign to a few of the great powers the duty of treaty-drafting. Those states not represented on the drafting committee had little opportunity to know what was in a treaty and why. Consequently, when agreement was reached among the great powers, the smaller Allied nations had little more opportunity to examine or amend the treaties than did the defeated Germans.

We had to devise a system that would facilitate agreement among the major powers and at the same time provide the smaller states with ample opportunity to express their views.

Fortunately, the procedure initiated by Secretary Hull and carried out by Secretary Stettinius in the establishment of the United Nations organization provided good precedent. The accomplishments at San Francisco demonstrated the wisdom of the earlier conversations at Dumbarton Oaks and at Yalta where the big powers had reached agreement on the more important points at issue.

Ben Cohen and I prepared the plan for the creation of the Council of Foreign Ministers. When I presented it to President Truman for his consideration, we suspected what later we found to be true: the Soviet Union did not wish to act promptly on a German treaty. We knew that because of the many serious problems presented, and because there was no German government, some delay was inevitable. But we thought a start should be made promptly and that our experience with the Italian and Balkan treaties would make it easier for us to agree on Germany's problems.

I visualized for him the council's operation, in these terms: The council would consider first the treaties with Italy and the Balkan enemy states because these were the least controversial. The Foreign Ministers would agree on certain general principles and appoint deputies to draft treaties based on these principles. The Foreign Ministers, shortly thereafter, would take up the German treaty, agree on fundamental problems such as frontiers, and local governments, and then appoint different deputies to begin drafting a German settlement. The peace treaties based on these general agreements would then be presented to all the United Nations for their consideration and amendment in the same way the Dumbarton Oaks proposals were reviewed at the San Francisco Conference. A similar course ultimately would be followed for Japan.

After consideration the President approved the plan. This was shortly before I became Secretary of State. The President submitted our memorandum to the State Department for comment. The Department officials had been thinking along similar lines and recommended the procedure.

It was a good theory. But it was faulty in one assumption. I had assumed that at the end of hostilities an era of peace would be so deeply desired by those nations that had fought the war in unity that the inevitable differences of opinion could be resolved without serious difficulty.

It is true that following Yalta we had been somewhat disillusioned. Such things as the Bern incident and the Soviet violation of the agreements on Poland and Rumania warned us that in the days to come we would encounter serious differences and would have to overcome deep-seated suspicion. However, fresh in our minds were the words of President Roosevelt's last message to Prime Minister Churchill, based upon his experience with the Russians, that such difficulties would straighten out.

Today it is easy for one to say that President Roosevelt's advice and our assumption were not warranted. It is a trite but true statement that "hindsight is better than foresight." But, if one can recall the attitude of the people of the United States toward the Soviets in the days immediately following the German surrender, he will agree that, as a result of our sufferings and sacrifices in a common cause, the Soviet Union then had in the United States a deposit of good will, as great, if not greater than that of any other country. It is little short of a tragedy that Russia should have withdrawn that deposit with the recklessness and the lack of appreciation shown during the last two and a half years. Our assumption that we could cooperate, and our patience in trying to cooperate, justify the firmness we now must show.

Our optimism certainly was not lessened by the speed with which the proposal to establish the Council of Foreign Ministers was approved at the conference table. Both Churchill and Stalin asked questions on our inclusion of China on the council; the Russian delegation continued to oppose the admission of France to the ranks of the great powers. When Churchill suggested that the Foreign Ministers consider whether the council should be composed of four or five members, Stalin quickly added, "or three members."

The Foreign Ministers met the following morning, and we agreed that China's part should be limited to Far East problems and those of world-wide importance. Mr. Molotov reiterated the view that France should participate in the drafting of only the Italian and the German treaties. We finally agreed that each treaty should be drafted by the states which signed the armistice with that particular enemy, and, that in the case of Italy, France would be regarded as a signatory of the armistice.

We submitted our recommendations to the chiefs of state that afternoon. Churchill inquired about a phrase stating that the council should draft treaties "with a view to their submission to the United Nations." I explained that this was required by the Declaration of the United Nations, which all of us had signed. Stalin then made a statement which carried a significance that we did not appreciate until later months. The inclusion of such a phrase in the document, he said, made no difference as "the three powers would represent the interests of all."

With this brief exchange, the proposal of the American delegation for the creation of a Council of Foreign Ministers charged with the responsibility of preparing peace treaties became the first approved act of the Berlin Conference.

The high state of our hopes is indicated by my notes of a luncheon conversation with Mr. Molotov on July 24. We discussed plans for the first meeting of the council to be held in London in September. I expressed the belief that we should organize the council and agree upon directives to guide our deputies and their staffs in the preparation of treaty drafts. I then added that the Ministers should be able to finish their work in about ten days, and that the effective performance by the deputies of their work would keep our subsequent meetings as short. Mr. Molotov appeared to be very pleased with this view. We discussed the appointment of deputies, the relationship of the council to the United Nations and the desirability of beginning work on the Italian treaty upon our return home. On all these points we appeared to be in complete accord.

We went to the meeting of the heads of governments encouraged by our apparent agreement. The debate that followed perhaps should have stifled my optimism, but it didn't. It dealt with another of the proposals that President Truman had presented at the opening meeting of the conference—the implementation of the Yalta Declaration on Liberated Europe.

Our paper stated flatly that the obligations assumed in the Yalta Declaration had not been carried out. A continuation of this situation, it went on, would be regarded throughout the world as evidence of lack of unity and would undermine confidence in the sincerity of the jointly proclaimed aims. We proposed joint action in reorganizing the governments of Bulgaria and Rumania to permit participation of all democratic groups as a prelude to establishing diplomatic relations and concluding peace treaties. We also suggested that our

three states should help the interim governments in holding "free and unfettered elections."

The discussions that churned around this paper and the issues it raised are worthy of note. They form the background for many weary hours of negotiating.

Stalin's initial response to our paper was simply that the Soviet Union had a proposal of its own to present on the subject. Molotov presented it at the meeting of the Foreign Ministers the next morning. It was devoted largely to a severe attack on Greece. Eden angrily termed the attack a "travesty of fact," pointing out that international observers, including representatives of the Soviet Union, had been invited to observe the Greek elections. Unfortunately, the same could not be said of Rumania or Bulgaria, he added. And he concluded by saying that the British Government "took the gravest exception" to the charges in the Soviet paper, and the matter could only be reported to the Prime Minister.

Mr. Molotov replied that the charges were directed only against the Greek Government. He asserted that the British had more representatives in Rumania and Bulgaria than the Soviet Union, and, citing British and American press reports as evidence, he charged that there were greater excesses in Greece than in either Rumania or Bulgaria.

My contribution to this exchange was to repeat a statement which I was to make many times. It is one which, I fear, Mr. Molotov never fully understood or believed. "The United States," I told him, "sincerely desires Russia to have friendly countries on her borders, but we believe they should seek the friendship of the people rather than of any particular government. We, therefore, want the governments to be representative of the people. If elections are held while there are restrictions not only on newspaper and radio correspondents but upon our own governmental representatives as well, the American people will distrust any government established as a result of such an election. We do not wish to become involved in the elections of any country, but, because of the postwar situation, we would join with others in observing elections in Italy, Greece, Hungary, Rumania and Bulgaria."

This discussion contains arguments heard scores of times during ensuing months. Whenever the Soviets were faced with an issue that annoyed them or placed them on the defensive it was standard operating procedure for them to gather up a sheaf of British and American press reports from Greece and launch a counterattack. Mr. Molotov always seemed ready to enjoy the blessings of other nations' free press.

A few days later our paper came up for discussion again, providing an interesting demonstration of the Soviet bargaining technique.

"The Soviet Union," Molotov said, "can not agree to the supervision of elections. I can understand, though, that other Allies want better facilities for their representatives in these countries. Now that the war is at an end, there is every reason to give greater freedom both to these representatives and to the press. They will have every opportunity to be informed fully regarding the elections."

Having stated an opposition and a promise, he then lodged a complaint that the Soviet representative on the Allied Control Council in Italy was not receiving proper attention. He followed these parries and thrusts with an offer to discuss our proposal regarding elections *if* we would agree to accord diplomatic recognition to Rumania and Bulgaria.

Eden explained that formal recognition was constitutionally impossible for Britain until peace was concluded. I told him that our recognition of a country had to be based on our own estimate of it rather than on its value as a bargaining point. But Mr. Molotov is a difficult man to discourage and the effort to effect a trade of diplomatic recognition in return for the

ends we desired went on and on.

Most of the Soviet bargaining effort was centered on Italy. We had asked for modification of Italy's armistice terms in recognition of her help in the war against Germany and of her declaration of war against Japan. We had proposed that the drafting of an Italian peace treaty be the first order of business for the Council of Foreign Ministers.

Both Generalissimo Stalin and Mr. Molotov were determined that no favor should be granted to Italy that was not also granted to Hungary, Rumania and Bulgaria. One essential difference was pointed out to them constantly: all foreign representatives were free to travel about in Italy and report their observations. During one of these exchanges, Mr. Churchill was stating that the British mission in Bucharest had been "penned up with a closeness approaching internment," when Stalin broke in to ask him how he could make such unverified statements.

Mr. Churchill reddened slightly; he said that the Generalissimo would be astonished at the catalogue of difficulties encountered by the British mission. "An iron fence has come down around them."

"All fairy tales," Stalin exclaimed, and maintained that British representatives in Rumania were accorded the same courtesies received by Soviet officials in Italy.

Not until the end of the conference, when we linked this question to that of reparations, did we secure Soviet acceptance of Section 10 of the protocol. This stated, first, the desirability of concluding peace treaties and resuming normal relations with all five countries. It then stated that the three powers "have included the preparation of a peace treaty with Italy as the first among the immediate important tasks to be undertaken by the new Council of Foreign Ministers." It then referred to the other four countries, in a way that permitted concurrent preparation of peace treaties with them if this were found feasible. We met the problem of recognition with the statement that "the three govern-ments agree to examine each separately in the near future, in the light of conditions then prevailing, the establishment of diplo-matic relations with Finland, Rumania, Bulgaria and Hungary to the extent possible prior to the conclusion of peace treaties with those countries."

The problem of the press was met by this statement: "The three governments have no doubt that in view of the changed conditions resulting from the termination of the war in Europe, representatives of the Allied press will enjoy full freedom to report to the world upon developments in Rumania, Bulgaria, Hungary and Finland."

I must admit we did have some doubt, but this was the strongest commitment for freedom of the press that we were able to achieve after many hours of discussion devoted to the issue.

In the meantime, the Soviet Union had placed on the table a second series of charges against Greece in obvious retalia-tion for a British paper directed against Yugoslavia. When agreement was finally reached on the foregoing section of the protocol, Mr. Bevin pointed out that the agenda carried two papers against Greece and one against Yugoslavia. He proposed that all three be dropped. Stalin quickly replied "Yes, welcome." It was a good demonstration of the seriousness with which some of the charges and counter-charges were made.

Another irritant running throughout the conference was the question of American- and British-owned industrial equipment in Rumania that had been seized by the Russians. As an example of the Soviet conception of property rights, it was a forewarning of the difficulties we were to encounter on reparations. Before the war American and British firms had substantial holdings in Rumanian oil enterprises in-volving the ownership of highly valuable equipment. The Germans, of course, con-fiscated this equipment when they overran Rumania; our people assumed that when

Rumania was liberated this equipment naturally would be returned to them. We were amazed to find, however, that the Red Army had carried off much of the equip-ment as war booty and insisted on, the right to a large quantity of what remained. We could not admit that the Russians had a right to take, as war booty, property owned by their Allies. Stalin, Molotov and Vyshin-ski all stoutly maintained that this equip-ment did not belong to our nationals but was German property which they had a right to confiscate. Some of it had been bought in Germany before the war by American and British interests. But the Soviets insisted that since the property was German in origin it did not belong to us.

Mr. Vyshinski presented much of the Russian case. He is an able and aggressive lawyer. When he sits across the table look-ing at you with his cold, gray, piercing eyes and arguing his case with relentless precision, it is easy to understand his selec-tion as Chief Prosecutor in the Soviet Union's great "purge" trials.

The question of ownership became fairly technical in such problems as equip-ment replacement and identification. Only after long argument were we able to ap-point Soviet-American and Anglo-Soviet committees of experts to investigate the legitimacy of our claims.

On the opening day of the conference, Stalin announced his desire to discuss the question of trusteeship, stating that the Soviet Union "would like some territory of the defeated states." His delegation accordingly submitted a paper proposing that the Soviet Union be named trustee of one of the Italian colonies. The Atlantic Charter was a forgotten pledge. He wanted territory—indicating his conception of a trusteeship.

When the item was reached on the agenda, Mr. Churchill was reluctant even to discuss it. The President immediately made clear our belief that it was a matter for the peace conference and the United Nations but that no bars should be raised against discussion. Thereupon, Mr. Churchill delivered an impassioned statement.

"Britain," he said, "expects no gain out of this war. We have suffered terrible losses. Our losses have not been so heavy in human life as those of our gallant Soviet Ally. We have come out of the war, however, a great debtor in the world. There is no possibility of our regaining naval equality with the United States. We built only one capital ship during the war and lost ten or twelve. But in spite of the heavy losses we have suffered, we have made no territorial claims—no Königsberg, no Baltic states, nothing. We therefore approach the question of the colonies with complete rectitude.

"The British, of course, have great interests in the Mediterranean," Mr. Churchill added, "and any marked change in the status quo will need long and careful consideration," and he asked the Generalissimo to state what it was the Soviet Union desired.

"We would like to learn if this meeting will consider whether Italy is to lose her colonies," Stalin replied. "In that event, we can decide to what states they should be transferred for trusteeship."

"I had not considered the possibility of the Soviet Union desiring to acquire a large tract of the African shore," Mr. Churchill declared. "If this is the case, it will have to be considered in relation to many other problems." The question, he said, properly belonged to the peace conference and the ultimate administration of the colonies was a matter for the United Nations.

The President finally intervened. He suggested that the question be referred to the Foreign Ministers for further discussion, and there was a noticeable relaxation of tension around the big table as this suggestion was accepted.

When the Foreign Ministers met to consider it, Mr. Molotov immediately proposed that a definite determination be made of the future status of these colonies. I reminded him of President Truman's declaration that such a decision could be made only in connection with the peace treaties. When I pointed out that work would begin on them within one month, he agreed to wait.

The Soviet desire to reach into the Mediterranean was more modestly but nonetheless importantly expressed in connection with the control of the Dardanelles. Mr. Churchill first raised the issue. He had discussed it previously with the Generalissimo and now he expressed once again his willingness to join in a revised agreement that would insure free passage through the Straits for both the naval and the merchant ships of the Soviet Union in peace or in war. He felt it important, however, that Turkey should not be alarmed unduly, and pointed to the concern aroused by Russia's requests for the provinces of Kars and Ardahan, and for a naval base in the Straits.

"This," Mr. Churchill said, "has led Turkey to fear for the integrity of her empire and her power to defend Constantinople."

Both Stalin and Molotov explained that the request for the provinces had resulted from Turkey's proposal to the Soviet Union of a treaty of alliance. They contended that, aside from the fact that these provinces had been part of Russia under the Czar, the Soviet Union was justified, when entering into a treaty of alliance, to fix the boundaries it would thereafter be obliged to defend. The Montreux Convention, Stalin described as "inimical" to the Soviet Union since it gave Russia the same rights granted the Japanese Emperor. Turkey, he maintained, was too weak to give any effective guarantees of free passage and it was, therefore, only right that the Soviet Union should be enabled to defend the Straits.

"The American government will agree to a revision of the Montreux Convention," the President said. "We believe, however, that the Straits should be a free waterway open to the whole world and guaranteed by all of us."

That presented the issue. The Soviets wanted the free navigation of the Straits guaranteed by the Soviets, or by the Soviets and Turkey. This meant their armed forces would be on Turkey's soil. We wanted the free navigation of the Straits guaranteed by the United Nations.

The thinking of the Soviet leaders in connection with the Dardanelles is unrealistic. For a hundred years Russia has coveted this section of its neighbor's territory. A hundred years ago the fortifications they now seek would have been of great military value. Today, without complete air superiority, their fortifications in the Straits would be of little value.

At this point, President Truman declared he was convinced that a great step toward ending Europe's recurring wars could be taken if the barriers to free passage of goods and vessels could be eliminated. He then presented the proposal we had prepared providing for free and unrestricted navigation of inland waterways.

This proposal, Stalin said, he was not prepared to discuss, since it had not been on the agenda. Despite several subsequent efforts by the President and by me, the best we could obtain was an agreement to refer the proposal to the Council of Foreign Ministers for later consideration. When it came to drafting the communique of the conference, Stalin objected to any mention even of this action, giving no reason other than that it was unnecessary and that the communique was already too long.

On July 25, the conference recessed, because the votes cast in the British election several weeks earlier were to be counted the following day. Mr. Churchill had brought the leader of the Opposition, Mr. Clement R. Attlee, to the conference, so that there would be continuity of representation regardless of the outcome of the election.

The day before the two Britons left for home to hear the results, I asked Mr. Churchill what he thought of his chances of remaining in office. He said he had no idea of the result but that the people who professed to know about elections had been betting that the Conservative Party would maintain a sizeable majority of the seats in the House of Commons. He felt very confident of victory. Mr. Attlee, on the other hand, impressed me as believing that his party would make a fine showing but would be defeated.

It made an interesting point that in the midst of our wrangling over how elections should be conducted in the liberated areas, these two leaders, weeks after the votes had been cast in England and by the armed forces overseas, were entirely unaware of the landslide that had taken place to sweep the Labor Party into power. The result was a surprise to all of us who had discussed the matter with them.

When the new Prime Minister returned to Potsdam, he brought Ernest Bevin to succeed Anthony Eden as Foreign Minister. As personalities, Attlee and Bevin differ from Churchill and Eden about as much as it is possible for people to differ. Mr. Attlee, in appearance and certainly in manner, gives one the impression of being a university professor. In speaking, he makes no pretense of oratory but presents his ideas clearly and carefully. He is exceedingly modest; there is nothing of the actor in him, and it is difficult to picture this earnest, serious man having great appeal for masses of people.

Soon after their arrival, Mr. Attlee and Mr. Bevin called on the President and the four of us discussed the work of the conference. The President mentioned the Soviet demand for East Prussia and indicated on a map the changes in the boundary lines of Germany, Poland and the Soviet Union that thus would be effected. Mr. Bevin immediately and forcefully presented his strong opposition to those boundaries.

His manner was so aggressive that both the President and I wondered how we would get along with this new Foreign Minister. Some time later I told Mr. Bevin of the impression he had made on us at our first meeting, adding that we soon came to admire his bluntness and directness. He rather enjoyed my statement. And indeed it did not take me long to learn to respect highly his fine mind, his forthrightness, his candor, and his scrupulous regard for a promise. I have not only a high regard for his ability but a genuine affection for him as a man.

Britain's stand on the issues before the conference was not altered in the slightest, so far as we could discern, by the replacement of Mr. Churchill and Mr. Eden by Mr. Attlee and Mr. Bevin. This continuity of Britain's foreign policy impressed me. Later, in London, an incident occurred which demonstrated that I was not the only one so impressed. During the session of the United Nations General Assembly, Mr. Bevin made an important speech on British foreign policy. An Englishwoman, who had followed foreign affairs closely and who, naturally, had contrasted Ernest Bevin's bulk of at least 250 pounds with Anthony Eden's tall slender frame, sat in the gallery with an American friend listening to Mr. Bevin's speech. During the course of it, she turned to her companion and remarked, "Anthony Eden is making a good speech, but he seems to have gotten a little stout."

With the arrival of the new British leaders, the conference resumed and we started work in earnest on the most difficult issue before us—Germany.

We had arrived in Potsdam to face what amounted to a *fait accompli*, so far as the Polish-German frontier was concerned. Prior to Yalta, the three powers had agreed to divide Germany into four zones of occupation, and they had made a positive declaration in Section VI of the Yalta Protocol that the final delimitation of the western frontier of Poland should await the peace conference. Although the protocol would seem to permit no misunderstanding, we learned before leaving the United States for Germany that, without any consultation either with the United Kingdom or with the United States, the Soviets had transferred all the German territory east of the Neisse River to Poland for administration.

Both President Truman and Prime Minister Churchill promptly asked for an explanation of this unilateral action in establishing, for all practical purposes, another zone. Such a course, the President maintained, not only was contrary to agreement but would make the settlement of problems such as reparations far more difficult.

The Soviet defense was that the Germans had fled before the Russian armies, and, since it was necessary to have some government in the area, they had permitted Poland to take over its administration. Generalissimo Stalin agreed that no one of the powers had the right to create a new zone, but said that the Soviet government had to be assured of stable conditions in the rear of the Red Army. He then admitted that Poland was actually removing from this area substantial amounts of coal, which we contended certainly should be considered part of reparations payments.

The President asked how the reparations issue could ever be settled "if part of the German territory is gone before we reach agreement on what reparations should be."

Stalin remarked that everything the President said was irrelevant since "no frontiers had been ceded at the Crimea Conference except for the provisions that Poland would receive territory."

"The western frontier question is open," Stalin said, "and the Soviet Union is not bound."

The President repeated: "You are not?"

"No," Stalin replied.

We were concerned also by the huge

displacement of population resulting from this action of the Soviets. Although Stalin claimed "no single German remained in the area to be given to Poland," an area that had a prewar German population of nearly nine million, our information indicated that there were at least two million Germans left there. Later, representatives of the Polish government admitted the presence of approximately a million and a half Germans, but contended that many of them would leave voluntarily if the area were assigned to Poland.

President Beirut of Poland argued his country's claim to eastern Germany at a meeting of the Foreign Ministers on July 24. He pointed out that, if all the area they asked were given them, Poland would still be smaller in total area than before the war because, in accordance with the Crimea decision, 180,000 square kilometers of territory in the east would be transferred to Russia. He asserted, however, that the eastern German area would give Poland a sounder economy and a more homogeneous population.

Mr. Churchill had pointed out that this Soviet-supported plan would take nearly one-fourth of the arable land within Germany's 1937 frontiers. Not only would the German food supply be cut, he stressed, but more than a million Germans would be forced into the western zones, "bringing their mouths with them."

Time after time, in discussing the claims of Poland and the question of recognizing the existence of Polish administration of the area during the occupation, the President repeated that there could be no transfer of territory until there was a peace conference. In addition, we specifically refrained from promising to support at the German Peace Conference any particular line as the western frontier of Poland.

Our deliberate avoidance of a promise on the Polish border is emphasized by the promise we did make in the protocol about the transfer of the city of Königsberg to the Soviet Union, when we said: "the

President of the United States and the British Prime Minister have declared that they will support the proposal of this conference at the forthcoming peace settlement."

To remove even an excuse for Poland or the Soviet Union to claim that the line had been established or that there was any promise to support a particular line, the Berlin Protocol declared: "The three heads of government reaffirm their opinion that the final delimitation of the western frontier of Poland should await the peace settlement."

In the light of this history, it is difficult to credit with good faith any person who asserts that Poland's western boundary was fixed by the conferees, or that there was a promise that it would be established at some particular place.

We had recognized from the outset, however, that we would have to accept for the time being the Polish administration of this part of the Soviet zone. It was an accomplished fact and we could not force the Russians to resume the responsibilities they had voluntarily resigned. However, no agreement even on the temporary administration was reached until we came to grips with the issue of reparations.

Ever since Yalta the great variance between the Soviet Union and ourselves on the subject of reparations had been apparent. We agreed that reparations should be obtained through payments "in kind" rather than in currency. But the meetings of the Commission on Reparations between the Yalta and Potsdam meetings had demonstrated that our agreement extended no further.

There was, first of all, the figure of twenty billion dollars, with one-half, or ten billion dollars, to go to the Soviet Union. Mr. Maisky had advanced this figure at Yalta and President Roosevelt had accepted it as a "basis for discussion" in the Reparations Commission. When the commission met at Moscow repeated efforts by our representative, Mr. Edwin Pauley, failed to elicit from Mr. Maisky any data to support this figure. At Potsdam, both Generalissimo Stalin and Mr. Molotov kept pressing for the establishment of a definite figure. We finally succeeded in eliminating from the agreed declaration any mention of a total amount either in terms of dollars or tonnages of equipment.

The major impasse at the Moscow Reparations Commission meetings arose from our insistence that there could be no reparations from current output until Germany exported enough goods to pay for essential imports. Here, too, we were guided by our experience in World War I when American loans paid for German purchases of raw materials, which were then converted into goods for delivery to other countries as reparations payments. We were determined that we would not again pay for Germany's reparations and, therefore, maintained that necessary imports and advances must constitute a first charge against any German production available for export.

Our desire to treat the reparations issue as part of the over-all economic planning struck a snag of reality. We had expected that no property other than war booty would be removed from Germany by any of the armies of occupation without a strict accounting so that its value could be charged against whatever reparations program was later agreed upon. But, even before the conference opened, we had received reports that the Soviet army was removing property and equipment that could in no sense be classified as war booty. Some of these reports were such that we were reluctant to believe them. But there was little room for doubt after our arrival in Germany where we not only received eye-witness accounts but ourselves encountered corroborating evidence.

The house assigned to the President and his party had been the home of a motion picture executive who, we were told, had been taken to Russia. His wife was acting as charwoman in one of the homes assigned to other members of the American delegation. "The Little White House" had been completely stripped of its furnishings, but had been refurnished for the conference with furniture taken from still other homes.

Assistant Secretary Clayton and Mr. Pauley were shown a point on the line between the American and Russian zones where the Soviets, before the dividing line was finally fixed, had taken machinery from a plant which eventually was left in our zone and moved it into their area not more than two-hundred yards from the line. There it was left in an open field. The International Telephone and Telegraph Company's plant in Berlin, they found, had been stripped of nearly all its machinery. They visited other plants where rayon, ice and optical instruments had been made, and observed similar conditions.

Mr. Pauley had discussed the matter at length with Mr. Maisky, who admitted that the occupying power could not rightfully remove property without accounting to the other powers unless that property could be classified as war booty. Mr. Maisky tried to devise a definition of war booty that would include furniture, bath fixtures, silverware, coal, and other nonmilitary supplies. He found it an impossible task.

Finally, at a meeting of the Foreign Ministers on July 23, I asked Mr. Molotov whether it was true that the Soviet authorities had taken large quantities of equipment and materials, including even household goods, out of their zone.

"Yes, this is the case," Mr. Molotov replied. If it was worrying me, he went on, he would agree to deduct from their reparations plan a suitable figure to cover removals already made and he suggested 300 million dollars as a proper amount. When I objected, he quickly responded with an offer to reduce their reparations claims from ten to nine billion to cover removals already made "and thus dispose of the question."

But at Paris, at New York and at

Moscow in the spring of 1947, Molotov was again demanding ten billion dollars.

Further complicating the problem of property removals was Poland's action in eastern Germany, where, Stalin admitted, the Poles were taking coal from the Silesian mines. This area, Mr. Molotov maintained, "must of necessity be considered differently."

We considered these practical problems in our delegation at considerable length. We knew that, if reparations were to be drawn from all Germany we would have to demand an accounting from the Soviets. We were sure they could not even approximate an accurate valuation of what had been taken, and we realized that the effort to establish and maintain such an accounting would be a source of constant friction, accusations and ill-will.

Mr. Clayton, Mr. Pauley and I concluded that the only way out of the situation was to persuade each country to satisfy its reparations claims out of its own zone. I discussed this idea with former Ambassador Joseph E. Davies and he, too, thought it was the solution. Then, with the approval of the President, I arranged for a private interview with Mr. Molotov on July 23.

The United States, I said, was "deeply concerned" at the development of the reparations issue. We had always favored the adoption of a policy by which the three powers would treat the entire German economic question as a whole, but we did not see how the Soviet Union's position on war booty, removals, and so on, could be reconciled with an over-all reparations plan. We were very much afraid, I stressed, that "the attempt to resolve these conditions in practice would lead to endless quarrels and disagreements between the three countries at a time when unity between them is essential." Therefore, under the circumstances, we believed it wise to consider the possibility of each country's taking reparations from its own zone.

Approximately 40 per cent of the value of "industrial equipment deemed unnecessary for a peace economy" was located in the Soviet zone. We proposed that 10 per cent of such industrial equipment in the western zones be given to the Soviets. If the Soviets desired certain additional equipment or materials from the British or American zones, these could be exchanged for food or coal needed for the German population in the west.

Mr. Molotov promised to give this proposal to Generalissimo Stalin for his consideration.

The day before Mr. Attlee and Mr. Bevin were to arrive, Mr. Molotov returned to the subject with the complaint that we were seeking to reverse a decision made at Yalta by not accepting the twenty-billion dollar total reparations proposal. I tried many ways to help him understand that acceptance by Roosevelt "as a basis for discussion" was not a commitment.

"If you ask me for a million dollars and I tell you I will discuss it," I told him, "it does not mean I will write a check for it." That didn't get the point over. So I pointed out that we not only had accepted the proposal as a basis for discussion but that Mr. Pauley had been in Moscow for thirty-five days and discussed it; then he had come to Berlin and we had continued to discuss it, and for the many reasons I had previously explained to him we had decided, after this discussion, that the figure was not practical.

As soon as Mr. Attlee and Mr. Bevin returned I visited them and, after several hours' discussion, obtained their agreement in principle to our proposal. The next day the President and I arranged to see Generalissimo Stalin and Mr. Molotov, but the Generalissimo was ill with a cold. Molotov came.

We declared our agreement to an equal division of the German fleet and merchant marine among the three powers, for which the Russians had been pressing very vigorously since the beginning of the conference. We urged him to accept our plan for reparations. Mr. Molotov thereupon announced that the Soviet Union was prepared to accept our proposal "in principle" but wished to settle certain "details." The major "detail" was the amount of equipment that would be turned over to the Soviet Union from the Ruhr and he suggested two billion dollars' worth as an appropriate amount!

We explained that the placing of a dollar value on the equipment was impossible and we could only agree to offer a certain percentage of the equipment to be declared available for reparations. Mr. Molotov was most insistent about having a total dollar value set because otherwise "a percentage figure would be meaningless."

During this conversation he asserted that the Economic Committee had not done so well. I knew this was a criticism of his representative, Mr. Maisky, for his inability to justify in some way the removals from the Soviet zone. But I did not realize how serious a matter it is for a Soviet representative to fail to have the right answers. Since that criticism, Mr. Maisky, who had served as Ambassador at London for ten years and spoke English fluently, has not been seen at a conference.

On July 31, I told Mr. Molotov there were three outstanding issues: reparations, Poland's administration of a part of the Soviet zone, and our paper entitled "Admission to the United Nations" dealing with Italy and the Balkan states. I submitted a proposal containing the only concessions we were willing to make and requested that Mr. Molotov present the three proposals to Generalissimo Stalin so that they might be discussed at the afternoon session. I told him we would agree to all three or none and that the President and I would leave for the United States the next day.

When the conference opened that afternoon the President immediately suggested that the three proposals be discussed and called on me to present them. I did so, emphasizing that it was all one proposition. Generalissimo Stalin expressed dis-

approval of "the tactics of Mr. Byrnes," in asking for consideration of the three proposals at one time. I replied that we had been considering them one at a time for three weeks; that we were now making concessions in one solely for the purpose of reaching a compromise on the three in order to bring the conference to an end. Therefore, we insisted on this procedure. The Generalissimo renewed his protest and then began to bargain. First, he suggested a fantastic increase in reparations. Then, he proposed that the amount of capital equipment to be removed from the western zone in return for products such as food, coal, timber, and so on, be increased from 12 per cent to 15 per cent. I said if he would withdraw his other demands and agree to the other two proposals in dispute, we would agree to the 15 per cent. He agreed and the conference ended shortly thereafter.

Molotov dropped, for the time being at least, his proposal for the joint administration of the Ruhr, a major objective of the Soviet Union in western Europe. Agreement quickly followed on such matters as the economic principles to govern the occupation of Germany, including the compact to treat the country as an economic unit; the orderly transfer of German population; and the revision of the Allied Control Council procedure in Rumania, Bulgaria and Hungary to meet, in part, some of the requests made in our paper on implementing the Yalta Declaration on Liberated Europe.

We agreed to urge our representatives to act promptly on the procedure for the trial of major war criminals. It would take some of the joy out of war if the men who started one, instead of a halo around the head, got a rope around the neck.

Note that nowhere in the Potsdam Protocol is there any provision for the payment of reparations from current production. All prior discussions were superseded by the formal reparations agreement at Potsdam. The Soviet Union's renewal one year later of its demand for ten billions of dollars of reparations from current production and its continued use of German labor are inexcusable.

There is even less justification for requiring Germany to pay reparations out of current production when it is considered that the prewar value of taxable property in the Silesian area alone, which is only a part of the region now administered by Poland, was 11,300,000,000 dollars. Poland invariably argues that it is entitled to this area because of the 180,000 square kilometers of its territory east of the Curzon Line transferred to Russia by the Yalta decision. In addition there is East Prussia, which we have pledged to the Soviet Union and which had taxable property valued at two and a half billion dollars. The resources of these areas certainly should be considered as part of the reparations settlement.

Even if the figures were less generous, I think we should realize that, modern war being what it is, it is shortsighted and futile for any country to seek approximate compensation for losses it has sustained.

Because Generalissimo Stalin made so clear in the discussion of reparations at Potsdam that he "disliked the tactics of Mr. Byrnes," I thought he was seriously offended. It was therefore a surprise and a good indication of Russian appreciation of firmness in negotiating that just before the final gavel was to fall on the Potsdam Conference he asked the President for permission to say a few words about "Mr. Byrnes who has worked harder perhaps than any of us."

"He has brought us together in reaching so many important decisions," Stalin added.

The President expressed the hope that the next time the Big Three met it would be in Washington.

"God willing," Stalin replied.

The conference ended in good spirits. But the American delegation that headed for home probably was less sanguine than the one that had departed from Yalta. Events had shown that agreements reached in conference must be hammered out on the hard anvil of experience. We thought, however, that we had established a basis for maintaining our war-born unity. Our efforts in relation to eastern Europe had been less successful than we had hoped. We had failed to exempt Italy from reparations. We thought we had succeeded in the case of Austria. We felt we had made genuine progress in the agreements about Germany, although there was ample ground for our fears that it would be a long time before we could get the Soviets to start work on a German settlement. Nevertheless, we believed our agreement on reparations enabled us to avoid denouncing their unilateral action in removing people and property from their zone.

Certainly, no one of us suspected that the first treaties of peace would be concluded only after sixteen more months of almost continuous negotiation. We considered the conference a success. We firmly believed that the agreements reached would provide a basis for the early restoration of stability to Europe.

The agreements did make the conference a success but the violation of those agreements has turned success into failure.

Expansion
in Europe
1945–1953

X

THE PRIORITY OF POWER IN ACTION

WALT WHITMAN ROSTOW

W. W. Rostow is perhaps the most articulate exponent of the theory that all Soviet policy has been guided predominantly by the calculations of leading Bolsheviks about what actions would best preserve or increase their power at home and abroad. It is his conviction that certain characteristics of Russia's history, Marxian theory, and the Communist leaders' personalities converge to make the principle, which he calls the "priority of power," the ruling one. As he expounds it, this theory is much more sophisticated than the simple belief that Lenin and his successors were motivated solely by a lust for power. It has attracted many adherents. In the excerpts printed here, Rostow discusses the Soviet Union's expansion into what are now her European satellites. Professor Rostow worked in the United States Office of Strategic Services 1941–45, and served as Assistant Chief in the Division of German-Austrian Economic Affairs in the State Department during 1946–47. He has taught history at Oxford and Cambridge, and since 1950 has been Professor of Economic History at the Massachusetts Institute of Technology. Among his most important books on international affairs are: *The American Diplomatic Revolution, the Prospects for Communist China* (with others), *An American Policy in Asia* (with R. W. Hatch), *A Proposal: Key to an Effective Foreign Policy* (with M. F. Millikan), and *The United States and the Diffusion of Power.*

THE course of Soviet foreign policy since 1945 is so close upon us that it is difficult to view it in a firm historical perspective. In general it would appear that Stalin saw in the aftermath of World War II unique opportunities for extending the power and influence of the Soviet regime. The ground-force positions attained or negotiated in the course of the war, the temporary elimination of Germany and Japan as independent elements of power in the world political arena, the weakness of Western Europe, the rise of powerful nationalist movements in Asia and the Middle East, and especially the success of the Chinese Communists have all presented possibilities of some attraction to the Politburo. These possibilities have been exploited within a framework set by the Soviet appreciation of American military strength and weakness. Stalin avoided the risk of U. S. strategic air attack; but he

Reprinted from *The Dynamics of Soviet Society* by W. W. Rostow, pp. 148–152, 153–165. By permission of W. W. Norton & Company, Inc., and Martin Secker & Warburg, Ltd. Copyright 1952, 1953 by Massachusetts Institute of Technology.

exploited to the full U. S. postwar demobilization and the inhibitions on the use of U. S. military force imposed by American and Western coalition politics.

In their determination to make the most of the practical possibilities available, the ideological background and, perhaps more important, the historical experience of the Russian Communist leaders have probably played a part. The theories of Marx and Lenin place a peculiar importance on war as a historical instrument for creating the conditions for revolutionary advance. More particularly, it has not been forgotten in the Kremlin that the Bolshevik opportunity to seize power in 1917 arose directly from a situation of weakness created by a protracted war. In addition it has probably not been forgotten that anti-Communist forces proved capable of rallying and re-establishing themselves to a degree which proved disappointing to the Bolsheviks in the years after World War I. It seems likely that these elements of ideology and remembered history joined with the long institutionalized posture of Soviet hostility to the external world to produce a policy of aggressive exploitation of opportunities after World War II.

In keeping with previous performance, the Soviet regime has pursued what it has believed to be its power interests in various parts of the world on an *ad hoc* basis, adjusting to potentialities and limitations as they have emerged. The fundamental facts about the postwar world, as opposed to the position before 1939, would appear to be:

1. The potentialities for the extension of Soviet power were vastly increased.

2. The increase in Soviet (as in U. S.) power has placed the Soviet Union in a position where its own actions are of such influence on the world environment that they help significantly to determine the environment and the issues which confront the Soviet Union.

It is no longer rational for the Soviet Union (or the U. S.) to behave as if the world environment it confronts is independently determined, and to construct its foreign policy on a series of specific reactions to events as they arise. There is, however, no conclusive evidence that the criteria for Soviet foreign policy have altered or that a systematic plan is serving as the touchstone for day-to-day Soviet foreign policy decisions.

Nevertheless, the shifting from the essentially defensive pursuit of power from a relatively weak base, which characterized the Soviet position from 1918 to 1941, to its offensive posture after 1945 in a world arena in which the Soviet Union is a major power base constitutes an enormous historical transition. It has raised, in particular, the following fundamental issues:

1. The degree to which major war should be risked by the Soviet regime in pursuit of its objective of enlarged external power.

2. The extent to which reliance should be placed on conventional diplomacy in expanding Soviet power, as opposed to the use of Communist parties and other instruments of subversion and internal interference abroad.

3. The manner in which relations should be conducted with Communist regimes abroad, whether indigenously generated or installed in power by the Soviet Union.

4. The shielding of the internal Soviet control system from the impact of enlarged relations with the non-Soviet world.

A full view of postwar Soviet foreign policy in the light of these central issues lies outside the scope of this essay, involving, as it would, Soviet actions throughout the world. In general it may be said that, under Stalin's direction, the Politburo has:

—firmly disciplined its pursuit of external power within the limitation that major war be avoided;

—attempted, as in the inter-war years, to use both diplomatic and subversive techniques simultaneously, shifting the relative weight attached to each in different areas at different periods of time, and accepting the political costs of this evident ambivalence;

—accepted, with the possible exception of China (up to the present), the political losses consequent upon the continued exercise from Moscow of direct absolute power in Communist areas abroad, rather than permit the development of partially independent Communist regimes;

—taken extraordinary measures to limit the direct knowledge and experience of its citizens concerning the outside world, and heightened its effort (begun before 1939) to associate the regime with historic xenophobic Russian nationalism.

It is a theme of this essay that, while the external expansion of Soviet power holds a priority second to the maintenance of the regime's internal control, the maximization of external power over time is a persistent goal of the Soviet rulers. What, then, are the roots of this posture of aggression?

First, it is doubtful that the Soviet regime is operating by a schedule or timetable of world domination or has so operated from the moment it abandoned its hopes of detonating world revolution through the catalytic agency of Russia's November Revolution. However, Marx's and Lenin's analysis of the course of future world history still exerts, after a fashion, a hold on the minds of Soviet leaders. It will be recalled that, while Lenin made his peace with Germany at Brest-Litovsk, and while the new regime was unprepared to take major risks to aid the later revolutionary efforts of German Communists, still the notion of world revolution was not wholly or cleanly abandoned for the long run. More important, perhaps, than its persistence as an ideological residue, this conception became institutionalized in the ties of the Soviet regime to the Communist parties of the world by means of the Comintern. These ties have been used in the interests of the Soviet national state—often

at the expense of the progress of Communism abroad. Nevertheless, the ingrained habits of thought of the regime have steadily looked to an expansion of its world power, even though this expansion is not an overriding priority nor governed by a fixed plan; and these habits of thought have their origins in the original ideological conception of Communism's world triumph. This conception constitutes in its present modified form, like government ownership and operation of industry, one of those ideological elements which converged with the pursuit of Soviet power, and thus it has survived.

Second, and more important, the internal stability of the regime has come to be judged dependent on the maintenance within the Soviet Union of the view that the external world is hostile, which, in turn, justifies Soviet hostility. Even if this Soviet hostility were a pure position of propaganda disassociated from aggressive Soviet moves abroad (which it has never been), it would tend to set in motion reactions which would, in turn, give an element of substance to the propaganda. Chronic hostility and the insecurity that goes with it lead to actions of aggression. Psychologically, in part, it may be that Soviet aggression is defensive rather than offensive, based on fear as well as hope. In the end, for practical purposes, and notably in the context of the residuum of ideological aggression discussed above, Soviet hostility is to be judged positively aggressive, even if partially based on an insecurity which in the end stems from overriding concern with the maintenance of the regime's domestic base. For there is no evidence that any action of assurance or appeasement by the external world is likely to give that sense of security to the regime which would lead its present leaders to settle down; and there is considerable evidence that weakened positions in the external world will be fully exploited by the Soviet regime. If this analysis is correct, the ultimate source of the regime's insecurity lies in its relation to its own peoples, and this relationship is not easily susceptible to reconciliation by initiatives from the outside world.

Third, the habits, now firmly bureaucratized, for handling power within the Soviet Union condition the external behavior of the regime. The exercise of domestic power is based on attitudes and methods of as nearly total control as modern techniques permit. These attitudes and methods make it difficult if not impossible for the present regime to operate comfortably in the situations of diffused or shared authority which a firm structure of world order demands. In Germany and Eastern Europe, notably, as well as in disarmament negotiations in the United Nations, the somewhat musclebound stage of Soviet internal evolution has certainly contributed in recent years to behavior which, by any objective test, is to be judged aggressive.

The picture which thus far emerges, then, is of a regime which is prepared to exploit fully such possibilities for expanding its power as the world scene may offer but which is limited consciously in its pursuit of power by the desire to avoid major war and limited unconsciously by the institutionalized methods to which it is attached both in conducting its foreign relations and in controlling its own society. How these now deeply ingrained methods and responses have combined with the altered power position of the postwar world is illustrated by the evolution of events within the European satellites since 1945.

*   *   *

The military evolution of World War II presented the Soviet Union with immense opportunities to extend its power westward. The immediate postrevolutionary dream of a communized Europe came alive again. After the success at Stalingrad (if not earlier) the Soviet leaders, despite their preoccupation with the winning of the war, turned their thoughts to postwar possibilities for Soviet-dominated Communism. Not

only Marxism itself but their own experience had engraved on their minds the potentialities offered them in war-weakened societies.

Even the quite specific question of Soviet Russia's relations to a Communist Eastern Europe was not new. Stalin, in 1918, against the background of the nationality problem about which he was then in correspondence with Lenin, had written from Tsaritsin:[1]

For the nations constituting the old Russia, our (Soviet) type of federation can and must be regarded as of the greatest assistance on the road towards international unity. The reasons are obvious: these national groups either had no state organization in the past or had long ago lost it, so that the Soviet (centralized) type of federation could be grafted on without any special friction.

The same cannot be said of those national groups not included in the old Russia as independent formations but having developed a specific state organization of their own, and which, if they become Soviet, will perforce have to enter into some State relation with Soviet Russia. Take for instance a future Soviet Germany, Poland, Hungary or Finland. It is doubtful whether these nations, who have their own State, their own army, their own finances, would, after becoming Soviet at once agree to enter into a federal relationship with Soviet Russia of the Bashkir or Ukrainian type . . . they would regard federation of the Soviet type as a form of reducing their national independence and as an attempt against it.

I do not doubt that the most acceptable form of rapprochement to these nationalities would be confederation. . . . I am leaving out the backward nationalities, e.g. Persia, Turkey, in relation to whom or for whom Soviet type of federation and federation in general would be still more unacceptable.

Bearing all this in mind, I think that it is indispensable to include at some point in your minutes on the transition forms of rapprochement between the workers of the

[1] J. Stalin, letter to Lenin of June 12, 1920, quoted in Lenin, *Collected Works*, 3d Russian ed. (Moscow, 1935), Vol. 25, note 141, p. 624.

various nations the mention of *confederation* (alongside federation). Such an amendment would lend your proposals more elasticity, enrich them with one more transition form of rapprochement as described, and would render State rapprochement with the Soviet easier to the national groups which did not previously form part of old Russia.

It would be wholly unwarranted to assume that the Soviet Union simply decided, as a matter of fixed plan, to implement Stalin's "confederation" policy of 1918 after 1945. There were complex problems of Allied negotiation over Germany in which the Soviet Union exhibited, for a time, some evident uncertainty. There was the question of the strength of U. S. postwar armaments and its rate and degree of demobilization. The regime had to establish the degree of importance the United States would attach to maintaining Eastern Europe outside the Soviet orbit. There was the question of Western Europe's political evolution, with its potentialities, in 1945–48, for an extension of Communism far beyond the limits reached by the Soviet armies.

As in . . . other cases of Soviet policy . . . the clear-cut result over time probably emerged from a series of particular short-run decisions, the upshot of which was a policy of absolute and intimate Soviet control over the areas where such control could be established. It may emerge, when evidence is more complete, that 1948 marked a distinct stage in the process, where the long-run implications of the emerging position were faced and crystallized in actions and institutions difficult to reverse. The controlled areas have, in the end, come down to those where Soviet or Soviet-dominated troops were present or where their weight could be made felt without incurring the risk of a major war. The transition to a pattern of control, in the image of the present internal Soviet system, from different initial positions, is, looking backward, remarkably uniform.

THE PROCESS OF TAKE-OVER

Soviet Russia proclaimed itself the liberator—in fact the only liberator—from the scourge of Nazism in Eastern Europe. Nazi collaborators who were also judged potential enemies of the new regimes were ruthlessly denounced wherever possible, as were certain other actual or believed enemies; all recollection of prewar conditions was branded as reactionary; the "right people" (not necessarily old Communists but rather those considered most pliable) were installed in key positions of power, often by direct order of the Soviet military command; and certain popular measures, such as land reform, were credited to the Soviet liberators and the parties sympathetic to them. Gradually the East European countries acquired controllable police and military forces and began increasingly to resemble their "liberators" in administrative structure.

At the same time the cultural, social, and economic transformation which had been crystallized in the Soviet Union during the prewar decade was imposed by the newly powerful governors with the confidence of a long-established firm opening branch offices. The familiar features of post-1928 Russia appeared: purges, shock troops, forced collectivization, rapid increase in heavy industry, "kulaks," "economic sabotage," "deviation," mechanically uniform propaganda, and so on. And, within a relatively few postwar years, the familiar instruments were employed to yield, under forced draft, a kind of copybook version of modern Soviet society.

The most striking feature of Eastern Europe since the war has been the uniformity of its development. Although the tempo of sovietization varied with the conditions of the several potential satellites, all went through more or less the same three stages. Only in Yugoslavia, which up to 1948 had appeared the model state of the new Soviet Empire, has the result deviated significantly from the standard form.

The first stage was a period of real coalition governments. Yugoslavia, which was not liberated by the Red Army as such, and which had the nucleus of a national government organization on the spot at the end of the war, went through this stage almost imperceptibly; Czechoslovakia, closest to the West both geographically and culturally, remained in it for nearly three years.

In every case several political parties combined in a government, based on Western parliamentary institutions, to form a coalition dedicated to a program including a purge of Fascists and collaborators, fairly radical social reforms such as the break-up of large landed estates, political freedom, and a foreign policy friendly to both the Soviet Union and the Western Allies.

During this first stage real freedom of speech and assembly prevailed except in the matter of criticizing the Soviet Union or its policies. Over other matters there was generally no censorship. Within the coalitions, however, the Communists managed to secure certain decisive positions from which they were able to exert power in the most effective way. With these levers of power—in general the key posts in the interior ministry (for the security police), the army general staff, and the information ministry—the Communists, aided by the threat of the Red Army, were gradually able to remove their strongest enemies, to make opposition to themselves increasingly impotent, and to build up a largely dependable administrative staff.

The second stage in the sovietization of Eastern Europe was a series of bogus coalition governments in which non-Communist parties were still represented in the government but only by members chosen by the Communists, not by the parties themselves. The peasant and bourgeois parties were driven into opposition which, though not yet illegal, became increasingly difficult. Newspapers could still be published, but their distribution, particularly in rural areas, was restricted. Sometimes the government would censor a newspaper; more often the printer's union would "indignantly refuse to print the reactionary calumnies against the peoples' authorities." Riots were frequent, meetings were broken up while the police preserved its "objective attitude," and government by intimidation, if not yet terror, prevailed. The end of stage two (which only Czechoslovakia seems to have skipped) marked the end of the transition to the full-fledged "People's Democracy," i.e., the stage of total control by Communist regimes approved by Moscow.

In the third stage, attained in all the East European states by 1948, all opposition was suppressed, its leaders were either exiled or arrested, and a completely disciplined united front control was achieved. Where there was a Social-Democratic movement, it was forcibly fused with the Communists in some kind of united party. Features of stage three have been purges, liquidations, spy trials, and forced labor.

The countries of Eastern Europe which fell within the Soviet Union's orbit after World War II differed in their political, social, and economic history and current structure. Poland had been the joint victim of Germany and Russia, and had, throughout the war, maintained a strong independent underground. Yugoslavia had fought Hitler before the Soviets were in the war, and the partisans of Tito had developed into something like a mass movement. Hungary and Rumania had fought on the German side; and Bulgaria had been allied to Germany though not at war with Russia. Czechoslovakia had been split into the Czech state, occupied by the Germans, and Slovakia, ruled by a semi-independent German sympathizer. But in the end Soviet policy has come to impose its system, with comparatively little variations, upon all of the states—allied or conquered, industrial or agrarian, monarchical or republican, Catholic or Orthodox.

Poland presented perhaps the most difficult task of absorption for the Soviet regime. On top of a centuries-old tradition of Polish-Russian animosity, Soviet Russia had amassed a record of atrocities against the Poles, beginning with the Hitler-Stalin Pact, and including the probable murder of the flower of the Polish officer corps at Katyn. The tragic razing of the city of Warsaw (July–August 1944), while the Soviet army stood outside and watched the Germans destroy the rebels and their city, was not forgotten. The burning hatred of Germany in postwar Poland, and its desire to industrialize, were, perhaps, the only major political assets the Russians had in dealing with that country. The manner in which the Soviet regime has implemented its control of Poland is, therefore, instructive of the pattern of domination everywhere.

On December 31, 1944 the Soviet-sponsored Lublin Committee declared itself the Provisional Government of Poland. It was recognized five days later by Stalin. After long wrangling among the Big Three, and finally after a Hopkins mission to Moscow (June 1945), the Western Allies compromised on a coalition government of five separate parties, with Mikolajczyk, the former exile leader, as one of the vice-premiers. But the period of "Red Army liberation" had been skilfully used by the Lublin government not only to occupy key positions in the administration but also to infiltrate the other parties as well.

The Ministry of the Interior was divided in two at the start, with Public Administration (routine bureaucratic matters) under Kiernik, a follower of Mikolajczyk, and Security (secret political police, internal security corps, and militia) under a Communist, Radkiewicz.

What was left of the army was also controlled, at least at the top, by Communists, and included many who had served in the Red Army.

The third crucial position occupied by the P.P.R. (Polish Workers Party—Communist) was the Ministry of Regained Territories (the Oder-Neisse territory), set up under separate administration under Gomulka, out of the hands of Kiernik. Since the territory was comparatively rich in industrial and agricultural opportunities, and since a complete resettlement was called for after the Germans were expelled, enormous possibilities for patronage and subjection were available to Gomulka, who was also at that time Secretary of the Polish Communist Party.

The regime was confronted in the early stages of its rule by some guerilla actions by unreconciled members of former underground groups. Later, when the police forces had been organized, the existence of guerilla bands was exploited as a justification for general repressive measures. After Mikolajczyk's original Peasant Party had been taken over by the Communists, two leaders of the new Polish People's Party, which he then established, were murdered. Mikolajczyk's protests and demands for investigation showed his "lack of confidence in the Minister of Security." A subsequent trial brought a suitable confession from an underground agent.

Mikolajczyk was able to hold a Party congress in January 1946, and resisted pressure to join the government bloc. Though Mikolajczyk's Polish People's Party (P.S.L.) was nominally in the government, delegates were arrested, meetings broken up, and party offices raided. The press continuously denounced Mikolajczyk as a British agent, and the P.S.L.'s own paper rations were cut drastically. In the plebiscite of June 1946 the government announced a majority of 68 per cent on the one disputed question—but according to Mikolajczyk the results would have been 83 per cent in his favor had there not been arrests and falsification.

From this time on the government moved quickly. To prepare for the parliamentary elections of January 1947, the "safe" western territories were given excessive electoral representation. Mikolajczyk and his followers were incriminated by the confessions of certain political prisoners who asserted they were foreign agents. Two bogus parties were set up to drain off the peasant vote toward Communist-controlled groups, thousands of P.S.L. members were (at least temporarily) arrested, and "voluntary open voting" took place in many districts. The resulting parliament, overwhelmingly backing the government bloc, passed a new provisional constitution in February 1947. Finally in the fall of 1947 Mikolajczyk, informed that he was about to be arrested, gave up the uneven struggle and left Poland secretly. The only other "independent" party left in Poland, the satellite Socialist party, completed the operation in 1948, when, in response to a demand for "workers' unity," it merged with the Communists to form a Polish United Workers' Party, purged, in the meantime, of all unreliable elements. By the end of 1948 all effective power was concentrated in this United Party. Poland was an almost completely communized state, operating with fully unified police and other controls.

In Hungary the Soviet task was easier because there was no large non-Communist underground and because potential rivals could simply be treated as former enemies in the light of their recent Nazi connections. Yet the occupying forces and their Communist allies actually sponsored the establishment of four differing parties, which would govern in a National Liberation Front. In Hungary, where land reform was a major factor, the Agriculture Ministry was a crucial lever of power for the Communists. Soon, too, they managed to gain control of the economic and political police, though the Minister of the Interior himself was only a sympathetic member of the National Peasant Party.

There was a free election in Budapest in the fall of 1945, resulting in a large anti-Communist majority. But eventually, with the interference and threatened interference of the Russian Commander, Marshal Voroshilov, a four-party bloc was maintained with a Communist in full control of the Interior Ministry. Thereupon the

bureaucracy, widely regarded as overstaffed was purged; the Communists managed to use this opportunity to conduct the purge on criteria of political reliability. Denunciation of peasant leaders and suppression of their journals began in earnest.

The detailed story of Hungary need not be rehearsed here. Pressure on nonconformists, including Premier Nagy, increased as the police was strengthened, and trials and confessions became more common. Early in 1947 Kovacs, the Secretary General of the Small Farmers Party, was mentioned in connection with activity against the Soviet Union, and was seized by Russian soldiers. In May, Nagy was denounced on the strength of alleged testimony of Kovacs and was forced to resign.

An election in August 1947, conducted under police supervision, gave the Communist party 22 per cent and their dummy-party allies another 38 per cent. By June of 1948 the government, now fully in Communist hands, felt strong enough to nationalize Catholic schools, and six months later Cardinal Mindszenty was arrested. After fusion of the two "proletarian parties" had taken place in 1948, the Hungarian Workers' Party had undisputed control and was able to stage a 90 per cent election in April 1949.

Rumania and Bulgaria deviated only in detail from this pattern. In Rumania Vishinsky asserted Russia's will as early as February 1945, and the broadening of the government's base, in accordance with the Moscow Conference of the Big Three Foreign Ministers (December 1945), made no substantial difference in the degree of Soviet control. Ministries of Interior, Justice and National Economy remained in trusted hands. The first manipulated election took place in November 1946 and, though opposition was not yet illegal, trials, purges, and confessions were common thereafter. In the fall of 1947 the Social Democratic Party was absorbed into the "United Workers' Party"; then King Michael, who had in any case wielded virtually no power, was forced to abdicate; and in March 1948, the renamed People's Democratic Front won its parliamentary election—405 to 9.

In Bulgaria, the first stage was over by the spring of 1945, when the Agrarian and Social Democratic parties were captured by Communists. The first terror-ridden election was held in November 1945, and throughout 1946 parties other than the Fatherland Front were terrorized. One by one, opposition leaders were tried and sentenced, and in 1948 the fusion of workers' parties took place. By the time of the Tito-Comintern split, Bulgaria claimed to be the most advanced of the Peoples' Democracies, as indeed it was in terms of the stages through which it had passed toward "confederation."

Yugoslavia and Czechoslovakia present the two extremes of variation in the pattern of sovietization of the satellites. Yugoslavia, which had its own indigenous National Liberation Front during the war, never passed through the first stage of real coalition government; while Czechoslovakia, possessing strong cultural links to the West, remained in the first stage until the coup of February 1948. But even the special features in these two countries do not substantially alter the essential uniformity of Soviet operations in Eastern Europe—until, that is, the Titoist break in the summer of 1948.

The Communist Party of Yugoslavia chose to hide its identity behind the People's Front, of which it was merely the directing nucleus, and to assign the Interior Ministry at first to an Orthodox priest. But by October 1945, the last opposition paper was suppressed, and a month later a 96 per cent election was held. Beginning with Mihailovic's trial in the spring of 1946, "treason," and not opposition, became the standard Yugoslav crime.

In Czechoslovakia the Communists, though aided until December 1945 by the presence of the Red Army, did not attempt to seize power immediately. The popular strength of the Communist Party (38 per cent at the free elections of May 1946) may have led to the decision to seek real popular support, and no doubt Gottwald, the Communist chief, sought to pose as a patriotic democratic leader.

Yet despite the freedom enjoyed in Czechoslovakia in 1945–48 (only the uranium mines were Soviet-controlled), the actual power position of the Communist Party was extremely strong. Finance, Interior, General Staff, Information (including the Union of Czech Youth and Radio Prague), Agriculture, and Border Areas (controlling confiscated German holdings) were directed by Communists in the provisional government; and, after the 1946 elections, Gottwald became Premier.

The rule of law and absence of serious abuses prevailed up to the summer of 1947, though popular tension was great, and acute internecine warfare was conducted between the Communist and non-Communist ministries. The Czech reaction to the Marshall Plan and the growing (but still secret) crisis with Tito probably were decisive in determining Stalin's decision to enforce more direct control by means of a *coup d'état*. The power at the disposal of the Czech Communists was ample to overcome the divided and unsure opposition of Beneš, Masaryk, and other Czech democratic leaders; and in February 1948, with a rather limited effort, the Gottwald regime was able to transform itself into a stage-three satellite government. Communist gangs, armed factory workers, and police occupied "opposition" ministries; resisters were arrested or fired upon, and all parties, newspapers, and unions were instructed to "cooperate" with the regime. Less than a month after the start of the coup, Jan Masaryk, former foreign minister and bearer of a great Czech name, was found dead in a courtyard. New elections yielded the customary 90 per cent majority in May, and on June 6, President Beneš, seeing that he could do nothing amid the series of purges, arrests, and new laws, resigned.

Just as the first Bolshevized state, Yugoslavia, was breaking away from the Soviet bloc, the last was bolted securely into place.

INSTITUTIONS IN THE SOVIET IMAGE

By the summer of 1948 the pattern of political seizure had been evolved and carried out in all the East European satellites. At the same time, an economic and institutional framework, modeled ever more closely on that of the Soviet Union, had been taking shape. Because of the varying degrees of Communist control up to 1948, this transformation did not correspond precisely to the stages of political development. But the pattern of economic changes in Eastern Europe illustrates how the historical experiences of the Soviet regime were consolidated, telescoped, and applied in the Soviet Union's first large-scale foreign venture.

In general, the economics of all the satellite states were made to conform as much as possible to the needs of the Soviet economy, and those countries upon whom the Soviet Union had reparations claims were harshly exploited. Roughly, those countries which had the most inequitable distribution of land before the war, such as Hungary, went through the greatest agrarian transformations, while those which had been most industrialized—for example Czechoslovakia—suffered the least economic dislocation. In this transformation Russian confiscation of German property played a major part, the Soviet Union taking over and enlarging the positions of economic power the Germans had held.

Among the peasants the standard plan in all the states comprised, first, a distribution of large landed estates among the peasantry, then a kind of transitional "NEP" stage, during which the main aim was to organize a more efficient system of exchange between town and village; and finally large-scale collectivization and liquidation of substantial landowners (kulaks).

The first step, expropriation of large estates and German property, took place in all the countries by legislative decree. Where there were large Church holdings, however, as in Hungary, land reform was not completed until 1947–48.

The second stage presented the Soviet regime with the same problems that it had faced at home in the 1920's, i.e., the factories, now concentrating on capital goods, could not produce unless the workers were fed; and the farmers were reluctant to sell their crops without being able to buy the products of industry. The solution was generally the same as it had been in Russia: fixed crop quotas which had to be delivered to the state at low prices, and allowance of a margin, dependent on the size of the harvest, which could be sold on the free market. In contrast to Russia, however, machine tractor stations were introduced before large-scale collectivization, both to increase production and to increase control over the peasantry.

Warned by the terrible experiences of the Soviet Union, the satellite planners seem to have proceeded slowly thus far on the third agricultural stage. That collectivization is definitely a part of the program for Eastern Europe has been shown, however, by such moves as the establishment of "Centralized co-operatives" and "Peasant self-help," particularly on redistributed lands.

Industrial planning has also been based largely on the Soviet model. All the satellite countries adopted short recovery plans and then embarked on Five- or Six-Year Plans for industrialization. Yugoslavia undertook its plan in 1947, Czechoslovakia and Bulgaria in 1949, and Hungary and Poland in 1950. Although private property was not outlawed as such, industry, banking, and wholesale trade had been effectively transferred to government control by the end of 1948.

In all the satellites planning seems to have been more ambitious than expert, and more in the nature of production targets than precise schedules. The rate of investment to national income sought has been high everywhere, but has not always been attained. Consumer-goods production in general has been reduced absolutely as well as relatively. Trade unions have been introduced even where they were comparatively unknown before the war, but these have had only the characteristic Soviet functions of stimulating productivity, increasing the size of the labor force, and disciplining the workers. The familiar Russian "heroes of labor," "shock workers," medals, Stakhanovite movements, and "socialist competition" are common in Eastern Europe, notably since 1948, when longer-term efforts to integrate the area into the Soviet economy became more general and explicit.

The whole structure of the satellite states cannot be examined here. Where Soviet examples were available, as in the organization of propaganda, police, or military institutions, they were closely followed by the satellite governments. Where there was no easily applicable model, as in the Church question, action seems to have been hesitant and uneven from country to country, although in general the attempt has been made to win Orthodox support for the regime and to suppress or intimidate the Catholic Church. What can be observed over-all is a remarkably unimaginative application of the bureaucratized techniques developed out of the Soviet evolution and applied by force—in defiance of popular feeling, in defiance of Marxist doctrine of history, and, in the end, in defiance of such authentic national Communist movements as existed within the area.

THE COMINFORM, TITOISM, AND THE
DYNAMIC CONSEQUENCES OF
THE TAKE-OVER

In the summer of 1947 the Kremlin chose to organize its satellite Communist parties, plus the French and Italian Communist parties, into the Communist Information Bureau. In part the Cominform was a response to the Marshall Plan, in that it promised increased economic integration to the East European states. In part it was an additional technique for binding the subject nations closer together by a means which appeared other than Soviet fiat. Certainly it constituted notice that Eastern Europe was not to be regarded as a group of separate states but rather as part of a unified power system.

This decision to tighten still further the degree of Soviet control met actual or believed opposition from a group of relatively strong Communist leaders whose loyalty to Moscow was unquestioned but who had held to, or were believed to have held to, the conception of nationally oriented Communist states. They were judged inappropriate agents for the stage of bureaucratized control over the satellites into which Soviet policy moved in 1948. Whether, or in what proportion, this stage represents a reflex to gathering Western strength, an instinctive desire to tidy up on the part of habit-dominated bureaucrats, or a conscious transition toward full incorporation of the satellites into the Soviet Union it is impossible to say on present evidence. In any case, this new phase has been marked by Tito's successful defiance in 1948, and by the unsuccessful abortive, or suspected resistance (or dissidence) of Gomulka in Poland, Kostov in Bulgaria, Patrascanu in Rumania, Rajk in Hungary, and Clementis and Slansky in Czechoslovakia. While there have been some substantive policy disagreements between the satellites and Moscow (for example, on East-West trade, the idea of Balkan Federation, and the rate of collectivization), it is evident that all real conflicts have been over the degree and character of Soviet control. Both sides, particularly in the case of Yugoslavia, built up after the event ideological differences to justify their positions on this issue of power distribution. Here again the politics of postwar Soviet Europe has followed the model of prewar Soviet internal politics.

The Cominform has been, essentially, a sideshow in the latest stage of satellite control. Its central feature has been more or less direct control by Moscow over the armed forces, secret police, and party bureaucracies of the individual states. Moreover, it has become clear, at least since 1948, that even in matters of local Balkan policy, such as negotiations between Bulgaria and Yugoslavia, Soviet Russian interests are made paramount.

In Yugoslavia Tito was strong enough politically and militarily within his country, and so located geographically, that he could hold out against the power, short of invasion, that Stalin could mobilize against him. In these circumstances, but not in his motivations, Tito was unique among the Eastern European postwar Communist leaders. For Tito the issue became one of his own life as well as that of his regime; and the correctness of his decision to resist Soviet control has been borne out by the fate of other potential or alleged Nationalist Communists who "recanted."

It is evidently now the bias of Soviet policy to choose virtually complete direct management over such areas as it controls rather than wider, more dilute influence. In terms of this bias, the loss of Yugoslavia was perhaps inevitable and even proper. Though the Titoist defiance has certainly injured the cause of world Communism, the advantage to the Kremlin of retaining the impression of absolute vigor in enforcing its will and tolerating no insubordination or even institutional variety in the region it still dominates may have, thus far, outweighed the loss of one satellite. Tito, continuing within the Cominform on his own terms, might well have disrupted the coherence of Soviet control. His elimination was essential to the new stage of which the placing of a Russian Marshal, Rokossovsky, in command of the Polish armed forces, in the fall of 1949, and his subsequent (1952) elevation to the post of Vice-Premier, is perhaps the most striking symbol.

NEW ASPECTS OF WORLD CONFLICT

ANDREI ZHDANOV

In early 1947 the Truman Doctrine and the Marshall Plan proclaimed the determination of the United States to resist further Soviet expansion. In September of the
same year a conference of Communist parties met in Poland for the purpose of organizing
the Cominform (The Information Bureau of Communist and Workers' Parties), ostensibly an agency that would coordinate the policies of the several national parties, but
actually an effort to replace the Comintern organization that had been publicly "dissolved" in 1943. Andrei Zhdanov, Stalin's deputy to the conference and a leading member
of the Politburo, presented a detailed analysis of international developments since
the war. Zhdanov divided the world into two hostile camps. On the one side were the
"imperialist aggressors" and "capitalist warmongers" led by the United States; on the
other were the "freedom-loving democracies" led by the Soviet Union. All loyal Communists were summoned to unite in the struggle against "The American Plan for the
Enthrallment of Europe." Because of Zhdanov's high position his speech may be said
to represent an official expression of Soviet party and government views in 1947 and the
years immediately following.

I. THE POSTWAR WORLD SITUATION

THE end of the Second World War
brought with it big changes in the world
situation. The military defeat of the bloc
of fascist states, the character of the war
as a war of liberation from fascism, and
the decisive role played by the Soviet Union
in the vanquishing of the fascist aggressors
sharply altered the alignment of forces between the two systems—the Socialist and
the Capitalist—in favor of Socialism.

What is the essential nature of these
changes?

The principal outcome of World War
II was the military defeat of Germany and
Japan—the two most militaristic and aggressive of the capitalist countries. The
reactionary imperialist elements all over
the world, notably in Britain, America and
France, had reposed great hopes in Germany and Japan, and chiefly in Hitler Germany: firstly as in a force most capable of
inflicting a blow on the Soviet Union in
order to, if not having it destroyed altogether, weaken it at least and undermine its
influence; secondly, as in a force capable

of smashing the revolutionary labor and
democratic movement in Germany herself
and in all countries singled out for Nazi
aggression, and thereby strengthening capitalism generally. This was the chief reason for the prewar policy of "appeasement"
and encouragement of fascist aggression,
the so-called Munich policy consistently
pursued by the imperialist ruling circles
of Britain, France, and the United States.

But the hopes reposed by the British,
French, and American imperialists in the
Hitlerites were not realized. The Hitlerites
proved to be weaker, and the Soviet Union
and the freedom-loving nations stronger
than the Munichists had anticipated. As
the result of World War II the major forces
of bellicose international fascist reaction
had been smashed and put out of commission for a long time to come.

This was accompanied by another
serious loss to the world capitalist system
generally. Whereas the principal result of
World War I had been that the united
imperialist front was breached and that
Russia dropped out of the world capitalist

From Andrei Zhdanov. "The International Situation," delivered at the Founding Conference of the
Cominform, September 1947, in *The Strategy and Tactics of World Communism* (Wash., D. C.: U. S.
Government Printing Office, 1948), Supplement I, pp. 212–222, 227–230.

system, and whereas, as a consequence of the triumph of the Socialist system in the USSR, capitalism ceased to be an integral, world-wide economic system, World War II and the defeat of fascism, the weakening of the world position of capitalism and the enhanced strength of the anti-fascist movement resulted in a number of countries in Central and Southeastern Europe dropping out of the imperialist system. In these countries new, popular, democratic regimes arose. The impressive lesson given by the Patriotic War of the Soviet Union and the liberating role of the Soviet Army were accompanied by a mass struggle of the freedom-loving peoples for national liberation from the fascist invaders and their accomplices. In the course of this struggle the pro-fascist elements, the collaborators with Hitler—the most influential of the big capitalists, large landowners, high officials and monarchist officers—were exposed as betrayers of the national interests. In the Danubian countries, liberation from German fascist slavery was accompanied by the removal from power of the top bourgeoisie and landlords, compromised by collaborating with German fascism, and by the rise to power of new forces from among the people who had proved their worth in the struggle against the Hitlerite conquerers. In these countries, representatives of the workers, the peasants and the progressive intellectuals took over power. Since the working class had everywhere displayed the greatest heroism, the greatest consistency and implacability in the struggle against fascism, its prestige and influence among the people have increased immensely.

The new democratic power in Yugoslavia, Bulgaria, Rumania, Poland, Czechoslovakia, Hungary and Albania, backed by the mass of the people, was able within a minimum period to carry through such progressive democratic reforms as bourgeois democracy is no longer capable of effecting. Agrarian reform turned over the land to the peasants and led to the elimina-

tion of the landlord class. Nationalization of large-scale industry and banks, and the confiscation of the property of traitors who had collaborated with the Germans radically undermined the position of monopoly capital in these countries and redeemed the masses from imperialist bondage. Together with this, the foundation was laid of state, national ownership, and a new type of state was created—the people's republic, where the power belongs to the people, where large-scale industry, transport and banks are owned by the state, and where a bloc of the laboring classes of the population, headed by the working class, constitute a leading force. As a result, the peoples of these countries have not only torn themselves from the clutches of imperialism, but are paving the way for entry onto the path of Socialist development.

The war immensely enhanced the international significance and prestige of the USSR. The USSR was the leading force and the guiding spirit in the military defeat of Germany and Japan. The progressive democratic forces of the whole world rallied around the Soviet Union. The socialist state successfully stood the strenuous test of the war and emerged victorious from the mortal struggle with a most powerful enemy. Instead of being enfeebled, the USSR became stronger.

The capitalist world has also undergone a substantial change. Of the six socalled great imperialist powers (Germany, Japan, Great Britain, the U.S.A., France and Italy), three have been eliminated by military defeat (Germany, Italy and Japan). France has also been weakened and has lost its significance as a great power. As a result, only two great imperialist world powers remain—the United States and Great Britain. But the position of one of them, Great Britain, has been undermined. The war revealed that militarily and politically British imperialism was not so strong as it had been. In Europe, Britain was helpless against German aggression. In Asia, Britain, one of the biggest of the imperialist powers, was unable to retain hold of her colonial possessions without outside aid. Temporarily cut off from colonies that supplied her with food and raw materials and absorbed a large part of her industrial products, Britain found herself dependent militarily and economically, upon American supplies of food and manufactured goods. After the war, Britain became increasingly dependent, financially, and economically, on the United States. Although she succeeded in recovering her colonies after the war, Britain found herself faced there with the enhanced influence of American imperialism, which during the war had invaded all the regions that before the war had been regarded as exclusive spheres of influence of British capital (the Arab East, Southeast Asia). America has also increased her influence in the British dominions and in South America, where the former role of Britain is very largely and to an ever increasing extent passing to the United States.

World War II aggravated the crisis of the colonial system, as expressed in the rise of a powerful movement for national liberation in the colonies and dependencies. This has placed the rear of the capitalist system in jeopardy. The peoples of the colonies no longer wish to live in the old way. The ruling classes of the metropolitan countries can no longer govern the colonies on the old lines. Attempts to crush the national liberation movement by military force now increasingly encounter armed resistance on the part of the colonial peoples and lead to protracted colonial wars (Holland-Indonesia, France-Viet Nam).

The war—itself a product of the unevenness of capitalist development in the different countries—still further intensified this unevenness. Of all the capitalist powers, only one—the United States—emerged from the war not only unweakened, but even considerably stronger economically and militarily. The war greatly enriched the American capitalists. The American

people, on the other hand, did not experience the privations that accompany war, the hardship of occupation, or aerial bombardment; and since America entered the war practically in its concluding stage, when the issue was already decided, her human casualties were relatively small. For the U.S.A., the war was primarily and chiefly a spur to extensive industrial development and to a substantial increase of exports (principally to Europe).

But the end of the war confronted the United States with a number of new problems. The capitalist monopolies were anxious to maintain their profits at the former high level, and accordingly pressed hard to prevent a reduction of the wartime volume of deliveries. But this meant that the United States must retain the foreign markets which had absorbed American products during the war, and moreover, acquire new markets, inasmuch as the war had substantially lowered the purchasing power of most of the countries. The financial and economic dependence of these countries on the U.S.A. had likewise increased. The United States extended credits abroad to a sum of 19,000 million dollars, not counting investments in the International Bank and the International Currency Fund. America's principal competitors, Germany and Japan, have disappeared from the world market, and this has opened up new and very considerable opportunities for the United States. Whereas before World War II the more influential reactionary circles of American imperialism had adhered to an isolationist policy and had refrained from active interference in the affairs of Europe and Asia, in the new, postwar conditions the Wall Street bosses adopted a new policy. They advanced a program of utilizing America's military and economic might, not only to retain and consolidate the positions won abroad during the war, but to expand them to the maximum and to replace Germany, Japan and Italy in the world market. The sharp decline of the economic power of the other capitalist states makes it possible to speculate on their post-war economic difficulties, and, in partic-ular, on the postwar economic difficulties of Great Britain, which makes it easier to bring these countries under American con-trol. The United States proclaimed a new frankly predatory and expansionist course.

The purpose of this new, frankly ex-pansionist course is to establish the world supremacy of American imperialism. With a view to consolidating America's monopoly position in the markets gained as a result of the disappearance of her two biggest competitors, Germany and Japan, and the weakening of her capitalist partners, Great Britain and France, the new course of United States policy envisages a broad pro-gram of military, economic and political measures, designed to establish United States political and economic domination in all countries marked out for American expansion, to reduce these countries to the status of satellites of the United States and to set up regimes within them which would eliminate all obstacles on the part of the labor and democratic movement to the ex-ploitation of these countries by American capital. The United States is now en-deavoring to extend this new line of policy not only to its enemies in the war and to neutral countries, but in an increasing de-gree to its wartime allies.

Special attention is being paid to the exploitation of the economic difficulties of Great Britain, which is not only America's ally but also a long-standing capitalist rival and competitor. It is the design of Amer-ica's expansionist policy not only to prevent Britain from escaping from the vise of economic dependence on the United States in which she was gripped during the war, but, on the contrary, to increase the pres-sure, with a view of gradually depriving her of control over her colonies, ousting her from her spheres of influence, and re-ducing her to the status of a vassal state.

Thus the new policy of the United States is designed to consolidate its monop-oly position and to reduce its capitalist partners to a state of subordination and dependence on America.

But America's aspirations to world supremacy encounter an obstacle in the USSR, the stronghold of anti-imperialist and anti-fascist policy, and its growing in-ternational influence, in the new democra-cies, which have escaped from the control of Britain and American imperialism, and in the workers of all countries, including America itself, who do not want a new war for the supremacy of their oppressors. Ac-cordingly, the new expansionist and reac-tionary policy of the United States envis-ages a struggle against the USSR, against the labor movements in all countries, in-cluding the United States, and against the emancipationist, anti-imperialist forces in all countries.

Alarmed by the achievements of So-cialism in the USSR, by the achievements of the new democracies, and by the post-war growth of the labor and democratic movement in all countries, the American reactionaries are disposed to take upon themselves the mission of "saviors" of the capital system from Communism.

The frank expansionist program of the United States is therefore highly reminis-cent of the reckless program, which failed so ignominiously, of the fascist aggressors, who, as we know, also made a bid for world supremacy.

Just as the Hitlerites, when they were making their preparations for piratical ag-gression, adopted the camouflage of anti-Communism in order to make it possible to oppress and enslave all peoples and pri-marily and chiefly their own people, Amer-ica's present-day ruling circles mask their expansionist policy, and even their offen-sive against the vital interests of their weaker imperialist rival, Great Britain, by fictitious considerations of defense against Communism. The feverish piling up of armaments, the construction of new mili-tary bases and the creation of bridgeheads for the American armed forces in all parts of the world is justified on the false and pharisaical grounds of "defense" against an imaginary threat of war on the part of the USSR. With the help of intimidation, bribery and chicanery, American diplomacy finds it easy to extort from other capitalist countries, and primarily from Great Britain, consent to the legitimization of America's superior position in Europe and Asia—in the Western Zones of Germany, in Austria, Italy, Greece, Turkey, Egypt, Iran, Afghanistan, China, Japan, and so forth.

The American imperialists regard themselves as the principal force opposed to the USSR, the new democracies and the labor and democratic movement in all countries of the world, as the bulwark of the reactionary, anti-democratic forces in all parts of the globe. Accordingly, literally on the day following the conclusion of World War II, they set to work to build up a front hostile to the USSR, and world democracy, and to encourage the anti-popular reactionary forces—collaborationists and former capitalist stooges—in the European countries which had been liberated from the Nazi yoke and which were beginning to arrange their affairs according to their own choice.

The more malignant and unbalanced imperialist politicians followed the lead of Churchill in hatching plans for the speedy launching of a preventive war against the USSR and openly called for the employment of America's temporary monopoly of the atomic weapon against the Soviet people. The new warmongers are trying to intimidate and browbeat not only the USSR, but other countries as well, notably China and India, by libellously depicting the USSR as a potential aggressor, while they themselves pose as "friends" of China and India, as "saviors" from the Communist peril, their mission being to "help" the weak. By these means they are seeking to keep India and China under the sway of imperialism and in continued political and economic bondage.

II. THE NEW POSTWAR ALIGNMENT OF POLITICAL FORCES AND THE FORMATION OF TWO CAMPS: THE IMPERIALIST AND ANTI-DEMOCRATIC CAMP, AND THE ANTI-IMPERIALIST AND DEMOCRATIC ONE

The fundamental changes caused by the war on the international scene and in the position of individual countries has entirely changed the political landscape of the world. A new alignment of political forces has arisen. The more the war recedes into the past, the more distinct become two major trends in postwar international policy, corresponding to the division of the political forces operating on the international arena into two major camps; the imperialist and anti-democratic camp, on the one hand, and the anti-imperialist and democratic camp, on the other. The principal driving force of the imperialist camp is the U.S.A. Allied with it are Great Britain and France. The existence of the Atlee-Bevin Labor Government in Britain and the Ramadier Socialist Government in France does not hinder these countries from playing the part of satellites of the United States and following the lead of its imperialist policy on all major questions. The imperialist camp is also supported by colony-owning countries, such as Belgium and Holland, by countries with reactionary anti-democratic regimes, such as Turkey and Greece, and by countries politically and economically dependent on the United States, such as the Near-Eastern and South-American countries and China.

The cardinal purpose of the imperialist camp is to strengthen imperialism, to hatch a new imperialist war, to combat Socialism and democracy, and to support reactionary and anti-democratic pro-fascist regimes and movements everywhere.

In the pursuit of these ends the imperialist camp is prepared to rely on reactionary and anti-democratic forces in all countries, and to support its former adversaries in the war against its wartime allies.

The anti-fascist forces comprise the second camp. This camp is based on the

USSR and the new democracies. It also includes countries that have broken with imperialism and have firmly set foot on the path of democratic development, such as Rumania, Hungary and Finland. Indonesia and Viet Nam are associated with it; it has the sympathy of India, Egypt and Syria. The anti-imperialist camp is backed by the labor and democratic movement and by the fraternal Communist parties in all countries, by the fighters for national liberation in the colonies and dependencies, by all progressive and democratic forces in every country. The purpose of this camp is to resist the threat of new wars and imperialist expansion, to strengthen democracy and to extirpate the vestiges of fascism.

The end of the Second World War confronted all the freedom-loving nations with the cardinal task of securing a lasting democratic peace sealing victory over fascism. In the accomplishment of this fundamental task of the postwar period the Soviet Union and its foreign policy are playing a leading role. This follows from the very nature of the Soviet Socialist state, to which motives of aggression and exploitation are utterly alien, and which is interested in creating the most favorable conditions for the building of a Communist society. One of these conditions is external peace. As embodiment of a new and superior social system, the Soviet Union reflects in its foreign policy the aspirations of progressive mankind, which desires lasting peace and has nothing to gain from a new war hatched by capitalism. The Soviet Union is a staunch supporter of the liberty and independence of all nations, and a foe of national and racial oppression and colonial exploitation in any shape or form. The change in the general alignment of forces between the capitalist world and the Socialist world brought about by the war has still further enhanced the significance of the foreign policy of the Soviet state and enlarged the scope of its activity on the international arena.

All the forces of the anti-imperialist and anti-fascist camp are united in the effort to secure a just and democratic peace. It is this united effort that has brought about and strengthened friendly cooperation between the USSR and democratic countries on all questions of foreign policy. These countries, and in the first place the new democracies—Yugoslavia, Poland, Czechoslovakia and Albania, which played a big part in the war of liberation from fascism, as well as Bulgaria, Rumania, Hungary and to some extent Finland, which have joined the anti-fascist front—have proved themselves in the postwar period staunch defenders of peace, democracy and their own liberty and independence against all attempts on the part of the United States and Great Britain to turn them back in their course and to bring them again under the imperialist yoke.

The successes and the growing international prestige of the democratic camp were not to the liking of the imperialists. Even while World War II was still on, reactionary forces in Great Britain and the United States became increasingly active, striving to prevent concerted action by the Allied powers, to protract the war, to bleed the USSR, and to save the fascist aggressors from utter defeat. The sabotage of the Second Front by the Anglo-Saxon imperialists, headed by Churchill, was a clear reflection of this tendency, which was in point of fact a continuation of the Munich policy in the new and changed conditions. But while the war was still in progress British and American reactionary circles did not venture to come out openly against the Soviet Union and the democratic countries, realizing that they had the undivided sympathy of the masses all over the world. But in the concluding months of the war the situation began to change. The British and American imperialists already manifested their unwillingness to respect the legitimate interests of the Soviet Union and the democratic countries at the Potsdam tripartite conference, in July 1945.

The foreign policy of the Soviet Union

and the democratic countries in these two past years has been a policy of consistently working for the observance of the democratic principles in the postwar settlement. The countries of the anti-imperialist camp have loyally and consistently striven for the implementation of these principles, without deviating from them one iota. Consequently, the major objective of the postwar foreign policy of the democratic states has been a democratic peace, the eradication of the vestiges of fascism and the prevention of a resurgence of fascist imperialist aggression, the recognition of the principle of the equality of nations and respect for their sovereignty, and general reduction of all armaments and the outlawing of the most destructive weapons, those designed for the mass slaughter of the civilian population. In their efforts to secure these objectives Soviet diplomacy and the diplomacy of the democratic countries met with the resistance of Anglo-American diplomacy, which since the war has persistently and unswervingly striven for the rejection of the general principles of the postwar settlement proclaimed by the Allies during the war, and to replace the policy of peace and consolidation of democracy by a new policy, a policy aiming at violating general peace, protecting fascist elements, and persecuting democracy in all countries.

Of immense importance are the joint efforts of the diplomacy of the USSR and that of the other democratic countries to secure a reduction of armaments and the outlawing of the most destructive of them—the atomic bomb.

On the initiative of the Soviet Union, a resolution was moved in the United Nations calling for a general reduction of armaments and the recognition, as a primary task, of the necessity to prohibit the production and use of atomic energy for warlike purposes. This motion of the Soviet government was fiercely resisted by the United States and Great Britain. All the efforts of the imperialist elements were concentrated on sabotaging this decision by erecting endless and fruitless obstacles and barriers, with the object of preventing the adoption of any effective practical measures. The activities of the delegates of the USSR and the other democratic countries in the agencies of the United Nations bear the character of a systematic, stubborn day-to-day struggle for democratic principles of international cooperation, for the exposure of the intrigues of the imperialist plotters against the peace and security of the nations.

This was openly demonstrated, for example, in the discussion of the situation on Greece's northern frontiers. The Soviet Union and Poland vigorously objected to the Security Council being used as a means of discrediting Yugoslavia, Bulgaria and Albania, who are falsely accused by the imperialists of aggressive acts against Greece.

Soviet foreign policy proceeds from the fact of the coexistence for a long period of the two systems—capitalism and socialism. From this it follows that cooperation between the USSR and countries with other systems is possible, provided that the principle of reciprocity is observed and that obligations once assumed are honored. Everyone knows that the USSR has always honored the obligations it has assumed. The Soviet Union has demonstrated its will and desire for cooperation.

Britain and America are pursuing the very opposite policy in the United Nations. They are doing everything they can to renounce their commitments and to secure a free hand for the prosecution of a new policy, a policy which envisages not cooperation among the nations, but the hounding of one against the other, violation of the rights and interests of democratic nations, and the isolation of the USSR.

Soviet policy follows the line of maintaining loyal, good-neighbor relations with all states that display the desire for cooperation. As to the countries that are its genuine friends and allies, the Soviet Union has always behaved, and will always behave, as their true friend and ally. Soviet foreign policy envisages a further extension of friendly aid by the Soviet Union to these countries.

Soviet foreign policy, defending the cause of peace, discountenances a policy of vengeance towards the vanquished countries.

It is known that the USSR is in favor of a united, peace-loving, demilitarized and democratic Germany. Comrade Stalin formulated the Soviet policy towards Germany when he said: "In short, the policy of the Soviet Union on the German question reduces itself to the demilitarization and democratization of Germany. The demilitarization and democratization of Germany is one of the most important guarantees for the establishment of a solid and lasting peace." However, this policy of the Soviet Union towards Germany is being encountered by frantic opposition from the imperialist circles in the United States and Great Britain.

The meeting of the Council of Foreign Ministers in Moscow in March and April 1947 demonstrated that the United States, Great Britain and France are prepared not only to prevent the democratic reconstruction and demilitarization of Germany, but even to liquidate her as an integral state, to dismember her, and to settle the question of peace separately.

Today this policy is being conducted under new conditions, now that America has abandoned the old course of Roosevelt and is passing to a new policy, a policy of preparing for new military adventures.

III. THE AMERICAN PLAN FOR THE ENTHRALLMENT OF EUROPE

The aggressive and frankly expansionist course to which American imperialism has committed itself since the end of World War II finds expression in both the foreign and home policy of the United States. The active support rendered to the reactionary, anti-democratic forces all over the world, the sabotage of the Potsdam decisions which call for the democratic reconstruction and demilitarization of Germany, the protection given to Japanese reactionaries, the extensive war preparations and the accumulation of atomic bombs—all this goes hand in hand with an offensive against the elementary democratic rights of the working people in the United States itself.

Although the U.S.A. suffered comparatively little from the war, the vast majority of the Americans do not want another war, with its accompanying sacrifices and limitations. This has induced monopoly capital and its servitors among the ruling circles in the United States to resort to extraordinary means in order to crush the opposition at home to the aggressive expansionist course and to secure a free hand for the further prosecution of this dangerous policy.

But the crusade against Communism proclaimed by America's ruling circles with the backing of the capitalist monopolies, leads as a logical consequence to attacks on the fundamental rights and interests of the American working people, to the fascization of America's political life, and to the dissemination of the most savage and misanthropic "theories" and views. Dreaming about preparing for a new, a third world war, American expansionist circles are vitally interested in stifling all possible resistance within the country to adventures abroad, in poisoning the minds of the politically backward and unenlightened American masses with the virus of chauvinism and militarism, and in stultifying the average American with the help of all the diverse means of anti-Soviet and anti-Communist propaganda—the cinema, the radio, the church, and the press. The expansionist foreign policy inspired and conducted by the American reactionaries envisages simultaneous action along all lines:

1) strategical military measures,
2) economic expansion, and
3) ideological struggle.

Realization of the strategical plans for future aggression is connected with the desire to utilize to the utmost the war production facilities of the United States, which had grown to enormous proportions by the end of World War II. American imperialism is persistently pursuing a policy of militarizing the country. Expenditure on the U.S. army and navy exceeds 11,000 million dollars per annum. In 1947–48, 35 per cent of America's budget was appropriated for the armed forces, or eleven times more than in 1937–1938.

On the outbreak of World War II the American army was the seventeenth largest in the capitalist world; today it is the largest one. The United States is not only accumulating stocks of atomic bombs; American strategists say quite openly that it is preparing bacteriological weapons.

The strategical plans of the United States envisage the creation in peacetime of numerous bases and vantage grounds situated at great distances from the American continent and designed to be used for aggressive purposes against the USSR and the countries of the new democracy. America has built, or is building, air and naval bases in Alaska, Japan, Italy, South Korea, China, Egypt, Iran, Turkey, Greece, Austria, and Western Germany. There are American military missions in Afghanistan and even in Nepal. Feverish preparations are being made to use the Arctic for purposes of military aggression.

Although the war has long since ended, the military alliance between Britain and the United States and even a combined Anglo-American military staff continue to exist. Under the guise of agreement for the standardization of weapons the United States has established its control over the armed forces and military plans of other countries, notably of Great Britain and Canada. Under the guise of joint defense of the Western Hemisphere, the countries of Latin America are being brought into

the orbit of America's plans of military expansion. The United States government has officially declared that it has committed itself to assist in the modernization of the Turkish army. The army of the reactionary Kuomintang is being trained by American instructors and armed with American material. The military circles are becoming an active political force in the United States, supplying large numbers of government officials and diplomats who are directing the whole policy of the country into an aggressive military course.

Economic expansion is an important supplement to the realization of America's strategical plan. American imperialism is endeavoring like a usurer, to take advantage of the postwar difficulties of the European countries, in particular of the shortage of raw materials, fuel and food in the Allied countries that suffered most from the war, to dictate to them extortionate terms for any assistance rendered. With an eye to the impending economic crisis, the United States is in a hurry to find new monopoly spheres of capital investment and markets for its goods. American economic "assistance" pursues the broad aim of bringing Europe into bondage to American capital. The more drastic the economic situation of a country is, the harsher are the terms which the American monopolies endeavor to dictate to it.

But economic control logically leads to political subjugation to American imperialism. Thus the United States combines the extension of monopoly markets for its goods with the acquisition of new bridgeheads for its fight against the new democratic forces of Europe. In "saving" a country from starvation and collapse, the American monopolies at the same time seek to rob it of all vestige of independence. American "assistance" automatically involves a change in the policy of the country to which it is rendered: parties and individuals come to power that are prepared, on directions from Washington, to carry out a program of home and foreign policy suitable to the United States, (France, Italy, and so on).

Lastly, the aspiration to world supremacy and the anti-democratic policy of the United States involve an ideological struggle. The principal purpose of the ideological part of the American strategical plan is to deceive public opinion by slanderously accusing the Soviet Union and the new democracies of aggressive intentions, and thus representing the Anglo-Saxon bloc in a defensive role and absolving it of responsibility for preparing a new war. During the Second World War the popularity of the Soviet Union in foreign countries was enormously enhanced. Its devoted and heroic struggle against imperialism earned it the affection and respect of working people in all countries. The military and economic might of the Socialist state, the invincible strength of the moral and political unity of Soviet society were graphically demonstrated to the whole world. The reactionary circles in the United States and Great Britain are anxious to erase the deep impression made by the Socialist system on the working people of the world. The war-mongers fully realize that long ideological preparation is necessary before they can get their soldiers to fight the Soviet Union.

In their ideological struggle against the USSR, the American imperialists, who have no great insight into political questions, demonstrate their ignorance by laying primary stress on the allegation that the Soviet Union is undemocratic and totalitarian, while the United States and Great Britain and the whole capitalist world are democratic. On this platform of ideological struggle—on this defense of bourgeois pseudo-democracy and condemnation of Communism as totalitarian—are united all the enemies of the working class without exception, from the capitalist magnates to the Right Socialist leaders, who seize with the greatest eagerness on any slander-

ous imputations against the USSR suggested to them by their imperialist masters. The pith and substance of this fraudulent propaganda is the claim that the earmark of true democracy is the existence of a plurality of parties and of an organized opposition minority. On these grounds the British Laborites, who spare no effort in their fight against Communism, would like to discover antagonistic classes and a corresponding struggle of parties in the USSR. Political ignoramuses that they are, they cannot understand that capitalists and landlords, antagonistic classes, and hence a plurality of parties, have long ceased to exist in the USSR. They would like to have in the USSR the bourgeois parties which are so dear to their hearts, including pseudo-socialistic parties, as an agency of imperialism. But to their bitter regret these parties of the exploiting bourgeoisie have been doomed by history to disappear from the scene. . . .

* * *

The Soviet Union unswervingly holds the position that political and economic relations between states must be built exclusively on the basis of equality of the parties and mutual respect for their sovereign rights. Soviet foreign policy and, in particular, Soviet economic relations with foreign countries are based on the principle of equality, on the principle that agreements must be of advantage to both parties. Treaties with the USSR are agreements that are of mutual advantage to both parties, and never contain anything that encroaches on the national independence and sovereignty of the contracting parties. This fundamental feature of the agreements of the USSR with other states stands out particularly vividly just now, in the light of the unfair and unequal treaties being concluded or planned by the United States. Unequal agreements are alien to Soviet foreign trade policy. More, the development of the Soviet Union's economic relations with all countries interested in such relations demonstrates on what principles normal relations between states should be built. Suffice it to recall the treaties recently concluded by the USSR with Poland, Yugoslavia, Czechoslovakia, Hungary, Bulgaria and Finland. In this way the USSR has clearly shown along what lines Europe may find the way out of its present economic plight. Britain might have had a similar treaty, if the Labor Government had not, under outside pressure, frustrated the agreement with the USSR, the agreement which was already on its way to conclusion.

The exposure of the American plan for the economic enslavement of the European countries is an indisputable service rendered by the foreign policy of the USSR and the new democracies.

It should be borne in mind that America herself is threatened with an economic crisis. There are weighty reasons for Marshall's official generosity. If the European countries do not receive American credits, their demand for American goods will diminish, and this will tend to accelerate and intensify the approaching economic crisis in the United States. Accordingly, if the European countries display the necessary stamina and readiness to resist the enthralling terms of the American credit, America may find herself compelled to beat a retreat.

IV. THE TASKS OF THE COMMUNIST PARTIES
IN UNITING THE DEMOCRATIC, ANTI-FASCIST,
PEACE-LOVING ELEMENTS TO RESIST THE
NEW PLANS OF WAR AND AGGRESSION

The dissolution of the Comintern, which conformed to the demands of the development of the labor movement in the new historical situation, played a positive role. The dissolution of the Comintern once and for all disposed of the slanderous allegation of the enemies of Communism and the labor movement that Moscow was interfering in the internal affairs of other states, and that the Communist parties in the various countries were acting not in the interests of their nations, but on orders from outside.

The Comintern was founded after the first world war, when the Communist parties were still weak, when practically no ties existed between the working classes of the different countries, and when the Communist parties had not yet produced generally recognized leaders of the labor movement. The service performed by the Comintern was that it restored and strengthened the ties between the working people of the different countries, that it elaborated theoretical questions of the labor movement in the new, postwar conditions of development, that it established general standards of propaganda of the ideas of Communism, and that it facilitated the preparation of leaders of the labor movement. This created the conditions for the conversion of the young Communist parties into mass labor parties. But once the young Communist parties had become mass labor parties, the direction of these parties from one center became impossible and inexpedient. As a result, the Comintern, from a factor promoting the development of the Communist parties began to turn into a factor hindering their development. The new stage in the development of the Communist parties demanded new forms of contact among the parties. It was these considerations that made it necessary to dissolve the Comintern and to devise new forms of connection between the parties.

In the course of the four years that have elapsed since the dissolution of the Comintern, the Communist parties have grown considerably in strength and influence in nearly all the countries of Europe and Asia. The influence of the Communist parties has increased not only in Eastern Europe, but in practically all European countries where fascism held sway, as well as in those which were occupied by the German fascists—France, Belgium, Holland, Norway, Denmark, Finland, etc. The influence of the Communists has increased especially in the new democracies, where the Communist parties are among the most influential parties in the state.

But the present position of the Communist parties has its shortcomings. Some comrades understood the dissolution of the Comintern to imply the elimination of all ties, of all contact, between the fraternal Communist parties. But experience has shown that such mutual isolation of the Communist parties is wrong, harmful and, in point of fact, unnatural. The Communist movement develops within national frameworks, but there are tasks and interests common to the parties of various countries. We get a rather curious state of affairs: the Socialists, who stopped at nothing to prove that the Comintern dictated directives from Moscow to the Communists of all countries, have restored their International; yet the Communists even refrained from meeting one another, let alone consulting with one another on questions of mutual interest to them, from fear of the slanderous talk of their enemies regarding the "hand of Moscow." Representatives of the most diverse fields of endeavor—scientists, cooperators, trade unionists, the youth, students—deem it possible to maintain international contact, to exchange experience and consult with one another on matters relating to their work, to arrange international congresses and conferences; yet the Communists, even of countries that are bound together as allies, hesitate to establish friendly ties. There can be no doubt that if the situation were to continue it would be fraught with most serious consequences to the development of the work of the fraternal parties. The need for mutual consultation and voluntary coordination of action between individual parties has become particularly urgent at the present juncture when continued isolation may lead to a slackening of mutual understanding, and at times, even to serious blunders.

In view of the fact that the majority of the leaders of the Socialist parties (espe-cially the British Laborites and the French Socialists) are acting as agents of United States imperialist circles, there has devolved upon the Communists the special historical task of leading the resistance to the American plan for the enthrallment of Europe, and of boldly denouncing all co-adjutors of American imperialism in their own countries. At the same time, Communists must support all the really patriotic elements who do not want their countries to be imposed upon, who want to resist enthrallment of their countries to foreign capital, and to uphold their national sovereignty. The Communists must be the leaders in enlisting all anti-fascist and freedom-loving elements in the struggle against the new American expansionist plans for the enslavement of Europe.

It must be borne in mind that a great gulf lies between the desire of the imperialists to unleash a new war and the possibility of engineering such a war. The peoples of the world do not want war. The forces that stand for peace are so big and influential that if they are staunch and determined in defense of peace, if they display fortitude and firmness, the plans of the aggressors will come to grief. It should not be forgotten that all the hullabaloo of the imperialist agents about the danger of war is designed to frighten the weak-nerved and unstable and to extort concessions to the aggressor by means of intimidation.

The chief danger to the working class at this present juncture lies in underrating its own strength and overrating the strength of the enemy. Just as in the past the Munich policy untied the hands of the Nazi aggressors, so today concessions to the new course of the United States and the imperialist camp may encourage its inspirers to be even more insolent and aggressive. The Communist parties must therefore head the resistance to the plans of imperialist expansion and aggression along every line—state, economic and ideological; they must rally their ranks and unite their efforts on the basis of a common anti-imperialist and democratic platform, and gather around them all the democratic and patriotic forces of the people.

A special task devolves on the fraternal Communist parties of France, Italy, Great Britain and other countries. They must take up the standard in defense of the national independence and sovereignty of their countries. If the Communist parties firmly stick to their position, if they do not allow themselves to be intimidated and blackmailed, if they act as courageous sentinels of enduring peace and popular democracy, of the national sovereignty, liberty and independence of their countries, if, in their struggle against the attempts to economically and politically enthrall their countries, they are able to take the lead of all the forces prepared to uphold the national honor and independence, no plans for the enthrallment of Europe can possibly succeed.

THE YUGOSLAV EXCEPTION

YUGOSLAV, COMINFORM, AND SOVIET CORRESPONDENCE

Soviet techniques of expansion in Eastern Europe and the views of Stalin about the rights and duties of other Communist nations vis-à-vis the USSR could hardly be more strikingly illustrated than they are in the following extracts from correspondence between the Communist Party of the Soviet Union and that of Yugoslavia. Of particular interest in this record of conflict are the gross accusations leveled at the Yugoslavs, the abusive tone of each Soviet note, Stalin's unorthodox views on national sovereignty, and his insistence that dissent from his directives constitutes treason to the cause of international communism. Finally, the role of the Cominform as executor of Soviet policy is clearly demonstrated by its formal "excommunication" of the Yugoslav Communist leaders.

FROM A LETTER BY THE YUGOSLAV PREMIER, J. B. TITO, TO SOVIET FOREIGN MINISTER, V. M. MOLOTOV, OF MARCH 20, 1948

ON March 18, General Barskov[1] advised us of the receipt of a telegram from Marshal Bulganin, Minister of National Defense of the USSR, informing us that the Government of the USSR had decided to withdraw immediately all military advisers and instructors with the motivation that they were "surrounded by an uncom-

radely attitude," namely, that they were not treated in a friendly way in Yugoslavia.

Of course, the Government of the USSR may recall its military specialists whenever it chooses to do so, but the reasons stated by the Government of the USSR for this decision amazed us. After examining, on the basis of this charge, the attitude of lower officials in our country towards the Soviet military advisers and instructors, we were completely convinced that such an explanation of their withdrawal was out of place, that throughout their stay in Yugo-

[1] General Alexey Nikolayevich Barskov, Chief of the Soviet military advisers in Yugoslavia.

From *White Book on Aggressive Activities by the Governments of the USSR, Poland, Czechoslovakia, Hungary, Rumania, Bulgaria and Albania towards Yugoslavia* (Beograd: Ministry of Foreign Affairs of the Federal People's Republic of Yugoslavia, 1951), pp. 57–78.

slavia the attitude towards them was not only good but brotherly and most hospitable, as is customary with regard to Soviet people in the new Yugoslavia. This is, therefore, strange and incomprehensible to us and affects us deeply, since we do not know the real cause of this decision of the Government of the USSR.

Furthermore, on March 19, 1948, I received a visit from the Chargé d'Affaires Armyaninov who informed me of the contents of a telegram in which the Government of the USSR ordered the withdrawal from Yugoslavia of all civilian specialists as well. The reasons stated for this decision are incomprehensible to us and astonish us. It is true that Minister Kidrič's assistant, Srzentić,[2] declared to your Commercial Representative, Lebedev,[3] that by decision of the Government of the FPRY,[4] they were not authorized to give important economic information to anyone and that Soviet people should apply for such information to higher levels, i.e. to the CC of the CPY[5] or to the Government. Srzentić also told Lebedev to apply for the information he was interested in to Minister Kidrič. Your people were told long ago that official representatives of the Soviet Government could get all important necessary information directly from the leaders of our country.

Such a decision was made by us because of the fact that the officials in our Ministries were giving necessary and unnecessary information to anyone whomsoever. Consequently, various people disclosed State and economic secrets which could, and some did, reach the hands of our common enemies.

We have no special agreement, as stated in the telegram, respecting the right of our people to give various kinds of information of an economic nature without the authorization of our Government or the CC to the Soviet people engaged in economic matters, with the exception, however, of the information the latter might need in performing duties assigned to them.

Whenever the Ambassador of the Government of USSR, Comrade Lavrentiyev, requested necessary information from me personally, I always gave it to him without reserve and so did the other responsible leaders. We would be very surprised if the Soviet Government did not approve of such an attitude on our part from the point of view of State interests.

* * *

FROM A LETTER BY THE CENTRAL COMMITTEE OF THE COMMUNIST PARTY OF THE SOVIET UNION (BOLSHEVIKS) TO THE CENTRAL COMMITTEE OF THE COMMUNIST PARTY OF YUGOSLAVIA, OF MARCH 27, 1948

With respect to the matter of the recall of military advisers, the sources of our information are statements made by the officials of the Ministry of the Armed Forces and communications from the advisers themselves. It is a known fact that military advisers were sent to Yugoslavia, after repeated requests by the Yugoslav Government, in a considerably smaller number than requested by the Yugoslav Government. Consequently, the Soviet Government had no intention to impose its advisers upon Yugoslavia.

Later, however, the Yugoslav military leaders, including Koča Popović[6] ventured to state that it was necessary to reduce the number of Soviet military advisers by 60 per cent. Different reasons were given for this statement: some said that the Soviet military advisers were very expensive for Yugoslavia; others contended that the Yugoslav Army did not need to adopt the experience of the Soviet Army; others

[2] Vojislav Srzentić, Assistant of the President of the Economic Council of the FPRY.

[3] Ivan Mihailovich Lebedev, Commercial Representative of the USSR in Beograd.

[4] Federal People's Republic of Yugoslavia.

[5] Central Committee of the Communist Party of Yugoslavia.

[6] Koča Popović, Colonel General, Chief of the General Staff of the Yugoslav Army.

again declared that the regulations of the Soviet Army were stereotyped and inflexible and that they were of no value to the Yugoslav Army; others, finally, made very plain allusions to the effect that the Soviet military advisers were being paid for nothing, since they were of no use. . . .

As the Yugoslav Government did not check these attempts to discredit the Soviet Army, it bears the responsibility for the situation that was created.

* * *

The sources of our information in respect to the recall of Soviet civilian specialists are mainly the reports of the Soviet Ambassador in Beograd, Lavrentiyev, and the statements of the specialists themselves. Your statement to the effect that Srzentić allegedly told our Commercial Representative Lebedev that the Soviet people should apply to the Central Committee of the CPY and to the Yugoslav Government for economic information, in no way corresponds to reality. Here is Lavrentiyev's communication of March 9th:

Srzentić, Kidrič's assistant in the Economic Council, declared to the Commercial Representative Lebedev that there was a Government decision prohibiting State officials and institutions from giving any economic data to anyone whomsoever. Therefore, regardless of the earlier agreement, he could not give Lebedev the data concerned. The State security organs have been ordered to implement control in this matter. Srzentić also said that Kidrič himself intended to speak of this with Lebedev.

From Lavrentiyev's statement it appears, first, that Srzentić did not even mention the possibility of obtaining economic information from the CC or the Yugoslav Government. And in general, it would be ridiculous to imagine that it is possible to apply to the CC or the Government for every item of economic information. There are regular economic bodies in Yugoslavia from which Soviet people used to obtain the necessary economic information.

Lavrentiyev's statement, furthermore, shows something contrary to what you allege—viz. that the Soviet representatives in Yugoslavia are under surveillance by the Yugoslav security organs.

It is not superfluous to mention that we meet with a similar practice of surveillance over Soviet representatives only in bourgeois countries, and not in all of them at that.

We must also note that the Yugoslav security organs shadow not only the representatives of the Soviet Government but also the representative of the CPSU(B) in the Cominform, Comrade Yudin.[7]

It would be ridiculous to imagine that the Soviet Government can agree to keep its civilian specialists in Yugoslavia under such conditions as have been created for them.

Evidently, here again the responsibility for the conditions created lies with the Yugoslav Government.

These are the reasons which compelled the Soviet Government to recall its military and civilian specialists from Yugoslavia.

* * *

FROM A LETTER BY THE CENTRAL COMMITTEE OF THE COMMUNIST PARTY OF YUGOSLAVIA TO J. V. STALIN AND V. M. MOLOTOV, OF APRIL 13, 1948

It was clearly expressed and established at the plenum of the CC of the CPY that S. Žujović and A. Hebrang, members of the CC of the CPY, were chiefly to blame for giving incorrect and slanderous information to Soviet representatives in Yugoslavia both regarding alleged statements made by certain leading people, and our Party in general. By giving such inaccurate and slanderous information they wanted to conceal their anti-Party activities and the tendencies and attempts on their part,

[7] Pavel, F. Yudin, member of the CC of the CPSU (B) [Communist Party of the Soviet Union (Bolshevik)], and its representative in the Information Bureau of some Communist Parties.

which had been manifested much earlier, to disrupt the unity of the leadership and the unity of the Party in general. Besides, information given by such people can be neither impartial, nor well-intentioned, nor accurate, and it usually has definite purpose. In this case the information has the aim of doing harm to the leadership of our Party, i.e. the new Yugoslavia; of aggravating the already hard task of developing the country, of preventing the fulfilment of the Five Year Plan and, by this token, the realization of Socialism in our country. We cannot understand why the Mission of the USSR has to this day not attempted to verify such information—first by contacting responsible people in our country, or by trying to obtain an explanation either from the CC of the CPY or from the Government. We consider the giving of such information as anti-Party as well as anti-State activity, because it has a negative effect on the relations between our two countries.

No matter how deeply one might love the country of Socialism, the USSR, one should under no circumstances feel less love for his own country, which is also building Socialism, in this case the Federal People's Republic of Yugoslavia, for which hundreds of thousands of its most progressive men have given their lives. We know very well that this opinion prevails in the Soviet Union as well.

We are extremely surprised that this matter was not brought up while Kardelj, Djilas and Bakarić were in Moscow as delegates of our Party and Government.[8] Your letter shows that your Government was in possession of this, and similar, information before our delegation came to Moscow. We think that both the question of the treatment of military and civilian specialists and other ones as well could

have been put to our delegation then.

We consider that our Government should have been informed through this delegation, or even earlier in some way, that the Soviet Government was not satisfied with the attitude of our people towards the Soviet specialists and that this matter should be settled in one way or another. Thus it came to pass that the Government of the USSR, by its decision to withdraw military and civilian specialists, placed before us an accomplished fact and in doing so caused us unnecessary difficulties.

As regards the withdrawal of Soviet military specialists, we do not see any other reason which might have induced the Government of the USSR to do this, except our decision to reduce their number to the minimum owing to financial difficulties. As early as 1946 the Yugoslav Premier, Tito, officially informed the Ambassador of the Soviet Government, Lavrentiyev, that for several reasons it was almost impossible for us to pay such high salaries to Soviet military specialists and he asked him to notify the Government of the USSR of this and of our wish that it should alleviate the conditions relative to the salaries of specialists. Ambassador Lavrentiyev transmitted the reply of the Soviet Government that the salaries could not be reduced and that we were free to act as we thought proper. Tito immediately told Lavrentiyev that we should, therefore, have to reduce the number of the above-mentioned specialists as soon as it would be possible to do so without great detriment to the training of our Army. The salaries of the Soviet specialists were four times as high as the salaries of our army corps commanders and three times as high as the salaries of our Federal Ministers. The commander of an army corps, with the rank of Lieutenant General or Colonel General, at the time

---

[8] The Delegation of the Government of the FPRY and of the CPY visited Moscow in the second half of February 1948, at the invitation of the leadership of the USSR in order to consider questions regarding relations between Balkan and Danubian coun- tries. During these talks the Soviet leadership expressed dissatisfaction because of rapprochement among Balkan and Danubian countries outside the scope determined by the Soviet leadership and consented to by it.

received from 9–11,000 dinars a month, while a Soviet military specialist with the rank of Lieutenant Colonel, Colonel or General received 30–40,000 dinars. At the same time our Federal Ministers received a salary of 12,000 dinars a month. Naturally, we felt this was not only financially burdensome, but also politically incorrect, because it gave rise to misunderstanding among our people. Consequently our decision to reduce the number of Soviet military specialists results only from the reason we have stated and from no other reasons. On the other hand, we do not exclude the possibility that some of our people made some inappropriate remarks. In such cases we should have been forwarded verified evidence and then we would undoubtedly have taken steps to prevent this happening in the future. We should also mention here that certain Soviet specialists did not always behave as they should and that this caused dissatisfaction among our people. Such behavior probably provoked, against our wishes and orders, various remarks which were later distorted and in such distorted form forwarded to the Command of the Soviet Army. We, however, consider these to be matters of such slight significance that they ought not to impair our State relationships.

* * *

The assertions in your letter that our state security organs shadow the Soviet specialists and other Soviet people do not correspond to facts. No one has ever brought decisions of such a nature nor is it true that Soviet representatives are shadowed. This is somebody's arbitrary information. It is even less true that officials of the Soviet Government and Comrade Yudin of the Cominform were subjected to such surveillance.

We cannot understand who found such slanders necessary, slanders which misled the Government of the USSR. We should like to be given concrete facts on this case as well.[9]

On what grounds is it contended in the letter that there is no democracy in our Party? Perhaps on the basis of information from Lavrentiyev? Where did he get such information? We consider that he, as Ambassador, is not entitled to seek information from anyone on the work of our Party,—this is not his business. Such information can be obtained by the CC of the CPSU(B) from the CC of the CPY.

* * *

If you were to ask us if there is anything causing dissatisfaction with you, we would openly have to say that there are several reasons for which we are dissatisfied. What are these reasons? It is impossible to enumerate all these reasons in this letter, but we shall mention several of them. First, we consider it improper for organs of the Soviet intelligence to recruit citizens in our country, which is heading for Socialism, into their intelligence service. This we can look upon only as being aimed against the interests of our country. This is being done despite the fact that our leading men and State security organs protested against it and brought it to your knowledge that we could not allow this. Our army officers, various officials and those who have a hostile attitude towards the new Yugoslavia are inveigled in this way.

We have proofs that certain organs of the Soviet intelligence service, while thus inveigling our Party members, cast suspicion upon our leaders, undermine their authority, make them appear incompetent and untrustworthy. For example, Colonel Stepanov did not hesitate, as early as 1945, while inveigling one of our good comrades attached to the Central Code Department in our State Security apparatus, to defame, and express suspicion of, all our leading men—admitting that "for

---

[9] The Government of the USSR, neither before nor after the delivery of the above-mentioned letters, ever offered any concrete facts to the Government of the FPRY in confirmation of its assertions.

the present Marshal Tito was working correctly." Such instances have continued to the present day. This also means that such inveigling is not being conducted with the purpose of fighting against some capitalist country and so we must inevitably come to the conclusion that this inveigling is destroying our internal unity, undermining confidence in our leadership, demoralizing our men, compromising our leading men and becoming a source of daily false information. Such a manner of proceeding on the part of the organs of the Soviet intelligence service cannot be termed loyal and friendly towards our country which is heading for Socialism and is the most faithful ally of the USSR.

We cannot agree to have the Soviet intelligence service create its intelligence network in Yugoslavia. We have our State security and our intelligence service for fighting against various foreign capitalist elements and the class enemy within the country, and if the Soviet intelligence organs need information or aid of this nature, they may get it whenever they want it, just as they have been getting it from us so far.

There are more such and similar matters with which we are not satisfied. But ought this to be a reason for the deterioration of our mutual relations? No. These are matters which can be eliminated or explained.

* * *

FROM A LETTER BY THE CENTRAL COMMITTEE OF THE COMMUNIST PARTY OF THE SOVIET UNION (BOLSHEVIKS) TO THE CENTRAL COMMITTEE OF THE COMMUNIST PARTY OF YUGOSLAVIA, OF MAY 4, 1948

Concerning the recall of Soviet military advisers from Yugoslavia. In its letter of March 27, 1948, the CC of the CPSU(B) stated the reasons for the recall of the Soviet military advisers declaring that the information of the CC of the CPSU(B) was based on the complaints of these advisers against the hostile attitude of the Yugoslav officials towards the Soviet Army and its representatives in Yugoslavia. Comrades Tito and Kardelj completely deny the justifiability of these complaints. The question arises: why should the CC of the CPSU(B) have more faith in the mere words of Comrades Tito and Kardelj than in the repeated complaints of the military advisers of the USSR? On what grounds? The USSR has military advisers in almost all the countries of people's democracy. We cannot but stress that so far we have not had any complaints from our military advisers in these countries. This accounts for the fact that we have had no disagreements in these countries in connection with the work of the Soviet military advisers there. We have had complaints and disagreements of this nature only in Yugoslavia. Is it not clear that this circumstance is to be explained only by the particular and hostile regime to which the Soviet military advisers are subjected in Yugoslavia?

Comrades Tito and Kardelj refer to heavy expenditures in connection with the maintenance of Soviet military advisers in Yugoslavia, and point out that Soviet Generals in Yugoslavia receive, in dinars, three to four times as much as Yugoslav Generals and that, in their opinion, this fact might have given rise to objections on the part of the Yugoslav military personnel. But, firstly, the Yugoslav Generals, in addition to dinars, also receive other allowances in kind: lodging, supplies, food and the like. Secondly, the salary received by the Soviet Generals in Yugoslavia fully corresponds to the amount of money received by the Soviet Generals in the USSR. Naturally, the Soviet Government could not consent to a reduction of the salary of Soviet Generals sent to Yugoslavia.

It is possible that expenditures for the Soviet Generals in Yugoslavia were heavy for the Yugoslav budget, but, if this were the case, the Yugoslav Government should have addressed a timely proposal to the

Soviet Government to take a part of the expenditures upon itself. The Soviet Government would certainly have consented to this. However, the Yugoslavs took another course: instead of solving the situation in a friendly manner, they began to slander our military advisers, to call them parasites, to discredit the Soviet Army, and the Yugoslav Government addressed itself to the Soviet Government only after a hostile atmosphere had been created around the Soviet military advisers.

It is easy to understand that the Soviet Government could not reconcile itself to such a situation.

Concerning the Soviet civilian specialists in Yugoslavia.—In its letter of March 27, 1948, the CC of the CPSU(B) communicated the reasons for the withdrawal of civilian specialists from Yugoslavia. In this case, the CC of the CPSU(B) relied on the complaints of the Soviet civilian specialists and on the reports of the Soviet Ambassador in Yugoslavia. These reports show that both the Soviet civilian specialists and the representative of the CPSU(B) in the Information Bureau, Comrade Yudin, had really been placed under the surveillance of the State security organs of Yugoslavia. Comrades Tito and Kardelj deny in their letter the justifiability of these complaints and communications, contending that the Yugoslav state security organs do not watch Soviet people in Yugoslavia. But why should the CC of the CPSU(B) believe the mere words of Comrades Tito and Kardelj, and not the complaints of Soviet people, among them Comrade Yudin? The Soviet Government has many civilian specialists in all the countries of people's democracy and yet it receives no complaints from its specialists, nor has it any disagreements with the Governments of those countries. The question arises: why did these disagreements and conflicts break out in Yugoslavia only? Is it not because the Yugoslav Government introduced a special regime for the Soviet people in Yugoslavia, including Comrade Yudin?

It is easy to understand that the Soviet Government could not reconcile itself to such a situation, and was therefore compelled to recall its civilian specialists from Yugoslavia.

* * *

Concerning the Soviet Ambassador in Yugoslavia and the Soviet State.—In their letter of April 13, 1948, Comrades Tito and Kardelj write: "We consider that he (the Soviet Ambassador), as Ambassador, is not entitled to seek information from anyone on the work of our Party. This is not his business."

We consider that this statement of Comrades Tito and Kardelj is fundamentally incorrect, anti-Soviet. As can be seen, they place the Soviet Ambassador, a responsible Communist who represents, in Yugoslavia, the Communist Government of the USSR before the Yugoslavia Communist Government, on an equal footing with an ordinary bourgeois Envoy, with an ordinary official of a bourgeois State, whose duty is to undermine the foundations of the Yugoslav State. It is hard to conceive that Comrades Tito and Kardelj could have come to such an absurd notion. Do they realize that such an attitude towards the Soviet Ambassador means the denial of friendly relations between the USSR and Yugoslavia? Do they realize that the Soviet Ambassador, a responsible Communist, the representative of a friendly country which liberated Yugoslavia from the German occupation, has not only the right but also the duty to discuss from time to time with the Communists of Yugoslavia all the questions they might be interested in? How can these simple and elementary things be subjected to doubts, if, of course, the position of friendly relations with the Soviet Union is still adhered to?

For the information of Comrades Tito and Kardelj we should say that, contrary to the Yugoslav model, we do not consider the Yugoslav Ambassador in Moscow as a simple official; we do not place him on an equal footing with bourgeois envoys and we do not deny him the right to seek information from anyone on the work of our Party. On becoming Ambassador, he did not cease to be a Communist. And we treat him as a comrade and a Communist worker. He has acquaintances and friends among the Soviet people. Does he "collect" data on the work of our Party? Probably he does. Well, let him "collect." We have no reason to conceal the shortcomings in our work from comrades. We ourselves reveal them in order to eliminate them.

We consider that such an attitude by the Yugoslav comrades towards the Soviet Ambassador cannot be considered accidental. It derives from the general attitude of the Yugoslav Government owing to which the Yugoslav leaders often do not see the difference between the foreign policy of the USSR and the foreign policy of the Anglo-Americans; they identify Soviet foreign policy with the foreign policy of the English and Americans and consider that Yugoslavia should pursue the same policy towards the Soviet Union as towards the imperialist countries, Great Britain and the U.S.A.

* * *

Comrades Tito and Kardelj accuse Soviet men of allegedly recruiting Yugoslav citizens into their intelligence service. They write:

We consider it improper for organs of the Soviet intelligence to recruit citizens in our country, which is heading for Socialism, into their intelligence service. This we can look upon only as being aimed against the interests of our country. This is being done despite the fact that our leading men and state security organs protested against it and brought it to your knowledge that we could not allow this. Our army officers, various officials and those who have a hostile attitude towards the new Yugoslavia are inveigled in this way.

We declare that this assertion of Comrades Tito and Kardelj, which is full of hostile offenses against the Soviet repre-

sentatives in Yugoslavia, does not at all correspond to reality.

It would be odd to request that the Soviet people who work in Yugoslavia fill their mouths with water and neither talk nor chat with anyone. The Soviet representatives are politically advanced people and not simply employees hired to work for pay without the right to take an interest in what is being done in Yugoslavia. It is natural that they address Yugoslav citizens, ask questions, desire to obtain explanations and the like. Only an incorrigible Sovietophobe could consider these talks as attempts to inveigle people, even people who "have a hostile attitude" towards the new Yugoslavia, into the intelligence service. Only anti-Soviets can imagine that the leaders of the Soviet Union are less concerned with the integrity and inviolability of the new Yugoslavia than is the Politbureau of the CC of the CPY.

It is typical that we meet with such absurd charges against Soviet People in Yugoslavia only.

It appears to us that these ugly charges against Soviet people have been fabricated in order to justify the activity of the state security organs of Yugoslavia who are exercising surveillance over the Soviet people in Yugoslavia.

* * *

FROM THE RESOLUTION "CONCERNING THE SITUATION IN THE COMMUNIST PARTY OF YUGOSLAVIA," PASSED AT THE COMINFORM SESSION OF JUNE 1948 IN RUMANIA, IN THE PRESENCE OF THE MOST RESPONSIBLE STATE AND PARTY LEADERS OF THE USSR AND EASTERN EUROPEAN COUNTRIES, OPENLY CALLING UPON THE PEOPLES OF YUGOSLAVIA TO REBEL AGAINST, AND OVERTHROW, THEIR LEGAL GOVERNMENT

The Information Bureau, composed of the representatives of the Bulgarian Workers' Party (Communists), Rumanian Workers' Party, Hungarian Workers' Party, Polish Workers' Party, the Communist

Party of the Soviet Union (Bolsheviks), Communist Party of France, Communist Party of Czechoslovakia and the Communist Party of Italy, upon discussing the situation in the Communist Party of Yugoslavia and announcing that the representatives of the Communist Party of Yugoslavia had refused to attend the meeting of the Information Bureau, unanimously reached the following conclusions:

The Information Bureau notes that recently the leadership of the Communist Party of Yugoslavia has pursued an incorrect line on the main questions of home and foreign policy, a line which represents a departure from Marxism-Leninism. In this connection the Information Bureau approves the action of the Central Committee of the CPSU(B), which took the initiative in exposing this incorrect policy of the Central Committee of the Communist Party of Yugoslavia, particularly the incorrect policy of Comrades Tito, Kardelj, Djilas and Ranković.

The Information Bureau declares that the leadership of the Yugoslav Communist Party is pursuing an unfriendly policy toward the Soviet Union and the CPSU(B). An undignified policy of defaming Soviet military experts and discrediting the Soviet Union, has been carried out in Yugoslavia. A special regime was instituted for Soviet civilian experts in Yugoslavia, whereby they were under surveillance of Yugoslav state security organs and were continually followed. The representative of the CPSU-(B) in the Information Bureau, Comrade Yudin, and a number of official representatives of the Soviet Union in Yugoslavia were followed and kept under observation by Yugoslav state security organs.

All these and similar facts show that the leaders of the Community Party of Yugoslavia have taken a stand unworthy of Communists, and have begun to identify the foreign policy of the Soviet Union with the foreign policy of the imperialist powers, behaving toward the Soviet Union in the same manner as they behave toward the bourgeois states. Precisely because of this anti-Soviet stand, slanderous propaganda about the "degeneration" of the CPSU(B), about the "degeneration" of the USSR, and so on, borrowed from the arsenal of counter-revolutionary Trotskyism, is current within the Central Committee of the Communist Party of Yugoslavia.

The Information Bureau denounces this anti-Soviet attitude of the leaders of the Communist Party of Yugoslavia, as being incompatible with Marxism-Leninism and only appropriate to nationalists. . . .

It is a completely intolerable state of affairs when the most elementary rights of members in the Yugoslav Communist Party are suppressed, when the slightest criticism of incorrect measures in the Party is brutally repressed.

The Information Bureau regards as disgraceful such actions as the expulsion from the Party and the arrest of the Central Committee members, Comrades Žujović and Hebrang, because they dared to criticize the anti-Soviet attitude of the leaders of the Yugoslav Communist Party, and called for friendship between Yugoslavia and the Soviet Union.

The Information Bureau considers that such a disgraceful, purely Turkish, terrorist regime cannot be tolerated in the Communist Party. The interest of the very existence and development of the Yugoslav Communist Party demands that an end be put to this regime. . . .

Unable to face the criticism of the Central Committee of the CPSU(B) and the Central Committees of the other fraternal Parties, the Yugoslav leaders took the path of outrightly deceiving their Party and people by concealing from the Yugoslav Communist Party the criticism of the Central Committee's incorrect policy and also by concealing from the Party and the people the real reasons for the brutal measures against Comrades Žujović and Hebrang. . . .

In view of this, the Information Bureau expresses complete agreement with the estimation of the situation in the Yugoslav Communist Party, with the criticism of the mistakes of the Central Committee of the Party, and with the political analysis of these mistakes contained in letters from the Central Committee of the Communist Party of the Soviet Union (B) to the Central Committee of the Communist Party of Yugoslavia between March and May, 1948.

The Information Bureau unanimously concludes that by their anti-Party and anti-Soviet views, incompatible with Marxism-Leninism, by their whole attitude and their refusal to attend the meeting of the Information Bureau, the leaders of the Communist Party of Yugoslavia have placed themselves in opposition to the Communist Parties affiliated to the Information Bureau, have taken the path of seceding from the united socialist front against imperialism, have taken the path of betraying the cause of international solidarity of the working people, and have taken up a position of nationalism.

The Information Bureau condemns this anti-Party policy and attitude of the Central Committee of the Communist Party of Yugoslavia.

The Information Bureau considers that in view of all this, the Central Committee of the Communist Party of Yugoslavia has placed itself and the Yugoslav Party outside the family of the fraternal Communist Parties, outside the united Communist front and consequently outside the ranks of the Information Bureau.

* * *

The Information Bureau considers that the basis of these mistakes made by the leadership of the Communist Party of Yugoslavia lies in the undoubted fact that nationalist elements, which previously existed in a disguised form, managed in the course of the past five or six months to reach a dominant position in the leadership of the Communist Party of Yugoslavia and that, consequently, the leadership of the Yugoslav Communist Party has broken with the international traditions of the Communist Party of Yugoslavia and has taken the road of nationalism.

Considerably overestimating the internal, national forces of Yugoslavia and their influence, the Yugoslav leaders think that they can maintain Yugoslavia's independence and build socialism without the support of the Communist Parties of other countries, without the support of the people's democracies, without the support of the Soviet Union. They think that the new Yugoslavia can do without the help of these revolutionary forces.

Showing their poor understanding of the international situation and their intimidation by the blackmailing threats of the imperialists, the Yugoslav leaders think that by making concessions they can curry favor with the Imperialist states. They think they will be able to bargain with them for Yugoslavia's independence and gradually get the people of Yugoslavia oriented on these states, that is, on capitalism. In this they proceed tacitly from the well-known bourgeois-nationalist thesis that "capitalist states are a lesser danger to the independence of Yugoslavia than the Soviet Union."

The Yugoslav leaders evidently do not understand or, probably, pretend they do not understand, that such a nationalist line can only lead to Yugoslavia's degeneration into an ordinary bourgeois republic, to the loss of its independence and to its transformation into a colony of the imperialist countries.

The Information Bureau does not doubt that inside the Communist Party of Yugoslavia there are sufficient healthy elements, loyal to Marxism-Leninism, to the international traditions of the Yugoslav Communist Party and to the united socialist front.

Their task is to compel their present leaders to recognize their mistakes openly and honestly and to rectify them; to break with nationalism, return to internationalism; and in every way to consolidate the united socialist front against imperialism.

Should the present leaders of the Yugoslav Communist Party prove to be incapable of doing this, their job is to replace them and to advance a new internationalist leadership of the Party.

The Information Bureau does not doubt that the Communist Party of Yugoslavia will be able to fulfill this honorable task.

FROM THE STATEMENT OF THE CENTRAL COMMITTEE OF THE COMMUNIST PARTY OF YUGOSLAVIA OF JUNE 29, 1948, FOLLOWING THE COMINFORM RESOLUTION CONCERNING THE SITUATION IN THE CPY

The Resolution of the Information Bureau "Concerning the Situation in the Communist Party of Yugoslavia" has a background, as is obvious from its contents.

Its basis is formed by the letters of the CC of the CPSU(B) addressed to the CC of the CPY. The first of these letters, dated March 27 of this year, in which the CC of the CPSU(B) brought forth its accusations against the CC of the CPY was simultaneously dispatched by the Central Committee of the CPSU(B) to all the other member Parties of the Cominform without the CC of the CPY being informed thereof. After this, a letter from the CC of the CP of Hungary was received through the CC of the CPSU(B) which supported the attitude of the CC of the CPSU(B) on all points. The letter of the Hungarian CC was also sent to the other Parties. After this, similar letters were received by the CC of the CPY from the other member Parties of the Cominform as well, with the exception of the Italian and French. The CC of the CPY points out that those Parties adopted the basic standpoint of the CC of the CPSU(B) without hearing the opinion or any counter-argument on the part of the CC of the CPY. After this letter from the CC of the CPSU(B) and the above-mentioned letters from the other Central Committees, as well as after the reply of the CC

of the CPY to the Central Committee of the CPSU(B) dated April 13 of this year, the CC of the CPY received other letters from the CC of the CPSU(B) (of May 4th and 22nd), which took more or less the same line as the first letter. The Resolution of the Cominform "Concerning the Situation in the CPY" is essentially a recapitulation of these letters from the CC of the CPSU(B). . . .

As can be seen from the statement addressed by the Politbureau of the CC of the CPY to the session of the Cominform annexed herewith, the CC of the CPY could not agree to a discussion on the basis of such accusations on the part of the Central Committee of the CPSU(B) founded on slanders, fabrications and ignorance of the situation in Yugoslavia, until the actual state of affairs was established and falsities were separated from actual objections on principle, whether on the part of the Central Committee of the CPSU(B) or on the part of any other Central Committee of the member Parties of the Cominform.

In connection with the publication of the above-mentioned Resolution of the Cominform, the Central Committee of the Communist Party of Yugoslavia states the following:

The criticism contained in the Resolution is based on inaccurate and unfounded assertions and represents an attempt to destroy the prestige of the Communist Party of Yugoslavia, both abroad and in the country; to create confusion among the masses in the country and in the international workers' movement; to weaken the unity of the CPY and its leading role. It is therefore even more surprising that the CC of the CPSU(B) refused to investigate on the spot the validity of its assertions as proposed in the letter of the CC of the CPY dated April 13, 1948. . . .

The CC of the CPY asserts that none of the leaders consider that Yugoslavia, in the struggle for the building of Socialism and the preservation of independence, does not need the help of the countries of people's democracy and of the USSR. Only people who have lost all contact with reality could assert anything of this kind. The CC of the CPY must in this connection emphasize that the extension of this aid and cooperation does not depend on it alone, but also on the countries of the people's democracy and the USSR. The CC of the CPY considers that this aid must be linked up with the internal and foreign policy of Yugoslavia and in no case with the fact that the CC of the CPY could not accept unfounded charges based on untruth.

The assertions that the Yugoslav leaders are preparing to make concessions to imperialists and to bargain with them about the independence of Yugoslavia—are a complete invention and belong among the grossest slanders against the new Yugoslavia.

The CC of the CPY must, however, point out that, in certain countries of people's democracy, a whole series of unprovoked acts have been committed by Party and State organs, acts which are insulting to the peoples of Yugoslavia, their State and State representatives, and which lead to a weakening of cooperation, and deterioration of relations with Yugoslavia. The CC of the CPY does not consider itself bound to pass in silence over similar acts in the future.

The CC of the CPY does not consider that it has in any way impaired the unity of the Communist front by refusing to discuss mistakes for which it is not responsible. The unity of this front is not based on the admission of invented or fabricated errors and slanders, but on the fact of whether or not the policy of a party is actually internationalist. One cannot, however, ignore the fact that the Cominform departed from the principles on which it was based and which provide for the voluntary adoption of its conclusions by every Party. The Cominform, however, not only compels the leaders of the CPY to admit errors which they have not committed, but even calls the

members of the CPY to rebellion within the Party, to shatter the unity of the Party. The CC of the CPY can never agree to a discussion about its policy on the basis of inventions and in an uncomradely spirit, without mutual confidence. Such a basis is unprincipled and in this and only in this sense the CC of the CPY considered that it was not on an equal footing in the discussion and that it could not accept a discussion on this basis. Further, in connection with the above, the CC of the CPY resolutely rejects the accusation that the Communist Party of Yugoslavia had become nationalistic. By its entire internal and foreign policy, by its struggle in the course of the War of National Liberation especially, and by the just solution of the national question in Yugoslavia, the CPY has given proofs of the exact opposite.

The greatest historical injustice has been done by the above-mentioned unjust charges against our Party, our working class and working masses, the peoples of Yugoslavia in general, and their unselfish and heroic struggle.

The Central Committee of the CPY is aware of the fact that the charges of the CC of the CPSU(B) against the CC of the CPY will be seized upon by enemy propaganda for the purpose of slandering the Soviet Union, Yugoslavia and other democratic countries. The CC of the CPY, however, declares that it bears no responsibility for all these happenings because it did not give rise to them by any of its acts.

The Central Committee of the Communist Party of Yugoslavia calls upon the party membership to close its ranks in the struggle for the realization of the Party line and for even greater Party unity, and it calls upon the working class and other working people in the People's Front, to continue even more persistently their work in building our Socialist homeland. This is the only way to prove in practice that the mentioned charges are unjustified.

The United Nations and Stalin's Death 1945–1953

THE SOVIET UNION IN THE UNITED NATIONS

R U P E R T   E M E R S O N   A N D   I N I S   L.   C L A U D E,   J R.

To its most optimistic adherents the United Nations is an embryo world government working mightily to establish a permanent and peaceful international order. To some less hopeful observers the UN is a talking shop where Soviet propagandists, masquerading as statesmen, block all progress by endlessly prating about the false virtues of communism and unjustly attacking the West. Avoiding these extremes, the authors of the following article examine the basic characteristics of sovereign states, the limitations of international organization, and the Soviet Union's role in the UN from 1945 to 1952. In the process they clear up a number of dangerous popular misconceptions. Professor Rupert Emerson, the senior author represented here, is now Professor of Government and Member of the Faculty of the Graduate School of Public Administration at Harvard University. He has been Director of the Division of Territories and Island Possessions in the Department of the Interior (1940–41), Coordinator of Inter-American Affairs (1941), Assistant Administrator, Lend Lease (1943), and Director of Liberated Areas in the Bureau of Foreign Economic Administration (1944–45). His principal published works are: *State and Sovereignty in Modern Germany, Malaysia, Representative Government in Southeast Asia,* and *From Empire to Nation: The Rise of Self-Assertion of Asian and African Peoples.* Inis L. Claude, who is Associate Professor of Political Science at the University of Michigan, has published *National Minorities: An International Problem* and *Swords into Plowshares: The Problems and Progress of International Organizatton.*

In the present climate of opinion it is customary to view the attitudes and actions of the USSR in the United Nations—as elsewhere—as dictated only by malice and evil.[1]

[1] "The position that the Soviet Union has taken toward the United Nations—her wild use of the veto, the frustration of orderly meetings by endless and pointless discussion, the vilification and diatribes directed against all people who do not agree

Since the gravest issues of peace and war may hinge upon the assessment which

with her, the withdrawal of her representatives from the various organs of the United Nations—are all based not upon a conviction that the United Nations is inadequate and should be strengthened but are based upon an effort to frustrate and discredit any other pattern of world organization than that of world communism." Frances H. Russell, "Toward a Stronger World Organization," Department of State, *Bulletin,* XXIII, 221.

From R. Emerson and I. L. Claude, Jr., "The Soviet Union and the United Nations, An Essay in Interpretation," *International Organization,* VI (1952), 1–26. By permission of *International Organization,* and the authors.

is made of the Soviet attitude, it is essential to seek an understanding of the ideas and forces which have shaped it. We have, therefore, attempted in the first place to assess the Soviet position as Moscow *may* see it, in some instances deliberately giving the benefit of the doubt, where doubt plausibly enters in, to the Soviet side; but the elements of explanation which have inevitably intruded themselves reflect the western frame of reference. The word "may" is in italic since this is necessarily an essay in interpretation; Soviet pronouncements obviously cover only part of the story and have their strong propaganda implications and limitations.

It seems clear that the position and role of the Soviet Union in the United Nations are in many respects markedly different from those of most other Members. The actions and policies of the Soviet bloc and the opposing policies adopted by other countries, primarily in response to the Communist challenge, have served to make Moscow and its satellites a kind of permanent (and often isolated) opposition in the United Nations. We suggest that it is plausible to assess Soviet attitudes toward and in the United Nations as compounded not only of bad faith but also of objectively valid and reasonable positions and of positions which are subjectively valid and reasonable, given the hold of Communist dogma on the Soviet mentality and the power-political character of present international relations.

No such assessment can be undertaken profitably without making certain preliminary assumptions as to the basic stand of the USSR in world affairs. For Moscow as for other capitals the role assigned to international organizations is essentially dictated by the over-all objectives of domestic and foreign policy and cannot be assumed to have an independent value in itself. If it be assumed that the only significant Communist goal is the immediate overthrow, by whatever means may be available, of the non-Communist world, then

the detailed examination of Soviet attitudes toward the United Nations has little if any significance, since they could add up to no more than the tactics and strategy of destruction. If, however, there is some measure of validity in the oft-repeated theory of the peaceful coexistence of the two spheres, then international organizations can have significance as instruments for the harmonization of the policies of the bipolar world.

At least for the purposes of this article we propose to adopt the following assumptions. The Soviet Union and Communists throughout the world are dedicated fundamentally to the proposition that Communism must and will have a global sweep, transforming the capitalist and pre-capitalist world in its own image. This transformation is by no means necessarily an immediate matter, although the Communist would obviously prefer it sooner rather than later. In the interim there is a vast amount of construction and consolidation to be undertaken in the Soviet Union and its satellites, and it is preferable that this be undertaken in the time of peace. There is nothing whatsoever to indicate that the Politburo has ever been tempted by notions of the desirability of war for its own sake as were the Nazis and Fascists; in fact, the Soviet leaders, who were even ready to make their peace with Hitler, have been characterized by a sober and realistic appraisal of the opposing forces and have shown no inclination to be seduced by the lure of martial adventures. On this basis it is reasonable to think that although war would be by no means excluded for them as a calculated instrument of policy, as witness Korea, the Soviet authorities would be unlikely to assess the present balance of forces as giving them a clear guarantee of victory in global war without the disruption of their own system and power. It is, of course, conceivable that the growing strength of the west and the encroaching circle of hostile bases would persuade them of the necessity of a desperate gamble for survival, but it is more probable that they would seek means of accommodation to permit peaceful coexistence until the inexorable laws of Marxism, aided by their persistent prodding, swing the balance more clearly in their favor. On this hypothesis, the United Nations can be assumed to have for them a positive value not only as a listening-post and as a forum from which to spread dissension but also as a meeting ground for the great opponents.

One highly important consequence of these assumptions is that the Soviet Union, unlike some of its rivals, is wholly unencumbered by any illusion as to the possibility or even the desirability of realizing the concept of one world—unless, of course, it be a world dominated by Communism. Peaceful coexistence is an interim measure only and has as its premise the fundamental antagonism of the parties to it, each seeking the ultimate disappearance of the other. It is groundless Utopianism to think that the United Nations or any other international organization can now be utilized as the instrumentality to achieve world solidarity directed toward commonly shared goals and ideals. For the Communist leaders it is not world brotherhood which can be produced from the machineries of the United Nations, but the watchful maintenance of an uneasy peace which each side will use to strengthen its own position. With appropriate citations from Lenin, they have regularly poured out their scorn on the naïve or scheming bourgeois enthusiasts for pacifism and for world government. In contrast to the widespread tendency in private if not in governmental circles in the west to view the United Nations and its specialized agencies as an embryonic form of world government which should be encouraged to grow, the Soviet leaders see it as a treaty relationship between the powers which should be held within a strict construction of its contractual terms.

Although there are sharp limitations on the powers and functions with which the United States is in fact prepared to endow international organizations, there is a general assumption in principle that an extension of the range of the United Nations or the specialized agencies is in itself a good thing; to hand over a problem to the United Nations for a solution is to take a generous step in the interest of a higher world community. The Soviet view of such matters is normally almost precisely the opposite. The expansion of the domain of the United Nations is feared as an encroachment on the sovereignty and "reserve powers" of its Members, and the transfer of decision or management to international agencies is suspected as an unsubtle attempt by the United States to conceal its imperialist manipulation of the world behind a transparent international screen. In Soviet eyes, when the United Nations oversteps its narrowly defined competence beyond the range of the veto, it is a hostile coalition which dances to the tune of its Fascist-capitalist paymasters. In Marxist theory the state is not a neutral arbiter but a product of class antagonisms and class domination, and international organizations must similarly embody the fundamental Marxist facts of life.

As Vishinsky has denied that a court can be conceived as an instrument of justice above classes and apart from politics, so the USSR has shunned arbitration and is alone among the major powers in not being willing to make even a formal bow toward the optional clause of the Statute of the International Court of Justice.

Indeed, somewhat to the bewilderment of those who looked to the international labor movement as the dependable champion of a future international society, the USSR has for present purposes become the most ardent advocate of sovereignty and the doctrine of domestic jurisdiction, whatever long-range views of the consolidation of a Communist world may be. Over and over again Soviet spokesmen in the United Nations and outside it have asserted their devotion to sovereignty, stressing its sanctification by the Charter, and holding it up as a shield of the rights of small nations and as a protection for the Soviet Union itself and for the new peoples' democracies on its frontiers against the insatiable greed of the imperialists. Far from being considered a retrograde idea, the concept of sovereignty is consistently defended as a "weapon of struggle of progressive-democratic forces against reactionary imperialist forces," the limitation of which would represent a victory of capitalism over the Communist world.

In the course of the first Indonesian case, and at other occasional points when it suited their book, Soviet representatives have suggested that sovereignty has its limits, but their standard position, if one ignored their treatment of the satellites and the practice of the Cominform, is an all-out defense of sovereignty as a bulwark of their present achievements and an instrument for the further advancement of their cause in the world. A resounding rendition of this line with all the stops pulled out was given by Andre Zhdanov at the organizing meeting of the Cominform in September, 1947:

> One of the lines taken by the ideological campaign that goes hand in hand with the plans for the enslavement of Europe is an attack on the principle of national sovereignty, an appeal for the renouncement of the sovereign rights of nations, to which is opposed the idea of world government. The purpose of this campaign is to mask the unbridled expansion of American imperialism which is ruthlessly violating the sovereign rights of nations. . . . The idea of world government has been taken up by bourgeois intellectual cranks and pacifists. . . . Under present conditions imperialist countries like the USA, Great Britain and the states closely associated with them become dangerous enemies of national independence and the self-determination of nations, while the Soviet Union and the new democracies are a reliable bulwark against encroachments on the equality and self-determination of nations.[2]

[2] *The Strategy and Tactics of World Communism,* House Document 619, 80th Cong., 2nd Sess., Supp. 1, pp. 222–223,

As Zhdanov's polemics indicate, the notion of the sovereign equality of states is closely linked to the doctrine of sovereignty. But in somewhat awkward juxtaposition to equality there is the proposition which is even more important for the Soviet Union that the great powers must be endowed with special rights. All states are equal, but, like the pigs in *Animal Farm*, the great powers are more equal than others. In his keynote speech to the General Assembly on September 18, 1947, Vishinsky linked the two principles in this fashion: the strengthening of the United Nations is only possible on the basis of a respectful attitude toward the sovereign equality of nations and a consistent and unconditional observance of the principle of unanimity among the great powers, which is a guarantee of the protection of the interests of all members of the United Nations, great and small.

In the light of other Soviet statements and actions it may be assumed that the hard core of the Communist position is to be found in the conviction that serious matters of international politics should be settled by negotiations between the great powers, on the basis of the unanimity principle. It is they who bear the burdens of the world and possess preponderant force, and on their united action must rest the responsibility for shaping the world they are to defend and maintain. There is every reason to think that the Soviet statesmen see the United Nations as essentially a gathering point for the great powers, each protected by the unanimity rule, with the lesser states trailing behind on sufferance. The Soviet demand that peace treaties be based on agreement among the great and submitted to the small for their grateful acquiescence is cut from the same cloth.

Theoretical arguments aside, the Soviet position is clearly influenced by the practical consideration of the overwhelming majority of votes—largely brought into being by the tactics and obstreperousness of the Soviet Union itself—by which the Communist bloc finds itself confronted on virtually every issue of consequence. Looking at the world either in power terms or in terms of the great opposing ideologies, this situation is an obviously intolerable one for the USSR if votes are to be the deciding factor. From the Soviet standpoint, it is not a matter of very marked consequence whether the customary forty- or fifty-odd to five division is the result of American economic and political pressure or the free decision of the voting states; the effect in either case is the same rolling up of a steam-roller majority against the Soviet bloc and in favor of the west. The clash over the admission of Argentina at San Francisco was a painful demonstration to Soviet delegates of the voting strength of the Latin American bloc, and it must remain a constant irritant that twenty states with a total population of less than 150,000,000 and with relatively little effective power in world affairs are able to muster a vote four times that of the Soviet bloc. The growing solidarity of the Marshall Plan-Atlantic Pact countries with the outside support they can always attract renders hopeless any significant proposal from the Communist camp, even though there be some defections among the non-Communist states.

The issue which this situation raises is a very serious and basic one for international organizations: what is the proper role and significance of voting in such bodies? The Soviet Union insists that the only way to move ahead on basic issues is by unanimous agreement among the powers, whereas the western states, sure of their majority, have time and again forced to a vote proposals to which Soviet spokesmen have expressed unyielding opposition. Given the basic Communist presumptions as to the hostility of the two spheres and as to the nature of the United Nations as a treaty relationship among sovereign states not creating anything of the order of a superstate, the only result of such votes is the highly important one of establishing agreement among the states outside the Soviet bloc. As the Soviet leaders see the world, a majority in the United Nations, no matter how arithmetically overpowering, represents no distillation of the moral and political conclusions of mankind as a whole but only the manipulated votes of a hostile capitalist-dominated coalition to which only as much attention is due as the danger it may carry for the USSR.

As a former Director-General of ILO[3] has pointed out, voting in an international body does not have the same function as in a democratically elected parliament: "An international conference is a negotiating rather than a legislative body." If there is no agreement among the negotiators, the formal registering of votes is likely at best to have no more than propaganda significance and at worst to be a serious irritant. A smashing victory of fifty-five votes to five is very remote from rendering the overwhelming verdict of "one world" when the five in opposition are the Soviet Union and its European satellites backed by the unrecorded vote of Communist China. It is, at least in power terms, half the world against the other half; and it is gravely to be doubted that if the United States, remaining convinced of the fundamental rightness and ultimate victory of its position, were in the perpetual and artificial minority it would be much more inclined cheerfully to accept its ballot box defeats than is the Soviet Union.

"A majority, of course, is a majority," Vishinsky pointed out to the Political Committee of the Assembly on October 10, 1950. "Arithmetic is arithmetic. But no arithmetic can solve questions pertaining to matters very far removed from arithmetical problems." And it is impossible to evade the conclusion reached by the Secretary-General in his first report to the General Assembly—that the United Nations is not equipped to act as a referee between the great powers: "It was founded upon the basic assumption that there would be agreement among the permanent members of

[3] ILO: The International Labor Organization—Ed.

the Security Council upon major issues."

If it is in fact impossible to secure such agreement, then we should not fool ourselves into thinking that we are making notable progress in the organization of the world as a whole, by a series of votes taken over the determined opposition of one of the major partners and its satellites.

Having examined in general terms the outlook of the USSR toward the United Nations, the task now is to explore the practical application of this outlook by focusing upon a few key topics, selected for the light they cast on the Soviet attitude.

The Security Council and the veto. It is obvious that the Soviet Union regards the Security Council as the all-important center of the United Nations both because of the Kremlin's emphasis on the great powers and because of its apparent conviction that the one really significant function of international organizations under present conditions lies in the realm of high politics. As a very broad generalization it may be said that aside from Security Council matters (many of which, of course, also have increasingly strong Assembly reverberations), Soviet delegates have rarely played a significantly positive role, but have rather reacted to, attacked, and sought to gain propaganda advantage from proposals submitted by others. In such matters as human rights, colonial and trusteeship affairs, and some of the problems particularly involving underdeveloped peoples they have taken an active part but the initiative has normally come from elsewhere. Insisting that the Security Council is the foundation of the United Nations, the USSR has been constantly preoccupied with protecting the primacy and maintaining the prerogatives of that organ.

If the Security Council is, in Soviet eyes, the foundation of the United Nations, the principle of unanimity is "the paramount principle which constitutes the cornerstone of the very foundation;"[4] noth-ing has been of more basic importance to the USSR than the use and defense of the veto. Lacking the votes to carry anything other than pious resolutions of good will through either the Security Council or Assembly, the Soviet Union has inescapably fallen back upon the veto as the principal weapon for its self-protection. If others look with shocked dismay at the freedom with which Gromyko, Vishinsky, and Malik have bandied the veto about, they themselves profess to be unabashed and unashamed; and in their interpretation it is, of course, not they who are abusing the veto but their opponents who have abandoned the principle of unanimity, the fundamental importance of which the latter never questioned during the negotiations which led to the conclusion of the Charter. On October 10, 1950, in the Assembly's Political Committee, Vishinsky met head on the charge of an abuse of the veto as causing the paralysis of the Security Council:

The veto, they say, has been applied 50 times! But, Mr. Dulles, it may well be applied 150 times in such conditions, because it is a means of self-defense against the pressure, the dictation which the states that believe themselves to be strongest and mightiest, and therefore capable of securing the realization of their own plans . . . by one means or another, are trying to exercise against other states in international affairs. . . . The cause of what we are now considering, namely, the difficulties in the Security Council, is the violation of the fundamental principle of every international organization, namely, the obligation which lies upon all its members to strive for coordinated action, to respect the state independence, the state equality, the sovereign equality of all the members of the organization, and to refrain from attempts to dictate in international affairs, to impose one's will by hook or by crook.[5]

The Soviet use of the veto has been too

---

[4] Vishinsky, in speech to the Political Committee of the General Assembly, October 10, 1950. *Speeches by A. Y. Vishinsky at the Fifth Session of the General Assembly of the United Nations* (USSR Embassy, Washington, 1950), p. 82.

[5] *Ibid.*, p. 81.

frequently examined to require extensive treatment here, but a few major points may be brought out. Obviously, the veto cannot be scrutinized in isolation. The extent and manner of its use are a function of existing international tensions and hostilities; Moscow inevitably sees it as one of the weapons of the cold war and not improperly measures its use of this weapon against the majorities by which the west seeks to override Soviet claims and positions. If the western powers rely mainly upon their steady majorities, they nevertheless hold to the right of veto in the United Nations as a protection in crucial matters, and they establish the principle of unanimity in some features of their own regional organizations —as witness NATO and the Council of Europe. Lofty moral judgments and ideological comparisons are perhaps out of place here, as Moscow maintains. In a world still ridden by power politics governments use their voting privileges to promote and conserve their interests. Votewise, the USSR is weak in the United Nations, and the west is strong; the strong do with their votes what they can, and the weak do what they must.

It is possible to view the Soviet use of the veto with either shocked surprise or pleased astonishment as to the relative moderation which has been shown. If the former is markedly the more prevalent attitude, the latter is at least worth examining. Soviet spokesmen have repeatedly asserted that one of the principal functions of the veto is to prevent the formation within the United Nations of hostile aggregations "of those who want to disrupt the Organization in order to have a free hand in the implementation of their aggressive plans," and more particularly to prevent the United Nations from becoming an outright tool of the State Department. That there has been an increasingly strong and effective consolidation of the anti-Communist forces within and outside the United Nations is clear, regardless of the question whether or not this consolidation is essentially a re-sponse to the aggressive moves and intentions of the Communists themselves. In such circumstances, it would be naïve to expect the Kremlin not to exploit and defend against all tampering the political instrument which it finds firmly embedded in the Charter, even though the veto has proved ineffective in preventing the formation of an anti-Communist bloc.

Of the 47 vetoes brandished by the USSR, no less than 22 have been invested in blocking the admission to United Nations membership of states outside the Communist orbit; but it certainly cannot be ignored that in more recent years Soviet delegates have urged the blanket admission of all candidates except south Korea—a position similar to that initially taken by the United States in 1946. Despite the International Court's majority opinion against conditioned votes in the membership sphere, it is not unreasonable to contend that the universality for which the Secretary-General has several times spoken has greater merit than the game of political sniping which has blocked the gates of the United Nations to a substantial number of states. Here, surely, is an instance where it is justifiable to stack up the use of majority votes against the use of the veto on virtually even terms.

For the rest it is an interesting hypothesis that the Soviet Union has on the whole confined its veto to matters fairly directly within its own sphere of interest and has limited its expression of disapproval in other spheres to the device of abstention. Writing off the very early Syria-Lebanon veto as one which came before Moscow had had time to make a full assessment of its strategy in the new United Nations environment, it is striking how uniformly the vetoes have been restricted to the Soviet orbit, particularly if Moscow's long concern with Spain be held to justify Spain's inclusion in this category. On this basis, 17 of the 25 non-membership vetoes relate to areas of special Soviet concern: 4 on the Spanish question, 6 on Greece,

1 on Albania (Corfu Channel Question), 2 on Czechoslovakia, 1 on Berlin, and 3 on Korea. Five more can be added in relation to the control of atomic energy and the reduction of armaments, unquestionably matters of vital concern to the USSR; and one was devoted to blocking the re-election of Trygve Lie after his unequivocal stand on armed action by the United Nations against Communist aggression in Korea. There is left only the veto exercised in the Indonesian case, which came after the final settlement had been reached and had no significant effect on future developments.

To round out the record it is highly important to take a look not only at the vetoes which have been cast but also at those which have *not* been cast. It is from these that the argument in favor of Soviet moderation can be most effectively developed. In any number of instances other than those concerning direct Soviet interests, the Soviet viewpoint has been overridden on matters of importance where it would take a brave or foolhardy man to say that the Soviet contentions were uniformly wrong; e.g., the demand in the Indonesian case that the Netherlands withdraw its forces to the position occupied before the "police action." In another series of instances the USSR has been barred from the participation in Security Council commissions or committees which its status as a great power and permanent member of the Council might have seemed to imply. Thus, through one device or another, Moscow was unrepresented on the subsidiary bodies set up to deal with Palestine, Indonesia, and Kashmir, although it must certainly be taken as an off-setting item that it declined to take its allotted place in the bodies dealing with Korea or, after the first round, with Greece. These reiterated rebuffs to the Soviet Union have been met not by the veto but by abstentions which have been explicitly accepted—in this instance on the basis of a loose interpretation of the Charter—as not involving the principle of unanimity. Against this background it is difficult to resist the conclusion that the Kremlin is operating in terms of a deliberate policy of indicating disapproval, but not blocking United Nations action outside its own immediate sphere of interest, and of conserving the veto for the protection of that sphere.

The Permanent Opposition. The American public, convinced of its own righteousness, has become equally convinced that the Soviet use of the veto has had the malicious and successful intention of thwarting the potential good works of the United Nations. The Kremlin's analysis must be a very different one. From the Soviet standpoint there is little in the record of United Nations organs dealing with matters of political importance to encourage abandonment or even a paring down of the veto. It has become a normal part of that record that any Soviet proposals which are not regarded as completely innocuous are rejected, and there has been a steady procession of actions which override firm Soviet positions or directly challenge the USSR in what it regards as its own sphere. Indeed, as the United Nations and the cold war have simultaneously developed, it is hardly too much to say that in many respects the United Nations has become a reflection or even an instrument of the policies of the western powers, almost always supported by a large majority of the other Members. If in one sense the United Nations continues to be a "neutral" organization of which the USSR is a member in good standing, it is also true in a perhaps even more significant sense that it is now committed to any number of positions flatly opposed to those taken by the Soviet bloc.

The inability of the USSR to secure adoption of its programs and resolutions is a general phenomenon which may be illustrated by reference to the dramatic highlights of the fifth Assembly, held under the shadow of the Korean war and with the issue of the representation of Communist China before it. In addition to its defeat on the Chinese issue, the Soviet Union here

suffered two other defeats on major pro-
grammatic proposals which embodied an
array of basic Communist positions. The
entire program proposed by Vishinsky
in the debate of the Secretary-General's
twenty-year peace program was rejected
paragraph by paragraph, and substantially
the same fate met the several points contained in his "Declaration on the removal
of the threat of a new war. . . ." Since these
proposals fairly effectively covered the
waterfront so far as the basic stand of the
USSR in the United Nations is concerned,
their rejection can appropriately be seen
as a repudiation of virtually the entire outlook of the Communist bloc.[6]

The debates or actions challenging or
overriding the Soviet Union in regard to
matters within what it regards its own
sphere are by now so numerous that it is
possible to do no more than list a few significant examples. Such challenges range
from the relatively insignificant problems
of Soviet wives of foreigners through
charges of Soviet exploitation of slave
labor and denial of the right of the Soviet
bloc to nominate the "Eastern European
representative" in the elected contingent
of the Security Council, to the almost incredible spectacle of a United Nations in
which there is Soviet support for north
Korea and Communist China in their war
with armed forces representing the authority of the United Nations itself. The challenge to Soviet freedom of action inherent
in the United Nations system found its first
expression no later than the second meeting
of the Security Council when the Iranian
charges of Soviet interference were taken
up. Almost simultaneously there began

the United Nations' long-continued concern
with the threat to the security of Greece
posed by neighboring Soviet satellites. The
problem of Korea was taken up by the
Assembly, despite vehement Soviet objection; only a Soviet veto prevented further
United Nations investigation of the Communist coup in Czechoslovakia; the allegations of peace treaty violations by Bulgaria,
Hungary, and Rumania were accepted by
the Assembly; and Communist China was
kept outside the United Nations fold while
the Assembly hesitantly considered Nationalist China's charges of Soviet threats to the
political independence and territorial integrity of that country.

The Kremlin has undoubtedly found
in the United Nations an effective forum in
which to air in unmeasured terms its bitter
view of the western powers; the latter, on
the other hand, have been able to go much
further in shaping the United Nations as a
responsive vehicle of their foreign policies.
From the Soviet point of view, the western
use of majority tactics for political purposes is fully equivalent to the Soviet use of
minority tactics. Certainly the regularity
of voting defeats in the United Nations has
done nothing to create enthusiasm for abstract majoritarianism among Soviet leaders; on the contrary, these experiences have
intensified the Soviet conviction that the
veto, which preserves a limited area of
invulnerability to outvoting tactics, must
be upheld.

*Innovations in the Structure of the
United Nations.* The assault on the Soviet
Union's Charter-based veto power of obstruction has assumed many forms. Frontal
attack on the veto, which the remaining

---

[6] These proposals covered, among other things: the
reaffirmation of the unanimity principle in the Security Council, the unconditional prohibition of
atomic weapons and the determination that the first
government to use such weapons should be branded
a war criminal, a reiteration of the demand for
equality in the armed forces to be made available
under Art. 43, condemnation of war propaganda, a
demand for a new peace pact to be entered into by
the Big Five, the reduction of the armed forces of
the great powers by one-third, the provision of tech-

nical assistance through the United Nations without strings attached to it, and the development of
international trade without discrimination and
without interference in the domestic affairs of
states.

It is not without interest that a number of speakers expressed their agreement with one or more of
these points, but indicated their refusal to go along
with them because of distrust of the general Soviet
position and because of the propagandistic setting
in which they were presented.

Big Four are themselves prepared to modify but not abandon, has perhaps been less significant than methods of indirection. In its structural improvisations the west has indulged in occasional *ad lib* readings of the score of the United Nations symphony with the purpose and effect of elevating the majority-controlled General Assembly to a new role in political and security affairs and thereby minimizing the obstructive value of the Soviet veto in the Security Council. On the other hand, it has been a constant preoccupation of Soviet delegates to maintain the primacy and prerogatives of the Security Council unimpaired and to insist upon a strict interpretation of the relevant Charter articles. Here as elsewhere where it served their purpose the Communists have appeared as the legalistic champions of the letter of the Charter. They have combatted the various efforts to magnify the role of the Assembly at the expense of the veto-clad Security Council, suggesting from time to time that if changes of this type, substantively if not formally weakening the Security Council, are to be introduced into or tacked onto the United Nations system they should be funnelled through the proper channel of Charter amendment—a channel neatly blocked by the veto. It is in regard to this category of Soviet grievances—innovations in the United Nations structure—that the contention of illegality has been most cogently applied by the USSR. Three major items may be listed under this heading, apart from the general and unsuccessful attempts to secure a formal limitation on the use of the veto.

Not the least significant of these was the action of the Assembly in 1950 in bypassing the Security Council and continuing Trygve Lie in office as Secretary-General for an additional three year term despite the bitter protests of the Soviet bloc. Although a case can be made for the political necessity of retaining Mr. Lie and, more dubiously, for the legality of the method devised to achieve that end, it is obvious that the already slight possibilities of effective Soviet cooperation in the United Nations are inevitably lessened when its symbolic and administrative head is maintained in office over the opposition of the USSR. The other two items concern more directly the building up of the Assembly at the expense of the Security Council: the creation of the Interim Committee or Little Assembly in 1947, and the passage of the Uniting for Peace resolution in 1950. Both these actions were proposed by the United States primarily to meet the situation posed by the Soviet use of the veto, and hence hit at the vitals of the Soviet position in the United Nations. Both were vehemently attacked by the Soviet Union as not only offensive but also illegal.

In the case of the Interim Committee, the mountain labored to produce something of a mouse. It has made some useful studies and in the Korean dilemma of 1948 it reluctantly agreed to support the American desire for supervised elections in south Korea alone, but it has realized neither the hopes of its sponsors nor the fears of its opponents. Although there are other reasons for its relative insignificance, the continued boycott by the Soviet bloc has undoubtedly been a major cause of the unreadiness to submit important political issues to it!

The Uniting for Peace resolution, adopted by the Assembly on November 3, 1950, by 52 votes against the 5 votes of the Soviet bloc (with India and Argentina abstaining), was, of course, phrased in general terms and named no names. There could, however, have been no uncertainty as to where the finger currently pointed, in view of the circumstances of the United Nations action in Korea and Secretary of State Acheson's explicit designation, in introducing the proposal, of "the new imperialism directed by the leaders of the Soviet Union" as "the root of our trouble." The veto came in for equally explicit treatment. Acknowledging the primary responsibility of the Security Council for the maintenance of peace, Mr. Acheson continued:

But if the Security Council is not able to act because of the obstructive tactics of a permanent member, the Charter does not leave the United Nations impotent. The obligation of all members to take action to maintain or restore the peace does not disappear because of a veto. . . . The General Assembly can and should organize itself to discharge its responsibility promptly and decisively if the Security Council is prevented from acting.[7]

Certain features of this resolution, as it progressed through the Political Committee, proved reasonably acceptable to the USSR, notably the possibility of special sessions of the Assembly and the establishment of a Peace Observation Commission on which the Soviet Union even accepted membership; but the features striking more seriously at the Security Council and the veto were far beyond the Communist pale. In essence, the action which the Assembly took, guided by the experience of Korea, was to establish at least the potentiality of an international force to be used against an aggressor by Assembly recommendation when and if the veto blocked Security Council action—and the outstanding potential aggressors then in sight were the members of the Soviet bloc.

The effect of this resolution was to achieve within the broader framework of the United Nations a loose approximation of the type of organized opposition to Soviet imperialism which NATO represents in a tighter and more limited frame.[8] This and other limited alliances, constructed under American leadership as counters to the close-knit body of Soviet alliances have been somewhat nominally linked to the United Nations through the loopholes of Articles 51 and 52 of the Charter (and with considerable disregard for the inconvenient Article 53). The Soviet Union may fear that the ultimate effect of the Assembly's resolution will be to facilitate the formal attachment of the United Nations to the kite of NATO and other regional alliances, flown from Washington. What appears to the western world as a mutual aid and security system, forced upon us by a Communist drive for world supremacy and designed to advance the principles of the United Nations, must from the vantage point of the Kremlin be seen as a menacing and mounting accumulation of armed might to be used for the evil purposes of capitalist imperialism and in violation of the United Nations' basic premises, albeit with the probable sanction of the United Nations, ill-gotten from the Assembly as a result of the "Acheson Plan."

The cumulative effect of the largely American inspired modifications of the United Nations structure has been to reduce the capacity of the Soviet bloc to protect itself in the United Nations from the votes of a hostile majority. Looking back, the Soviet Union may well be inclined to question the good faith of the United States in accepting the product of the negotia- -tions at San Francisco in 1945. Surely the Soviet delegation left that conference with the impression that the United States accepted the principle of great power unanimity in matters of high politics and Charter amendment. The USSR can cite the official report of Secretary of State Stettinius to the effect that the delegates consciously created a "separation of powers" system, giving the General Assembly functions quite distinct from those of

---

[7] Speech to plenary session of fifth General Assembly, September 20, 1950. Department of State, *Bulletin*, XXIII, pp. 524–525. Soviet representatives, as strict constructionists, can argue that a negative decision of the Security Council, reached as the result of a veto, is quite as valid and decisive as an affirmative decision, and that to shift a matter to the General Assembly at that stage is to repu-

diate a Security Council decision made in conformity with Article 27 (3).

[8] NATO: The North Atlantic Treaty Organization; its members are: Belgium, Canada, Denmark, France, Greece, Iceland, Italy, Luxembourg, Netherlands, Norway, Portugal, Turkey, the United Kingdom, the United States, and West Germany— Ed.

the Security Council, and that they intended to make it impossible for the Assembly to "invade the functions which have been specifically assigned in security matters to the Security Council. . . ." That the breaches of this principle have been occasioned primarily by the policy and tactics of the Soviet Union itself is unlikely to be an explanation acceptable to Moscow.

Disarmament and the Creation of an International Force. Of the verbal devotion of the Soviet Union to drastic disarmament and the abolition of the atomic weapon there can be no question, but the sincerity and significance of that devotion are matters of bitter dispute, particularly in view of the high level at which Soviet armaments have been kept. In the United Nations as in the League, the USSR has played the role of champion *par excellence* of the thesis that, among the things needful for the maintenance of peace, disarmament heads the list, and that the way to disarm is to disarm. Its most recent proposal to this effect was the insistence in the General Assembly in 1950 that the great powers reduce their present armed forces immediately by one-third of their effectives, a proposal which was further elaborated in the succeeding Assembly.

Moscow's disarmament proposals have habitually been greeted with much the same suspicion and hostility with which Moscow itself views all proposals emanating from the west. No major Soviet proposal can be accepted at face value and without searching scrutiny of the motives concealed behind it; disarmament projects are seen as traps for the unwary, designed to strengthen the USSR's relative power position. More particularly, it is contended that, even granted effective Soviet compliance with a disarmament agreement, the natural Communist weapons—the sabotage, intrigue, and revolution of its fifth columns—are sharpened by disarmament. Moreover, the Soviet wealth in manpower would be unimpaired by disarmament, while the more highly mechanized forces of the west would

be cut down and retarded. At all events there has been no disarmament on an international basis since the Washington Conference of 1921–22, and the sincerity of Moscow's protestations has been left untested because of the unreadiness of the other powers to get down to serious business on the terms which the Kremlin has from time to time laid down.

The opposing stands on the international control of atomic energy have been so frequently and searchingly examined that there is no occasion to submit them to detailed review here. Furthermore, given the present state of the cold war, the elaborate and far-reaching schemes for international control initiated by the United States and developed in the United Nations seem to date from remote past, and it requires no vast cynicism to suspect that these schemes are now almost as unlikely to secure acceptance and implementation from Washington as from Moscow. Although the USSR has declined to accept the United Nations majority plan and has generally operated obstructively, it has from time to time made not inconsiderable concessions and has put forward its own counter-proposals for control and inspection, coupled always with the demand for immediate and complete prohibition of the atomic weapon.

Were the general international scene less bleak, it is at least open to argument that the door is not irretrievably closed to further negotiation and compromise.

If the chances of securing disarmament and atomic energy control at this juncture are infinitesimal, the prospects of building up internationally available forces under Chapter VII of the Charter must be written off as non-existent. Given the general outlook of the Kremlin, it is inconceivable that it could place faith in an international police force under international command, and there is little in the record to encourage the view that the USSR actually desires to see Article 43 brought to life. Its specific plan for identical forces to be contributed by the Big Five and the restrictions and conditions which it has sought to impose on their location and use had no ring of eager anticipation about them. The derision and hostility with which the Soviet delegates greeted the Secretary-General's proposal for a United Nations guard force, protesting an invasion of sovereignty as well as of the Security Council's domain and alleging American domination of the United Nations, laid bare their distaste for international machinery of this type not subject at least to their negative control. But it must also be recognized that, whatever the particular positions of the USSR on the subject, a global international force does not make realistic sense in a world divided down the middle.

Economic and Social Affairs. The concern of the USSR with the economic and social, as opposed to the high political, activities of the United Nations has been relatively slight. It is noteworthy that Molotov, speaking at the opening plenary session of the San Francisco Conference in 1945, made no mention of the economic and social role of the new world organization. The uncharitable critic may content himself with observing that Moscow obviously did not want to promote general well-being in the world: welcoming chaos and distress, it hoped to exploit such conditions for its own purposes. However, other explanations are worth considering. A good Marxist can scarcely attach much significance to functionalism as a device either for ameliorating the ills of society or for preventing war. The Marxist cure involves the elimination of capitalism, not the development of cooperation within a predominantly capitalist family of nations. There was, indeed, a fundamental unrealism in expecting a Communist regime to assist its principal rivals in bolstering up a non-Communist world, whose demise it sought, by reformist methods which it overtly regarded as both futile and fraudulent.

It must be remembered that the Communists considered themselves a chosen people, and, by the same token, a peculiar people. They might cooperate under certain circumstances for peace and security, but they could hardly feel at home in a capitalist International Bank or Monetary Fund or expect to find intellectual fellowship in UNESCO.[9] The Communist states, lonely and peculiar in a bourgeois world, had little incentive to join in its economic and social arrangements, and had reason to be cautious about undertaking obligations to open their books to or to be guided by the policies of international agencies to whose basic orientation they were opposed and in whose good will they had no faith.

Although Soviet indifference or hostility to economic and social cooperation has never been absolute, it has been the dominant trend. The USSR joined in the Bretton Woods and Hot Springs conferences, was a full-fledged member of UNRRA, and has played a continuing and significant role in ECOSOC; but of the specialized agencies it has been a member only of WHO from which it withdrew in 1949, and of the more limited technical bodies, UPU, ITU, and WMO.[10] Even on the face of the record, Soviet cooperation has been sharply limited; if one looks beneath the surface, the extent and nature of cooperation are even more dubious. In some measure the character of Soviet participation in UNRRA gave a clue to what might develop later. It was at least conceivable that the USSR, as one of the original members of the Big Four of the Central Committee, would take an active and positive part in shaping the organization and policies of a benevolent agency which could have an important role in the making of the postwar world. In fact, the USSR to a surprising

[9] UNESCO: United Nations Educational, Scientific, and Cultural Organization—Ed.

[10] UNRRA: United Nations Relief and Rehabilitation Administration; ECOSOC: Economic and Social Council; WHO: World Health Organization; UPU: Universal Postal Union; ITU: International Telecommunication Union; WMO: World Meteorological Organization—Ed.

degree confined its role in UNRRA to either promoting its own interests and those of its more direct clients or blocking programs which seemed to impinge adversely on those interests. The creative work of building and managing UNRRA was left in the hands of the United States, United Kingdom, Canada, and a few others.

As far as the specialized agencies are concerned, the earlier Soviet attitude of cautious aloofness has gradually turned into studied and hostile rejection, based in large part on the charge that they have become tools of the United States and its cohorts and have been prostituted to the purposes of capitalist imperialism. In ECOSOC the Soviet delegates have from time to time struck out at the specialized agencies and sought to prevent their being used as working partners in a division of labor with the United Nations itself. In particular there has been sharp criticism of the referral of items to ILO as a device for evading Soviet participation in their consideration or for pigeonholing issues with which the United Nations itself should deal.

One striking feature of the Soviet attitude has been the failure to contribute "one red ruble" to international efforts for the relief, reconstruction and development of war-devastated and underdeveloped regions. Communist delegates have repeatedly pleaded for full-scale international administration of such activities, asserting their desire to bar the intrusion of political motives; and many impartial observers would agree that the United States and others have not made the fullest use of United Nations machinery or adequately divorced their generosity from politics. But the fair words of the USSR have been matched by no equivalent actions. They have not only taken no part in such programs as those of UNICEF and technical assistance, but have also discouraged international relief and development activities in the satellites and have wholly failed to channel their own contacts of this type with the satellites through international agen-

cies.[11] Their record has been one of the vilification of the motives of others and non-participation on their own part. Putting itself forward as the champion of the underprivileged, the USSR has functioned mainly as a kind of Marxist Cassandra, warning against capitalist exploitation in the guise of assistance.

Two segments of the economic and social concerns of the United Nations deserve special mention because of the more positive attitude taken toward them by the Soviet Union. In the Economic Commission for Europe the USSR appears to have found a body dealing with matters of immediate and vital interest to itself and the European satellites. If it has utilized the formal meetings of ECE for propaganda purposes—for example, as a forum in which to condemn the Marshall Plan—it has collaborated effectively with the specialized committees and technical staff which have been the focal points of ECE's contribution.[12] ECE has also served as a natural setting, though by no means the only one, for the expression of disaffection with the American efforts to cut western trade with the Soviet bloc down to the barest possible bones.

The embattled issue of human rights has likewise provided numerous occasions for the USSR to present its views and launch its attacks. There has been here an obvious clash between the basic concepts and values of a liberal and a Communist society, and each side has seized upon the issue as a heaven-sent instrument to expose the sins and evils of the other. The persistence and vigor with which Soviet voices have been raised in the field of human rights must be peculiarly suspect because of the low level of such rights within the USSR, but it is also clear that Moscow has had a theme of wide appeal in its attacks upon the American aversion to internation-

[11] UNICEF: United Nations International Children's Emergency Fund—Ed.

[12] ECE: Economic Commission for Europe, a regional commission of ECOSOC—Ed.

ally established economic, social and cultural rights and to curbs on freedom of expression for quasi-Fascist groups. Similarly the Soviet Union has found wide support for its contention that any covenant on human rights must not be limited in the scope of its territorial application by the complexities of federalism or colonial status. Characteristically, however, Moscow combines the demand for a broad definition and full territorial applicability of human rights with adamant insistence that there be no attempt at international implementation or enforcement. This stand is an integral part of the pattern of jealously guarded sovereignty and of the fear that international machinery would be used to undermine the Soviet regime.

With few exceptions the record of Soviet participation in the United Nations' handling of economic and social affairs is a bleak one. It becomes even more bleak when there is added the conviction of many who have earnestly sought agreement with Soviet delegates that the latter display a monotonous concern to propagandize and to block rather than to make the system work. As to the weight of the different components entering into the Soviet attitude there can be only guesswork. One of the components is undoubtedly the fundamental incompatibility of the Communist and non-Communist goals and outlooks, a problem which is not eased by the preponderance of Anglo-American influence in these spheres. Perhaps the most significant element in relation to at least some of the agencies is that effective membership would involve the exchange of information, creating a series of rifts in the iron curtain which guards the secrecy of every aspect of Soviet life.

It is not evident that Soviet obstruction and non-participation have been crucially important negative factors in the economic and social work of the United Nations, but it can scarcely be maintained that the USSR has made a genuine effort to promote international advance. In truth, the basic requirements for collaboration—some sense of common purpose and some readiness to pool experience and programs —are gravely lacking.

Colonialism. Despite early optimistic hopes that effective collaboration might be developed between western states and the Soviet bloc in an international attack upon the evils of colonialism, the degree of actual collaboration has been relatively meagre. The United Nations system for trusteeship and non-self-governing areas is at best only a compromise with anti-colonialism, and the cautiously evolutionary reformism which it represents is not such as to lend it great significance in Soviet eyes, save perhaps as an invitation to inject a disturbing finger into the colonial pie and to agitate for more drastic measures. Repudiating the charges of colonialism within their own system, the Communists fundamentally deny the validity of any colonialism and stand for a radical interpretation of the doctrine of self-determination. It is not without moment that in its onslaughts in this realm the USSR can count on the support of a considerable number of peoples who, from recent experience, share their abhorrence of any colonial relationship.

The USSR has from the outset contended for an expansion of international control and for recognition of speedy independence as the only appropriate goal for dependent peoples. The actual working out of the trusteeship system has been under constant attack from the Soviet Union despite its surprising acquiescence to the United States proposal for a strategic trusteeship over the former Japanese mandated islands. On grounds of alleged illegalities and improprieties in the first batch of trusteeship agreements the USSR declined to take its seat in the Trusteeship Council, but after more than a year of absence decided to participate, perhaps because of the reference to the Council of some of the issues of Palestine. In the Council and in the Assembly it has been an ardent champion of the rights of the inhabitants of the trust territories and an indefatigable critic of the administering authorities. To the suggestion that it might practice what it preached by placing the Kurile Islands under trusteeship, the USSR has turned a deaf ear, but it did at an early stage make an unwary move to take over Tripolitania.

In the implementation of Chapter XI of the Charter the Soviet Union has consistently pressed for the broadest possible extension of the powers of the United Nations, reaching clearly beyond the meagre confines of the authority actually granted to the United Nations. In this instance the customary restrictive interpretation of the Charter is abandoned, as are the otherwise sacrosanct doctrines of sovereignty and domestic jurisdiction. Seeking to establish an international accountability of wide range, the USSR has pressed for reports by the colonial powers on all aspects of their administration and has proposed that the United Nations should not only examine petitions and hear witnesses but also send inspection missions into the field.

Peculiarly in the colonial sphere the Communist bloc can hit at a vulnerable point in the armor of the free world and at a point where many are afflicted by a bad conscience. The attacks of Communist spokesmen on the arming and fortification of trust territories, the assimilation of such territories to neighboring colonies, and the generally slow rate of progress have not infrequently had sound merit behind them. There are few who would claim that the colonial record of the powers has been such as to make them immune from criticism and attack. Regrettably the intransigence of the Soviet assault and its failure to take into account some of the actual difficulties confronting the colonial administrator, as well as the deep distrust of Soviet motives, have had the effect of rendering its criticism far less useful than it might otherwise have been and of producing a united front of an almost equally intransigent character among colonial powers and their adherents. Denying that the United Nations system

can work effectively toward the ideals it espouses, the USSR has opened itself to the accusation of seeking to assist the inevitability of its failure.

Soviet Officials and Representatives in the United Nations. Some measure of the extent and nature of Soviet interest in the United Nations may be found in a glance at the people whom the USSR has made available to the United Nations, either as members of the Secretariat or as delegates, and the way in which they have conducted themselves.

In the Secretariat the extraordinary feature is the trifling number of officials who have come from the Soviet Union despite the efforts of the Secretary-General and others to secure a more adequate geographical distribution from this important part of the world and of the United Nations. Whereas other countries have shown great eagerness to secure adequate representation in the Secretariat, Moscow has resisted all blandishments to make more personnel available—as it has also, in keeping with the iron curtain policy, resisted any direct recruitment. Of the total number of 1,018 employed at headquarters in the Secretariat in 1949 in grade 8 or above, only 14 are listed as coming from the Soviet Union. Granted that there may well be difficulties in discovering large numbers of persons who are qualified for international employment without stripping the home services and other international assignments, it is impossible to escape the conclusions that the Kremlin has no very high regard for the bulk of the operations of the United Nations and that it fears to expose any large number of its subjects to the contamination of the west. Of the few officials who have come from the Soviet Union it appears to be the general report that they have done their work competently and have conducted themselves correctly but there is the general sense that to a greater extent than is true for others in the Secretariat they remain tied to their own government. The totalitarian nature of the

Communist system makes it impossible for Soviet citizens to have the same measure of freedom as international servants as citizens of the western democracies.

In the Assembly and Security Council the official representation of the Soviet Union has been kept at a high level, including the appearance of such personalities as Molotov and Vishinsky, and in the other bodies Soviet representation has been at least at a competent and adequate level, generally equivalent to that of other members. The distinctive features of this representation have been its isolation from the rest of the United Nations community (which is also characteristic of the Soviet members of the Secretariat) and the rigidity of the instructions under which it operates. While the Soviet diplomats have solemnly or jovially made the rounds of the cocktail parties and the official banquets, it is almost unheard of that they have entered into an easy give-and-take above the level of small talk or even approached the point of unburdening their souls. As the Soviet Union has lived apart from its non-Communist neighbors in the world, so the Soviet delegates coming to the United Nations have lived to themselves and have unbent to virtually no one.

In negotiations they have adhered rigidly to their instructions and have given no evidence that compromise and adjustment were contained within their code unless orders to that effect came through from Moscow. All too often they have left their fellow negotiators with the impression that their basic purpose was not to reach agreement on a commonly acceptable course, but to delay, obstruct, and propagandize, perhaps rejecting at the end a decision on which many weary hours or days of efforts to meet their points had been invested. The performance of Malik as president of the Security Council in August, 1950, brought this problem vividly home to millions. And it need scarcely be added that the tone and temper of the Soviet representatives has brought the language and manners of international intercourse to a new low.

Perhaps the most surprising thing about the attitude of the USSR toward the United Nations is the bare fact that it has remained a member of an organization which is in basic respects so remote from what it set out to be—in Stalin's view it was to be an agency primarily devoted to preventing a renewed outburst of German or Japanese aggression—and which operates in a world so different from that in which it was created. A long road has been travelled since the days when the unanimity of the great powers was assumed to be the cornerstone of peace, and when the veto was accepted as the realistic recognition that if the great powers fell out among themselves no currently conceivable international organization could prevent war on the grand scale.

Instead of collaboration among the wartime allies in the tasks of peace there is open hostility between the Soviet bloc and an increasingly closeknit coalition of the western powers, a coalition brought into being to meet the challenge of a Soviet imperialism which was in evidence even before the end of the war. Warfare in Korea, repeated testing of atomic weapons, continued partition of Germany, and a Japanese peace settlement to which neither the USSR nor China is a partner are outward symbols of the collapse of the dream of a world moving peacefully forward under the aegis of the United Nations. The USSR has ringed itself with satellite states and the mainland of China has joined the Communist fold; the challenge has been taken up by the west, which has embarked on a vast and coordinated arms program, has erected a series of bases pressing in close upon the Soviet frontiers, and now seeks to throw the military force of Germany and Japan into the balance. The United Nations itself has in some measure become an instrument of the anti-Communist coalition, and, outside the United Nations, the leaders of the coalition have established mutual aid and security systems which Moscow, without unduly straining its imagination, must inevitably inscribe on its books as hostile alliances.

It is a curious partnership, yet the Soviet Union has not withdrawn from the United Nations, presumably calculating, as it did earlier on different grounds in relation to the League, that its interests are better served inside than out. Although the net balance in favor of staying in must have declined as the years have passed and new regional groupings have cut in on the global centrality of the United Nations, there is no reason to assume that the calculations were peculiarly subtle or Machiavellian. The United Nations is a meeting place of the statesmen of the world and significant international business is transacted in its chambers, corridors, and cocktail lounges. As a great power, as an expanding power, and as a threatened power, the USSR could not afford to be absent from it—a lesson which the Soviet withdrawal during the early stages of the Korean war must have reinforced.

Through its membership in the United Nations the Soviet Union gains a platform from which it can propagandize to its heart's content, exposing the sins and mistakes of its opponents and extolling its own role as the self-appointed champion of the oppressed and exploited. By working with the neutralists and the anti-imperialists it can exploit to the full the actual and potential rifts in the majority which normally opposes it. By safeguarding and using the veto, it can in some measure impede the process of transforming the United Nations into an effective anti-Communist agency. As the leader of its own peace crusade, which has been so largely characterized by the incitement of hatred against all who do not follow the Communist line, it can utilize both its membership and its particular activities in the United Nations as a demonstration of its professed devotion to peace.

From the Soviet standpoint these are not small advantages but since they accrue wholly to the Communist account it is of greater importance for the free world that the USSR, if our original working assumption is justified, presumably looks to the United Nations as one of the instrumentalities for the prevention of a third world war which could spell ruin for the Kremlin's regime. There is good ground for belief that under present circumstances the Soviet Union finds its version of peaceful coexistence preferable to war, but it is essential to recognize that this version is based on an explicit division of the world into spheres which might collaborate for limited purposes in the United Nations but could never merge into the western concept of one world.

Apart from the Communist faithful there would be a large measure of unanimity on the proposition that the USSR has done very little to advance, and much to thwart, the brave hopes of building a world community through the United Nations. The failure of the Soviet Union to join in making the United Nations system work cannot be thrown back upon the western powers even though it be conceded that they have from time to time sinned against both the USSR and the United Nations. If the Soviet Union had seen fit to operate differently in the world at large and in the United Nations in particular—in brief, if it had sought to enter into the cooperative relationships on which any world order must rest—it would have encountered a very different reception from that accorded its actual policies, whereas there is the gravest doubt that more cooperative efforts on the part of the west would have markedly changed the basic attitudes of the Kremlin.

To say this is by no means to dismiss the United Nations as a futile gesture of non-existent good will, or to relegate it to the role of an armed alliance against the Communist bloc. The free world is confronted by a threefold and often contradictory task. It must build through the United

Nations structure the largest measure of world community which it can secure, wherein it can expect little, if any, Soviet cooperation. It cannot evade the problem of utilizing and equipping the United Nations to accomplish its major purpose of maintaining international peace and security in face of the threat of further Communist aggression. But it must at the same time preserve the United Nations as a global organization within whose framework the cold war, through negotiation and compromise, might begin to be translated into a peaceful coexistence which would at least be nearer peace than war. In this task there remains hope of Soviet cooperation.

STALINISM AND THE WORLD CONFLICT

ROBERT C. TUCKER

Robert C. Tucker, now a professor of government at Indiana University, was for eight years with the American Embassy in Moscow as editor of the Anglo-American Joint Press Reading Service. He has also been a consultant to the Rand Corporation. In the article reprinted here, he argues that a significant factor in the determination of postwar Soviet foreign policy is what he terms the "Stalinist mentality" of the men involved in policy-making. These men, he believes, suffer from a sort of collective neuroticism, and transfer personal "animosities, ambitions, and obsessions" to their thinking about foreign policy. Professor Tucker's article is an outstanding example of recent efforts to discover the determining factors of Soviet policy by means of psychological analysis.

THE observer of international affairs who traces the course of the great East-West conflict which emerged in the aftermath of the second World War sooner or later finds himself face to face with the problem of its underlying causes. This is a problem of much greater difficulty and complexity than that which arises in explaining the majority of international conflicts. The existence of a multitude of sovereign states, each pursuing its own national self-interest in a highly interdependent world, inescapably gives rise to friction and conflict between states of varying degrees of seriousness. However, the sources of these conflicts usually lie close to the surface of events and are not difficult to discern. They are generated by objective collisions of national interests and tend to subside when and if the particular situations which cause them are satisfactorily resolved.

The postwar conflict between Russia and the Western democracies has been a conflict of a different order. While most international conflicts arise out of local issues, the issue here is not one that can be localized. Like external symptoms of an organic disease, the many different conflicts which have broken out on the surface of East-West relations since the end of the war, ranging from the deadlocks in negotiation and the cleavages in the United Nations to the grim trials of strength in Berlin and Korea, have been phenomena of a secondary character stemming from and reflecting a conflict down deep in the

From R. C. Tucker, "Stalinism and the World Conflict," *Journal of International Affairs*, Vol. VIII, No. 1 (1954), pp. 7–20. By permission of the *Journal of International Affairs*.

sources of events. This *basic conflict* and its causes will form the theme of the discussion that follows.

There is a general observation which must first be made in order to place the problem in its proper perspective. The basic conflict has been essentially one-sided both in its origin and in its driving force. Surveying the sequence of events beginning in 1944 and 1945, we see the Soviet government acting from the outset as though there were an East-West conflict in prospect or in progress, while Western diplomacy kept operating for some time on the premise that this was not, or at any rate need not be, the case. The attempts of the Western powers to restore independence to liberated states and enlist Soviet cooperation in administering occupied territories encountered growing difficulties. At every key point of East-West contact—in the negotiations between heads of state and foreign ministers, in the relations between Soviet and Western representatives in the capitals of East European countries, in the dealings between the occupation authorities in Germany, Austria and Korea—Western representatives encountered multiplying signs of Soviet aggressiveness and intransigence. Only gradually and reluctantly did the leaders of Western policy come to the conclusion that the Kremlin's policies were forcing upon the democracies a new struggle of deadly earnestness and consequence. Defensive countermoves were called for and appeared in various forms—the program of aid for Greece and Turkey and, at a later date, rearmament and the Atlantic Pact. In Moscow these countermoves were presented to the Russian public as evidence of the West's aggressive intentions toward a peaceful U.S.S.R. and as justification for the sacrifices which were demanded of the Russian people in order to build up the Soviet war machine. However, the fact remains that all through the period of conflict the Soviet posture has been offensive and the Western posture defensive. The source of the basic conflict lay in the East, and the conflict was joined by the Western powers because they had no alternative; it was imposed upon them. Hence we must look to Soviet policy for an explanation of the origin of the cold war.

The basic conflict grew out of the aggressive policies followed by the Soviet government after the war, but it would not be entirely accurate to say that these were its root cause. To get at this root cause we must probe into the state of mind of the men who were responsible for the decision to follow these policies. The prime mover of the conflict is the mentality of which postwar Soviet foreign policy has been a projection. We do not know at the present time just how great the influence of Stalin's individual personality was in the shaping of postwar Soviet policies, although there is reason to believe that his was a dominant role. Let us, at any rate, designate the mentality underlying the basic conflict as "Stalinist," leaving aside the question of the extent to which it represents an individual or a collective phenomenon.

The "Stalinist mentality" is one which appears to have very strong affinities with a common variety of neurotic condition known to psychology as the "aggressive type." This condition has been analyzed in detail in the works of the late Dr. Karen Horney, and at this point we shall digress briefly to describe some of its characteristics. It stems, like all neuroses, from a "basic anxiety," which Dr. Horney defines as a feeling of being isolated in a world conceived as potientially hostile.[1] The aggressive type responds in the spirit of a struggle. He seeks safety through being tough and strong and through gaining power and control over others so that they will no longer have the capacity to hurt him. This involves him, so to speak, in a private "cold war" against people around him, most of whom will not readily submit to the total domination which is the only

[1] Karen Horney, *Neurosis and Human Growth* (New York, 1950), p. 18.

kind of relationship with others affording him a sense of security and satisfaction. In keeping with these trends, he develops a philosophy of life which looks upon the world as the arena of a ruthless struggle of all against all. This reinforces his tendency to value strength above all else as the equipment for successful living. In this struggle of all against all, taking the offensive appears to him to be the best defense: "To hit back or—preferably—to hit first appears to him (logically!) as an indispensable weapon against the crooked and hostile world around him. It is nothing but intelligent, legitimate self-interest."[2] The attitude of persons of this type toward other people is permeated with a fundamental animosity which runs the entire gamut from covert distrust to violent outbursts of vindictive rage. The neurotic not only harbors this permanent animosity toward others but, what is equally important, assumes that others harbor the identical feeling toward him: "He is convinced that everybody at bottom is malevolent and crooked, that it is only wisdom to regard everyone with distrust until he has been proved honest. But even such proof will readily make room for suspicion at the slightest provocation."[3] It is important to note that all this tends to set in motion a process of impairment of the neurotic's personal relations which grows worse and worse in a vicious circle. In other words, whether or not others actually do regard him with the hostility which he imputes to them, his own hostility and the aggressive behavior springing from it will eventually tend to turn them against him in self-defense. This, however, merely reinforces him in his conviction that they were hostile toward him all along, and he responds with still greater hostility and still more aggressive behavior, which tends to arouse an even stronger reaction against him, and so on. If we transpose this process from the

sphere of personal relations to the sphere of political relations, we will have a fairly faithful representation of the inner dynamics of the postwar conflict between Russia and the West up until the time of Stalin's death.

Returning now to the "Stalinist mentality," let us now observe several significant ways in which it parallels or reflects a neurotic condition of the type which we have described here in highly simplified terms. It is not difficult to see the parallel between the neurotic's "basic anxiety," derived from the feeling of being isolated in a hostile world, and the Stalinist picture of Russia as an isolated fortress of socialism besieged on all sides by an angry host of capitalist states bent on closing in upon it and destroying it at the first convenient opportunity: here we have the familiar doctrine of "capitalist encirclement." Although on the surface this is an ideological construction rather than a psychological attitude, the tremendous adherence to the doctrine in the face of events and facts which go to invalidate it points to the need for a psychological interpretation. On the one hand, we find that the entire wartime experience of Russian alliance with two mighty "capitalist" states, the United States and Great Britain, failed to unseat the belief in a hostile capitalist encirclement, which re-emerged in Soviet writings as soon as the war was over. On the other hand, we find this same belief being maintained years later in the face of an entirely new set of facts which clearly called for some modification of it. In August, 1951, the theoretical organ of the Soviet Communist Party, *Bolshevik*, reported that readers were suggesting in letters to the editor that it was no longer justified to speak of a "capitalist encirclement" in view of the fact that the U.S.S.R. was now bordered largely by countries with Communist regimes. Such a view, replied this authoritative voice of Stalinism, was entirely mistaken: "Certain comrades have erroneously construed the establishment of a people's-democratic sys-

2 *Ibid.*, p. 206.
3 *Ibid.*, p. 199.

tem in a number of countries bordering on the U.S.S.R. as liquidating the capitalist encirclement. Evidently, these comrades have looked upon the capitalist encirclement as a purely geographical conception, which is, of course, entirely wrong."[4] In January, 1953, this same journal, now published under a new name, *Kommunist*, made the still more striking statement that "so long as capitalism remains in the principal capitalist countries, it would be wrong to speak of the liquidation of the capitalist encirclement."[5] All this points to the conclusion that the concept of a capitalist encirclement fulfills certain powerful psychological needs rooted deep in the Stalinist mentality.

Secondly, the neurotic's conception of the world as the arena of a struggle of all against all is the foundation of Stalinism as a philosophical creed. The Stalinist mind views struggle and warfare as the most fundamental and pervasive attribute not only of human existence but of the universe itself, which is seen as operating according to the dialectical law of the "struggle of opposites." History is seen as revolving around the struggle of classes. The Soviet Union is pictured as locked in mortal combat with the forces of capitalism as a consequence of its historic mission as the "first shock-brigade" in the modern day class struggle between the proletariat and the bourgeoisie. The notion of struggle as the essence of life likewise pervades the Stalinist image of the world beyond the Soviet borders. The world is seen as a tissue of "contradictions" pitting not only class against class and group against group in each individual country but also colonies against metropolitan countries and each metropolitan country against all others. And even inside the supposedly monolithic Soviet society, the Stalinist mind sees development as proceeding through "non-antagonistic contradictions" which never-

theless necessitate a ceaseless "struggle of the new against the old." The obsession with the notion of warfare and struggle is the source of Stalinism's furious rejection of every manifestation of "reformism," a philosophy which implies that improvement in human affairs can on occasion come about by peaceful means.

Thirdly, the profound hostility which permeates the neurotic's attitude toward persons around him and especially toward actual or potential rivals in the competitive struggle has a counterpart in the underlying unfriendliness or animosity toward foreign governments which is such a familiar feature of the Stalinist mentality. This is a primary source of the deviousness and secretiveness which the Soviet government customarily displays in its dealings with foreign governments and their representatives. For reasons of policy, expressions of animosity have to be kept in check in certain areas of foreign relations, such as Soviet relations with other Communist states. However, as the experience of Tito and other foreign Communist leaders has shown, the animosity itself and the suspicion and distrust which it breeds are always lurking in the background of these relations even if no sign of it appears upon the surface. No such restraint is operative in Soviet relations with "capitalist" states except during periods of temporary alliance dictated by tactical imperatives, such as the period of the Soviet-German pact and the period of the wartime coalition with the Western democracies. In this sphere free rein can be, and is, given to the underlying animosity, with the result that hostility builds up to an explosive intensity against the foreign government or governments which happen at any given time to be in the forefront of opposition to Soviet policy, as the United States government has been in recent years. One important corollary of this basic animosity is the need to believe that foreign governments are actuated by an equally deep or even deeper animosity toward the Soviet Union. It is therefore an

---

[4] *Bolshevik*, No. 16, 1951, p .61.

[5] *Kommunist*, No. 2, 1953, p. 19.

unshakable article of the Stalinist faith that the capitalist world is plotting the destruction of the Soviet system, that the motives of bourgeois governments in their dealings with Moscow are sinister and hostile and that any friendly gestures they may make are hypocritical. This makes it seem imperative for the Soviet government and people never to relax their "revolutionary vigilance," which connotes an attitude of always remaining suspiciously on the lookout for machinations by potential enemies who are assumed to exist in every quarter, including the U.S.S.R. itself.

One final neurotic trait which has its counterpart in the Stalinist mentality is the worship of material strength and the profound fear of being or seeming weak in any respect. (One recalls in this context the famous question attributed to Stalin: "How many divisions has the Pope?") In internal policy this attitude manifests itself in a willingness to subordinate every other consideration, including the morale of the Soviet people, to the one overriding goal of amassing economic and military strength. The obsession with strength also shows up in the vast amount of public attention bestowed upon the Soviet armed forces, and in the glorification of the power and might of the Soviet state which became such a prominent theme of Soviet propaganda writings durng the postwar years. It is interesting to observe in this connection how Soviet propaganda found itself in something of a quandary in its "peace campaign" of recent years. Although the "peace" propaganda was anything but peaceful in tone, the Soviet authorities were apparently afraid that the outside world might suspect elements of Soviet weakness behind it. In this campaign, therefore, it became the rule for Soviet press articles to conclude with an emphatic warning that the Soviet Union's desire for peace was not to be construed as a sign of weakness or fear of war. The anxious emphasis upon this point is a good illustration of Stalinism's need always to be and appear strong. To the Stalinist mentality the only formula for security is overwhelming material strength.

Certain broad lines of policy flow logically from the psychological attitudes and the image of the world discussed above. In domestic affairs an all-out effort to build up a position of impregnable economic-military strength is obviously indicated. In foreign policy the need to cope with an international environment regarded as implacably hostile dictates an aggressively competitive course of conduct calculated to weaken and divide Soviet Russia's adversaries and simultaneously to expand the orbit of Soviet power and influence whenever an opportunity to do so presents itself. The logical long-range goal of this foreign policy is world hegemony, which means a global preponderance of power in terms of territory, population, resources, and military potential. Nothing less than this would seem to the Stalinist mentality to provide Russia with effective insurance against potential attempts of the hostile environment to crush and destroy it. In other words, the establishment of predominant control over the international environment is seen as the only possible means of coming to terms with it. Three main strategies recommend themselves in this ceaseless drive to better Russia's relative position in the competitive struggle. Firstly, Russia should encourage and support pro-Soviet movements and other oppositional tendencies in foreign states and their dependencies so as to weaken these states as much as possible and keep them off balance. Secondly, it should endeavor to exploit and accentuate the discords between opponent-states in order to obstruct them from joining forces against it. And thirdly, it should seek whenever possible to incorporate neighboring countries or territories within the Soviet orbit in order to bring a greater and greater area of the hostile international environment under control. We may call these three lines of action the strategies of harassment, division, and expansion. For each of the strategies the Communist ideology provides an elaborate doctrinal rationalization. The strategy of harassment is rationalized as "support for the foreign proletariat and its class organization in the struggle to realize their legitimate demands and for the national-liberation struggle of the oppressed peoples in the colonial rear of imperialism." The strategy of division is rationalized in terms of "contradictions rending the camp of imperialist powers." And the strategy of expansion finds ideological justification in the proposition that the Soviet Union, as the base and homeland of a world-wide proletarian revolution, must give its support to other peoples in their "revolutionary struggle for liberation from imperialist bondage." Viewed through the binoculars of Marxist-Leninist doctrine, the expanding periphery of Soviet power appears as the outward growth of the world revolution.

With reference to the strategy of expansion, the question arises as to the methods which appear to the Stalinist mentality as feasible for the purpose of extending Soviet control over neighboring countries and territories. The international environment, as we have said, is regarded as implacably hostile, but it is also regarded as extremely powerful and dangerous. Therefore, the constant quest for opportunities of Soviet expansion is combined with a certain elementary tactical caution in the Kremlin lest any reckless aggressive act on its part mobilize all the potentialities of the capitalist encirclement for destructive action and bring down catastrophic consequences upon the Soviet Union. An open act of Soviet armed aggression, regardless of how successful in attaining its immediate objective, would upset the strategy of division and bring about the always feared prospect of a showdown with a solid phalanx of capitalist powers ranged against Russia. This tends to impose a limitation upon the means which the Soviet government is willing to employ to effectuate the strategy of expansion. Recognition of this limitation is reflected in the formula of "peaceful coexistence" of the two opposing

systems. To the Stalinist mentality "peaceful coexistence" does not mean that the two worlds can live together in amity, but merely that total war should be excluded as a means of resolving the conflict between them, all lesser means being legitimate. In fact, "peaceful coexistence" is the Stalinist euphemism for the state of no-war-no-peace for which the West has coined the phrase "cold war."

Although these considerations militate against a sudden "adventurist" move of a military nature which would risk all the fortunes and gains of the Soviet regime on one whirl of the wheel of chance, they do not rule out various moves of a more limited character in the pursuit of the strategy of expansion. One such move which appeals powerfully to the Stalinist mind is the war by proxy in which the Soviet Union adopts the pose of a neutral power while Communist-led forces subservient to it battle for control of new territory. The classic example of such an operation is the war in Korea. Secondly, opportunities for Soviet expansion present themselves whenever there is any internationally acceptable excuse for the Soviet Union to move its armed forces into neighboring countries, as there was in the final phase of the defeat of Germany in 1944. In situations of this kind the strategy of expansion dictates the use of every possible means to perpetuate Soviet control over the occupied territories. The most common means is the organization of Communist-dominated puppet regimes through which control can be exercised indirectly even if the Soviet occupation forces are eventually withdrawn. So long as Soviet policy operates within the outer limits of caution previously mentioned, possibilities of expansion are broadly limited to these two types of action. There are, however, exceptional situations in which internal subversion can accomplish the purpose without an outright military occupation (as in Czechoslovakia) or in which native Communist movements succeed in capturing control of countries by largely independent military action (as Yugoslavia and China). As the Tito affair has shown, cases of the latter type pose for the Soviet regime the new and disturbing problem of consolidating and perpetuating its control over the victorious native Communist movement. Techniques of infiltration are used to reinforce the ties of ideological allegiance to the Soviet Union.

Surveying the postwar course of Soviet policy in the light of this interpretation of its moving springs, we can understand that the opportunities for expansion implicit in the Soviet occupation of Eastern and East-Central Europe were irresistibly attractive to the Stalinist mentality, especially in conjunction with the immediate postwar weakness of the regimes in Western Europe and the precipitate withdrawal of American armed might. As Stalin implied by his speech of February 9, 1946, in which he charted an internal policy of concentration on building up Russia's military-economic potential, it was understood in Kremlin circles that Soviet expansion was incompatible with continued good relations with the Western democracies. However, the Stalinist mind could see no particular disadvantage in a break with the West because, as we have suggested, it assumed that in any event the real attitude of the Western powers toward Russia was at bottom crooked, malevolent, and self-seeking. Since no amount of Soviet "good behavior" could alter this basic fact, the only logical course for the Soviet government to take was, in this view, to seize the initiative and consolidate its position in preparation for the duel for power which must inevitably result. The developing crisis of East-West relations found fresh focal points in the countries subjected to a divided occupation —Germany, Austria and Korea. The Stalinist power reflex operated here as in countries wholly occupied by Soviet forces with the result that temporary boundaries of military occupation zones hardened into quasi-permanent lines of partition. Far from contemplating an eventual withdrawal

of Soviet power from these advance outposts, Stalinist thinking was dominated by the idea of employing them—especially East Germany and North Korea—as bases for the incorporation of the remaining parts of the partitioned countries into its power system. As the initial moves in this pattern of Soviet expansion were carried out, the inevitable signs of Western hostile reaction (Churchill's Fulton speech, for example) were seized upon in Moscow as evidence that the Western attitude toward Russia had been hostile from the very beginning, and Soviet propaganda unloosed its campaign of vitriolic recrimination against the Western powers which in so many ways set the tone of the postwar period. Hostility and tension mounted in the pattern of a vicious circle.

During the critical years of 1946 and 1947 there appears to have taken place in the Kremlin a momentous reassessment of the entire international situation in the light of postwar developments. Some of these developments were the westward advance of Soviet power into the heart of Europe, the temporary disappearance of Germany and Japan from the ranks of the powers, the instability of the postwar governments in continental Western Europe, the unforeseen seriousness of the economic disorganization of the European economy as a result of the war, and of the detachment of East European resources from it, and the widespread ferment and unrest in Asia leading to the disintegration of European colonial empires and the weakening, in particular, of the British position in world affairs. Reflecting on these events, the Stalinist leadership reached the conclusion that the time for a decision in the long-range Russian bid for a global preponderance of power was already at hand, contrary to the previous assumption that it would come at some indefinite point in the future. The fact that such a reassessment did occur was almost clearly demonstrated by the theoretical attack launched in May, 1947, against the dean of Kremlin economists, Eugene Varga, who had predicted, on the basis of an unusually empirical-minded investigation carried out during and immediately after the war, that the capitalist system contained the prerequisites for at least a decade of "relative stabilization" after the second World War. Varga's rather complacent picture of the slow steady march of a socialist economic revolution which would in due time prevail throughout most of the world was thrust aside, and in its place appeared the Stalinist apocalyptic vision of a life-and-death struggle between two opposing world camps centered respectively in Soviet Russia and the United States of America. The capitalist camp—gravely weakened by the war, shot through with domestic strife in every country, beset by insoluble economic problems, and wallowing in inter-capitalist contradictions—was viewed as being incapable of pulling itself together and bringing about a new period of "relative capitalist stabilization" comparable to that achieved in the nineteen twenties after the first World War. As a result of the second World War the scales of world power had come into even balance and now they were tipping in favor of the Soviet bloc. This appraisal called for a maximum effort to weight the scales decisively in the direction they were tipping. It dictated a policy not of conservative restraint in foreign affairs combined with consolidation of positions already won, but of bringing relentless aggressive pressure to bear upon the international environment in order to effect a further and radical improvement of the Soviet position at the expense of the rival camp. The main lines of this new Stalinist appraisal were visible in Zhdanov's address at the founding meeting of the Cominform in September, 1947, and in Molotov's anniversary speech of November 6, 1947, which closed with the resounding cry: "We live in an age when all roads lead to Communism!"

Out of this reassessment of the international position emerged a whole series of offensive moves in Soviet foreign policy which were aimed either at enlarging the sphere of Soviet control or harassing Russia's opponents. This inaugurated a second and increasingly bitter period of the basic conflict, which lasted from 1947 until Stalin's death in March 1953. During the early part of this new period the principal focus of Soviet pressure lay in Europe. Outstanding among its manifestations were the civil war in Greece, the creation of the Cominform, the desperate drive to obstruct the European Recovery Program, the seizure of Czechoslovakia, and the whole sequence of Soviet policy moves in Germany which culminated in the blockade of Berlin. In the face of ever stiffening Western resistance, as shown in the Atlantic pact, rearmament, the airlift, and the new stability which the American aid programs helped to create in Greece, Turkey, and Western Europe (a resistance which was powerfully abetted by Tito's revolt against Stalinist methods of controlling the Soviet satellite), the European phase of the Soviet offensive finally slowed down to a virtual halt. There was, however, no corresponding diminution of the impulse behind it. Meanwhile, the Communist victory in China offered a convenient opportunity to shift the main focus of expansionist pressure to East Asia where the situation in many lands favored the use of the war by proxy as the principal method of Soviet expansion. The Asian phase of the grand offensive came to a bloody but inconclusive climax in the Soviet war by proxy in Korea.

Stalinism's supreme effort, undertaken from 1947 onward to prevent a new "relative capitalist stabilization" and to alter decisively the world balance of power by all means short of a general war, was a failure at virtually every key point with the notable exception of China, where the Communist success was a triumph for Russia but hardly a direct product of Russian policy. The effort did, however, generate an enormous amount of international tension and set in motion certain processes which adversely affected the Soviet position. These were the endeavors of countries outside the orbit of Soviet control but inside the far larger orbit of Soviet ambition and animosity to set their affairs in order, strengthen themselves, and band together in defensive coalitions, like the Atlantic and Balkan pacts, and schemes for economic integration like the European coal-steel community. This meant that even in the absence of a general war the different elements of the Stalinist strategy had come into conflict. More specifically, the ruthless pursuit of the strategies of harassment and expansion had finally goaded the free world into a posture of unity and strength which made it much less vulnerable to the strategy of division than it had been previously. Nevertheless, so long as Stalin lived, no disposition was manifested in Moscow to acknowledge this fact or to revise Soviet policies in the light of it. On the contrary, Stalin maintained stubbornly in *Economic Problems of Socialism in the U.S.S.R.* that the contradiction between the leading capitalist states not only continued to exist but were "in practice" even more potent than the contradictions between the two world camps. What were the implications of this remarkable statement? In the present writer's view, Stalin was covertly arguing here against anonymous Soviet advocates of a policy of greater restraint which would allow international tension to subside and might induce the free world to abandon its dangerous new unity. He was saying in effect that this unity was merely superficial and could not long withstand the divisive tendencies inherent in the capitalist system, the unvoiced inference being that it was unnecessary to relieve the pressure and reduce the tension in order to disunite Russia's adversaries. Stalin was thus blinking the fact that different elements of the Stalinist strategy had come into conflict and was insisting that the Soviet government should persevere in the policies which it had been following since 1947. Although this interpretation is speculative, there is a certain amount of indirect evidence to support it,

particularly in the Soviet ideological writings of the period immediately following the Nineteenth Party Congress. Stalin's aggressive "shock-brigade" speech at the closing session of the Nineteenth Congress certainly gave no inkling of an intention to decrease world tension, nor did the whole series of post-Congress events in Moscow, including the preparation for a new purge trial based on the trumped-up "doctors' plot." Although the Soviet government embarked upon no spectacular new act of expansion during this period, neither was there any easing of pressure or release of international tension until after Stalin died. It is particularly noteworthy in this connection that the third anniversary of the signing of the Sino-Soviet treaty of alliance was marked by the publication in *Pravda* of an article by Mao Tse-tung in which he promised that the war in Korea would be waged on for years if necessary until the winning of "complete victory."

The death of Stalin came at a time of crisis for the postwar Stalinist foreign policy. The actions taken from 1947 on had failed to achieve a radical alteration of the world balance of power in favor of the Soviet bloc but did, on the other hand, produce a situation in which further efforts to realize this bold design were fraught with greater danger to the continued maintenance of formal peace between the Soviet Union and the Western coalition. There were indications that the crisis was apparent to some more realistic minds in Moscow and that they had advocated—without success—the idea of calling at least a temporary halt to the march of Soviet expansion in order to allow the war danger to subside and encourage the Western coalition to drift apart. Some of the foreign policy moves taken in Moscow since March of 1953 lend themselves to interpretation on the hypothesis that this "realistic" assessment prevailed among the new rulers of Russia once Stalin was out of the way. The reversal of Stalinist policy in Korea, implicit in the speedy conclusion of an armistice on UN terms after Stalin died, would fit in with such an interpretation, as would a number of other steps taken to reduce tension. On this hypothesis, the present period would constitute a lull in the basic conflict, a respite allowed by the new Soviet leadership while it concentrates upon internal affairs and upon the consolidation of international positions already won. Whatever its duration, the lull would represent no more than a change of tactics, leaving the long-range goal of Soviet foreign policy unchanged and the strategies for its achievement unimpaired.

While there is no firm evidence to support a more hopeful interpretation of Russian foreign policy after Stalin, the possibility that time will bring a deeper change, a change not merely of pace but of direction, should not be dogmatically ruled out. The analysis presented here suggests that the driving forces behind the basic conflict between Soviet Russia and the Western democracies have been subjective in origin. Stalinism's postwar offensive against the free world was not simply an effort to promote the national or imperial interests of Russia as a great power, although elements of national self-interest were prominent in it. Nor, on the other hand, was it a messianic quest to actualize an ideological image of the world, although ideological constructions have undoubtedly played a part in the determination and especially in the formulation of Soviet policy. It represents, in a deeper sense, the translation into foreign policy of the animosities, ambitions, and obsessions characteristic of a neurotic personality. This focuses attention upon the personalities of the men in power in Russia both before and after Stalin's death, and enhances the potential importance of shifts in the locus of power within the Soviet hierarchy. It seems highly probable that Stalin, who wielded autocratic power in Russia for upwards of two decades, furnished the principal inspiration for the neurotic phenomenon which we have called the Stalinist mentality, although the foundations upon which he built were provided by history. The mentality can survive the man and live on in the policies of his successors, whose habits of political thought, after all, were formed and molded very largely under Stalin's personal influence. Nevertheless, the passing of Stalin may have opened up possibilities, which did not exist while he lived, for a change in the mind of Stalinism.

Such a change would mean in essence that the judgments, deliberations, and actions of the men in power in Russia would no longer be dominated by a pathological psychology. The evolution away from this psychology would be manifested, firstly, in a drastic decline of the intense and pervasive hostility which appears to be the deepest mark of the spirit of Stalinism; secondly, in a fundamental relaxation of the aggressive pressure against the international environment which stems as a strategic necessity from this hostility; and thirdly, in a loosening of the compulsive rigidity of Stalinist thinking and behavior, which ultimately derives from the same source. The relaxation of aggressive pressure would not then be a mere tactical maneuver. It would signify the abandonment of the conviction that the only way to come to terms with the international environment is to secure control over it—the abandonment, in other words, of the drive to dominate the world. The basic conflict which the drive for world domination has generated would consequently tend to subside. Such an evolution would not be marked by any dramatic act of ideological heresy, although the resultant loosening of Stalinist rigidity would very probably lead to changes in the ideological sphere as well as in others (as the example of post-Stalinist Yugoslavia shows). Nor would it produce any sudden desire on the part of the Soviet leadership to withdraw from foreign affairs into a position of national isolation. On the contrary, the concept of Russia's interests as a great power with manifold positions to defend and claims to assert in foreign affairs would come to the fore for the first time as the driving force behind Soviet foreign policy. In view of the present geographical spread of Russian power and influence, this means that very many thorny issues would remain to be resolved. However, with the subsiding of the basic conflict which has imparted to all these issues a profoundly malignant character, they would no longer be impervious to the devices of reason and the resources of diplomacy.

Developments in the Far East 1945–1953

THE SINO-SOVIET ALLIANCE

HOWARD L. BOORMAN

As an official of the United States Department of State, Howard L. Boorman worked in Peiping from 1947 to 1950 and in Hong Kong until late 1954. Since 1955 he has been Director of the Research Project on Men and Politics in Modern China, at Columbia University. In the following pages he discusses Sino-Soviet relations up to 1953, and hazards some well-educated guesses concerning the significance of events about which we have very little detailed evidence.

THE eruption of Chinese Communist power in Eastern Asia has led to a radical shift in the world balance of power. As early as 1950, it was apparent that the new and compulsive political entity which styles itself the People's Republic of China was to be the heart of an extraordinarily difficult problem in world politics. The protracted war in Korea and the Communist conquest of northern Vietnam have confirmed the strategic imbalance created by the recrudescence of Chinese power in Asia. Neither the armistice agreements which put an end to hostilities in these two areas nor the persistent efforts of non-Asian nations to bolster present barriers to Communist expansion in Asia have yet given hope that a new situation of balance and stability between the contending forces has been attained.

Nor can the problem be understood by analyzing its purely Chinese dimensions in isolation. Communist China is firmly allied with one of the two strongest military and industrial powers in the world, and it has, in general, pursued its national and international objectives in coordination with the Soviet Union. Communist China has also come to play an increasingly significant role within the coalition of the world's two great Communist powers athwart the Eurasian land mass. Formerly it was possible and profitable to discuss the Soviet impact on the Western world. Now one must ponder the still broader problem: the Sino-Soviet impact on the world.

Is the Moscow-Peking axis unbreakable? What is Communist China's role within the Sino-Soviet alliance? Will mainland China find Russian backing sufficient

From Howard L. Boorman, "The Sino-Soviet Alliance: The Political Impact," in H. L. Boorman, A. Eckstein, P. E. Mosely, and B. Schwartz, *Moscow-Peking Axis: Strengths and Strains* (New York: Harper, for the Council on Foreign Relations, 1957), pp. 1–13. By permission of the Council on Foreign Relations, Inc.

297

to help it achieve its own lusty desires and ambitions?

Answers to these broad questions must be sought if the non-Communist world is to formulate effective policies for meeting the most ruthless challenge of our day. Viewed in perspective, the emergence of the Sino-Soviet alliance as the most dangerous coalition in the world has been neither abrupt nor accidental. If its intrusion into the world's consciousness has been jarring, the development itself is actually the result of a series of particular events—sometimes unnoted or misinterpreted by contemporary observers—which have gradually merged into a reasonably distinct total pattern. Thus, to understand the potentialities of the Moscow-Peking axis we must review what is now known of relations between the Russians and the Chinese Communists during the past few years, and we must examine how far the general aims of Chinese Communist foreign policy and the specific requirements of the alliance coincide or diverge.

PEKING AND MOSCOW

Russia and the Chinese Communists before 1949

Two decades ago, after the Chinese Communists had carried out their epoch-making Long March from Kiangsi to the remote hills of northwest China, reliable information about their relations with the Russians became exceedingly elusive. Mao's followers displayed a careful orthodoxy in their theoretical statements and a respectful deference toward Moscow, and they executed a thorough-going program aimed at building up a tightly disciplined Communist party along strict Leninist lines. Yet, in retrospect, one cannot point to a large body of concrete data bearing upon the political or personal contacts of the Chinese Communist leaders with Stalin and the contemporary top leadership of the Soviet Union.

Even later, following the Japanese sur-render in 1945 and the emergence of Mao Tse-tung and his followers from the caves of Yenan, the Communist march to total power in China left behind few clues as to the precise nature of Russian support or influence. In fact, in this respect the years between 1945 and 1949 are particularly obscure, even for the specialized student of relations between the Soviet and Chinese Communist Parties.

There had been collaboration in Manchuria between the Russian units which appeared there after the war against Japan had been won in the Pacific and the Chinese Communist forces which speedily made their way overland to that critical arena of conflict. Yet the extensive Russian removal of important industrial equipment from an area which was so soon, as it turned out, to come under complete Communist domination raises the question as to the degree of confidence with which the Russians viewed their Chinese counterparts in the immediate postwar period. A few years later, in the discussion groups organized in China to implant the new revolutionary creed, there was no question more difficult for a Chinese Communist political commissar to answer satisfactorily than the query: If the Russians are really such good fellows and such superior disciples of Marx and Lenin, why did they behave like a mob of hoodlums in Manchuria in 1945–46?

During the years following the Japanese surrender, when the Chinese Communists were fighting their way to power, their own political line with respect to the Soviet Union was both consistent and correct. Their radio station in northern Shensi paid dutiful homage to Moscow, and Liu Shao-ch'i's essay, *On Internationalism and Nationalism*, published in November 1948, supported the Soviet stand in the Tito apostasy of that year. It is debatable whether the Chinese Communists had organized their diplomatic assumptions into a coherent whole as early as the end of 1948, at a time when they were still pre-occupied with the military aspects of the civil war then being fought in China. In any case, it seems clear that the senior leaders of the Chinese party viewed their orientation toward Moscow as both necessary and, in terms of their own interests, highly desirable. In July 1949, even before the establishment of the new National Government in Peking, Mao Tse-tung formally outlined the Chinese Communist position with respect to Sino-Soviet relations. His "lean-to-one-side" speech announced forthrightly that the new regime would base its policies on close cooperation with the Soviet Union, not with the non-Communist "imperialist" world.

Until 1949, while the Chinese Communists were fighting for victory, the Soviet attitude toward the National Government of China was ambiguous. At the official level, it was scrupulously proper. The Russians continued to maintain formal diplomatic relations with the National Government, the sworn enemy of the Communists in China. At the operational level, the Soviet attitude was cynical and enigmatic. As late as 1949, the Soviet ambassador in China continued to negotiate with the National Government over important economic and transportation concessions in Sinkiang, apparently with a view to obtaining for Russia a special position in the province during the very months when the Chinese Communist armies were driving rapidly into the northwest.

The scanty evidence regarding conversations and agreements between the Russians and the Chinese Communists during 1947–49 is both incomplete and contradictory. It is relatively simple to sketch the broad outlines of the design, but difficult to fill in the fine detail. Possibly official Soviet representatives in China were not always *au courant* of developments in the Communist-controlled areas of the country in which they were stationed. And it is probable that Stalin, much farther removed from the rapidly changing circumstances in the hinterland of China, was not adequately prepared for the new political situation which was then being created by the startling military advance of the Chinese Communist armies as they drove southward and westward from Manchuria.

Certainly the balance in the Sino-Soviet Communist Party relationship was now drastically altered from what it had been a generation before, in the 1920's, when the Chinese Communist Party was young, inexperienced, and firmly under Moscow's direction. By 1949, Chinese Communism had grown into a vigorous and self-confident force which, if not yet fully mature, was clearly enjoying the brash assurance of late adolescence. It possessed a tightly knit political organization, then numbering over 3 million members, and a battle-toughened army of over 1.5 million men. During the two decades when it had been growing to this stature, the Communist Party of China had probably been less under direct Soviet control than Communist parties elsewhere. Its revolutionary armies were native to the soil and had not required active support from the Soviet Red Army to plan their campaigns or win their battles. By 1949, the Chinese Communist leaders possessed a background of practical political and administrative experience in their own country far more extensive than that which the leaders of the Bolshevik revolution in Russia had possessed in 1917 or even in 1921.

Stalin and the New Ally in Peking: 1949–1953

The Central People's Government of the People's Republic of China was formally established on October 1, 1949. The Soviet Union at once accorded it recognition, and the large Russian embassy on Legation Street, closed since the Chinese Communist occupation of Peking, reopened for business. Early in October, N. V. Roshchin—who had served as Soviet ambassador to the National Government of China as recently as May 1949, when he departed for Moscow—arrived in China again as the first foreign diplomat accredited to the new Communist regime there. Mao Tse-tung, in turn, dispatched the first Chinese Communist ambassador to Moscow.

The establishment of formal diplomatic relations and the exchange of official representatives, while noteworthy, were nevertheless routine. Neither these developments nor the tidy political slogans which poured unceasingly from Peking could provide adequate answers to the basic security and ideological problems involved in the new phase of contacts between the Russians and the Chinese Communists. It was left to Mao Tse-tung himself to travel to the Soviet Union to discuss these issues personally with Stalin. Mao's mission to Moscow underscored the fact that, for a prominent Communist, he was still in a decidedly irregular position. Ruler of the most populous Communist nation, he had never visited Russia, spoke no Russian, and had had relatively little contact with the Russians. His journey to negotiate with Stalin at the end of 1949, when the Soviet dictator was already seventy, was Mao's first venture outside his native China and, to date, his only pilgrimage to the Mecca of world Communism.

It was doubtless an extraordinarily difficult period of negotiation for the two Communist leaders in Moscow, for both were tough political realists, not vague theorists. It is probable that Stalin, increasingly rigid in his later years, viewed Mao Tse-tung as an Asian and an inferior. Mao, for his part, knew very well that Stalin's failure, two decades earlier, to understand the realities of the Chinese political situation had led Moscow in 1927 to issue unrealistic directives to the Chinese Communists and had resulted in staggering Communist losses at the hands of the Kuomintang. Whether Stalin and Mao reviewed the past or discussed the theory and practice of Communist revolution in Asia is uncertain. All the effusive propaganda about Sino-Soviet friendship could not, however, conceal the probability that the

negotiations must have been devoted, essentially, to hardheaded practical bargaining. Mao Tse-tung stayed in Moscow for nine weeks—from December 16, 1949, until February 17, 1950—at what was one of the most important Communist conferences of the postwar period.

On February 14, 1950, a joint communiqué announced the conclusion of three new Sino-Soviet agreements, signed in the Kremlin by the late A. Y. Vyshinsky, then the Soviet Minister of Foreign Affairs, and Chou En-lai, the Chinese Communist Foreign Minister.

The first was the Sino-Soviet Treaty of Friendship, Alliance, and Mutual Assistance, the foundation stone of the new alliance between the two major Communist powers. This treaty is valid until 1980 and may be further extended by mutual consent. Its focus is Asia; its nucleus is a military alliance ostensibly directed against defeated Japan. In it, Moscow and Peking agree to take all necessary measures to prevent the resumption of aggression on the part of Japan "or any other state that may collaborate with Japan directly or indirectly"—a clear reference, in this context, to the United States. If either Communist China or the Soviet Union is attacked by Japan "or any state allied with it" and thus becomes involved in a war, the other party will immediately render military and other assistance by all means at its disposal.

The second agreement covered the respective rights of the Russians and the Chinese Communists in Manchuria, the major border area in which both have significant strategic interests. It stipulated:

That the principal railroad network in Manchuria, the Chinese Changchun railway, would continue to be operated under joint Sino-Soviet administration (as had been provided earlier in the agreement signed between Moscow and the National Government of China in August 1945).

That the important naval base, Port Arthur, would also continue to be "jointly used," with Russian troops garrisoned there (as they had been since 1945), and would be employed to support joint military operations in the event of war with Japan or any country allied with Japan. Both of these arrangements—that concerning the Chinese Changchun railway and that concerning Port Arthur—were to be terminated upon the conclusion of a peace treaty with Japan or at the end of 1952, whichever came earlier.

That the administration of Dairen, the principal port at the southern end of the Chinese Changchun railway, was confirmed as belonging entirely to the Chinese. Since 1945, it had been under Soviet control.

The third agreement dealt with Russian financial assistance to Communist China. The Russians granted a credit which, at the official rate, amounted to U.S. $300 million, at an interest rate of one per cent per year. This credit arrangement covered the five-year period from 1950 through 1954, with one-fifth, or U.S. $60 million, to be made available annually. Communist China was to use this loan to pay for deliveries of industrial and railway supplies from the Soviet Union: equipment for electric power stations, metallurgical and engineering plants, mining equipment, railway and other transport equipment, rails, and "other materials for the restoration and development of the national economy." China was to repay the credit in ten equal annual installments, the first at the end of 1954 and the last at the end of 1963.

At the same time, the Soviet and Chinese Communist governments exchanged notes covering two other matters. The treaty and other agreements concluded on August 14, 1945, between the Soviet Union and the National Government of China were now declared null and void, and the independent status of the Mongolian People's Republic (Outer Mongolia) was guaranteed by both governments.

The developing alliance between the Soviet Union and Communist China was extended by other agreements signed in the spring of 1950. These provided for the establishment of a network of Sino-Soviet joint-stock companies to operate in the borderland areas of China:

Two companies to undertake the exploitation of nonferrous and rare minerals, and petroleum in Sinkiang (Chinese Turkestan), the vast province in the far northwest of China adjacent to Russian Central Asia;

A civil aviation company to operate flights between Peking and the Soviet Union via Manchuria, Outer Mongolia, and Sinkiang;

A company to build and repair ships at Dairen, the commercial port adjacent to Port Arthur in southern Manchuria.

And, in the spring of 1950, the two Communist allies completed initial negotiations on trading arrangements under which the Soviet Union was to supply industrial equipment while Communist China would, in return, export raw materials.

The forging of the Moscow-Peking axis was thus well begun before the outbreak of the Korean war in mid-1950 and the ensuing Chinese Communist intervention, in October. From 1950 through 1952, the government in Peking was in the difficult position of having to push through its initial programs of political unification and economic rehabilitation at home, while at the same time deeply involved in a costly and risky military engagement in Korea. Viewed from one standpoint, the Korean war was useful to the Communists in China, for it permitted them to consolidate domestic controls and mobilize human and material resources more rapidly than would otherwise have been politically feasible. In the midst of a war, internal opposition, or even criticism, could be dealt with as treason committed in favor of the "imperialists." By mid-1952, however, there were indications that the rulers in Peking were more anxious to push forward with their internal development programs than to continue what were for them increasingly pointless military operations which were also placing a severe strain upon scarce resources.

The war in Korea served to test Sino-Soviet relations. The alliance provided substantial Russian assistance to the modernization of the Chinese Communist forces. It also furnished a useful deterrent to more ambitious proposals, such as the bombing of Chinese bases in Manchuria, on the part of the United Nations forces.

Caution suggests that the interpretation of the diplomatic history of the Korean war be left to the future, since the present evidence is as overabundant as it is incomplete. Sino-Soviet relations during the Korean conflict are, in many respects, still a riddle. At times, Russian and Chinese moves seemed perfectly timed to present a common Communist front. Yet there were instances in the United Nations negotiations where, it would appear, the Russians failed to take complete advantage of tactical opportunities favorable to them and made only inconclusive gestures toward advancing Chinese interests. Certain it was, in any event, that Communist China felt by mid-1952 that the point of diminishing returns had been reached in Korea.

Further high-level political discussions between the Russians and the Chinese were now required. The most pressing problem was the joint consideration of issues outstanding under the agreements of February 1950 on the Chinese Changchun railway and Port Arthur. Thus, in the early autumn of 1952, a delegation headed by Chou En-lai flew to Moscow for new negotiations with the Soviet leaders. In mid-September, an official communiqué outlined the areas of agreement. The Soviet government was to transfer to China, with full title and without compensation, all Russian rights in the joint management of the Chinese Changchun railway and all property belonging to it. A second exchange of notes declared that the Chinese government "suggests and asks the Soviet government to agree to postpone the withdrawal of

Soviet troops from the jointly-used Chinese naval base of Port Arthur" until peace treaties had been concluded between the Communist governments and Japan. This exchange of notes, incorporating Peking's "request" and Moscow's "agreement," was retroactively made a component part of the Sino-Soviet Treaty of 1950.

Implementation of these revised arrangements proceeded on schedule. The transfer of the Manchurian rail network from joint Sino-Soviet to full Chinese control was carried out at a formal ceremony in Harbin at the end of 1952. This was a significant event in the Communist bloc, as it marked one of the first instances in Stalin's post-1945 career when the Russians had voluntarily relinquished valuable economic rights once they had been acquired. While giving up its control over the principal railway in Manchuria, Moscow tightened and prolonged its hold on the important Far Eastern naval base of Port Arthur. In view of the generally unsettled situation in the Far East and the continued military stalemate in Korea, it is possible that Communist China, possessing only a tiny naval force of its own, may have felt in the autumn of 1952 that the continued garrisoning of Soviet forces there was actually desirable from the standpoint of its national security. The terminology of the notes exchanged was nevertheless of interest in indicating the deliberate care apparently taken to demonstrate that the extended stay of Russian forces in Port Arthur was at China's request and by China's grace. The net result, in any event, was that the Soviet Union continued to maintain its own military and naval establishment at a major base within Chinese territory.

The negotiations of August and September 1952 also touched upon the issue of Outer Mongolia. The three governments — "with a view to strengthening their mutual economic and cultural ties" — worked out a tripartite Sino-Soviet-Mongol agreement on the construction of a new strategic rail link, through the Mongolian People's

Republic, to connect the rail systems of the Soviet Union and Communist China. This agreement, concluded in 1952, was not announced publicly by the Communists until two years later, in October 1954.

It seems likely that Chou En-lai's negotiations in Moscow must also have dealt with the Korean war, which was dragging into its third year with no clear indication of an armistice, and with no slackening of Communist military commitment in Korea. There was, however, no public mention of this subject, nor of Sino-Soviet economic relations, although it was clear that the issue of long-term Russian assistance was of pressing concern to the Chinese Communists as they prepared to move into their first Five-Year Plan of "large-scale economic construction," scheduled to begin in 1953. Indeed, after Chou En-lai and some of his delegation had returned to Peking late in September 1952, other experts and advisers who had accompanied him to Moscow stayed behind, apparently to continue detailed economic negotiations which lasted well into the following year.

An event of major significance in the Communist world at this time was the Nineteenth Congress of the Communist Party of the Soviet Union, held in October 1952. The first since 1939, this Congress was an important general gathering of Communist parties, with many sending their most senior leaders to Moscow for the occasion. The Communist Party of China was represented by Liu Shao-ch'i, who offered the official greetings of the Chinese party to the Congress at the session of October 8.

That Mao Tse-tung should have selected Liu Shao-ch'i to speak for the Chinese Communist Party at the Soviet party Congress was not surprising, for Liu had clearly established his pre-eminence as deputy to Mao in the realm of party affairs in China. This was Liu's first trip to Moscow since the distant days when he had studied there as a neophyte of the Comintern from 1920 to 1922, and it would be

interesting to speculate on his personal impressions and reactions to the changes which had taken place in the Soviet capital. On his 1952 trip Liu remained in Moscow for slightly over three months. Yet his return to Peking in mid-January 1953 was accompanied only by the briefest of official announcements which told nothing except that he had been met at the airfield by virtually the entire membership of the Political Bureau of the Chinese Communist Party. Nor did Peking make any subsequent statements regarding his trip, the subject of his negotiations, if any, with the Russians, or the degree of success of his mission. That this visit, the most extended stay in Moscow of any key member of the Chinese Communist Political Bureau since 1950, was devoid of significance is doubtful. There would seem little reason—aside from medical consultation—for a senior Communist with the manifold responsibilities which Liu had in Peking to linger in the Soviet Union for over fourteen weeks except for the purpose of conducting serious discussions. The fact that his extended sojourn in Moscow took place during the final months of Stalin's life offers grounds for speculation. But the visit was, and remains, an enigma.

Many aspects of the relations between Moscow and Peking during the Stalin period are still obscure. It is not clear, for example, how far Stalin may have attempted to go in penetrating the internal control apparatus of the Chinese Communist dictatorship. It is, however, reasonably clear that he was reluctant to cast the People's Republic of China in what might be construed to be a co-starring role on the international Communist stage.

But if the director was aging and obdurate, Communist China—the youthful aspirant from the East—was both resilient and realistic, confident that its very energy would ensure general recognition in the end. Whatever Mao Tse-tung's private estimates may have been during these years, he apparently felt it important during the final weeks of Stalin's life to lay public emphasis upon the essential solidarity of the Sino-Soviet bloc in checking any "aggressive moves of imperialism" in the Far East; upon the lack of strain in Moscow-Peking relations; and upon the continuing Russian support for Peking in the pursuit of the basic—still unattained—national goals of China.

A DECADE OF SOVIET POLICY IN ASIA

RODGER SWEARINGEN

Rodger Swearingen is Professor of International Relations and Coordinator of Research at the School of International Relations, University of Southern California. During World War II he served in the Far East as a Japanese language officer and was with the occupation in Tokyo. In the postwar years he worked in the State Department and was a Fellow at the Harvard Russian Research Center. He is co-author (with Paul F. Langer) of *Red Flag in Japan*. In this article, he traces the shift from the moderate interest in South and Southeast Asia, which characterized Soviet policy in the years immediately after the war, to the creation of the Sino-Soviet axis and the early exploration of its implications for communist theory and tactics around the world.

Two developments of the past decade have far-reaching implications for Soviet foreign policy, especially in Asia. One, the emergence of Communist China as a second Communist power-center certainly must be ranked in the annals of Far Eastern history as among the most significant events of the twentieth century. The other development is, of course, the death of Stalin and the new look in Soviet policy—the war of smiles, vodka parties and economic assistance. To be sure there have been tactical turns in the past but never before such a sharp curve nor so fast a driver.

At the twentieth Party Congress, in February, 1956, the Soviets claimed an economic level sufficient to permit technical and economic assistance to undeveloped countries "with no strings attached." The Soviets have, in fact, already launched an impressive economic offensive in South and Southeast Asia and in the Middle East. By denouncing Stalin and by attributing the terror and failures of the Soviet system to him, Moscow has sought to destroy the Western argument that when you sup with the Devil you should use a very long spoon.

In Asia, the Soviets today are in the strongest strategic position in their history. They are the ones who operate from a position of strength. But in the Far East, as elsewhere, postwar Soviet victories have come either as a direct consequence of negotiation with the United States (the Soviet takeover of Sakhalin and the Kuriles following the Yalta agreements, for example) or in areas where Soviet armies controlled the situation: in Manchuria and North Korea. The recent loss of northern Indochina only strengthens the case: victory came to the Communists when the Viet Minh Communist forces with techni-

From Rodger Swearingen, "A Decade of Soviet Policy in Asia, 1945–1956," *Current History*, Vol. XXXII, No. 186 (February 1957), pp. 89–96. Copyright 1957 by Current History, Inc. and used with their permission.

cal, logistic and organizational support from the Chinese Communist army were able to maneuver the French and the Vietnamese into an untenable position. This point must be balanced immediately by Undersecretary of State Walter Bedell Smith's wise observation following the Geneva Conference that "diplomacy has rarely gained at the conference table what cannot be gained or held on the battlefield."

Postwar Soviet Asian policy may be conveniently divided into four main periods. The first period, 1945 to 1947, was one of lingering wartime semi-cooperation and reconstruction. It extended from the Yalta Conference of February, 1945, to the formation of the Cominform in October, 1947. The second period, 1948 to 1949, was a militant, aggressive phase which followed the establishment of the Soviet Cominform in Eastern Europe and began to change in character with the establishment of the Chinese People's Republic in the fall of 1949 although the militancy persisted for a time. The third period, 1950 to 1953, represents the years of readjustment during which the Moscow-Peking axis became a reality with a number of implications for international Communist theory and tactics in Asia. The period extended roughly from the creation of the Chinese People's Republic to Stalin's death. The fourth and final period, 1953 to the present, may be characterized as one of "peaceful co-existence" and calculated cordiality.

Two very practical considerations, and two wrong assumptions appear to have substantially influenced Soviet Asian policy during the initial postwar period. The practical considerations were (1) the relative weakness of the Soviet power position and (2) Western domination of the Asian scene. On the first score, not only did the Soviets require time to recover from the serious economic effects of the war, but the basic Soviet economy in the important coal and steel area totaled only about one-half United States production while the United States enjoyed a monopoly of atomic weapons and a preponderance of air and naval power.

With respect to the second point, Western domination of Asia, the policy limitations inherent in the situation in Asia could hardly have escaped—and the record suggests did not escape—the Soviet leaders. The Pacific was a United States lake controlled by a powerful United States Navy and loaded with formidable United States airbases. United States influence and military forces in China were substantial. The British controlled India and Burma. The restoration of Western dominance in Southeast Asia, once Japan had been eliminated, seemed inevitable.

Against this background, the Soviets appear to have made two basic assumptions. Both proved wrong. They assumed that once the war was over, the capitalist United States would immediately drop any pretense of cooperation and revert to the Soviet conception of the standard capitalist-imperialist pattern, which would mean a forceful United States anti-Soviet policy in Asia. It may be argued that such a policy was, in fact, pursued by the United States —or more correctly by General MacArthur —in Japan and South Korea.

Early postwar American policy in China, however, does not seem to have been motivated by fears of the Soviet Union nor of Chinese communism, while the degree of official optimism in the United States in 1945 regarding the prospects for genuine cooperation with the Soviet Union in the postwar decade now appears considerably greater than the circumstances justified.

It is ironic that the Soviets, on theoretical or ideological grounds, should have judged United States wartime cooperation as an insincere deviation from the norm prompted by necessity while the United States, virtually ignoring Soviet theory and ideology, tended to take Soviet wartime semi-cooperation at face value, assuming that it would continue into the postwar era.

The Soviets appear to have made a second wrong assumption: every indication points to the fact that the Soviet leaders must have underestimated the strength and potential of the Chinese Communists and assumed that it would be some years before the Communists in China could expect significantly to influence the situation in Asia. If accepted, these realities and assumptions may explain the character of Soviet Asian policy during the early postwar years.

First Period, Lingering Wartime Cooperation, 1945–1947

When Churchill, Roosevelt and Stalin met at Yalta in February, 1945, for political and ideological reasons already suggested, the policy alternatives open to the Soviets in Asia must have seemed rather few, indeed. The Yalta Agreement of February 11, 1945, formed the basis of Soviet postwar Asian policy for almost five years. It stipulated that the Soviets would enter the war against Japan two or three months after Germany surrendered provided that (1) the status quo in Outer Mongolia (the Mongolian People's Republic) would be preserved, (2) the former rights of Russia violated by Japan's attack in 1904 would be restored—that is, Southern Sakhalin returned, the commercial port of Dairen internationalized under Soviet control, Port Arthur leased as a naval base, and the Chinese-Eastern Railroad and the South-Manchurian Railroad, providing the outlet to Dairen, jointly operated by a Soviet-Chinese company and (3) the Kurile Islands would be handed over to Russia.

A top secret record of the Roosevelt-Stalin Meeting of February 8, 1945, was released by the State Department a decade later. One or two points are amusing and suggestive. When the President advanced the idea of a 20-year trusteeship for Korea, Marshal Stalin replied, "The shorter the period the better," and then inquired whether any foreign troops would be stationed in Korea. "The President," we are told, "replied in the negative, to which Marshal Stalin expressed approval."

The President also said he had in mind a trusteeship for Indochina, noted that the French had done nothing to improve the natives since they had the colony, and stated that General de Gaulle had asked for ships to transport French forces to Indochina. Stalin then inquired where de Gaulle was going to get the troops. The President replied that de Gaulle said he was going to find the troops when the President could find the ships, but the President added that up to the present he had been unable to find the ships. At this point Stalin must have been really confused. What new, subtle game were the imperialists playing?

The Soviet Union entered the Pacific War on schedule two weeks before the surrender, breaking a five-year neutrality pact with Japan. Soviet forces swept over Manchuria, thereby both placing Moscow in a position to assist the Communists in China directly and assuring Soviet participation in the postwar peace settlements in Asia. About the same time, the Soviet Union concluded a treaty of friendship and alliance with the Nationalist Government of China.

No useful purpose would be served by attempting to review the complicated developments in China through 1947 even if space should permit. At least four elements of Soviet policy stand out: (1) The Soviets stripped Manchuria of more than two billion dollars worth of industrial equipment, suggesting possibly both the pressure of economic demands at home and the fact that Moscow policy-makers did not anticipate an early Communist victory in China; (2) The Soviets turned over or allowed to fall to Chinese Communist forces in the area millions of pieces of captured Japanese military equipment and weapons; (3) The Soviets maintained diplomatic relations with the Nationalist government and denied any ties with the Chinese Communists; (4) The Soviets set up an extensive indoctrination program for the thousands of Japanese prisoners of war captured in Manchuria.

Soviet military operations against the Japanese in Korea began on August 12, 1945, as, in effect, an extension of the Soviet offensive in Manchuria, based upon a purely military understanding that the Soviets would accept the surrender of Japanese forces north of the thirty-eighth parallel. Once the Soviet forces occupied the northern portion of the country, they refused permission for United States observers to enter Soviet territory, brought in a number of Soviet and Chinese Communist trained Koreans to help organize the politics and economy of the area and immediately began to build a "Korean people's army" as the first steps towards incorporation of the area into the Soviet bloc. All agreements, so-called negotiations on Korea, and Soviet statements in the United Nations and elsewhere strike one as rather meaningless in view of this observable, unchanging Soviet policy.

With respect to Japan, the initial Soviet effort was, of course, directed toward obtaining as great a share as possible in the postwar control of the country. At a meeting with Harry Hopkins on May 29, 1945, Stalin said that he expected that the Soviet Union would share in the actual occupation. When the United States refused to accept such a proposal, the Soviets next demanded a direct role in the policy-making function and running of the occupation. This too was overruled, and the Soviets settled for a lesser, advisory role. As it turned out, the occupation of Japan from the outset was essentially an American venture with General Douglas MacArthur calling the tune and tolerating little interference from Moscow or from Washington, for that matter.

Perhaps because of problems at home, involvements elsewhere, especially in Eastern Europe, and the distance from the area, the Soviet Union displayed little direct interest in South and Southeast Asia during the initial postwar period. In the absence of any degree of Soviet initiative, Communist policy in the immediate postwar years continued to reflect the wartime pattern of cooperation, essentially the old Comintern, 1935, united front line. This strategy regarded imperialism and feudalism as the Communist's main enemies.

Accordingly, a two-stage revolution was prescribed which called first for a bourgeois-democratic revolution to prepare the ground for the subsequent proletarian-social revolution. In India, Burma, Thailand, Indochina, the East Indies and the Philippines for the first several postwar years, independent Communist activity was played down. Communists, a number of them Moscow-trained, cooperated with nationalist movements and sought to maneuver themselves into key positions in the new governments, national parties, labor unions and student groups.

Second Period, Militant Phase,
1948 and After

With the formation of the Cominform in October, 1947, Soviet world policy took a firm and aggressive turn. These were the years of Communist attacks on American planes, the Soviet coup in Czechoslovakia, the Berlin airlift. Before long the new militant line became evident also in Asia.

In China, as elsewhere, toward the end of 1947, Soviet policy and propaganda became increasingly anti-American in character. The Soviet press began to speak of the traditionally aggressive nature of American Far Eastern policy, harking back to the 1844 treaty with China and Perry's expedition to Japan and pointing accusingly to the annexation of Hawaii and the Philippines. A statement by Mao Tse-tung on December 25, 1947, spoke of the Soviet Union in glowing terms and contained a vicious attack on the United States as being primarily responsible for the continuation of the Chinese civil war.

As the military and economic position of the Chinese Nationalist government deteriorated during 1948, the Soviet government nevertheless maintained official relations with that government while Soviet propaganda continued to reflect surprising restraint. In a speech on the thirty-first anniversary of the Russian Revolution, Molotov referred to the growth of the "liberation movements" in Asia but made no mention of the Chinese Communist successes. Even after the capture of Peking by the Communists on January 31, 1949, Moscow continued to maintain diplomatic relations with the Chinese Nationalist Government.

The Soviet Union was, in fact, the only nation to send its ambassador south with the Chinese government after it had been forced to retire to Canton. At the same time, the Soviets officially closed their consulates in the Communist-occupied territory, though the staffs are known to have remained active in the area. Soviet negotiations with the Chinese Nationalist Government on economic matters, notably with regard to Sinkiang, appear to have continued right up to the very end.

The Soviet government maintained diplomatic relations with the Chinese Nationalist Government through the spring of 1949 when the Soviet Ambassador, Roshchin, went to Moscow for consultations. He did not return, and the Soviets, of course, recognized the new Government of the Chinese People's Republic immediately upon its establishment, September 30, 1949.

Why did the Soviet Union pursue in China what on the surface appears to be such a contradictory policy, that of continuing to maintain diplomatic relations with the Nationalist Government, long after it became clear that the Communists were winning? The answer is probably that even in retrospect and viewed objectively the policy pursued by the Soviets in postwar China was the best alternative available to them. Any other policy would have denied the Soviets access to Nationalist-controlled areas, thereby removing an important intelligence and propaganda potential. It would have ended negotiations with the Nationalists where the Soviets apparently hoped to squeeze all they could out of the situation, and it certainly would have opened the Soviets to the charge of interfering in the internal affairs of China. The avoidance of this latter charge and possible reaction it could evoke from the United States appears to have been one of the keystones of initial postwar Soviet China policy.

The Soviets failed to unite Korea on their terms, but developed a trained force of some 200,000 North Korean troops in contrast to about 50,000 ill-equipped police in the South. Then they launched their new independence and anti-American campaign by declaring in September, 1947, that if the Americans agreed that all foreign troops should be withdrawn at the beginning of 1948, the Soviets would agree also. When further negotiations broke down, the division into two Koreas was, in effect, crystallized by the formation through the good offices of the United Nations of a Republic of Korea, with its capital in Seoul, and the creation by the Soviets of a "Korean Democratic People's Republic" with headquarters in Pyongyang. Both Korean governments applied unsuccessfully in February, 1949, for admission to the United Nations. Following the Soviet lead, the United States, despite opposition from the South Korean Government, completed the withdrawal of occupation forces during the first half of 1949, leaving a military mission of 500 men to assist in organizing the country's defense forces. The stage was set for the North Korean attack.

With respect to Japan, as has been suggested, there was little the Soviets could do directly. The situation was controlled by the United States. The principal Soviet objective remained to bring an end to the

American occupation and to increase pro-Soviet and Communist sentiment in Japan. The principal organization mobilized for this purpose was, of course, the Communist Party of Japan. Under these circumstances, the Soviet shift to a more aggressive policy in 1948 had somewhat less effect on Soviet Japanese policy than, let us say, policy in South and Southeast Asia.

More active Soviet interest in South and Southeast Asia was first evidenced towards the end of 1947 in a speech by Zhdanov at the opening conference of the Cominform, in which he called for Communist support for the national liberation movements. This was followed by an article by Zhukov in *Bolshevik* emphasizing the same theme. Mao Tse-tung, after praising the purposes and power of the Soviet bloc, asserting that "the superiority is already with us," and noting the significance of developments in Europe, told the Central Committee of the Communist Party of China at the end of 1947: "All anti-imperialist forces of the various eastern countries should now unite to oppose the oppression of imperialism and the reactionaries within each country, taking as the objective of their struggle the liberation of the more than a billion oppressed peoples of the East." The new Soviet policy was discussed at the Communist-sponsored Calcutta Youth Congress in February 1948, and the following month the new aggressive line was confirmed by the Second Congress of the Communist Party of India.

The Moscow "Left" aggressive strategy considers capitalism and the native bourgeoisie enemies at least as important as imperialism and feudalism. Accordingly, the concept of the need for a bourgeois-democratic revolution was dropped in favor of an early socialist revolution, a "united front from below," direct action.

Throughout South and Southeast Asia, Communists abandoned their earlier practice of cooperation with the non-Communist Left; leaders of the nationalist parties were denounced as traitors to their followers and within six months of the announced change, terrorism and insurrections began or were intensified in India, Pakistan, Burma, Malaya, Indonesia, Indochina and the Philippines.

Third Period: Adjustment to the New Dimension, 1950–1953

Moscow was clearly impressed and possibly even surprised by the swiftness of the Communist victory in China. The emergence in Asia of a second Communist power-center with a population of more than 550 million added a new dimension to Soviet foreign policy and must have raised all sorts of questions in Moscow as it did in the West.

Both in terms of power politics and ideology, reappraisal and reallocation of roles and missions seemed in order. Power-wise, the Soviet position in Asia was vastly superior to that enjoyed by Moscow at the end of the Pacific war. While the United States forces had been dismantled during the first five postwar years, the Soviets had used the time to build. By 1950, the Soviet Union is thought to have had air, submarine and troop superiority in the Far East—a combination which at the time publicly worried the United States Navy. Moreover, whatever decisive superiority may have been implicit in the United States' early monopoly of the atomic bomb began to evaporate when the Soviets exploded a nuclear device in 1949, several years ahead of responsible Western estimates.

In China, Nationalist forces had disintegrated and retreated to Formosa, while the Chinese Communist armies were gaining in strength and confidence almost daily. Peking was, of course, dependent on Moscow in the economic and military fields. The Soviet build up was continuing in North Korea. The decision to attack South Korea is presumed to have been made during the Mao-Stalin talks in Moscow in January and February of 1950 after apparently deciding that neither forces in being nor Western policy were strong enough to prevent a cheap and quick Communist military victory.

Significant changes related to foreign policy also characterized the ideological front—especially with respect to the employment of ideology as a tactical weapon in Asia. Maoism appears to have been authorized by Moscow for colonial areas and for all of the Asian Communist Parties. The end of violence and a shift to peaceful Maoism occurred in India, Burma, Pakistan, Ceylon and Indonesia during 1951. In Indochina, Malaya and the Philippines, the Maoist armed struggle strategy was still employed as late as 1952 when in the latter two cases observers began to note decreasing militant activity and increasing propaganda for peace, though the anti-American campaign remained a dominant theme.

While Moscow was thus able to challenge the West throughout Asia virtually on its own terms without risking a single Soviet soldier, there was always the possibility that the exuberant Chinese Communists might go too far and plunge the world into war. After all, the defense of Communist China was tied to the Soviet Union by the treaties of 1950 which singled out Japan, and, by implication, the United States.

Stalin must have been aware of the dilemma. This would explain the Malik hint in 1951 that the Communists were ready to call off the Korean war. By that time, it will be recalled, the United Nations were going over to the offensive in Korea and United States military leaders and Congress were becoming increasingly impatient with the indecisive situation. There was, in short, the real possibility that the war might be expanded to Manchuria. The Soviets in such a case might have been forced to choose, in effect, between abandoning their Chinese allies and war with the United States.

The emergence of the Moscow-Peking axis did not immediately affect basic Soviet policy toward Japan, although the Japanese Communist Party was encouraged to take a more positive position in support of the Korean war with riots, sabotage and militant activity. The role of Peking in Communist policy and propaganda towards Japan soon became increasingly conspicuous.

Basic Soviet policy towards Japan was rather clearly set forth at the time of the San Francisco Peace Treaty Conference, when the Soviets demanded in substance:

1. Confirmation of the Cairo, Yalta and Potsdam agreements, especially that Japan give up permanently to the Soviet Union claim to Sakhalin and the Kurile Islands.

2. Formosa to go to Communist China.

3. United States troops to be withdrawn from Japan within 90 days.

4. Signatory powers to the treaty to include the Chinese People's Republic and the Mongolian People's Republic.

5. Removal of obstacles to the strengthening of "democratic tendencies" among the Japanese people.

6. Prohibition against Japan's entering into any coalitions or military alliances directed against any of the Powers which had taken part in the war against her.

7. Strict limitations of armed forces and prohibition against the manufacturing or possession of atomic bombs and a wide range of conventional heavy weapons.

8. The straits around the Japanese islands to be demilitarized and open only to the naval vessels belonging to Powers adjacent to the Sea of Japan, namely, Japan, the Soviet Union, Communist China and Korea.

It may be noted that during the ensuing four years the Soviet Union did not reestablish diplomatic relations with Japan nor retreat from this very firm position despite a propaganda policy which emphasized peace and cooperation.

Fourth Period: Co-existence, Collective Peace, 1953–1956

The period since Stalin's death has witnessed a mellowing of Soviet behavior and propaganda though not, as has been suggested, any apparent change in Soviet objectives or, for that matter, any fundamental concessions on major policy questions. The Geneva spirit has its limitations. We seem to be back essentially where we started, in the 1945–1947 era of semi-cooperation and popular front tactics with one obvious difference: the emergence of a Communist China and the consolidation of the Moscow-Peking axis places an additional effective foreign policy weapon in Soviet hands.

Current Soviet foreign policy objectives in Asia may be characterized as (1) strengthening of the Moscow-Peking axis, (2) removal of United States influence and power, military bases and regional security groupings, (3) neutralization of the area, particularly the key countries of Japan and India, and (4) destruction of the Western alliance and, where it still exists, of Western unity. There is no reason to assume that the long-range goal of Soviet domination has changed.

On Japan, Soviet policy remains firm though the propaganda line has been altered in the direction of reasonableness, less emphasis on the negative, anti-American theme, more emphasis on the positive themes of peace and the need to regularize relations with the Soviet Union and with Communist China. Negotiations between Tokyo and Moscow looking toward the reestablishment of diplomatic relations between the two nations, which opened in London in June, 1955, were concluded in Moscow in October, 1956, after Prime Minister Hatoyama had, in effect, made concessions on virtually every point.

With respect to Korea, Soviet policy since Stalin has likewise been to stand pat, to build up North Korea (in direct violation of the provisions of the armistice agreements) and to wait for and to encourage the disintegration of the present regime in the South or its abandonment by the United States while at the same time apparently permitting North Korea to remain in the Chinese sphere of influence and interest.

Likewise, the questions of the status of Formosa and the offshore islands and a seat for Communist China in the United Nations have been handled more gently by the Soviets and the Chinese Communists since the important Afro-Asian Conference at Bandung, Indonesia, in 1955. The new line is to rally supporters for the Soviet position by a show of reasonableness. In Asia, especially, the Communist collective peace campaign contrasts sharply—as is no doubt the intention—with the United States program of military bases and collective security.

Northern Indochina was added to the Moscow-Peking bloc in the summer of 1954. Since that time it has been clear that despite protestations of peaceful intentions, the Communists are only biding time, looking toward the eventual acquisition of South Vietnam, Laos and Cambodia. It is, in fact, there in South and Southeast Asia that the three related recent developments in the Communist sphere are producing the most significant alterations in Soviet Asian policy. The developments are: (1) The growing power, prestige and initiative of the Axis' junior partner, Communist China; (2) The downgrading of Stalin, and (3) The Soviet economic offensive.

The exact division of labor between Moscow and Peking in the foreign relations area is not clear. Peking appears to be increasing the scope of its activities, particularly in the political and cultural realms. Asian Communist Party relations now seem to be handled largely through Peking. Military and strategic questions which might involve the Soviet Union directly appear to be another matter. Some observers saw in the revised Soviet-Chinese Communist agreements of 1954 a weakening of the Moscow-Peking axis.

Dr. Philip Mosely of the Council on Foreign Relations wisely cautions against attributing too much autonomy to Peking: "Those who believe that the Moscow and Peking centers can be separated from each other," he said recently, "must first prove that each of the centers would judge itself better able, in separation or even in conflict with each other, to achieve its own goals." There is, of course, a wide area of agreement between Moscow and Peking foreign policy goals in Asia and they share a similar, Marxist view of mankind and of the world.

Whatever hope Peking may entertain of building the strong economic foundation of a new empire in Asia clearly depends, for the time being, on assistance from the Soviet Union. Economically and militarily, Peking needs Moscow. Politically and militarily, Moscow must find it convenient to have an Asian ally to argue the Soviet position or fight the Soviet battle in the East.

The renunciation of Stalin and the Soviet economic offensive, now under way on a large scale, may be viewed as two sides of the same coin. Bulganin and Khrushchev are saying to Nasser and Nehru and to others in the Afro-Asian area, "We will help you build your countries, no strings attached. And if there were risks in the past in dealing with the Communists, they are gone—with Stalin." Communist China supports this Soviet Asian policy with the appealing themes of Asia for the Asians, co-existence, trade, and collective peace.

And if you ask, but what has really changed—the basic Soviet position on disarmament, the refusal to unify or to hold free elections in Eastern Germany and North Korea, the enslavement of Eastern Europe, the totalitarian character of the regimes and systems in Russia and China? The answer is that on fundamentals the Soviets have not changed. But the argument is irrelevant—many Asians are impressed!

THE NEW STRATEGY OF INTERNATIONAL COMMUNISM

JOHN KAUTSKY

Theories about Soviet foreign policy, whether soundly-based upon empirical evidence or produced by free-flying excursions into the realm of abstract reason, are essential tools for our study. Some collapse under the first critical examination, while others stand for decades; but even the poorest theories may perform a useful catalytic function by forcing men who disagree to construct new, more acceptable theories. By considering the problem from many sides and examining all possible interpretations of the available evidence, we gain an understanding of the multitude of issues and forces involved and the nature of their interplay in the formation of policy. Here, John Kautsky, author of *Moscow and the Communist Party of India,* presents his theory about recent Soviet policy[A new communist strategy, he believes, was developed by Mao Tse-tung during the war years, in the struggle to win China; it was then taken over by Soviet policymakers, who have made it the principal strategy of international communism (i.e., Soviet foreign policy) around the world] To say the least, Kautsky's theory is provocative, intelligently developed, and quite revolutionary in some of its conclusions.

COMMUNIST international organizations and Communist parties the world over tend to follow a single strategy, which is always determined primarily by the needs of Soviet foreign policy paramount at the time. Corresponding to the requirements of the Soviet Union's "cold war" against the United States, a new strategy has gradually been adopted by international communism since 1947. Often non-Communist observers and sometimes even the Communists themselves seem unaware of the novelty of this strategy and they frequently obscure it by the use of terms more descriptive of older strategies, such as "united front" and "popular front." It is the purpose of this essay to distinguish sharply between the various Communist strategies with a view to clarifying the characteristic features of the new strategy. It would, of course, be both easy and tempting to document and enliven such an attempt with innumerable examples from history and quotations from Communist literature. However, it would go beyond the intended scope of this brief analysis to do more than draw the broadest generalizations from the record of thirty-five years of international communism.[1]

The central problem of Communist strategy has always been to determine who is, at any time, to be considered the principal enemy and consequently what classes should be accepted as allies of communism and what type of alliance should be entered into with them. These three factors, and especially the latter two, furnish the crucial distinctions between different Communist strategies. Two alternative solutions of this problem formed the bases of the two strategies followed by international communism

[1] It may also be noted that to a large extent Communist terminology is used in the following discussion of the distinguishing characteristics of the various Communist strategies, since it is both derived from and intended to be applied to the analysis of Communist writings. It must be remembered that, though quotation marks will be omitted for the sake of simplicity, the meaning to be attached to such terms as imperialism, feudalism, bourgeoisie, socialism, or national liberation is that given to them by the Communists.

From John H. Kautsky, "The New Strategy of International Communism." *The American Political Science Review*, Vol. XLIX, No. 2 (June 1955), pp. 478–486. By permission of The American Political Science Association.

during its first thirty years as an organized movement. In the Communists' own terminology, we may refer to them here simply as the "left" and the "right" strategies. The "left" strategy, which can perhaps be called the classical strategy of communism and is often erroneously thought to be still in effect, considered capitalism as its main enemy. Even in underdeveloped areas, the native bourgeoisie was looked upon as an enemy on a par with foreign imperialism and native feudalism, i.e., the landlords and the nobility. This strategy envisaged the socialist revolution as its immediate goal. Even in societies which, according to the Marxian schema of historical stages, had not yet traversed the capitalist stage, the next revolution was presumed to lay the basis for socialism and to merge with or even skip some of the phases of the so-called bourgeois-democratic revolution.

This "left" strategy was an attempt to form a "united front from below." It was based on appeals to workers and also poor peasants and petty bourgeois elements, both as individuals and in local organizations affiliated with socialist or "bourgeois" parties, or in the underdeveloped countries, the so-called bourgeois-nationalist movements. The appeals were designed to induce the rank and file to leave these parties and to join the Communists, either directly or by cooperating with them in "united action." Such appeals were therefore always coupled with violent denunciations of the top leaders of the other parties as servants of the bourgeoisie and of imperialism and as traitors to the interests of their rank-and-file followers. Similar tactics were followed in the trade union field in pursuance of this "left" strategy.

The "right" strategy of communism, on the other hand, regarded as its main enemy not capitalism as such but fascism and similar movements and, in underdeveloped areas, feudalism and foreign imperialism. The professed immediate aim of this strategy was the establishment or defense of democracy or national liberation, to which social revolution had to be subordinated. It therefore looked forward to a revolution in two stages: first a bourgeois-democratic revolution directed against fascism or imperialism and feudalism, followed later by a proletarian-socialist revolution directed against the bourgeoisie and capitalism, with the Communists participating in the first as well as in the second.

Not being anti-capitalist, the "right" strategy called for an alliance of the Communist party with other parties, which were recognized as anti-fascist or anti-imperialist and anti-feudal and which might include both labor and bourgeois parties.[2] Its most important characteristic, which easily distinguished the "right' strategy from the other Communist strategies, was thus that it involved a united front "from above," a "top alliance" with other parties arrived at in agreement with their national party leadership. Similar alliances or even mergers of Communist trade unions with socialist and nationalist trade unions were also advocated as part of this policy.

It is clear then that the "left" and "right" strategies were designed for diametrically opposite objectives: the united front from below was intended to weaken and split the very groups with which the Communists sought to enter an alliance when they were committed to a united front from above. The unfortunate fact that the Communists referred to both of these strategies as "united front" policies has given

[2] The "popular front" was broad enough to embrace both of these, while the "united front from above," in the narrower sense of this term, was an alliance of the Communist party only with a labor or socialist party. In practice this distinction is not too important, for the really difficult decision for Communists was to ally themselves with any strong party and particularly with their most hated enemies, the democratic socialists. Since these latter are, in any case, regarded as lackeys of the bourgeoisie, once this decision was made, it was easy and usual to extend the alliance to at least some left-wing bourgeois parties. We may therefore overlook the distinction here and refer to both the popular front and the united front from above by the latter term.

rise to much confusion and can obscure shifts from one to the other. The fact is all too often overlooked that, in a sense, Communists always follow a united front policy. To state no more than this, as is frequently done, without distinguishing between the united fronts from above and below, is merely to inform us that they, like all political parties, seek to increase their strength.

Different as the two strategies were, it must be emphasized that under both of them the Communist party insisted that it was a proletarian party, representing the interests of the workers and of the poor peasantry and petty bourgeoisie, but not those of the capitalists. It remained basically anti-bourgeois even when it entered into alliances with certain bourgeois parties and groups in a united front from above.

Until after the Second World War, the "left" and the "right" strategies were essentially the only ones pursued by international Communism. Both found application during the early 1920's. Then the "left" strategy was followed throughout the late twenties and early thirties. It was replaced about 1935 by the "right" strategy, which remained in use until 1947, interrupted only by a return to the "left" strategy during the period between the conclusion of the Stalin-Hitler Pact in August 1939 and the Nazi invasion of Russia in June 1941. During the war, however, the Chinese Communists under the leadership of Mao Tse-tung developed a strategy which is fundamentally different from the two traditional ones, though it combines certain of their features.

As it has since come to be applied by international communism, this new strategy, like the "right" one, singles out foreign imperialism and, where applicable, feudalism, as its main enemy. Also like the "right" strategy, therefore, it expects the revolution to take place in two stages: first as an anti-imperialist struggle for national independence or an anti-feudal bourgeois-democratic revolution, and only later as a socialist revolution. The range of forces to be united under Communist leadership, consequently, also corresponds to that grouped in the united front from above and particularly the popular front embracing the so-called "bloc of four classes," i.e., the proletariat, the peasantry, the petty bourgeoisie, and the anti-imperialist sections of the bourgeoisie. To some extent, this union is to be attained by the methods of the united front from above, i.e., by a "top" alliance with other parties, but these are generally parties weaker than the Communist party and frequently fronts set up by the Communists. Principally the new strategy follows the method of the united front from below of the "left" strategy. The large parties, which more or less actually represent the classes to be united and with which the Communists would be allied in a united front from above under the "right" strategy (e.g., the socialist, liberal, and Christian-Democratic parties in the West and the nationalist parties, like the Kuomintang and the Indian Congress, and the socialists in the underdeveloped areas) are denounced as traitors to the interests of these classes and as servants of foreign imperialism. The same policy is applied by the Communist trade unions.

The Communist party (alone or in conjunction with its "united front" of subsidiary and front-parties) now claims to represent the interests of the entire peasantry and the anti-imperialist capitalists, as well as those of the proletariat, the poor peasantry, and the petty bourgeoisie. Having confined their appeal under both traditional strategies to these latter three "exploited" groups, the Communists were able to attract sections of these groups only through the united front from below. However—and this is crucial—they could seek the support also of sections of the bourgeoisie and of the entire peasantry only through the united front from above. It is because of the radical innovation of appealing directly to the interests of all four classes that the new strategy can apply the method of the united front from below to a range of groups so wide that it could formerly be encompassed only in the united front from above.

We need not be concerned with the theoretics according to which the bourgeoisie is divided into a pro-imperialist and an anti-imperialist wing.[3] What matters is merely that the dividing line between the friends and enemies of the Communist party is now drawn not short of the bourgeoisie but bisecting it. In practice, of course, the division is made not so much along economic or sociological lines, as is implied by the terms used to describe the two sections, but along political lines. Those business men who, for whatever reasons, are willing or likely to be willing to follow the lead of the Communist party are considered anti-imperialist capitalists. Those who are and are likely to remain opposed to the Communists, even if they have no ties with foreign interests and have only small businesses, are condemned as allies and servants of imperialism. Just as the working class is frequently made synonymous with the Communist party, so here too the Marxist materialist conception of history is turned upside down; class affiliation is deduced from ideology rather than vice versa.

As the new strategy was developed in China by Mao Tse-tung and more recently in some countries of Southeast Asia, its most important characteristics appeared to be not the appeal "from below" to the bourgeoisie, but reliance on the peasantry rather than the industrial working class as a mass base in the struggle for power and resort to guerrilla warfare. This has tended to obscure the fact that it is, fundamentally, the essentials of this new strategy that are being applied by international communism throughout the non-Communist world to-day. Actually, neither of the two specifically Chinese features is an essential characteristic of the new strategy. In China, the peasants were the Communist party's main target; elsewhere other groups can be substituted, as has been the case not only in the West, but also in Japan and to some extent even in India. On the other hand, some reliance on the peasantry is not a new Communist policy. In practically none of the underdeveloped countries have the Communists in any real sense of the word been a working-class party. Rather they have been largely intellectuals seeking a popular base where they could find it. In this search, even under the old "right" and "left" strategies they have never looked exclusively to the industrial working class (which in its Marxian sense of an urban stratum cut off from its rural moorings has, at least until recently, been virtually non-existent in most underdeveloped countries). Instead, they have also sought out the petty bourgeoisie and at least some sections of the peasantry who can easily be characterized as exploited classes in underdeveloped countries. They have attempted to conceal this fact, just as Maoism has in China, by speaking of working-class hegemony, which always means their own hegemony. In other words, they substituted themselves for the working class by a process of mental transposition.

Similarly, the use of armed force is neither characteristic of the new strategy alone nor does it necessarily accompany that strategy. Obviously important as it is, the use or absence of violent methods does not constitute the basic distinction among Communist strategies, which is rather, as we have seen, to be found in the extent and type of alliances made by the Commu-

---

[3] The terminology used in Communist literature to describe the various sections of the bourgeoisie is not always consistent. Those capitalists who are only slightly or not at all tied to imperialism and can thus help form the "bloc of four classes" are generally called the "national," "medium," "middle," or "liberal" capitalists or bourgeoisie (although the term "national" may also be used simply as a synonym for "native"), while that section of the bourgeoisie which is regarded as a firm ally of imperialism is referred to variously as "comprador," "bureaucratic," "big," or "monopolistic."

nists with non-Communist elements.[4] Attempts to identify one or the other of the three strategies with a "hard" or "soft" line, though frequently made, are therefore misleading. Thus it is often implied that the "right" strategy is necessarily coupled with a "soft" line. It is, of course, true that under many circumstances an alliance between the Communist party and labor and bourgeois parties is inconceivable where the Communist party engages in violent activities. But in other circumstances its allies too may be engaged in or approve of such activities as, for example, during the Spanish Civil War, the wartime resistance in Western Europe, or colonial revolts against the mother country. On the other hand, the "left" strategy, while easily adaptable to armed violence, need not necessarily employ that tactic. Thus it was, with certain exceptions, used peacefully in Western Europe before 1935. Finally the new strategy too, though developed in conjunction with guerrilla warfare, can also be combined with a "soft" line, as is illustrated by the present tactics of the Communists not only in Western Europe and Latin America, but also in India and Indonesia. Each of the three strategies can be applied in a violent or a peaceful manner. The use of armed force is a matter not of strategy but of tactics, which can be changed according to conditions while the strategy remains unchanged; it can even be in effect in some parts of a country while peaceful methods are applied in others at the same time.

The essential characteristic of the new strategy, which distinguishes it from both its "left" and its "right" predecessors, is its direct appeal "from below" (i.e., not through bourgeois parties) to the bourgeoisie. This appeal is made quite openly; it is defended on theoretical grounds and is expressed in propaganda emphasizing the interests held in common by workers and capitalists as against the foreign imperialists. Unlike reliance on the peasantry or on armed force, it is startlingly new to Communists. The proposition that the Communist party, the party of the exploited toilers, represents also the interests of the capitalists, who are, by Marxian definition, the exploiters, that the two classes between which the class struggle is supposed to be raging can be united in the Communist party, is hardly traditional Communist doctrine. It can, however, be considered an extraordinary but logical extension of "proletarian internationalism," i.e., the identification of the interests of the proletariat everywhere with those of the Soviet Union: the party of the proletariat is to unite all classes, regardless of their class interests, provided they are opposed to imperialism, meaning the United States. In short, the class struggle has been replaced by the cold war.

Indeed, if the "left" strategy was the strategy of anti-capitalism and the "right" strategy that of anti-fascism, the new strategy is the strategy of anti-Americanism. Before 1947 the new strategy as it had been developed in China was of little interest to Moscow and probably was hardly known there. With the beginning of the cold war, however, the "right" strategy of cooperation with the principal bourgeois and labor parties and with the governments formed by them was given up, since these were generally pro-American. During the following years, which also saw the rise to prominence of the Chinese Communists and their strategy in the world of international communism, there was some difference of opinion in Moscow and in some Communist

---

[4] A simple and perhaps oversimplified test to determine which of the three strategies the Communists pursue at any one time consists of the following one or two questions: Are the Communists making a serious attempt to form an alliance with the top leadership of the socialist party? If the answer is yes, they are following the "right" strategy; if it is no, a second question must be asked: Are there any capitalists among the groups to whose interests the Communists are appealing? If the answer to this question is no, they are following the "left" strategy; if it is yes, they are adhering to the new strategy.

parties as to whether the "left" or the new strategy was to replace the discarded "right" one. It soon became clear, however, that the "left" alternative, by regarding capitalism as an enemy, unduly limited the range of the Communists' potential supporters to the so-called exploited classes— the workers, the poor peasantry and some petty-bourgeois elements—while in Moscow's eyes there was no reason, except the negligible one of Marxist theory, why exploiters too should not be mobilized on its side against the United States. The "left" strategy, though traditionally "internationalist," even entailed the serious danger that each Communist party would concentrate on the bourgeoisie in its own country as its main enemy rather than on Moscow's chief opponent, the United States, thus, from the Soviet point of view, "fighting the wrong war against the wrong enemy at the wrong time."

The new strategy, on the other hand, is admirably suited to the needs of Soviet foreign policy. Under it the Communists frankly invite the cooperation of "all classes, parties, groups, organizations, and individuals," including capitalists and even feudal elements, the sole test of their eligibility being friendliness to the Soviet Union and antagonism to the United States. Thus this strategy, like the "left" and "right" ones in earlier periods, has gradually been adopted by international communism throughout the non-Communist world. It is obvious that this is true in Asia, where the Communist parties have been urged by both Peking and Moscow to take the "Chinese path," in some countries in its violent, in others in its peaceful form. It is also the case in the other underdeveloped areas and particularly in Latin America, where the Communists openly employ the strategy

of the bloc of four classes, including the "national bourgeoisie." However, since the Communists depict even the countries of Western Europe as colonial spoil of "American imperialism," a strategy containing the essential elements of the new strategy has come to be applied in these countries too. This is clear from the Communist parties' concentration on the United States rather than capitalism as their main enemy and their call "from below" for cooperation with all elements, regardless of class, coupled with attacks on the governments and leading parties who would be their allies in the united front "from above" of the "right" strategy. The so-called "peace" movement with its anti-American appeal to all classes, the emphasis in Communist propaganda on the injury done by "American imperialism" to the national economy and the interests of labor and capital alike, and the outright attempts to attract capitalists by vistas of East-West trade, notably expressed by the Moscow Economic Conference of 1952, are all manifestations of the new strategy in evidence as much in the West as in the underdeveloped areas.

That the new strategy of communism involves a radical departure from Marxism is obvious and has already been indicated. It is, however, only a logical development of Leninism. The doctrines of Mao Tsetung, even better than Lenin's prototype, serve to elucidate the implications of Leninism. To Marx and Engels the working class itself was the revolutionary agent, as it was matured by the inevitable historical and social development. The party, along with the trade unions, was conceived to be only a tool of the class in its class struggle and it could not, therefore, any more than the unions, rely on elements which, by Marxian definition, were the enemies of the workers.

---

[5] While, as we mentioned, the approach of the new strategy to other parties is generally one "from below" (i.e., antagonistic), this can, in conformity with the dominant anti-American motive behind the strategy, be changed to one "from above," where a party becomes sufficiently anti-American and pro-Soviet, as has happened in Indonesia and under the Arbenz regime in Guatemala, thus constituting a return to the "right" strategy in relation to that party. The Communist party's direct appeal to the bourgeoisie, however, is likely to continue in any case.

Lenin, however, took the crucial step of divorcing the party from the class, shifting the emphasis from the latter to the former as the agent of an essentially no longer inevitable historical development, and in effect making the working class the tool of the party. Once this step was taken, there was no longer any reason why some other class could not also become the tool of the party. This can be the peasantry, as it was in China and to some extent in Russia, but it can even be the capitalists, as is now possible under the new strategy. From the Marxist emphasis on the working class we have, via Lenin's reliance on the party, now arrived at a party, independent of all classes and representing none, seeking a base for the realization of its own ambitions in any class where it can find support. The end of Marx's party—the class struggle—has been abandoned for the means—the party in its quest for power.

Improved Manners and "Peaceful Coexistence" 1953–1956

POST-STALIN POLICY IN WESTERN EUROPE

ROBERT F. BYRNES

Professor Byrnes is Chairman of the Department of History and Director of the Russian and East European Institute at Indiana University. He has taught at Rutgers and Columbia Universities, at Swarthmore College, and has written and edited numerous valuable works on French and Russian history and the Soviet Union's European satellites. Here he presents a thoughtful analysis of the many alarms and excursions that occurred in Soviet foreign policy between Stalin's death (March 5, 1953) and late 1955. The domestic turbulence of these years was reflected in the Communists' foreign policy; violent, frequent, but superficial changes made it extremely difficult for observers to discern the more fundamental and subtle changes. Professor Byrnes clearly identifies the important developments and evaluates their significance.

STALIN'S successors inherited a policy which was global and which reflected Stalin's personal ambitions, the accumulated baggage of Russian history and of the Marxist-Leninist-Stalinist philosophy, domestic problems and pressures, and critical situations around the world, such as stalled armistice negotiations in Korea, a new administration in Washington which talked of liberation, and a divided France wrestling with the problems posed by Western German economic recovery and with plans for bringing Western Germany into the Western community. Both Stalin and his successors considered Western Europe their primary political target, but they defined Soviet policy toward this crucial area with other world problems in mind. Moreover, Stalin's successors must have been at least as impressed as some Western observers by the magnitude of the succession problem and by the growing demands of the new Soviet élite.

STAGES OF SOVIET POLICY

The history of Soviet foreign policy has been marked by extraordinary tactical switches, most notably by the sudden reversal in policy toward Nazi Germany in August 1939. This history and the great vacuum left by the charismatic Stalin have naturally increased the attentiveness with which Western observers have searched for

From Robert F. Byrnes, "Soviet Policy Toward Western Europe Since Stalin," *The Annals of The American Academy of Political and Social Science*, CCCIII (January 1956), pp. 166–178. By permission of The American Academy of Political and Social Science.

sharp changes. Fundamentally, there has been no great change in Soviet policy toward Western Europe since Stalin's death. There has been little change in Soviet tactics, although the apparent variations have been numerous and sometimes spectacular. However, in its general emphasis, Soviet policy toward Western Europe has increasingly favored the carrot more and the stick less. In addition, the general line has been softer, subtler, and more persuasive than it was under Stalin.

During the twenty-three months in which Malenkov was Premier, there were no concessions to the West, although the tone of the Soviet Union was more mild than it had been under Stalin. The Korean armistice negotiations were finally concluded on July 27, 1953, reducing the divisive issues affecting relations between the United States and its European allies, but these conflicts were soon replaced by problems deriving from Indochina and Formosa. The Berlin and Geneva conferences early in 1954 demonstrated that Molotov still deserved his reputation and his nickname.

With the demotion of Malenkov, in February 1955, some Western observers, who had been impressed by his apparent reasonableness and occasional civilities, feared that the "final" opportunity to negotiate with the Soviet Union had been lost. However, the regime led by Khrushchev and Bulganin has maintained the principal lines of Soviet foreign policy as well as the little amenities. The most coarse anti-American propaganda has disappeared, and Soviet policy toward the West has been more flexible, moderate, and skillful. The Soviet Union in the spring of 1955 finally accepted the Austrian State Treaty, and the Soviet leaders in June 1955 made a sensational pilgrimage to a Yugoslav Canossa to admit error in past Soviet policy toward Tito. At the Geneva conference, in July 1955, they exuded friendliness and good fellowship in a meeting designed to take advantage of and to extend the new "atmosphere" so that negotiations on the basic issues might be undertaken in a friendly spirit. In September 1955, after a Soviet initiative, diplomatic relations were opened between Moscow and Bonn, which the Russians had previously denounced as a Nazi stooge of the United States.

The recent changes do emphasize the eternal problem: Is there now a genuine shift in Soviet policy toward Western Europe? Do the recent reversals on details conceal a genuine change on matters of substance or are they merely skillful tactical maneuvers? Are we at least witnessing a gradual trend which will ultimately produce a basic modification? Available evidence suggests that there has been no basic change in Soviet policy or goals, although the tactics used are now different. The Soviet rulers are simply adjusting to life without Stalin and to a new phase in post-war relations, one which assumes a temporary political and military stalemate, avoidance of war between the great powers, and continuation of the cold war by political and economic means which do not involve increasing the likelihood of general war.

SOVIET GOALS

The primary aim of Soviet policy, of course, is the defense of the Soviet Union and of the Soviet empire. With regard to Western Europe, the unspoken Soviet goal is Soviet control, which would swing the world balance of power clearly to the advantage of the Soviet Union. To attain this goal, the Soviet leaders seek to oust United States forces and bases and to destroy all the organizations and institutions established to promote Western unity. They seek to destroy the North Atlantic Treaty Organization, to dissolve the ties between Western Germany and its allies, and to incorporate Western Germany into a unified Germany under Soviet rule, which would enable the Soviet Union to control all of Europe. The Soviet leaders have a keen appreciation of the crucial significance of Germany and of the role of Western Germany in the Western European Union. They also have understood more clearly than most Western Europeans the political importance of the European Defense Community and of the European Political Community as means of damping and extinguishing the Franco-German conflict, directing the spiritual, economic, and military forces of Western Europe into new channels, and creating a political unity which could resist Soviet influence, pull Britain, Canada, and the United States more firmly into European affairs, and serve as a magnet to draw satellite Europe from the Soviet grip.

BASES OF SOVIET POLICY

The principal Soviet means to attain these great goals are sometimes not noticed and usually not mentioned, because at the same time they constitute the bases of Soviet power. The basic Soviet weapon is the industrial and military power of the Soviet Union, which Stalin's successors have been just as assiduous as he to strengthen. The Soviet rulers denounce others for seeking to negotiate from a "position of force," but Soviet industrial and military power provides the base from which Soviet policy operates. The impressive growth of the Soviet economy has had a noticeable impact upon the underdeveloped countries, some of which consider the Soviet rise to power a model. However, its effect has been just as powerful upon the governments and peoples of Western Europe, which has lost to the United States and the Soviet Union its role as world leader and which in its relative weakness and decline feels naked and defenseless before growing Soviet power and Soviet ruthlessness in the use of that power. Indeed, if the Soviet economic program is successful, within a generation or so Western Europe may be forced "irrevocably into a position of complete dependence"

upon either the Soviet or the American industrial and power complex.[1]

Since the death of Stalin, several waves of Soviet speeches and decrees have signaled an apparent reversal of established policy and a heavy increase in capital investment for the production of consumers' goods. However, the industries producing capital goods and military equipment have retained their priority and still receive the lion's share of capital investment. Indeed, in the budget announced on February 3, 1955, by Minister of Finance Zverev, the funds allotted to heavy industry were more than double those assigned to agriculture and light industry combined. Expenditures for defense in 1955 were increased by almost 12 per cent over those of 1954, and the Soviet military capability continues to grow. The hearty but false emphasis on consumers' goods was designed to ease the transition from Stalin to the new regime, to placate the Soviet upper classes, and to persuade the non-Communist world, especially Western Europe, of the peaceful intentions of the Soviet rulers.

Soviet control over East-Central Europe and the gradual but inexorable reshaping of this critical area along Soviet lines constitute the second fixed base for Soviet policy toward Western Europe. The brutal division of Europe and the presence of Soviet and satellite forces at the waist of Europe have placed Western Europe in jeopardy and form the core of the threat under which it lives. Moreover, Soviet control of Eastern Germany and Soviet ability to prevent the unification of Germany block the Western program for unity and grant the Soviet Union a disruptive weapon of enormous power in Germany and in all of Western Europe.

The third established base of Soviet power is the international Communist movement, which controls hundreds of thousands of Communists and which leads

[1] Philip E. Mosely, "Can Moscow Match Us Industrially?" *Harvard Business Review*, Vol. 33 (1955), p. 103.

millions of dupes around the world in support of Soviet policies. Every government in Western Europe, particularly the weak and unstable governments of France and Italy, is sensitive to the various forms of pressure which the Soviet government generates through its network of organizations and its vast propaganda system. These also exploit the philosophical vacuums which exist in many parts of the world by peddling the Soviet philosophy, one of the Soviet Union's most potent weapons. The Soviet rulers almost certainly believe that the road to Paris lies through Hanoi and that the channel to power in Western Europe runs through the Sea of Confusion and Despair. Consequently, the international Communist movement exerts pressures in manifold ways, from colonial revolution to incessant propaganda for "peace," and its instruments include civil war in Indochina and Malaya, the World Peace Council, Soviet Friendship Societies, the French Communist party, and the World Federation of Trade Unions.

GENERAL RELAXATION OF TENSION

Western success in rebuilding the economic, political, and military power and unity of Western Europe and the containment of Soviet expansion in Western Europe have forced the Soviet Union to revise its tactics. Even before Stalin's death, greater emphasis was being placed upon political warfare in all its forms and upon softening resistance to expansion. The new Soviet leaders emphasize those actions in Soviet domestic policy which may help persuade the Western observer in particular that the Soviet system is thawing. At the same time, in their policies toward foreign governments and peoples, they have introduced civilities and amenities to obtain a relaxation of Western vigilance.

Domestic policy

Within the Soviet Union, these steps have been restricted to a major amnesty shortly after Stalin's death, another amnesty in September 1955, occasional emphasis upon the rights of Soviet citizens, a small, gradual increase in the production of consumers' goods, and increased access to the products of foreign culture. This approach became most marked in the summer of 1955, when tourist traffic into and out of the Soviet Union widened to a trickle. All of these steps, plus the so-called "New Course" in East-Central Europe, were designed to convince Western Europeans that the Soviet menace had evaporated and that the Western program for military strength and unity should be abandoned.

The amenities

With regard to Soviet policy toward Western Europe itself, the steps taken have generally been small. Indeed, most of them have been simple conciliatory gestures and have merely marked Soviet adoption of the minimum standards of civilized life. They included allowing Russian wives of foreigners to leave the Soviet Union to join their husbands, allowing Swedish and Danish trawlers to fish within twelve miles of the Baltic states' coast and returning some prisoners of war. The Soviet Union "interceded" with its Far Eastern allies on behalf of civilian prisoners, and it helped to make possible the conclusion of the Korean truce. On May 30, 1953, in a note published July 19, 1953, the Soviet Union renounced its claims to Turkish territory and to special privileges in the Dardanelles. It has also resumed "normal" diplomatic relations with Greece, Israel, and Yugoslavia. The norm of Soviet practice and the eagerness with which the West hopes for change were both illustrated by the wild flurry of speculation concerning Soviet policy when Malenkov, in August 1954, picked a bouquet of flowers for a member of a visiting British Labor delegation. As someone remarked, Western observers often seem to believe that the appearance of *petits pois à la française* on a Kremlin menu marks a new policy toward France.

Current Soviet tactics are well illustrated by the action of the Supreme Soviet during the last year or so in encouraging representatives of various parliamentary bodies to exchange visits with "the Soviet parliament." In February 1955, it voted to join the Interparliamentary Union, and delegates of the Supreme Soviet attended the forty-fourth annual conference of the Union at Helsinki in August. Official delegations of the parliaments of Britain, Finland, Sweden, India, Syria, Yugoslavia, and Japan have already visited Moscow, and the parliaments of Belgium, France, Austria, Italy, and Canada have accepted invitations. While this procedure exposes some of the Soviet élite to the wholesome influence of Western parliamentary tradition, it also opens up an important new propaganda avenue for the Soviet Union. Above all, it enables the Supreme Soviet to pose as a genuine parliament, thus helping to persude Western Europeans that the Soviet Union is governed by law and that there is no Soviet menace.

Peace campaign

This approach is a fundamental part of the Soviet campaign for "peace" and for "peaceful coexistence." The Soviet rulers remember clearly the immense advantage Lenin obtained in 1917 by his campaign for immediate peace, and they appreciate that an opponent of this campaign is easily labeled a warmonger. Moreover, their approach to "all men of good will" for peace and "friendship among nations," their emphasis upon noble emotions and high principles, and their attacks upon Western alliances and bases and upon alleged barbarous American practices have a strong appeal in this nuclear age not only to neutralists, but even to strong anti-Communists affected by fear of nuclear war. The Soviet demands for immediate prohibition of the use and manufacture of nuclear weapons, for a reduction in conventional arms and effectives to agreed levels, and for control machinery to be created at a later date have had little effect upon *informed* opinion throughout the world but have been important propaganda weapons for weakening *popular* resistance to Soviet policy. As such, the spurious Soviet "peace" campaign constitutes a deadly threat to Western unity and vigilance.

Trade

In its efforts to convince the world that it wants peace and wishes to strengthen peaceful relationships, the Soviet Union has sought to break Western controls over the export of strategic goods, to persuade Western Europeans that the Soviet empire constitutes a vast untapped market, and to create divisions within Western Europe over trade policy. This Soviet program has been waged on several levels—the completion of short-term bilateral trade agreements, political campaigning within the United Nations Economic Commission for Europe, and general propaganda. For example, the trade agreement signed with France in July 1953 was negotiated more quickly than the one signed with Italy in November of that year, and the Soviet Union purchased some items from France rather than Italy because France and the French vote on the European Defense Community were important Soviet political targets.

The Soviet Union has been especially skillful in dangling lucrative orders before Western businessmen. For example, Kabanov, the Minister of Foreign Trade, in February 1954 told a group of British businessmen visiting Moscow that the Soviet Union was prepared to place orders in Britain for more than a billion dollars between 1955 and 1957. About half of the goods he listed were under strategic controls, but this appeal for "normalization of Anglo-Soviet trade" stimulated British industrial and commercial appetites and strengthened criticism of Western controls. Moreover, such promises created a sensation in Western Germany, where fear is strong that Britain may gain a lead in

Soviet trade. Dangling the same lure before West Germans, especially after the visit of Adenauer to Moscow, will worry the British and increase competition for Soviet markets.

The Russians had shown an interest in ECE even before Stalin's death, and on January 30, 1953, the ECE announced that the Soviet Union had agreed to participate in a conference on East-West trade, although in September 1952 it had refused a similar invitation. In the various ECE conferences the Soviet representatives have given especial priority to "removal of obstacles to foreign trade" and to denunciation of the United States as the power responsible for the COCOM (Consultative Group Coordinating Committee) strategic controls.

This theme has been a favorite one for Soviet political warriors, and they have declared Western strategic controls responsible for the decline after 1949 in trade between Western Europe and the Soviet empire. This campaign ignores the facts of this trade, which had declined before strategic controls were established. The Soviet Union has reorganized the economic structures of the countries of East-Central Europe and has tied their trade strings to Moscow. Moreover, these states now lack supplies of grain and timber for export to the West. Indeed, on balance the Soviet Union and its satellite states even imported foodstuffs in 1954. In addition, while the COCOM states pruned the strategic list in August 1954, exports from the Soviet empire remain under complete control. Finally, Soviet abrogation of trade with Yugoslavia in 1948 and with Australia in 1954 demonstrated that Soviet trade controls are used for political reasons in a way which is not possible in the West.

Western Communist parties

Western Communist parties as instruments of the Soviet Union are used to support the impression that the Soviet Union is not a threat and that each national Communist party is just another political party. Thus, in 1953 the French party abandoned the forceful program which had led to incidents such as the Ridgeway riots in May 1952, and began to work for a "patriotic national front." Jacques Duclos on October 22, 1953, indicated that the party was prepared to join with any other Frenchmen in a national campaign to end the war in Indochina, to prevent German rearmament, and to hasten general disarmament. The Communists have cooperated closely with the Radical Socialists and the Gaullists, especially against EDC. On June 8, 1954, Thorez proclaimed that it was "orthodox Communist doctrine" to accept allies wherever they could be found, and persistent efforts have been made for a united front with the Socialists or a popular front with other political groups. The Communist effort to infiltrate political, religious, educational, and labor organizations in particular has been quite successful, especially in France, where the use of *la douce parole* works as effectively for the Communists as it did for Philip the Fair centuries ago.

International organizations

The new Soviet leaders use international organizations to carry political warfare against Western Europe. The primary forum since 1945 has been the United Nations. In addition, the Soviet Union joined the United Nations Educational, Scientific and Cultural Organization in April 1954. In July 1955 it announced it would resume active participation in the World Health Organization, from which it had withdrawn in 1949, that it would become a member of the International Bureau of Education, and that it would contribute two million rubles in kind and services to the United Nations Children's Fund. These steps, and the participation of the Soviet Union and some of its satellites in the International Labor Organization, not only provide new forums but also help convince other states and peoples that the Soviet Union is a normal state seeking to attain its goals in normal ways.

DIPLOMACY: AUSTRIA

The principal Soviet weapon against Western Europe during the past thirty months has been Soviet diplomacy, which has been generally used with great effectiveness to attain Soviet goals or to prevent the United States and the Western European states from attaining their aims. This can be seen most clearly in the long Western struggle to obtain freedom and independence for Austria and unification for Germany. In the case of Austria, the Soviet Union in the spring of 1955 finally yielded, at a high price and in return for other advantages which it estimated then outweighed the benefits to be derived from continuing to block the treaty.

At the close of the Moscow Conference on November 1, 1943, the United States, the United Kingdom and the Soviet Union had issued a joint declaration pledging the re-establishment of "a free and independent Austria." All but five articles of the Austrian State Treaty had been agreed to by 1949. However, Austria was not freed until the spring of 1955, even though the foreign ministers dealt with the Austrian State Treaty in six conferences between 1947 and 1953 while over the same years their deputies had held more than 260 meetings. The Soviet policy was clearly based on the desire to retain troops in Austria, to prevent Austria from joining the West, to obtain economic profit from the Soviet zone, and to use Austria as a bargaining counter on the German and other issues.

The long period of Soviet recalcitrance reached its depths at the Berlin conference of the foreign ministers, in February 1954, when Molotov proposed that the Austrian treaty be linked to an agreement on German unification and that the withdrawal of foreign troops from Austria be postponed until a peace treaty with Germany had been concluded. He even refused to sign the Austrian State Treaty when the three Western powers agreed to accept the Soviet version of the five articles which had been in dispute since 1949.

The Berlin conference of 1954 was preceded and followed by minor concessions to the Austrian government, such as the note on June 30, 1953, announcing that the Soviet Union would assume all Soviet occupation costs as of September 1. However, the pressures on Austrian government and police officials remained sharp and strong, and the Soviet Union refused to discuss reducing its heavy claims upon the Austrian economy.

Signature of Austrian treaty

However, the Soviet policy toward Austria was suddenly reversed in March 1955, when Molotov announced that the Austrian treaty was not dependent upon a German treaty. He also proposed preliminary negotiations between Austria and the Soviet Union on the basis of withdrawal of all foreign troops from Austria and an Austrian undertaking not to join any military alliance or to allow military bases on Austrian territory. With this Soviet reversal, the way was opened to the signature of the Austrian treaty, on May 15, 1955. This treaty gave Austria its freedom and independence; prohibited *Anschluss* with Germany, foreign alliances, and foreign bases; provided for the withdrawal of foreign troops within ninety days of ratification; and provided for substantial payments by Austria to the Soviet Union as the price of its freedom. These payments include delivery of $150,000,000 in Austrian goods over six years, in return for handing back the ex-German assets seized by the Soviet Union; the delivery of 1,000,000 tons of crude oil a year for ten years from the oil fields and refineries of eastern Austria; and purchase of the Soviet-controlled Danube Shipping Company for $2,000,000.

Signature of the Austrian State Treaty removed the Soviet grip from Austria and marks a step backward for the Soviet forces in Central Europe. However, Western troops have also left Austria, and Austria has now been neutralized. The Soviet Union added to its laurels as a peacemaker, since the final initiative came from Molotov and the treaty was concluded after a visit of Chancellor Raab to Moscow. Moreover, Austria will remain in economic bondage to Moscow for a full decade. The Kremlin obviously hopes to draw Austria into its orbit through trade bonds and to make of Austria a kind of Central European Finland. Finally, the Soviet leaders obviously hope that this will serve as a precedent for achieving a united neutralized Germany and for forcing the withdrawal of American troops from Europe.

Diplomacy: Germany

The Soviet leaders recognize Germany as the key to Europe, and they intend in one way or another, sooner or later, to bring all of Germany under Soviet control. In this, they are simply continuing a policy which Stalin set in motion. Soviet control over Eastern Germany has given the Soviet Union the power to veto any program for the unification of Germany which it does not find acceptable. It has been clear since the end of World War II, and the Soviet leaders made it brutally plain to Adenauer and the West in Moscow in September 1955, that the Soviet Union intends to retain control over Eastern Germany and to force Western Germany and the West ultimately to sue for unification on Soviet terms. To attain this great goal, the Soviet Union has used both pressure and guile, varying its tactics and its themes as circumstances required but always keeping the main goal in view and utilizing simultaneously every type of technique.

The extraordinary reconstruction and economic recovery of Western Germany, since 1949 in particular, its rapid rise to political respectability, and the program for a European Defense Community incorporating Western Germany led the Soviet Union until September 6, 1953, to concen-

trate upon defeating Adenauer. After his victory in the election, the Soviet Union concentrated until late summer 1954 upon influencing the French vote on EDC. The French failure to ratify EDC was only a brief victory, because the London and Paris agreements provided a substitute which was weaker, but still too strong from the Soviet point of view, in the form of Western European Union, West German sovereignty, and West German membership in NATO. After these agreements had been ratified, the Soviet leaders again shifted gears, widened their smiles, opened diplomatic relations with the West German government, and inaugurated another period in Soviet European policy.

Eastern Germany

Eastern Germany is an important pawn in Soviet policy toward Western Europe, and the Soviet leaders like to believe that the existence of a "socialist" state in Eastern Germany exerts a magnetic influence upon Western Germany. However, Soviet control, the vast economic and political contrasts between Eastern and Western Germany, and the fraudulent elections, especially those of October 17, 1954, handicap the Soviet Union. The steady flow of refugees from Eastern Germany—over two million have "voted with their feet" by fleeing to West Berlin and Western Germany—daily indicts Soviet rule and cripples the Soviet effort to make Eastern Germany a magnet.

In the spring of 1953, following the decision of the Soviet leaders that the puppet state needed more attractive window dressing, the Pankow government announced a series of minor reform measures, such as returning confiscated waste land to farmers, increasing the production of consumers' goods, reducing labor controls, relaxing the drive for collectivization, and correcting tax collection methods. This program was upset by the June riots, which weakened the Soviet line for the September elections in Western Germany and which underlined the basic Soviet dilemma. The June riots in the East and the continued economic and political progress in Western Germany have led the Soviet leaders to increase their efforts to reward, strengthen, and dignify the German Democratic Republic. Thus, during the last few months of 1953 the Soviet Union returned about 10,000 prisoners of war to Eastern Germany. As of January 1, 1954, reparations payments to the Soviet Union ceased, firms taken over by the Soviet Union were returned to German control, and occupation costs were limited to not more than 5 per cent of the East German national income. On March 25, 1954, the Soviet government announced that it would henceforth treat Eastern Germany as a sovereign state, with "freedom to make decisions according to its own views in domestic and foreign affairs." Following the Adenauer trip to Moscow and the opening of diplomatic relations between Moscow and Bonn, the Soviet government, on September 20, 1955, granted full sovereignty to the German Democratic Republic, including control of civilian traffic between West Germany and West Berlin and the right to rearm and to play a full role in the Warsaw Pact.

As the campaign to whitewash and dignify the government of the German Democratic Republic progressed, Eastern Germany began to play a more prominent role in the Soviet plan. Its leaders frequently appealed to the French government and to groups of Frenchmen to defeat EDC and WEU. Intensive efforts were made to increase the range of contacts with West German technicians and officials on matters concerning trade, transport, sport, and cultural affairs. The program for "all Germans around one table" sought to bring workers, churchmen, athletes, newsmen, women, and above all elected representatives together for friendly discussions. Threats to force West German officials and representatives to meet with Communists were also used, most notably in the spring of 1955, when the German Democratic

Republic levied enormous increases in dues on West German vehicles using Soviet-zone roads.

France

Soviet policy toward Western Germany and the Soviet design for neutralizing Western Europe are generally defined with one eye on France. Soviet policy toward France has emphasized both Soviet economic and military power and Soviet "peace" proposals. At the same time, the Soviet Union has exerted pressure on France through Indochina. It has appealed to the traditional French fear of Germany and to the old French policy of cooperating with Germany's eastern neighbors to prevent German revival and expansion.

Thus, Soviet propaganda in France through all of its outlets emphasized the dangers courted by Western policy toward Germany and the great virtues of the Franco-Soviet treaty of alliance of 1944. Great efforts were made to improve relations between France and the Communist governments of Poland and Czechoslovakia. For example, just before the final debate on EDC, Poland offered France a treaty of alliance and mutual assistance. The legislatures of Poland, Czechoslovakia, and Eastern Germany in December 1954 appealed to the French National Assembly not to ratify the Paris agreement on West German rearmament. At the same time, the Soviet government several times warned both France and the United Kingdom that the London and Paris agreements flagrantly violated the Franco-Soviet and Anglo-Soviet treaties and that ratification would lead the Soviet Union to annul the treaties. When this threat did not succeed, the treaties were annulled by the Presidium of the Supreme Soviet on May 7, 1955. Only one month later, the carrot reappeared, when Molotov at a luncheon in Paris referred to the need to forget the past, expressed a wish for more frequent and direct contact with French leaders, and invited Pinay and Faure to Moscow.

German unification

The Western powers have sought to rebuild Western economic and political strength and to create a new unity to resist Soviet pressure and to lead toward a stable and peaceful future. General Western success and the recovery of Western Germany have thus raised to a new level questions concerning German unification and the position of a united Germany in Europe. The Western states propose free elections throughout Germany under a law drafted and promulgated by the four occupying powers and supervised by them; the convocation of a national assembly; the drafting of a constitution and the preparation of peace treaty negotiations by this assembly; the adoption of the constitution and the formation of an all-German government; and the signature and entry into force of the peace treaty. The heart of the Western position lies in free elections. As Bidault pointed out to Molotov at Berlin, "From a democratic point of view, it seems obvious that it is elections which create governments and not governments which create elections."

To counter the Western program, the Soviet Union has stood fast behind a policy which seeks controlled elections and Communist control over all of Germany. This position has been stated quite clearly a number of times, notably in a Soviet note to France, Britain, and the United States on August 16, 1953, again at the Berlin conference in January and February 1954, and during and after the Geneva conference in July 1955. Fundamentally, although this is always concealed and denied, the Soviet Union has no intention of accepting free elections. Soviet policy on German unification emphasizes the following: representatives of the governments of both Eastern and Western Germany should participate in any conference discussing German unification and a German peace treaty; an all-German provisional government, created by the parliaments of the two Germanies with the cooperation of "democratic par-

ties and organizations," should draft an electoral law and prepare "free and secret elections" for a national assembly and should help prepare and sign a German peace treaty; all occupation forces should leave Germany after the signature of the peace treaty; German armed forces should be limited to those required for internal security and frontier patrol; and no foreign bases should be allowed. The heart of the Soviet position lies in the precedence granted to the formation of a German government over elections, which would be rigged by the government.

European "security"

The bald Soviet program for controlled elections leading to German unity under communism has been both sweetened and concealed by Soviet proposals for the withdrawal of all occupation forces and for the establishment of a European "security" system. Soviet suggestions that occupation forces be withdrawn are frequently reiterated, but this campaign for a neutralized Germany and an exposed Europe has generally had little effect.

The proposal for a European "security" system first appeared in January 1953, but it was presented in more elaborate form at the Berlin conference early in 1954 and has since become a standard Soviet prop. Fundamentally, this proposal is a device for removing American influence and power from Europe and for providing an ostensible substitute to NATO. In effect, it constitutes a system of "Europe for the Europeans," with the Soviet Union of course counted as a European state and with the United States belatedly recognized as one also. The pact is open to all European states "without regard to their social systems," to both German governments, and later to a reunified Germany. It specifically binds its members "not to enter any coalition or alliance." When these proposals were rejected as a plan to divide Germany for fifty years and to neutralize Western Europe, Molotov on March 31,

1954, proposed that the Soviet Union and "other European countries" join NATO to give it "a really defensive character" and to preclude German's being drawn into military groupings.

Soviet policy since WEU

During the past nine months or so, Soviet policy has paid particular attention to four simultaneous lines. The first of these has emphasized Soviet power and resolution and the consequences of Western refusal to abandon NATO and WEU. The Soviet Union has not threatened war— indeed, it has prated of peace—but it has reiterated that ratification of WEU would lead to the annulment of the Franco-Soviet and Anglo-Soviet treaties, to the creation of an Eastern European parallel to NATO, and to the "permanent" division of Germany. When the threats failed, the treaties were annulled. The Soviet Union and its satellites, in May 1955 at Warsaw, then "formed" a military organization under Soviet command. Finally, the opening of diplomatic relations with Western Germany and the grant of full "sovereignty" to Eastern Germany in September underlined that the West had reached a stone wall on German unification, unless it surrendered to Soviet terms.

The second emphasis has been upon the proposed Soviet European "security" system. This is offered as a substitute for NATO and WEU, as a device for bringing the two Germanies into one organization, and as a means of obtaining Western recognition of the Soviet position in East-Central Europe. It has little appeal, except to Communists, but there is some danger that it will be confused with Western plans being developed to win Soviet approval to German unity within Western union.

The third accent, and currently the most noticeable one, is upon the general relaxation of tensions. While the Soviet leaders have not concealed their goals, they have at the same time adopted a friendly, cheerful, benevolent pose to lull their op-

ponents into carelessness and slumber. This tactic was most marked at the Geneva "summit" conference, where all of the ideas came from the West and where the Soviet leaders concentrated upon spreading an atmosphere of cordiality and friendliness.

Finally, Soviet policy stresses relations with Western Germany. The establishment of diplomatic relations between Moscow and Bonn was foreshadowed by a Moscow radio broadcast on January 15, 1955. It sent a shiver of fear through the West, which remembers August 1939, which notes with apprehension the age and importance of Adenauer, and which worries over the power of German nationalism as unification is delayed and as the two Germanies are driven into closer relationships with each other.

In other words, with regard to Germany, the Soviet leaders apparently have settled down for the long haul. While exuding good cheer and cordiality, broadcasting the virtues of peaceful coexistence and buying apparent virtue at little price through ceding their Porkkala base to Finland, they will seek to isolate and overthrow Adenauer or to wait until his death or retirement creates a new political situation in Western Germany. In the meantime, they will strive in every way to push the two Germanies into closer contact. As these relationships improve, the structure of the East German state will probably be revised along ostensibly federal lines, and Soviet policy will concentrate upon weakening the center parties in Western Germany, strengthening the left-wing Socialists, the neo-Nazis, and the nationalists, and working for a National Front in both Germanies. In short, the Soviet leaders will probably rely upon this approach, as well as on increased trade between Western Germany and the Soviet empire under a new Rapallo, a Western economic and political crisis, the desire for "peace," and the carelessness or impatience of the West, to bring about German unification on Soviet terms.

OUTLOOK

Soviet policy toward Western Europe since the death of Stalin has been marked by the same failures which attended Stalin's efforts. The Communists have failed to prevent or even seriously to hinder the economic and political recovery of Western Europe from the depths of 1945 and 1947. NATO continues to thrive, though its foundations seem perilously military and fragile and though it is wracked by occasional conflicts between members and by growing reluctance to meet its high annual costs. The Western European Union has been established, with Western Germany a member. Above all, the United States has maintained its forces and its commitments, in Western Europe.

While the Soviet leaders have failed to attain their goals, they have achieved some successes and they have made some progress toward undermining Western unity and resolution. The Soviet Union contributed heavily to the French refusal to ratify EDC through its skillful political warfare in France and through the continuing influence of the French Communist party. While the size of the Communist parties and of Communist-controlled organizations in Western Europe has continued to decline steadily, neutralism, pacifism, and nationalism, stimulated by the Communists, have grown, undermining the foundations of Western resolution and strength. The skillful Soviet effort to persuade Western Europe that the Soviet Union is not a threat and that the high costs of defense are not necessary has softened the Western program and made the great alliance hesitate. The Geneva conference in particular has influenced popular opinion, and the smiles and bouquets of Krushchev and Bulganin are weakening Western persistence far more than did the arrogance and ruthlessness of Stalin. In this general approach toward relaxation, the Soviet leaders have clearly inherited Stalin's great ability to create a success out of a series of failures.

Problems on both sides

Both Western Europe and the Soviet Union face serious problems. The West suffers now from its own achievements, and its prosperity and security seem so solid that vigilance slackens. Western stability and unity depend to a large degree on the solidity of economic foundations, and the economies of several of the key states and of the area in general are somewhat vulnerable. In addition, Western recovery depends to a great degree upon the survival of democracy in Western Germany, still naturally a suspect neighbor. Finally, in its present moods, Western Europe is increasingly vulnerable to the current Soviet political warfare tune. There is some danger that the populace in one of the links which make up Western Europe will succumb to the lure of neutralism or even to a Soviet European "security" pact which would relax the vigilance of the West, lead to a serious reduction in forces, and divide the allies as they were divided during the 1930's by the Nazis. Indeed, there is some likelihood that those who stand for strength and vigilance will be hounded as was Churchill in the 1930's.

In other words, the West provides vulnerabilities and opportunities to the Soviet leaders for exploitation. However, at the same time Soviet policy must continue to operate under serious handicaps. To begin with, the Soviet record cannot be erased. In addition, while Soviet control over Eastern Europe provides a great addition to Soviet power, a strategic area of great value, and a prime source of Soviet political influence in Western Europe, at the same time it constitutes a disadvantage. This is particularly so in the case of Eastern Germany, whose true status is exposed daily by a flood of refugees and which falls ever further behind Western Germany in every index.

Moreover, while the Soviet Union can play one tune in France and another in Germany, it cannot forever be all things to all people without paying a penalty.

Finally, while the current policy of smiles and cooperation helps to undermine Western vigilance, at the same time it corrodes the vitals of Communist political power.

A system which is based on conflict and war requires tension and feeds on struggle. No system is more vulnerable to relaxation than a totalitarian state.

POST-STALIN POLICY IN ASIA

HAROLD H. FISHER

One of America's most experienced analysts of Soviet affairs, Harold H. Fisher is now Professor of International Relations at San Francisco State College. In 1921–22 he served as an officer of the American Relief Administration in Eastern Europe and Russia. For many years he was Chairman of the Hoover Institution on War, Revolution, and Peace, and Professor of History at Stanford University. He has traveled widely throughout Asia. Among his published works are *The Famine in Russia*, *The Bolshevik Revolution* (with others), *The Bolsheviks and the World War*, and *The Communist Revolution*. Professor Fisher's examination of complex events in the different nations of Asia leads him to the conclusion that while the long-range strategic objectives of Soviet policy remained unchanged after Stalin, a series of new and effective tactics were developed.

SOVIET policy in Asia has changed in the two and one-half years since Stalin's death. The aims of Soviet policy, however, remained unchanged. The Soviet Communists and all who take their orders or follow their example still hope to prevail upon the peoples of Asia to follow the Communist lead and use Communist methods to achieve peace, progress, and equality. The degree to which the Soviet Union has changed its policies to gain this end depends on the extent to which one interprets the policies of the local Asian Communist parties as actually policies ordered, suggested or approved by the leaders of the Communist Party of the Soviet Union who direct all Soviet policy. For example, what about the decisions of the Third Congress of the Communist party of India at Madurai, December 27, 1953 to January 3, 1954? At this meeting the veteran British Com-

munist, Harry Pollitt, attempted, in the name of Moscow and the international Communist movement, to persuade the Congress to accept an anti-American and pro-British line. Or take the purges of 1954–55 carried out by the Chinese Communists against the ex-Manchurian boss Kao Kang, the Marxist writer Hu Feng, and many others. Were these Soviet-directed policies or policies of the Communist party of China adopted in imitation of the Communist Party of the Soviet Union? Was Chou En-lai carrying out a Soviet policy in Asia when he took part in the Bandung Conference in April 1955 and announced that the Chinese People's Government wanted peace with the United States and was willing to negotiate?

The relations of Communist parties in power or seeking power to the CPSU and to each other are in many respects secret;

From Harold H. Fisher, "Soviet Policy in Asia Since Stalin," *The Annals of The American Academy of Political and Social Science*, CCCIII (January, 1956), pp. 179–191. By permission of The American Academy of Political and Social Science.

in some respects they are open but complex. It is not easy to tell just where to draw the line between policies that have been ordered by the Kremlin and those that Asian Communists have adopted in the belief that such policies were in harmony with the international line of the CPSU. The purpose of this paper is not to explore the murky and treacherous area of Communist inter-party relations but to take note of some of the actions of Communist governments and parties in Asia that are of enough importance to justify the belief that they were approved or ordered by the Communist Party of the Soviet Union and so in some measure reflect Soviet policies.

RECENT CHANGES ENUMERATED

The changes that have been most striking in respect to Asia during the two and a half years are briefly these:

In Asia as elsewhere, the Soviet government and the Communist parties have emphasized the aim of peaceful coexistence between regimes based on different political and ideological systems, the development of trade and the export of technical assistance in international affairs instead of wars of liberation and other forms of international class war. In domestic affairs the Communist parties have advocated "united fronts" against imperialism combined with peaceful and legal competition with the nationalist parties instead of guerrilla wars, civil wars, sabotage, and other openly illegal activities. Before Malenkov's demotion in February 1955, the Communists continued the virulence of their attacks on the United States. The "thaw" in the attitude toward the West introduced by Khrushchev and Bulganin in Europe was felt also in Asia but the temperature there did not climb as fast or as high as at the summit conference in Geneva.

In Korea, where the Communists had used the most irritating and offensive devices to stall the armistice negotiations for two years, on July 27, 1953, six months after Mao-Tse-tung had said the war would be waged for years if necessary, they suddenly agreed to conditions that differed but little from what had been offered time and time again during the embittered negotiations.

At Geneva on July 21, 1954, after their sensational Vietminh victory at Dienbienphu, May 7, the Communists signed three agreements bringing to an end a war that had been waged in Indochina for seven years and seven months, a war which the Communists seemed to be winning.

In the Formosa Strait the Communists continued until the spring of 1955 to threaten to "liberate" the great and beautiful island and its offshore neighbors by force. They underscored the seriousness of these threats by intermittent bombardment of the Quemoy and Matsu islands and by troop movements and the building of air installations on the mainland opposite the strait. Tension in the Formosa Strait area was intense during the winter of 1954–55. The Tachens were evacuated by the Nationalists in February and an informal "cease-fire" status had almost been reached by the time of the Bandung Conference (April 18–24, 1955). There the Communist Premier, Chou En-lai, declared that the Chinese people did not want a war with the United States and that his government was willing to negotiate on the question of relaxing the tension in the Formosa Strait. As a sequel to these declarations and the backstage negotiations that had preceded them, a conference began in Geneva on August 1, 1955, between Ambassador U. Alexis Johnson of the United States and Ambassador Wang Ping-nan of the People's Government.

The principal Communist parties seeking power in South and Southeast Asia and Japan made significant changes in tactics. These changes did not follow the same pattern in every country, but they reflected the same general swing again from the "left," "hard" policies of civil and guerrilla war, sabotage, terror and intensified class struggle toward the "right" or "soft" policies of peaceful coexistence between classes as well as between nations. Instead of fighting the nationalist parties, which governed the newly independent states, the Communists, at different times in different places, tried to make peace with the nationalists and draw them into "people's democracy fronts" consisting of all democratic, "antifeudal," anti-imperialist forces.

The violent period had followed, in most cases, the founding of the Cominform in 1947, the development of the "Zhdanovshchina" in the USSR, and the mounting successes of the Chinese Communists spreading out from their territorial base in North China.

Indonesia and India

In Indonesia in September 1948, where the situation of the new Indonesian republic was desperate, the Communists tried to establish a territorial base by seizing the city of Madiun, the third largest in the republic. The people did not follow the Communists, and the revolt was a bloody, costly failure. In 1952 the Indonesian Communist party switched from attacking the nationalists to trying to join them in a national front. The Communist party gained sufficient strength to help bring down one ministry and to give essential aid to Dr. Ali Sastroamidjojo's nationalist ministry from 1953 to 1955. This "united front from above" tactic has increased the prestige and influence of the Communists, who made a strikingly impressive showing (about 22 per cent of the votes) in the first elections of the Republic of Indonesia in late September 1955.

The fortunes of the Communist party of India have followed a curve similar to that of their Indonesian comrades. Like the Indonesians, the Indian Communists made terror and civil war their official policy in 1948 at the Second Party Congress, which followed a Communist-inspired conference sponsored by the World Federation of Democratic Youth and the Inter-

national Union of Students in Calcutta in February. Having seized the leadership of a peasant uprising in the Telengana district, the Indian Communists had, for a time, a territorial base, but they were unable to expand its area as the Chinese had done at Yenan. The Indian government forces liquidated the Telengana base, and in 1950 the Communists were told by Moscow that in trying to follow the "Chinese path" they had gone astray. They were directed to postpone armed rebellion and guerrilla war and to compete for popular support with the Indian Congress and Socialist parties by organizing legally a broad united front like the Chinese coalition of four classes. In the first Indian general election at the end of 1952, the Communists elected twenty-three deputies to the national Parliament, becoming the second largest party after the Congress party, which elected 362.

The surprising strength shown by the Communists in the general elections of 1952 did not prove that the new tactics were irresistible, for in February 1955 the Communists were decisively defeated in elections in Andhra, a new state in which the party was believed to be exceptionally strong.

Soviet Communist policy in Indonesia and India and also in Burma has been to divert the local Communist parties not only away from armed revolt but also away from out-and-out attacks against the nationalist parties in power, parties that are believed to be neutralist. The chief political enemies of the Communists are the Socialist parties and those parties such as the Masjumi in Indonesia which have a religious background or are suspected of a willingness to regard the United States as a friend rather than as the leader of a new imperialism.

Philippines and Malaya

In the Philippines and Malaya the Communists had launched a guerrilla war when Moscow gave them the signal in 1948. These guerrilla wars were costly, but the Communists kept them going after they had changed their tactics elsewhere. The guerrilla wars never grew into civil wars. In May 1954, Luis Taruc, the leader of the Hukpalahaps, surrendered, and on June 23, 1955, the leaders of the Malay People's Liberation Army sued for peace. The British rejected this proposal of an armistice and offered amnesty to those Communists who gave themselves up. The Communist party of Malaya made a new peace offer on September 24, 1955, to end the eight-year war or, as it is called in Malaya, "the emergency." Tengku Abdul Rahman, the chief Minister of the Federation of Malaya, with the approval of the British High Commissioner, agreed to meet the Communist leader, Chin Peng.

Burma and Ceylon

Burma, Ceylon, and Japan have had legal Communist parties — Burma has had the dubious distinction of having two competing Communist groups and Ceylon three. In Ceylon and Burma the Communist movement has been too much divided and too badly led to be as useful an instrument of Soviet policy as in India and Indonesia. It has perhaps also been hampered by the opposition of the Buddhist faith. In Burma the orthodox Communist party followed the "Calcutta line" after 1948, engaging in guerrilla warfare and other kinds of violence while trying to follow the "Chinese path." As elsewhere, these tactics failed and as in the neighboring states, the Communist party of Burma began to change its tactics. A pro-Soviet Burma Workers' and Peasants' party was set up to carry on legal united-front political activity. This was in line with the revised Soviet policy before and after Stalin's death. As with India and Indonesia the Soviet Union prefers to cultivate the good will of the Burmese government as a member of the "peace area" rather than to encourage the local Communists to try to destroy that government.

Japanese Communist party

In Japan, Soviet Communist policy has followed a different timetable. The Communist party of Japan, organized in 1922 and suppressed in 1934, was reborn in 1945 during the American occupation, when SCAP[1] restored "political, civic, and religious freedoms" and encouraged the revival of political parties. From the return from Yenan of the veteran leader, Sanzo Nosaka, in January 1946, to January 1950, the party followed the line of peaceful, democratic activity, trying to appear as "the lovable Communist party." In 1949 the party elected thirty-five members of the national Diet and launched a drive to "acquire a million Bolsheviks." Encouraged by Communist victories in China and by directives from Moscow, and perhaps in anticipation of the approaching crisis in Korea, the Communists in 1950 changed their tactics and launched a series of strikes and acts of violence and sabotage. Nosaka's peaceful revolution formula was denounced by the Cominform. Especially violent demonstrations took place in 1952. In the face of official retaliation and public resentment the Communists failed to elect a single deputy to the Diet in the elections of October 1952.

A year later, seven months after Stalin's death, the Japanese Communists again changed their tactics in accordance with the policies laid down by Moscow for the other Asian parties. The new program called for a united front based on the slogans "anti-America, anti-Yoshida, and anti-rearmament" and for repudiation of the San Francisco Peace Treaty and other agreements with the United States. The program also included opposition to foreign military bases, withdrawal of foreign troops, restoration of normal and friendly political and trade relations with the Soviet Union and Communist China, freedom of travel, speech, assembly, and association (not permitted in Communist countries), and opposition to the Pacific military alliances (such as existed or were proposed between the United States and various

[1] SCAP: Supreme Command Allied Powers—**Ed.**

Pacific nations including Japan).] In Japan, as in India and Indonesia, the new policy does not mean that the Communist parties have abandoned and destroyed their underground and military apparatus.

Soviet-Japanese relations

Along with Communist party activities the Soviet Union has used diplomacy and propaganda to persuade the Japanese that economic survival, political independence, and national security depend on eliminating American military establishments in Japan and Okinawa, the re-establishment of normal trade and diplomatic relations with the Chinese mainland and the Soviet Union, the realization of Japanese neutrality outside the orbit of the American imperialists and alongside the "peace area" that the Peking government, with Soviet support, is working with Premier Nehru to create in Asia. The USSR has used more tangible inducements, including the possibilities of much needed raw materials, the repatriation of war prisoners, a new fishing agreement that would extend Japanese fishing grounds, the possible return of the Habomai and Shikotan Islands between Hokkaido and the Kuriles, and the possible support of Japan's admission to the United Nations. Behind these agreeable possibilities are less agreeable ones — the nearness of Russian air and naval bases, which the Japanese are never allowed to forget.

Soviet-Japanese peace treaty negotiations began in London in June 1955 and after four months were suspended. The Soviet conditions for the restoration of normal relations appear to have been little affected by the changes at the Soviet summit since 1953. They were the same as those presented at the San Francisco conference in 1951. The Soviet negotiators required Japan: (1) to recognize Soviet sovereignty over southern Sakhalin and the Kuriles; (2) to take no part in a military pact aimed at countries opposed to Japan in the Pacific war, that is, to annul the Japanese-American Security Treaty; (3) to

demilitarize the straits of Tsugaru, Soya, Nemuro, and Tseushima; (4) to agree to extended cultural relations; (5) to agree not to interfere in each other's domestic affairs; and (6) to waive reparations claims.

NEW TACTICS OR NEW STRATEGY?

Does this important tactical change mean merely that the Communists have concluded that more flies can be caught with sugar than with vinegar? Or does it mean that the Communists in the last decade have worked out a new strategy? Professor John H. Kautsky makes the interesting suggestion[2] that Mao Tse-tung has combined the best features of the two traditional Communist strategies: the "left" or "hard" tactics advocating "united front from below" and the "right" or "soft" based on "united front from above." According to this formula, the Communist party is not only the party dedicated to the leadership of the toiling and exploited masses in their struggle against the bourgeoisie but also the party dedicated to the leadership of the bourgeoisie against foreign imperialists. Mr. Kautsky sums it up this way: "Indeed if the 'left' strategy was the strategy of anti-capitalism and the 'right' strategy that of anti-fascism, the new strategy is the strategy of anti-Americanism."[3]

There is no doubt that after Stalin's death and until about the time of the Bandung Conference, the Communists tried to persuade the Asians that the worst enemies of peace and progress were not the native middle-class nationalists but the American "colonizers" who, *Pravda* charged,[4] had promoted a terrorist organization, the name of this terrorist band being the Salvation Army! Later, particularly after Khrush-

[2] "The New Strategy of International Communism," *American Political Science Review*, Vol. 49, No. XLIX, 2 (June 1955), pp. 478–486.
[3] *Ibid.*, p. 484.
[4] September 22, 1953.

chev and Bulganin became their chief Soviet spokesmen, anti-Americanism became less virulent. Peking got in step with Moscow—lagging a bit—and began to talk more about "peaceful liberation," and the virtues of trade and less about germ warfare and other atrocities.

Time will tell whether the acceleration of this tendency since Stalin's death means, as Mr. Kautsky believes, that "the class struggle has been replaced by the cold war" as the basic Communist strategy or whether, as it appears to me, this is a significant change in tactics rather than in basic strategy, a change designed to fit present conditions in, and aspirations of, underdeveloped countries. It does not appear to me to mean the abandonment of the strategy based on the Marxist theory of the class struggle, the Leninist theory of imperialism, and the Stalinist theory of the general crisis of capitalism. Under the banner of "proletarian internationalism," the encouragement of class consciousness and class struggle, the promotion of the allegedly inevitable divisions, rivalries, and conflicts between non-Communist nations, and coordination and mutual aid between Communist parties of all countries are still basic features of the strategy of the world Communist movement. The new tactics greatly lessen the danger of a new total war; they make possible the gradual transformation of a cold-war coexistence into a competitive coexistence. There is always the possibility that such a coexistence may continue indefinitely and that the competition of political and economic systems will lead to the modification of both rather than to their mutual destruction.

POST-STALIN EVENTS

Stalin's death did not appear to have any important effect on Sino-Soviet relations. The Chinese Communists paid the expected tribute to the departed and accepted the principle of collective leadership for the Soviet Union and the world Com-

munist movement without, however, adopting it for China. Mao Tse-tung became the most eminent of living Communists after Stalin's death, but China's needs and dependence on the Soviet Union were too great to allow Mao to claim the prerogatives of his pre-eminence even if he had any inclination to do so. China continued "leaning to one side," seemingly undisturbed by the fact that Beria, one of the collective leaders, was accused of treason by his comrades, condemned, and shot and that another collective leader, Malenkov, the first among the equals, confessed his inadequacy, was demoted, but was allowed to live. Behind the Chinese Communists' prompt and dutiful acceptance of these changes, the fact remained that three years after Stalin's death the prestige of the Russian leadership had fallen in Asia as that of the Chinese leaders, particularly Mao Tse-tung and Chou En-lai, had risen. It is possible that the warmth with which Khrushchev promoted peaceful coexistence may have been the result of the desire to regain for the Communist fatherland the prestige and policy initiative among the Communists that had been seriously compromised by the loss of Stalin, the Beria scandal, and Malenkov's failure to keep the power he had inherited.

Korean armistice

The Korean armistice and exchange of war prisoners showed several things of which the Kremlin was forced to take note. For one thing, neither the Communists nor the United Nations was willing to pay the cost in lives and other ways to try to unify Korea by victory on Korean soil. Neither side was ready to run the risk of a general war by spreading the fighting to the Communist "sanctuaries" in China or to the United Nations sanctuaries in Japan. The non-Korean belligerents wanted more to end the fighting than to unify Korea. The Communists must have wanted very badly to end the fighting or they would not have agreed to the voluntary repatriation of prisoners. They opposed this with all the means at their command short of continuing the war and finally agreed to the loss of face involved in the refusal of over 74 per cent of the Chinese "volunteers" to return to the fatherlands the Communists were in the process of transforming.

The Communists turned on the full force of their propaganda to obscure by extravagant claims of victory the bleak fact that they had failed in their major objective to win all of Korea by force, that they had provoked a successful application of the principle of collective action, under UN auspices, against aggression, and that they had caused the United States to speed up its rearmament and redouble its efforts to strengthen regional security and economic aid against direct and indirect aggression.

The war in Indochina

As the Korean crisis subsided into a stalemate, the war in Indochina, which had been treated as a brush fire or a fringe war for several years, suddenly seemed on the point of spreading throughout Southeast Asia. To what degree the stalemate in Korea enabled the Chinese Communists to increase their aid to Ho Chi Minh is not clear, but it is a fact that the Vietminh successes increased in range and significance after the Korean cease fire. It is also true that the regime of Bao Dai had lost prestige and the power of resistance and that both the funds and the morale of the French had been all but exhausted in a war that they could afford neither to win nor to lose. The United States seemed to be faced with the unpleasant choice of seeing all of Indochina fall into Communist hands or of intervening as in Korea, but without such a clearly drawn issue and against the prevailing opinion in Asia and in the North Atlantic Treaty Organization.

Geneva Conference, 1954

At the four-power conference in Berlin in February 1954, the foreign ministers of France, the United Kingdom, the Soviet Union, and the United States agreed to meet at Geneva on April 26 to discuss Korean questions and peace in Indochina.

Representatives of nineteen countries met at the Geneva Far Eastern Conference on April 26, 1954, to discuss these matters. The Russians again tried to have the Chinese People's Government given a status of equality with the Big Four but, largely through the opposition of the United States, failed. The plan for unification of Korea on the basis of free elections made no headway in the Conference chiefly because of conditions and obstacles presented by the North Korean regime, supported by the representatives of the Soviet Union and the Chinese People's Government. The Communists, who had been declared aggressors by the UN, took the line that the UN was the aggressor and should therefore be excluded from all responsibility for the proposed elections. This line had about the same relation to reality as the myth about the Chinese "volunteers" who in complete formations and with full equipment and logistical support had joined the Korean War. If the Communists of the Soviet Union did not originate this argument, they supported it. Korea remained divided, with the elections as far off as ever. So far as Korea is concerned, Soviet policy since Stalin has been to hold to the present division, build up North Korea militarily and economically, wait confidently for the disintegration of the present regime in the Republic of Korea or its abandonment by the United States and permit North Korea to remain in the sphere of interest of China.

The Communists had much greater success in that part of the Geneva meeting that dealt with Indochina. They were in a much stronger position, because the Vietminh forces, aided by China which in turn was aided by the Soviet Union, were winning victories. Their forces captured Dienbienphu on May 8, while negotiations were going on. The French, upon whom resistance largely depended, were weary and divided. The Vietnam nationalists were at odds among themselves and with the French.

Vietminh captures Dienbienphu in Indochina

The Americans, to whom both the French and the Vietnamese looked for material and moral support, were unwilling to intervene in force and so become involved in another "Korea," and they were reluctant for domestic political reasons to negotiate with the Vietminh and the Chinese Communists, with whom it was necessary for somebody to negotiate if the seven years' war in Indochina were to be ended. Neither the French nor the Americans came to Geneva with a program, much less a joint program, except the admirable but unrealistic objective of a free, united, and democratic Indochina, an objective that might have been realized only if the Vietminh had been losing instead of winning the war.

The Communists appeared to be willing to accept a stalemate of the Korean type. Since United States politics and policy prohibited Mr. Dulles from talking either peace or war with the Communists, the leadership and the laurels of the conference were taken by Sir Anthony Eden and Mr. Molotov, who served as presidents, and by Mr. Chou En-lai, who showed great skill in making the best use of the advantageous military and diplomatic position of the Communists and of the awkward predicament of their opponents, who were made to appear as opposed to peace and incapable of war.

Provisions on Indochina

On July 21, 1954, the representatives of the governments directly concerned signed agreements which included three provisions: All of north Vietnam from the Chinese border to approximately the seventeenth parallel was left under the control of the regime headed by Ho Chi Minh, now known as the Democratic Republic of Vietnam. Vietnam south of the parallel remained under the state of Vietnam, at that time headed by Bao Dai, the Emperor in absentia, who was soon succeeded by Ngo Dinh Diem, as the de facto head of the Vietnam government. The United States agreed to respect these terms but not to be responsible for their enforcement, which was left to a commission of Polish, Canadian, and Indian members under Indian chairmanship. The independence of Laos and Cambodia was recognized, and Laos was in effect divided like Vietnam when the Communist, Vietminh-led Laotian rebels, known under the ancient name of Pathet Lao, were given special status in three provinces, a status which they have since maintained with arms. The conference reaffirmed the unity of Vietnam (North and South) and agreed that its future status should be decided by a free and secret election to be held in July 1956.

COMMUNIST CHINA AFTER GENEVA

With the prestige gained by military success in Indochina and by diplomatic successes at Geneva the Communists intensified the propaganda of peaceful coexistence, and at the same time the Chinese Communists kept up the tension in the Formosa Strait by military activity and by threats to liberate the island of Formosa from alleged American occupation.

The five principles of Chou En-lai and Nehru

On June 28, 1954, Premier Chou En-lai and Pandit Nehru proclaimed their "five principles" of international conduct as a sound basis for peaceful coexistence among the nations of Asia. These principles had been the basis of the Sino-Indian agreement on Tibet of April 29, 1954. The five principles were: (1) nonaggression, (2) noninterference, (3) mutual respect, (4) equality and mutual benefit, (5) peaceful coexistence. There was, of course, nothing new about these principles. As a matter of fact, seventeen years before, on July 16, 1937, Secretary of State Cordell Hull, in different words, had covered all of these principles and in addition that of disarmament in his six "fundamental principles of international policy." They all are excellent proposals and all of them have been violated by the Communists, who committed flagrant aggression in Korea, interfered in every Asian country, and showed the utmost contempt and disrespect for the new governments set up by national and socialist parties of East and South Asian countries.

The joint promulgation of the five principles, however, had a great effect in Asia, for several reasons. They were proclaimed to be the basis of a "peace area" to which Red China and India and later Burma and Indonesia belonged. The USSR not only approved the "peace area" but, in effect, joined it by claiming that these were the very principles on which Soviet policy had been founded. The announcement was well timed, since it was issued while the Geneva talks were going on and world attention was focused on peace or war in Asia. The fact that Chou was a cosigner of the declaration seemed to suggest that the Communists might have turned over a new leaf and given up their aggressive program of liberating other Asians from their chosen leaders. The fact that Nehru was a cosigner seemed to suggest that the dangers of Red aggression and subversion could be eliminated if there were only enough confidence and good will to meet the Communists halfway.

Attitudes to U. S.

In contrast to this shining example of peaceful coexistence between "peace-loving" Communists and peace-loving non-Communists, all Communist parties and some neutralists following the Soviet lead in representing the United States as the imperialist aggressor and "colonizer" and the chief obstacle to peaceful coexistence. They denounced the Southeast Asia Treaty Organization formed under United States leadership at Manila in September 1954 as what *Pravda* later described as "the aggressive SEATO pact" and a "military conspiracy of the colonizers in Asia."[5] Vyshinskii carried the campaign in the

[5] May 20, 1955.

United Nations with a demand that something be done about American aggression against China.

Sino-Soviet relations

During the autumn of 1954 and the winter of 1955, while there was still much talk of war in Southeast Asia, Sino-Soviet relations appeared to reach a greater degree of intimacy and mutual admiration than ever. Following in the footsteps of the Soviet elder brother, the Chinese People's Congress, on September 20, adopted the Constitution of 1954, which was based on the Common Program and the two Organic Laws adopted in 1949. But it also borrowed many of the provisions and some of the language of the Stalin Constitution of 1936. The new organic law proclaimed the successful resistance to United States aggression and "indestructible friendship with the great USSR and the People's Democracies." The Chinese Communist party followed Soviet example in another way by launching a purge as the elder brother had done so often in Stalin's time. On the fifth anniversary of the Chinese Communist assumption of state power, the Soviet Union announced that all Soviet forces would be withdrawn from the Port Arthur naval base and all installations handed over free to the People's Government. This transfer took place on May 24, 1955.

The Chinese Communists gained more prestige than the Russians from the events in Korea and Indochina, and from Chou En-lai's diplomacy at Geneva and among China's Asian neighbors. These achievements may have strengthened Peking's position in dealing with Moscow and underscored the fact that China was not a satellite but a partner of the USSR. In February 1955 Molotov paid his Chinese comrades the honor of including China with the USSR as heads of the camp of Communism. The Soviet official statement accords the Chinese the honor of being referred to as the "great" Chinese people, an honor otherwise reserved for the "great Soviet people."

That China was still a junior partner of the Communist axis was clear from the fact of China's dependence on the Soviet Union for economic and technical aid in both civilian and military development programs. Three years after the Sino-Soviet Treaty of Friendship and Mutual Aid, China's trade with the Soviet bloc had grown from 26 per cent of the total to 72 per cent. In 1953 and again in 1954, when Khrushchev and Bulganin visited Peking, the Russians made economic and political agreements reflecting both China's growing prestige and her growing needs. The dissolution of the joint Sino-Soviet stock companies and the supply of more technicians were promised. But China's import needs were vastly greater than could be supplied by the USSR.

It is suggested that one immediate effect of China's increase in prestige and needs is to cause the Soviet Union to retain China's warm partnership "at the expense of weaker European countries," which have been forced to help foot the bill for China's economic development.

BANDUNG CONFERENCE

The Soviet Union strongly approved of the Bandung Conference, and the Communists did their best to make the most of the occasion to convince the Asians and Africans and, in fact, the world at large, that the Soviet and Chinese parties that had previously supported and directed sabotage, guerrilla, and civil wars against the Asian governments were now wholly dedicated to the proposition that countries having different political and social systems could and should exist peacefully side by side. Large Soviet and Chinese delegations with representatives of fourteen other countries attended an unofficial coexistence conference on April 10 at New Delhi as a kind of warming up for Bandung.

President Soekarno's speech

In his speech opening the conference, President Soekarno referred to two events of the past. One was the conference in Brussels by the League Against Imperialism nearly thirty years before. He observed that many distinguished delegates who were present at Bandung had attended the Brussels meeting to discuss their fight for independence. President Soekarno did not mention the further interesting fact that the League Against Imperialism was actually a "front" organization set up under the guidance of the Comintern to establish contact with leaders of Asian nationalist movements such as Pandit Nehru and Soekarno himself. Neither the League Against Imperialism nor the Comintern exists today, but the leaders of the Communist movement have revived their policy of cultivating contact with Asia nationalist leaders.

President Soekarno also mentioned the fact that the Bandung Conference was opening on April 18, the anniversary of Paul Revere's ride on April 18, 1775, and "the opening of the American War of Independence, the first successful anticolonial war in history."

Premier Chou En-lai

Premier Chou En-lai did not salute the Americans as pioneers in the struggle against colonialism, but his references to the United States as solely responsible for the tensions in the "Taiwan area" and in connection with SEATO were made in language much more restrained than had been customary in Communist comment on American policy and national character.

In urging the Asian-African delegates to seek common ground in spite of different ideologies and different social systems, Premier Chou said that two groups of Asian and African countries had gained independence since the war. One group consists of countries led by Communists, the other group of countries like India, Burma, and Indonesia, which are led by nationalists. "Is there any reason," asked Mr. Chou En-lai, "why we cannot understand and respect each other and give support and sympathy to each other?" The Premier failed to mention one important reason why such understanding and support would be difficult, the fact that in all of the countries of the second group the Communists have tried to overthrow and destroy the independent regimes set up by the nationalists. Did he expect that Asians and Africans who had been exposed to Communist conspiracy, abuse, and violence would have forgotten so soon? In any case, other members of the conference repaired the omission and pointed out to the Chinese delegate that Africans and Asians were exposed to more than one kind of imperialism.

Premier Chou replied with courtesy and restraint. He proposed that if "peaceful coexistence" were tainted with Communism the words "Live together in peace" be substituted. He suggested that two more principles be added to the five promulgated by Premier Nehru and himself: (6) "respect for the rights of people of all countries to choose freely a way of life as well as political and economic systems"; (7) "abstention from doing damage to each other." Far more significant was a remark later in his speech. Instead of the familiar "hate America" routine he said: "As to relations between China and the United States, the Chinese people do not want to have war with the United States. We are willing to settle international disputes by peaceful means." Chou En-lai did not, of course, admit that the problem of Formosa was an "international dispute" but he substituted "talk" for "war" as a method of dealing with differences between the United States and the People's Government.[6] This suggestion of negotiation instead of forceful liberation and the general moderation of his tone added to his prestige and con-

tributed to the success of his diplomacy, opening the way for the talks begun in Geneva on August 1, 1955, by Ambassadors U. Alexis Johnson and Wang Ping-nan.

CHINESE-INDONESIAN TREATY

The Premier of the People's Government gave tangible evidence of Red China's good intentions toward her neighbors by announcing at Bandung his government's willingness "to solve the problem of dual nationality of overseas Chinese with governments of the countries concerned." A treaty was negotiated with Indonesia in which Peking recognized the right of the Indonesian residents of Chinese descent to choose whether to become citizens of China or of Indonesia. This treaty, intended to be the model for similar treaties with other Soviet-East Asian countries, was perhaps also intended to diminish Chinese Nationalist influence among the 12,000,000 overseas Chinese, but even so it appeared to be a step in the right direction in an old and troublesome problem.

U.S.–PEKING TALKS AT GENEVA

Soon after the summit conference, talks began at Geneva at the ambassadorial level between Messrs. Johnson and Wang. After a month of talks the Peking government agreed to release the Americans whom they had seized and condemned as spies. This bandit style of diplomacy was practiced in more primitive societies where foreigners were seized and held for ransom. In the present case, as in Soviet negotiations with the Germans and Japanese, the ransom for the prisoners was some diplomatic concession to Communist demands. Communist concessions on repatriation, however, relieved tensions on a problem that the Communists had deliberately created. Neither at Bandung nor at Geneva had the Communists changed their position on basic Asian issues.

---

[6] This and preceding quotations are from *Selected Documents of the Bandung Conference: Texts of Selected Speeches and Final Communiqué of the Asian-African Conference, Bandung, Indonesia, April 18–24, 1955*, distributed by the Institute of Pacific Relations.

COMMUNIST OBJECTIVES

As several observers have noted, there has been much elbow rubbing and bending and much champagne and vodka drunk in the name of peaceful coexistence, but peaceful coexistence remains in the Communist ideology not an end but a means. The new tactical objectives are these: (1) to take advantage of the Asians' desire to make technological and social progress in the shortest possible time; (2) to exploit the Asians' hope of preventing their countries from becoming the battleground of the struggle between the two great power systems; (3) to prevent the West from making use of its greater resources in technology, capital, and the creative initiatives of a free society. Soviet support of the "peace area" based on the "five principles," the offers of technical and military aid not only to the Communist bloc but to the nations of South Asia and the Middle East, and the efforts to identify Soviet policy with that of the Arab-Asian bloc and the Bandung nations generally in opposition to colonialism —these are practical applications of the new tactics.

REVOLT AND SUPPRESSION IN EASTERN EUROPE

MADAN GOPAL GUPTA

Madan Gupta is a professor of political science at Allahabad University, India. He has published several books on Indian history and political theory in Hindi, and is also the author of a number of studies in English on international relations and Indian political developments. His description and analysis of events in Poland and Hungary from 1956 to 1958 are of particular interest because of Professor Gupta's nationality and India's present international position. He examines this phase of the East-West conflict from the point of view of a "neutral," attempting, so to speak, to reach an objective judgment from "outside." Whether this "neutrality" helps him to weigh up the forces at work in Poland and Hungary more accurately than a Western or Soviet observer might do is an open question. Each side, of course, would charge him with being naïve for failing to believe its "true" interpretation. The fact remains that millions of people in Southeast Asia, the Middle East, Africa, and elsewhere are sympathetic to one or another "neutralist" version of Soviet policy.

THE Western and Soviet explanations of the revolt in East Europe in 1956 differ widely. The Western argument is that the foremost factor in this was economic. The economic dislocations in Eastern Europe resulting from war-connected transfers or contributions to the Soviet Union, dismantlement and removal to the Soviet Union of industrial plant equipment, Soviet confiscation of German and Italian assets in Eastern Europe, the flow of reparation payments to the U.S.S.R. and People's Democracies, financial contributions toward the maintenance of Soviet occupation troops had created chaotic conditions. The joint stock companies, the unrestricted Soviet utilization of East Europe's transportation facilities, and the patterning of new industries in the countries of this region after the Soviet model had caused hardships. The bilateral trade agreements between them and the U.S.S.R. had led to a series of unequal trade relations in which the Soviet Union was invariably the winning partner. Prices paid by Moscow for satellite imports tended to be lower than prices prevailing on the world markets, while the average prices of Soviet exports to Eastern Europe were frequently higher. The bargaining power of the U.S.S.R., which could

From Madan Gopal Gupta, *International Relations Since 1919* (Allahabad, India, 1958), II, 315–331. Reprinted by permission of the Chaitanya Publishing House and M. G. Gupta.

operate fully through the mechanism of bilateral agreements, manifested itself also in Moscow's frequent role as a trade debtor within the orbit. This imposed upon the satellites the additional burden of carrying short-term commercial credits free of interest. For instance, Poland's prices of coal deliveries to the U.S.S.R. in exchange for Soviet shipments of German reparations to Poland were generally 90% below world market rates. In Poland as well as in Hungary the bulk of the people, so runs the Western argument, were being driven to desperation by intolerable conditions, low wages, long hours, shortage of food, shortage of housing, shortage of consumer goods. As Mr. W. N. Ewer put it: "Their economic position, so far from improving has been deteriorating, to the point at which hardship without hope had become unendurable." In short, it was a revolt against Communism.

Secondly, it is suggested that the revolt of the Poles and the Hungarians was against Russian domination and was largely inspired by national feeling as well as by national tradition. All of the East European countries, it is argued, have a national history and have some memories of national greatness. This national past is associated with religious faith. Again, there was not merely a nationalism of the masses, but as Hugh Seton-Watson has put it, there is also the nationalism of the leaders. The swift and massive industrialization created a new ruling class—"a state bourgeoisie"—possessing many of the moral and intellectual characteristics of the private bourgeoisie elevated by the industrial revolution in the early stages of West European capitalism. And these leaders naturally resented foreign domination. It is true that nearly all the countries of Eastern Europe with the exception of East Germany are Slav in race and language and thus there is some link and identity of interest between them and Russia. But it should not be forgotten that it was largely the Soviet security interests, the position of great military

strength which the Soviet Union had in 1944–45 in the region, and "some of the old Czarist ambitions to spread out, more especially over the Slav areas" which led to the communization of these areas. As Mr. Nehru wrote on his return from Moscow in July 1955: "It (the Soviet Union) also had the desire to protect itself in the future by having as many friendly countries as possible next to its borders. The easiest way to have a friendly country appeared to them to have a communist regime there under their patronage." The desire to liberate themselves from the Soviet patronage therefore was natural. On this showing, therefore, the revolt both in Hungary and Poland can be said to be an essentially nationalist movement.

Thirdly, it is pointed out that the post-Stalin New Look in Russia, the normalization of relations with Yugoslavia, and the process of liberalization in People's Democracies were major causes of revolt in Hungary and Poland. Thus Richard Lowenthal has argued: "The major common factor in the background of both the Polish and Hungarian events was clearly the weakening of Soviet authority both within the international communist movement in general and within the satellite states in particular. That weakening, which has proceeded slowly and gradually ever since the death of Stalin and the loosening of economic and police controls in the satellites, was greatly accelerated by two major events: the Belgrade Declaration of 1955 by which the Soviet rulers recognized Yugoslavia's right to her 'own road to socialism' and the 'secret' Khrushchev attack on Stalin at the Twentieth Congress of the C.P.S.U." Khrushchev's disclosure and condemnation of Stalin's methods of rule and conduct of foreign policy combined with the relaxation policy at home, a peace offensive abroad and the rehabilitation of Tito naturally led to a weakening of Soviet control which "found visible expression in the astonishing outburst of free criticism in the Polish communist and non-party press, in the openly critical discussions conducted before ever larger audiences of writers, students and young officers in Budapest." All these factors, it is further argued, prevented the Soviet Union from successfully reasserting its authority at least in Poland, for the use or open threat of force would have jeopardized Soviet efforts to woo the "uncommitted nations" and would have caused renewed friction with the Yugoslavs.

On the other hand, the Soviet explanation of East European revolt is that imperialist and reactionary Polish underground agents, taking advantage of certain economic difficulties, incited serious disturbances in Poland. Similarly, about Hungary it is suggested that "internal and international reactionary and counter-revolutionary forces launched an attack on socialist gains" and "attempted to utilize the pent-up resentment of the masses of the working people who rightly called for an improvement in the country's guidance and for a rise in the living standards of the population." The Soviet Union also alleged that the former government and party leadership of Hungary headed by Rakosi and Geroe had made "grave mistakes in resolving the problems of socialist construction both in questions of policy and in the field of economic and cultural construction. The Rakosi-Geroe leadership and government bodies showed a lack of vigilance and overlooked both the spread of just resentment among the people and the ever-growing subversive conspiratorial activity of the counter-revolutionary elements."

What, in fact, is the objective explanation? Is it correct to attribute all this to the personality cult and to the system associated with it? It is suggested that if "Stalinism" was wrong and responsible for creating discontent, the process of de-Stalinization and the manner in which it was carried out was responsible for stirring it. It has been certainly carried out "in a somewhat disingenuous fashion, without taking the progressive movement in the world into confidence." Moreover, it has been applied "unequally." The break with Stalinism in Moscow at the 20th Party Congress should have been synchronized organically and not merely in an *ad hoc* series of improvisations, with a complete overhaul of the whole structure of the foreign relations of the Soviet Union. Nothing of the kind was done. While the Soviet Union undertook a reorientation with the West and "normalization of relations" with Yugoslavia, the framework of Soviet relationship with the People's Democracies was left almost untouched, and for this a heavy price had to be paid. This might be due to the fact that the Soviet Union was badly informed of the state of affairs in these countries as the "information often came from sycophantic sources who, over the years had become rather like the countries in the story of the Emperor's clothes."

It is against this background that we will briefly summarize the Polish and the Hungarian revolts and their after-effects.

THE POLISH REVOLT

Soon after the death of Stalin, a movement towards liberalization and relaxation had begun in Poland. In October 1953, Beirut declared at a plenary meeting of the Polish Party's Central Committee that the party's aim must be "a rapid rise in the living standards of the working people in town and countryside." Investment in agriculture was to be 45% greater in 1955 than in 1953, and investment in consumer goods, housing and social welfare about one-third greater. Aid was to be given to individual peasants as well as to collective and state farms. Detailed plans were to be discussed at a party congress, announced for mid-January 1954. In the religious sphere, however, the struggle continued and in September 1953, Cardinal Wyszinsky was arrested. The Soviet security system also remained tight, possibly because they did not wish to take any chance. Poland, it was realized, lies on the main line of communication with East Germany, where the Soviet weakness had been decisively demonstrated in the workers' uprisings of June 1953. But in April 1954 the Polish Council of Art and Culture condemned the principles of dictation from above, restrictions on the artists' freedom of expression and discouragement of experimentation. In January 1955, the communist Workers' Party Central Committee decided to democratize the security police and to restrict its supreme power. In May, "a soul-searching criticism of managerial and trade union practices" was undertaken and at the same time "the personality cult" came under fire. In February 1956 the 20th Party Congress released powerful forces and the objective of independence from Soviet control was evolved. A demand for freedom for the growth of realism, and schools of art other than socialist, and increased cultural contacts with the West grew and the Polish press started discussing frankly the past practices of parliamentary life in Poland. On March 12, Beirut, leader of the Polish Party, died and his death marked the end of one-man dictatorship in Poland. "There arose a dualism in the Warsaw ruling system, with control divided between the party on the one hand—under the leadership of Edward Ochab, Beirut's successor—and the government on the other hand—headed by Premier Josef Cyrankiewicz." In April for the first time in many years key economic and social problems were discussed publicly and the government promised a number of economic and social reforms. About 200,000 persons were given amnesty. Many Stalinists were removed from the government and were replaced by adherents of Cyrankiewicz' liberation policy. The pro-Stalin critics were ignored. Earlier on March 27, 1956, Jerzy Morawski, Secretary of the Polish United Workers Party had published an article on "the lessons of the 20th Congress of the C.P.S.U." and condemned Stalinism. On April 7, Ochab acknowledged "the painful and bitter truth about the mistakes of Joseph Stalin." On

April 23, Cyrankiewicz addressed the Sejm and expressed his government's firm determination "to carry to the end the investigation concerning those guilty of breaches of the rule of law, of applying illegal investigating methods and of concocting trials." On April 29, Ochab writing in *Pravda* on Lenin's rules and principles of Party life, returned to the theme of the anti-Stalin campaign. Meanwhile, trade unions in Poland were getting stale and they had lost contact with and the cooperation of the laboring masses. Abuses and malpractices were rampant. The state railroads had not issued since 1951 the clothing due to their workers as partial pay. There was evidence of managerial misuse of the enterprise funds allocated to improve the workers' standard of living. The Polish labor resources were thus practically exhausted. The rigorous labor legislation was rigorously enforced and appeals against misuses went unheeded. This was roughly the background of the riots in Poland.

On June 17, 1956 an International Fair opened in Poznań. On June 28, workers of the *ZISPO* factory (locomotives and heavy machinery) and other plants staged "a demonstration which turned into a riot and finally a pitched battle between the rioters and armed detachments of the police." On June 29, the riots were quelled and a government delegation headed by Cyrankiewicz arrived on the spot. The Government attributed the riots to the "imperialist agents and the reactionary underground . . . trying to use the economic difficulties and shortcomings at several Poznań enterprises to incite outbursts against the people's rule." The same day the *Trybuno Ludu* carried an editorial, "Provocation," and cast aspersions on "one of the American fanatics of the cold war," and Cyrankiewicz issued a proclamation to the people of Poznań and charged the "imperialist centers" with exploiting "the dissatisfaction of a portion of the workers and laborers of Poznań, caused by the difficult material conditions of the working population." Thus the immediate conclusion drawn was that vigilance against "the class enemy from within and subversion by agents from abroad" could not be relaxed. On July 1, *Pravda* declared that "hostile agents carried out a crude provocation in Poznań." The same day the Yugoslav official view was released that "the true meaning of the Poznań disorders must be sought in the attempt of reactionary forces to compromise the process of domestic development in Poland and after long years of Stalinist deformation is now following the path of democratization and concern for the people's everyday needs."

Soon after, however, the Polish official view started changing and the *Trybuno Ludu* made a distinction between "a legal strike movement by the Poznań workers" and "the illegal acts of violence" which followed, and suggested that there had been two entirely different movements in Poznań and that all began with a perfectly legal demonstration of workers and in a later phase, hostile forces entered and transformed the demonstration into "an armed provocation." On July 18–28 the Central Committee of the Polish United Workers Party held its 7th plenary session and in a resolution declared that "the Poznań events cannot be treated in isolation from the situation in the country. . . . Dissatisfaction in many workers' centers is being accentuated by prolonged and frequently soulless dealing with the first demands and grievances of the working men. This leads to the upsetting of proper relations between the different sections of the working class and the party and the people's power; it gives birth to feelings of mistrust and disappointment." On July 19, Ochab spoke out and completely repudiated the original explanation of the Poznań riots: "In investigating the reasons for these occurrences it would be wrong to have mainly in view the machinations of provocateurs and imperialist agents. Rather one must first look for the social roots of what happened." This change must have disturbed Moscow. On July 20, a Soviet delegation headed by Bulganin and Zhukov came to Poland for the celebration of the 12th anniversary of Poland's liberation from Nazi occupation. On July 21, Bulganin in his address revived the theory of imperialist instigation: "The recent events at Poznań, provoked by enemy agents, serve as additional proof that the international reaction has still not abandoned its delirious dreams of restoring capitalism in the socialist countries. We cannot forget this for a second. The Western frontiers and Silesia are now for ever Polish."

The Soviet leaders, however, failed in their effort to revive the legend of imperialist instigation of the Poznań riots and in another resolution the Polish Central Committee admitted that "in the course of implementation of the 6-year Plan several disproportions occurred in our national economy" and "that discontent was due to disillusionment over the unfulfilled hopes for a substantial improvement in the standard of living."

Gomulka comes to power. In order to escape from these difficulties, the Polish Government and Party resorted to two methods. One was to promise a swift change of course followed by the dismissal from office of the responsible economic ministers in order to allay discontent. The other was to initiate talks with Wladyslaw Gomulka and to reinstate him as a party member. It may be mentioned that Gomulka was purged in 1949 (after conflict between Tito and Stalin) for advocating an "independent Polish approach to socialism." Through his punishment, imprisonment and opposition to forced collectivization, he had become "a symbol of resistance to Moscow." The attempt to reinstate Gomulka was naturally unwelcome to the old Stalinists in Poland and to the Soviet Union, which would not permit anti-Stalinism to such an absurd degree. Nevertheless, on August 4, 1956, the Politburo of the P.U.W.P. restored "to comrade Gomulka his rights as a party member." The next step was to entrust him with party leadership in order to stem the rot. But Gomulka held the trump cards and he chose to move them correctly. He laid down his terms: no economic demagogy, abandonment of forced collectivization and enforced agricultural deliveries, devolution of the M.T.S., decentralization of economic planning and acceptance of workers' control, reorientation of Polish-Soviet relations on a basis of equality, and removal of Soviet stooges from the party leadership. In September these demands were conceded. On October 15, the Politburo of the P.U.W.P. decided to call the 8th session of the Central Committee on October 19. The Central Committee met that day and co-opted Gomulka. He was re-elected as Secretary-General of the P.U.W.P. and Beirut's co-workers were removed from their positions.

New Poland: October 1956—April 1958. The day the 8th session of the Central Committee met, a Soviet delegation led by Khrushchev, Kaganovich, Mikoyan and Molotov came to Warsaw to discuss with the Polish party leaders "current problems of interest for the two parties." They were obviously annoyed at the turn of events in Poland. It was reported that they called Gomulka a traitor and ordered Soviet troop movements from various parts of the country in the direction of Warsaw. The Poles, however, stuck to their guns and all that the Soviet leaders could obtain from the Poles was an agreement that a delegation of Polish leaders would go to Moscow "in the nearest future" to discuss with the Soviet leaders "problems of further strengthening the political and economic cooperation" between their countries and "of further consolidating the fraternal friendship and coexistence of the P.U.W.P. and the C.P.S.U." The Soviet leaders left Warsaw on October 20 . On October 20–21, Gomulka resumed the party leadership, removed the Soviet stooges from it and made changes in the army. Meanwhile trouble in Hungary

had begun, to which we will turn shortly.

About new Poland, three points deserve special attention. *First,* since Gomulka came to power, the process of liberalization has gone quite far, though not as far as in Yugoslavia. *Secondly,* the relations between Poland and the U.S.S.R. have been uneasy but correct. Poland is, therefore, a symbol of national communism and in spite of the fact that it remains a part of the Warsaw Pact, it can no longer be regarded as part of international communism. *Thirdly,* the relations of Gomulka's Poland with the West have become closer and more friendly than ever since 1945.

So far as the process of liberalization is concerned, Gomulka soon after assumption of power broadened the popular base of the Sejm and a new electoral law was passed. In his speech on October 20, 1956, he had outlined his program in detail (See *National Communism and Popular Revolt in Eastern Europe,* edited by Paul E. Zinner, pp. 197-234). The stress on heavy industry has since been replaced by emphasis on consumer goods. Forced collectivization has been abolished. Collectives have been allowed to dissolve and repressive measures against private farming have been withdrawn. The educational system has been liberalized; Press censorship has been relaxed; free dissemination of foreign literature has been allowed. The experiments in Yugoslavia as well as Mao's "hundred flowers" have had a catch in Poland. Private initiative is encouraged. The secret police has been neutralized and "the dogma—the official ideology—has completely disintegrated under repeated onslaughts from the reawakened intellectuals, from disillusioned youths, from minds finally freed from the silence of fear. Common sense, experimentation and pragmatism are taking its place." Nor does the party maintain "the monolithic facade" so marked a feature of totalitarianism. It is true that Poland is not a democracy. Parliamentary institutions are lacking and rule of law is also missing. There is no rule by the people and a minority decides what is objectively good for the people. Indeed, one authority has described Gomulka's regime as "a Government of National Defense." It has all the contradictions that such a concept implies. There is intellectual freedom but there is also party control. Hatred of Russia exists side by side with military and political alliance with Moscow. It holds an anti-religious ideology yet it has granted the Catholic Church rights denied to it in "pluralistic and democratic" countries, e.g. freedom of religious instructions in the public schools.

So far as the Polish relations with the Soviet Union are concerned, for the most part they have been uneasy. We have noted that Khrushchev had invited the Polish leaders to Moscow on October 20, 1956. The visit came off in November. It should be remembered that the background of Polish-Soviet relations has been rather unhappy and the Polish people's experience with their Soviet neighbors since 1939 can have done nothing to improve matters. Indeed, it might even be said that the Poles have become accustomed to equate their hatred of communism with their dislike of all things Russian. Nor has the Polish Communist Party had any reason to feel particularly attached to the "mother land of the Revolution. Gomulka's task was really difficult to contain the widespread and potentially violent anti-Soviet feeling of the Polish people, while preventing the Russians from using force to retain their position." He wanted to terminate Soviet economic exploitation and political domination without having a complete break with Moscow. The negotiations at Moscow and their results should be appreciated in this context. These yielded an agreement limiting the number, location and movements of Soviet troops within the borders of Poland and providing for Soviet expenditure on their stay in Poland. The Polish debts in the nominal amount of about 2 billion rubles, run up by earlier Soviet credits were cancelled outright and Poland was granted a new advance on goods in the amount of about a third of this sum. The Poles were left free to accept economic aid from the West. Shortly after, negotiations were actually started between Poland and the United States. The concessions which the Poles gave to the Soviet Union were especially valuable for the latter at that moment particularly because just then in Hungary the Nagy government had brought Soviet prestige in jeopardy. For the Poles the alliance with the Soviet Union was valuable "not only because the U.S.S.R. is the only great power to guarantee the Oder-Neisse frontier, but also because the repudiation of this alliance and Poland's secession from the Warsaw Pact is the one thing the Kremlin would not tolerate." For the Soviet Union it was more risky and more difficult to relax their ideological hold over Poland than to surrender some of their economic privileges. For the Poles there was the fear of Germany, West German rearmament and the German demand for alteration of the provisional Oder-Neisse boundary. From the Soviet standpoint a Soviet guarantee of this boundary would "keep Warsaw tied to the Soviet bloc." The Polish independence is therefore precarious. They are friendly to Kadar's Government in Hungary and yet they opposed Soviet intervention there. In a vote on this question in the General Assembly, the Polish representative for the first time in many years dissociated himself from the stand of the Soviet Union by abstaining from voting. On the one hand, Gomulka says that "the road to socialism pursued by the U.S.S.R. under specific conditions is neither fully necessary nor entirely suitable for other nations"—a thesis of National Communism. On the other, he maintains that "Our party most resolutely condemns everything directed against the unity of the socialist camp, everything that undermines Polish-Soviet friendship"—a thesis of unity of the Socialist Camp. In this light one can better appreciate the Polish adherence to the Moscow Declaration of November 22, 1957, to which we earlier referred.

In maintaining this precarious balance, the Poles have been helped not only by Yugoslavia but also by China. The Chinese formula "Let all flowers blossom, let diverse schools of thought contend" is a very useful argument in support of Poland's National road to Socialism which consists of Workers' Councils, increased administrative autonomy, greater freedom to the peasants and emphasis on cooperation, agreement with the Church, greater political freedom, cooperation with the West and friendship with the Soviet Union and its allies. Poland is not as independent of Moscow as Yugoslavia because Gomulka is not as strong in his party as Tito was in his, because of the greater entrenched power of the Catholic Church in Poland, because of the Soviet support—a very valuable support indeed—for the Polish frontiers and because the U.S.S.R. would not tolerate as free a Poland as Yugoslavia. Thus sandwiched between the Germans and the Russians, the Poles can hardly afford a really independent foreign policy. Nevertheless, the Polish relations with the West since November 1956 have been remarkably good. Trade with the German Federal Republic has been considerably expanded. The U. S. loan of 200 million dollars was obtained in the summer of 1957 and credits have been obtained from France and the U. K. As a result of the pressure of public opinion, the convicts at the Poznań trial were released and a "real basis for an exchange of ideas between the Polish legal profession and the legal opinion of the non-communist world developed."

THE HUNGARIAN REVOLT

The Hungarian revolt of October 1956 was essentially a liberal nationalist uprising against Stalinist communism and foreigners' control, led by the workers and youth, and was ultimately crushed by a combination of such factors as lack of honest local leadership, the enormous might of the Soviet troops and tanks, general panic and confusion caused by the Suez crisis, un-

certainty of a presidential election year in the United States, and the general ineffectiveness of the United Nations. We have summarized in a previous chapter the situation in Hungary from 1945 to 1952. During this period Hungary had grown into a People's Democracy. Rajk had been executed in 1949 as a Titoist and the Stalin constitution had been adopted in 1950. When, therefore, Stalin died, there emerged a spontaneous urge for relaxation and the New Course was at once adopted. Ten days after the Berlin revolt—on June 27-28, 1953 —the principle of collective leadership was accepted. Hitherto M. Rakosi was the Secretary-General of the Party as well as the Premier. Now, the former post was abolished and was replaced by a secretariat of three so that Rakosi had to share power with two others. On July 2, he ceased to be the Prime Minister and Imre Nagy (the Hungarian Malenkov) was appointed to this office in order to raise the living standards of the industrial workers, to revise the Labor Code, to increase the production of consumer goods, and to slow down the compulsory collectivization of agriculture. But Rakosi (still the Secretary-General) and Geroe—the principal protagonist of economic planning—were rather opposed to these measures announced by Nagy on July 4, and the regime, therefore, felt shaky. Discipline was undermined, peasants started leaving the co-operatives and party ranks were confused. Rakosi and Nagy, therefore, were forced to restate the new policy and no more was now heard of increased freedom in religion and in small trade and the promises made by Nagy remained unfulfilled. In 1954, however, the liberalization process went ahead, crop quotas were reduced, peasants were granted cuts in income tax. By March 1955, Rakosi prevailed on the Soviet Union to dismiss Nagy for "having gone too far with his new course." This was followed by a tightening of control, except that criticism within the Party and comparative freedom of expression continued. In November, Nagy was expelled from the party. Towards the latter half of 1955 a most significant manifestation of intellectual unrest occured against the maintenance of rigid, arbitrary and stifling party controls over literary activity. The communist students organized the Petofi Circle (after the name of the Hungarian Poet and patriot Alexander Petofi, 1823–49), which in course of time became a center of intellectual ferment. In February 1956, the 20th Party Congress unleashed powerful forces. The first effect of these forces was visible on March 29, 1956, when Rajk's name was restored to grace and Janos Kadar, a former ally of Rajk, was released from prison. In May, anti-Stalinism had gone so far ahead that Rakosi was openly criticized in the Press and on July 18, he was replaced as party chief by Ernoe Geroe. Although Geroe was a no less rigid Stalinist than Rakosi, the former at once called for reconciliation with Tito. In June, the Poznań riots had occurred and on July 21, Mikoyan came to Budapest in order to curb a further extension of the Poznań spirit. In September, a directive is reported to have been sent by the Soviet government emphasizing the leading role of the U.S.S.R. This annoyed Tito and this in turn brought Khrushchev to Belgrade and then Tito to Yalta on September 30 for talks in which Geroe also joined. Meanwhile the intellectual climate of the revolt was being prepared and the Petofi Circle evolved the demand for the rehabilitation of Nagy who had became the symbol of reform and freedom. Gomulka's advent in Poland gave a further impetus to the revolutionary tendencies and the progress of de-Stalinization.

On October 3, the Central Committee of the Hungarian Workers Party (H.W.P.) announced the decision to pay "last respects to comrades who, as a result of political trials in past years, have been innocently condemned and executed." On October 6, Rajk was disinterred and given a public funeral with honors, while an estimated 200,000 Hungarians marched beside his coffin. On October 10, the Government praised Tito for his fight against "Stalinist tyranny," and on October 13, Nagy was reinstated in the party. On the same day Gen. Mihaly Farkas, former secret police Chief under Rakosi was arrested for having violated "socialist legality." On October 14, a Hungarian delegation under the leadership of Ernoe Geroe departed to Yugoslavia to formalize the terms of friendly cooperation between the two countries. On October 20, about 3,000 students of the University of Szeged broke with the communist youth organization and the same day the party organ declared the need for a "Hungarian way to socialism." Nagy was restored to the Academy of Sciences and the Budapest radio welcomed the rehabilitation of Gomulka. On October 22, the Petofi Circle formulated demands for greater personal and national freedom including the demand that all trade agreements with the Soviet Union be made public and relations with it be established on a basis of equality. Popular demonstrations in Gyor called for the release of Cardinal Mindszenty, for the withdrawal from Hungary of all Soviet troops and for the return of Nagy. The demonstrations organized by the Petofi Circle acquired a mass character on October 23 and the Ministry of Interior had to lift the ban on public assembly under pressure of the demonstrators.

Stages of Revolt. Four clear phases of the Hungarian Revolt can be easily traced: (a) From October 23, 1956 to October 29, ending with the defeat of the Soviet attempt to crush the revolt. (b) From October 29 to November 3, when Hungary had freed itself from the Soviet control. (c) From November 4 to November 11, when the second Soviet intervention began and ended. (d) From November 11, 1956 to early January 1957, when the passive resistance stage of the revolution came to an end and the pre-revolt pattern was restored.

The disturbances which began in Budapest on October 23, rapidly spread to the entire country. Geroe's broadcast of October 23, protesting against nationalist excesses and defending the Soviet-Hungarian relations, and the police firing at the demonstrators converted the demonstrations into "violent and uncontrollable riots." In the night of October 23–24, the Hungarian Central Committee met and decided to call in Nagy to head the government. At the same time, without Nagy's knowledge, Geroe requested help from the Russians under the Warsaw Pact. On October 24, Hegedus resigned and was replaced by Nagy and the Soviet-Hungarian troops were sent to suppress the riots. On October 25, Mikoyan and Suslov flew into Budapest, ousted Geroe as party secretary and acceded to Nagy's assumption of office. Kadar was appointed as party secretary. It was decided that Nagy would announce "a series of concessions promising withdrawal of Soviet troops from the city of Budapest" and a review of Soviet-Hungarian treaties. On October 26, Nagy recognized the justice of some of the demands of the demonstrators and ascribed the unrest to "mistakes and crimes" of the last ten years, and promised complete Soviet military withdrawal from Hungary. On October 27, he announced his new coalition cabinet including Tildy and Kovacs and next day he conceded victory to the rebels and announced that negotiations had begun with the Soviet Union about the withdrawal of Soviet troops. On October 29, the political police was dissolved and the Soviets began to withdraw from Budapest as requested. On October 30, Nagy denied responsibility for calling in the Russian troops on October 24 and announced that they would completely withdraw from Budapest on October 31. The Hungarian Air Force command published an ultimatum giving the Soviet troops 12 hours to leave Budapest. Free elections were promised by Nagy.

On October 30, it must have been realized in Moscow that the despatch of Soviet troops on October 24 had aggravated the situation in Hungary. That day a remarkable statement was drafted and released the next day under the caption "Settlement of Relations Between Socialist States." In this the Soviet government expressed readiness "to discuss together with the governments of other socialist states measures ensuring further development and strengthening of economic ties among the socialist countries in order to remove any possibility of violation of the principles of national sovereignty, mutual benefit and equality in economic relations." The Soviet government also raised the point of recalling its advisers from the People's Democracies and expressed its readiness "to review with the other socialist countries which are members of the Warsaw Treaty the question of Soviet troops stationed on the territory of the above-mentioned countries." Referring to the Hungarian situation the statement said: "Having in mind that the further presence of Soviet military units in Hungary could serve as an excuse for further aggravation of the situation, the Soviet government has given its military command instructions to withdraw the Soviet military units from the city of Budapest (and) is prepared to enter into negotiations with Hungary and other members of the Warsaw Treaty on the question of the presence of Soviet troops on the territory of Hungary."

On October 31, it was confirmed that the Soviet troops had left Budapest. The same day Cardinal Mindszenty was released. From October 29 to November 3, Hungary had come to its own. Nagy formed his new coalition cabinet including the representatives of the Socialist Democrats and the Petofi Party. Local councils were formed in every factory, municipality, city and county. Workers' Councils had taken over the factories, and demands for independence of the Soviet control were raised. Old political parties were re-established. The communists were feeling isolated. Press censorship was removed. But the rift between Nagy and Kadar was widening, the cleavage between people and party had become final. "Nagy had chosen the people, and Kadar the party."

The renewed Soviet intervention. On October 31, Mikoyan and Suslov again came to Budapest and discovered that the revolution in Hungary was almost complete. On November 1, Nagy demanded of the Soviet Ambassador to Hungary that Soviet troops newly arrived be immediately withdrawn, gave notice to terminate Hungarian adherence to the Warsaw Pact, declared Hungarian neutrality, and requested the U.N. Secretary General to place the question of Hungarian neutrality on the next agenda of the General Assembly. The same day Tildy told Mikoyan that the Warsaw Pact would in any case be repudiated by Hungary, and Mikoyan and Suslov met Kadar. It was, presumably, in this meeting that the decision to form a new government by Kadar which would invite Soviet military intervention, was taken. This decision must have also been induced by the diversion of world opinion to events in the Middle East. On October 30, the Anglo-French ultimatum was delivered to Cairo and in the context of the possible reactions in the United States and in Afro-Asian countries to this ultimatum the Soviet leaders could be sure "that the shock which the use of force in Hungary would cause would be substantially mitigated throughout the world." Possibly Eden's own decision to attack Egypt at this time might have been influenced by the same logic. In any case the two events seem to be interrelated and acted and reacted on each other. On November 2-3 substantial additional Soviet forces moved into Hungary. The Austrian border was sealed. As late as November 3, Radio Budapest announced that in a joint committee of Soviet military leaders and the representatives of the Hungarian Government that day the Soviet delegation had promised that no further moves of Soviet troops would take place across the Hungarian frontier.

On November 4, the Soviet troops attacked Budapest, Nagy was deposed and took refuge in the Yugoslav embassy. Kadar was appointed Prime Minister. He made promises of amnesty of coalition and popular front governments and withdrawal of Soviet troops. The armed resistance of Hungarian troops lasted for six days. From November 11 onward, passive resistance was offered by the industrial workers. Kadar could not fulfill the promises he made. On November 22, Nagy was abducted by the Soviet authorities in spite of the safe conduct Kadar gave him. The revolutionary councils were dissolved and workers' councils were made illegal on December 8. On December 28, the Writers' Union was suspended. On January 11, the Csepel armed rising was suppressed.

Hungary, 1957–58. In January, Khrushchev, Malenkov and Chou En-lai visited Budapest and in order to allay the world opinion roused against the U.S.S.R., a policy of compromise was laid down. The Government was still "too weak to ignore the mood of the masses." The Yugoslavs had been shaken by recent events and the policy of rapprochement received a jerk. But by March 1957 there came a shift and regimentation and Soviet control was reestablished. On March 20, a Hungarian delegation led by Kadar came to Moscow and held talks with the Soviet leaders for a week. A Soviet-Hungarian Treaty was signed on March 27 under which the Soviet Union agreed to deliver goods valued at 1,010 million rubles, a long term credit for 1957 amounting to 750 million rubles of which 200 million is in convertible currency. On March 28, a joint declaration was issued which affirmed that the two governments deemed it "absolutely necessary that Soviet troops should be temporarily stationed in Hungary" and that negotiations on the subject would soon begin. On May 27, a Soviet delegation led by Gromyko and Zhukov came to Budapest and signed with Hungary the agreement the same day. It reaffirmed the Moscow Declaration of

March 28 and provided for the Hungarian courts jurisdiction over Soviet soldiers in the cases of civil and criminal offences. It makes no reference to the number or location of Soviet troops or to the date of their withdrawal. The agreement is to remain in force as long as Soviet troops are stationed in Hungary. On April 2, Kadar left no doubt on the point and declared that "Soviet troops will remain here as long as their presence is needed." The Russian language has again become compulsory in schools. Collective farms have been revived and taxes on the peasantry have been increased. On August 1, 1957, a flat 10% cut in industrial wages was effected and the workers in a number of factories were ordered to pay back unjustified wage increases. The rebels were arrested and under the martial law decrees of December 8 and December 12, 1956, hundreds of them have been executed. In September 1957 a Hungarian diplomatic offensive in the Near East began to forestall the United Nations General Assembly debate. In November, elections were held and the Communists won 99.7% votes. On December 18, 1957, Hungary and the Soviet Union signed a new agreement on economic and technical aid, under which Hungary received a long term credit of 300 million rubles. On April 2, 1958, a Soviet Party and Government Delegation led by Khrushchev came to Budapest to attend the 13th anniversary of the country's liberation from Nazi invaders. Khrushchev declared on April 3 that "the October–November events in Hungary were 'a test of Soviet-Hungarian friendship,'" and Kadar and Premier Ferene Muennich assured their guests that "Hungary will remain loyal to proletarian internationalism."

The Soviet view of Hungarian revolt. The Soviet view of the events in Hungary is entirely different. They argue that the former leadership of Hungary was responsible for gross mistakes and abuses in general political questions and economic policies, that the demonstrations of October 23 against these mistakes were "quite legitimate" but that soon "reactionary fascist elements tried to exploit this healthy movement for their purposes in an attempt to wreck the people's democratic system and to overthrow it." The use of Soviet troops stationed in Hungary under the Warsaw Treaty and at the express request of the Hungarian Government was proper and valid. Nevertheless, to prevent an aggravation of the situation the Soviet Union decided to withdraw their troops on October 29, 1956. Soon after, however, the reactionaries, internal and external, started a murder campaign, "hanging upright patriots on the lamp posts in the streets of Budapest," and pushed the Nagy Government which had lost control of the situation further and further on to the road of "conniving at rebellion." A "Hungarian Committee" was set up in Vienna to render assistance to the rebels. Nagy being a traitor, honest patriots like Kadar quitted his government and, supported by the people, formed a popular government which requested the Soviet Union, on November 4, for assistance in repulsing the onslaught of the fascist forces. The Soviet Union's intervention was perfectly valid because (*a*) it had been sought by a friendly country, (*b*) the Soviet Union had treaty obligations under the Hungarian Peace Treaty, to which U.S.A. and U.K. were parties, to suppress fascism in Hungary, and (*c*) because the Soviet Union could not have allowed the victory of reaction on her border. It is further argued that the role of the U.S.A. in these events has been abominable, that the U.S. Congress had authorized the training of special personnel for guiding the resistance movement, for propaganda and infiltration in East Europe, and had sanctioned "hundreds of millions of dollars" not for refugee relief but for "feeding the subversive activities." The Soviet Union, therefore, rejected the allegations of aggression, genocide, and deportation as "stinking newspaper canard picked up on a junk heap of refuted misinformation" and denied the competence of the U.N. to act on the Hungarian developments. With the handling of the Hungarian developments by the United Nations, we will deal in a later chapter.

Conclusions. Meanwhile we can draw useful conclusions from this survey of events in East Europe. Whatever the truth in the Soviet allegations of subversion financed and instigated by the United States, it is certain that if certain reactionary forces had not come to dominate the uprising in Hungary and if Nagy had been more energetic and less hesitant in acting against these forces, the Soviet Union would have acted in the spirit of the Declaration of October 30. The Soviet decision to intervene on November 4 must have really been a difficult decision and "the Soviet leaders could not have been unaware of the golden opportunities of propaganda it would offer to all the Cold Warriors of the world." The alternative to intervention

appeared to be counter-revolution to the Soviet leaders and, therefore, intervention appeared to be a lesser evil. This substantiated the view of Mr. Nehru expressed in July 1955 about East European countries:

Whether these countries are strong or weak, it seems exceedingly unlikely that any change will come to them by external pressure, apart from war and its results. In fact, the whole idea of "liberating" them, as expressed in America, really makes it more difficult for any change to come there peacefully. The Soviet Union will resist to the utmost any pressure tactics in regard to these states because if they go outside its influence, this will endanger the Soviet Union's security. It is possible, however, and indeed probable, that if there is a marked improvement in world tensions and the cold war ceases, then internal developments and changes will take place in these East European states. The Soviet Union may well withdraw its armies where they exist and its political domination will also become less, though its influence will remain.

NEW INTEREST IN THE MIDDLE EAST

WALTER Z. LAQUEUR

A prolific and discerning journalist, Mr. Laqueur is author of *Communism and Nationalism in the Middle East* and *The Soviet Union and the Middle East.* He has also published numerous shorter studies dealing with Soviet foreign relations, and is editor of *Soviet Survey,* a quarterly journal dedicated to the study of cultural and social developments in the Soviet Union. In the article reprinted here, he describes the swift proliferation of Soviet relations with Middle Eastern nations during 1955 and speculates upon its causes. Of particular importance is his summary of the advantages and limitations which surround Soviet policy-makers attempting to win influence among nations long subjected to the rule of Western "imperialist" powers. To Laqueur the Soviet moves in the Middle East represent nothing more than "power politics pure and simple."

AFTER the second World War the Soviet political line had for some years been to keep aloof from Middle Eastern affairs and to maintain an attitude of studious unconcern in relation to that quarter. As a result, not a few Western observers have

From W. Z. L., "Soviet Policy in the Middle East," *The World Today*, Vol. II, No. 12 (December 1955), pp. 519–529. Reprinted by permission of *The World Today* and Walter Z. Laqueur.

tended to forget that this apparent unconcern could be no more than a transient phenomenon in view of Russia's geographical proximity to the Middle East and her traditional interest in it. It has been too easily forgotten that throughout the nineteenth century, and even longer ago, the Near and Middle East was Russia's main sphere of interest and expansion, and the "Oriental question" was one of the main bones of contention between the Powers for more than a hundred and fifty years. Then, as now, Russian policy aimed at launching or strengthening anti-Turkish movements in the peripheral areas. It was to that end that Baron von Thonus (the earliest predecessor of Mr. Daniel Solod, now Russian Ambassador in Egypt) was sent to Cairo by Catherine II. (The end of his mission was unfortunate: he was strangled in prison on the orders of Ibrahim Pasha who, in an official communiqué the next day, "deeply regretted" the sudden death of the Russian consul.) Trenchant observations on Russia's Oriental policy were made, from opposite vantage points, by Karl Marx and Friedrich Engels in their articles on the Crimean War and by Dostoevski in his *Diary of a Writer*. Marx, in particular, noted the incessant territorial progress made by Russia since the time of Peter the Great, and expressed the view that Russia was superior to the West in tenacity and in the application of clever political stratagems.

After 1917 the Bolshevik leaders renounced Tsarist imperialism; in subsequent years, too, when the original anti-imperialist ardour had long since disappeared, the Middle East continued to be of little interest to Moscow in view of its reduced political importance and the absence of a strong Communist or nationalist revolutionary movement in that part of the world. In the wake of the second World War some attempt was made to gain a foothold there: this could be seen, for example, in the demand for the cession of several Turkish provinces (and pressure on Turkey in general), and in the U.S.S.R.'s reluctance to evacuate its positions in Northern Persia.

It is difficult to say in retrospect whether the Russian retreat from the Middle East in 1946 was merely the tactical response to Western pressure or formed part of a settled policy. There can be no doubt that Soviet absence from the Middle East paid handsome dividends in 1949–52: Soviet and Communist propagandists could point to the sharp contrast between Moscow's policy of "hands off" and "Western Imperialist" attempts to "organize" the area and draw the various countries into all kinds of suspect "defence" blocs. These Western activities tended to fan smouldering anti-Western resentment and to antagonize the Arabs, most of whom were psychologically quite unprepared to understand the situation: the Soviet danger was in their eyes some mythical invention, or perhaps a clever stratagem, of American and European "Imperialists" desirous to perpetuate their rule in the Middle East. As a result, Soviet prestige grew.

THE NEW OFFENSIVE OPENS

These developments were undoubtedly highly agreeable to Moscow. But prestige is only something in the nature of a prerequisite in international politics: it helped Moscow up to a point, but no further. It did not prevent, for instance, the Turko-Iraqi alliance of January–February 1955, which subsequently, following the adhesion of Persia, Pakistan, and Britain, resulted in the construction of the famous "northern tier" of States allied to the West. The emergence of this defensive alliance was viewed in Moscow with far greater concern than was realized in the West at that time: in retrospect it appears quite clear that Moscow then realized that a more active Soviet policy would be needed from now on in the Middle East. Prestige alone would not be enough to promote Soviet interests in that part of the world. It was, as subsequently emerged, the turning point in Soviet Middle Eastern policy. *Izvestia* published on 17 April 1955 a statement of the Soviet Ministry of Foreign Affairs on the Middle Eastern situation which at the time attracted little attention but which in effect announced the change in Soviet Middle Eastern policy. It began by stating that "the situation in the Middle East has greatly deteriorated of late," and ended with the declaration that the Soviet Union would, "in the interests of peace," do everything to develop closer relations with the countries of the Middle East.

The Soviet Middle Eastern offensive was foreshadowed in another field, little remarked at the time by Western observers: the revival of Soviet Middle Eastern studies and the important revaluation of ideas undertaken at the same time in the Middle Eastern field. The study of the contemporary East had virtually come to a standstill as the result of the purge of the nineteen-thirties and had not been revived throughout the 'forties. It was only in the winter of 1954/5 that fresh impetus was given to Soviet Oriental studies. After a break of eighteen years Soviet Eastern experts were again given a magazine of their own (*Sovetskoe Vostokovedenie;* the first issue appeared by a coincidence in April 1955, the same month in which the Foreign Ministry's statement on the Middle East was published). There was a sudden flood of new books and studies, and the official party bi-weekly, *Kommunist*, not yet satisfied, in May 1955 called for a fresh upsurge of interest in the Middle Eastern field, for more and better books and more Oriental experts. This revival was anything but academic; it was a direct reflection of the growing Soviet interest in the Middle East. It amounted to a great deal more than the mere publication of so many new books or periodicals, and coincided with a far-reaching tactical revaluation of Russia's estimates concerning some of the Middle Eastern States.

Changing Soviet comment on Egypt may serve as an illustration. In 1954 the leading Soviet Egyptian expert, Mrs. L. Vatolina, had characterized the Nagib-Nasser regime as "madly reactionary, terrorist, anti-democratic, demagogic," etc. A year later, in another work published by the Soviet Academy of Science on the peoples of Africa, the Anglo-Egyptian treaty of July 1954 was defined as "contrary to the national interests of Egypt and the other Arab countries." The Egyptian Government was again attacked for its un-democratic character, and it was stated rather ominously that "the Egyptian toilers would still have to fight many a struggle before the victory of real democracy." Communist criticism became even more violent following the execution of Muslim Brotherhood leaders and the arrest of Communist militants in Egypt throughout the winter of 1954/5. But in the late spring and early summer of 1955 this attitude was radically modified. In June the Cairo leaders were being praised by Moscow radio for their stand against Western defence pacts and for neutralism, and in early July they were commended for the support given to the Sudan, "which played an important part in the liberation of the Sudanese people." Colonel Nasser received a pat on the back, for "dressed in the simple uniform of a lieutenant-colonel he had contributed a great deal to the success of Bandung, supporting the principle of peaceful coexistence." The same Soviet source soon after stated even more emphatically that "both Egypt and the Soviet Union stand squarely on the platform of peace and oppose the policy of aggression. Common to them is the deep desire to live in peace."

This change in the Soviet attitude was not, of course, due to any sudden realization in Moscow that some grievous ideological mistake had been committed *vis-à-vis* Egypt. The new line was the outcome of a number of factors: a more elastic approach; an endeavour to introduce a more active Soviet policy in relation to the Middle East; and, lastly, the realization that certain common interests between Moscow and Cairo had in fact emerged. Syria might have served as an alternative jumping-off ground for Russian policy in the Middle East: Syrian Communists had considerable, if indirect, influence on their country's foreign policy at the time. But Syria is not a central factor in Middle Eastern politics, and consequently the choice fell on Egypt. Ideologically, such a rapprochement presented no particular difficulty for Moscow; Stalin and his disciples have carried out more difficult manœuvres in their time.

Soviet emissaries found in Cairo a political climate highly propitious to their plans. The Cairo leaders deeply resented the fact that they had lost their predominant status in the Arab world, following the transfer of the centre of political and military gravity in the direction of the "northern tier." To pursue a Great Power policy has been the one constant urge among Cairo policy-makers; and Soviet assistance in their eyes offered the double chance of regaining supremacy in the Arab League and making Egypt a leading African Power. Soviet leaders were little concerned about the motives influencing the Egyptian junta. In the nineteen-twenties and the early 'thirties Comintern officials had warned against making use of the bourgeois nationalist movements in Asia and Africa which desired closer relations with the U.S.S.R. merely in order to play off the West against the Soviet Union and vice versa, thus strengthening their own position. But the international situation had changed during the past thirty years; the Soviet Union itself had grown in strength and experience, and was now willingly prepared to take upon itself that calculated risk. Few if any political leaders have ever succeeded in getting the better of Moscow in a deal: it appeared unlikely, to put it mildly, that Gamal Abdul Nasser and his colleagues would succeed where more sophisticated and experienced statesmen had failed. Lastly, it has to be recalled that certain striking affinities exist between the Communist regime and other twentieth-century dictatorships, and that they are closer to each other than to the democracies: there is a surprising similarity between the anti-Western propaganda of the Soviet Union, Nazi Germany, and present day Egypt. This too may have contributed to a certain extent to a rapprochement between the two regimes.

Since the spring of 1955 the new Soviet line in the Middle East has been reflected in increased political, economic, and cultural activity in that part of the world. Soviet "cultural missions" and sports clubs (mainly footballers and weight-lifters) toured Egypt, Syria, and the Lebanon. Among the Arab delegations which have recently visited the U.S.S.R. were a Syrian parliamentary group (in July 1955), a Syrian scientists' mission, and an Arab Women's delegation. Hassan el Bakouri, Egyptian Minister of Waqfs, visited China, and Fathi Ridvan, Egyptian Minister of Communications (at one time co-founder of the fascist "Misr-al-Fatah") went to Hungary and Czechoslovakia. Soviet and Chinese Muslim pilgrims came to Mecca in July and visited Al Azhar in Cairo. The Orthodox Patriarch of Antioch, Alexander III, went to Moscow with several other Syrian and Lebanese bishops on another goodwill tour. But Alexander Tahan had been known as a friend of the Soviet Union for many years, whereas Christoforos II, Patriarch of Alexandria and all Egypt, who also went to Moscow in the summer of 1955, had not previously been known as a sympathizer. All this—and the list could be prolonged—does not perhaps add up to much in comparison with Soviet activities in Europe. But the Middle East had been neglected by the Communist bloc for some time and there was something of a novelty in all these visits.

ECONOMIC RELATIONS

The state of affairs in the economic field has given rise to various misconceptions. Recently there has been a Soviet trade drive in the Middle East, but its scope has been limited and its political impact restricted. Eastern bloc imports from the Middle East (including Greece and Yugoslavia) increased in 1954 by about 56 per cent over the 1953 figure, while exports to the Middle East increased by about 26 per cent. But a closer scrutiny of the figures shows that in comparison with 1952–3 the increase was far less marked (24 per cent for exports and 10 per cent for imports). It also shows that trade relations with Greece and Persia have developed at a swifter pace than those with the Arab States who were the main object of Soviet wooing. In the autumn of 1955 the Soviet bloc took about 16–20 per cent of Egyptian cotton exports, which was considerably more than the 1953/4 average (9 per cent) but not much more than the amount taken by Communist countries in 1952/3 (16 per cent). But the situation in this field has changed recently as a result of the arms deal with the Soviet bloc in consequence of which, it is reported, Egypt will have to mortgage most of her cotton and rice crops for the next few years.

Czechoslovakia and Hungary have made great efforts to get larger slices of the Egyptian market, and the Soviet pavilion has made much impression at successive Damascus affairs. Egypt has trade agreements with most of the satellite countries, including a tripartite agreement with Rumania and the U.S.S.R. according to which the latter supplies petroleum products at prices 15 per cent below the world market. Egypt also has a new trade agreement with Communist China, and negotiations between several Arab States and other Eastern bloc countries are pending. Significant for the political character of these trade relations is the fact that almost all Middle Eastern countries can at present show an export surplus in their trade with the Communist bloc.

Nevertheless, it would be wrong to compare the Soviet trade offensive with the German drive in the Balkans in the late 'thirties. Communist possibilities are more restricted: the Soviet Union cannot offer a wide range of finished products, and it needs to import less in the way of raw materials. Its underlying aim, according to all evidence, is to gain the maximum political advantage as the result of the minimum economic investment. The trade drive is mainly governed by political, not economic, considerations, and trade relations are therefore frequently artificial. No attempt has been made so far to gain a monopoly for the Soviet Union (as the Germans did in the Balkans); rather the aim has been to attain some commanding positions by a few well-chosen investments.

The same goes for the recent Soviet offers to give the Arab countries economic aid and equipment and building materials to cover their needs in all aspects of economic development, including the $250-million project of the Aswan dam, a plan which has intrigued Egyptian rulers for more than a generation. It is difficult to comment on these reports, if only for the reason that no details have been made known so far, apart from those which have emanated from Middle Eastern capitals (as yet unconfirmed by Moscow) and which have therefore to be taken with due caution. It is a well-known fact that Soviet industry, like that of other countries, is now in the throes of a second technological revolution demanding enormous investments. It is no secret either that Soviet industry has been unable to give all the help needed by China, and it is therefore unlikely that it can undertake and carry out major new obligations elsewhere. The assistance promised to the Middle Eastern countries would therefore appear to be of psychological rather than material importance. It strengthens, for instance, the bargaining position of the Egyptian Government *vis-à-vis* the World Bank and the West in general; and for this, admittedly, the Egyptian Government has reason to be grateful to Moscow.

THE EGYPTIAN-CZECH ARMS DEAL

But on the whole it is difficult not to regard trade relations (like the new cultural and religious ties) as minor developments, sideshows to the main events which are taking place on the political scene. The negotiations leading to the arms deal with the Soviet bloc apparently took place in Cairo in July and according to some reports were initiated by the Soviet Union. D. P. Shepilov, editor-in-chief of *Pravda* and of recent months a prominent figure in Soviet foreign policy, came to Cairo in July to take part in the Liberation celebrations and on that occasion declared that "the sentiments of the Soviet people are wholly on the side of the Egyptian People's aspirations." Several days later it was officially announced that Premier Nasser had been invited by the Soviet Government to visit the U.S.S.R. In late August rumours of a Communist-Egyptian arms deal began to spread, and provoked comment from Mr. Dulles. The Israeli Minister in Moscow, when he asked for information, was told that these reports were inventions and that no negotiations were in train, nor had the U.S.S.R. even considered selling arms. But there was an ominous postscript: the Soviet Union, he was given to understand, regarded the sale of arms needed for the defence of the purchasing State or for internal security measures as a normal commercial transaction.

By the end of September the news of the arms deal could no longer be kept secret. It was first revealed by Gamal Salem, a member of the Cairo junta, on a trip to India, and subsequently confirmed by the Egyptian Government. Soviet press and radio for some time tried to play down these "exaggerated reports," stating that there was no ground for Western anxiety. But in view of the evident concern in the West this approach was discontinued after some days, and *Pravda* on 2 October carried a short official statement concerning the agreement which reiterated that "each

State has the legitimate right to look after its own defence and to buy weapons for its defence requirements from other States on the usual commercial terms." Elsewhere the Soviet press published attacks against the West from Arab sources, according to which the U.S.A., Britain, and France were criticized for not having supplied more arms to the Arab States and for having stipulated all kinds of "conditions," such as the demand for guarantees that the arms supplied would not be used for aggressive aims.

According to the evidence available, Soviet leaders had some misgivings as to the impression which their policy would make in the West. The fact that Czechoslovakia, not the Soviet Union, was chosen to carry out the "commercial transaction" points to that. The statements of Arab leaders were as a rule reported in full in the Soviet press, but the anti-Israeli attacks were usually censored. And the anti-Western polemics on Middle Eastern issues in the Soviet press ceased on the eve of the second Geneva conference: there was no wish to shelve a new policy that had proved so successful, but there was no desire either to see the Soviet Middle Eastern offensive become the subject of close international scrutiny.

By comparison, all other developments in Soviet-Middle Eastern relations since early October 1955 have been of lesser importance: Moscow's denial that arms had been offered to Israel was a matter of routine. The Middle Eastern situation being what it is, it was sufficient to supply arms to only one of the rival camps in order to promote Soviet interests in the area: arms supply to both sides would have created complications and raised unnecessary suspicions of foul play. Persia's adhesion in mid-October to the Turko-Iraqi pact provoked emphatic and dire, if unspecified, threats in Moscow, and the Governments belonging to the defence pact were described as the "lickspittle of the colonizers."

As a counterpoise, Soviet activities in other countries were stepped up: diplomatic relations with Saudi Arabia were re-established, the Soviet-Yemen pact of 1927 was renewed, negotiations for diplomatic contacts with the Sudan and Libya were started, and arms were offered Afghanistan, Syria, and Saudi Arabia—all within the second half of October.

REASONS FOR THE NEW OFFENSIVE

Soviet policies in the Middle East have been successful in recent months, and Soviet designs in that area are fairly transparent. Nevertheless, at least in the early days of the Soviet offensive, several conflicting interpretations were put forward by Western observers in explanation of its motives and background. It transpired only gradually that, far from removing the dangers of local wars, the Geneva conference of July 1955 had actually increased them. For once it became plain that a global war was ruled out by both sides, it became far less dangerous than before for interested parties to engage in local conflicts. The Communist leaders have apparently drawn the obvious conclusions from this new situation. But part of Western public opinion has continued to believe that the "spirit of Geneva" meant that the Communist world had abandoned the idea of promoting Communism and Soviet interests by force outside the present frontiers.

Others argued that the recent Soviet moves in the Middle East had come merely as a reaction to Western defence schemes in that part of the world, that it was a defensive rather than an offensive action. It may be true that the establishment of the "northern tier" hastened the Soviet drive in the Middle East, but it is extremely unlikely that Moscow would in any case have "neglected" the Middle East in its global plans for much longer. If the Soviet arms supply to Egypt and the other recent moves constituted a defensive action, it would

seem to follow that the Soviet leaders might be ready to join the Western Powers in their endeavour to maintain peace and stability in the Middle East—to sign a declaration, for instance, guaranteeing the *status quo*. But such a hypothesis appears unrealistic; Soviet diplomats may of course prefer not to close altogether the door to diplomatic negotiations with the West with a view to removing the "northern tier"— while still maintaining the Soviet positions. Basically, however, Russia has nothing to gain and much to lose from the preservation of the *status quo* in the Middle East. The assistance to Egypt is given at present for the very same reason that Israel was supported in 1948: that it appears to be the factor most likely now to upset the political balance in the Middle East.

Another fairly widespread misconception is the assumption that ideological considerations are somehow involved in so far as the Soviet Union is concerned. But Soviet policy in the Middle East (where no influential Communist parties exist) is almost entirely free from ideological motivation; it is power politics pure and simple. If we disregard for a moment the propaganda slogans, it would appear that the Soviet policy-makers like one Middle Eastern country as much as another. But they like even more conditions conducive to the spread of Communism and of Soviet influence. Such conditions come into being (as the experience of the last forty years has shown) mainly in the wake of war, when State machinery is weakened—and not only in the State that loses the war. Stalin in his last pamphlet reiterated the thesis of the "inevitable armed conflicts" within the Western camps. His heirs would be less than faithful to the teachings of both Lenin and Stalin if they failed to exploit such a promising situation as the Arab-Israeli conflict. Russia has no vested interest in the victory of Egypt in a possible war, despite the assistance rendered: on the contrary, it may be imagined that the conditions for the growth of Communism in a defeated Egypt or Syria would be more favourable than in an Israel which has lost a war. But be that as it may, if Egypt should prevail in the arms race against Israel it will be owing to Soviet help, and Soviet prestige will increase enormously. Conversely, if Egypt should be defeated for a second time, Communism (and thus, indirectly, the Soviet Union) will again be the main beneficiary. It is a case of heads I win, tails you lose.

FUTURE PROSPECTS

Soviet penetration in the Middle East offers great prospects, but there are, at present, certain limitations to it. Soviet actions in that region tend to jeopardize to a considerable extent the "climate of confidence" which Soviet diplomats have with much effort created in Europe. Soviet policy-makers appear to be ready to accept this risk to a certain extent, and they are disinclined to give up what must appear to them a most promising line of action. But it is possible that in the face of Western pressure Soviet action might become more cautious; little may change in substance, but its openly hostile character in relation to the West might probably be concealed. For similar reasons it is unlikely that the Soviet bloc will take an openly hostile stand *vis-à-vis* Israel: Jewish public opinion in the West—and, perhaps, to a certain degree behind the Iron Curtain too—will not be needlessly antagonized by Moscow.

Basically, however, all signs point to the likelihood that the present Soviet offensive in the Middle East will be continued. Even if it should not come to a local war, Russia's alignment with Egypt, and to a lesser degree with Syria and Saudi Arabia, is highly important for Moscow because it may disrupt Western defence schemes. These pacts may be the prototype of a new form of alliance in specific Middle Eastern style. True, neither the local Communists nor the democratic liberal elements figure in this "popular front" inspired from above. But the political effect may well be similar. When the European Socialist movements tried to counter Communist attempts to subvert their parties during the "Popular Front" period they had at least some experience and an organization to operate with. Middle Eastern leaders have neither the same experience of Communist theory and practice nor a political organization to enable them to stand up to their present allies. What they have by way of ideological equipment is woefully insufficient to compete with the vast appeal of Communism in backward areas. The Egyptian leaders are beyond doubt perfectly honest in their protestations that they want Communist arms, not ideas. But the very idea that they will be able to get the one without the other points either to megalomania or to an extraordinary degree of naiveté and lack of experience and political imagination—and perhaps to both. There are historical reasons for all this, and the U.S.S.R.'s policy has astutely exploited them. In its blueprints Egypt and Syria have become the "weakest link" in the non-Communist chain. It would be difficult to deny the validity of this assumption.

TECHNICAL ASSISTANCE

WALDEMAR A. NIELSEN AND ZORAN S. HODJERA

In the years after Stalin's death Soviet policy-makers perfected a new tactic for winning the so-called "uncommitted" nations of the world to the communist camp. Combining their theories of the inevitable course of world revolution with lessons learned from the technical and economic assistance programs of the Western nations and with the Soviet bloc's growing economic strength, they launched a series of their own aid programs. Since then, these programs have multiplied and have been successful enough to encourage Soviet leaders to challenge the West to world-wide economic competition. This new tactic is one of the principal techniques now used in the battle for influence in Asia, Africa, and Latin America. Since the Communists have scored some very real victories, while enjoying an inordinate amount of favorable propaganda for their efforts, it is important to understand the unique qualities, capabilities, and limitations of their programs.

DURING 1958, the program of the Sino-Soviet bloc countries to enlarge and deepen their economic relations with the less-developed Free World countries moved steadily forward.[1] In the twelve month period, 601 million dollars of new credits and grants were extended for industrial equipment and technical assistance. The expansion of trading relationships proceeded in parallel. Trade and payments agreements with non-Communist countries increased from 149 with 28 countries at the end of 1957 to 177 with 31 countries at the end of 1958. Bloc trade promotion delegations were active, particularly in the Middle East and Southeast Asia, and well-financed exhibitions of bloc products were to be seen at trade fairs in many countries. Bloc trade with the less-developed countries increased steadily from 1953 through 1957. In the first half of 1958 bloc exports to the less-developed countries continued to rise at a significant rate, but imports showed a decline, reflecting in part the drop in world prices of some of the major commodity components.

An integral element of Soviet bloc credit agreements is the provision of technical assistance, and this aspect has shown a particularly sharp growth during 1958 In the latter half of 1957, 1,585 bloc technicians worked for one month or more on economic assignment in less-developed countries outside of the Soviet sphere. In the last six months of 1958, this total rose to 2,800.[2] Table 1 shows the breakdown by various countries and regions.

TECHNICAL ASSISTANCE: SOVIET STYLE

As used by the bloc countries, the term technical assistance means essentially the provision of experts or training for compensation from a contracting government, often in conjunction with credit sales of

[1] Because of the extent to which their economic and technical assistance efforts are co-ordinated as well as because of the political ties which bind them together, the bloc countries in this analysis are considered as a unit.

[2] Totals exclude bloc personnel engaged purely in trade promotion, regular members of embassy staffs, and the considerable number of technicians engaged in military assistance projects; inclusion of the latter would raise the total by another 50 per cent.

From Waldemar A. Nielsen and Zoran S. Hodjera, "Sino-Soviet Bloc Technical Assistance—Another Bilateral Approach," *The Annals of The American Academy of Political and Social Science*, CCCXXIII (May 1959), 41–49. By permission of The American Academy of Political and Social Science.

Table 1	ESTIMATES OF SOVIET BLOC ECONOMIC AID PERSONNEL IN SELECTED COUNTRIES JULY–DECEMBER 1957 AND JULY–DECEMBER 1958*

COUNTRIES	SECOND HALF 1957	SECOND HALF 1958
Middle East and Africa	555	1,105
Egypt	360	535
Ethiopia	0	25
Iran	5	10
Syria	110	275
Turkey	15	60
Yemen	55	200
Sudan	10	0
South and Southeast Asia	915	1,635
Afghanistan	445	600
Burma	60	120
Cambodia	30	50
Ceylon	5	40
India	260	555
Indonesia	105	265
Pakistan	0	5
Latin America	55	45
Argentina	50	45
Brazil, Chile, Mexico	5	0
Europe	60	15
Yugoslavia	50	10
Greece	10	5
Total**	1,585	2,800

* Data are based on unclassified information, unpublished as of February 1959, collected by United States Government agencies.

** Figures, which are rounded to nearest 5, include only bloc personnel on economic assignment for one month or more during the six-month period.

equipment. This type of training and expert assistance resembles that of Western private firms in connection with construction contracts and the sale of industrial equipment abroad. In the United States technical assistance is normally understood to mean expert advice and training given by one country to another—over and above the ordinary flow of technicians and training growing out of commercial trade and contracts.

In discussing Soviet bloc technical assistance, because of the fundamentally different character of Communist economic conceptions, we are obliged to warp further the meaning of an already somewhat unclear term. In all comparisons of bloc and Western technical assistance it must be remembered that the Western total, to be comparable with bloc figures, should include not only government-financed activity but also that of private foundations and voluntary organizations, plus a very large amount of privately organized commercial exchange.

Because bloc technical assistance arrangements are embedded in the credit agreements between bloc countries and the less-developed Free World countries, the content and characteristics of these agreements must be reviewed in some detail.

Typically, Soviet credits are for a period of twelve years and bear an interest rate of $2\frac{1}{2}$ per cent, which is considerably below that charged by the World Bank and the United States Export-Import Bank. Satellite credits are sometimes for shorter periods and carry interest rates higher than those of the USSR. There is commonly a grace period before repayment begins, and repayment can often be made in goods or in local currency. World market prices are used generally as a yardstick for setting the value of bloc equipment to be delivered, but in the case of services the cost to the recipient country of bloc technicians is considerably below the going rate for comparable experts from the Western countries.

The bloc has concentrated its economic efforts in the Middle East, Africa, and

South and Southeast Asia. Within these areas it has been further concentrated: Egypt, Syria, Yemen have received 97 per cent of the economic aid to the Middle East and Africa; Afghanistan, India, and Indonesia have received 82 per cent of the aid to South and Southeast Asia. Although numerous cultural delegations have gone to the countries south of the Sahara in Africa and despite various aid offers, no major assistance agreements in this region have yet been concluded.[3] In Latin America, there have been a number of offers of technical assistance and credit, but until recently activity has been very limited. However, one of the major developments of 1958 was the signing of the first major agreement in the Western Hemisphere, a

[3] Subsequent to the time of preparation of this article, February 1959, important bloc credits to Iraq and Guinea have been reported.

100 million dollar credit to Argentina. In Europe, Yugoslavia was involved in a web of economic arrangements with the other Communist countries while a member of the bloc. In 1948, however, the Soviets broke all assistance agreements. In 1956 new credits were extended totalling 464 million dollars of which 300 million dollars have subsequently been indefinitely postponed, canceled, or allowed to expire.

In general, bloc credits have been focused on the financing of specific development projects, particularly in basic industries such as steel and textiles and in overhead investments like irrigation works, power, roads, and communications. To a much smaller extent they have involved equipment for the production of consumer goods and for agricultural development. Table 2 indicates the type and range of projects financed in three selected countries.

Table 2

SOVIET BLOC CREDIT AND TECHNICAL ASSISTANCE PROJECTS IN THREE SELECTED FREE WORLD COUNTRIES*

RECIPIENT FREE WORLD COUNTRY	SUPPLYING BLOC COUNTRY	PROJECT
Egypt	*East Germany*	High-tension line
	Hungary	El Tabbin power station Nile River bridge Small revolving bridges (3)
	Poland	Oil storage tanks (21) Swing bridges
	USSR	Atomic Energy laboratory Oil research plant Textile factories (3)
	Czechoslovakia	Ceramics factory Water filtration plant Shoe factory Cement plant

* Source: Unclassified data, unpublished as of February 1959, collected by official United States agencies.

RECIPIENT FREE WORLD COUNTRY	SUPPLYING BLOC COUNTRY	PROJECT
Egypt	*Czechoslovakia*	Bridges (9) Bicycle factory
Afghanistan	*USSR*	Silos, flour mill, and bakery Road paving, Kabul Asphalt factory, Kabul Salang Pass road Bagram airfield Jungalot machine shop complex Physics and chemical laboratory Naghlu hydroelectric project Kabul fertilizer plant Pul-i-Khumri II hydroelectric project Herat and Pul-i-Khumri vehicle repair shops Mazar-i-Sharif glass factory Kabul airport Darunta irrigation project Sardeh, Palto, and Khawar irrigation dams Oil storage tanks (3) Port of Qizil Qala Petroleum exploration
	Czechoslovakia	Jabal-us-Seraj cement plant Pul-i-Khumri cement plant Kabul brick and tile kiln Kandahar fruit cannery Kabul and Herat tanneries Kabul shoe factory Baghlan cheese factory Coal mining equipment
India	*USSR*	Bhilai steel plant Heavy machine building plant Powerplant for lignite project Korba coalfield development Optical glass factory Petroleum exploration Bombay Technological Institute (partly UN, partly bilateral) Oil drilling
	Czechoslovakia	Sugar refinery, Panipat Sugar mill, Assam Cement plant, Assam Sugar refinery, Madras Thermal power station Foundry forge project

RECIPIENT FREE WORLD COUNTRY	SUPPLYING BLOC COUNTRY	PROJECT
India	*Poland*	Sugar refinery, Tanjore Equipment for manufacture of electric motors
	East Germany	Textile machinery Raw film factory
	Rumania	Petroleum refinery Oil drilling

TYPES OF TECHNICAL ASSISTANCE

In the large majority of bloc credit agreements, provision is made for Soviet style technical assistance, that is the hiring of specialized services by the contracting country. Most commonly, experts are used to assist in preliminary engineering surveys, to supervise construction, and to direct the installation of equipment. Agreements have sometimes provided for basic resource surveys, the training of operating personnel either in the Free World country or in the bloc countries, economic advisory services, and mineral prospecting.

Scientific and educational facilities have been financed as special projects in a few cases. Among the more important examples are an atomic energy laboratory and an oil research plant in Egypt and an institution for advanced technical training in India. In Burma, the Soviets agreed to build and equip a complete scientific institute. According to a Russian announcement, the project would provide living accommodations for 1,000 students, apartments for the faculty and staff, a 500-seat assembly hall, a 100,000-volume library, reading rooms, restaurant, sports grounds, swimming pool, and 18 fully equipped laboratories.

Because the available data are fragmentary, and because of definitional problems, estimates of the value of bloc technical assistance are necessarily crude. In mid-1958 Joseph Berliner judged the cumulative total, 1953–58, to be in the order of magnitude of 5 to 10 million dollars. Since some forty technical assistance missions had then been identified, he assumed a total of 80 to avoid underestimating, assumed the cost of each to be $100,000, and arrived at a rough figure of 8 million dollars as a basis for his estimate.

If one were to add the value of scientific apparatus and training facilities, the cumulative total would increase by some 3 or 4 million dollars.

A quite different approach would be to calculate the current rate of technical assistance by taking the number of personnel and imputing a value to their services. The figures in Table 1 do not include technicians who worked abroad for less than one month nor do they give extra weight to those working for periods longer than one month. A monthly average of 600 for the most recent period in which data are available would therefore be a conservative estimate. Assuming a minimum direct cost of $500 per month for salary, maintenance and travel, the current monthly rate would approximate $300,000, or $3,600,000 per year. Assuming a monthly value of services at the approximate cost of maintaining an American technician abroad, namely $1,250, the current monthly value of bloc technical assistance would be $750,000 or an annual rate of $9,000,000. The actual cost of these services in local currency to the recipient less-developed countries is probably somewhere between these two extremes.

In summary, the bloc economic assistance effort has clear differences in scope and content from that of the United States government: In world-wide terms, the bloc program is much smaller; it is highly concentrated geographically in contrast to the widely dispersed United States program; it is almost entirely on a credit basis whereas the United States program is on a grant basis; and it is focused on individual industrial projects whereas the United States effort supports general development programs and agricultural development as well.

Important as these differences are, there are other and even more fundamental contrasts in organization, technique, and objectives.

ORGANIZATION AND OVER-ALL CO-ORDINATION

Since 1953, the Soviet Union has repeatedly reorganized its system for administering foreign aid and technical assistance, each time raising the responsible agency to higher status and more comprehensive authority. At the present time, and since July 1957, such programs are directed by the State Committee for External Economic Relations of the Soviet Council of Ministers. The Committee, which reports directly to the Council of Ministers, includes top level officials and is not a subordinate element of the Ministry of Foreign Affairs nor of any of the economic ministries. Its operating staff is organized on both a geographic and a functional basis. It probably administers military as well as economic assistance; it has sections for scientific and technical cooperation; it includes several foreign trade agencies which have been transferred to it from the Ministry for Foreign Trade.

In the past, such co-ordination as has been required within the bloc has apparently been handled directly between Moscow and the various agencies of the satellite countries dealing with foreign economic and technical matters. In recent months, however, it appears that plans have been laid for a greater degree of co-ordinated bloc economic policy and operations for the seven-year period, 1959–65. From meetings of the Council on Mutual Economic Assistance (CEMA) in Warsaw in late 1958, there emerged reports of extensive discussion of means of creating a single, unified economy in the area, including the concentration of research and development activities and of training activities for scientists and specialists from all countries. Apparently, consideration has also been given to the co-ordination of plans in the several bloc countries in bidding for major contracts for new factories and installations in the less-developed countries.

Although many details of the structure and procedure for planning, co-ordinating, and administering bloc economic assistance are not known, it is clear that essential co-ordination has been achieved and that the arrangements have functioned adequately. The bureaucracy in the USSR and the bloc has been able to act with speed, flexibility, and on occasion, finesse. Cooperation and participation by the satellites has been achieved and political, military, propaganda, and economic policies have been successfully orchestrated.

TECHNIQUES OF NEGOTIATION

In economic dealings with the non-Communist less-developed countries, the Soviets have largely cast aside traditional methods of diplomacy. Preparatory contacts have taken a variety of informal channels—offers contained in speeches by delegates to the United Nations, in official newspaper articles, in propaganda broadcasts, in interviews at diplomatic receptions, in public letters from Soviet leaders, and so forth. With a fine sense of theatre, the basic negotiations have often been conducted by top Communist officials on state visits abroad. Such visits have often been timed at a moment of emergency in the economy or foreign policy of the recipient country. And in the old tradition of oriental potentates, handsome gifts have frequently been distributed to sweeten the general atmosphere of negotiations—a sports stadium to Burma, autobuses to Afghanistan, tractors to India, jet airliners to Syria and Egypt.

Once preliminary negotiations have been completed, concrete steps to implement the agreement are taken promptly. For example, Bulganin and Krushchev visited Afghanistan in mid-December 1955 and a general aid and technical assistance agreement was concluded in three days, the Soviet Union pledging a loan of 100 million dollars. By the first of March 1956 the implementing agreement was signed specifying the individual projects to be financed. In May, the first equipment and experts began to arrive.

During the same period, incidentally, Afghanistan decided to establish diplomatic relations with Communist China, began trade negotiations with Czechoslovakia, and joined the Soviet Union in a declaration calling for general disarmament and a ban on atomic weapons.

LOCAL ADMINISTRATION OF BLOC TECHNICAL ASSISTANCE

In the local administration of aid and technical assistance, the bloc countries follow methods and conceptions radically different from those commonly employed by the American government. First, the assistance is provided on a project-by-project basis. The recipient country is not required to develop a general plan or framework for developing in terms of which specific projects have to be justified. Second, bloc negotiators tend to confine their action to the acceptance or rejection of individual project proposals from the recipient country, whereas United States operations missions typically become involved in the whole development planning process. Third, bloc technicians and experts as required are brought in for a specific project and in the great majority of cases remain only for a few weeks. Fourth, they usually live as a group in a location near the project and have little direct contact with their embassy in the country. Fifth, the bloc embassies do not maintain resident staffs of economists and develop-

ment experts as is the case with American embassies in less-developed countries. Finally, it appears that the bloc countries do not require detailed accounting of the use of funds and comprehensive progress reports.

COMPETENCE AND BEHAVIOR OF BLOC TECHNICIANS

From various kinds of evidence— newspaper reports, impressions of American technicians who have worked in the underdeveloped areas, official American reports, estimates of United Nations officials dealing with technical assistance, and statements by representatives of recipient countries—it seems clear that bloc technicians who go abroad are fully qualified in their particular specialties. Here and there, as in the case of a sugar refinery project in Indonesia, there seems to have been some mismanagement. But generally their performance seems to be equal to that of their Western counterparts.

Contrary to some widely circulated reports, bloc technicians on the whole do not seem to have superior linguistic skills. There are exceptions, as in Afghanistan where apparently a high proportion of the Soviet technicians were brought from Turkestan, Kazakhstan and Uzbekistan, where languages related to those in Afghanistan are spoken. But ordinarily Soviet technicians are not specially trained in the language of the countries to which they are sent. They generally rely on interpreters and frequently use the Western language which is best known in the foreign locality.

In personal behavior, they have impressed people in the recipient countries as hardworking and serious, even to the point of being dull and wooden in personal relationships. On the whole, there appears to be little contact between the bloc specialists and the citizens of the less-developed countries apart from the work situation.

The evidence available is not conclusive that Soviet technicians have been used for espionage or agitation. On the contrary, although they have probably been expected to prepare the kind of economic intelligence reports which most countries expect of their experts who travel abroad, it seems that the Soviets prefer to leave delicate political functions to professionals.

SCHOLARSHIP AND EDUCATIONAL EXCHANGES

From a political as well as economic point of view, one of the interesting elements of bloc technical assistance has been the training of nationals from the less-developed countries in schools in the Communist bloc. In part this exchange is related to projects built with bloc credits, as in the case of several hundred Indian engineers and technicians being trained in the Soviet Union for work at the huge Bhilai steel plant. And in part it is based on bilateral educational exchange agreements administered separately from the technical assistance programs.

Since 1954, scholarships in increasing numbers have been offered by the Soviet Union and the other Communist nations. Although there was a generally hesitant reaction when such offers were first made, the rate of acceptance has increased and the number of students from Free World countries going to the bloc for training in 1958 was double that for 1957. By Free World standards, however, the total volume remains small. Foreign students in the Soviet Union in 1958, including those from bloc countries, totaled 15,000, or a little more than $1/3$ of the 43,391 foreign students in the United States during the period. Of the Soviet total, it is reported that some 2,000 were from less-developed countries, principally Africa, the Middle East, and Asia; of the United States total, 27,000 came from Asia, Latin America, the Middle East, and Africa.

A noteworthy aspect of bloc educational exchanges is the concerted effort made in a few selected countries. The United Arab Republic, where the USSR, Rumania, Hungary, Czechoslovakia, and East Germany all made special scholarship offers in 1958, is one focus of attention. Another is Algeria, from which students have traditionally gone to French universities for advanced training. They have experienced progressively greater difficulties as the Algerian war has intensified and the Soviet Union, East Germany, Czechoslovakia, and Communist China have all come forth in recent months with attractive scholarship offers for study in the East.

ECONOMIC, PSYCHOLOGICAL, AND POLITICAL RESULTS

Bloc aid programs are only five years old. The bloc countries are still evolving their policies and experimenting with techniques. It is thus much too early to make any definitive assessment of results; but some tentative conclusions can be ventured.

From an economic viewpoint, a few of the projects financed, such as the paving of streets in Kabul, seem to have little more than propagandistic justification. But the great bulk of the assistance has gone for overhead investment and basic industrial projects, which are the economic sectors where the most serious bottlenecks to development frequently are found. These are at the same time the sectors which yield the greatest external economies over the long run and which make possible the most marked increases in productivity. On the whole, the list of bloc financed projects is creditable, and economic benefits to the recipient countries are undeniable. Moreover, given the relatively minor scale of bloc assistance, there is probably not much lost by operating on a project-by-project basis without attempting to fit each action into an overall development plan.

However, because of the enormous needs of Asia and the Middle East for development capital, needs which are compounded by rapid population growth, bloc assistance on the present scale cannot have decisive economic effect. On the other hand, the psychological and political consequences may be considerable. By the very act of providing assistance the Soviet Union and the bloc countries have neutralized the criticism of being indifferent to the needs of impoverished areas of the world, an awkward posture in which their refusal to provide aid prior to 1953 had placed them. Also, at a time of growing Soviet prestige because of industrial advance and military and scientific achievement, foreign economic assistance has added an appearance of respectability and responsibility to the naked fact of power.

At every step the bloc countries have been alert to the propaganda possibilities of economic assistance and have tailored the terms of agreements to fit local sensibilities and situations. Administrative methods as well have been designed to minimize frictions with the recipient country and to reenforce the theme of "aid without strings." Through extensive publicity, concentration on visible and sometimes spectacular projects, and high geographical concentration in key countries, widespread popular awareness and approval has been created.

Whether more sophisticated leadership elements in the less-developed countries have been equally well impressed is another matter. Within the past year there have been two cases, Yugoslavia and Finland, in which the Soviet Union in headlong fashion attempted to exploit trade and aid relationships for political purposes. Perhaps as a consequence, public figures in a number of the countries which are major recipients of aid have indicated uneasiness about the aims and methods of Soviet policy. In Indonesia, in 1957, parliamentary doubts about the wisdom of accepting further bloc assistance delayed ratification of Soviet aid agreement. Nehru in 1958 for the first time publicly expressed fundamental concern and disagreement with the philosophy of Communism. Nasser in the United Arab Republic in early 1959 began a vigorous roundup of Communist elements.

But such signs of possibly increasing resistance far from cancel the long-range and subtle political gains which the Communist countries may reap. Their aid has been useful in stirring anti-Western sentiment in the Middle East, in embarrassing and diminishing the prestige of pro-Western governments, and in encouraging others to take a more neutral position in the East-West conflict. Their programs are spreading consciousness of Soviet strength and capability, familiarity with bloc equipment, and use of the ruble as an international currency. Hundreds of technicians trained in the bloc countries are returning home each year having acquired in addition to new skills a new ideological perspective. Bloc financed industrial projects in recipient countries have given local Communist party organizations new talking points, new encouragement, new prestige.

The patience of Communist leaders in awaiting long-range rewards is re-enforced by deep doctrinal convictions. They believe the present governments in the less-developed countries eventually will be overwhelmed and are convinced that nothing less than Communist regimes with totalitarian methods of rigid planning and compulsory sacrifice by the populations can succeed in producing a rapid rate of development. Second, imbued as they are with Marxist conceptions of the social and political effects of industrialization, they undoubtedly attach importance to the concentration of assistance in the industrial sector in order to encourage the growth of a labor class and trade unions in the less-developed countries which in turn, they are confident, will generate revolutionary pressures.

Given the continuing vulnerability of the less-developed Free World countries, the mixed but still considerable success of bloc aid to date, and the clear capacity of the bloc to extend the scale of such activity in the future, it is likely that the economic front may become more active and important in the next phase of the cold war.

A Balance of Terror

XV

THE DEVELOPING PARTNERSHIP: CHINA AND THE SOVIET UNION

ALLEN S. WHITING

Allen S. Whiting is one of the most talented young American political scientists now concerned with unraveling the secrets of Sino-Soviet relations. He studied at Cornell as an undergraduate and received his Ph.D. from Columbia University. From 1953 to 1955 he carried out research on Sino-Soviet relations in Taiwan, Hong Kong, and Japan. He has taught at Northwestern and Michigan State Universities, and is presently a member of the Social Science Division of the Rand Corporation at Santa Monica, California. Among his published works are: *Soviet Policies in China, 1917–1924, Dynamics of International Relations* (with Ernest B. Haas), and *Sinkiang: Pawn or Pivot?* (with General Sheng Shih-ts'ai). Communist China's steadily increasing authority in the Moscow-Peking axis, her growing influence upon Soviet policy, and the connotations of this dynamic process for the future, pose questions of very grave significance for the Western world.

TEN years ago, Mao Tse-tung declared, "Internationally we belong to the anti-imperialist front, headed by the Soviet Union." Formal founding of the Sino-Soviet alliance in 1950 initiated military, economic, and political implementation of his words. Neither changes in the Kremlin nor turbulent events in East Europe have shaken Mao from his 1949 conviction that "the Chinese people must either incline toward the side of imperialism or toward that of socialism. There can be no exception to this rule. It is impossible to sit on the fence. There is no third road."

In the intervening years, the People's Republic of China has grown from a dependent Soviet satellite to a major partner in the Moscow-Peking axis. Particularly since the death of Stalin in 1953, this transformation in Peking's status, both inside the bloc and in the world at large, has seemed to justify Mao's abandonment of the traditional Chinese policy of "using barbarians against barbarians" in favor of "leaning to one side."

To be sure, Peking has paid for its gains. Approximately 2.4 billion dollars in Soviet credits consumed between 1950 and 1957 require payment with interest over the next decade. Virtually all of the 211

From Allen S. Whiting, "Dynamics of the Moscow-Peking Axis," *The Annals of The American Academy of Political and Social Science*, CCCXXI (January 1959), 101–111. By permission of The American Academy of Political and Social Science.

industrial projects based on Soviet deliveries are covered by Chinese exports. Politically, by aligning with Moscow, Peking lessened its chances for recognition from the United States and thereby for admission to the United Nations. But without attempting to strike a comprehensive balance, certain observations strengthen the conviction that Peking's gains in the alliance far outweigh its losses.

GAINS FROM THE ALLIANCE

The strategic payoff in the military realm is impressive. No other policy could have provided Mao with the largest and most modern air force in Asia only ten years after seizing power. For a nation which produced its first automobile in 1958, the 1,800 jet fighters and bombers provide important proof of Soviet support. Nor could China's scant and scattered petroleum resources sustain this force without large fuel deliveries from the Soviet bloc.

On the ground, the process of re-equipping and modernizing with Russian tanks, artillery, and transport has drastically transformed the poorly trained and inadequately armed masses of Chinese infantry who fought in Korea. Even greater changes may lie in store as a consequence of the Soviet alliance. In 1958, Foreign Minister Ch'en Yi predicted, "We will have atomic weapons in the future." Should Moscow open its nuclear stockpile to Peking, a new impetus might be afforded the drive toward Chinese Communist ascendancy in Asia.

The bedrock of Sino-Soviet military unity is the pledge of mutual assistance in case of outside attack. First enunciated in the Treaty of Friendship, Alliance, and Mutual Assistance Between the USSR and the People's Republic of China, signed on February 14, 1950, this guarantees that "in the event of one of the High Contracting Parties being attacked by Japan or States allied with it, and thus being involved in a state of war, the other High Contracting Party will immediately render military and other assistance with all the means at its disposal." While not explicitly operative against the United States and United Nations forces in Korea, this guarantee undoubtedly deterred American strategists from striking at Peking's sanctuary in Manchuria when Chinese Communist "volunteers" hurled General MacArthur's troops back from the Yalu River to the thirty-eighth parallel.

On September 7, 1958, Nikita Khrushchev dropped the qualifications covering mutual assistance in the 1950 treaty and declared flatly, "An attack upon the People's Republic of China . . . is an attack upon the Soviet Union." This unprecedented Soviet support for Peking came in a letter to President Dwight D. Eisenhower during the crisis over the Taiwan Strait. On September 19, 1958, Khrushchev amplified this pledge by threatening nuclear retaliation against any country which employed nuclear weapons against Communist China. Thus the Sino-Soviet Alliance provides Peking both with minimal military security in case of war and with vital political leverage for atomic blackmail.

In the realm of economics, the alliance has also served Mao's interests. Credits, technical assistance, and imports from Moscow made possible the striking gains of the First Five-Year Plan indicated in Table 1.

Table 1 INDUSTRIAL OUTPUT OF MAINLAND CHINA, 1952–1957

PRODUCT	1952	1957
Coal (*million tons*)	63.5	128.0
Electric power (*billion kilowatt-hours*)	7.3	19.0
Iron (*million tons*)	1.9	5.9
Steel (*million tons*)	1.4	5.2
Cement (*million tons*)	2.9	6.7

With more than half of the original 211 industrial and construction projects "to be supplied from the Soviet Union" remaining in the Second Five-Year Plan, China's proclaimed goal of "overtaking Great Britain in fifteen years" clearly depends upon continuing Russian cooperation in trade, if not in aid. No Soviet credits have been announced since 1956. Moscow's share of Peking's foreign trade, however, exceeds 50 per cent. This provides a valuable source of imports, as well as an outlet for exports. Outside the bloc, China's shortage in foreign exchange is matched by its lack of large marketable export surpluses. Furthermore, Peking has given politics priority over economics in determining its relations with capitalist countries. This has kept trade with Japan and Great Britain below the level otherwise possible. These constraints upon China's trade outside the bloc make the Moscow-Peking axis a valuable asset for Mao's program of industrialization.

Training of China's managerial and scientific cadres has also depended largely upon Russian resources. From 1950 to 1957, more than 7,000 Soviet advisers worked in China at various times. While they appear insignificant against the population of 600 million, their impact was far out of proportion to their number. These Soviet specialists directed principal construction projects, such as the massive Yangtze River bridge. In addition, they supervised indigenous personnel in on-the-job training programs, especially in the burgeoning industrial base of Northeast China (Manchuria). Mass translation of Soviet technical journals, and intensive training programs for thousands of Chinese engineers, scientists, and skilled workers in the Soviet Union provide further impetus for the "leap forward" from agrarian backwardness to modern industrialization.

Symbolic of this leap, as well as of Moscow's assistance in making it possible, was the revelation by Kuo Mo-jo, President of the Chinese Academy of Sciences, that "Chinese scientists are determined to get China's artificial earth satellite into the sky at an early date. . . . The earlier that day comes, the better." Kuo's statement, hailing Sputnik III, admonished Chinese scientists to "study" Soviet achievements closely. A Chinese satellite might answer non-party criticism of "Marxist-Leninist science" prominent in the "rightist attack" of 1957. The political impact elsewhere in Asia might be even more significant, especially on Taiwan and among the overseas Chinese.

THE ROLE OF IDEOLOGY

Few of these gains could have been foreseen by Mao Tse-tung in 1949. His commitment to the Russian alliance was primarily ideological, albeit reinforced by his perception of American commitment to Chiang Kai-shek in the civil war. Whatever may have been the strains of negotiating with Stalin in 1950, or in mediating between "great power chauvinism" (Russian) and "narrow nationalism" (Polish) in 1956–57, the mystique of "socialist unity against the imperialist camp" undoubtedly dominates Peking's view of world affairs.

But while the ideological component preceded in time the military and economic interaction in the Moscow-Peking axis, it alone is insufficient to explain the ties that bind. In fact, "universal application of the fundamental laws of Marxism-Leninism," championed by both partners, has not prevented important divergencies on both domestic and foreign policy. Certain consistent ideological differences between the Soviet and Chinese Communists can be discerned over the past three decades. Yet the degree to which these differences have influenced the political interaction of the two elites varies sharply from time to time.

These differences have been described by Peking as "contradictions between socialist countries, between communist parties [which are] not basic . . . not the result of a fundamental clash of interests between classes but of conflict between right and wrong opinions or of a partial contradiction of interests." The first decade of the Moscow-Peking axis suggests that, in this respect, relations between Communist partners resemble those between capitalist states in the existence of conflicting national interests. The degree to which Peking may succeed in pressing its interests against those of Moscow depends upon four variable factors: the relative stability of the two elites in terms of domestic opposition; the relative influence of the two elites within the Communist bloc; the degree of Chinese dependence upon Russian assistance; and the prevailing power relationship between the Communist bloc and the "imperialist camp" as seen from Moscow and Peking. Thus it is not ideology alone which conditions relations between Moscow and Peking. In fact, ideology may be subordinated to military and economic factors so far as the resolution of differences is concerned.

Brief comparison of Peking's policy and position of 1949–50 with that of 1956–57 illustrates this point. During the first period, Mao supported the expulsion of Tito from the Cominform, muted his own claims to ideological innovation, and paid homage to Stalin's unfailing genius. Close reading of Chinese Communist writings of the period, however, revealed implicit differences with Moscow. If too obvious, such differences frequently were suppressed in later editions.

Mao's disagreements arose in part from his independence of Stalin in winning control of the Chinese Communist Party (CCP) in the 1930's and of all China in the 1940's. Suppression of disagreement was a necessary result of his utter dependence upon Stalin to maintain power after 1949. Rebuilding the shattered Chinese economy and restraining "imperialist aggression and its running-dog Chiang Kai-shek" necessitated reliance upon Russia. If Stalin's personal price for assistance was complete acceptance of Moscow's views, at least on the public record, Mao's inferior power compelled acquiescence.

The emergence of differences after Stalin's death, notably in the East European crisis of 1956–57, followed changes in these critical factors. First, stability of the Soviet elite was uncertain following the Twentieth Party Congress, while no comparable struggle for power appeared in the Chinese Communist Party. Second, Khrushchev dealt Soviet bloc leadership a heavy blow in his de-Stalinization speech at the Congress. Third, China's dependence on Russian support had declined, especially in the economic realm, from the earlier years. Finally, no crisis threatened the bloc from without, and in some respects the Soviet military position was becoming increasingly favorable in comparison with that of the United States.

These developments offered Mao more political leverage against Russian policies than had been available during the Stalin period. This transformation of China from satellite to partner is reflected in the changing image of the Moscow-Peking axis found in Western analyses. In 1950, many observers believed that Chinese intervention in the Korean crisis was forced upon Mao by Stalin. In 1958, an equally substantial core of opinion believed Khrushchev's attack on Tito to have been forced by Mao.

Setting aside such speculation for the moment, one final observation on the role of ideology might be made. It was more than ideological conviction which caused Peking to intervene in the bloc dispute of 1956, in contrast with its position in 1948. Intervention served Chinese military, economic, and political interests. Any breach of bloc unity affects Chinese military security both in the encouragement it offers "the imperialist camp" and in the burdens it places upon Soviet military forces. While Peking and Moscow agree on the need for bloc unity, however, they have differed on the means of attaining this end.

Furthermore, China's economic progress depends in part upon the reliability of planned deliveries from East Europe. Increased Soviet commitments to tide over unstable regimes may also reduce the availability of Russian economic assistance for China. Finally, Peking's prestige at home and abroad is involved with bloc developments. To cite specific instances, in 1956 Chinese university students voiced "shock" and "dismay" over Soviet military intervention in Hungary. The consequent turmoil in intellectual circles posed problems for the Chinese Communist Party throughout the summer of 1957. Meanwhile in the United Nations, Burmese denunciation of the Russian military move coincided with Chou En-lai's tour of Southeast Asia. Chou, who was then both Premier and Foreign Minister, was publicly and privately pressed to explain his support for the use of foreign troops to intervene in domestic affairs.

This indicates that ideology alone did not prompt Chinese participation in the struggle between East Europe and the Soviet Union in 1956. It further suggests that changes in the Chinese position on this problem in 1957–58 came from equally serious military, economic, and political considerations, especially since these changes were incompatible with past ideological expressions. A brief review of the 1957–58 developments, therefore, may indicate the nature of these considerations and thereby throw light on subsequent Chinese policy in other areas.

CHINESE VIEWS ON BLOC RELATIONS

Although the Twentieth Party Congress of February 1956 proclaimed the possibility of "different paths to socialism," the Poznań crisis in July and the Polish and Hungarian ferment of September and October made the question of Soviet controls over satellite developments a central issue. Vacillation and division in Moscow between "hard" and "soft" lines contrasted with Peking's position which fell midway between the confederative and the unitary approach to bloc relations. Chinese comment attacked extreme champions of independence as "bourgeois nationalists," at the same time rejecting complete Soviet domination as "great-power chauvinism."

Three points appeared at issue: the limits of Soviet prerogative vis-à-vis other bloc countries; the limits of deviation from Soviet practice by other bloc countries; and the means of achieving unanimity or of maintaining differences within the bloc. In brief, the Chinese formula called for keeping dissent confidential within the bloc while tolerating divergent views. This approach had characterized the CCP's approach to past differences with Moscow over theoretical and practical issues. It was succinctly stated by Chou En-lai in March 1957, two months after his successful repairing of relations between Warsaw and Moscow:

. . . All the socialist countries take Marxism-Leninism as their guiding philosophy, which constitutes the basis of our unanimity on questions of principle. Yet this does not mean that all socialist countries, while being unanimous on principles, have also identical views on all questions at all times. Compared with the main aspect of our unanimity on principles, our differences on certain questions are after all of secondary importance. Moreover, these differences can be resolved and, on the common basis of Marxism-Leninism, a unanimity can be reached gradually through comradely discussions and consultation. Even if no unanimity can be reached for the time being, it would also be normal to reserve the differences while upholding our solidarity.

The consistency with which Peking promoted this policy despite varying reactions in Moscow was manifest in the authoritative reports of Mao's encouragement to Gomulka throughout 1956–57, contrasted with Khrushchev's personal opposition to Gomulka both before and after the Hungarian uprising. It was evidenced in the more moderate criticism of Yugoslav statements on Hungary in *Jen Min Jih Pao*, compared with *Pravda*. Similarly Politburo member P'eng Chen's conciliatory visit to Belgrade came a few weeks before Soviet suspension of credits to Tito's government in February 1957. Only on the question of Hungary did Moscow and Peking present a unanimous front, established after differing domestic reports on the early stages of the revolt.

Formal enunciation of Sino-Soviet agreement on bloc relations, in the joint communiqué of January 19, 1957, asserted, "The Socialist countries are independent and sovereign states and relations between them are based upon the Leninist principle of national equality." The statement reiterated the famous Panch Shila or "five principles" of the Sino-Indian agreement of 1954, "complete equality, respect for territorial integrity, independence, sovereignty, and non-interference in each other's internal affairs." The last point in particular symbolized the nub of Polish-Soviet problems in 1956–57. The context of the statement, which was issued upon Chou En-lai's departure from Moscow, suggested that Chinese mediation had assured Gomulka's survival against internal and external "Stalinist" pressures.

Thus the need for intervention in bloc affairs coincided with Peking's ability to intervene, reflected in the previously discussed increase in military, economic, and political power. The results were favorable; Peking's mediation appeared to cement ties between Warsaw and Moscow. Soviet acquiescence in Gomulka's leadership, despite his appeasement of the Polish peasantry and the Catholic Church, was reciprocated by Gomulka's insistence upon party leadership and his careful, consistent attack against "revisionism." The consequent reduction of tensions within Poland, paralleled throughout East Europe in the spring and summer of 1957, furthered both Soviet and Chinese strategic and economic interests. Finally, acceptance of the Chinese formula for bloc relations elevated Peking's prestige both inside and outside the bloc, without impairing the basic unity of the Moscow alliance.

THE MOSCOW CONFERENCE, NOVEMBER 1957

Suddenly the Chinese formula was abandoned and pressure for conformity with Soviet policy reapplied throughout East Europe. In September, the Communist Party of the Soviet Union theses for the November celebration of the fortieth anniversary of the Bolshevik revolution warned that "those who stress the national peculiarities of each country marching to socialism" were "fundamentally opposed to Marxism-Leninism." Resisting this pressure, Gomulka, writing in *Pravda* on November 5, restated his past argument for "a specifically Polish road to socialism that accorded with our own concrete conditions." The next day, Khrushchev and Mao, in that order, delivered parallel injunctions to the Supreme Soviet against "revisionism." The Soviet leader warned: "The dream of the enemies of socialism is that communists should start looking for some completely new, artificial road to socialism for each individual country. . . . This is one of the chief dangers and we must wage the most resolute fight against it." Mao followed, declaring, "At present, the urgent task is to oppose revisionist deviations." Gomulka, as third speaker, did not echo these remarks.

Gomulka's position was a curious one. Repeatedly in Poland he had already attacked "revisionism." His expressions on the need for bloc unity carried no less conviction than did those of other bloc leaders. Yet within the context of the November conference, he appeared unwilling to subscribe to the positions enunciated by Khrushchev and Mao. The precise nature of the stakes for which he was playing remains obscure. However, his differences with the Sino-Soviet position, particularly in choice of emphasis, are apparent.

Gomulka's article in *Pravda* reiterated the 1956 formula for bloc relations, stressing "the Leninist principles of complete equality, mutual respect, independence, and sovereignty." Mao, however, signaled a major shift from the earlier Chinese position, making no reference to "equality" or "independence" for bloc members in his Moscow remarks. Dropping the 1956–57 term "socialist commonwealth of nations" with its confederative connotations, Mao evoked the more traditional image of "the socialist camp" in a militant defense of Soviet leadership:

The socialist force has surpassed the imperialist force. Our socialist camp should have a leader, and this is the Soviet Union. The enemy also has a leader, and this is America. If there is no leader, the strength will be weakened.

Mao's argument for Soviet leadership paralleled Khrushchev's attack against revisionism in the reference to external threat. Here, too, the Sino-Soviet partners differed from the Polish leader in their emphasis upon the danger of war. Gomulka nowhere at the conference attacked "U.S. imperialism," but claimed hope in "the strengthening of the peace-loving forces and in there being greater chances for the preservation of peace." He justified reduced Polish industrial investments and other deviations from Soviet practice in part because of the absence of "imperialist and civil wars . . . and the threat of intervention" which had faced the early Soviet regime. By implication, no such threats now faced the bloc.

Mao, however, warned of "imperialist wolves" who "put their hope in war." Threats from "U.S. imperialists" in Hungary, Syria, Egypt, and Taiwan won special attention. His address to the Supreme Soviet made no reference to "the broad peace area" or to "the contradictions within the imperialist camp." He did not repeat the theme of 1956–57 that "war is no longer inevitable" and did not echo the foreign policy analyses of Ch'en Yi and Chou En-lai of the same period which saw "the relaxation of tension" prevailing in international relations. Just as Mao followed the lead of the Soviet Communist party and Khrushchev in redefining bloc relations, so

too he supported the bellicose Soviet posture during the recent Syrian crisis by focusing on the threat of war.

The November 1957 conference produced two documents. The first was a "declaration" signed by twelve bloc delegations, the Yugoslavs abstaining. The second, a "peace manifesto," won support from sixty-four Communist parties, including the Yugoslavs. The "declaration" was more important, its compromise nature manifested in its inclusion of essential elements from both the Polish and the Sino-Soviet positions. Postconference comment diluted the appearance of unanimity with each side stressing those aspects which reflected its original stand. Increased Soviet attention to "revisionism" after November suggested Belgrade as the obvious target, in view of Tito's refusal to attend the conference and Yugoslav failure to support the declaration. Gomulka's position, in retrospect, appears to have made Warsaw also subject to pressure from the new Sino-Soviet line.

To the knowledge of the writer, no anticipation of Mao's shift on the problems of bloc relations and revisionism had appeared in the Chinese press, not even in the articles written for the November anniversary. Polish and Yugoslav sources subsequently claimed surprise at the extent of Sino-Soviet unanimity in supporting firmness within the bloc and harshness towards nonbloc countries, and offered no credible explanation for the phenomenon.

To be sure, political tensions in China seemed explosive during June and July 1957, with open criticism of the party's domestic and foreign policy from influential government and intellectual spokesmen. Yet the "antirightest struggle" of August and September appeared to have suppressed opposition. Serious as was the damage to Mao's experiment in resolving "nonantagonistic contradictions" through "blooming and contending," it seemed insufficient to cause so sudden and far-reaching a reversal of policy. Nor did Tito's refusal to attend the conference compel renewed pressure upon Gomulka. The Polish leader had shown no basic change in policy from the spring of 1957. At that time, Cyrankiewicz's visit to Peking had prompted an announcement from Mao of a return trip to Warsaw. Mao's unannounced cancellation of the visit was never explained, but at the time was not interpreted in Warsaw as evidence of displeasure.

1958 ATTACK ON YUGOSLAV "REVISIONISM"

The import of the new Moscow-Peking line became apparent in 1958. In March, publication of the draft program for the Seventh Congress of the League of Yugoslav Communists (LYC) reopened much of the controversy which had underlain the Moscow meeting. The Soviet rebuttal in *Kommunist* in mid-April, though mild in tone, signaled a wide range of disagreement on important points of domestic and foreign policy. Bloc delegations boycotted the LYC Congress, despite some modification in the draft program. Following the adoption of the program, amidst pointed Yugoslav speeches bitterly referring to 1948, the bloc stepped up the attack. On May 5, *Jen Min Jih Pao* called the program "out and out revisionist" and went beyond previous Soviet comment in approving the 1948 Cominform resolution as "basically correct."

Space precludes a detailed review of the massive campaign which followed. The lines were consistent with those apparent in November, however. On the one hand, Sino-Soviet attacks pursued the themes of "unity of the socialist camp," "the danger of war," and "revisionism," in order to link Tito's acceptance of American aid with the idea that his position undermined the bloc. On the other hand, Polish comment belatedly and temperately criticized specific points of the LYC program but limited the area and means of the dispute. While Moscow suspended economic credits to Belgrade, Warsaw continued to negotiate economic exchange with the Yugoslavs. When Budapest linked Nagy's execution with alleged Yugoslav provocation of the Hungarian uprising, signs of Polish displeasure contrasted with official Chinese "joy" at the announcement. Khrushchev's personal attacks against Tito won belated response from Gomulka, with no Polish endorsement for "Soviet leadership" and with typical Polish emphasis upon "independence" and "equality" embodied in the "socialist commonwealth of nations."

Thus the 1956–57 political proximity between Warsaw and Peking against Moscow now changed into a Moscow-Peking union against Warsaw. This union was obscured by the staggered timing of the statements from the two capitals, as well as from apparent Chinese initiative in increasing the intensity of attack. It seems likely, however, that both these phenomena were pre-arranged, alternating the source of pressure upon Belgrade while gradually increasing it. The alternative image of Mao forcing Krushchev's hand, even to the point of compelling suspension of Soviet credits to Tito, does not take account of the relative power of the two leaders, much less of the probable pattern of Chinese behavior in such circumstances.

"EAST WIND OVER WEST WIND"

This leaves unexplained the reason for Mao's major shift in November 1957. Conceivably he agreed to abandon the previous moderate policy in reaction against the combined pressures of domestic criticism from "bourgeois rightists" and of continued East European dissension from "revisionists." More than doctrine was at stake. At home the challenge to Chinese Communist leadership struck at the foundations of political power. In East Europe the challenge to Soviet leadership struck at the foundations of strategic power. Should Tito's wooing of Gomulka prompt the Poles to emulate the Yugoslavs and bargain between the United States and the Soviet Union without commitment to either side, China's strategic and economic interests in bloc unity would be jeopardized.

These interests appear, as in the past, to have played the more immediate role, making ideological concern a secondary, albeit contributing, factor. On November 17, 1957, Mao offered a new formulation proclaiming the strategic ascendancy of the socialist over the "imperialist" camp, "East Wind prevails over West Wind." His phrase, which keynoted Chinese propaganda throughout 1957–58, was linked with the Moscow conferences and Soviet earth satellite launchings as "proving" the superior strength of the Soviet bloc. *Jen Min Jih Pao*, on November 22, amplified Mao's words to include Soviet intercontinental ballistic missile accomplishments. Mao's proclamation of "a new turning point" in the relation of forces was reiterated in Chinese statements from this point forth.

To be sure, previous Chinese editorial comment had hailed both ICBM and Sputnik developments as marking the superiority of socialism over capitalism and the "smashing rebuff" to "hopes of imperialists who seek to start a new war." Yet it is possible to discern a difference between propagandistic reactions following closely on the heels of Soviet announcements, and authoritative analyses from high government spokesmen laying down major policy lines. In this regard, it is of interest that Mao's initial references in Moscow to the Sputnik hailed it in an exclusively scientific reference to "man's conquest of nature"; his strategic emphasis came only two weeks later. This shift brought Mao into line with the evaluation of Soviet weapons developments voiced by Soviet Air Marshal Vershinin and Premier Khrushchev during the Syrian crisis of September and October 1957. In short, the evidence suggests a Chinese willingness to exploit Russian accomplishments for at least political propaganda, but that the final decision to do so at the highest level came only after consultation in Moscow.

One other development must be noted. On November 5, a high level Chinese military mission suddenly departed from Peking for Moscow, too late to attend the Russian celebration. The group stayed in the Soviet Union for three weeks, reportedly attending reviews and inspecting military installations. Its composition, however, and the timing of its flight suggest that Mao required wider military assistance in problems under review than was afforded by the Minister of National Defense, Marshal P'eng Te-huai, who accompanied Mao initially.

Is it possible that Mao agreed to support Khrushchev politically on the question of bloc relations with the hope or expectation of sharing in the new Soviet acquisition of military strength? The image of such bargaining requires considerable refinement before serious consideration can be given this hypothesis. At the very least, however, it suggests that a new Soviet willingness to give political support for Chinese moves in Asia was agreed upon, perhaps including Soviet statements concerning the use of nuclear arms under certain contingencies as a deterrent to possible moves by the United States. From this minimal level of agreement which assumes only political moves by Moscow, Mao may have anticipated the sufficient possibility of a later expansion of Soviet support to have left the question of actual Sino-Soviet sharing of nuclear weapons to another time. Alternatively, increased Russian assistance in launching a Chinese satellite would have domestic as well as foreign benefits for Peking worthy of Mao's reciprocal political support against Khrushchev's "revisionist" opponents.

Such speculation answers no questions but may make more plausible the hypothesis of Chinese political leverage operating upon Russian policy within certain conditions and under certain limitations. The year following the November conference reinforced this possibility. In the change of policy towards East Europe, Mao Tse-tung appeared to gain nothing, while losing prestige not only within the bloc but among uncommitted non-Communist countries as well. Khrushchev, however, increased Russian bloc dominance in appearance, if not in reality.

The situation seemed reversed in the crisis in Taiwan Strait. Here it was Khrushchev who steadily increased Russian commitment to a situation whose immediate benefits accrued only to China. The Soviet leader risked much of his "summit-conference" posture, and, in the last analysis, appeared to risk Soviet military involvement over a situation which had little direct bearing on Russian interests. Thus it is only in the general sense that Russian and Chinese interests converge in maximizing the pressures upon both bloc and nonbloc targets through exploitation of Soviet weapons. In specific instances, the divergence of interest is sufficiently great to compel the question: how has agreement been reached for co-ordinating policy?

The problem of plumbing Sino-Soviet secrecy was aptly demonstrated by the Khrushchev-Mao meeting in Peking of July 30 to August 3, 1958. First, the secrecy of the meeting was well kept, to judge by the surprised reaction of Western chancelleries, although its participants included not only the two chiefs of state but also Chou En-lai, Wang Chia-hsiang, Minister of Foreign Affairs Ch'en Yi, and Minister of National Defense P'eng Te-huai on the Chinese side, with Soviet participants including Minister of Defense Marshal Rodin Y. Malinovsky, acting Minister of Foreign Affairs V. V. Kuznetsov, and B. N. Ponomarev. Secondly, the lengthy statement issued upon conclusion of the four-day conference consisted mostly of propaganda themes current in Communist media on such issues as summit conferences, the Middle East crisis, and Yugoslav "revisionism." No mention was made of Taiwan or the offshore islands, although this problem was immediately to raise international tensions to heights unequaled since the early days of the Korean crisis.

Yet the abundance of published materials which flow from Peking and Moscow may provide clues as to the differences of policy between the two partners. By testing various hypotheses concerning these differences and their resolution against the course of succeeding events, we improve our understanding of the dynamics of the Moscow-Peking axis. The task of uncovering Russian and Chinese intentions separately is difficult enough. But the greater problem of determining the interaction of Russian and Chinese policy poses the basic challenge for those concerned with the fate of the Arab-Asian world which borders this formidable alliance.

NUCLEAR POWER—THE GREAT DETERRENT

HERBERT S. DINERSTEIN

The great German military writer Karl von Clausewitz believed that war was simply "the continuation of state policy by other means," and so it has been during the first sixty years of the twentieth century. But in the new era of nuclear fission, intercontinental missiles, and satellites orbiting the earth, war threatens to be incredibly destructive for victor and vanquished alike; indeed the advent of a Third World Conflict promises to end what man calls "civilized life." Nevertheless, national states continue to prepare for war, and include the possibility of war in the calculations which accompany their formulation of foreign policy. Rival great powers move from stalemate to stalemate in their frantic search for new means of attack and defense, with each side hoping to discover the ultimate weapon against which there can be no retaliation. Herbert S. Dinerstein, an eminent specialist in Soviet affairs and a staff member of the Rand Corporation, has spent almost a decade studying Soviet military policy and its relationship to politics. Here he traces the development of Soviet theory about the way to fight and win a war in the space age.

SOME months after Stalin died, the chief theoretical organ of the Soviet Ministry of Defense, *Voennaia mysl'* (*Military Thought*), carried an article by Major General Talenskii that opened the first real discussion on military theory in the Soviet Union for twenty-five years. Since 1945 this journal has been intended only for Soviet military officers.

Talenskii rejected Stalin's formula concerning the permanently operating factors, asserting that it was not a basic law of war. He advanced a basic law that, he argued, was an improvement over Stalin's formula because it did "not exclude the possibility of a decisive defeat within a a limited time . . . given the existence of certain conditions." For the first time since 1945 a Soviet publication had envisaged a possible war of the future essentially different from World Wars I and II. There could be decisive defeat in a limited time. This did not mean that a single campaign with nuclear weapons would be decisive or that measures could not be taken to reduce the likelihood that the nuclear phase would be decisive. The inconclusiveness of Talen-

skii's article was not important. What was important was the attention it focused on a new basic issue.

The discussion, initiated at least ostensibly by Talenskii, produced ten articles of comment and forty letters combined in a single article, together with a summation and an official resolution of the issues by the editors. These writings reveal how novel was the serious consideration of these theoretical issues. Obviously no official line on the subject existed. Some argued that Stalin's idea of the permanently operating factors was still perfectly satisfactory; others said that "surprise . . . might in certain conditions even determine the outcome of the war," a clear rejection of Stalin's view that transitory factors cannot be decisive. Such diversity of views on matters of basic importance had not been possible in the Soviet Union for a generation. There seems to be no doubt that this was a real, and not a staged, discussion, for there was considerable irrelevance and some of the disputants failed to discern the main issues, concentrating on peripheral ones.

Several major conclusions emerged

From H. S. Dinerstein, *War and the Soviet Union* (New York, 1959), pp. 9–27. By permission of Frederick A. Praeger, Inc.

and the editors of *Military Thought* established these, in a sense, as a new official line in an article of April, 1955, which closed the discussion. The new line characterized the doctrine of permanently operating factors as inadequate on the whole, although valid in some contexts. The formula first dropped out of sight and then, in 1957, was explicitly abandoned as more confusing than helpful.

Talenskii's chief verbal innovation was his emphasis on the *armed conflict* as the crucial aspect of warfare. A strange innovation! Surely a law of war ought to deal with war. But the number of objections raised by Soviet commentators to this simple proposition reveals the significance of Talenskii's approach in the Soviet context. Not only did he put the armed conflict in the forefront of his treatment, but he insisted that the same principles of war affected both parties in the armed conflict. His opponents complained that it was anti-Marxist, that is, theoretically and morally wrong, to apply the same social laws to two radically different social systems. Capitalist states organized differently and seeking different goals could not command the loyalty of their own peoples over an extended period and had perforce to try for quick conclusions. The wars conducted by a socialist state were just by definition and therefore enjoyed the enthusiastic support of the population, which besides worked within a more rational economic framework. Talenskii and his supporters accepted the importance of these differences but insisted on maintaining at the center of attention an armed conflict whose laws applied equally to both contending sides.

In emphasizing combat at the expense of economics and morale, Talenskii made it possible to assess justly the role of nuclear weapons. Once discussion was freed from the confines of the permanently-operating-factors formula, the obvious implications of the existence of nuclear weapons followed almost automatically. Plainly, if one country's nuclear campaign

were successful in destroying a large proportion of the armed forces, industry, and cities of another country, the attacker might gain an irreversible advantage. The Soviet theorists did not follow some Western ones who have proceeded to argue that the initial nuclear campaign itself would end the war; they contended merely that the success of the nuclear campaign *could* mean ultimate victory. This view, now official doctrine, puts an unprecedented emphasis on the importance of surprise. As a corollary, the Russians argued that the advantage of surprise might be denied to the enemy if foreknowledge of his intentions were obtained and defensive action were taken to reduce the likelihood that his nuclear blow would decide the war. From a defensive as well as from an offensive standpoint, the importance of the factor of surprise had grown greatly in Soviet eyes.

If the advantages that the offense may gain from achieving surprise are so great, every power that recognizes this fact must experience a temptation to pre-empt the initiative when the outlook for peace is unpromising. Generally, Soviet writers have gone no further than to say, and only rarely, that surprise is a two-edged weapon, but in the more restricted columns of *Military Thought,* written for officers, we find the plain statement that the Soviet Union has to be prepared to deal a forestalling blow so as to deprive the enemy of the advantage of surprise. The image called up is that of a quick blow against the enemy, who is poised to strike, before he can launch his own attack. While the capacity to deliver such a blow is officially advocated, the writers who express official views hasten to add that this policy should not be confused with that of preventive war. In this context the term "preventive war" may be taken to indicate a war initiated in order to forestall a remote possibility of enemy attack at some indefinite time in the future. In this sense, the term may be distinguished from "pre-emptive war," defined as a war initiated in order to forestall an attack that is believed to be imminent. Whatever the intention of the Soviet leaders, in public statements they would automatically deny that preventive war could be their policy. Preventive war and warmongering have become identified with each other in Soviet propaganda, and consequently it cannot be admitted that a socialist government would even consider preventive war.

The professional discussion of these matters was subsequently reflected in the public press, and it was even more obvious that the realistic military thinkers had won the day. Changes in the Soviet military posture over the next two years seemed to reflect the changes in theory. The military consequences of the new theory will be treated in more detail at a later stage. Meanwhile, what of its political consequences?

The main political result of the reappraisal of nuclear weapons was the improved prospect that the Soviet Union would not have to fight a major war unless she chose to do so. In the past, nations had often been deterred from making war because they feared that they would lose more than they gained. The experience of France and Great Britain during and after the First World War strongly suggested that in modern wars the cost of victory might be so great as to bring about a relative decline in the power of the victors. This paradox, however, could not be erected into an axiom as the Second World War made clear. From that conflict the United States and the Soviet Union emerged much stronger than before, both absolutely and relatively, in spite of vast expenditures by the former and great devastation of the latter. In the past the conclusion that war did not pay was pragmatic rather than axiomatic. Today, however, nuclear weapons could destroy more in a few days than years of large-scale war had destroyed in the past. The belief that war did not pay would now act as a deterrent to a potential warmaker whether or not he expected to win an ultimate military victory.

Such a belief was much less likely to be held in Stalin's time, when official doctrine held that the air battle, with the use of nuclear weapons, would be more important than ever before, but still not decisive. That doctrine put a ceiling, as it were, on the potential destructiveness of nuclear weapons. As long as the enormous destructive possibilities of nuclear weapons were less than fully admitted, it was difficult to advance the hypothesis that other nations, or even one's own, would be deterred from initiating nuclear war because the costs— win or lose—would be too high.

In estimating Western intentions from the Stalinist point of view, the Soviet analyst had to assume that the capitalist powers would make a last desperate effort when they saw political dominance passing to communism. Nuclear weapons, however, introduced a fresh consideration into this old dogma. Unless the capitalists could reconcile themselves to suffer the destruction produced by nuclear weapons, they would prefer gradual decline to nuclear war. Under the Stalinist formula, the Soviet analyst might conclude that the capitalists would be deterred from making war if they felt that victory was in doubt. After the reappraisal of nuclear weapons, however, it was legitimate to argue that capitalism might be deterred from making war, irrespective of its chances of victory.

The belief that the capitalist powers would probably not attack the Soviet Union brought with it a profound modification of the traditional fear that national catastrophe was possible sooner or later. The country must continue, of course, to ensure itself against catastrophe by building up its military strength, but the constant preoccupation with impending disaster was no longer justifiable.

The Soviet analyst, however, could scarcely admit that he lived in a relatively secure new world until he was assured that the Soviet Union really had the nuclear power to deter the United States and that the United States recognized the existence of that power. Evidence on these points is presented in later chapters.

The new Soviet position rested on the possession of nuclear weapons and the ability to deliver them. It was simple enough to count the nuclear weapons in the Soviet stockpile, but it was difficult to be sure that the Soviet Union had the capacity to deliver against the United States a punishing retaliatory blow, if the latter attacked first. Nothing less than this capacity constituted an adequate deterrent. The ability to strike a first blow could constitute only a threat, not a deterrent.

In estimating the probable effects of a Soviet retaliatory blow the Soviet analyst had to consider a great many variables. He had to establish the probable weight of the American first strike, for which he depended on a knowledge of the numbers, efficiency, and strategic uses of American aircraft and weapons. He had to decide how far the weight of the American blow would be reduced by effective warning and defense measures. Having made due allowance for these factors, he had to calculate the effectiveness of a Soviet counterstrike.

The ability of the Soviet striking force to employ what power it still retained depended on many imponderables. If one assumed that the American attack aimed to reduce the size of the Soviet striking force, then the destructiveness of individual weapons became an important factor. Would the American force bring a large or a small number of hydrogen bombs? How effective would the Soviet chain of command be after an American blow?

This list of factors required for an estimate of the retaliatory capability of the Soviet Union could be extended, but it is probably clear already that it was extremely difficult for Soviet planners to determine the precise moment when the Soviet Union acquired a retaliatory capability adequate to her requirements for deterring an American attack. There seems to be little question that the Soviet Union did not have such a capability in 1950, or that she does

have it in 1958. Even if one had all the facts available to both Soviet and American military planners, one could not fix with certainty a point in time when the Soviets acquired a deterrent nuclear capability. For deterrent capability is, so to speak, in the mind of the deterrer. One can, as it happens, learn within reasonable limits the period when the Soviet planners decided that their military power met the requirements of deterrence.

In March, 1954, some persons in the Soviet Union stated quite unmistakably that the Soviet Union possessed a deterrent capability. The best known of these were Malenkov and Mikoian. That they were sincere in their opinions is made probable by the fact that other persons publicly disagreed with them. Once again one had the feeling that a genuine debate was in progress. Those who opposed Malenkov's views repeated the old shibboleth about capitalist encirclement of the Soviet Union and indicated quite clearly that they did not accept the fact of Soviet deterrent capability, at least as of that moment. The most notable in this group were Khrushchev, Bulganin, Kaganovich, and Molotov. Only a directed verdict could have produced uniformity in statements of opinion on the subject, but at this early date such a verdict was not forthcoming. At this time, as we shall see, differences of opinion about military and other matters extended into the highest ranks of the Soviet leadership.

It is interesting, but by no means surprising, that the Soviet military leaders were not among the first to shout that the age of Soviet nuclear deterrence had arrived. While some civilian leaders believed that the mere possession of nuclear weapons and aircraft constituted a deterrent capability, military leaders by virtue of their experience did not make this mistake of oversimplification. Moreover, the caution and conservatism characteristic of military leaders in powerful countries must have delayed the recognition that so important a change had really taken place.

If the United States did not know that the Soviet Union could answer an air-nuclear attack in kind, she could not be deterred from making such an attack merely by fear of retaliation. It only takes one party to commit an act of aggression; it requires an unspoken agreement between two to deter such an act. For the doubters, including the military, it was extremely important to determine whether the United States was framing her policy on the assumption that an American attack on the Soviet Union would result in a level of damage to the United States that her leaders would find unacceptable. The answer to this question was bound to make a tremendous difference in the Soviet sense of security. True, the Marxist might reason that the United States would refrain from making war on the Soviet Union because one group of capitalists wanted peace, because the population had not yet been properly prepared for war, because of contradictions in the relationships among capitalist countries, or because the capitalist military establishment was not yet ready. Under any of these hypotheses, however, the Soviet Union was secure against attack only as long as the restraining factors existed. By their very nature, these factors were transitory. Only the capitalist fear of unacceptable retaliation could be counted on to provide the desirable degree of security.

Had the United States been deterred, either transitorily or permanently, from launching war against the Soviet Union? The indicators were contradictory and confusing.

The United States had not minimized the importance of nuclear weapons while she possessed a monopoly of them and had frequently stated that these weapons constituted a deterrent to aggression. Yet during the Korean War, the only major act of Soviet-sponsored aggression in the period when the United States had a clear superiority in nuclear weapons and delivery capability, the United States exercised restraint.

Far from being willing to engage the Soviet Union directly with nuclear weapons, America was clearly anxious to avoid any expansion of the war. This was true of both the Democratic and Republican administrations.

Thus far the omens were favorable to the Soviet Union, but the situation was not clear cut. While those in power in the United States were relatively cautious about committing American resources to the Far Eastern conflict, several military and political leaders urged the expansion of the war in Asia and the use of nuclear weapons against China, even at the risk of precipitating a war with the Soviet Union. The Korean War may well have forced on the Soviet military leaders a heightened awareness of how exposed they were to a nuclear attack if the Americans decided to make one.

The Korean War ended early in President Eisenhower's first term of office. The new President expressed his abhorrence of nuclear war. In a major speech of December, 1953, he began to advance his conviction that current weapons development made general war unthinkable. The leaders of the Soviet Union might well have regarded the President's remarks as evidence that their own possession of nuclear weapons was already effectively deterring the United States from making war against them.

In January, 1954, however, Secretary of State Dulles announced the latest policy of the National Security Council. The United States would meet aggression with "massive retaliation at places and times of our own choosing." Since the issue of massive retaliation in response to a massive Soviet attack was not in question, the Secretary's announcement seemed to mean that the United States might initiate a nuclear exchange with the Soviet Union if provoked by less than an all-out attack on her own positions. This interpretation implied that the United States would not be deterred by the Soviet nuclear capability from greeting local aggression with an all-out nuclear attack. But the almost instantaneous reaction of America's British ally to the Dulles statement made it obvious that the United States could not use British bases without British permission. For this and other reasons, as later chapters will show, the Soviet Union concluded that probably the United States either could not or would not use nuclear weapons against her under the provocation of limited Soviet aggression.

Since no major act of Soviet provocation comparable to the attack on South Korea has occurred since Dulles's speech of January, 1954, no real test of the readiness of the United States to execute the policy of massive retaliation has been possible.

The very idea that it was possible to count on nuclear weapons to provide immunity from attack by the United States (capitalist hostility being axiomatic in the Soviet mind) opened up many seemingly attractive vistas for the Soviet Union. First, the Soviet leaders could hope to gain parity with the United States in the newest weapons much more rapidly than in conventional armaments, where the industrial mobilization base was of prime importance. Even by optimistic estimates the Soviet Union would require decades to approach American industrial potential capacity. To achieve parity in nuclear weapons, however, might take only a matter of years.

In the months after Stalin's death, Malenkov and some others contended that possession of nuclear weapons could assure the Soviet Union of immunity from American attack, if the country concentrated on the deterrent aspects of military posture. Under such a program military expenditures could be kept at a level that would permit the Soviet Union to use its resources to raise the standard of living at home. Other Soviet leaders, notably Khrushchev, were hostile to these ideas and branded reliance on a deterrent posture as a policy of complacency which could lead to dis-

aster. After a little time the second group prevailed.

A theoretical distinction, never precise, has long been made between a military posture that will deter the enemy from undertaking war and one designed to bring war to the enemy, destroy his forces, and occupy his territory. One might say that the second is an extension of the first. With the advent of nuclear weapons, the distinction has survived but its character has changed. Soviet military and political thinkers have addressed themselves to present-day problems with this distinction in mind. Their conclusions may be more readily understood if, at this point, a few general observations about military deterrence are introduced.

Traditional deterrents against a war of the opponent's choosing can be divided into three categories. First, an overwhelming military superiority residing in one power group will deter other powers from a calculated decision to attack that group. In 1907, France increased her ability to deter a hostile Germany by entering into the Triple Entente of Great Britain, France and Russia, for the combined might of the three countries seemed to exceed Germany's. The existence of this alliance, however, failed to deter a German attack on France. But neither side, as it turned out, had an overwhelming superiority over the other.

In the First World War victory was believed to depend on the rapid destruction of the enemy's military forces, an obvious maxim of war. When the front lines bogged down, the wearing effects of blockade and attrition began to play a role. Had German statesmen been faced in mid-1914 with Allied military forces unequivocally superior, and therefore clearly able to defeat an invader, one can scarcely doubt that they would have been deterred from making war. In such a case the deterrent force and the warmaking force are one and the same. The theoretical distinction between them does not apply. A marked superiority in over-all fighting capacity has been the most common deterrent to aggression on the part of the weaker powers, as it has been a frequent cause of aggression on the part of the stronger.

The second type of deterrent may be called the "sturdy rampart." For centuries England's island position, combined with an effective naval force, deterred invasion and facilitated successful military campaigns on the Continent. Similarly, the mountains of Switzerland have protected her independence for seven centuries. In each of these examples we find an excellent natural barrier supplemented by appropriate military measures. A favorable combination of geographical position and military art is required to make such a deterrent effective. Unfavorable changes in the military art may deprive a natural rampart of impenetrability, and hence of deterrent value. To be effective as a deterrent, the rampart need not discourage all attempts to breach it; it need merely prevent their succeeding. But the failure of such an attempt is likely to deter future attacks.

Where a strong natural rampart exists, the military forces required to deter a presumptive aggressor are far from identical with those required to destroy the opponent's military forces. The former are usually organized for purely defensive purposes and hence are incapable of inflicting strategic defeat on a powerful enemy. Great Britain, for example, could seldom bring war to a European enemy and defeat his land forces without the assistance of continental powers that possessed large armies.

Besides water and mountain barriers, sheer physical distance may act as a deterrent to war. Ancient Rome and China, for example, could not come to grips with each other. In this connection the transportation facilities possessed by the potential aggressor are bound to affect his decision to make war over great distances, as well as the drain on his other resources that such a war would entail.

The sturdy-rampart type of deterrent seems to be obsolete in the nuclear age. Only extraordinary developments in the art of defense seem likely to make its revival possible. At present such developments are not in sight.

The third type of deterrent is that of "disproportionate cost" and is of great antiquity. Here the presumptive aggressor is deterred because he decides that the game is not worth the candle. A potential aggressor is persuaded not to initiate a war because the cost of victory seems likely to exceed its value. As one might expect, this type of deterrent has often been used by the weak against the strong. It is, indeed, a variant of the first type. While overwhelming military superiority (the first type) will deter relatively weak powers from aggression, the latter may in turn protect themselves from strong powers by possessing and publicizing their ability to inflict an unacceptable level of damage on the attacker.

There is a certain similarity between this type of deterrent and those factors that may induce a strong power to abandon a war against a weaker one. Among such factors one may include difficulty of access to the weaker power's territory and military forces, unfavorable or strange fighting conditions, and guerrilla activity. All these factors played a part in Great Britain's abandonment of the American Revolutionary War, in spite of her obvious ability to continue it. In 1783 and again in 1814, the United States gained surprisingly favorable terms from the British. Indeed the granting of such terms by the British would be inexplicable if one were to take into account only the military forces that each contestant could muster. In view of the limited military forces that the British could transport to, or raise in, the North American Continent, however, and of the difficult fighting conditions imposed by wooded terrain on soldiers trained in the formal maneuvers of the parade ground, the Americans could exact from the British a price for continuing to fight that the latter found disproportionate to what they hoped to gain from the war.

Today the principle of disproportionate cost has become one of paramount importance. Considerations related to this principle have become the major deterrent to large-scale war involving the use of nuclear weapons. In the First and Second World Wars, though the destruction of the enemy's economic base began to play a larger role than before, the major strategy of the contestants was to destroy the enemy's military forces. Today and in the future, however, a war in which nuclear weapons are extensively employed will result in wholesale destruction of life and economic assets. Under modern conditions, damage to the economic base of each contestant is bound to be a major consequence of all-out war. Whether or not such destruction will be a major strategic aim of the contestants, it may well be the consequence of an effort to destroy numerous and widely dispersed targets in the opponent's country by the employment of megaton weapons. Such destruction is even more likely if the delivery vehicle is a ballistic missile, for the inaccuracy of fire of such missiles must be compensated by a large radius of destruction if the target is to be destroyed. Hence arises the thought that no potential aggressor can reasonably hope for victory in general war at a cost acceptable to himself. Thus the principle of disproportionate cost has become the major deterrent to nuclear war. To a greater extent, perhaps, than ever before the great powers are deterred from a head-on clash more by the threat of destruction to their economic resources and population than by the threat to their military forces. This historic change in the relative weight assigned to the various deterrent factors has blurred whatever practical significance once resided in the distinction between forces designated primarily to deter the enemy and forces designed primarily to destroy his military forces.

Before 1945 certain military arrange-

ments were often valuable both as deterrents to aggression and in active defense should war break out. The numerous coastal guns placed on American shores in the nineteenth century were clearly meant to deter a possible invader; they were certainly not meant to carry the war to the enemy. The Dutch preparations for flooding before World War II were not intended primarily to destroy the enemy's forces, but to deter him from attempting an invasion of the Netherlands. The French fortress system built before World War I was meant to deter an invasion across the Franco-German border.

Each of these deterrent devices could be used in a defensive role in the event that deterrence failed. Although the American coastal artillery never fired a shot in anger, the flooding of Dutch lands briefly delayed the advance of the German invaders. For nearly a century before 1914 the British navy not only maintained the Pax Britannica but deterred others, at least until 1898, from attempting to compete for mastery of the world's oceans. In the First World War the navy was an essential element in Britain's fighting forces. Thus it is clear that the deterrent role of a given military arrangement is seldom, if ever, its only role. Nevertheless, the distinction between a deterrent force and a warmaking force is worth maintaining, if only as a tool for analyzing the motives behind a country's development of this or that kind of military power. Consider, for example, the case of the huge German naval program of 1900. Since Germany, from a military point of view, was essentially a land-locked power, observers supposed that the intended role of the new Germany navy was offensive rather than deterrent or defensive. It was not possible to detect such a distinction in the case of the British navy.

Considerations such as the above suggest that there has more frequently been an identity between the requirements of defense and deterrence than between those of offense and deterrence. Since the development of nuclear weapons, however, the relationship between offensive capabilities and deterrence has become much closer. Conversely, a large investment in defensive arrangements may very well indicate not *primarily* a desire to deter nuclear attack, but rather a form of insurance against retaliation. Where this is true, the heavy investor in defense may well be hoping to reduce the risks of initiating offensive action. As we shall see in a later chapter, the Soviet Union has invested a great deal more in measures of active and civil defense than the United States.

Why have nuclear weapons brought about this change in the mutual relationships of offensive, defensive, and deterrent capabilities? An answer has already been suggested above. The major consequence of nuclear war (and therefore the major deterrent to its initiation) is the destruction of population and economic resources; hence the tendency to devote ever more attention to minimizing this destruction, should war break out, by the development of defensive systems.

In the chapters that follow we shall present evidence indicating that the Soviet position is based on reasoning similar to the above. The group around Malenkov, which tended to rely on mutual deterrence as a guarantee of prolonged peace, was stigmatized as complacent and defeatist: complacent because they thought that Soviet nuclear weapons precluded a war not of Soviet choosing; defeatist because they did not believe in the possibility of surviving a nuclear war. The Soviet Union would suffer fearful destruction, answered Khrushchev, but it would win the war.

Khrushchev's theoretical and political victory over Malenkov had immediate practical consequences for Soviet military planning. No Soviet leader had opposed the building of long-range aircraft and missiles, weapons that were at once of offensive and deterrent value. Khrushchev's insistence on the possibility of victory in a nuclear war, however, demanded still more

expensive additions to the Soviet military posture. Should deterrence fail, the country must have a defensive system capable of minimizing destruction. There is a more or less definite limit to what a country can usefully spend on offensive nuclear weapons; there seems to be no limit to the returns from added increments of expenditure on defense against such weapons. This discrepancy is a direct consequence of the unprecedented destructive potential of modern weapon systems. The great destructiveness of individual weapons requires active defense to destroy a very high percentage of the delivery vehicles. The marriage of nuclear weapons to high-speed aircraft and missiles makes a low rate of interception futile. Even an inadequate defense, however, is extremely expensive to build and maintain.

The Soviet decision to prepare to fight a war if need be, rather than to rely on the effectiveness of deterrence, involves enormous expenditures and sets severe limits on the non-military sector of the country's economy. The condition of the Soviet peoples, therefore, is directly and powerfully affected by the present military policies of the Kremlin.

* * *

Once it had been decided that the major mission of the Soviet armed forces was to fight a full-scale war if the need arose, the choice of strategies open to the planners was automatically narrowed. If war came the Soviet aim was victory, and the well-understood characteristics of nuclear weapons made it necessary to conceive of victory primarily in terms of the survival of a substantial proportion of the population and the economy. Now that nuclear weapons make wholesale devastation of the homeland an almost inescapable concomitant of war, the destruction of the enemy's military forces can no longer be *in itself* the main object of military operations. That mission has now become the means to a more fundamental end, namely the preservation of that proportion of one's own population and economic resources that one believes to be compatible with "victory." The Soviet strategy, therefore, is to destroy the enemy's military forces before those forces can destroy Soviet population and cities. This strategy has the greatest promise of success if the Soviet Union is able to initiate the use of nuclear weapons. If the Soviet leaders believe that the United States is about to attack, they must try to effect a pre-emptive nuclear assault. A retaliatory attack on their part might come too late to achieve the main object of any major war, the salvation of the Soviet population and economic wealth.

Such a pre-emptive strategy requires that the Soviet Union get timely and un-equivocal warning of the enemy's intention to attack. It may be said that the cold-blooded planning of a preventive war would obviate the necessity for warning.

Soviet strategic plans, then, demand the ability to destroy a large part of the presumptive enemy's warmaking force at its bases, to knock out such elements of this force as may reach the Soviet Union, and to minimize by civil-defense measures the effects of the weapons that get through the active defenses. Such requirements necessitate a striking force able to hit with con-siderable precision. The more the targets to be destroyed have been "hardened," the greater the required precision of delivery. Underground installations protected by thick concrete must receive near-direct hits.

An important role in this over-all strategy has been assigned to ground forces, at least for the next decade. If the main object of the war is to protect the Soviet population, enemy missiles moved to new bases in Western Europe after the initiation of hostilities will constitute a major men-ace. The surest way of eliminating them is to occupy the ground. A rapid Soviet advance across Europe is therefore essen-tial for the successful execution of the whole Soviet strategy.

The present Soviet strategy, as out-lined above, is designed for a period when the Soviet Union has no retaliation-proof capability. But if that country should con-tinue to develop its warmaking capability to the point where its high-yield weapons have great accuracy and reliability, and if its presumptive opponents should fall be-hind, the strategy of the initial blow may become much more attractive to the Soviet leaders than it is now. As soon as such a blow seems to promise immunity from re-taliation, the Soviet planners will have greater freedom in making major military decisions.

At present, however, the planners must rely on the least of several evils, namely their ability to get in a first blow upon receipt of warning, though not necessarily with the hope of eliminating retaliation. At best this means, for the Soviet Union, that the enemy chooses the time for initiating hostilities; at worst it means that the Soviet homeland may be devastated if warning comes too late. Nevertheless, the Soviet Union has to aim for the expected advan-tages of getting in the first strike, should war threaten. Without the power to oblit-erate the enemy's striking force by a single, all-out blow, the Soviet Union would court destruction by launching a nuclear strike "out of the blue." Such a strike would be insane, and we have no reason to think that the present Soviet leaders are anything but shrewd and calculating. For this very prac-tical reason, their professed abhorrence of "preventive war," that is, of the cold-blooded planning of all-out war, is no doubt sincere.

Should the Soviet Union ever acquire what her leaders consider a retaliation-proof capability, the world situation will alter radically. One need exercise little imagination to visualize the dangers in-herent in such a development. No one can say that the acquisition of such a vastly improved capability would induce the pres-ent Soviet leaders to plan a cold-blooded "preventive" war. In such circumstances, however, the United States would have to fear constantly that the Soviet Union might be tempted to initiate war in the conviction that the first blow would decide it.

For a few years the United States possessed a monopoly of both nuclear weapons and delivery vehicles. Yet there was no general war. This seemingly hopeful analogy departs from the hypothetical situation just described in two important respects. First, for much of the earlier period the Soviet leaders did not really believe that the employment of nuclear weapons could decide the outcome of war. Second, in this period the Soviet Union did not possess the capability of making *any* kind of nuclear strike against the United States. This fact emphasizes the principal danger in one power's gaining a retaliation-proof strategy. That power's presumptive enemy will possess the capability of making a first nuclear strike. The weaker power is bound to consider that making a first strike, in its own time and without specific provocation, may well be the best insurance against national extinction. Hence an imbalance of this unprecedented kind is likely to lead to an unprecedented danger of all-out war.

Should the Soviet Union ever acquire a retaliation-proof capability, she would have to consider the possibility that any small international crisis might be the occasion for the execution of an American nuclear strike. For the Russians would surely argue that a desperate American attempt to reap the benefits of surprise and priority was more likely now that the United States lacked the power to recover from an initial Soviet blow. Hence, the Soviet leaders would feel tempted, on grounds of reason and prudence, to plan an obliterating strike in their own time and without any specific provocation.

PEACEFUL COMPETITION OR DESTRUCTION

NIKITA KHRUSHCHEV

Nikita Khrushchev became Secretary General of the Communist Party of the Soviet Union in 1953 and Chairman of the Council of Ministers of the USSR in 1958. His position of leadership and the vigorous role he has played in foreign affairs make him one of the best of all possible sources on the purposes and practices of Soviet foreign policy. He takes great pains to emphasize the unity of purpose in Soviet policy since 1917, insisting constantly that his policies are dictated by the principles of Marxism-Leninism. In the following extract from an important address made in late January 1959, he rings all the changes of theoretical argument while surveying the international situation in every corner of the globe. Presenting his interpretation of international affairs in a speech designed for both domestic and international circulation, he employs every slogan or catchword that might appeal to the "uncommitted," "neutralist," and "colonial peoples" and pounces enthusiastically upon every opportunity to berate the "imperialist aggressors" of the West. This is a typical and classic expression of current Soviet views on world problems and how to solve them.

In the West they say that we have issued a "challenge." Well, if they like the word, let us consider that we have. But it is a challenge *to compete in peaceful economic development and in raising the people's living standard.* By carrying out the October Revolution our people challenged capitalism, but it was not a military challenge, it was a challenge to peaceful competition. If our people had to develop war industry, it was only to be prepared to repulse armed attack, the threat of which has always hung over our country. Our chief aim was and is peaceful development and improvement of the people's welfare. (*Prolonged applause.*)

We want to compete not in the arms race and the production of atomic and hydrogen bombs and missiles, but in the production of manufactured goods, meat, butter, milk, clothing, footwear and other consumer goods.

Let the people judge for themselves which system best satisfies their requirements and let them judge each system duly!

The Peaceful Policy of the U.S.S.R. and Questions of International Relations.— The seven-year plan is a fresh expression of the Leninist peaceful policy of the Soviet Union. Fulfillment of this plan will play a tremendous role in solving the fundamental problem of our time—the preservation of world peace.

The significance of the plan lies, first, in that it is imbued with the spirit of peace. A state which undertakes a huge program of building new factories, plants, power stations, mines and other enterprises, which allocates almost 400,000,000,000 rubles for housing and communal construction and sets the goal of considerably raising the living standard of the people—that state is oriented toward peace, not war.

Secondly, fulfillment of the plan will so greatly increase the economic potential of the U.S.S.R. that, along with the growth of the economic potential of all the socialist

From Nikita Khrushchev, "Report to the Extraordinary XXI Congress of the Communist Party of the Soviet Union: On Control Figures for Development of the U.S.S.R. National Economy in 1959–1965," *Pravda*, Jan. 28, 1959, as translated in *The Current Digest of the Soviet Press*, Vol. XI, No. 4 (March 4, 1959), pp. 19–25. Reprinted by permission of *The Current Digest of the Soviet Press*, published at Columbia University by the Joint Committee on Slavic Studies appointed by the Social Science Research Council and the American Council of Learned Societies.

countries, it will ensure a decisive advantage for peace in the correlation of forces in the international arena, and thus there will arise new, even more favorable conditions for averting a world war, for preserving peace on earth.

The conclusion drawn by the 20th Party Congress that war is not fatally inevitable has been completely justified. Today we have to reaffirm this conclusion with even more reason. There are now tremendous forces capable of rebuffing the imperialist aggressors and defeating them if they should unleash a world war.

What new factors will be introduced into the international situation with the fulfillment of the economic plans of the Soviet Union, of all the socialist countries of Europe and Asia? As a result of this *there will be created real possibilities for eliminating war as a means of settling international issues.*

Indeed, when the U.S.S.R. becomes the world's leading industrial power, when the Chinese People's Republic becomes a mighty industrial power and all the socialist countries together will be producing more than half of the world's industrial output, the international situation will change radically. The successes of the countries of the socialist camp will unquestionably exert a tremendous effect on strengthening the forces of peace throughout the world. One need have no doubt that by that time the countries working for the strengthening of peace will be joined by new countries that have freed themselves from colonial oppression. The idea that war is inadmissible will take still firmer root in the minds of peoples. The new balance of forces will be so evident that even the most die-hard imperialists will clearly see the futility of any attempt to unleash war against the socialist camp. Relying on the might of the socialist camp, the peace-loving nations will then be able to compel the militant circles of imperialism to abandon plans for a new world war.

Thus there will arise a real possibility of excluding world war from the life of society even before the complete triumph of socialism, even with capitalism existing in part of the world.

It may be said: But capitalism will still exist, hence there will still be adventurers who might start a war. That is true, and it must not be forgotten. As long as capitalism exists there may always be people who "in the face of common sense" will want to plunge into a hopeless venture. But by doing so they will only bring nearer the ultimate downfall of the capitalist system. Any attempt at aggression will be stopped short and the adventurers put where they belong. (*Prolonged applause.*)

Such, comrades, are the perspectives seen as we discuss our plans.

Permit me to turn to specific problems of the international situation. Without discussing all the international problems, I wish to touch on only the more vital of them.

Correct solution of the German problem is of great importance to the preservation of peace and the security of nations. As is known, German imperialism launched world wars twice in the first half of the 20th century. Now, with the help of the monopolists of the U.S.A., Britain and the other participants in the aggressive North Atlantic Pact, West Germany is turning into the principal nuclear and missile base of NATO. Even now West Germany is already beginning to play a prime role in that aggressive bloc. Some politicians of Western countries are evidently thinking of again directing the German threat eastward, forgetting that German militarism also knows the way to the West.

A situation is taking shape in which German militarism may draw mankind into a world war for the third time. When we point to the serious danger arising in connection with the arming of West Germany, we are answered that West Germany is allegedly under control within the NATO framework and hence is no longer dangerous. But all can now see that militarism and revanchism have raised their heads in West Germany and menace the peaceful nations.

The Federal German Republic is one of the countries whose ruling circles are for continuing the "cold war," for carrying on the so-called policy of "positions of strength." Chancellor Adenauer pursues that policy most zealously. He is one of the chief opponents of any kind of agreement designed to reduce international tension and end the "cold war." This stand of Adenauer's has the support of influential circles in Western states and of countries which are dependent upon the United States and the Federal German Republic because they want to obtain credits from them, or for other reasons.

The threat presented by German militarism compels the peaceful states, particularly West Germany's neighbors, to take necessary measures.

For many years the Soviet Union has consistently sought to help Germany's peaceful democratic development in accordance with the Potsdam agreements and to prevent the revival of militarism. But all Soviet moves have met with the stubborn resistance of the ruling circles of the U.S.A., Britain, France and West Germany.

In view of the mounting military danger from the Federal German Republic, the Soviet Union has recently made a number of new proposals on the German problem. We suggest undertaking a gradual reduction of foreign troops in Germany, or, better still, their complete withdrawal. We stand for establishment of a "zone of separation" of armed forces. The farther apart they are, the greater will be the guarantee against clashes and conflicts. The Soviet Union is prepared to withdraw its forces not only from Germany, but from Poland and Hungary, where they are stationed under the Warsaw Treaty, if all the NATO countries will withdraw their troops to their national boundaries and abolish military bases situated in other countries.

The Soviet Union supports the plan of the Polish People's Republic for creating an "atom-free zone" in Europe and for reducing conventional armaments in that zone.

Last November the Soviet government turned to the United States, Britain and France with a proposal to put an end to the remnants of the occupation regime in Berlin and make West Berlin a demilitarized free city. This solution of the Berlin problem corresponds to the interests of peace in Europe and would help to reduce international tension.

Conclusion of a German peace treaty would be the fundamental solution of the German problem. There is nothing to justify the fact that to this day, fourteen years after the end of the war, no peace treaty has been signed between Germany and the countries with which it fought. That, in effect, benefits the people who stand for continuing the "cold war." It is used by the Western powers to keep their troops in the heart of Europe, to maintain an atomic bridgehead there and to prepare a new war, highhandedly employing Germany and her people as pawns.

The draft peace treaty proposed by the Soviet Union combines guarantee of the rights of the German people, their full sovereignty and every opportunity for peaceful democratic development with necessary measures for preserving the security of nations and maintenance of peace in Europe. Conclusion of a peace treaty with Germany would immediately relieve tension in Europe. It would establish a reliable legal basis and cut the ground from under the revanchist trend in West Germany; it would rid the German people of foreign occupation and enable them to decide for themselves all questions of domestic and foreign policy.

For its part, the Soviet Union will spare no effort toward conclusion of the peace treaty and will work for it consistently and tirelessly. Conclusion of a peace treaty would lead also to solving the Berlin problem on a peaceful and democratic basis, would ensure turning West Berlin into a free city with the necessary guarantee of noninterference in its affairs. The United Nations should be enlisted in enforcing this guarantee. We want to conduct negotiations on all these problems so as to find a sensible solution for them. Our proposals are in line with this purpose, they lead to eliminating many of the causes of tension in the relations among states in the heart of Europe, and they will help to strengthen peace.

Conclusion of the peace treaty will signify a big step forward toward German reunification, now hindered by the existing international tension, particularly the tension in the relations between the two German states.

It must be clearly understood that the reunification of Germany is entirely and completely a matter for the German people themselves. Since there are two sovereign states today and neither can be eliminated without setting off a world war, the reunification of Germany can be achieved only through negotiations between the German Democratic Republic and the Federal German Republic. There is no other way. (*Applause.*)

All sensible people realize that the peaceful reunification of Germany cannot be achieved by abolishing the socialist gains of the German people in the German Democratic Republic. The unification of Germany on the terms proposed by Adenauer would jeopardize European security, since it would mean the spread of militarism, revanchism and reaction to the whole territory of Germany. One should likewise not expect to unify Germany by abolishing the regime existing in the Federal German Republic.

It would be wrong to impose on the Germans conditions for the reunification of their country: Let the Germans settle the issue among themselves. Therefore we support the slogan of the democratic circles of Germany, "Germans, sit down around one table!"

Western propaganda cries loudly that the Soviet Union allegedly opposes German reunification on the basis of free elections. We have never objected and do not object to free elections. But, again, the question must be settled by the Germans themselves. We want all questions of German reunification to be solved by agreement between the two German states, and not as Adenauer wants it, that is, through pressure by foreign powers, through their interference in the internal affairs of the German people and by swallowing up the German Democratic Republic.

To make reunification of Germany easier for the two German states, we support the wise proposal of the government of the German Democratic Republic to form a confederation as a first step toward establishing a permanent connection between the German Democratic Republic and the Federal German Republic, and creating all-German agencies. If there is any other way whereby the two German states could come to agreement on reunification, we are prepared to cooperate in it.

In this connection, the role of Chancellor Adenauer, who fears German reunification on a peaceful and democratic basis, must be mentioned once again. His position is utterly incomprehensible. It is contrary to common sense and to the interests of the German people. Adenauer is the leader of the Christian Democratic Party. It would appear that he should be guided by the evangelical principles of which his party loves to talk so much. (*Laughter in the hall.*) Yet in actuality this "Christian" holds a cross in one hand and wants to take an atom bomb in the other. He counts most of all on the bomb, although such an attitude is far from consistent with either the evangelical precepts or solution of the national problem of the German people. Herr Adenauer is an elderly and experienced man. How can he fail to see that nuclear weapons are possessed not only by his allies, but by the Soviet land, too? It must not be forgotten that these are weapons that can cause great loss of life. And since West Germany is being turned into an atomic base, its population will be the first to suffer in the event of an armed conflict.

If Herr Adenauer were really pious, it would appear that, by Christian precepts, he should show concern for the hereafter, for "getting into Heaven." (*General laughter.*) But, to judge by Herr Adenauer's actual deeds, it must be said bluntly that he has no hope of going to Heaven. (*Stir in the hall.*) According to sacred writ, such deeds [as his] lead to an entirely different place—fiery Gehenna. (*General laughter.*)

In another part of the globe—the Far East—the United States' aggressive policy toward the Chinese People's Republic and other peace-loving states is the fundamental source of tension. Not long ago the whole world watched with alarm as America's aggressive actions threatened to turn into a terrible armed conflagration. Only the resolute actions of the Chinese People's Republic and other peace-loving forces averted this menace.

The Pacific Ocean area has become the main proving ground for American atomic weapons.

All this creates urgent concern for averting war, particularly atomic war, in this part of the globe. The chances appear to be better here than elsewhere, because the Soviet Union, the Chinese People's Republic, the Korean People's Democratic Republic, the Democratic Republic of Vietnam, and also India, Indonesia, Burma and other states in that region are championing the cause of peace. Their joint stand for prohibition of the atomic weapon and nuclear tests could be of decisive help for preserving peace in the Pacific. Initiative by these countries would be supported by the people of Japan and other countries of the Pacific basin. *A zone of peace, above all an atom-free zone, can and must be created in the Far East and the entire Pacific basin.*

All progressive mankind can be pleased with the course of events in the countries of the Near and Middle East. We greet the national liberation movement of the Arab peoples and the other peoples of Asia and Africa who have shaken off colonial oppression. The ousting of troops of the imperialist colonialists from a number of countries in that region has been a big triumph of the Arab peoples and of all the peace-loving forces. But it must not be thought that the possibility of a sharpening of the situation there is excluded, because the colonialists, driven out of the colonies, will never reconcile themselves to their defeat. The Western powers, above all the United States and Britain, are trying to set some Arab states against others, are weaving a web of intrigue in Iraq and other Arab countries. They are looking for weak spots in order to divide the liberated peoples, particularly the peoples of the Arab East.

When a people wages a struggle for national independence against the colonialists, all patriotic forces join in a united national front.

This was the case, for example, in the period of struggle by the Egyptian and other Arab peoples for liberation from oppression by the imperialist colonialists. In Egypt the result of mobilization of all the national forces was successful conduct of the struggle to expel the colonialists from the country and to nationalize the Suez Canal company. The national liberation of Egypt was hailed by all progressive mankind. A reactionary clique which served the imperialists was overthrown in Iraq and an independent republic was established. The Soviet people and the people of the other socialist countries actively supported the just struggle of the Arab peoples. Prominent leaders of that movement— President Gamal Abdel Nasser of the United Arab Republic and Abdul Karim el Kassem, head of the government of the Iraq republic—won the warmest regard of Soviet people.

After the colonialists are ousted and the nationwide tasks are solved in the main, the peoples seek a solution to the social problems raised by life: above all to the agrarian and peasant problem and the problems of labor's struggle against capital. Social processes arise within the ranks of the national liberation movement, processes which inevitably engender diverse opinions about the paths of further development of their states.

Our country, like the other socialist countries, has supported and will support the national liberation movement. The Soviet Union does not interfere and has no intention of interfering in the internal affairs of other countries, but we cannot fail to state our attitude toward the fact that a campaign is being conducted against progressive forces in some countries under the spurious slogans of anti-Communism. Since there recently have been statements in the United Arab Republic against the ideas of communism and accusations were leveled at Communists, I, as a Communist, consider it necessary to declare at the Congress of our Communist Party that it is wrong to accuse Communists of helping to weaken or divide national efforts in the struggle against imperialism. On the contrary, there are no people more resolute and loyal to the struggle against colonialists than the Communists. (*Stormy, prolonged applause.*) There are no forces more resolute in the struggle against imperialism than the forces of communism. It is no accident that the imperialists are aiming the spearhead of their struggle against the Communist movement.

The struggle against Communist and other progressive parties is a reactionary undertaking. An anti-Communist policy does not unite national forces, it divides them and consequently weakens the efforts of the whole nation in defending its interests against imperialism. It is wrong to accuse the Communists of acting against the national interests of the Arab peoples. It is likewise naïve to equate Communism and Zionism. Everyone knows that Communists, including those of Israel, are fighting against Zionism.

It is irrational to see "Communist intrigues" in everything. Problems of social development must be analyzed more deeply. There are objective laws of social development. They tell us that nations contain classes with divergent interests. After imperialist oppression is eliminated in the colonial countries the workers want shorter working hours and higher wages; the peasants want more land and an opportunity to enjoy the fruits of their labor; both workers and peasants want political rights. But the capitalists want greater profits, the landowners want to keep their land. The progressive forces seek development of their country along the path of social progress, they strive to strengthen its national independence and to protect it from imperialist intrigues. Domestic reactionary forces, often incited from abroad by the imperialists, wage a struggle against this.

These processes in the countries which have freed themselves from imperialist oppression arise not by the will and wish of one or another party, but because there are classes and they have divergent interests. We, as Communists, and all progressive persons, too, naturally sympathize with those who are fighting for social justice. (*Prolonged applause.*)

We do not conceal the fact that we and some of the leaders of the United Arab Republic have divergent views in the sphere of ideology. But our position coincides with theirs in questions of the struggle against imperialism, of strengthening the political and economic independence of countries that have freed themselves from colonialism, and of the struggle against the war danger. The differences in ideological views should not impede the development of friendly relations between our countries and the cause of joint struggle against imperialism. (*Applause.*)

Agents of imperialist states, traveling about the Middle and Near East, want to frighten certain people with communism, hoping thereby to gain influence for the imperialists and to support reactionary forces. For this reason the people there must be on guard against imperialist intrigues.

The countries which have achieved their national liberation need and will continue to need the support of the socialist countries and of all progressive people. The Soviet Union and the other socialist countries are strengthening friendly relations with the countries that have liberated themselves from colonial oppression; they are giving them assistance and will continue to do so.

The imperialists use their economic relations with the underdeveloped countries as instruments of blackmail and extortion; they saddle these countries with military and political conditions. Our country bases its relations with all states on complete equality and cooperation, with no conditions of a military or political nature. We do not engage in charity. The Soviet Union gives help on a fair commercial basis. The socialist countries help underdeveloped countries to establish their own industry, whereas the United States tries to sell them consumer goods that have failed to find a market at home. The seven-year plan opens up new possibilities for Soviet economic cooperation with the industrially underdeveloped countries.

A new stage has been reached in this struggle of peoples for their freedom and independence; the national liberation movement is developing in all the colonial and dependent countries. The peoples of Latin America have increased their struggle against American imperialist oppression. The peoples of Asia and Africa are in ferment. Peoples who have won their national freedom want to decide their destinies themselves. Now they need peaceful conditions more than ever. The great powers must pledge to respect as sacred the sovereignty of the nations of the Arab East and Africa, to abstain from the use of force in settling disputes and from interference in the internal affairs of these states. In place of the powder keg where they play with fire,

a zone of peace and free national development must be established.

Measures necessary for relaxing tension in the various regions must be combined with the struggle for general improvement in the international climate.

The task of tasks today is to break the impasse on *the disarmament issue.* The armaments race continues, swallowing up ever more financial and material resources. To raise funds for the production of armaments, the governments of the capitalist states allocate the lion's share of their budgets for militarization and pursue a policy of plundering the working people, operating on the principle: "I may go in tatters, but wearing a saber." (*Stir in the hall.*)

The need to ban tests of atomic and hydrogen weapons is particularly urgent. Now that all have recognized the possibility of detecting atomic explosions [occurring] at any point on the globe, there is no reason to delay settlement of the problem of banning tests of nuclear armaments. The peoples of all countries demand a stop to these tests, which contaminate the world atmosphere with harmful radioactivity. And this demand must be met.

We act upon the principle that relations among states with different social systems must be based on peaceful coexistence. We and the ruling circles of the capitalist countries have different views, different outlooks. We shall never change our views and cherish no illusions that our class adversaries will change their ideology. But this does not mean we should go to war because of our divergent views. In each country it is the people themselves who determine their own destiny and choose the direction of their development. The Soviet Union does not want to force anyone to take the Soviet path. We guide ourselves entirely by V. I. Lenin's principle that revolutions cannot be exported.

Would it not be better for the heads of states with different social systems to conclude, and to do so as soon as possible, that, since we share one planet, and not too large a planet by today's technological standards, it is better to live on it without elbowing one another and not to threaten one another constantly by shaking fists in the form of atomic or hydrogen bombs? We must learn to settle disputes by peaceful negotiation.

It is time to realize that threats are bound to fail when it is a matter of the Soviet Union and the socialist camp, and to acknowledge the fundamental changes that have taken place in the world strategic situation.

Today everyone recognizes the successes attained by Soviet science and technology, which have blazed man's trail into outer space. These achievements demonstrate the capacities of the Soviet Union, of the world socialist system. It is quite obvious that if the Soviet Union can send a rocket hundreds of thousands of kilometers into outer space it can send powerful rockets to any part of the globe without a miss. (*Applause.*)

However, we draw quite different conclusions from these facts than those drawn by certain circles in the West. The latter view each achievement of science and technology principally from the standpoint of the military advantage that it represents. When the first atomic bomb was developed in the United States, American ruling circles immediately came forth with claims to world domination.

Such intentions are alien to the Soviet Union. We do not use the historic achievements of Soviet science and technology to carry out a belligerent policy or to dictate our will to other states. We use them to redouble our efforts in the struggle for world peace. And now, when the advantage in rocket technology is on our side, we again propose to the United States, Britain and France: Let us ban for all time the testing, production and use of atomic, hydrogen and rocket weapons, let us destroy all stockpiles of these lethal weapons, let us use this supreme discovery of human

genius exclusively for peaceful purposes, for the welfare of man. Our government is prepared to sign an agreement to this effect at any time. (*Prolonged applause.*)

The only sensible policy for the great powers is to turn to a peaceful settlement of international problems and to universal disarmament.

More than a year ago the Soviet government proposed a conference of heads of government of countries of East and West. Since then, through the fault of the Western powers, no progress has been made on this matter. But we consider it our duty to the peoples of all countries to work for this conference, on which all who want peace and security pin so much hope.

We have repeatedly had occasion to point to the heavy responsibility borne by the two great powers—the Soviet Union and the United States—for preserving the peace. As concerns the Soviet Union, it has more than once expressed its sincere desire to normalize relations with the United States, and has confirmed this with deeds. The Soviet Union proposed a 50-year pact of nonaggression, extensive reciprocal trade, promotion of cultural relations, etc. But in every instance we came up against either outright refusal or veiled resistance.

Our two countries have never had and do not have any territorial claims against one another. There are no grounds for clashes between our peoples, yet the relations between the U.S.S.R. and the U.S.A. have long been abnormal.

We know that among the politicians, financiers, Senators and newspaper publishers in the U.S.A. there are many who are interested in keeping relations on this level. But the number of adherents of friendly, good-neighborly relations with the Soviet Union is growing in America. The reception accorded A. I. Mikoyan in the United States is vivid confirmation of this. His visit turned into a manifestation of the American people's friendly feeling for the people of the Soviet Union. Most of the Americans whom he met expressed sincere and outspoken sympathies for the Soviet people and their desire for friendship and peaceful cooperation with the Soviet Union. Among them were persons of diverse political and religious views and from many ranks of society, including scientists, cultural workers, businessmen and broad strata of the public. Evidently most Americans no longer believe the anti-Soviet propaganda that the bourgeois reactionary newspapers conduct in the U.S.A. The attempts made by some elements to organize provocational acts during Comrade Mikoyan's visit were a total failure, for these elements do not reflect the sentiments and views of the American people.

We welcome the efforts of all those Americans who favor ending the cold war and support peaceful coexistence and cooperation among all countries. Sympathies for the American people, whose industrial genius and efficiency are known to the whole world, are strong in our country.

There are, of course, many difficulties along the path of peaceful coexistence. In taking this path, both sides have to show a great inclination toward mutual understanding, great restraint and, if you wish, great patience. (*Applause.*)

Extensive *development of world trade* could play a big part in relaxing international tension and strengthening mutual confidence.

In spite of all the obstructions that are erected, the trade between the Soviet Union and the capitalist countries of Europe and America almost tripled between 1950 and 1958. We have built up a good business with Sweden; long-term trade agreements have also been concluded with France and Italy, and trade with other countries is expanding.

The economic program of peaceful construction in the U.S.S.R. in 1959–1965 opens up broad prospects for the development of Soviet foreign trade with all countries. We can at least double the volume of foreign trade.

We offer the capitalist countries peace-ful competition, and our offer goes beyond the seven-year plan. We are drawing up a long-term plan for U.S.S.R. development covering fifteen years. This plan, too, is based on the principles of peaceful development and peaceful economic competition.

As the peoples of all countries see, *our plans are plans of peaceful construction. We call on all peoples to intensify the struggle for the preservation and strengthening of peace. For our part, we shall do everything in our power to ensure peace throughout the world.* (*Stormy, prolonged applause.*)

Communist Construction in the U.S.S.R. and the International Working-Class Movement.—Comrades! Our seven-year plan is a powerful moral support for the international workers' and Communist movement, for all democratic forces, in their struggle against reaction and imperialism. By winning new victories in building communism, the Soviet people will be performing their internationalist duty to the world working class.

There are now Communist and Workers' Parties in 83 countries, with a total membership of more than 33,000,000. This is a tremendous triumph of Marxism-Leninism, a great achievement for the working class. (*Prolonged applause.*)

Reactionaries of all hues have waged dozens of campaigns against communism. But nothing can throttle the Communist movement, for it springs from the class struggle of the proletariat, of all the working people, and expresses their interests. Many Communist Parties in the capitalist countries now confront great difficulties. Reaction is launching a new, frenzied offensive against them, which, we are confident, will end in another failure, while our fraternal parties will emerge stronger and firmer from the tests. (*Prolonged applause.*)

In organizing the offensive against the working-class and Communist movement, international reaction is resorting to social demagogy, to deceiving the masses with fairy tales about the so-called "free world." The imperialist ideologists try to dress up the antipopular capitalist ways. Prominent bourgeois leaders claim in almost their every speech that the capitalist countries of the West are the "free countries" and the capitalist world is the "free world."

There is indeed freedom in the capitalist countries, but for whom? Not, of course, for the workers, who have to hire themselves out to the capitalists on any terms to avoid finding themselves in the huge army of persons "free" of work. And not for the peasants, over whom there hangs the constant threat of being "freed" of their farms through ruin. And not for the intellectuals, whose creative work is squeezed in the toils of material dependence upon the moneybags and "thought control" by assorted loyalty committees. Freedom in the capitalist countries exists only for those who have money and, consequently, power.

The politicians and ideologists of the "free world" like to portray themselves as champions of the religious ethic. But they ought to know full well from the religious legends about Christ that when he saw the traders and moneylenders and money-changers haggling in the temple he took a whip and drove them from the temple. (*Stir in the hall.*) If the capitalists have recourse to religious ethic, why have they turned the society in which they rule into a paradise for the rich and a hell for the poor? And this in spite of the Christian parable that says that it is easier for a camel to go through the eye of a needle than for a rich man to enter into heaven! The "free world" is the kingdom of the dollar, of profit-making and unbridled speculation, of harsh exploitation of millions of people to enrich a handful of monopolists.

There was a time when, in the struggle against feudalism, bourgeois revolutions proclaimed the alluring slogans of equality, fraternity and liberty, but the bourgeoisie proclaimed them primarily to elbow aside the aristocracy and pave the way for capi-

tal. As it built up its power, the bourgeoisie discarded slogans more and more.

Although they continue to make use of the slogans of equality, fraternity and liberty, the imperialists resort more and more frequently nowadays to outright dictatorship. Sinister signs of an onswell of reaction and fascism are appearing in the capitalist countries. This is the reactionary path taken by West Germany, where the Communist Party has been banned, democratic forces are persecuted, and fascist and revanchist organizations are given free rein. The trend toward open dictatorship has taken form in France, where the democratic freedoms and the gains of the masses are being trampled. The onslaught of reaction in France, a country known for its democratic traditions, causes alarm to all advocates of democracy and progress. The military coups in Pakistan and Thailand have shown that an attack is developing against the democratic gains of peoples who have won national independence. The forces of reaction are being activated also in a number of other capitalist countries.

Thus we have not isolated instances, but a clear-cut general tendency, characteristic of many countries of the capitalist world.

The reactionary forces are resorting to the old, antipopular method of wiping out democratic ways and setting up "strong-arm" governments. But today, as in the period when fascist dictatorship was established in Italy and Germany, the tendency toward open dictatorship of the monopoly bourgeoisie is a sign not of strength, but of weakness of the bourgeoisie. At the same time it must not be forgotten that under an unlimited dictatorship reaction has a better chance of spreading repression and terror, of suppressing any opposition movement, of propagandizing the masses to suit its ends of infecting them with the poison of chauvinism, and of freeing its hands for military gambles. For this reason, the people must be vigilant, ever ready to repel the offensive of reaction and the menace of a resurgence of fascism.

In the minds of millions of people fascism is usually associated with the names of Hitler and Mussolini. But the possibility must not be ruled out that fascism will revive in other forms than the old ones that have already discredited themselves in the eyes of the peoples.

Now that a powerful socialist camp exists, now that the workers' movement has great experience in the struggle with reaction and the working class is better organized, the peoples have greater possibilities of blocking the advance of fascism. The broadest strata of the people, all democratic, genuinely national forces, can and must be united against fascism. In this connection it is very important to overcome all sectarian narrowness, which can be a hindrance to mobilization of the masses for the struggle against reaction and fascism. The unity of the democratic forces, above all of the working class, is the most reliable barrier to the fascist danger.

Who holds back the cause of unity of the working class? Imperialist reaction and its henchmen in the workers' movement, such anti-Communist-minded leaders of Social-Democracy as Guy Mollet and Spaak. We know all these chieftains of anti-Communism by name and it is not on them that we count when we speak of unity of working-class action. Most of those in the ranks of the Social-Democratic Parties are supporters of peace and social progress, although they hold a different view of the way to achieve these goals than do we Communists. It is in the struggle against reaction and fascism that Communists and Social-Democrats should find a common language. It is time for the representatives of all the trends in the labor movement, after throwing out the mountebanks of anti-Communism, to sit down around one table and work out a mutually acceptable platform for joint action by the working class in defense of its interests, in defense of peace.

Imperative for further successes of the Communist and Workers' Parties are ideological and organizational strengthening of their ranks, increased solidarity on the basis of Marxism-Leninism and firmer fraternal international ties.

The conferences of representatives of Communist and Workers' Parties in November, 1957, demonstrated the complete unity of views of the fraternal parties. The conference declaration[1] was unanimously approved by all the Communist and Workers' Parties and became a charter of international unity of the world Communist movement. The declaration condemned revisionism as the principal danger and also dogmatism and sectarianism. Life fully proved the declaration's conclusions to have been correct. And we are guided by them now.

After the November conferences there occurred a further consolidation of forces within each Communist Party, and the whole international Communist movement became even more firmly rallied. The revisionists did not succeed in turning a single fraternal party off the Marxist-Leninist path. Only miserable, small groups of opportunists and individuals who lost their heads under the fire of the class enemy followed the revisionists. This scum that had polluted the pure fount of the Communist movement rose to the surface in the course of the struggle and was cast out.

The revisionists' contentions have been disproved by life, by the practice of the working class struggle and by the entire course of social development. The fundamental theses of revisionism have been refuted—the theses of a change in the nature of capitalism, of crisis-free development of capitalism, of a peaceful evolution of capitalism into socialism, and so forth.

The international Communist movement has condemned the outlook and poli-

[1] *Current Digest of the Soviet Press*, Vol. IX, No. 47, pp. 3–7.

cies of the Yugoslav revisionists. The leaders of the League of Communists of Yugoslavia try to present matters as though the Marxist-Leninist parties had begun an ideological struggle against them because they refused to sign the declaration. This claim is utterly false. It was the Yugoslav leaders who countered the declaration by coming forth with their revisionist program, in which they attacked the Marxist-Leninist stand of the international Communist movement. One asks: Could Marxists have ignored these facts? Of course not. Therefore all parties that take Marxist-Leninist positions came forth with principled criticism of the program of the League of Communists of Yugoslavia.

Our position on the views of the Yugoslav leaders is clear. We have set it forth repeatedly in all frankness. But the Yugoslav leaders twist and turn, falsify, and dodge the truth.

The Yugoslav leaders try to conceal the essence of their differences with the Marxist-Leninists. This is that the Yugoslav revisionists deny the necessity of international class solidarity and abandon working-class positions. They try to convince all and sundry that there are two blocs, two military camps, in the world. Yet everyone knows that the socialist camp, embracing the socialist countries of Europe and Asia, is not a military camp, but a community of equal peoples in the struggle for peace and for a better life for the working people, for socialism and communism. (*Stormy applause.*) The other camp is the camp of the imperialists, seeking at any price to preserve the system of oppression and violence, and confronting mankind with the menace of war. We did not imagine these camps; they took shape in the course of social development.

The Yugoslav leaders claim that they stand aside from blocs and above the camps, although in actuality they belong to the Balkan bloc, consisting of Yugoslavia, Turkey and Greece. The latter two countries, as is known, are members of the aggressive NATO bloc, while Turkey belongs, moreover, to the Baghdad Pact. The leaders of the League of Communists of Yugoslavia greatly resent our telling them that they are sitting on two stools. They claim that they are seated on their own, the Yugoslav stool. But for some reason the Yugoslav stool is greatly supported by the American monopolies! And this position "outside of blocs," this neutrality that the leaders of the League of Communists of Yugoslavia advertise so much, carries a distinct odor of the American monopolies, which nourish "Yugoslav socialism." The history of class struggle contains no instance of the bourgeoisie materially or morally encouraging its class enemy and helping to build socialism.

The best test of the course taken by a country's leadership is the progress made in developing the national economy and advancing the cultural level and well-being of the people. We Soviet Communists consider our path to socialism, pointed out by the great Lenin, to be the right one. Following it, the Soviet Union has scored victories that amaze the whole world. All the people's democracies have followed the path of the October Revolution, Lenin's path, and they too have achieved remarkable successes.

Who achieved the least results? That very party, that very country, whose leaders extol their so-called Yugoslav path as the only right one. The people reason thus: The best way is the way that makes possible maximum economic and political results quickly. If one compares the living standards of the peoples of the socialist countries, one finds that, according to the published economic data, the standard is rising much more slowly in Yugoslavia. Yugoslav practice itself refutes the theoretical "discoveries" of the Yugoslav revisionists.

If Yugoslavia lags in her development, if she does not walk but staggers along the socialist path, the responsibility for this lies entirely on the revisionist, anti-Marxist line of the Yugoslav League of Communists leadership, which has its own particular view of the role of the Party in building socialism. The Yugoslav revisionists minimize the Party's role and in effect reject the Leninist doctrine that the Party is the guiding force in the struggle for socialism.

The Marxist-Leninist parties observe with alarm what is happening in Yugoslavia. At the price of great sacrifice, the fraternal peoples of Yugoslavia, with Soviet support, liberated themselves from German and Italian occupation, overthrew the rule of their own bourgeoisie, and took the path of socialism. Yet now the policy of the Yugoslav leaders, aimed at opposing Yugoslavia to the socialist camp and the international Communist movement, may lead to the loss of the socialist gains made by the Yugoslav people.

We have the very friendliest feelings for the fraternal peoples of Yugoslavia, for the Yugoslav Communists, heroes of underground and partisan struggle. On many questions of foreign policy we speak a common language. We shall continue to develop trade with Yugoslavia on a reciprocal basis. We shall seek to cooperate with Yugoslavia on all the questions of the anti-imperialist and peace struggle on which our attitudes shall coincide.

How will matters stand in the Party sphere? Everything will depend on the League of Communists of Yugoslavia. Its leaders have isolated themselves from the international Communist movement. Therefore, it is up to the Yugoslav League of Communists to make a turn toward rapprochement with the Communist Parties on the basis of Marxism-Leninism; this would be also in the interests of the Yugoslav people themselves.

The Communist movement has dealt revisionism crushing blows. But revisionism is not dead yet. It must be borne in mind that imperialism will seek in every way to support and activize the revisionists.

There is also the need to combat dogmatism and sectarianism, which impede the development of Marxist-Leninist theory and its creative application and cause the Communist Parties to lose contact with the masses. Lenin's behest to strengthen the ties with the masses, to give the utmost heed to the voice of the masses and to march at the head of the masses is sacred to all us Communists.

As regards relations among the fraternal parties within the international Communist movement, we have always followed Lenin's presentation of the matter. Lenin taught us that these relations are erected upon the basis of equality and independence of the national detachments of the international working class, upon the principles of proletarian internationalism. It is precisely because all the Parties have equal rights that they have established relations of trust and voluntary cooperation, that, as component units of the single great army of labor, they voluntarily and consciously seek united action.

All the Communist Parties are independent and work out their own policy, proceeding from the particular conditions in their respective countries; they have scored successes in their activity, are steadily extending their influence, increasing the number of their followers and winning prestige among all strata of the people.

The ideologists of imperialism and the revisionists who take their cue from them strive by every method to undermine the growing influence of the Communist Parties and spread the false assertion that the Communist movement is "the work of Moscow" and that the Communist and Workers' Parties are dependent upon the Communist Party of the Soviet Union. The Yugoslav revisionists, who allege that our party seeks "hegemonism" over other parties, show particular zeal. They have even included in their program the thesis of "hegemonism." The revisionists assert that our party interferes in the internal affairs of other countries and seeks to control the other Communist Parties. The reactionaries express particular gratefulness to the Yugoslav revisionists for this slander.

All who are familiar with the Communist movement will have no difficulty in smashing the falsehoods concocted by the international reactionaries and revisionists.

It is ridiculous to think that a political party of the working class, often numbering hundreds of thousands and sometimes millions of members, could be organized in any country from somewhere abroad. No one will believe that, for example, the Italian Communist Party of 2,000,000, the French of almost 500,000, the Indonesian of 1,500,000, the Indian of nearly 300,000 and the other fraternal parties were "made in Moscow" and that their members are "foreign agents."

The Communist Parties arose not because some single center "planted" them in all countries. Such miracles do not happen. The history of the development of society shows that Marxist parties come into being with the appearance and growth of the working class. This means that the Communist movement arose as an objective necessity, that it was born of the very conditions of life of the working class in each country. There are classes in all the capitalist countries and consequently there are political parties of the working class and they will exist as long as the working class exists. (*Stormy applause.*) In the same way, it is naïve to think that the millions of people in the Communist Parties can be told from abroad what to think today and what to do tomorrow.

It is said that the "dependence" of the Communist and Workers' Parties on Moscow is corroborated by statements to the effect that the Communist Party of the Soviet Union stands at the head of the international Communist movement. In making this claim, the well known thesis is cited from the declaration of the Moscow conference that "the camp of socialist states is headed by the Soviet Union."

The Communists of the Soviet Union and of all the other countries consider that this statement was a tribute to our country and the working class that, under the leadership of the Communist Party headed by the great Lenin, was the first to carry out the socialist revolution, the first to take power. (*Prolonged applause.*) In more than forty years a long and difficult path of struggle and victories has been traversed and a powerful state, bulwark of all the socialist countries and of the world Communist movement, has been established. (*Stormy applause.*)

We express sincere gratitude to the fraternal parties for this recognition of the historic role of the Soviet Union and the Communist Party of the Soviet Union. (*Stormy, prolonged applause.*)

At the same time, it must be emphasized that complete equality and independence have existed and do exist for all the Communist and Workers' Parties in the Communist movement and for the socialist countries in the socialist camp. In actuality the Communist Party of the Soviet Union does not control any parties, the Soviet Union does not control any other country. There are no "superior" or "subordinate" parties in the Communist movement. All the Communist and Workers' Parties are equal and independent, all of them bear responsibility for the destinies of the Communist movement, for its failures and successes. (*Applause.*) Each Communist or Workers' Party is responsible to the working class, to the working people, of its country, and to the whole international workers' and Communist movement. In the struggle for the interests of the working class, for socialism, the Communist Parties combine the universal tenets of Marxism-Leninism with the specific historical and national conditions in their countries. Only a Marxist-Leninist party connected with the working class, with the people of its country, is able to know the specific conditions of the struggle; it alone can work out a political line suiting these conditions and taking account of the traditions of the workers' movement of the given country.

And this is so in reality. All the Communist and Workers' Parties exist and struggle on the basis of complete independence and the principles of proletarian internationalism, of voluntary cooperation and mutual assistance. This is how our party understands the nature of the relations among the fraternal parties. (*Applause.*)

As regards the Soviet Union, its role, as is known, consists not in controlling other countries, but in having been the first to blaze the trail to socialism for mankind, in being the most powerful country in the international socialist system and the first to have entered the period of extensive building of communism. (*Stormy applause.*)

The Communist Party of the Soviet Union was molded by Lenin in the spirit of proletarian internationalism. We Soviet Communists not only have studied Marxism-Leninism, but have defended it in struggle against enemies of all kinds. Guided by this teaching, the Soviet people, headed by the Communist Party, built socialism in grim struggle and are advancing confidently toward communism. (*Applause.*)

We have always followed and will continue uncompromisingly to follow the great international teaching of Marx, Engels and Lenin. Figuratively speaking, our Communist Party regards itself as one of the advanced detachments of the world Communist movement, the detachment which is first to take the heights of communism.

And on our way to these heights we shall not be stopped by an avalanche or landslide; nobody can make us turn off the path of advance toward communism. (*Stormy applause.*)

We have always held and still hold that one cannot retire to one's national "domain" and withdraw into one's shell. We think that the might of the international Communist movement must be further reinforced in accordance with the principles adopted by all the fraternal parties in the Moscow declaration. Concern for the solidarity and strength of our ranks is the supreme internationalist duty of each Communist or Workers' Party. *Success in the national cause of the working class is inconceivable without the international solidarity of all its detachments.* (*Prolonged applause.*)

We are unified by the great common purpose of liberating toiling mankind, of fighting for universal peace. We have one common concern—concern for the welfare of the peoples, for their prosperity and security, their happy future, which can be achieved only along the paths of socialism. We are united by the great teaching of Marxism-Leninism and by the struggle to put it into practice. We shall always keep the ideological weapon of Marxism-Leninism pure, we shall fight against opportunists, against revisionists of all shades, we shall always be loyal to the working class. In this we see our international duty to the world Communist and workers' movement. (*Stormy, prolonged applause.*)

Bibliography

A sizeable number of works dealing with various aspects of Soviet foreign policy have been published in English. This bibliography, in no way exhaustive, presents a selective list of some of the more useful materials available. It should be noted that the valuable sources of the extracts printed in the previous pages are not repeated here, since full citations accompany each extract or article.

More extensive listings are presented in the successive editions of *Foreign Affairs Bibliography* (New York, 1933, 1945, 1955), which cover the period from 1919 to 1952. For later years see Henry L. Roberts' "Recent Books on International Relations," in each issue of *Foreign Affairs*, Donald Wasson's "Source Materials" on international relations in the same quarterly, and the *International Political Science Abstracts*. The *Monthly Catalogue of U. S. Government Publications* lists many useful materials, only a few of which are mentioned below. The Rand Corporation's *Index of Publications* catalogues its own studies of Soviet affairs, and the monthly *United Nations Documents Index* provides an exhaustive guide to United Nations publications. Finally, many of the specialized studies listed below contain valuable bibliographies dealing with the problems or areas they examine.

Current Soviet diplomatic documents and speeches are regularly published or summarized in *The New York Times*. The *Current Digest of the Soviet Press*, edited by Leo Gruliow and published each week by the Joint Committee on Slavic Studies, contains full and reliable translations or summaries of official pronouncements, speeches, and important articles.

Some of the most authoritative studies on Soviet foreign policy appear in "learned" journals dedicated to such widely diversified topics as history, political science, international relations, and international organization, or to one or another geographical or cultural area of the world. The reader may glean a sample list of the most important of these journals by examining the sources of the articles listed below.

DOCUMENTS

BISHOP, DONALD GORDON, *Soviet Foreign Relations: Documents and Readings.* Syracuse, 1952.

BRANDT, CONRAD, JOHN F. FAIRBANK, AND BENJAMIN I. SCHWARTZ, *A Documentary History of Chinese Communism.* Cambridge, Mass., 1952.

DEGRAS, JANE, *Calendar of Soviet Documents on Foreign Policy, 1917–1941.* London, New York, 1948.

DEGRAS (continued), *The Communist International, 1919–1943*, Vol. I: *1919–1922*. New York, 1956; Vol. II: *1923–1928*. New York, 1960.

——————, *Soviet Documents on Foreign Policy*, 3 vols. (covering 1917–1941). New York, 1951–1953.

DIMITROV, GEORGI, *Selected Speeches and Articles*. London, 1951.

——————, *The United Front*. London, 1938.

EUDIN, XENIA, AND ROBERT C. NORTH, *Soviet Russia and the East, 1920–1927*. Stanford, 1957.

EUDIN, XENIA, AND HAROLD H. FISHER, *Soviet Russia and the West, 1920–1927*. Stanford, 1957.

FARRELL, ROBERT BARRY, *Jugoslavia and the Soviet Union, 1948–1956: An Analysis with Documents*. Hamden, Conn., 1956.

Finnish Blue Book: The Development of Finnish-Soviet Relations During the Autumn of 1939. New York, 1940.

Foreign Relations of the United States: Diplomatic Papers. Washington. *Russia, 1918*, 3 vols., 1931–1932; *Russia, 1919*, 1937; *The Soviet Union, 1933–1939*, 1952; *The Conferences at Malta and Yalta*, 2 vols., 1955. In addition to these specialized volumes the annual volumes contain valuable sections under the headings "Russia" or "The Soviet Union."

GANKIN, OLGA H., AND HAROLD H. FISHER, *The Bolsheviks and the World War: The Origin of the Third International*. Stanford, 1940.

LASERSON, M. M., "The Development of Soviet Foreign Policy in Europe, 1917–1942: A Selection of Documents," *International Conciliation*, No. 386 (January 1943).

LASKY, MELVIN J., *The Hungarian Revolution: A White Book*. New York, 1957.

LENIN, V. I., *Collected Works*. New York, 1927-1945.

MOLOTOV, V. M., *Problems of Foreign Policy: Speeches and Statements, April 1945-November 1948*. Moscow, 1949.

ROTHSTEIN, ANDREW, *Soviet Foreign Policy During the Patriotic War: Documents and Materials*, 2 vols. New York, 1946.

ROYAL INSTITUTE OF INTERNATIONAL AFFAIRS, *Documents on International Affairs* (multi-volume work). London, New York, 1923—.

RUBINSTEIN, ALVIN Z., *The Foreign Policy of the Soviet Union*. New York, 1960.

SHAPIRO, LEONARD, *Soviet Treaty Series*, 2 vols. (covering 1917-1939). Washington, 1950–1955.

SLUSSER, ROBERT M., AND JAN F. TRISKA, *A Calendar of Soviet Treaties, 1917–1957*. Stanford, 1959.

SONTAG, RAYMOND J., AND JAMES S. BEDDIE, *Nazi-Soviet Relations 1939–1941; Documents from the Archives of the German Foreign Office as Released by the Department of State*. Washington, 1948.

SOVIET UNION, *Documents and Materials Relating to the Eve of the Second World War*, 2 vols. Moscow, 1948. Vol. I: *Materials from the Archives of the German Ministry of Foreign Affairs (1937–1938)*; Vol. II: *The Dirksen Papers (1938–1939)*.

The Soviet-Yugoslav Dispute. London, 1948.

STALIN, J. V., *Foundations of Leninism*. Moscow, 1939.

——————, *Problems of Leninism*. Moscow, 1947.

——————, *Works*, 13 vols. Moscow, 1952–1955.

Stalin's Correspondence with Churchill, Attlee, Roosevelt and Truman, 1941–1945. New York, 1958.

WILBUR, C. MARTIN, AND JULIE LIEN-YING HOW, *Documents on Communism, Nationalism, and Soviet Advisers in China, 1918–1927.* New York, 1956.

ZINNER, PAUL E., *National Communism and Popular Revolt in Eastern Europe: A Selection of Documents on Events in Poland, and Hungary, February–November 1956.* New York, 1956.

MEMOIRS

BARMINE, ALEXANDER, *One Who Survived.* New York, 1945.

BESIEDOVSKII, G. Z., *Revelations of a Soviet Diplomat.* London, 1931.

BUCHANAN, SIR GEORGE, *My Mission to Russia and Other Diplomatic Memories,* 2 vols. Boston, 1923.

CHIANG KAI-SHEK, *Soviet Russia in China: A Summing-up at Seventy.* New York, 1957.

CHURCHILL, WINSTON S., *The Second World War,* 6 vols. Boston, 1948-1954.

DEANE, JOHN R., *The Strange Alliance.* New York, 1947.

DIRKSEN, HERBERT VON, *Moscow, Tokyo, London: Twenty Years of German Foreign Policy.* London, 1951.

EDEN, ANTHONY, *Full Circle: The Memoirs of Anthony Eden.* Boston, 1960.

FRANCIS, DAVID R., *Russia from the American Embassy: April 1916-November 1918.* New York, 1921.

GRAVES, WILLIAM S., *America's Siberian Adventure, 1918–1920.* New York, 1931.

HILGER, GUSTAV, AND ALFRED G. MEYER, *The Incompatible Allies: A Memoir-History of German-Soviet Relations, 1918–1941.* New York, 1953.

KHOKHLOV, NIKOLAI, *In the Name of Conscience.* New York, 1959.

KRIVITSKY, WALTER G., *In Stalin's Secret Service.* New York, 1939.

LANE, ARTHUR BLISS, *I Saw Poland Betrayed.* Indianapolis, 1948.

LOCKHART, R. H. BRUCE, *British Agent.* New York, London, 1933.

NAGY, FERENC, *The Struggle Behind the Iron Curtain.* New York, 1948.

STANDLEY, WILLIAM H., *Admiral Ambassador to Russia.* Chicago, 1955.

STETTINIUS, EDWARD R., *Roosevelt and the Russians.* New York, 1949.

TRUMAN, HARRY S., *Memoirs,* 2 vols. New York, 1955–1956.

BOOKS

ALLEN, ROBERT LORING, *Middle Eastern Economic Relations with the Soviet Union, Eastern Europe, and Mainland China.* Charlottesville, Va., 1958.

BARGHOORN, FREDERICK C., *The Soviet Cultural Offensive.* Princeton, 1960.

————, *The Soviet Image of the United States.* New York, 1950.

————, *Soviet Russian Nationalism.* New York, 1956.

BELOFF, MAX, *Soviet Policy in the Far East, 1944–1951.* New York, London, 1953.

BERLINER, JOSEPH S., *Soviet Economic Aid.* New York, 1958.

BILIANKIN, GEORGE, *Maisky: Ten Years Ambassador.* London, 1944.

BLACKETT, P. M. S., *Atomic Weapons and East-West Relations.* New York, 1956.

BORKENAU, FRANZ, *The Spanish Cockpit.* New York, 1937.

————, *European Communism.* New York, 1953.

BRANDT, CONRAD, *Stalin's Failure in China, 1924–1927.* Cambridge, Mass., 1958.

BRENAN, GERALD, *The Spanish Labyrinth,* Cambridge, 1943.

BROWDER, ROBERT, *The Origins of Soviet-American Diplomacy.* Princeton, 1953.

CARR, EDWARD HALLETT, *The Soviet Impact on the Western World.* New York, 1947.

————, *The Twenty Years' Crisis, 1919–1939.* London, 1946, 1948.

CATTELL, DAVID T., *Communism and the Spanish Civil War.* Berkeley, 1955.

————, *Soviet Diplomacy and the Spanish Civil War.* Berkeley, 1957.

CHENG, TIENFONG, *A History of Sino-Russian Relations.* Washington, 1957.

CHILDS, JOHN L., *America, Russia, and the Communist Party in the Postwar World.* New York, 1943.

CHURCHILL, WINSTON S., *The Aftermath: The World Crisis, 1918–1928.* New York, 1929.

CLAUDE, INIS L., JR., *Swords into Plowshares.* New York, 1956.

COLUMBIA-HARVARD RESEARCH GROUP, *USSR and Eastern Europe* (A Study Prepared at the Request of The Committee on Foreign Relations, United States Senate). Washington, D. C., 1960.

DALLIN, ALEXANDER, *German Rule in Russia, 1941–1945.* New York, 1957.

————, ed., *Soviet Conduct in World Affairs.* New York, 1960.

DALLIN, DAVID J., *The Changing World of Soviet Russia.* New Haven, 1956.

————, *Russia and Postwar Europe.* New Haven, 1943, 1944.

————, *Soviet Espionage.* New Haven, 1955.

————, *Soviet Foreign Policy After Stalin.* Philadelphia, New York, 1961.

————, *Soviet Russia and the Far East.* New Haven, 1948.

————, *Soviet Russia's Foreign Policy, 1939–1942.* New Haven, 1942.

DAVIDSON, W. PHILLIPS, *The Berlin Blockade: A Study in Cold War Politics.* Princeton, 1958.

DEAN, VERA, *The United States and Russia.* Cambridge, Mass., 1948.

DENNETT, RAYMOND, AND JOSEPH E. JOHNSON, eds., *Negotiating with the Russians.* Boston, 1951.

EMBREE, G. D., *The Soviet Union between the 19th and 20th Party Congresses, 1952–1956.* The Hague, 1959.

FEIS, HERBERT, *Churchill-Roosevelt-Stalin.* Princeton, 1957.

————, *Between War and Peace: The Potsdam Conference.* Princeton, 1960.

FELLER, A. H., *The United Nations and World Community.* Boston, 1952.

FISCHER, LOUIS, *The Soviets in World Affairs,* 2 vols. Princeton, 1951.

FISCHER, RUTH, *Stalin and German Communism.* Cambridge, Mass., 1948.

FISHER, HAROLD H., *The Communist Revolution: An Outline of Strategy and Tactics.* Stanford, 1955.

FREUND, GERALD, *Unholy Alliance: Russian-German Relations from the Treaty of Brest-Litovsk to the Treaty of Berlin.* New York, 1957.

GURIAN, WALDEMAR, *The Soviet Union: Background, Ideology, and Reality.* Notre Dame, 1951.

HALLOWELL, JOHN N., ed., *Soviet Satellite Nations: A Study of the New Imperialism.* Gainsville, Fla., 1958.

HILL, RUSSELL, *Struggle for Germany.* New York, 1947.

ISAACS, HAROLD R., *The Tragedy of the Chinese Revolution.* Stanford, 1951.

KAUTSKY, JOHN H., *Moscow and the Communist Party of India.* Cambridge, Mass., and New York, 1956.

KENNAN, GEORGE F., *Russia Leaves the War*. Princeton, 1956.
——————, *The Decision to Intervene*. Princeton, 1958.
——————, *Russia, the Atom, and the West*. New York, 1958.
——————, *Soviet Foreign Policy, 1917–1941*. New York, 1960.
KIRKPATRICK, EVRON M., ed., *The World-Communist Propaganda Activities in 1955*. New York, 1956.
KISSINGER, HENRY A., *Nuclear Weapons and Foreign Policy*. New York, 1957.
KOCHAN, LIONEL, *Russia and the Weimar Republic*. Cambridge, 1954.
KONOVALOV, SERGE, *Russo-Polish Relations: An Historical Survey*. Princeton, 1945.
KULSKI, WLADYSLAW W., *Peaceful Co-existence*. Chicago, 1959.
LANGER, PAUL F., AND RODGER SWEARINGEN, *Red Flag in Japan: International Communism in Action, 1919–1951*. Cambridge, Mass., 1952.
LAQUEUR, WALTER Z., *Communism and Nationalism in the Middle East*. New York, 1956.
——————, *The Soviet Union and the Middle East*. New York, 1959.
LASERSON, MAX M., *Russia and the Western World*. New York, 1945.
LEITES, NATHAN, *A Study of Bolshevism*. Glencoe, Ill., 1953.
LENCZOWSKI, GEORGE, *Russia and the West in Iran, 1918–1948: A Study in Big Power Rivalry*. Ithaca, 1949.
LINDSAY, MICHAEL, *China and the Cold War: A Study in International Politics*. [Carlton] Melbourne Univ. Press, 1955.
LIPPMANN, WALTER, *The Communist World and Ours*. Boston, 1959.
McLANE, CHARLES B., *Soviet Policy and the Chinese Communists, 1931–1946*. New York, 1958.
McNEILL, WILLIAM H., *America, Britain, and Russia: Their Cooperation and Conflict, 1941–1946*. New York, 1954.
MEYER, ALFRED G., *Leninism*. Cambridge, Mass., 1957.
MOORE, HARRIET LUCY, *A Record of Soviet Far Eastern Relations, 1931–1942*. New York, 1942.
MOSELY, PHILIP E., *The Kremlin and World Politics: Studies in Soviet Policy and Action*. New York, 1960.
NETTL, J. P., *The Eastern Zone and Soviet Policy in Germany, 1945–1950*. London, New York, 1951.
NORTH, ROBERT CARVER, *Moscow and Chinese Communists*. Stanford, 1953.
OVERSTREET, GENE D., AND MARSHALL WINDMILLER, *Communism in India*. Berkeley, 1959.
ROBERTS, HENRY, *Russia and America: Dangers and Prospects*. New York, 1956.
ROSSI, ANGELO, (pseud.), *The Russo-German Alliance, August 1939-June 1941*. Boston, 1951.
ROSTOW, W. W., *The Prospects for Communist China*. New York, 1954.
RUSSELL, BERTRAND, *Common Sense and Nuclear Warfare*. London, 1959.
SCHNEIDER, RONALD M., *Communism in Guatemala: 1944–1954*. New York, 1959.
SCHWARTZ, BENJAMIN I., *Chinese Communism and the Rise of Mao*. Cambridge, Mass., 1951.
SCOTT, JOHN. *Duel for Europe: Stalin versus Hitler*. Boston, 1942.
SETON-WATSON, HUGH. *Eastern Europe between the Wars*. London, 1945.
——————, *The East European Revolution*. London, 1952.
——————, *Neither War Nor Peace: The Struggle for Power in the Postwar World*. New York, 1960.

SHOTWELL, JAMES T., AND M. M. LASERSON, *Poland and Russia, 1919–1945*. New York, 1954.

SLESSOR, SIR JOHN, *The Great Deterrent*. New York, 1958.

SNELL, JOHN L., ed., *The Meaning of Yalta*. Baton Rouge, 1956.

——————, *Wartime Origins of the East-West Dilemma over Germany*. New Orleans, 1959.

SNOW, EDGAR, *The Pattern of Soviet Power*. New York, 1945.

STRAUSZ-HUPÉ, ROBERT, with William R. Kintner, James E. Dougherty, and Alvin J. Cottrell, *Protracted Conflict: A Study of Communist Strategy*. New York, 1959.

SHERWOOD, ROBERT E., *Roosevelt and Hopkins: An Intimate History*. New York, 1948.

Survey of International Affairs, 1920–1954. London, New York, 1927–1958. Other volumes in preparation.

SYROP, KONRAD, *Spring in October: The Polish Revolution of 1956*. New York, 1958.

TANG, PETER S. H., *Russian and Soviet Policy in Manchuria and Outer Mongolia, 1911–1931*. New York, 1959.

TANNER, VAINO, *The Winter War: Finland Against Russia, 1939–1940*. Stanford, 1950.

TARACOUZIO, T. A., *The Soviet Union and International Law*. New York, 1935.

——————, *War and Peace in Soviet Diplomacy*. New York, 1940.

TARULIS, ALBERT N., Soviet Policy toward the Baltic States. Notre Dame, 1959.

TOMASIC, D. A., *National Communism and Soviet Strategy*. Washington, 1957.

TOMPKINS, PAULINE, *American-Russian Relations in the Far East*. New York, 1949.

TROTSKY, LEON, *The First Five Years of the Communist International*. New York, 1945.

ULAM, ADAM B., *Titoism and the Cominform*, Cambridge, Mass., 1952.

U. S. DEPARTMENT OF DEFENSE, *The Entry of the Soviet Union into the War against Japan*. Washington, 1955.

U. S. DEPARTMENT OF STATE, *The Sino-Soviet Economic Offensive in the Less Developed Countries*. Washington, 1958.

U. S. SENATE, Special Committee to Study the Foreign Aid Program, *Tensions within the Soviet Union*, Document No. 41, 82nd Congress, 1st Session, May 24, 1951.

——————, Spec. Com. to Study the Foreign Aid Program, *A Study: Foreign Assistance Activities of the Communist Bloc and Their Implications for the United States*, 85th Cong., 1st Sess., March 1957.

——————, Subcommittee on Technical Assistance Programs, *Soviet Technical Assistance*, 84th Cong., 2nd Sess., 1956.

UTLEY, FREDA, *Last Chance in China*. Indianapolis, 1947.

WARTH, ROBET D., *The Allies and the Russian Revolution*. Durham, N. C., 1954.

WEI, HENRY, *China and Soviet Russia*. New York, 1956.

WEINBERG, GERHARD L., *Germany and the Soviet Union, 1939–1941*. Leyden, 1954.

WHEELER-BENNETT, JOHN W., *The Forgotten Peace: Brest-Litovsk, March 1918*. New York, 1939.

——————, *Munich: Prologue to Tragedy*. New York, 1948.

WHITING, ALLEN S., *Soviet Policies in China, 1917–1924*. New York, 1954.

——————, AND SHENG SHIH-TS'AI, *Sinkiang: Pawn or Pivot?* East Lansing, Mich., 1958.

WILLOUGHBY, MAJOR GENERAL CHARLES A., *Shanghai Conspiracy: The Sorge Spy Ring*. New York, 1952.

WU, AI-CH'ÊN, *China and the Soviet Union: A Study of Sino-Soviet Relations*. New York, 1950.

Yakhontoff, Victor A., *Russia and the Soviet Union in the Far East.* New York, 1931.
————————, *USSR Foreign Policy.* New York, 1945.
Zabriskie, E. H., *American-Russian Rivalry in the Far East: A Study in Diplomacy and Power Politics, 1895–1914.* Philadelphia, 1946.

ARTICLES

Acheson, Dean, "The Illusion of Disengagement," *Foreign Affairs*, XXXVI, No. 3 (April 1958), 371–382.
Alexander, Robert J., "Brazil's CP: A Case Study in Latin American Communism," *Problems of Communism*, IV, No. 5 (Sept.-Oct. 1955), 17–26.
Allen, Robert L., "Economic Motives in Soviet Foreign Trade Policy," *Southern Economic Journal*, XXV, No. 2 (Oct. 1958), 189–201.
————————, "United Nations Technical Assistance: Soviet and East European Participation," *International Organization*, XI, No. 4 (Autumn 1957), 615–634.
Anderson, Albin T., "The Soviets and Northern Europe," *World Politics*, IV, No. 4 (July 1952), 468–487.
Arciniegas, G., "Communism in Latin America: A Problem for the Immediate Future," *Journal of International Affairs*, VIII, No. 1 (1954), 86–95.
Aubrey, Henry G., "Sino-Soviet Aid to South and Southeast Asia," *World Politics*, XII, No. 1 (Oct. 1959), 62–70.
Ballis, W. B., "The Pattern of Sino-Soviet Treaties, 1945–50," *The Annals of The American Academy of Political and Social Science*, Vol. 277 (Sept. 1951), 167–176.
Barghoorn, Frederick C., "Nationality Doctrine in Soviet Political Strategy," *The Review of Politics*, Vol. 16 (July 1954), 283–304.
————————, "The Soviet Critique of American Foreign Policy," *Journal of International Affairs*, V, No. 1 (Winter 1951), 5–14.
Beloff, Max, "No Peace, No War," *Foreign Affairs*, XXVII, No. 2 (Jan. 1949), 215–232.
————————, "Soviet Foreign Policy 1929–41: Some Notes," *Soviet Studies*, II, No. 2 (Oct. 1950), 123–137.
————————, "Soviet Policy in China," *Pacific Affairs*, XXIII, No. 2 (June 1950), 128–138.
————————, "The Theory of Soviet Foreign Policy," *Soviet Studies*, III, No. 4 (Apr. 1952), 345–350.
Black, Cyril B., "The Role of Diplomacy in Soviet Imperialism," in C. Grove Haines (ed.), *The Threat of Soviet Imperialism*, pp. 100–116. Baltimore, 1954.
————————, "Soviet Policy in Eastern Europe," *The Annals of The American Academy of Political and Social Science*, Vol. 263 (May 1949), 152–164.
Blackett, P. M. S., "Nuclear Weapons and Defence: Comments on Kissinger, Kennan, and King-Hall," *International Affairs*, XXXIV, No. 4 (Oct. 1958), 421–434.
Bruegel, Bedrich, "Methods of Soviet Domination in Satellite States," *International Affairs*, XXVII, No. 1 (Jan. 1951), 32–37.
Brzezinski, Zbigniew, "Ideology and Power: Crisis in the Soviet Bloc," *Problems of Communism*, VI, No. 1 (1957), 12–17.

BRZEZINSKI (continued), "The Politics of Underdevelopment," *World Politics*, IX, No. 1 (Oct. 1956), 55–75.

CAMPBELL, ROBERT W., "Some Recent Changes in Soviet Economic Policy," *World Politics*, IX, No. 1 (Oct. 1956), 1–14.

CARR, EDWARD H., "The Foundations of Soviet Foreign Policy," *International Spectator* (The Hague), X (Jan. 8, 1956), 6–25.

DALLIN, ALEXANDER, "Soviet Policy toward Eastern Europe," *Journal of International Affairs*, XI, No. 1 (Jan. 1957), 48–59.

————————, "The Soviet Stake in Eastern Europe," *The Annals of The American Academy of Political and Social Science*, Vol. 317 (May 1958), 138–145.

DALLIN, DAVID, "Communist Politics in the Western World," *The Annals of The American Academy of Political and Social Science*, Vol. 324 (July 1959), 2–7.

————————, "On the Nature of Soviet Imperialism: Communist Innovations," *Yale Review*, XLII, No. 3 (Mar. 1953), 343–350.

DEDIJER, VLADIMIR, "Albania, Soviet Pawn," *Foreign Affairs*, XXX (Oct. 1951), 103–111.

DINERSTEIN, HERBERT S., "The Revolution in Soviet Strategic Thinking," *Foreign Affairs*, XXXVI, No. 2 (Jan. 1958), 241–252.

DIPLOMATICUS, "Stalinist Theory and Soviet Foreign Policy," *Review of Politics*, XIV, No. 4 (Oct. 1952), 468–483.

DJILAS, H. E. M., "Yugoslav-Soviet Relations," *International Affairs*, XXVII, No. 2 (April 1951), 167–175.

DUCHACEK, IVO, "The Strategy of Communist Infiltration: Czechoslovakia, 1944–48," *World Politics*, II (Apr. 1950), 345–372.

FEIS, H., "The Three Who Led," *Foreign Affairs*, XXXVII, No. 2 (Jan. 1959), 282–292.

FISCHER, RUTH, "Ho Chi Minh: Disciplined Communist," *Foreign Affairs*, XXXIII, No. 1 (Oct. 1954), 86–98.

FRANKEL, J., "The Soviet Union and the United Nations," *Yearbook of World Affairs*, VIII (1954), 69–94.

FULLER, C. DALE, "Soviet Policy in the United Nations," *The Annals of The American Academy of Political and Social Science*, Vol. 263 (May 1949), 141–151.

GARTHOFF, RAYMOND L., "The Concept of the Balance of Power in Soviet Policy-Making," *World Politics*, IV (Oct. 1951), 85–111.

————————, "The Role of the Military in Recent Soviet Politics," *The Russian Review*, XVI, No. 2 (Apr. 1957), 15–24.

————————, "The Tragedy of Hungary," *Problems of Communism*, VI, No. 1 (1957), 3–11.

GLASER, WILLIAM A., "Theories of Soviet Foreign Policy: A Classification of the Literature," *World Affairs Quarterly*, XXVII (1956–57), 128–152.

GOODALL, MERRILL C., "Soviet Policy and India: Some Postwar Trends," *Journal of International Affairs*, VIII, No. 1 (1954), 43–51.

GOODMAN, ELLIOT R., "The Soviet Union and World Government," *Journal of Politics*, XV (May 1953), 231–253.

GOTTLEIB, W., "A Self-Portrait of Soviet Foreign Policy," *Soviet Studies*, III, No. 2 (Oct. 1951), 185–205.

GURIAN, W., "Permanent Features of Soviet Foreign Policy," in Hans J. Morgenthau and Kenneth W. Thompson (eds.), *Principles and Problems of International Politics*, pp. 265–288. New York, 1951, 1952.

HAMMEN, OSCAR J., "The 'Ashes' of Yalta," *South Atlantic Quarterly*, LIII (Oct. 1954), 477–484.

HEALEY, DENIS, "The Cominform and World Communism," *International Affairs*, XXIV (July 1948), 339–349.

HENDERSON, WILLIAM, "Communist Movements in Southeast Asia," *Journal of International Affairs*, VIII, No. 1 (1954), 32–42.

HEYMANN, HANS, JR., "Soviet Foreign Aid as a Problem for U. S. Policy," *World Politics*, XII, No. 4 (July 1960), 525–540.

HISTORICUS (GEORGE A. MORGAN), "Stalin on Revolution," *Foreign Affairs*, XXVII, No. 2 (January 1949), 175–214.

HODGMAN, DONALD R., "Soviet Foreign Economic and Technical Assistance," *Recent Soviet Trends*, Proceedings of a conference held at the University of Texas, Oct. 11–12, 1956, pp. 79–97.

HUDSON, G. F., "Mao, Marx and Moscow," *Foreign Affairs*, XXXVII, No. 4 (July 1959), 561–572.

————————, "Moscow and Peiping: Seeds of Conflict," *Problems of Communism*, V (Nov.-Dec. 1956), 17–23.

JACOBSON, H. R., "The Soviet Union, the U. N. and World Trade," *The Western Political Quarterly*, XI, No. 3 (Sept. 1958), 573–688.

JOHNSON, JOSEPH E., "The Soviet Union, the United States and International Security," *International Organization*, III (Febr. 1949), 1–13.

KENNAN, GEORGE F., "Disengagement Revisited," *Foreign Affairs*, XXXVII, No. 2 (January 1959), 187–210.

————————, "Peaceful Coexistence: A Western View," *Foreign Affairs*, XXXVIII, No. 2 (January 1960), 171–190.

KENNEY, CHARLES D., "Contemporary Soviet Foreign Policy: A Lesson in 'Creative Marxism' and 'Communist Morality,' " *World Affairs Quarterly*, XXVIII (Oct. 1957), 260–286.

KHRUSCHCHEV, NIKITA S., "On Peaceful Coexistence," *Foreign Affairs*, XXXVIII, No. 1 (Oct. 1959), 1–18.

KULSKI, W. W., "The Soviet System of Collective Security Compared with the Western System," *American Journal of International Law*, XLIV, No. 3 (July 1950), 453–476.

LANGER, PAUL F., "The Soviet Union and Japan," *Journal of International Affairs*, VIII, No. 1 (1954), 21–31.

————————, AND RODGER SWEARINGEN, "The Japanese Communist Party, the Soviet Union and Korea," *Pacific Affairs*, XXIII (Dec. 1950), 339–355.

LAQUEUR, WALTER Z., "The 'National Bourgeoisie,' a Soviet Dilemma in the Middle East," *International Affairs*, XXXV, No. 3 (July 1959), 324–31.

LAUCKHUFF, PERRY, "German Reactions to Soviet Policy, 1945–1953," *Journal of International Affairs*, VIII, No. 1 (1954), 62–73.

LENCZOWSKI, GEORGE, "Soviet Policy in the Middle East: A Summary of Developments Since 1945," *Journal of International Affairs*, VIII, No. 1 (1954), 52–61.

LI CHANG, "The Soviet Grip on Sinkiang," *Foreign Affairs*, XXXII, No. 3 (Apr. 1954), 491–503.

MACRIDIS, ROY, "Stalinism and the Meaning of Titoism," *World Politics*, IV, No. 2 (Jan. 15), 219–238.

————————, "Stalinism and the Pattern of Colonial Revolt," *The Western Political Quarterly*, VII (March 1954), 23–35.

MARKOV, M., "The Soviet Union and the Korean Question," *New Times* (Dec. 15, 1948), pp. 7–10.

MILLIKAN, GORDON W., "The Science of Soviet Politics," *Foreign Affairs*, XXXI, No. 3 (Apr. 1953), 472–485.

MORRIS, BERNARD, "The Cominform: A Five-Year Perspective," *World Politics*, V, No. 3 (April 1953), 368–376.

——————, "Communist International Front Organizations," *World Politics*, IX, No. 1 (Oct. 1956), 76–87.

MOSELY, PHILIP E., "Czechoslovakia, Poland, Yugoslavia, Observations and Reflections," *Political Science Quarterly*, LXIII (March 1948), 1–15.

——————, "Dismemberment of Germany: The Allied Negotiations from Yalta to Potsdam," *Foreign Affairs*, XXVIII, No. 3 (Apr. 1950), 487–498.

——————, "How 'New' Is the Kremlin's New Line?" *Foreign Affairs*, XXXIII, No. 3 (Apr. 1955), 376–386.

——————, "The Kremlin's Foreign Policy Since Stalin," *Foreign Affairs*, XXXII, No. 1 (Oct. 1953), 20–33.

——————, "Khrushchev's New Economic Gambit," *Foreign Affairs*, XXXVI, No. 4 (July 1958), 557–568.

——————, "Soviet-American Relations Since the War," *The Annals of The American Academy of Political and Social Science*, Vol. 263 (May 1949), 202–211.

——————, "Soviet Foreign Policy: New Goals or New Manners?" *Foreign Affairs*, XXXIV, No. 4 (July 1956), 541–553.

——————, "Soviet Policy and the (Korean) War," *Journal of International Affairs*, VI, No. 2 (Spr. 1952), 107–114.

——————, "Soviet Policy and the Revolutions in Asia," *The Annals of The American Academy of Political and Social Science*, Vol. 276 (July 1951), 91–98.

——————, "Soviet Policy in a Two-World System," *International Journal* (Toronto), III, No. 3 (Sum. 1948), 191–200.

——————, "Soviet Policy in the Two-World Conflict: Som......to." *Journal of International Affairs*, VIII, No. 1 (1954), 107–114.

——————, "Soviet Policy in the UN," *Proceedings of the Academy of Political Science*, XXII, No. 2 (Jan. 1947), 28–37.

——————, "The Soviet Union and the United States: Problems and Prospects," *The Annals of The American Academy of Political and Social Science*, Vol. 303 (Jan. 1956), 192–198.

NAIR, KUSUM, "Where India, China and Russia Meet," *Foreign Affairs*, XXXVI, No. 2 (Jan. 1958), 330–339.

OVERSTREET, GENE D., "Soviet and Communist Policy in India," *Journal of Politics*, XX, No. 1 (Febr. 1958), 187–202.

PYE, L. W., "Communist Strategies and Asian Societies," *World Politics*, XI, No. 1 (Oct. 1958), 118.

RIEBER, ALFRED, "Communist Tactics in France: 1945–1953," *Journal of International Affairs*, VIII, No. 1 (1954), 73–85.

ROBERTS, HENRY L., "The Crisis in the Soviet Empire," *Foreign Affairs*, XXXV, No. 2 (Jan. 1957), 191–200.

——————, "Soviet-American Relations: Problems of Choice and Decision," *Texas Quarterly*, I, No. 3 (1958), 101–109.

RUBINSTEIN, ALVIN Z., "Soviet Policy in ECAFE: A Case Study of Soviet Behavior in

International Economic Organization," *International Organization*, XII, No. 4 (Autumn 1958), 459–471.

————————, "Soviet Policy toward Underdeveloped Areas in the Economic and Social Council," *International Organization*, IX, No. 2 (May 1955), 232–243.

RUDZINSKI, A. W., "The Influence of the United Nations on Soviet Policy," *International Organization*, V, No. 2 (May 1951), 282–299.

————————, "Soviet Peace Offensives," *International Conciliation*, No. 490 (Apr. 1953), 177–225.

SACKS, MILTON, "Strategy of Communism in Southeast Asia," *Pacific Affairs*, XXIII (Sept. 1950), 227–247.

SANAKOYEV, S., "The Basis of the Relations between the Socialist Countries," *International Affairs* (Moscow), No. 7 (July 1958), 23–33.

SCALAPINO, R. A., "Neutralism in Asia," *The American Political Science Review*, XLVIII, No. 1 (Mar. 1954), 49–62.

SCHAPIRO, LEONARD, "Has Russia Changed?" *Foreign Affairs*, XXXVIII, No. 3 (April 1960), 391–401.

SCHOENFELD, H. F. A., "Soviet Imperialism in Hungary," *Foreign Affairs*, XXVI, No. 3 (Apr. 1948), 554–566.

SCOTT, N. B., "Soviet Economic Relations with the Under-developed Countries," *Soviet Studies*, X (July 1958), 36–53.

SHULMAN, MARSHALL D., "Changing Appreciation of the Soviet Problem," *World Politics*, X, No. 4 (July 1958), 499–511.

SKILLING, GORDON A., " 'People's Democracy' in Soviet Theory," *Soviet Studies*, III (July 1951), 16–33; III (Oct. 1951), 131–149.

SONTAG, RAYMOND J., "The Last Months of Peace, 1939," *Foreign Affairs*, XXXV, No. 3 (Apr. 1957), 507–524.

————————, "Reflections on the Yalta Papers," *Foreign Affairs*, XXXIII, No. 4 (July 1955), 615–623.

SPEIER, HANS, "Soviet Atomic Blackmail and the North Atlantic Alliance," *World Politics*, IX, No. 3 (Apr. 1957), 308–328.

SWEARINGEN, RODGER, "Japanese Communism and the Moscow-Peking Axis," *The Annals of The American Academy of Political and Social Science*, Vol. 308 (Nov. 1956), 63–75.

TARN, R. S., "Continuity in Russian Foreign Policy," *International Journal* (Toronto), V, No. 4 (Aut. 1950), 283–298.

TAURER, BERNARD, "Stalin's Last Thesis," *Foreign Affairs*, XXXI, No. 3 (Apr. 1953), 367–381.

TITO, J. B., "On Certain Current International Questions," *Foreign Affairs*, XXXVI, No. 1 (Oct. 1957), 63–77.

TRISKA, JAN F., "Model for Study of Soviet Foreign Policy," *The American Political Science Review*, LII (Mar. 1958), 64–83.

TUCKER, ROBERT C., "The Politics of Soviet De-Stalinization," *World Politics*, IX, No. 4 (July 1956), 550–578.

ULAM, ADAM B., "The Cominform and the People's Democracies," *World Politics*, III, No. 2 (Jan. 1951), 200–217.

————————, "Soviet Ideology and Soviet Foreign Policy," *World Politics*, XI, No. 2 (Jan. 1959), 153–172.

ULLMAN, RICHARD H., "The Davies Mission and United States-Soviet Relations, 1937–41," *World Politics*, IX, No. 2 (Jan. 1959), 220–239.

WANDYCZ, PIOTR S., "The Soviet System of Alliances in East Central Europe," *Journal of Central European Affairs*, XVI, No. 2 (July 1956), 177–184.

WHEELER, G. E., "Soviet Policy in Central Asia," *International Affairs*, XXXI, No. 3 (July 1955), 317–326.

WINNACKER, RUDOLPH A., "Yalta—Another Munich?" *Virginia Quarterly Review*, XXIV, No. 4 (Aut. 1948), 521–537.

WITTFOGEL, KARL, "Russia and Asia," *World Politics*, II, No. 4 (July 1950), 445–462.

WOLF, CHARLES, JR., "Soviet Economic Aid in Southeast Asia: Threat or Windfall?" *World Politics*, X, No. 1 (Oct. 1957), 91–101.

WOLFE, BERTRAM, "A New Look at the Soviet 'New Look,'" *Foreign Affairs*, XXXIII, No. 2 (Jan. 1955), 184–198.

"X" (GEORGE KENNAN), "The Sources of Soviet Conduct," *Foreign Affairs*, XXV, No. 4 (July 1947), 566–582.

ZINNER, P. E., "The Ideological Bases of Soviet Foreign Policy," *World Politics*, IV, No. 4 (July 1952), 489–511.

——————, "Soviet Policies in Eastern Europe," *The Annals of The American Academy of Political and Social Science*, Vol. 303 (J.... .... Underdeveloped Countries, *World Politics*, XI, No. 3 (Apr. 1959), 378–398.

——————, "Soviet Foreign Economic Policy," *Political Science Quarterly*, LXXIII, No. 2 (June 1958), 206–233.